The Three Jewels I

THE COMPLETE WORKS OF SANGHARAKSHITA include all his previously published work, as well as talks, seminars, and writings published here for the first time. The collection represents the definitive edition of his life's work as Buddhist writer and teacher. For further details, including the contents of each volume, please turn to the 'Guide' on pp.793–801.

FOUNDATION

1 A Survey of Buddhism / The Buddha's Noble Eightfold Path
2 The Three Jewels I
3 The Three Jewels II
4 The Bodhisattva Ideal
5 The Purpose and Practice of Buddhist Meditation
6 The Essential Sangharakshita

INDIA

7 Crossing the Stream: India Writings I
8 Beating the Dharma Drum: India Writings II
9 Dr Ambedkar and the Revival of Buddhism I
10 Dr Ambedkar and the Revival of Buddhism II

THE WEST

11 A New Buddhist Movement I
12 A New Buddhist Movement II
13 Eastern and Western Traditions

COMMENTARY

14 The Eternal Legacy / Wisdom Beyond Words
15 Pāli Canon Teachings and Translations
16 Mahāyāna Myths and Stories
17 Wisdom Teachings of the Mahāyāna
18 Milarepa and the Art of Discipleship I
19 Milarepa and the Art of Discipleship II

MEMOIRS

20 The Rainbow Road from Tooting Broadway to Kalimpong
21 Facing Mount Kanchenjunga
22 In the Sign of the Golden Wheel
23 Moving Against the Stream
24 Through Buddhist Eyes

POETRY AND THE ARTS

25 Complete Poems
26 Aphorisms and the Arts

27 Concordance and Appendices

COMPLETE WORKS 2 **FOUNDATION**

Sangharakshita
The Three Jewels I

EDITED BY KALYANAPRABHA

Windhorse Publications
17e Sturton Street
Cambridge
CB1 2SN
UK

info@windhorsepublications.com
www.windhorsepublications.com

Cover design by Dhammarati and Akasajoti
Cover images: Front: Sutra Covers with the Eight Buddhist Treasures, China, 1403–1424. Courtesy of the Metropolitan Museum of Art. Gift of Florence and Herbert Irving, 2015. Back flap: Sangharakshita, 1968. Courtesy of Clear Vision Trust.

Typesetting and layout by Ruth Rudd
Printed by Bell & Bain Ltd, Glasgow

British Library Cataloguing in Publication Data:
A catalogue record for this book is available from the British Library.

ISBN 978-1-911407-33-1 (paperback)
ISBN 978-1-911407-32-4 (hardback)

CONTENTS

Foreword, *Nagabodhi* xi
A Note from the Editor xix

THE THREE JEWELS 1

Preface to the Fourth Edition 7

Part I: The Buddha 9

1 Life and Records 11
2 The Bodhisattva Career 14
3 The Life 19
4 The Legends 31
5 Philosophical Interpretations 39

Part II: The Dharma 47

6 Approaches to Buddhism 49
7 The Essence of the Dharma 53
8 Doctrinal Formulas 58
9 Cosmology 62
10 The Wheel of Life 68

11 The Nature of Existence 80
12 The Human Situation 93
13 The Stages of the Path 101
14 The Goal 120

Part III: The Sangha 135

15 The Assembly of the Noble 137
16 The Glorious Company of Bodhisattvas 153
17 The Monastic Order 185
18 The Place of the Laity 202
19 Popular Buddhism 218

THE MEANING OF CONVERSION IN BUDDHISM 233

1 Introduction 237
2 Going for Refuge 240
3 Entering the Stream 250
4 The Arising of the *Bodhicitta* 266
5 The Turning About in the Deepest Seat of Consciousness 275

GOING FOR REFUGE 287

THE TEN PILLARS OF BUDDHISM 307

The Ten Precepts in Pali 311
The Ten Precepts in English 312
The Ten Positive Precepts 313

Introduction 315

Part I: The Ten Precepts Collectively 321

1 The Relation Between Refuges and Precepts 323
2 The Canonical Sources of the Ten Precepts 326
3 The Ten Precepts and Total Transformation 335

4 The Ten Precepts as Principles of Ethics 339
5 The Ten Precepts as Rules of Training 342
6 The Ten Precepts as '*Mūla-Prātimokṣa*' 344
7 The Ten Precepts and Other Ethical Formulas 349
8 The Ten Precepts and Lifestyle 351

Part II: The Ten Precepts Individually 355

1 The First Precept: The principle of abstention from killing living beings; or love 357
2 The Second Precept: The principle of abstention from taking the not-given; or generosity 364
3 The Third Precept: The principle of abstention from sexual misconduct; or contentment 370
4 The Fourth Precept: The principle of abstention from false speech; or truthfulness 374
5 The Fifth Precept: The principle of abstention from harsh speech; or kindly speech 379
6 The Sixth Precept: The principle of abstention from frivolous speech; or meaningful speech 381
7 The Seventh Precept: The principle of abstention from slanderous speech; or harmonious speech 383
8 The Eighth Precept: The principle of abstention from covetousness; or tranquillity 385
9 The Ninth Precept: The principle of abstention from hatred; or compassion 388
10 The Tenth Precept: The principle of abstention from false views; or wisdom 390

Conclusion 395

THE HISTORY OF MY GOING FOR REFUGE 397

1 Introduction 403
2 The *Diamond Sūtra* and the *Sūtra of Wei Lang* 407
3 U Thittila and *Pansil* 410
4 Going Forth 412
5 *Śrāmaṇera* Ordination 417

6 *Bhikṣu* Ordination 420
7 'Taking Refuge in the Buddha' 423
8 *A Survey of Buddhism* 427
9 Dhardo Rimpoche and *The Path of the Buddha* 434
10 Ambedkar and the ex-Untouchables 437
11 More Light from Tibetan Buddhism 440
12 *The Three Jewels* and Other Writings 447
13 Bodhisattva Ordination 454
14 Light from Vatican II 457
15 'The Meaning of Conversion in Buddhism' 460
16 Founding the Western Buddhist Order 466
17 The Wider Context 473
18 Levels of Going for Refuge 479
19 Going for Refuge Old and New 484
20 *Upāsaka* into *Dharmacārī* 489
21 Ambedkar and Going for Refuge 494
22 Conclusion 498

MY RELATION TO THE ORDER 505

EXTENDING THE HAND OF FELLOWSHIP 541

FORTY-THREE YEARS AGO 575

WAS THE BUDDHA A BHIKKHU? 615

Appendices 651
The Five Precepts 653
The Eight Precepts 654
The Ten *Śrāmaṇera* Precepts 655
Dr Ambedkar's Twenty-Two Conversion Vows 656
The Bodhisattva's *Saṃvara-śīla* or Sixty-Four Precepts 657

Notes 661
Index 759
A Guide to the *Complete Works of Sangharakshita* 793

FOREWORD

The cross-channel ferry had docked late so as we entered the Assembly Room at UNESCO's Paris headquarters the proceedings were already under way and up front a panel of besuited gentlemen was engaged in heated discussion. As unfussily as possible, we took our places and joined the 300 or so delegates to participate in this, the first session of the first International Congress of the European Buddhist Union.

This was June 1979, early days in the history of Western Buddhism and even earlier for the Friends of the Western Buddhist Order on whose behalf we'd accepted the invitation to attend. Our exalted surroundings, finessed by Sri Lanka's Ambassador to UNESCO, were a never-to-be repeated fluke but somehow helped us feel as if the Buddha-Dharma really had arrived in the sophisticated, post-industrial West.

But then, as we took in the proceedings on stage, we could feel ourselves being carried back to another era, another place. What was being discussed, even hotly debated, was the challenge involved in assembling the necessary elements of a traditionally exact ordination *sīmā*. ('Perhaps something could be done on a raft in the middle of a river?') Only then, they held, could we start ordaining *monks*. And our Western Buddhism must have monks; without monks there can be no Western Buddhism! Hence the priority given to this, the Congress's first agenda item.

It's not that we didn't know something about, or respect, the way most Buddhist schools had gone about things throughout history; our

Triratna (then FWBO) Community's approach to Dharma study had introduced us to the customs and teachings of a pretty wide range of them. And quite a few traditional schools, in their intact Eastern form, were gaining a following in the West. But to our Sangharakshita-trained ears the discussion seemed quaint, achingly peripheral to the fundamental project of helping people to discover the Dharma and live a viable Buddhist life as Westerners in the modern world.

As if to underline the point, before us was the spectacle of four men passionately engaged in a debate about the absolute prerequisite of a technically authentic and correct Theravāda monastic ordination ceremony – when few of the assembled delegates came from Theravāda communities, and when it was pretty obvious that none of the men on the panel showed any wish to become a monk himself. Perhaps mischievously, I couldn't help wondering whether, deep down, their dream of a Western Buddhist world graced and sanctioned by flocks of yellow-robed monks was rooted in the wish for a world in which they could cosily settle into the less demanding status as laymen.

I think that's when I first grasped just how radical was Sangharakshita's vision in founding a new kind of Buddhist order: ecumenical, free from the tectonic gulf between monks and layfolk, free from the spiritually deadening atmosphere of surface formalism he'd encountered so often in the East. The defining act of the Buddhist life, he held, is not to become a monk or nun and adhere routinely to the requirements of a particular branch of the tradition. Irrespective of cultural context or lifestyle, you are a Buddhist because and only because you '*go for Refuge to the Three Jewels*': whatever the conditions of your life you *commit* to engaging wholeheartedly with the ideal of Enlightenment, with the deepest implications of the Buddha's teachings and with the active pursuit of spiritual guidance and the highest possibilities of spiritual fellowship.

> I go to the Blessed One for refuge, to the Dhamma, and to the Community of monks. May the Blessed One remember me as a follower who has gone to him for refuge, from this day forward, for life.

Such exclamations erupt often and fervently from the pages of Buddhist scripture. They occur on occasions when the Buddha has ignited vision, faith, and an urge to 'live the life' in someone he's encountered. The words are always uttered in mid-epiphany – by householders as well as by those ready to drop everything and become full-time followers. And yet, by the twentieth century, the formula of 'Going for Refuge' had become just that, a formula of words in a dead language recited on ceremonial occasions as a subsidiary to the (equally formalized but status defining) recitation of ethical precepts.

The fact that the Going for Refuge is not a formula, much less subsidiary to anything else, seemed obvious to me and my friends. As members of Sangharakshita's order we'd grown up in an atmosphere suffused with the idea. And yet for Sangharakshita, the journey he'd taken towards reclaiming and articulating the Going for Refuge as the central and, crucially, *unifying* heart-principle of all Buddhist life had been a long and often lonely one.

The volume you hold in your hands is a record of that journey. The writings assembled here allow us to track not only the development of Sangharakshita's unfolding insight into the significance of Going for Refuge, but also his highly individual relationship with some of the Buddhist world's most deeply rooted assumptions. We can track, too, his deepening knowledge of and devotion to the Three Jewels (most comprehensively articulated in the book of that name), not just as a student and scholar but as one who *goes for Refuge* to them, even as one who shares the fruits of his journey with others.

In this lifetime at least, the journey began when as a very young man he read the *Diamond Sūtra* and realized, as he so often puts it, 'I was a Buddhist and had always been one.' But perhaps the time-bending manner in which Sangharakshita describes this moment warns us that the metaphor of a journey is only partly helpful. As he writes, in *The History of My Going for Refuge*:

> The full significance of that supremely important act became apparent to me only gradually as, over the years, I acted upon the imperfect idea of Going for Refuge which I already had and as, my idea of it being clarified to some extent, I again acted upon it and it was again clarified – the act becoming more adequate to the idea as the idea itself became clearer, and the idea becoming clearer as the act became more adequate.

For the purposes of this volume, and in an attempt to impose a little narrative neatness on things, we must locate the point at which Sangharakshita encountered a life-changing fork in the road. A few years after his ordination he discovered that one of the monks who'd participated in his ordination was impure with regard to some important monastic restraints. This was tantamount to discovering that his ordination, his longed-for entry into the life of a Buddhist monk, was technically invalid.

Of course, Sangharakshita could have quietly ignored his discovery, as others had doubtless done countless times over the centuries. But what was he to do or think in a Buddhist world so strongly preoccupied with the formalities of monastic lifestyles and technical correctness, in which the officiant at his ordination ceremony had spent more time correcting his pronunciation of Pāli words than explaining their significance?

It was no small thing. It mattered to Sangharakshita personally that his ordination was technically invalid. He had once longed for ordination, believing it to be the indispensable gateway to a truly Buddhist life, and after a series of false starts and challenges had realized, or thought he had realized, his ambition. But there was more. It was inconceivable that his experience was, throughout time, unique. And this carried the unavoidable implication that the entire monastic ordination tradition, and thus the rationale for the ubiquitous and categorical monk–lay divide, must be equally compromised.

I don't know how much the more personal dimension of his status as a Theravāda monk within a particular *nikāya* mattered to Sangharakshita by the time of this discovery. He was after all happily living as a sincere, committed Buddhist, soon to have his own vihara, surrounded mainly by Tibetan Buddhists, and working for the good of Buddhism in his own singular way. Maybe that's why Sangharakshita was able to recognize that, despite his lapses under the monastic rule, the so-called 'impure' monk who'd attended his ordination ceremony was without doubt living as a good Buddhist in his own way.

So what was he to make of this? As *Forty-Three Years Ago* and *Was the Buddha a Bhikkhu?* record, this event and the reflections it spawned, presented him with a series of challenges and questions he couldn't ignore. It was time, he realized, to put aside all assumptions – his own and many of the Eastern Buddhist world's, and ask himself again and again: what *does* it truly mean to be a good Buddhist?

'What relevance does this teaching have to the living of a spiritual life?' Over the years this was his subliminal mantra as he immersed himself in practice and Dharma study. In the service of a spiritual life, he realized, nothing can or should be taken for granted or accepted merely on the authority of tradition.

How then, he reflected, does a contemporary Buddhist extract spiritual nourishment from teachings delivered two-and-a-half millennia ago? It is axiomatic that the Buddha, Dharma, and Sangha occupy their central position, but how do we approach and engage with them right now? What does it *mean* to go for Refuge to the Buddha, to the Dharma, to the Sangha? *The Three Jewels, The Meaning of Conversion in Buddhism, Going for Refuge*: writings and lectures such as these bear witness to his increasingly creative, and when necessary critical, relationship with the Buddhist world around him.

The history of Buddhism is in large part a history of schools and sects, each with its own emphasis, favoured practices, even, sometimes, its own figures of devotion. As the Buddha-Dharma entered new eras, cultures, climates, and even villages, sects and schools had evolved that could seem to have little or nothing in common with each other. What then, was one to make of them?

Freed of dutiful allegiance to any one system or school, Sangharakshita could sense a kinship with them all, a kinship he could also sense that flowed between them. To his mind their disparate manifestations were not random or accidental but unified in origin and intention, ways in which the various *dimensions* of Going for Refuge (described in the talk, *Going for Refuge*) had been emphasized at different times by different people according to need and cultural disposition. Freed from their national boundaries, and approached intelligently in a consciously ecumenical spirit, what riches might their symbols, myths and practices bring to the treasure chest of possibilities awaiting its Western heirs? How might they enrich and balance the spiritual life of new generations in our highly networked global village?

The essentially binary arrangement of celibate monastics *vis-à-vis* lay-folk seemed as old as Buddhism itself, even enshrined in scriptural records. But might there be room for an entirely new kind of order, Sangharakshita wondered, one that is neither monastic *nor* lay, all of whose members are equally challenged to live an intense spiritual life? Could there be too, as he asks in *The Ten Pillars of Buddhism*, an essentialized moral code pertinent to all, whether or not living under a monastic rule? It is significant as an insight into Sangharakshita's sense of mission that he introduces this text not simply as a brief outline of the ethical precepts observed by members of his own order but as a tightly argued offering for the consideration of the entire Buddhist world.

By placing the Going for Refuge at the centre of things, and in recognizing that the act takes place at a range of levels and in an array of dimensions, so much became clear. It was as if Sangharakshita had transported himself and anyone who chose to follow him into a Buddhist realm in which it was possible to speak of 'Stream Entry' *and* the 'arising of *bodhicitta*', or refer to Akṣobhya *and* Aṅgulimāla, or address issues of the monastic *and* household life in the same company.

Seen this way, the Going for Refuge offers a lens through which the most profound insights, the most sublime visions of the entire Buddhist experience can speak to anyone who is making a sincere effort to live the Buddhist life, and can do so in a context and language that most appropriately and inspirationally meets their evolving needs.

We'll never know what might have happened had Sangharakshita not received his invitation to visit the UK in 1964. Nor can we imagine what might have happened had a falling out with his hosts not liberated him – as he came to see it – to embark on what was to become his major life's work in establishing the Triratna Buddhist Order and its encircling community of Friends and postulants. This is a project that has offered a proving ground for many of the ideas and principles outlined in this volume. It has also given him the platform from which many of the ideas expressed in these pages first saw light of day as talks or papers delivered to an assembly of the Order's '*dharmacārīs*' and '*dharmacāriṇīs*'.

This order of men *and* women, following a wide range of lifestyles, training under a fundamental *pāṭimokkha* of ten ethical precepts, many of them equally at home with the language of all three *yānas*, meeting regularly, meditating and studying together, even sometimes living and working together, all in an ambience of strong spiritual fellowship: this has become a living embodiment of Sangharakshita's vision. It is a Buddhist community in which Going for Refuge to the Three Jewels in all of its dimensions takes centre stage, where commitment is primary and lifestyle, though important, is secondary.

Since so much of the material gathered here speaks of the relationship between Sangharakshita's ideas and the traditional Buddhist world, and since the Triratna Buddhist Order has so many of its roots in the ideas expressed here, it seems appropriate to include in this volume a paper he delivered concerning his views on the Order's relationship with the wider Buddhist world. In *Extending the Hand of Fellowship* he visits some of the misunderstandings that can limit and confuse those relations. There is no disrespect intended. It's just that most Buddhist schools, as already noted, have evolved around a particular emphasis or specialization. Over the centuries, and often in geographical isolation, they have come to regard their angle of approach as the norm and sometimes even their way as the only way. So, while being respectful of their achievements, their discoveries and riches, Sangharakshita alerts us to the possibility that they might find it hard to understand our ecumenical approach and our very different kind of order. This is not to say that spiritual fellowship between us all isn't possible or desirable. But it will be most happily and appropriately enjoyed when we meet as practising Buddhists, as individuals rather than as representatives of our respective movements or traditions.

In *My Relation to the Order* Sangharakshita makes clear that friendship trumps institutional relationships even within a single Buddhist community like the Order he has established. Friendship can be 'horizontal', between spiritual equals, and it can be 'vertical' with those more experienced, more spiritually developed than ourselves. But it is friendship, truly human connection and communication, that matters rather than any institutional relationship. Perhaps, then, it shouldn't come as a surprise when we hear him speaking of his own place in the Order he's founded as that of a *friend*: nothing more, nothing less.

This emphasis on what really matters in communication between Buddhists echoes his emphasis on the Going for Refuge itself, to which all else, no matter how important as support, is secondary. It is here, now, and always the life-defining intention and direction behind our actions of body, speech, and mind, that really matters. 'How is this teaching, this ordination, this activity, this moment serving and expressing my deepest values and ideals?' To live this way is quite a challenge, isn't it?

The writings collected here display the energy and integrity with which Sangharakshita has tried to meet that challenge. I know that you, the reader, find yourself faced with words on a page, pixels on a screen. But as you read on just try to see Sangharakshita sitting alone in his study with pen poised over paper. Or see him standing at a lectern bringing forth these words, these ideas, into the world. Now as then he is sharing *with you* in friendship, as you sit here reading, his thoughts, his journey, his vision. This, he is saying, is what really matters.

Nagabodhi
1 January 2018

A NOTE FROM THE EDITOR

This second volume in the *Complete Works* series contains nine texts of very different lengths, their genesis ranging from articles written for an Indian encyclopedia to talks given to members of the Western Buddhist Order (now the Triratna Buddhist Order). A short explanatory note introduces each one. They are presented in the order in which they were composed with the exception of *Extending the Hand of Fellowship* which, along with *My Relation to the Order,* was originally envisaged as an extension to *The History of My Going for Refuge.* In the present volume the three texts follow on one from the other.

The editorial work has been mainly to create endnotes, in the first place providing a full reference for all quoted passages from Buddhist literature. Wherever possible I have given a reference to the particular translation quoted. Generally I have tried to give references to both the older translations of *suttas* and *sūtras* which Sangharakshita himself drew from, and to more modern ones which may be more accurate having the benefit of now many decades of scholarly work on Buddhist scriptures and their translation.

When a non-specific reference is made to the Buddhist tradition (such as 'in the Mahāyāna') I have tried to find a specific source in the *sūtras*, commentaries, and other works. For anyone interested in exploring further, I highly recommend the Sangharakshita Library at Adhisthana – Triratna's central location in Herefordshire, UK, and home to Sangharakshita – which contains thousands of books. They provide the background to the development of Sangharakshita's thought, his understanding of the Buddhist tradition, and his particular presentation of the Dharma.

Our policy is to give sources that are to be found in a printed book on the understanding that, although all things are impermanent, the Internet may be less reliable in the long term. At the same time I would like to acknowledge with gratitude *accesstoinsight* and other Buddhist and non-Buddhist Internet sites without whose help I might never have located some sources.

Two of the nine texts in this volume strike a more personal note: *The History of My Going for Refuge* and *My Relation to the Order*, both of which were originally delivered as papers to members of the Order. In the second of these in particular, Sangharakshita mentions developments in the Order and Movement he founded which were familiar to his auditors at the time but which may need explanation for readers of the *Complete Works*. Some endnotes, therefore, offer a glimpse into the history of the Triratna Buddhist Community and with a few brush strokes of fact try to evoke the times and the people who took a lead in setting up some of Triratna's institutions. I have done my best to check with those who were there, but should readers notice errors of fact, please inform the publisher so that corrections may be made in future editions.

As editor I have been dealing with words and letters, with sources of quotations and the like but in the end they are all only a vehicle for the transmission of the Dharma, the Buddha-Dharma which, though ungraspable – or precisely because ungraspable – is, as the *suttas* tell us, *kalyāṇa:* lovely – at the beginning, in the middle, and at the end. The texts in this volume, these communications from Sangharakshita, have contributed enormously to my own understanding of the Three Jewels, the Buddha, the Dharma, and the Sangha, and to communicating to me something of their loveliness. May it be so for all readers who come to these pages.

Kalyanaprabha
Great Malvern
1 March 2018

To help readers unfamiliar with Pāli and Sanskrit, plurals have been indicated by an -s suffix rather than employ the technically correct orthography.

The Three Jewels

THE CENTRAL IDEALS OF BUDDHISM

INTRODUCTORY NOTE

The Three Jewels began life as one of a series of articles on the heritage of Buddhism commissioned by the *Oriya Encyclopaedia,* one of a dozen or more regional language encyclopedias sponsored by the government of India. The editor of the *Oriya Encyclopaedia* was Dr Mansinha, the principal of a boys' college, whom Sangharakshita knew personally.

The first of these commissioned articles was to be an introduction to the Three Jewels of Buddhism: the Buddha, the Dharma, and the Sangha. It was composed in the second half of 1961 when Sangharakshita was based at his vihara in Kalimpong in the eastern Himalayas. In the course of writing the article considerably outgrew the purpose for which it had been commissioned and Dr Mansinha was obliged to drastically shorten it for inclusion in the *Encyclopoedia.*

The complete manuscript accompanied Sangharakshita to England in 1964. There, at the Hampstead Buddhist Vihara, the London headquarters of the English Sangha Trust where he was based for a couple of years, he wrote a preface and looked for a way to publish it as a book. At the suggestion of his old friend Lama Govinda, he wrote to Gerald Yorke, a reader for Rider and Co., the leading British publisher of books on Buddhism. *The Three Jewels* was accepted and appeared in 1967 with the subtitle 'an introduction to Buddhism'. (Gerald Yorke became a personal friend – but that is another story). An American edition was published by Anchor Books in 1970. The word 'modern' was added to the subtitle so it became 'an introduction to modern Buddhism' (a change not likely to have been advocated by the author since the Buddhism to which we are introduced through its pages is the *akāliko Dhamma*, the timeless teaching that is neither ancient nor modern). The second and third editions, published in 1977 and 1991 in the UK, this time by Windhorse Publications, bear the original subtitle. In 1998 Windhorse Publications produced a fourth edition for which Sangharakshita wrote a new Preface which we have included in this *Complete Works* edition. Another change was also made: the subtitle became 'the central ideals of Buddhism' which perhaps communicates most essentially what the book is about.

Sangharakshita describes the writing and publication of The Three Jewels *in* Moving Against the Stream, *Windhorse Publications, Birmingham 2003, chapter 31 (*Complete Works, *vol. 23); and in* The History of My Going for Refuge, *section 12, in this volume, pp. 447ff.*

I take my refuge in the Buddha, and pray that with all beings I may understand the Great Way, whereby the Buddha-seed may forever thrive.

I take my refuge in the Dharma, and pray that with all beings I may enter deeply into the sūtra-treasure, whereby our wisdom may grow as vast as the ocean.

I take my refuge in the Sangha, and pray that with all beings I may reign in great multitudes and have nothing to check the unimpeded progress of Truth.[1]

Avataṃsaka Sūtra

PREFACE TO THE FOURTH EDITION

During the last five decades interest in Buddhism has become widespread in the West. From being the closed preserve of professional orientalists, whose interest was largely linguistic and historical, and to whom Buddhism was little more than a particularly well-preserved mummy in the museum of Comparative Religion, the wise, compassionate, and vital teachings of the Buddha have started attracting the attention of an increasing number of sensitive and thoughtful people who, though having outgrown authoritarian creeds of every kind, are yet in search of a framework of psychological and spiritual reference ample enough to contain and elastic enough not to confine their aspirations. Whether choosing to describe themselves as Buddhists or not, those who feel 'at home' within the framework called Buddhism, and who settle down therein, in effect commit themselves to the realization of an ideal by following a certain way of life in the company of other people similarly committed. This is what is traditionally known as 'Going for Refuge' to the Three Jewels, an act which, though it may find ceremonial expression, is essentially a profound inner experience, a spiritual rebirth or 'conversion', as a result of which one's whole life is transformed and reoriented.

The Three Jewels are the Buddha, the Dharma, and the Sangha. By the Buddha or Enlightened One is meant not only the historical Śākyamuni, the founder of Buddhism, but the ideal of Enlightenment both in its universal aspect and its ultimate reality. The Dharma or

Doctrine is not only the sum total of the Buddha's teachings but the whole body of moral and spiritual laws, discovered and revealed by him, of which the doctrinal teachings form the conceptual formulation and practical exemplification. Similarly the Sangha or Assembly is the spiritual community of those who, following the Dharma, have attained the same levels of spiritual experience, or observe a common rule of monastic discipline, or simply the whole body of the faithful Going for Refuge to the Three Jewels – Enlightened and unenlightened, monastic and lay, real and nominal.

The Three Jewels are, therefore, of pivotal importance in Buddhism. Indeed, the Three Jewels are Buddhism.

Such being the case, it is astonishing that, although there have appeared in print numerous accounts of the life and teachings of the Buddha, both popular and scholarly, not a single work of importance has been dedicated to the Three Jewels as such, even though these constitute the triple object of the central act of the Buddhist life, from which all other acts derive their significance, and without reference to which Buddhism itself is unintelligible.

The present work is designed to remedy this deficiency. Originally written as a series of articles for the *Oriya Encyclopædia*, it subsequently reached a much wider audience when published in book form. May this new Windhorse edition be the means of opening the eyes of many more people to the multifaceted splendour of the Three Jewels.

Sangharakshita
Madhyamaloka
Birmingham
26 January 1998

PART I
THE BUDDHA

I
LIFE AND RECORDS

An account of Buddhism necessarily begins with the Buddha. Though he is not regarded by his followers either as prophet or incarnation of God, from him as the perfectly Enlightened and boundlessly compassionate teacher of all sentient beings proceeds the unique message of the Path to Enlightenment, and it is therefore his figure, either in its original human form or in various idealized hypostases, which dominates the entire history of Buddhism. His spirit, active not only during eighty years of earthly life, but now and for ever, permeates all subsequent developments of the Teaching, giving guidance in the midst of doubt and indecision, support in moments of crisis, and a fresh impetus in times of stagnation and decay. As the eagle in ancient legend draws strength from gazing at the sun, so both the individual Buddhist and the whole vast spiritual, cultural, and social movement we call Buddhism again and again derive inspiration from the recollection of the exemplary life of that most serene, dignified, wise, and loving of the sons of men. 'How pleasant is thy shadow, O Śramaṇa!'[2] cried Rāhula, the child of his humanity, and mankind itself might echo the exclamation.

Even if the Buddha is regarded merely from the historical point of view, his influence is unparalleled. Besides being the founder of Buddhism, a teaching that eventually won the allegiance of one-fourth of the human race, he reshaped Hinduism and profoundly modified Taoism, Confucianism, and Shintoism. Through Neoplatonism and Sufism respectively, Christianity and Islam received from him spiritual impulses which for centuries did much to temper the dogmatic harshness of these religions. Today the whole Western world is beginning to come under the influence of his teaching. Judged by these standards, Gautama the Buddha is the most conspicuous figure in the history of the human race.

But what do we actually know of his life? A handful of hard facts, a glittering mass of legends, and a body of abstruse disquisitions on his true nature, are practically all that remains. So far back in time does he stand, so high in attainment does he tower, that, as with some lofty mountain peak, the intervening depth of atmosphere, while enhancing the beauty of the spiritual colours of his career, would seem to blur the sharpness of the biographical outline. Yet despite the comparative paucity of biographical records as compared with doctrinal and disciplinary material in the Buddhist scriptures, we know considerably more about the Buddha than about either Jesus or Mohammed, while his historicity is indisputable.

Though no complete biography is found in the Tripiṭaka or 'Three Collections' of sacred traditions current in the early monastic communities, they do contain certain connected accounts of the Buddha's attainment of Enlightenment at Bodh Gaya and his *parinirvāṇa* at Kusinārā, as well as of the occurrences immediately preceding and succeeding these two great events. Incidents and anecdotes pertaining to the forty-five years in between are indeed not wanting, but the complete sequence is very difficult to determine with accuracy. Nevertheless, by having recourse to aesthetic and didactic, as well as to scientific, principles in the ordering of the vast material at their disposal, the ancient Buddhist writers were able to compile or compose five biographies of the Buddha.

Of these the mixed Sanskrit *Lalitavistara* or 'Extended [Account of the] Sports [of the Buddha]' – probably a Sarvāstivādin work which has undergone editing at Mahāyānist hands – is the most systematic. 'Its sonorous *gāthas*', says Dr Nalinaksha Dutt,

> are replete with bold imagery and its descriptive accounts in prose and poetry, though unrealistic, are calculated to produce faith and devotion for the Great Being.[3]

Even earlier is the *Mahāvastu* or 'Great Relation', a bulky and rather chaotic work, also in mixed Sanskrit, compiled from earlier materials probably 300 years after the *parinirvāṇa* and purporting to belong to the late Vinaya Piṭaka of the Lokottaravāda, a sub-school of the Mahāsāṃghika. Both these works depict the Buddha as an essentially transcendental being who, having gained perfection in previous lives, appears again among mankind out of compassion. Of more purely human interest, and even greater literary value, is the *Buddhacarita* or 'Acts of the Buddha' of Aśvaghoṣa, one of the supreme poets and dramatists of India, who flourished towards the end of the first century CE. Unfortunately the last fifteen chapters of this work, which was written in pure Sanskrit, have been lost in the original and are extant only in translation. A similar fate has befallen the whole of the *Abhiniṣkramaṇa Sūtra* or 'Discourse on the Great Renunciation', a work belonging to the Dharmaguptika – one of the eighteen early schools – and composed probably in mixed Sanskrit. Lastly there is the *Nidānakathā* or 'Connected Account' written in pure Pāli by way of introduction to the commentary on the *Jātaka* book and attributed to the eminent fifth-century Theravādin scholastic Buddhaghosa.

With the help of these biographies, as well as with that of the Pāli Tipiṭaka and such portions of its Sanskrit counterparts as are still extant, either in the original or in translations, it should be possible to give a sketch of the Buddha's career which would not be unacceptable even to the scientific historian. It will also be necessary to examine the significance of the legendary and mythological elements in which the traditional biographies abound, as well as to consider the metaphysical ponderings of the Buddhist doctors on the real nature of the Enlightened One. However, before dealing with his last life, in which he became the Buddha, we must direct our attention to those many former lives through which, as bodhisattva, the Great Being struggled towards his goal.

2

THE BODHISATTVA CAREER

Buddhism teaches rebirth. Not, indeed, in the sense of an unchanging immaterial entity (*ātman*) transmigrating from one physical body to another, but in a deeper, subtler sense. Just as, in the present existence, a preceding becomes the condition for a succeeding mental state, so in dependence on the last thought-moment of one life arises the first thought-moment of the next, the relation between the two lives, as between the two mental states, being one of causal continuity. The illustration appropriate to the case is not that of a man who changes from one set of clothes to another, the man himself remaining the while unchanged, but rather that of a flame which, in its advance, feeds upon successive bundles of fuel.

Popular expositions of the Dharma, including discourses attributed to the Buddha, do indeed sometimes make use of such terms as *ātman* and *punarjanman*;[4] but they are employed only by way of an accommodation to conventional modes of expression and are certainly not to be taken literally and made the starting point for a series of deductions about Buddhism. Advanced expositions make use of a more precise terminology. Instead of *ātman* they speak of *cittasantāna* or psyche-continuum (sometimes simply *santāna*), while *punarbhava*, 'again-becoming', replaces *punarjanman*, 'rebirth'.

To say that, at death, the psychical life ceases with that of the body is one extreme view; to say that any psychical element, such as an immortal soul, survives death unchanged is the other. Here, as elsewhere,

Buddhism follows the middle path, teaching that the 'being' of one life is neither exactly the same as, nor completely different from, the 'being' of another life. Though consenting to speak in terms of rebirth, it precludes misunderstanding by pointing out that there is no one who is reborn.

Unless this is clearly understood, we are likely to be misled by those who, on the basis of a very superficial acquaintance with Buddhism, maintain either that the Buddha contradicted himself by teaching the *anātman* doctrine *and* rebirth, or that he taught one of them but not the other. We may also be in danger of wondering whether the accounts of the Buddha's successive lives as a bodhisattva are not apocryphal!

This does not mean that we should fly to the opposite extreme and accept at face value the entire contents of the *Jātaka* books. As Rhys Davids has pointed out, only the verses of the Pāli *Jātaka* book belong to the Tipiṭaka. The 550 'birth-stories' are related in the commentary and are non-canonical.[5] The canonical birth-stories are found scattered throughout the *nikāyas* of the Sutta Piṭaka. In them the Buddha (or bodhisattva, as he then was) is depicted not as a bird or animal, as in the tales of the *Jātaka* commentary, but invariably as a famous sage or teacher of olden time – which is what we should have expected. The non-canonical tales of the *Jātaka* book commentary, which have delighted and inspired hundreds of generations of Buddhists, need not therefore be dismissed as worthless. Whether or not pertaining to the psyche-continuum of Gautama the Buddha himself, they do illustrate, often in an extremely moving manner, how the urge to Enlightenment is immanent in all forms and spheres of life, from the humblest to the highest, and manifests whenever a kind and intelligent action is performed.

Moreover, whatever our doubts about the authenticity of this or that particular tale may be, we should not forget that the Buddha did claim the power of remembering his previous existences as far back as he wished. This power, technically known as *pūrvanivāsānusmṛti*, 'recollection of previous abodes', constitutes one of the *abhijñās* or 'superknowledges' attained by him on the night of his Supreme Enlightenment.[6] It is attainable, albeit not to the same degree, by other beings also. In modern times – it is interesting to observe – attempts are being made, in various ways, to verify rebirth experimentally.[7] The attempt is of scientific rather than spiritual significance, as according to Buddhism the power of recollecting previous births, though developed in the higher stages of mental concentration, is not in itself a factor conducive to the attainment of Enlightenment.

All the *Jātakas*, canonical and non-canonical, in theory represent the Bodhisattva preparing himself for the attainment of Buddhahood by the practice of certain definite virtues afterwards called *pāramitās* or 'perfections'. In the earliest texts dealing with the subject, which are in Sanskrit, these are six in number: generosity (*dāna*), morality (*śīla*), patience (*kṣānti*), energy (*vīrya*), concentration (*samādhi*), and wisdom (*prajñā*). Four more were subsequently added to the list: skill in means (*upāya-kauśalya*), resolution (*praṇidhāna*), power (*bala*), and knowledge (*jñāna*). A later and less systematic list, apparently drawn up in imitation of the earlier one, is found in the Pāli literature of the Theravādins.

Each birth-story is designed to illustrate the Bodhisattva's practice of a particular perfection. In the well-known tale of the life in which he was Kṣāntivādin – 'Advocate of Patience' – for example, he preaches this virtue to a group of palace ladies, who in order to listen to the sermon leave their sleeping lord and master unattended. When the king wakes up and finds himself alone he is so enraged that he cuts off the preacher's limbs one by one, at the same time asking him, with each blow of the sword, whether he still advocates patience. Each time Kṣāntivādin replies that he does.[8] In the yet more popular tale of the king of the Śibis the Bodhisattva sacrifices an equivalent amount of his own flesh in order to ransom the life of a bird, thus practising the perfection of generosity.[9]

Most accounts divide not only Gautama's but any bodhisattva's career into three periods, each consisting of 10^{59} years. During the first he meets an Enlightened One (Buddhism teaches a plurality not only of lives but of inhabited worlds) and, inspired by his example, develops in his presence the will to Enlightenment (*bodhicitta*), resolves to attain Supreme Buddhahood for the good of all, and receives from him an assurance (*vyākaraṇa*) of final success. By the practice of the perfection of giving he attains the 'joyful stage' (*pramuditābhūmi*), the first of the ten stages of spiritual progress through which a bodhisattva must pass. In the second period he practises the perfections of morality, patience, energy, concentration, wisdom, skilful means, and resolution, thus traversing six more *bhūmis* and attaining the seventh. These are the 'immaculate' (*vimalā*), 'illuminating' (*prabhākarī*), 'blazing' (*arciṣmatī*), 'very difficult to conquer' (*sudurjayā*), 'face-to-face' (*abhimukhī*), 'far-going' (*dūraṅgamā*), and 'unshakeable' (*acalā*). In the third and last period he practises the perfections of power and knowledge, traverses the two remaining *bhūmis*, those of 'good thoughts' (*sadhūmatī*) and 'cloud of dharma' (*dharmameghā*), and becomes a Supreme Buddha for the benefit of all sentient beings.[10]

Though these and other similar details of the bodhisattva's career need not be understood too literally, or made articles of faith, once one has accepted the basic premise of 'again-becoming' they will seem neither fantastic nor improbable, and in outline at least should not be found difficult of acceptance. Buddhahood being in any case so hard of achievement it is but natural that the moral, intellectual, and spiritual equipment necessary to create a sound basis for its full realization and effective manifestation should take some time to accumulate and call for the energetic practice of virtues such as the *pāramitās* during not one but many lives.

In the case of 'our own' Buddha, as he is called, tradition tells us that countless ages ago, in another world-period, he was a Brahmin named Sumedha who, perplexed by the problems of existence and determined to find a way out, renounced his wealth and became a forest-dwelling hermit:

> At that time Dīpaṇkara Buddha appeared in the world, and attained enlightenment. It happened one day that Dīpaṇkara Buddha was to pass that way, and men were preparing the road for him. Sumedha asked and received permission to join in the work, and not only did he do so, but when Dīpaṇkara came Sumedha laid himself down in the mud, so that the Buddha might walk upon his body without soiling his feet. Then Dīpaṇkara's attention was aroused and he became aware of Sumedha's intention to become a Buddha, and, looking countless ages into the future, he saw that he would become a Buddha of the name of Gautama, and he prophesied accordingly. Thereupon Sumedha rejoiced, and, rejecting the immediate prospect of becoming an Arahant, as the disciple of Dīpaṇkara, 'Let me rather', he said, 'like Dīpaṇkara, having risen to the supreme knowledge of the truth, enable all men to enter the ship of truth, and thus I may bear them over the Sea of Existence, and then only let me realize Nibbāna myself.'[11]

After practising the *pāramitās* and traversing the *bhūmis* in the manner and for the period already described, the Great Being, now on the threshold of Supreme Buddhahood, is born in the divine realm called 'Contented' (*tuṣitadevaloka*), whence descending into the womb of Māyādevī and being born in the Lumbinī garden he not only appears for the last time in the world of men but becomes accessible to historical inquiry.

3
THE LIFE

According to traditions current in the days of Aśoka, who ascended the throne of Magadha in 274 BCE, the future Buddha was born at a spot midway between Kapilavastu and Devadaha. The dates given for the event in different Buddhist records vary considerably, but modern scholarship, working backwards from Aśoka, on the whole tends to place it at 563 BCE.[12] The Śākyas, the tribe or clan into which he was born, were a proud, independent people numbering perhaps 1,000,000 who inhabited nearly 2,000 square miles of territory at the foot of the central portion of the Himalayan Range, the northern part of the area now falling within the borders of Nepal and the southern forming part of India. Economically the Śākyas were a predominantly agricultural community; politically, like a number of other Northern Indian peoples in those days, they constituted a republic. Either at the time of the Buddha's birth or some later period his father Suddhodana, a well-to-do land-owning patrician, was serving a term as elected president of the public assembly at which was conducted the administrative and judicial business of the clan.

His mother dying shortly after his birth, Siddhārtha – 'The Accomplished One', as he was called – was reared by his maternal aunt Mahāprajāpatī, Suddhodana having taken both sisters to wife. By contemporary standards the education he received was a good one, consisting mainly of a grounding in the ethics and traditions of the clan, training in manly sports and knightly exercises, and instruction in such Brahminical lore as had by that time penetrated into Śākya territory. There is no evidence that he could read and write, and as in all 'primitive' communities such things as genealogies and ward-runes had to be learned by heart. The most significant event of his childhood was of the type loosely called mystical. Seated one day under a rose-apple tree, while his father was ploughing, he spontaneously experienced a state of purity, bliss, and peace so intense that years later, at a moment of supreme crisis, the recollection of it was able to exert a decisive influence upon the course of his career.[13] Meanwhile he grew up enjoying all the comforts and luxuries, pleasures and amusements, proper to his age and class. According to his own subsequent confession he was a youth delicate to the point of effeminacy, being sheltered with white umbrellas, wearing costly apparel, and making use of garlands, perfumes, and cosmetics. He spent each season at a different spot, Suddhodana having placed at his disposal three mansions, one for the summer, one for the winter, and one for the rains. At each mansion lotus pools were made for him wherein bloomed blue or white or red lotuses. The rainy season, which he spent surrounded by female musicians, was in particular given up to pleasure, and for four months at a stretch he did not stir out of doors.[14] Eventually, he was married, probably to more than one wife, and had a son. Yet despite so deep an enjoyment of worldly happiness he was not satisfied. The problem of existence tormented him. In particular he was obsessed by the pitiableness of the human predicament. Was there no way out for beings subjected to the miseries of birth, old age, disease, and death? Suddhodana, with whom he discussed the matter, was unable to answer his questions. He therefore resolved to follow the time-honoured practice of giving up family and possessions and going forth as a homeless wandering beggar in quest of Truth. In vain his father and foster-mother sought to dissuade him. One day, despite their tears and entreaties, he had his hair and beard cut off, donned the yellow robe, and went forth from the home into the homeless life.[15]

Journeying south-east from Kapilavastu and penetrating into the jungles of what is now the province of Bihar, he came across the hermitage of Ārāḍa Kāḷāma, a noted sage, who agreed to accept him as a pupil. What Siddhārtha learned from him we are not told, though from the fact that on the practical side his teaching culminated in the realization of a superconscious state termed *ākiñcanyāyatana* or 'sphere of no-thing-ness' we may infer that the sage's teaching was a theosophy of the Upanishadic type. Not satisfied with a merely theoretical grasp of the teaching, Siddhārtha applied himself to its realization, and in a short time succeeded in attaining whatever Ārāḍa Kāḷāma himself had attained. The noble-minded teacher, discerning his ability, thereupon invited him to share the leadership of the community. But feeling that beyond the sphere of 'no-thing-ness' there lay an even higher state, Siddhārtha refused to accept the generous offer and, instead, left Ārāḍa Kāḷāma's hermitage for that of Udraka Rāmaputra. With the help of this sage he attained an even higher state, that of *naivasaṃjñānāsaṃjñāyatana* or 'sphere of neither-perception-nor-non-perception'. But he felt that this too was not ultimate, and though his second teacher made the same offer as the first he resolved to continue his quest alone. Resuming his wanderings he passed through the kingdom of Magadha, and eventually reached a place called Uruvelā, on the outskirts of which he resolved to settle down. Thereafter followed six years of fearsome austerities. No ascetic, he subsequently declared, had outgone him in self-mortification, or was ever likely to outgo him. Nakedness, systematic reduction of food, exposure to extreme heat and extreme cold, retention of the breath until the body seemed on fire, together with every other repulsive and disgusting practice which the perverted ascetic imagination of the day had devised, did he compel himself to undergo in his search for Supreme Enlightenment.[16] Yet the great effort failed. Eventually, when he was almost dead from exhaustion, he suddenly recollected his childhood experience under the rose-apple tree. Was this the way to Supreme Enlightenment, he wondered? Convinced that it was, he abandoned his austerities and started taking proper nourishment again. Five fellow ascetics, who had gathered around him in the hope of sharing the Truth when he gained it, now left him in disgust, feeling that he had given up the search and returned to a life of ease. Undismayed by their defection, however, and with strength renewed, the Bodhisattva seated himself on a heap of grass beneath a *pīpal* tree with the firm resolve not to stir from his seat until Supreme Enlightenment had been attained. Night fell. During the first watch, having traversed the four *dhyānas* (see p. 110), he bent his purified and supple intelligence to the recollection of his former births, recalling in this way first hundreds, then thousands, and finally hundreds of thousands of previous existences. During the second watch, he saw with his superhuman divine vision beings vanishing from one state of existence and reappearing in another according to their good and bad deeds. During the third watch, having directed his mind to the destruction of the 'biases' (*āśravas*) towards sensuous experience (*kāma*), conditioned existence (*bhava*), and speculative opinions (*dṛṣṭi*), he realized the ineffable Truth and saw in its light the contingent and conditioned character of all mundane things whatsoever. In the resultant state of freedom and emancipation there arose the consciousness that rebirth had been destroyed and the higher life fulfilled.[17] When dawn came a Supreme Buddha sat beneath the tree.

The next few weeks, which were spent at the foot of various other trees in the neighbourhood, were devoted to the full assimilation of the Truth he had discovered. During this period he had three visitors, a haughty brahmin who came and asked the characteristics of a brahmin in the course of the second week, and two travelling merchants, Trapuṣa (Pāli Tapussa) and Bhallika, who turned aside from the road to pay their respects in the fourth week and who, after offering rice cake and honeycomb, took refuge in him and his Dharma, thus constituting themselves the first lay disciples.[18] In the fifth week, after initial hesitation on account of its extreme abstruseness, he decided out of compassion to make known to mankind the Truth he had penetrated.[19] His two former teachers having recently died, he determined to seek out his five fellow ascetics and preach first to them. Accordingly he set out on foot for the Deer Park near the ancient city of Benares, more than 100 miles away, where they were then residing. On the way he encountered a sceptical-minded Ājīvaka named Upaka to whom, in response to his enquiries, he declared that having gained knowledge by his personal exertions he had no teacher, being in fact himself the highest teacher, unequalled in the world of men and gods, the supremely Enlightened One. Unconvinced, Upaka walked on.[20] A week later the Buddha entered the Deer Park. Still thinking him a renegade from asceticism, the five ascetics agreed not to receive him with the customary remarks of respect. But so awe-inspiring was his demeanour that as he approached they involuntarily rose from their seats. It was only with much difficulty, however, that he succeeded in persuading them that, far from being a fallen ascetic, he was now the supremely Enlightened One. Convinced at last, they consented to listen to his teaching. He thereupon preached to them his first sermon, the *Dharmacakra-pravartana Sūtra* or 'Discourse Setting in Motion the Wheel of Truth', which according to the unanimous testimony of the most ancient records consisted in a brief statement of the Middle Way, the four noble truths, and the Noble Eightfold Path. One by one the five ascetics, beginning with Ajñāta Kauṇḍinya, realized the import of the teaching and received ordination from the Master, thus becoming the first *bhikṣus*.[21] Further conversions followed. Yaśa, a rich young man of Benares, became a monk after a midnight talk with the Buddha, while his parents became lay disciples. Before long, fifty-four of Yaśa's friends, all belonging to prominent merchant families of the city, had followed his example. Including the Buddha, there were now sixty-one *arhants*, or Enlightened beings, in the world.[22]

The Master then took a step of extraordinary and far-reaching importance. Addressing the sixty Enlightened disciples, he declared,

> I am delivered, monks, from all fetters, human and divine. You, monks, are also delivered from all fetters, human and divine. Go ye now, monks, and wander, for the gain of the many, for the welfare of the many, out of compassion for the world, for the good, for the gain, and for the happiness of gods and men. Let not two of you go the same way. Preach, monks, the Dharma which is lovely in the beginning, lovely in the middle, lovely at the end, in the spirit and in the letter; proclaim a consummate, perfect, and pure life of holiness. There are beings whose mental eyes are covered by scarcely any dust, but if the Dharma is not preached to them, they cannot attain salvation.[23]

He himself, he said, would go to preach at Uruvelā. Thirty pleasure-seeking young men whom he met on the way were converted to his teaching and received into the Order.[24] Uruvelā was at that time an important centre of the Jaṭilas, or fire-worshipping ascetics, 1,000 of whom resided in the area under the leadership of the three Kāśyapa brothers. Although the Buddha stayed for a considerable time with Uruvelā Kāśyapa, the eldest brother, for whose benefit he performed extraordinary feats of supernormal power, the stubborn fire-worshipper could not be converted. Despite the wonders he saw, he persisted in thinking himself holier than the Buddha. Eventually the Buddha had to tell him bluntly that he was neither holy nor on the path to holiness. Converted at last, Uruvelā Kāśyapa, together with his 500 followers, was received into the Order. Nāḍi Kāśyapa with 300 adherents, and Gayā Kāśyapa with 200, followed suit. Leading the thousand ex-fire-worshippers to Gayā Head, a neighbouring promontory, the Buddha preached to them one of the most famous and magnificent of all his discourses, the *Āditta-pariyāya Sutta* or 'Fire Sermon'.[25] At Rājagṛha, the capital of the kingdom of Magadha, whither he proceeded with his retinue of new followers, doubt arose in the minds of King Bimbisāra and the brahmins and householders of Magadha as to whether Uruvelā Kāśyapa had converted the Buddha or the Buddha Uruvelā Kāśyapa. Apprised of the facts of the case, they too took refuge in the Buddha, the Dharma, and the Sangha. King Bimbisāra, in fact, invited the Buddha and his disciples to lunch, after which he gifted to them the Veḷuvana or 'Bamboo Grove', a royal park situated outside the city gates. This was the first landed property to be donated to the Order.[26] Meanwhile Aśvajit, one of the original five ascetics, had converted Śāriputra, a follower of Sañjaya Belaṭṭhiputra, who had in turn converted his friend Maudgalyāyana. Together with 250 companions, all followers of the same teacher, they came to the Bamboo Grove for ordination. As he saw them coming from afar the Buddha predicted that the two friends would be his chief pair of disciples.[27] By this time so many converts had joined the Sangha that people started raising objections, saying that the Buddha had made parents childless, and wives to become widows, and that he was causing the destruction of families. They even made a gibing popular song about it. Telling the monks that the disturbance would die down after seven days, the Buddha gave them a stanza to chant in reply. Eventually all befell as he had predicted, and the circle of his adherents continued to expand.[28]

At this point the story of the Buddha's life, which had hitherto marched with epic sublimity from climax to climax, starts breaking up into incidents and episodes the chronological order of which it is impossible to determine. Though it is not difficult, indeed, to arrange the more important events chronicled in the most ancient records in a quite plausible sequence, the result would pertain not so much to the life as to the legend of the Master. Only as we approach the very end of his ministry do we find ourselves, chronologically speaking, on as firm ground as at its beginning. Yet however unsatisfactory from the narrative point of view the material at our disposal may be, the largely unconnected anecdotes and episodes of which it consists convey a definite unity of impression. Even making due allowance for pious exaggeration, in depth and extent of influence the Buddha was evidently, during his own lifetime, the most successful propagandist the world has ever seen, and the picture which jigsaw-puzzle-wise emerges is that of a vigorous spiritual movement in process of constant expansion, adaptation, and consolidation. If the events up to and immediately after the Enlightenment form as it were a single narrative line climbing graph-like from peak to peak of achievement, those of the remaining forty-five years suggest a number of lines radiating from a common centre of force. Though prose or verse narrative may suffice for the first, only painting, with its power of depicting a number of episodes simultaneously, could do justice to the second. Geographically, the area of the Buddha's personal influence in north-eastern India formed a rough triangle based upon Campā in the east and Kauśāmbī in the west, with Kapilavastu as the apex. Politically it included the kingdoms of Kosala, Magadha, and Aṅga, in each of whose capitals the Order had important foundations, and republics such as those of the Śākyas, the Kālāmas, the Mallas, and the Licchavis. In terms of present-day political geography the area covered comprises, approximately, distances 450 miles from east to west, by over 200 from north to south; from west of Allahabad in the Uttar Pradesh, to east of Bhagalpur in Bihar. Within this triangle, perhaps 50,000 square miles in extent, the social and cultural – to say nothing of the spiritual – influence of the Buddha was ubiquitous. Bimbisāra and Prasenajit, the rulers of Magadha and Kosala respectively, were his adherents, as were most of the leading republican families. Members of the wealthy trading class, like Anāthapiṇḍada and Viśākhā, both of whom built hostelries for the Order at Śrāvastī, declared themselves his followers and contributed lavishly to the cause.[29] Cultured brahmins, whether ritualists or free-thinkers, were in regular communication with him, and though not always converted to the Teaching were evidently aware of its prestige and popularity.[30] On his travels, which lasted for nine months of the year, the Buddha came in close personal contact not only with wandering ascetics of various types but also with peasants, artisans, shopkeepers, and robbers, with young and old, men and women, rich and poor, learned and ignorant. Men of all castes, from the lordly *kṣatriya* to the humble *śūdra*, poured into the Sangha, there to lose their separate designations, being thereafter reckoned simply 'monks who are sons of the Śākyan' (*śākyaputra-*

śramaṇas). So extraordinary was the Master's influence, that rival teachers, at a loss to account for his success, alleged that he charmed and attracted people by means of spells.[31]

In a sense they were right. The fascination of the Buddha's personality was unequalled. Diehard adherents of this or that sectarian teacher, after seeing him only once, behaved as if bewitched. Though sublime in his dignity, he was eminently approachable, combining aristocratic aloofness and democratic cordiality, freedom and reserve. So awe-inspiring was his presence that kings grew nervous as they approached, yet so compassionate that the broken-hearted fled to him for refuge as though by instinct. Fearlessness, equanimity, self-confidence, and energy were among his most outstanding characteristics. Whether expounding the Teaching to the dull-witted, or dealing with recalcitrant followers, his patience was unfailing. Practical difficulties connected with the organization and administration of the Sangha he met in a manner which suggested that Enlightenment did not exclude common sense. Moreover, as numerous episodes attest, he was not without a sense of humour. Yet despite these and many other human qualities he was at the same time so very much more than human that even his closest and most advanced disciples felt that in his true nature he transcended their understanding. Like the great ocean, the Tathāgata was unfathomable.

Fortunately the relative chronology of what, historically speaking, are the three most outstanding episodes of the Master's public career is clear from internal evidence, and with these we must bridge the gap between the end of the beginning of his ministry and the beginning of the end. The first centres on his return to Kapilavastu. Though at first displeased to see him begging – as was his custom – from door to door, Suddhodana eventually gave ear to his son's teaching and became a convert.[32] Ānanda and Devadatta, both cousins of the Buddha, joined the Order, as did a number of other young Śākyans.[33] Rāhula, sent by his mother to claim his inheritance, received instead of any mundane patrimony the gift of the Dharma, being admitted into the fellowship as a novice by Śāriputra and Maudgalyāyana. Several of the Buddha's admonitions to Rāhula survive in the Scriptures.[34] The scene of the second episode, which took place more than twenty years later, is the Licchavi capital Vaiśālī. Apparently on a recent visit to Kapilavastu the Buddha had refused the request of Mahāprajāpatī, his foster-mother, that women be allowed to go forth into the homeless life. She therefore cut off her hair, donned the saffron-coloured robes, and as though to present him with a *fait accompli* trudged with a number of other Śākyan women to Vaiśālī. But for all her tears the Buddha refused to admit her to the Order. Only on the intercession of Ānanda, who by that time had become his personal attendant, did he finally relent.[35] It is with reference to this episode that writers on Buddhism represent the Buddha as declaring that women having been admitted to the Order it would last in its integrity for 500 years instead of for 1,000. A closer examination of the text does not bear out this interpretation. What the Buddha in effect said was that the eight special conditions he had imposed upon Mahāprajāpatī were designed to prevent such a deterioration, which otherwise in the nature of things was bound to take place. Whatever lowering of standards might subsequently have occurred in the Sangha, there is no evidence whatever to suggest that it was in any way connected with the presence in it of women. The last episode, or rather series of episodes, took place in and around Rājagṛha in the closing decades of the Buddha's earthly life. Devadatta, who had already instigated Ajātaśatru to seize the throne of Magadha from his father Bimbisāra, suggested that the Buddha, being old, should make over the leadership of the Sangha to him and live in retirement. This suggestion the Buddha sternly rejected. Making use of his influence with Ajātaśatru, Devadatta thereupon plotted to kill the Master. First he hired assassins to lie in wait for him, then himself rolled down upon him a huge boulder, a splinter from which wounded him in the foot, and finally released against him a mad elephant. All these attempts miscarried. Having failed either to assume leadership of the Sangha or to remove the Buddha, Devadatta tried to create a schism and win over at least a section of the Order to his own side. But proving unsuccessful in this attempt also, he eventually died in despair. After his death the Buddha declared that Devadatta had come to grief because of evil desires and evil friends, and by his having come to a stop on the Way because he had attained the lower psychic powers.[36]

During the last six months of his life the Buddha sojourned at fourteen different places, beginning with the Gṛdhrakūṭa or 'Vulture's Peak' at Rājagṛha, and ending with the Sāl Grove of the Mallas at Kusinārā, where he attained *parinirvāṇa*. Aware that it was his last tour among his disciples, he missed no opportunity of instructing and admonishing them. At eleven out of the fourteen places he delivered a 'comprehensive religious discourse' which, since it occurs so many times, and under such circumstances, may be regarded as constituting the essence of his teaching. 'Such and such is right conduct (*śīla*),' the texts in brief report him as saying,

> ... such and such is meditation (*samādhi*), such and such is wisdom (*prajñā*). Great becomes the fruit, great the advantage of meditation, when it is set round with upright conduct. Great becomes the fruit, great the advantage of wisdom when it is set round with meditation. The mind set round with wisdom is set quite free from the biases (*āśravas*), that is to say, from the bias towards sensuous experience (*kāma*), towards conditioned existence (*bhava*), towards speculative opinions (*dṛṣṭi*), and towards ignorance (*avidyā*).[37]

Before the Buddha left Rājagṛha, Ajātaśatru, who was planning the destruction of the Vajjians, sent his minister to enquire whether the attempt would be successful. Recalling the seven conditions of welfare he had once taught them, the Master declared that so long as these conditions were observed by the Vajjians they would not decline but prosper. After the minister's departure he called together all the *bhikṣus* in the neighbourhood and taught them 'seven times seven conditions of welfare, less one', observing which the Sangha might be expected not to decline but to grow.[38] During the last rainy season retreat, which he spent at Beluva, a village near Vaiśālī, the Master fell ill; but thinking it would not be proper to pass away without addressing the disciples and taking leave of the Order he suppressed the sickness by sheer force of will and carried on. Shortly afterwards Ānanda hinted at the desirability of some final instructions regarding the Order. This suggestion the Buddha flatly repudiated.[39] It was enough that he had taught the Dharma; he did not imagine that he led the Sangha or that it was dependent on him. Let Ānanda and the rest be lamps unto themselves, refuges unto themselves; let them take the Dharma as a lamp, the Dharma as a refuge.[40] Such true disciples, practising mindfulness with regard to body, sensations, moods, and ideas could, either then or after he was dead, attain the very topmost height. But they should be willing to learn! At Vaiśālī, again calling the monks together, he exhorted them, in language reminiscent of the charge to the first sixty *arhants*, to make themselves masters of the truths he had taught, to practise them, meditate upon them, and spread them abroad,

> in order that pure religion may last long and be perpetuated, in order that it may continue to be for the good and happiness of the great multitudes, out of pity for the world, to the good and the gain and the weal of gods and men![41]

Bidding farewell to the pleasant groves and shrines of Vaiśālī, the Buddha, accompanied by a great number of monks, walked by easy stages to Pāvā, taking between two and three months to complete the journey and preaching as he went.

At Pāvā, at the hands of Cunda the metal-worker, he partook of his last meal, presumably in the forenoon. Unfortunately, some of the mushrooms with which he was served were poisonous, and the meal brought on a severe attack of dysentery. Nevertheless the Buddha pressed on to Kusinārā, though twice on the way he felt tired and had to rest. But physical debility did not prevent him from preaching. Pukkusa, a young Mallian, who had stepped aside from the road after seeing the Buddha resting at the foot of a tree, was converted as the result of a short discussion, and sending home for a pair of robes of cloth-of-gold robed the Buddha in one of them and Ānanda in the other. The Master also found time to think of Cunda the metal-worker, warning Ānanda that he was not to be allowed to suffer remorse or blame himself on account of the last meal.[42] Eventually the party reached the Sāl Grove of the Mallas at Kusinārā. Here, between two *sāl* trees, with its head to the north, there stood a stone couch. On this the Buddha lay down. As he did so untimely blossoms rained down upon him from the branches above. Ānanda, in his devotion, took this for an act of worship, and was delighted. But even at such a moment the Buddha would not tolerate sentimentality, and firmly reminded him that true worship of the Tathāgata consisted in following his teaching. Ānanda then enquired what they were to do with his remains. But more firmly and earnestly still the Master exhorted him that the monks should devote themselves to their own spiritual growth, leaving to the lay followers the honouring of his dead body. Despite such exhortations, however, Ānanda was so moved at the thought of the imminent departure of his beloved master that he went aside and wept, and had to be sent for by the Buddha who, after comforting him, predicted his speedy Enlightenment and praised him to the assembled brethren. He was then dispatched to inform the Mallas of Kusinārā that the *parinirvāṇa* would take place during the third watch of the night. The first watch was accordingly taken up with the visits of these republican folk, who came in large numbers to pay their last respects. In order to save time Ānanda introduced them family by family. During the second watch came Subhadra, a wandering ascetic, who, having heard that the Buddha was about to pass away, pleaded for an interview. Ānanda was unwilling that the Tathāgata should be troubled at such a time; but overhearing their conversation the Buddha ordered the man to be admitted. After a short discussion, in the course of which the Master roundly declared that true saints were found only where the Āryan Eightfold Path was found, and nowhere else, he too was converted and received into the Order. The third watch of the night was devoted to the brethren. After telling Ānanda that, after his death, they were to regard the Dharma and the Vinaya as their teacher, he urged them to declare whatever doubt or misgiving they had in their mind as to the Buddha, or the Dharma, or the Sangha, or the Path, or the Method. But none had any doubt, and the Buddha declared that even the most backward of them was assured of Enlightenment.[43] He then addressed them and said,

> Behold now, brethren, I exhort you, saying: 'Impermanent are all component things. With mindfulness strive on.'[44]

These were his last words.

4
THE LEGENDS

Modern writers on Buddhism in general believe that the traditional accounts of the Buddha's life consist of a substratum of historical fact upon which have been superimposed successive layers of 'legendary' material, and that their task is to separate the one from the other – it being assumed as self-evident that 'legendary' is synonymous with 'fictitious'. In adopting this procedure they are only partly correct. Though we have followed them to the extent of giving, in our short sketch of the Buddha's career, only such facts as are generally allowed to have survived the shakings of their sieve, this concession has been made only as a matter of convenience, not on principle. Far from being all of one kind, those elements in the traditional biographies which are dismissed as legendary are on the contrary found, on analysis, to comprise at least three distinct categories of material. To the first category belong episodes which are legendary in the common acceptation of the term, that is, which though represented as historical did not really take place; to the second, episodes which are treated as untrue because they violate certain scientific notions of what is possible and what impossible; to the third, those which, though presented in the form of external, historical events, in fact symbolize spiritual truths and experiences. A few examples of each of these categories, all of which are capable of subdivision, will help to make the distinction perfectly clear and demonstrate that the 'life' of the Buddha ought not always to be so sharply divided from the 'legend' as the learned have commonly supposed.

To the first category belong legends, or legendary elements, which are traceable to simple exaggeration, to interested invention, or to misattribution. Of these the first is the most innocent and easily detectable. In contrast to the Greek, the classical Indian mind was constitutionally prone to extravagance and exaggeration, especially when inflamed by religious devotion. This gave rise, for example, in the case of Buddhism, to a pronounced tendency to augmentation of the number of persons in attendance on the Buddha or converted as a result of his preaching. Thus if 1,250 monks are mentioned by an earlier text one of later date, dealing with the same episode, is sure to increase the number to at least 12,500. So much a habit does this multiplication of zeros become among the redactors of the canonical literature that in one of the 'Perfection of Wisdom' texts the Lord is represented as taking by way of example

> a mother who has many children, – five, or ten, or twenty, or thirty, or forty, or fifty, or one hundred, or one thousand.[45]

This tendency to numerical exaggeration, as well as to prolixity and discursiveness of all kinds, permeates the vast bulk of Buddhist canonical literature to so great an extent that the student may be pardoned for mistaking it for a characteristic of Buddhism itself. That this is by no means the case is demonstrated by the history of Buddhism in China, where the Chan or Dhyāna school in particular, reacting not against Indian Buddhism so much as against distinctively Indian modes of expression, supplies the corrective by creating, out of indigenous resources, a terser and more compact form of expression for the same spiritual truths.

As easily detected, though less innocent and less amenable to correction, are the legends attributable to interested invention. The 'interest' is often a nationalistic one. To this subdivision may be assigned those accounts, made so much of by certain modern writers belonging to the countries concerned, of the Buddha's personal visits to Sri Lanka and Burma.[46] For these visits there is not a shred of evidence. Yet to such an extent can scholarship be vitiated by national prejudice that even writers of repute insist on according these pious fictions the status of indubitable historic facts. Were they presented simply as an expression of an understandable wish for a closer link with the person of the

Buddha than that which history vouchsafes, little objection to these legends could be raised: they have their parallels in the belief that Christ visited Britain and in the pure Arabian descent alleged by some Indian Muslims. But when in all seriousness they are made the basis for a claim to spiritual pre-eminence in the Buddhist world they cannot be allowed to pass uncontradicted.

By misattribution, the third and last subdivision of the first category, is meant the relating about the Buddha of an incident which actually happened not to him but to some other person, usually a disciple. One of the most striking examples of this type of 'legend' is found in the Vinaya Piṭaka's account of how Yaśa, one of the earliest converts (see p. 23), abandoned home one night after seeing his dancing girls asleep in various unseemly and disgusting attitudes. This story the *Nidānakathā* relates of the future Buddha![47] It is also referred to in the *Mahāvastu*,[48] besides being recounted at length in Aśvaghoṣa's *Buddhacarita*,[49] where it forms one of the most admired passages in that noble poem. Some may, of course, argue that the episode was transferred from the Master's life to the disciple's. But against this must be weighed the fact that what appear to be the oldest and most authentic accounts of the Bodhisattva's renunciation make no mention of it whatever.[50]

The second category of legendary material includes all incidents in which the Buddha is represented as exercising supernormal powers, such as clairvoyance, clairaudience, and levitation, or as holding converse with non-human beings, *devas, brahmās, māras*, etc. Brought up as most of them were under the overt or covert influence of eighteenth-century rationalistic and nineteenth-century materialistic and agnostic modes of thought, the older generation of orientalists naturally discarded these incidents as pure invention, assuming it to be self-evident that in a universe governed by natural law they could not have taken place. Their modern counterparts are usually not so rash. Scientific thinking is now much less biased towards materialism than it was, and few scientists would be prepared to dogmatize on the limits of the possible. Some, indeed, are seriously investigating, by means of standard procedures, a variety of phenomena now classified under the heading of ESP. Rhine's experiments in this field are well known.[51] Unfortunately, however, due partly to the fact that in many cases the works of the older orientalists are still in circulation, and partly to the operation of a sort of cultural time-lag, whereby at least half a century elapses before an idea or discovery gets into general circulation, works on the Buddha and Buddhism continue to reflect modes of thought that have been definitely discredited. Even as late as 1948 there could appear a scholarly compilation from the Pāli canon that deliberately excises all references to the 'supernatural'.[52] This is not to say that tales of the Cock Lane Ghost[53] variety do not appear in Buddhist literature, or that every miracle and marvel reported in the Tripiṭaka is deserving of unlimited credence. One must follow a middle path between credulity and scepticism. Besides, it must not be forgotten that unlike Christianity Buddhism does not regard the 'miracles' of its founder as establishing either the truth of his teaching or the uniqueness of his personal spiritual attainments. Psychic powers such as those exhibited by the Buddha[54] are natural, not supernatural, and can be developed by anyone willing to practise the appropriate exercises. But they do not lead to liberation and Enlightenment. In the same way, *devas* and *brahmās*, however superior to humanity they may be, still belong to the natural world, and are subject to its laws. Though the showing of respect to them is traditional in most Buddhist lands, it is well understood that this practice does not conduce to the attainment of the ultimate goal of the Teaching. Once all these points are borne in mind it should not be difficult for us to adopt a more truly scientific attitude towards this category of 'legendary' material, not only so far as the traditional lives of the Buddha are concerned, but in regard to Buddhist literature generally. Even though unable to accept at their face value all 'legendary' episodes of this type, we are no longer justified in rejecting even the most absurd of them on *a priori* grounds. The Buddha's greatness had, perhaps, dimensions of which modern knowledge has as yet taken no cognizance.

True as this is of the second, it is still more true of the third and last category, consisting of those legends the significance of which is really not historical at all, but psychological and spiritual. Far from being either devotional effusions or flights of poetic fancy these legends in fact make up a symbolical biography of the Buddha no less important than the historical narrative with which, in the traditional biographies, it is interwoven, and upon the main episodes of which it constitutes a spiritual-cum-metaphysical commentary of the highest value. To disengage the symbolical from the historical elements is not always easy, however. The compilers of the traditional biographies do not seem to have made so absolute a distinction between fact and symbol as people do now, nor to have made it with such rigorous consistency, so that although some episodes are clearly historical, and some symbolical, others would seem capable of being not only either but both. But with such differences as these we are not now concerned. A systematic study of the symbolical biography of the Buddha, though one of the most fruitful works that could be undertaken, would require excursuses into Buddhist thought and spiritual practice, as well as into modern psychology, more extensive than are possible here. All we propose to do, therefore, is to cite a few representative episodes which, even if not self-evidently symbolical, are at least sufficiently simple to require the minimum of interpretation to establish our point.

The story of the four sights, of how Siddhārtha, issuing from his father's mansion, encountered for the first time an old man, a sick man, a corpse, and a monk, is recounted by all the traditional biographies[55] and occurs in most modern works. But though no episode is better known than this, few are less likely to be factually true. Its authenticity has indeed often been challenged, usually on the grounds of inherent improbability. How, it is asked, would it have been possible to keep a young man as ignorant of life as the story suggests? Is it really credible that until his twenty-ninth year Siddhārtha knew nothing of old age, disease, and death? Could he conceivably have never till then set eyes on a wandering mendicant, when saffron robes and begging-bowls were to be encountered at every street corner? These objections are unanswerable, and from the historical life of the Buddha the episode must certainly be deleted. But this does not mean it should be altogether discarded, or relegated to literary limbo along with Ossian and the Decretals of Constantine.[56] From a passage in the *Aṅguttara Nikāya*, which evidently constitutes the psychological basis of the story of the four sights, we can see that this episode belongs not to the historical but to the symbolical biography of the Buddha.

> Then, O monks, did I … think thus, 'an ignorant, ordinary person, who is himself subject to old age, not beyond the sphere of old age, on seeing an old man is troubled, ashamed and disgusted, extending the thought to himself. I too am subject to old age, not beyond the sphere of old age, and should I, who am subject to old age, not beyond the sphere of old age, on seeing an old man be troubled, ashamed, and disgusted?' This seemed to me not fitting.

> As thus I reflected on it, all the elation [*mada*, lit. 'intoxication'] in youth utterly disappeared.[57]

The same is then repeated of sickness and death. As E. J. Thomas pertinently remarks,

> It is easy to see how the above account can have been developed into the story of his actually meeting these objects, but not how, if the story is a real biographical event, it can have been converted into this abstract form.[58]

With the *Aṅguttara Nikāya* account before us, it becomes obvious that the compilers of the traditional biographies, or the oral sources on which they drew, after objectifying the psychological experience projected it into the world of external events in the vivid and colourful form of the well-known episode. Whether this was done of deliberate intent, for pedagogical reasons, or whether the minds of some early Buddhists were so constituted as to apprehend the spiritual truth of the Buddha's life more easily in concrete images and pictures than in psychological abstractions, it is perhaps fruitless to inquire. But that such transpositions did occur the present instance demonstrates.

Another well-known episode which is in reality the objectification of a psychological experience is that which took place immediately before the Great Enlightenment, when Māra launched against the tranquil figure beneath the bodhi tree his army of lusts, hatreds, and fears. The legends give long and vivid descriptions of this tremendous attack. Demoniacal figures, some monstrously deformed, swirl round the Bodhisattva with frightful noises in a vain attempt to disturb his meditation by swinging clubs, hurling rocks and uprooted trees, shooting arrows, and spitting flame.[59] A detonation of truth in the Bodhisattva's unconscious mind had clearly exploded thousands of emotional ideas and impulses. This does not mean, of course, that he might not have actually 'seen' the fragments of his own exploded unconscious spread out before him in the form of menacing or alluring shapes. All that we are not to imagine, as generations of less instructed Buddhists have perhaps imagined, is that Māra and his host appeared on the scene in gross material bodies. Vividly as they can at times be perceived, the basic reality of such externalized mental phenomena is psychological.

Also connected with the period of the Enlightenment, though its symbolism is more recondite, is the Mucalinda episode. During the third week after the Great Awakening, relate the traditional biographies, there came a great storm. For seven days and seven nights it rained. In order to protect the Buddha from the downpour, Mucalinda, the serpent king, wrapped his coils seven times round him and sheltered him with his hood. When the storm had subsided he appeared before the Buddha in the form of a beautiful sixteen-year-old youth and respectfully saluted him.[60] Some, of course, give a purely naturalistic explanation of this episode, regarding it as an instance of that remarkable power over animals which holy men often possess. But it must not be forgotten that the legends relating to the weeks (four in earlier, seven in the later accounts) spent by the Buddha in the neighbourhood of the bodhi tree immediately after the Enlightenment are concerned mainly with his spiritual experiences. In any case the appearance of the *nāga* king, an obviously symbolical motif, should put us on our guard against naturalistic explanations. The *nāgas* inhabit the depths of the ocean, where they dwell in marvellous palaces in which are heaps of priceless jewels and other treasures. They represent the upsurging energies of the unconscious, not in their negative destructive aspect (symbolized by Māra and his host) but in the positive creative aspect which makes available to the conscious mind treasures of beauty, insight, and understanding it did not dream it possessed. They are the forces of artistic and religious inspiration in general. Their king, Mucalinda, is the *kuṇḍalinī* or 'coiled-up' power, the latent spiritual energy which, according to a well-known system of yoga, resides in the lowest of the seven chakras or psychic centres in the human body. His wrapping himself seven times round the Buddha, laying one coil upon another (as frequently depicted in art), indicates the ascent of this energy through all these centres. The storm (which lasts for *seven* days) is the shower of bliss that descends into every part of the body as soon as the *kuṇḍalinī* reaches the topmost chakra. As for the beautiful youthful form finally assumed by Mucalinda, it represents the purely spiritual body into which the Buddha's exalted realization has transmuted the energies of his human personality, while the serpent king's bowing before him signifies the perfect serviceability of that body as the instrument of the Enlightened mind. All the symbols occurring in this episode are met with again and again in Buddhist literature, especially in Tantric works, one of the characteristics of which is to make systematic use of symbolism in connection with spiritual exercises and experiences. Further research will probably establish the fact that not only the Mucalinda episode but other incidents taking place immediately after the *sambodhi* represent not historic events but a symbolical unfolding of different aspects of the Buddha's Enlightenment.

For a simple example of a 'legendary' episode with a metaphysical rather than a psychological significance we shall have to go back to the Buddha's birth. In the traditional biographies symbolism here reigns supreme. Among other marvels it is related how the Bodhisattva, as soon as he was born, took seven steps, at each of which a lotus sprang up to support his foot.[61] Much could be said, of course, on the significance of the number of steps taken. At the moment, however, we are concerned with the lotuses. These beautiful flowers, it is well known, bloom with petals unstained by the mud and water out of which they grow. Hence in Buddhist literature (as at *Sutta-Nipāta* 71), and in Indian religious works generally, the lotus represents the state of living 'in the world, but not of it'. This being so, it is understandable that it should have been adopted as a symbol of their doctrine by those who, from an early period, perhaps even during the Buddha's own lifetime, regarded him not as a human but as a purely transcendental being who underwent the ordinary experiences of life in appearance only. Lotuses spring up as he takes his first seven steps to prevent him making direct contact with the earth, thus emphasizing that he was of transcendental origin from the very outset of his earthly career, being in truth not the product of this world but the irruption into it of transcendental reality in the form of an eternally enlightened personality.

5
PHILOSOPHICAL INTERPRETATIONS

To the extent that it keeps in touch with living experience Buddhist thought is always in the making. In the course of its development it resembles a great river which, having taken its rise high in the mountains, winds through thousands of miles of field, forest, and desert, receiving hundreds of tributaries on the way, until at last it comes to the end of its long journey and plunges into the sea. None of the doctrines of Buddhism, perhaps, is so novel that it is not foreshadowed, however faintly, in earlier teachings, and none so antiquated as to be incapable of further development. These remarks apply with particular force to our present subject. Nearly a thousand years after the *parinirvāṇa* the efforts of generations of saints and sages to fathom the Master's true nature culminated in the doctrine of the *trikāya* or 'three bodies' of the Buddha. Though other Indian schools of major importance also contributed to its development,[62] this doctrine was given full and definitive expression by the Yogācārins, or 'Practitioners of Yoga'. As elaborated by them, it is one of the finest flowers of Buddhist thought, combining profound philosophical meaning with the richest spiritual and artistic significance, and unless it is properly understood the *raison d'être* of much that is most precious in the tradition is likely to remain obscure. This does not mean that we cannot understand the *trikāya* doctrine without tracing it through the successive phases of its development, or following up every one of its numerous ramifications. What is essential is a grasp of the basic principle of the doctrine; once this is grasped the rest will follow.

Though comparatively simple, the principle on which the *trikāya* doctrine is based is perhaps best made clear with the help of an illustration. Three people are looking at a flower. One is a child, one a botanist, and one a poet. All that the child sees is an object of a certain shape with a pleasing bright colour. The botanist, while not failing to observe its shape and colour, sees that the flower belongs to a particular species, thrives best at a certain time, place, etc. The poet, though his eyes are as keen as the child's, and though he knows as much about botany as the botanist, is not so preoccupied with the colour of the flower or the formation of its leaves and petals. He sees that the flower is alive, joyously alive, even as he is alive, and that there works through the frail perfection of its leaves and blossoms the same spirit of life whose creative impulse he feels pulsing in the depths of his own being. Despite their great differences of vision, however, the child, the botanist, and the poet still all see the same flower, not three different flowers. The child's seeing is mere visual perception. This the botanist also has; but as he looks at the flower there comes into operation a faculty higher than perception – understanding – which enables him to see deeper into the reality of the flower than the child could. The poet has both perception and understanding, but when *he* looks at the flower there comes into operation a faculty higher than either, intuition, which enables him to see deepest of all, and not only to see but to feel, and even to become one with what he sees and feels.

In the same way, an ordinary person, a yogi, and one possessing *prajñā* or wisdom, look at the Buddha. The first, beholding either with his physical eyes (if a contemporary) or with his earthbound intelligence (if he merely hears or reads about the Buddha), perceives or forms the idea of a human, historical person subject – like himself – to the laws of time, space, and causation. He sees a Buddha whose existence is separated from his own by hundreds or thousands of years or miles, a Buddha who is born, grows old, and dies. In other words he sees the *nirmāṇakāya*, the first of the three bodies of the Enlightened One. Some canonical texts designate the body as the *rūpakāya*, or 'form body'; but when the Yogācārins systematized the *trikāya* doctrine they popularized the term *nirmāṇakāya*, 'created body' or 'body of transformation', found in other texts, probably because it reflected the widely current view that what appeared to be the Buddha's physical body was in reality a purely spiritual presence created by absolute compassion and projected into the world for the benefit of all sentient beings. In the present context it makes no difference which term is used, since even those holding transcendentalist views admitted that the Buddha's human body was perceived *as though* it was in all respects material. Most people, including even Buddhists, make use only of their physical senses and their earthbound intelligence. It is but natural, therefore, that the Buddha's *nirmāṇakāya* should be more widely known and better understood than his other bodies.

When the yogi looks at the Buddha it is with attention withdrawn from the senses, so that sense impressions are stopped and the external world no longer perceived. Unwholesome emotions such as greed, hatred, anxiety, ennui, and perplexity have been suppressed and the grosser forms of mental activity suspended, so that equanimity and concentration alone are present. In other words, the yogi sees not in the ordinary waking state but in the superconscious state of *samādhi*. Where the ordinary person sees the *nirmāṇakāya*, therefore, he sees the *sambhogakāya*, the second of the three bodies of the Enlightened One. According to one explanation the *sambhogakāya*, or 'body of mutual enjoyment', is so called because the vision of it is enjoyed by the bodhisattvas, those highly advanced beings who in both this world and other higher realms of existence practise the six or ten perfections, including *dhyāna-pāramitā*, the perfection of concentration. According to another it is the body 'enjoyed' by the Buddha himself as a result of all the good deeds he had performed and the knowledge he had accumulated during his countless lives as a bodhisattva.[63] These explanations do not exclude each other. Inasmuch as a literal translation fails to convey the full meaning of the term, *sambhogakāya* is also rendered as 'body of bliss' or 'glorious body'. The latter rendering is perhaps the best. The yogi, in his meditation, has transcended time and space, at least in the form that they are known to us, for he has transcended the mind which perceives things under the form of these two great categories. At the moment of his meditative experience, therefore, he sees the Buddha as actually present before him in that higher, wider, more spiritual dimension of space (or rather, of consciousness) which has been called 'the beyond within'. He sees him in a glorious form which, though human, is infinitely more majestic, brilliant, and beautiful than any mortal frame. This form is adorned with the thirty-two major and eighty minor 'marks', two standard sets embodying an ancient Indian conception of ideal beauty which the Buddhists, at an early date, took over from traditions concerning the *mahāpuruṣa* or superman and applied to their own more spiritual purposes. All yogis do not, of course, perceive the *sambhogakāya* Buddha in the same way. The brilliance of his form, seemingly made up of pure radiance, may be either dazzlingly white or suffused by a particular colour – red, blue, green, or golden yellow. His expression may be peaceful, fascinating, stern, or even (according to Tantric tradition) terrible. There are also a variety of *mudrās*, or postures of the hands, each of which has a meaning. One of the most important *sambhogakāya* forms is Amitābha, 'Infinite Light', also known as Amitāyus, 'Infinite Life'. These names indicate the universality of the *sambhogakāya*, the spiritual activity and influence of which are unlimited as regards both space and time. According to some sources, he exercises jurisdiction over 10,000,000,000 worlds, for the spiritual progress of all the sentient beings in which he is responsible.[64] The *sambhogakāya* Buddha is not, however, identical with the God of the theistic religions, being not the creator of the universe but only the teacher of its inhabitants, and to regard the *trikāya* doctrine as involving some kind of theistic development within the Mahāyāna is one of the most pernicious errors of which a student of Buddhism can be guilty. Other *sambhogakāya* forms are Vairocana, 'The Illuminator', Ratnasambhava, 'The Jewel-Born', Amoghasiddhi, 'The Unobstructed Success', Akṣobhya, 'The Imperturbable', and Vaiḍūryaprabha, 'Blue Radiance'. Despite what may appear to be the contrary testimony of Buddhist iconography, none of these forms is subject to spatial limitation in the ordinary sense, nor are they perceived in quite the same way as we perceive external objects or mental pictures. In the earlier stages of meditation Buddha-forms may indeed be perceived in this manner, and perceived very vividly; but these are usually images released from the subconscious mind, not glimpses of the *sambhogakāya*. Since the Yogācārins stressed the importance of meditation, and emphasized that a comprehensive view of reality should pay adequate attention to the nature of the world as perceived by the yogi in a state of *samādhi*, they were naturally more highly aware of the existence of the *sambhogakāya* than the followers of schools that emphasized either psychological analysis or dialectics. Historically, indeed, the contribution of the Yogācārins to the *trikāya* doctrine consists in their clearly distinguishing the *sambhogakāya* from the other *kāyas* and recognizing it as an independent body.

When one who possesses *prajñā* in its distinctively Buddhist sense of insight into the painful, transitory, and insubstantial nature of all conditioned things looks at the Buddha he sees him as the unconditioned absolute reality. As Buddhist thought developed, truth or reality naturally acquired a number of designations, according to the different angles from which it was viewed. Some of these, such as *śūnyatā*, or 'the voidness', indicated its transcendence over the world or phenomena; others, like *dharmadhātu*, 'realm of truth', its characteristic of totality and all-embracingness. *Tathatā*, 'suchness', revealed its unique indefinable essentiality; *tathāgatagarbha* its mysterious immanence. *Ālaya-vijñāna*, 'store consciousness', recognized it as the principle of potentiality; *nirvāṇadhātu*, 'sphere of extinction', viewed it as the support of the emancipated mind; while *bhūtakoṭi*, 'pinnacle of existence', drew attention to its aspect of consummation and completion. Reality may also be thought of as fully realized by the Buddha and therefore as revealed in and through him. It is this aspect which is known as the *dharmakāya*, 'body of truth or reality', or 'essential body', the third of the three bodies of the Enlightened One. Though the *trikāya* doctrine was systematically formulated long after the *parinirvāṇa,* the fact that there existed beyond the Buddha's human personality an unconditioned ineffable essence which constituted his true being was recognized from the beginning. Says the Master in the *Pārāyana-vagga* of the *Sutta-Nipāta*, one of the oldest portions of the Theravāda Pāli canon:

> There is no measuring of man,
> Won to the goal, whereby they'ld say
> His measure's so: that's not for him;
> When all conditions are removed,
> All ways of telling are removed.[65]

Similarly, in the *Saṃyutta Nikāya* he declares of himself:

> Since a Tathāgata, even when actually present, is
> incomprehensible, it is incpt to say of him – of the Uttermost
> Person, the Supernal Person, the Attainer of the Supernal – that

after dying the Tathāgata is, or is not, or both is and is not, or neither is or is not.[66]

Again, to the same effect, in the *Majjhima Nikāya*:

That material shape, that feeling, that perception, those impulses, that consciousness by which one, in defining the Tathāgata, might define him – all have been got rid of by the Tathāgata, cut off at the root, made like a palm-tree stump that cannot sprout again. Free from reckoning by material shape, feeling, perception, the impulses, consciousness is the Tathāgata; He is deep, immeasurable, unfathomable, as is the great ocean. 'Arises' does not apply, nor does 'does not arise', nor 'both arises and does not arise', nor 'neither arises nor does not arise'.[67]

The same idea is adumbrated in the great Mahāyāna *sūtras*, especially in those belonging to the *Prajñāpāramitā* or 'Perfection of Wisdom' corpus, where the bodhisattva is time and again urged to contemplate the Buddha not under his conditioned but under his unconditioned aspect. A passage from the *Vajracchedikā* bearing on this theme concludes with the well-known stanzas:

Those who by my form did see me,
And those who followed me by voice
Wrong the efforts they engaged in,
Me those people will not see.

From the Dharma should one see the Buddhas,
From the Dharmabodies comes their guidance.
Yet Dharma's true nature cannot be discerned,
And no one can be conscious of it as an object.[68]

In another passage from the same corpus the Buddha makes it clear that inasmuch as the *dharmakāya* constitutes his true personality this alone should be the object of the bodhisattva's recollection:

How does a Bodhisattva develop the recollection of the Buddha? He does not attend to the Tathagata through form, or feeling,

> etc. For form, feeling, etc., have no own-being. And what has no own-being, that is non-existent.... A Tathagata further should not be attended to through the thirty-two marks of a Superman,... nor should he be attended to through the effulgence of his halo, or through the eighty minor characteristics. And that for the same reasons as before.[69]

All these texts indicate that the *dharmakāya* is impersonal. This is denied, however, by Dr D. T. Suzuki, who in one of his early works maintains that it is personal.[70] This in effect nullifies the distinction between the *dharmakāya* on the one hand and the two remaining *kāyas* on the other. The texts which he quotes from the *Gaṇḍavyūha Sūtra* seem really to mean that inasmuch as it constitutes their ultimate reality whatever is predicated of the *nirmāṇakāya* and the *sambhogakāya*, including love, will, and intelligence, is indirectly predicated of the *dharmakāya*. In dealing with the *trikāya* doctrine, however, one must beware of being led astray by words. The *dharmakāya* is not impersonal in the sense that it utterly and completely excludes personality, for that would be to identify it with one of two opposite terms, whereas the truth of the matter is that, being non-different from absolute reality, the *dharmakāya* transcends all opposites whatsoever.

Having distinguished the *kāyas* one from another for purposes of exposition it is now necessary for us to reintegrate them into a living whole. The child, the botanist, and the poet of our illustration did not see three different flowers. They saw one flower. The difference lay in the greater or lesser extent to which they succeeded in penetrating into its reality and seeing it as it really was. In the same way the ordinary man, the yogi, and one possessing *prajñā* all see the same Buddha. All see the *dharmakāya*. But so gross is the ordinary man's perception, so darkened his mind by unwholesome emotions and erroneous views, that, like one almost totally blind who sees instead of the sun only a faint glimmer of light, he sees not the *dharmakāya* but the *nirmāṇakāya*. The yogi's perception is more refined. Disciplined by long practice of meditation, his mind has become freed from the grosser veils. When he looks at the Buddha through the subtle veils that remain the *dharmakaya* appears as the *sambhogakāya*. One with *prajñā* has removed all veils. He sees the Buddha as he really is. He sees the naked *dharmakāya*. Between him and the Buddha there is no difference. He has become the Buddha. That this is the correct interpretation of the *trikāya* doctrine is borne out by an important passage in *The Awakening of Faith in the Mahāyāna*, a Chinese work traditionally believed to have been translated from a Sanskrit original by Aśvaghoṣa. After saying that the *dharmakāya* has two aspects the text proceeds:

> The first one depends on the phenomena-particularizing-consciousness, by means of which the activity [the *dharmakāya*] is conceived by the minds of common people (*pṛthagjana*), *Śrāvakas,* and Pratyekabuddhas. This aspect is called the Body of Transformation (*nirmāṇakāya*).... The second aspect of the Dharmakāya depends on the activity-consciousness (*karma-vijñāna*) by means of which the activity is conceived by the minds of Bodhisattvas while passing from their first aspiration (*cittotpāda*) stage up to the height of Bodhisattvahood. This is called the Body of Bliss (*sambhogakāya*).[71]

Needless to say, it should not be thought that there is a hard and fast line of distinction between one *kāya* and another any more than there is between one colour in a rainbow and the next. Between the respective perceptions of the ordinary person, the yogi, and the one possessing *prajñā* there are innumerable gradations of perception. *Nirmāṇakāya* therefore merges into *sambhogakāya* and *sambhogakāya* into *dharmakāya* by imperceptible degrees. As actually three in number, the *kāyas* are no more than points abstracted from a line at regular intervals, like the inches marked on a foot-rule. This should help us remember that in the *trikāya* doctrine we have to deal not with an abstract metaphysical speculation but with an attempt to explain systematically the deepening spiritual experience of the devotee of the Buddha in his quest for absolute reality.

PART II
THE DHARMA

6
APPROACHES TO BUDDHISM

In the *Udāna* the Buddha relates the Parable of the Blind Men and the Elephant.[72] A number of men, blind from birth, are asked to feel the body of an elephant and then describe the beast. Those who felt the head declared it to be a pot, those who grasped the ear said it was a winnowing-basket, those who handled the tusk opined it was a ploughshare, and so on. Eventually, each one vehemently maintaining his own opinion, they began to quarrel and fight. The parable illustrates not only the one-sidedness of the sectarian teachers of the Buddha's own time, in connection with whom it was originally told, but also the wide divergences that can be noticed between the different approaches to Buddhism adopted by modern writers.

Until very recently three approaches were most common. They may be termed respectively the sectarian, the fundamentalist, and the encyclopedic. The basic error of the sectarian approach is that it mistakes the part for the whole. Quite early in the history of Buddhism, perhaps within a century of the *parinirvāṇa*, there arose within the Buddhist community circumstances which eventually led to the formation of different schools. Though differing on various doctrinal and disciplinary points, these schools shared a common tradition which united them to a far greater extent than their points of difference divided them. As time went on, however, and they started occupying different geographical centres, not only in India but throughout Asia, their differences gradually grew more pronounced. The result is that instead of consisting of one version of the Dharma only, Buddhism now comprises a number of different versions laid as it were side by side and overlapping in varying degrees. To identify Buddhism with one particular version, on whatever grounds, is ridiculous. As Dr Edward Conze says (we have quoted his words elsewhere, but they bear repetition),

> The doctrine of the Buddha, conceived in its full breadth, width, majesty and grandeur, comprises all those teachings which are linked to the original teaching by historical continuity, and which work out methods leading to the extinction of individuality by eliminating the belief in it.[73]

Unfortunately, some corners of the Buddhist world have not yet awoken to the truth of these words. Books, pamphlets, and articles continue to be produced which naively present a single branch as the whole tree. This is not to say that the branch is not a noble branch, nor that individual accounts of the different Buddhist schools are not needed. We refer to something quite different: the practice of presenting, as complete accounts of Buddhism, what are in fact expositions of the tenets of one school based on a highly selective reading of a single branch of the canonical literature, usually the Pāli Tipiṭaka. Some writers go to the extreme of explicitly repudiating as 'not the pure Dharma' all Buddhist traditions but their own.[74] Despite occasional absurdities of this kind, however, the sectarian type of approach to Buddhism is fortunately on the wane. Throughout the Buddhist world the conviction is steadily gaining ground that so far as the Dharma is concerned the truth, to apply the Hegelian dictum, is the whole.[75]

The fundamentalist approach is concerned with what the Buddha 'really' said. It has two forms. The first to some extent coincides with the sectarian approach which, in one of its forms, maintains even in the face of abundant internal evidence to the contrary that the Pāli Tipiṭaka consists entirely of the *ipsissima verba* of the Buddha. The second, the intellectually respectable form, is a product of modern scholarship, largely non-Buddhist. By means of textual criticism, comparison with archaeological and epigraphical evidence, etc., it endeavours to separate the passages belonging to earlier from those belonging to later strata of the canonical literature. Broadly speaking, this attempt has met with some success. The fundamentalist desires, however, a greater degree of certainty than the nature of the subject allows. Even if it is possible to isolate the most ancient texts, the problem of the relation of these to the oral tradition which preceded them and of this to the Buddha's own utterances remains insoluble. It is doubtful whether any known Buddhist text contains a line which preserves the Dharma in the same language or dialect in which it was originally expounded by the Buddha. The more strictly scientific methods are applied, the greater likelihood there seems to be that the fundamentalist will eventually be left with nothing but the Buddha's 'noble silence'. Some, indeed, horrified by the void confronting them, have sought to fill it with their own arbitrary constructions of what they imagine the Buddha 'really' taught. Both forms of fundamentalism commit the mistake of assuming that the Teaching is bound up with a certain form of words, and that unless these are known it cannot be properly understood. Though such an approach is ultimately self-destructive, as we have shown, it has recently been adopted by at least one earnest writer on Buddhism. However, instead of pursuing the approach to its logical conclusion, the Buddha's silence, he stops short at those parts of the Pāli Tipiṭaka he believes to be the most ancient and then reverts to the naive form of fundamentalism with regard to them.

The encyclopedic approach emphasizes breadth rather than depth of knowledge. It tends to confuse knowledge *about* Buddhism with knowledge *of* Buddhism. It is concerned more with facts than with principles, tries to see from without instead of feeling from within. For a century it has profoundly influenced, if not dominated, the world of non-traditional Buddhist scholarship. Since it is not an isolated phenomenon, but has its roots deep in the soil of the modern scientific outlook, whose general tendencies it exemplifies within its own special field, this approach is likely to remain important for some time to come. Provided its limitations are understood, and any mischief to which they might give rise guarded against, this is not necessarily a bad thing for Buddhism. Such scholarship has accomplished much useful work. Moreover, during the last decade it has been leavened and enlivened, in the case of one or two well-known writers, by elements of sympathy and understanding which were originally lacking. Nevertheless, this does not alter the basic fact that, owing to the vast extent of Buddhist literature, which includes thousands of works regarded as canonical, besides innumerable non-canonical works, its aim of achieving complete factual knowledge about Buddhism and from this inferring its nature is impossible of attainment.

The ideal approach to Buddhism incorporates elements from the sectarian, the fundamentalist, and the encyclopedic approaches, shorn of their imperfections. It has for basis an insight into the Dharma derived from the actual practice of a system of spiritual discipline which, owing to the specialized nature of such techniques, is necessarily that of a particular school – Japanese Zen, Tibetan Mahāmudrā, or the Thai '*sammā arahaṃ*' method. Despite this fact, it will be vividly aware and warmly appreciative of the multiple richness of the Buddhist tradition, and however firmly it may grasp a particular thread will never lose sight of its connection with the whole fabric. While accurately distinguishing earlier formulations of the Teaching from later ones, and even preferring the former for introductory purposes, it will not commit the mistake of treating the age of a formulation as the sole criterion of its spiritual authenticity, nor consider the Dharma to be limited to its verbal expressions. Depth will not, however, exclude breadth. Besides keeping abreast of developments in the field of non-traditional Buddhist studies, the ideal approach to Buddhism will not only take all Buddhism for its province but will enforce its conclusions by drawing upon as wide a range of scriptural reference as possible. Above all, it will be concerned to exhibit the living spirit of Buddhism.

7
THE ESSENCE OF THE DHARMA

Many students of Buddhism are at first staggered by the vastness of the field before them and bewildered by the abundance of material. This is natural. Like Christianity and Islam, Buddhism is not only a teaching but a culture, a civilization, a movement in history, a social order, in fact a whole world in itself. It comprises systems of philosophy, methods of meditation, rituals, manners and customs, clothes, languages, sacred literature, pagodas, temples, monasteries, calligraphy, poems, paintings, plays, stories, games, flower-arrangements, pottery, and a thousand other things. All this is Buddhist, and often immediately recognizable as such. Whether it be a stone Buddha seated cross-legged in the jungles of Anuradhupura, a Tibetan sacred dance, a cup of tea between friends in Japan, or the way in which a *bhikṣu* answers a question in London, everything is invisibly signed with the same mysterious seal. Sometimes it floats with the clouds between heaven and earth, shines in the rainbow, or gurgles over pebbles in the company of a mountain stream.

> Looked at, it cannot be seen; listened to, it cannot be heard.[76]

Sooner or later, however, the student tries to identify it. He wonders what it could be that gives unity to all these diverse expressions, so that however remote in space and time, and however different their respective mediums, one perfectly harmonizes with another, creating not the dissonance that might have been expected but 'a concord of sweet sounds'. Eventually a question shapes itself in his mind, and at last he enquires, 'What is the essence of the Dharma?'

The best answer to this question would be the 'thunder-like silence' with which Vimalakīrti, in the Mahāyāna *sūtra* that bears his name, answered the bodhisattva Mañjuśrī's question about the nature of reality.[77] Can we describe even the colour of a rose? But this apparently negative procedure the student would not find very helpful. Concessions must be made. Buddhism is essentially an experience. 'An experience of what?' Before answering this second question let us try to explain why, of all the words in the dictionary, 'experience' is the first term on which one falls back when compelled to abandon the 'thunder-like silence'. Unlike thought, experience is direct, unmediated; it is knowledge by acquaintance. Hence it is characterized by a feeling of absolute certainty. When we see the sun shining in a clear sky we do not doubt that it is bright; when a thorn runs beneath our fingernail we do not speculate whether it is painful. In saying that Buddhism is essentially an experience we do not suggest that the object of that experience in any way resembles the objects of sense-experience, nor even that there is an object at all. We simply draw attention to its unique unconceptualized immediacy. The relation between sense-experience and the one with which we are now concerned is merely analogical. For this reason it is necessary to go a step further and complete our definition by saying that the essence of the Dharma, of Buddhism, consists in a *spiritual* or *transcendental* experience. This is what in traditional terminology is called Enlightenment-experience.

Apart from conveying an impression of the subject having now been lost sight of in the clouds, the mere addition of these adjectives is inconclusive. They themselves need definition. But inasmuch as this will involve the use of terms even more abstract, more remote from concrete experience, such definition will set up a process of conceptualization as a result of which the reflection of Enlightenment-experience in our minds will be in danger of complete distortion, like the moon's reflection in a pond the surface of which the wind has chopped into waves. Concepts had therefore better be treated as symbols, the value of which lies not in their literal meaning so much as in their suggestiveness. They should be handled in the spirit not of logic but of poetry; not pushed hither and thither with grim calculation like pieces on a chessboard, but tossed lightly, playfully in the air like a juggler's multicoloured balls.

Approaching the subject in this spirit we may define Enlightenment-experience as 'seeing things as they are (*yathābhūta-jñānadarśana*)'. This is the traditional definition. Here also, it will be observed, the use of the word 'seeing' (*darśana*) – which primarily denotes a form of sense-perception – emphasizes not only the directness and immediacy of the experience but also its noetic character. Enlightenment-experience is not just a blind sensing of things, but, as the English word suggests, the shining forth of a light, an illumination, in the brightness of which things become visible in their reality. Such expressions should not mislead us into thinking that there is any real difference between the subject and the object of the experience, between the light and the things illuminated (which disposes of the second question raised above). Were it not for the fact that all words indicative of existence have for Buddhism a disagreeable substantialist flavour, it might even be preferable not to speak of Enlightenment as an experience at all but as a state of being. Fortunately other ways of surmounting the difficulty are available. The *Avataṃsaka Sūtra*, for instance, depicts the world of Enlightenment-experience as consisting not of objects illuminated from without but entirely of innumerable beams of light, all intersecting and intersected, none of which offers any resistance to the passage of any other.[78] Light being always in motion, this striking similitude has the additional advantage of precluding the notion that Enlightenment is a definite state in which one as it were settles comfortably down for good, instead of a movement from perfection to greater perfection in a process in which there is no final term, the direction of movement alone remaining constant.

If spiritual or transcendental experience is a state of seeing things as they are, its opposite, mundane experience, wherein all unenlightened beings are involved, must be one of seeing them as they are not. The cause of this blindness is twofold. Being a creature of desires, man is concerned with things only to the extent that they can be made to subserve his own ends. He is interested not in truth but in utility. For him things and people exist not in their own right but only as actual or possible means of his own gratification. This is the 'veil of passions' (*kleśāvaraṇa*). Usually we do not like to acknowledge, even to ourselves, that our attitude towards life is often no better than that of a pig rooting for acorns. Motives are therefore rationalized. Instead of admitting that we hate somebody, we say he is wicked and ought to be punished. Rather than admit we enjoy eating flesh, we maintain that sheep and cows were created for man's benefit. Not wishing to die, we invent the dogma of the immortality of the individual soul. Craving help and protection, we start believing in a personal God. According to the Buddha, all the philosophies, and a great deal of religious teaching, are rationalizations of desires.[79] This is the 'veil of (false) assumptions' (*jñeyāvaraṇa*). On the attainment of Enlightenment both veils are rent asunder. For this reason the experience is accompanied by an exhilarating sense of release. The Buddha compares the state of mind of one gaining Enlightenment to that of a man who has come safe out of a dangerous jungle, or been freed from debt, or released from prison.[80] It is as though an intolerable burden had at last been lifted from his back. So intense is this feeling of release from pain, suffering, conflicting emotions, and mental sterility and stagnation that many of the older canonical texts speak of the Enlightenment-experience exclusively in terms of freedom or emancipation (*vimukti*). One of them represents the Buddha himself as saying that even as the great ocean had one taste, the taste of salt, so his teaching had one flavour, the flavour of emancipation.[81] Besides a psychological aspect, *vimukti* has an intellectual and an existential aspect. In the first place it is a freedom from all theories and speculations about reality; and in the second, from any form of conditioned existence whatever, including 're-becoming' as a result of karma. The freedom into which one breaks through at the time of Enlightenment is not limited and partial, but absolute and unconditioned.

This introduces an aspect of Enlightenment-experience which is not always properly understood. Freedom, to be really unconditioned, must transcend the distinction between conditioned and unconditioned, *saṃsāra* and *nirvāṇa*, bondage and liberation, all of which are really mental constructions and, as such, part of the 'veil of assumptions'. Therefore there can in the ultimate sense be no question of escaping from the conditioned to the Unconditioned as though they were distinct entities. Or, to speak paradoxically, in order to be truly free one has to escape not only from bondage but from liberation, not only from *saṃsāra* into *nirvāṇa* but from *nirvāṇa* back into *saṃsāra*. It is this 'escape' or descent that constitutes the *mahākaruṇā* or 'Great Compassion' of the Buddha, which is in reality his realization of the non-duality of the conditioned and the Unconditioned as that realization appears from the viewpoint of the conditioned. The Enlightenment experience is therefore not only one of illumination and freedom but also of infinite and inexhaustible love, a love which has for object all sentient beings, and which manifests as uninterrupted activity in pursuit of their temporal and spiritual welfare.

8

DOCTRINAL FORMULAS

While it is possible to lose sight of the spirit of Buddhism among the multifariousness of its forms, it is no less possible to lose the spirit by repudiating the forms prematurely. The Buddha Amitāyus, 'Infinite Life', bears in his hands a jar containing the nectar of immortality. Jar without nectar is useless, but nectar without jar to contain it will only be spilled and wasted. After exhibiting as clearly as possible the spirit of Buddhism we have therefore to relate it to its doctrinal embodiment, as well as to indicate the origin, true nature, and proper function of that embodiment.

As already related, it was out of compassion that the newly Enlightened Lord decided to make known to mankind the Truth he had penetrated (see p. 22). Again, when a few months later he sent forth the sixty Enlightened disciples he charged them to go forth and proclaim the Dharma 'out of compassion for the world' (see p. 23). This love or compassion, which as we have just seen constitutes with illumination and freedom the essence of Buddhism, brings the Enlightened into communication, even into communion, with the unenlightened mind. The medium of this communication is the formulated Dharma. This consists in the first place of words and concepts. But the fact that these were not invented by the Buddha, and can be traced in the records of pre-Buddhist teachings, does not justify such sweeping conclusions as 'the Buddha was influenced by the Upanishads' or 'Buddhism is an offshoot of Hinduism'. One might just as well maintain that Shakespeare 'copied' his plays from obscure early Elizabethan dramatists on the grounds that he made use of the same words and drew upon the same general stock of ideas as they did. Whatever words and concepts constitute the formulated Dharma, it is in fact essentially a medium for the communication to mankind of a unique and ineffable experience, the Buddha's experience of illumination-freedom-love, as well as an attempt to induce all who heard the words and understood the concepts to participate in it themselves by having immediate and vigorous recourse to such methods as he in his wisdom could devise. As such the Dharma is not an end in itself but a means to an end. In the *Majjhima Nikāya* the Buddha compares his teaching to the raft used for crossing a great stretch of water, roundly declaring that to burden oneself with it after its work is done is sheer foolishness.[82] The comparison is doubly apposite. It brings out not only the more obvious point to which reference has just been made, but also the subtler one that although the Dharma is only a means it is an indispensable means. The point is important. Only too often do those with a merely theoretical understanding of the instrumental value of the Dharma assume themselves to be thereby exempted from the necessity of having effective recourse to it as the veritable Means of Enlightenment. This is to abandon the raft before one has even started crossing the water. A middle path should be followed. One must understand that a collection of sticks only constitutes a raft through the existence of the further shore, and it is only by means of the raft that the further shore can be actually reached. Spirit and letter are interdependent. Divorced from the living spirit of the Master's teaching, the letter of the Dharma, however faithfully transmitted, is dead, a thing of idle words and empty concepts: separated from its concrete embodiment in the letter, the spirit of the Dharma, however exalted, lacking a medium of communication is rendered inoperative. In writing about Buddhism one should therefore be careful to pay equal attention to both aspects. The ideal account would in fact show spiritual experiences crystallizing into concrete doctrinal and disciplinary forms and these resolving themselves back into spiritual experiences. Full justice would then be done both to the letter and to the spirit of the tradition.

What is true of the whole is no less true of its parts. For reasons mainly mnemonic and pedagogic, much of the recorded Dharma has come down to us in the shape of stereotype formulas and numbered lists of doctrinal terms. Thus we have the three characteristics (*tri-lakṣaṇa*), the four *āryan* truths (*catur-āryasatya*), the five groups (*pañca-skandha*), the six bases (*ṣaḍāyatana*), the seven factors of Enlightenment (*sapta-bodhyaṇga*), the Āryan Eightfold Path (*ārya-aṣṭāṇgika-mārga*), the nine transcendental states (*nava-lokottara-dharma*), the ten perfections (*daśa-pāramitā*), the twelve links (*dvādaśa-nidāna*), the thirty-seven wings of Enlightenment (*bodhipakṣyā-dharma*), and hundreds more. After the *parinirvāṇa* of the Buddha the drawing up of such lists, especially of mental states, became almost an obsession with a section of his followers, and though a reaction eventually set in, Indian Buddhism was hardly ever free from this tendency. The result is that having been compiled under such auspices almost the whole of the Hīnayāna and much of the Mahāyāna canonical literature has come down to us in an artificial, stereotyped form which, as one can see from short passages which proved unamenable to such treatment, is often at variance with the spiritual vitality of the message it enshrines. This is not to say that, given the conditions under which it had to be transmitted, the Dharma could have been handed down in any other manner, or that we should not feel profoundly grateful to the compilers and codifiers who gave it such an unattractive but durable shape. Yet for the student of Buddhism, and even more acutely for the writer, the existence of so many doctrinal formulas does constitute a problem. What is one to do with them all? Some writers, of course, ignore them, and give an arbitrary account of what they imagine the Buddha taught. Others, like the author of *Atthārasarāsī Dīpanī*,[83] which purports to be an aid to meditation, include as many as possible without giving a thought to what they really mean. The first procedure is justifiable only if, like the Buddha, one has oneself crossed to the Other Shore, and can speak out of the depths of one's own Enlightenment-experience; the second, if one is compiling a glossary of Buddhist terms. Once again a middle path should be pursued. For the student of Buddhism to try to understand the Dharma without having mastered at least all the more important doctrinal terms would be like a pianist attempting to play the *Moonlight Sonata* who had never bothered to practise any scales. Nevertheless scales are not sonatas, and the student should not commit the mistake of thinking that knowing by heart the doctrinal categories of Buddhism in Pāli or Sanskrit or any other language is the same thing as a true understanding of the Dharma. The balanced writer on Buddhism follows a similar course. While not obtruding doctrinal formulas ostentatiously on the reader for their own sake, he does not seek in his expositions to eschew the use of them altogether. The principal formulas he will delineate with precision and clarity, drawing attention to their importance for the history of Buddhist thought. At the same time instead of treating them so literally that they become as it were solid and opaque he will enable them to fulfil their true function by refining them to so high a degree of transparency that through them the radiance of the Enlightenment-experience shines with the minimum of obstruction.

9
COSMOLOGY

One of the most important doctrinal categories is that which divides all *dharmas*, as the Abhidharma tradition terms the ultimate elements of existence (reckoned by different schools as 172, 75, 84, or 100 in number), into two groups, that of *saṃskṛta-dharmas*, compounded or conditioned elements of existence, and that of *asaṃskṛta-dharmas*, elements which are uncompounded and unconditioned. The first of these, which comprises by far the larger number of terms, constitutes the whole phenomenal universe or cosmos of Buddhism. As this provides the background against which the formulated Dharma unfolds we shall attempt a rough sketch map of it before turning to consider, in a subsequent chapter, the 'marks' that are attached to it and which express its true nature. The second group, that of the unconditioned *dharmas*, includes Nirvāṇa. This topic will also be dealt with.

So far as grand outlines are concerned, the most striking fact about Buddhist cosmology is the extent to which it dwarfs the conceptions of the Semitic religions on the subject and the degree to which its vision of the universe resembles the one disclosed by the modern telescope. Until recently the Christian world believed that the universe consisted of seven concentric spheres, one within another like Chinese ivory balls, with the earth in the centre and the sphere of the fixed stars at the circumference, and further that this universe, which had been created by the fiat of the Almighty about 4,000 years BCE (some chronologists succeeded in working out the exact date) had an extension in space of about 10,000 miles. The corresponding Buddhist notions are by contrast of overwhelming sublimity. To begin with, the phenomenal universe is declared to be without perceptible limit in space or perceptible first beginning in time. Here *perceptible* is the operative word. As the list of the fourteen inexpressibles (*avyākṛtavastus*), one of the oldest doctrinal formulas, makes clear, the fact that the universe is not finite, either in space or in time, does not mean that it is infinite, or even that it is either both or neither.[84] Analysis reveals all these alternatives as self-contradictory, or, as we shall see later, space and time are not objective realities external to consciousness but part of the conditions under which it perceives things. However far in space one may go, therefore, in any direction, it is always possible to go still farther, for wherever one goes the mind goes too.

The Scriptures try to convey some conception of the inexhaustible vastness of space not by means of calculation but imaginatively. According to one similitude, even if a man were to take all the grains of sand in the river Ganges and, travelling north, south, east, or west, go on depositing one grain of sand at the end of every period of years equal in number to all the grains of sand, even after exhausting the whole river Ganges he would be no closer to reaching the end of space than he was at the beginning.[85] As even the most unimaginative reader of popular modern works on astronomy has probably felt, the contemplation of vistas such as these is not without effect on the mind. Growing up as they did with the transcendent immensity of space for background, the Dharma and its followers through the ages naturally developed a breadth and freedom of outlook which would have been impossible within the stuffy confines of the dogmatic Christian world-view.

Their awareness of the dimensions of the phenomenal universe did not, however, cause them to overlook what were, in comparison, matters of detail. Besides being of unimaginable breadth and depth, the cosmos mirrored in the Scriptures is filled with millions of world systems, each one containing ten thousand worlds. These world systems, which are described as disc-like, are distributed through space at unthinkably vast intervals. They resemble what modern astronomy terms spiral galaxies, consisting of thousands of millions of stars rotating round a common centre. The world system Buddhists called the *sahāloka* or 'world of tribulation' corresponds in part to the Milky Way, somewhere upon the outer fringes of which exists the solar system wherein our own earth 'spins like a fretful midge' among its sister planets.[86] The Scriptures reveal a number of other details also. Many worlds are inhabited by intelligent living beings who, according to the Mahāyāna *sūtras*, have Buddhas of their own from whom they hear the same Dharma that Śākyamuni Buddha preaches to the beings of the *sahāloka*. As might be expected, there is much traffic of Buddhas and bodhisattvas to and fro between different world systems.[87] Though these details are not necessarily untrue even if understood literally, they clearly indicate the universality of the Dharma, which can be practised wherever living beings endowed with intelligence are found, and the omnipresence of the Enlightenment-mind, which manifests wherever conditions are favourable.

As space is plotted out by the world systems so time is measured in *kalpas*. A *kalpa* is a length of time equivalent to the life-period of a world system, from its initial condensation to its final destruction by water, fire, or wind. Scholastics with a penchant for mathematics later on tried to work out a figure for this enormous stretch of time, and though the results they arrived at often differed they all agreed it amounted to thousands of millions of years. The Buddha, perhaps more wisely, had been content with a simile. Suppose, he said, there was a cube of solid rock four leagues square, and at the end of every century a man were to come and stroke it once with a fine piece of Benares muslin – the rock would be worn away before the *kalpa* came to an end.[88] Each *kalpa* is divided into four 'incalculable' *kalpas* corresponding to different phases of the involution and evolution of the world system and the progress and deterioration of the human race; each incalculable *kalpa* into twenty 'intermediate' *kalpas*, and each intermediate *kalpa* into eight *yugas* or 'ages'.

As the scale of events decreases and we come to what are, geologically speaking, our own times, certain discrepancies between Buddhist traditions and current scientific notions begin to appear. This hardly ever amounts to flat contradiction. Taking into account as it does the existence not only of the material universe but also of the subtle spiritual counterpart from which, by a process analogous to that of condensation, it emerged, Buddhism interleaves with the facts of science a set of spiritual facts of its own discovery. Thus while in no way denying the animal descent of man as a physical organism, it makes it clear that the emergence of *homo sapiens* is due to the conjunction of a descending spiritual order of personal existence with an ascending biological one. (This is the true meaning of the popular Tibetan belief that human beings are descended from the bodhisattva Avalokiteśvara and a female monkey.)

At the same time, we cannot ignore the fact that the Scriptures make a number of statements on geography, anatomy, and physiology, and other scientific subjects, that are plainly wrong. The Buddha, or whoever compiled and edited his words, was more concerned with the spiritual reality of his message than with the factual truth of the scientific references embedded in the language and culture which were his medium of communication. The statement 'King Charles was beheaded two hours after sunrise' is not invalidated by the fact that it is the earth, not the sun, which moves. Some modern readers are outraged by Buddhaghosa's account of the digestive processes and the internal organs.[89] Yet, far from being dependent on fifth-century misunderstandings of the subject, the spiritual exercises the great Theravādin commentator describes can just as well be practised on the basis of the most advanced scientific knowledge of human physiology. In any case, there is nothing in Buddhism that hinders us from discarding whatever obsolete science the Scriptures may contain, for while all schools held the Buddha to be omniscient as regards the Path and the Goal, the Tripiṭaka, unlike the Bible and the Koran, was never revered as being of divine origin, verbally inspired and hence infallible.

Before deciding that a given scriptural text is unscientific, however, we should make quite sure that we really know to what order of existence it pertains. Ridicule has often been poured on Buddhist geography, with its 'islands' and 'oceans' and its many-tiered Mount Sumeru, the abode of the gods, rising from the centre of the map. But despite the fact that Sumeru was sometimes identified with a particular peak in the Himalayan Range, it is clear that this apparently fantastic picture is meant as a description not of this earth only, but of a number of intersecting planes of existence the common axial principle of which is symbolized by Mount Sumeru, and of which our earth, represented by Jambudvīpa, 'The Rose-Apple Island', constitutes one plane.

This brings out the point that whereas the universe of science exists only in space and time, that of Buddhism exists also in depth. This depth is not physical but spiritual. According to ancient traditions basic to all schools, the phenomenal universe as distinct from the limited physical universe consists of three planes or spheres of existence (*lokas*), each 'higher' and subtler than the preceding one. First there is the *kāmaloka* or 'plane of desire' in which are included, besides the universe known to science, the various worlds inhabited by spirits, infernal beings, and the lower, earthbound orders of deities. Next comes the *rūpaloka* or 'plane of (subtle) form', which is inhabited by higher orders of deities imperceptible to ordinary human sense whose consciousness, though dissociated from 'matter', is still bound up either with one or with many spiritual forms. These deities are of various degrees of luminosity. Finally in the *arūpaloka*, the 'formless plane', dwell deities of the highest orders of all who, being free even from spiritual form, represent various dimensions of pure but still mundane consciousness. They are naturally of even greater luminosity. Like the first, the second and third planes are divided into a number of sub-planes, and their inhabitants distinguished by different names. Some of these names are indicative of the type or degree of radiance emitted by the class of deity concerned. Despite the detailed classifications found in some works, the higher one goes in the hierarchy of deities the more careful one should be not to think too literally in terms of groups and classes, for here, even more than with lower forms of existence, the ascent is continuous rather than by discrete steps, the lower being transformed into the higher mode of being without perceptible break.[90]

One classification, or rather principle of classification, however, is too relevant to be omitted. It is well known that through the practice of concentration the yogi attains certain superconscious states known as *dhyānas* (Sanskrit) or *jhānas* (Pāli). These are divided into two groups, a lower and a higher. Each group is in turn divided into four, the successive grades constituting the first group being distinguished according to the psychological factors variously present, and the classes which make up the second group (the psychological factors of which are those of the fourth lower *dhyāna*) being differentiated according to their respective objects. What concerns us here is the fact that the *dhyānas* comprising the first group are known collectively as *rūpa-dhyānas* and those comprising the second group as *arūpa-dhyānas*. There is thus a correspondence between *dhyānas* and *lokas*, the one representing the psychological, the other the cosmological aspect of existence. A *loka* is attained, and its inhabitants are seen, when the yogi succeeds in entering the corresponding *dhyāna*. This means that, existentially speaking, *dhyāna* is prior to *loka*, or that, as the first verse of the Pāli *Dhammapada* teaches, consciousness precedes and determines being.[91] (The double meaning of the word *saṃskāra*, which may stand either for the formative psychological factors or for things formed – in the latter case being equivalent to *saṃskṛta-dharma* – may conceal a reference to this idea.) Moreover, space and time being correlative, as soon as he attains a particular *loka* the yogi also begins to experience a new timescale. The Abhidharma tradition explains this by means of a table according to which the life-term in the *loka* of the deities called 'the four great kings' is 9,000,000 years, one day and night being equivalent to 50 years of human life, and so on up through the *lokas* as far as the plane of the supreme Brahmās, the highest deities of all, whose life-term is 16,000 *kalpas*.[92] Since ultimately it is consciousness that determines both space- and time-perception, and since the entire phenomenal universe exists nowhere save in space and time, it is evident not only that consciousness determines being but that in essence being is consciousness. In the language of the first verse of the *Dhammapada* the elements of existence are not only mind-preceded (*manopubbaṅgamā*) and mind-determined (*manoseṭṭhā*) but also made up or composed of mind (*manomayā*). Here is the germ of the doctrine, set forth in Mahāyāna *sūtras* such as the *Laṅkāvatāra* and *Sandhinirmocana*, and systematized by the Yogācāra school, that all conditioned things – world systems, planes, deities, and even Buddhas (as *The Tibetan Book of the Dead*, for example, explicitly teaches) – are in truth merely phenomena of the eternally radiant unconditioned reality of absolute mind.[93] The tantras express the same idea when, reverting to geographical symbolism, they identify Mount Sumeru with the spinal column in the human body.[94]

10

THE WHEEL OF LIFE

The laws in accordance with which individualized consciousness determines conditioned being are covered by the compendious term *karma*, while the actual process is elucidated in the complex of teachings pictorially represented in Buddhist art by the 'wheel of life' (*bhavacakra*).

So far as its usage in connection with Buddhism is concerned, the word 'karma' is often employed in a gravely erroneous manner. Some writers make it mean not only action, its literal meaning, but the result of action, for which Buddhist literature reserves separate terms such as *karma-vipāka* and *karma-phala*. Others use it in the sense of fate or destiny, sometimes even going so far as to maintain that according to Buddhism whatever happens to us, whether pleasant or painful, comes about as the result of previous karma. The confusion must be cleared up before the different types of karma are enumerated.

Though having the literal meaning of action, karma in this context invariably means act of volition. Thus we get the important equation karma = *cetanā* (volition) = *saṃskāras* ('formative' or rebirth-producing psychological factors). As opposed to Jainism, Buddhism maintains that involuntary actions, whether those of body, speech, or mind, do not constitute karma and therefore cannot bring about the results accruing to karma. This does not mean that such actions produce no results at all: the unintentional dropping of a brick on our own toes hurts no less than if we had done it deliberately, perhaps more so. It only means that unwilled actions do not modify character. The confusion arises because the fact that according to Buddhism there is a relation of 'cause' and 'effect' between karma, or act of will, and *karma-vipāka*, the fruit of that act in the form of pleasant or painful experience, has led some unwary students to jump to the conclusion that the law of karma and the law of cause and effect are synonymous. Karma (or more correctly karma and *karma-vipāka*) is only one particular type of cause-effect relation. The *Nikāya/Āgama* discourses represent the Buddha as repeatedly condemning the doctrine of fatalism and as declaring that though he teaches that every willed action produces an experienced effect he does not teach that all experienced effects are products of willed action or karma.[95]

This important distinction is elaborated in the formula of the five *niyamas*, or different orders of cause-effect or conditionality obtaining in the universe. They are *utu-niyama*, physical inorganic order; *bīja-niyama*, physical organic or biological order; *citta-niyama* (non-volitional) mental order; *karma-niyama*, volitional order; and *dharma-niyama*, transcendental order. To distinguish effects produced by one *niyama* from those produced by another is not always easy. Some effects, in fact, can be brought about by any *niyama*. Suppose there is a man suffering from fever. The complaint may be due to a sudden change of temperature (*utu-niyama*), to the presence of a germ (*bīja-niyama*), to mental strain or worry, or to tension due to experiences taking place in the *dhyānas* (*citta-niyama*), to the fact that in a previous life he had harmed someone (*karma-niyama*), or to chemical and cellular changes occurring in the body consequent upon transcendental realization (*dharma-niyama*).[96]

This doctrine has an important practical bearing. Critics of the Dharma sometimes allege that Buddhists are indifferent to human suffering, and take no steps to relieve it, because their religion teaches them to regard it as the result of past karma. However true this may be of Hinduism, which generally inclines to a fatalistic view of karma, or even of some less instructed Buddhists in Asian lands, the accusation certainly does not hold good in respect of the Buddha and his teaching. Buddhists are urged to make every effort to remove disease, privation, and want in all their ignoble, soul-crippling, life-destroying forms because not being Enlightened they cannot know by which *niyama* they have been brought about. Only after making every attempt to remove a certain condition, and finding that although other circumstances are favourable an unknown factor frustrates all our efforts, are we entitled to apply the method of residues and conclude that the condition is due to karma. In any case, it would be a mistake to regard the *karma-niyama* or any other *niyama* as an absolutely self-contained system. Despite the contrary impression sometimes created by modern Theravādin writers, the five *niyamas* not only all act one upon another, but are collectively acted upon and influenced by the higher and wider containing reality of the Universal Consciousness (*ālaya-vijñāna*).[97] Unless this is borne constantly in mind, the drily analytic manner in which such writers tabulate and chart the workings of karma may make us feel that we have to do not with the heart-throbs of a living human mind and character but with an intricate piece of dead mechanism.

The different types of karma are described in the Abhidharma literature with a wealth of illustrative detail.[98] Here we shall be briefly concerned only with the broad principles of classification. These are seven in number. Karmas may be grouped in accordance with their ethical status, the 'door' through which they act, the appropriateness of the resultant experiences, their time and relative priority of taking effect, the nature of their function, and the plane of existence on which they mature. Of these principles, the first is the most important, since this constitutes the basis of the rest. From the point of view of its ethical status or quality a volition (including its concomitant mental factors) is either wholesome (*kuśala*) or unwholesome (*akuśala*). Unwholesome volition is that rooted in greed (*lobha*), hatred (*dveṣa*), and delusion (*moha*) – another primitive formula – and wholesome volition that rooted in the opposite of these passions, that is to say rooted in contentment, love, and mental pellucidity. Each of these two types of volition can act either directly through the 'door' of the mind (the terminology is not to be taken too literally) or indirectly through the door of body or the door of speech.

On this fact are based two of the most important ethical findings of Buddhism. First, that a man will reap the consequences not only of what he has intentionally said and done, but also of what he has deliberately thought, or allowed himself to think, without giving it overt expression in word or deed. One who, in the vigorous language of the New Testament, looks at a woman to lust after her, not only has already committed adultery with her in his heart[99] but, under the operation of the *karma-niyama*, will one day suffer the consequences of adultery. This does not quite mean that we are no less answerable for a passing dirty thought than for the actual unwholesome deed. Volitions admit of varying degrees of intensity. A volition that fulfils itself in word or deed is generally stronger than one that does not, and a strong will obviously produces greater results than a weak volition. Whether wholesome or unwholesome, however, a mind-volition of the degree of intensity that normally results in word or deed or both will, even if denied overt vocal or bodily expression, undoubtedly bring about the same pleasant or painful experiences that the actual performance of the deed would have done. The point is illustrated by a number of charming traditional anecdotes, like that of the Chinese pilgrim about the old woman who worshipped a dog's tooth thinking it was the Buddha's, or the Zen story of the monk who carried a pretty girl across a stream and then forgot her while his more strait-laced companion 'carried' her in his mind all the way back to the monastery.[100] Tales such as these, which generations of Buddhists have found more illuminating than pages of psychological analysis, link the first with the second of the two important ethical findings based on the relation between volition and 'doors'.

On account of this second finding Buddhist ethics has been described as an ethics of intention. Words and deeds are wholesome or unwholesome, it says, not in themselves, but according to whether they are the expression of wholesome or of unwholesome volitions. Despite its formidable lists of rules, therefore, Buddhist ethics consists essentially in the cultivation of a morally healthy mental attitude towards life. The rules, whether those prescribed for the monk or those prescribed for the layman, merely represent the normal behaviour pattern of one in whom such an attitude is predominant.

Both ethical status and doors enter into the third principle of classification, that according to the appropriateness of the resultant experiences. In the *Cūḷa-* and *Mahā-kammavibhaṅga Suttas*, or Lesser and Greater Discourses on the Analysis of Volitions, the Buddha makes it clear that those who are given to the taking of life, cruelty, anger, envy, avarice, and pride, all of which are acts rooted in unhealthy volitions, will be reborn in states of suffering, or, if reborn as men, will be short-lived, diseased, ugly, despised, poor, and of mean descent. Contrariwise, those whose acts of body, speech, and mind are the opposite of these, being rooted in healthy attitudes, will be reborn in the blissful higher planes of existence, or, if reborn as men, will be long-lived, healthy, handsome, respected, wealthy, and of distinguished family.[101] Other texts give further examples of this type of correspondence. One declares stupidity to be the result of mental indolence, and intelligence of a desire to learn.[102] In the case of this principle of classification one should be careful not to pervert the Buddha's teaching by arguing that, for example, poverty is invariably the punishment for 'bad' and riches the reward of 'good' karmas performed in past lives, for this would be to fall a victim to the very misunderstandings that we have tried to clear up at the beginning of the section.

With regard to time and relative priority of effect, the fourth and fifth principles, the classification of karmas is in each case a fourfold one. A karma may ripen in the very life in which it was performed, in the next life, in a succeeding life, or, owing to the preponderance of 'counteractive' karma or to its being too weak, it may never ripen. The classification according to priority of effect refers not to the effects of karma in general but only to one kind of effect, that which we call rebirth, or, more correctly, rebecoming. From this point of view karmas are classified as 'weighty', 'death-proximate', 'habitual', and 'residual'. The *dhyānas* are all reckoned as healthy weighty volitions. Matricide, patricide, killing an *arhant*, wounding a Buddha, and creating a schism in the Sangha, together with erroneous opinions of the type negating the very possibility of a life dedicated to the attainment of Enlightenment, are all unhealthy weighty volitions. Death-proximate karma is the healthy or unhealthy volition occurring immediately before death, which may be the reflex of some previously performed healthy or unhealthy karma, or of something connected with it, or of a sign indicating the future plane of existence. Habitual karma is a healthy or unhealthy volition either repeatedly performed or performed once and repeatedly reflected upon. Authorities on the Abhidharma agree that as a factor determining the nature of the next rebirth a weighty karma, whether healthy or unhealthy, invariably takes precedence over death-proximate and habitual karmas. In the absence of a weighty karma, the determining factor is either a death-proximate or a habitual karma, the order of precedence being here a matter of dispute. Residual karma is a healthy or unhealthy karma not included in the previous three classes which has been performed once and which can determine rebirth only if it has been repeatedly reflected upon.

Karmas are also fourfold according to function, the sixth principle of classification. From this point of view they are either 'reproductive', 'supportive', 'counteractive', or 'destructive'. The first function produces the psychophysical 'personality' of the next birth and maintains it for the period of its existence; the second produces no effects of its own, but supports and strengthens those of a reproductive karma; the third, on the contrary, weakens the results of a reproductive karma; the fourth destroys them and produces effects of its own. Reproductive karma is likened to sowing seed, supportive to manuring and irrigating the field, counteractive to a hailstorm that spoils the crop, and destructive to a fire that consumes it and leaves only ash.

Though enumerated one after another, the thirty-two types of karma so far described are not mutually exclusive, for we have to deal not with a machine made up of a limited number of cogs and wheels, each with its own separate function, but simply with a play of healthy and unhealthy volitions that can be looked at from various points of view as represented by the principles of classification.

With regard to the plane of existence on which they mature, the seventh and last such principle, four classes of karma are distinguished: unhealthy volitions maturing in the four lowest, subhuman *kāmaloka* planes, namely those of the anti-gods (*asuras*), revenants (*pretas*), animals, and infernals, all of which are planes of misery; healthy volitions maturing in any one of the seven higher *kāmaloka* planes, namely the human plane, where 'joy and woe are woven fine',[103] and the six lowest divine realms, where there is only joy; healthy volitions (namely the four *rūpa-dhyānas*) maturing according to their degree of intensity in any one of the twelve higher divine sub-planes of the *rūpaloka*, where from the fourth sub-plane upwards even joy is transcended; and healthy volitions (the four *arūpa-dhyānas*) maturing in the four sub-planes of the *arūpaloka*. Counting the human plane and each of the three lowest *kāmaloka* planes (omitting that of the *asuras*) separately, and reckoning all the divine planes, lower and higher, as one plane, we get the *pañca-gati* or five 'goings' of sentient beings according to their karma as depicted in the five principal segments of the wheel of life. A sixth segment is often made by dividing that of the gods into two and allotting one half to the *asuras*.

According to the *Divyāvadāna* or 'Divine Heroic Feats [of the Buddha and his Disciples]', one of the best-known *avadānas* of the

Sarvāstivādins, the original model of the wheel of life was painted over the gateway of the Veḷuvana Vihāra at Rājagṛha on the personal instructions of the Master, who indicated exactly how the work should be done.[104] Whether or not of so ancient an origin, it undoubtedly figures on the wall of one of the rock-cut monasteries of Ajanta, and is still well known in Tibet, where it is often depicted inside temple porches for the edification of the faithful.

The wheel consists of four concentric circles. Working from centre to circumference, the first circle, which constitutes the hub of the Wheel, contains three animals representing the three poisons: a dove (or cock) for lust (*lobha*), a snake for hatred (*dveṣa*), and a pig for delusion (*moha*), each biting the tail of the one in front. They represent different aspects of egocentric volition which, whether in its subtle healthy or its gross unhealthy forms, keeps going the whole process of conditioned existence. The second circle is divided into two equal segments, one white and one black. In the former, human beings whose volitions were healthy joyfully ascend into the realm of the gods; in the latter, those whose volitions were unhealthy plunge terrified headlong into hell. The third circle is divided into six segments, one of each of the six classes of sentient beings already described. At the top is the realm of the gods, next (in clockwise order) the *asuras*,[105] then the animal kingdom, at the bottom the infernal regions, after that the plane of the *pretas*, and finally the human world. In each sphere of existence the bodhisattva Avalokiteśvara, representing the omnipresence of absolute compassion, appears in a differently coloured Buddha-form with insignia appropriate to the needs of its inhabitants. As a white Buddha he plays the melody of impermanence on a lute to the long-lived gods, as a green one brandishes at the warlike *asuras* the flaming sword of knowledge, which alone wins the true victory, as a blue one shows the animals a book, as a smoke-coloured one showers the infernal beings with ambrosia, as a red one regales the *pretas* with food and drink, and as a yellow one bears among men a staff and begging-bowl, symbolical of the holy life which they alone of the different classes of sentient beings are fully capable of leading.

The fourth and outermost circle of the Wheel is divided into twelve segments, each representing one of the *nidānas* or 'links' in the process of the *pratītya-samutpāda* or 'conditioned co-production' of the so-called individual stream of consciousness-volition as, appearing now in one, now in another of the six spheres, it twists round and round in the vortex of conditioned existence. The first two segments (again counting in clockwise order from the top) depict a blind man with a stick and a potter with wheel and pots. These represent *avidyā* and the *saṃskāras* ('ignorance' and the 'formative' psychological factors), which together constitute the karma-process of the past life and in dependence on which arises the result-process of the present life. This result-process is covered by the next five segments, which respectively depict: a monkey climbing a flowering tree; a boat with four passengers, one of whom is steering; an empty house with six apertures; a man and woman embracing; and a man with an arrow stuck in his eye. The monkey is *vijñāna*, consciousness; not in the widest acceptation of the term, but in the narrower sense of the initial flash of consciousness arising in the mother's womb at the moment of conception in dependence on the last flash of consciousness of the previous life. This *paṭisandhi* or 'relinking' consciousness, as it is technically called, is neither the same as nor different from the *cuti-citta* or 'death-consciousness' by which it is conditioned. Hence it does not constitute an unchanging, transmigrating entity. Though the requisite physical factors are present, in the absence of the relinking consciousness no conception can take place. The boat and its four passengers are the *skandhas*, the five 'groups' or 'heaps' into which Buddhism analyses the psychophysical personality. These are *rūpa* or body (the boat) and *vedanā* or feeling, *saṃjñā* or perception, the *saṃskāras* or volitional mental phenomena, and *vijñāna* or consciousness (the four passengers: consciousness is steering). They will be dealt with in Chapter 12. The empty house with six apertures stands for the six sense-organs (*ṣaḍāyatana*), mind being reckoned as the sixth, while the man and woman embracing represent contact (*sparśa*) in the sense of the mutual impingement of the sense-organs and the external world. The man with the arrow stuck in his eye depicts feeling (*vedanā*), whether pleasant, painful, or neutral. The eighth, ninth, and tenth segments of the circle show a woman offering a drink to a seated man; a man gathering fruit from a tree; and a woman great with child. These represent the karma-process of the present life. The woman offering drink to the seated man symbolizes thirst or craving (*tṛṣṇā*); the man gathering fruit from the tree grasping (*upādāna*); and the woman great with child 'becoming' (*bhava*) or conception. Though the Theravādins include the last of these three links in the karma-process of the present life, it ought really to be reckoned as the first link of the result-process of the next life. According to the Sarvāstivādins, who interpret the word differently, it refers to the *antarābhava* or period of 'intermediate existence' between two lives of which the *Bardo Thödol*, known in the West as *The Tibetan Book of the Dead*, paints a vivid picture. The eleventh and twelfth segments, representing the two links which constitute the result-process of the next life, show a woman in childbirth and a man carrying a corpse to the cemetery on his back. The first obviously illustrates birth, the second (old age, disease, and) death.

Thus after being divided into karma-processes and result-processes the twelve *nidānas* of the *pratītya-samutpāda* are distributed over the past life, the present life, and the future life. Herein it should be noted that ignorance and the formative psychological factors, the karma-process of the past, coincide with craving, grasping, and becoming, the karma-process of the present. Likewise consciousness, name and form, the six sense-organs, contact, and feeling, the result-process of the present, correspond with birth and death, the result-process of the future. In each life karma-process and result-process go on simultaneously, the result-process of the preceding coexisting with the karma-process of the succeeding existence. The karma-process in a way resembles the *Wille* and the result-process the *Vorstellung* of Schopenhauer's philosophy.[106] To summarize the message of the twelve segments: sentient existence consists of activities set up through spiritual ignorance; as a result, beings take rebirth as psychophysical organisms equipped with sense-organs by means of which they establish contact with the external world and experience pleasant, painful, and neutral sensations; developing a craving for the pleasant sensations, they try to cling on to the objects that produce them, which leads (according to the Theravādins) to fresh conception in a womb or (according to the Sarvāstivādins) to the plane of intermediate existence; in consequence of this they again have to undergo birth, old age, disease, and death.

Finally, peering over the rim of the outermost circle a fearsome monster wearing a headdress of skulls is shown clasping the Wheel with all its circles and segments in his teeth and between his arms and legs. This is Death or Impermanence. Outside the Wheel above the monster's head, floating on clouds to the right, the Buddha compassionately points out to sentient beings the way of release from conditioned existence.

The details of the Abhidharma discussion of karma and the

pratītya-samutpāda, a few of which have just been given, should not be allowed to obscure the great truth of which they are both expressions, namely that, on the level of individuality, consciousness precedes and determines being, and that being is therefore in essence consciousness. Consciousness-volition is of two kinds, individual and collective. As Takakusu, using a slightly different terminology, puts it:

> Individual action-influence creates the individual being. Common action-influence creates the universe itself.[107]

The wheel of life is the objectivization of the lust, hatred, and delusion in the mind of man. A modern writer, Ben Shahn, seems to have understood this more clearly than some scholars of Buddhism.

> In a monastery near the border of Tibet – where I went hoping it might be over the wall – I found a portrait of myself. Someone in saffron told me that it was called the Wheel of Life, the Round of Existence, but it was myself, exact and representational. There were all the many aspects of myself painted crude and clear: the pig, the lion, the snake, the cock, all animals, angels, demons, titans, gods and men, all heaven and hell, all pleasures and pains, all that went to make me, and all as it were, within the round of myself, within the wall, exactly as I had found it. All that I could be was within the enclosure of myself, all that I could do would only turn the Wheel around and around. There was no way out. I would go on and on, now up, now down, never ceasing, never changing. The mechanism was perfect. I had achieved perpetual motion: immortality.[108]

Huineng (Wei Lang), the sixth patriarch of the Chan or Dhyāna school in China, had given the same idea profounder and more succinct expression centuries earlier.

> The idea of a self (ātma) or that of a being is Mount Meru. A depraved mind is the ocean. *Klesha* (defilement) is the billow. Wickedness is the evil dragon. Falsehood is the devil. The wearisome sense objects are the aquatic animals. Greed and hatred are the hells. Ignorance and infatuation are the brutes.[109]

The universe referred to here, and depicted in the wheel of life, is of the kind known as an impure Buddha-field. As previously described (see p. 42), a *sambhogakāya* Buddha exercises jurisdiction over and is responsible for the spiritual progress of the inhabitants of one world system, which is therefore known as his Buddha-field. Such fields (*kṣetras*) of influence are of two kinds, pure and impure. An impure Buddha-field, like the one to which our own earth belongs, is inhabited by beings of all the six classes of existence. A pure Buddha-field contains only two of them, namely gods and men, and the conditions under which they live are infinitely more favourable to the attainment of Enlightenment than those of an impure Buddha-field. Some pure Buddha-fields come into existence as a result of the collective karma of divine and human beings of more than average spirituality; others are willed into existence by a particular bodhisattva who, out of compassion for sentient beings, vows to establish for their benefit a Pure Land whereof, after his Enlightenment, he will himself be the presiding Buddha. Both kinds of pure Buddha-field arise in dependence on a consciousness that, whether individual or collective, is not merely healthy but spiritually pure, for which reason they are not regarded as included in the three great planes of existence, the *kāmaloka*, the *rūpaloka*, and the *arūpaloka*, but as it were standing apart from and outside them all. As the *Vimalakīrti-nirdeśa* declares:

> If one wishes to reach the Pure Land, he must purify his mind. In accord with the purity of his mind, so will the Buddha-field be pure.[110]

Just as the impure mind, whether healthy or unhealthy, creates impure Buddha-fields, so the pure mind creates Buddha-fields that are pure. In the words of the *Avataṃsaka Sūtra*:

> All the Buddhalands rise from one's own mind and have infinite forms,
> Sometimes pure, sometimes defiled, they are in various cycles of enjoyment or suffering.[111]

Nevertheless it should not be thought that the six spheres of existence depicted in the wheel of life, and the various Pure Lands described in the

Scriptures, are no more than figurative expressions for what in essence are purely subjective mental states. The 'objective' world we perceive, with all its seas and mountains, trees, houses, and human beings, is in reality a state of mind. Contrariwise, what is in reality a state of mind can appear as an objectively existing world which those who inhabit it or, more precisely, those who have been or who are in the mental state correlative to it, can actually experience and perceive.

11
THE NATURE OF EXISTENCE

Now that we have explored the universe of Buddhism as it exists in space, time, and spiritual depth, as well as seen the way in which consciousness is involved in a process of perpetual objectification of itself to itself as one or another modality of sentient being, it is time to consider the 'marks' which attach to all conditioned existence and which express its true nature.

Besides provisionally distinguishing between *saṃskṛta-* and *asaṃskṛta-dharmas*, the conditioned and the Unconditioned, Buddhism, like the great metaphysical idealisms of the West, also distinguishes the conditioned as it exists in reality from the conditioned as it appears, that is, as presented to the senses and interpreted by the unenlightened mind. In reality conditioned existence is painful (*duḥkha*), impermanent (*anitya*), insubstantial (*anātman*), and ugly (*aśubha*). Owing to our habitual self-centredness and our deeply-rooted attachments, however, we imagine it to be pleasant (*sukha*), permanent (*nitya*), substantial (*ātman*), and beautiful (*śubha*), thus falling a victim to what are known as the four *vipariyāsas* or (mental) 'perversities'. Of course, most religious people, including even those who are nominally Buddhists, profess to regard the world as a vale of tears, a house of sorrow, a 'battered caravanserai'[112] in which man passes but one night and moves on; but observing them in the affairs of daily life one will be able to detect little difference, if any, between their behaviour and that of their admittedly worldly brethren, and it will soon transpire that the principles on which their actions are based, and which therefore constitute the real though concealed mainspring of their being, are usually the very opposite of the ones professed. They, no less than other men, live as though the world was on the whole a pleasant enough place, as though whatever they acquired could never be taken away from them, and as though they were going to live for a few centuries at least, if not for ever. Everyone will smile at the portrait, and perhaps recognize himself in it; but none but will continue to act as before. This is because the mental perversities are not just a matter of incorrect information, like thinking that the Buddha was born in China, but attitudes as deeply rooted almost as sentient existence itself. According to the Buddha's teaching they can be extirpated only by prolonged systematic meditation on the fact that the world as we know it is unreal. As an ancient and famous verse incorporated in the *Vajracchedikā Sūtra* exhorts us:

> As stars, a fault of vision, as a lamp,
> A mock show, dew drops, or a bubble,
> A dream, a lightning flash, or cloud,
> So should one view what is conditioned.[113]

In order to assist such meditation, *sūtras* like the *Laṅkāvatāra* and *ācāryas* like Asaṅga and Vasubandhu not only multiply such similes but explain them elaborately. Conditioned things are like stars, for instance, because having no real existence they cannot be got at or grasped; because they are insignificant in comparison with absolute reality, even as the stars in comparison with the vastness of space; and because when the Truth is realized it is no more possible to discern them than it is to see the stars after the sun has risen.[114] In their zeal to uproot the *vipariyāsas* both *sūtras* and *ācāryas* sometimes went to the extreme of declaring that the world was not only unreal but absolutely non-existent. According to the older and more widely accepted tradition, however, systematic meditation on the unreality of the world does not involve impugning its existence but consists in viewing it simply as painful, transitory, and insubstantial. These are the three 'marks' or 'characteristics' (*lakṣaṇas*) of conditioned existence with which we are now concerned. They correspond with the first, second, and third of the four mental perversities. The *locus classicus* of this most important doctrinal formula is *Dhammapada* verses 277–9, according to which the vision – by means of wisdom (*prajñā*) – that all *saṃskāras* are *anitya*, all *saṃskāras duḥkha*, and all *dharmas anātman*, constitutes the path of purity (*viśuddhi-mārga*).[115] As the third characteristic applies not only to the conditioned but also to the Unconditioned, in this case the all-inclusive term *dharma* is used instead of the word *saṃskāras*, which denotes only the conditioned. Sometimes a fourth *lakṣana*, 'Nirvāṇa alone is peace', is added to the original set of three.[116] This obviously applies only to the Unconditioned. For convenience of exposition we shall review the marks attaching to conditioned existence, and their corresponding mental perversities, not in the traditional order but in that of the ugly, the impermanent, the insubstantial, and the painful.

Aśubha, which means not only ugly but also horrid, disgusting, repulsive, or impure, is best understood by referring to the word from which it is derived by the addition of a negative prefix. *Śubha*, literally 'purity', really means beauty, though beauty of the spiritual rather than of the sensuous order. It is pure beauty in the Platonic and Neoplatonic sense of something shining in a world of its own above and beyond concrete things, which are termed beautiful only so far as they participate in its perfection. When Buddhism insists that all conditioned things are *aśubha*, it does not mean that we have to regard a flower, for instance, as essentially ugly, but only that in comparison with the beauties of a higher plane of reality those of a lower plane are insignificant. Beauty and ugliness are relative terms. We cannot really see the conditioned as *aśubha* until we have seen the Unconditioned as *śubha*. Similarly, within the conditioned itself, in order to see the ugliness and impurity of objects belonging to a lower plane it is necessary to ascend, in meditation, to one which is higher. This is the significance of the well-known episode of the Buddha's cousin Nanda and the heavenly nymphs:

> The Lord said to the venerable Nanda: 'You admit it is true that without zest you fare the Brahma-faring, that you cannot endure it, and that, throwing off the training, you will return to the low life. How is this?'
>
> 'Revered sir, when I left my home a Śākyan girl, the fairest in the land, with hair half combed, looked back at me and said: "May you soon be back again, young master." Revered sir, as I

am always thinking of that, I have no zest for the Brahma-faring, can't endure it, and, throwing off the training, will return to the low life.'

Then the Lord, taking the venerable Nanda by the arm, as a strong man might stretch out his bent arm or might bend back his outstretched arm, vanishing from the Jeta Grove, appeared among the Devas of the Thirty-Three. At that time as many as five hundred nymphs were come to minister to Sakka, the lord of devas, and they were called 'dove-footed'. The Lord asked the venerable Nanda which he thought the more lovely, worth looking at and charming, the Śākyan girl, the fairest in the land, or these five hundred nymphs called 'dove-footed'.

'O, revered sir, just as if she were a mutilated monkey with ears and nose cut off, even so the Śākyan girl, the fairest in the land, if set beside these five hundred nymphs called "dove-footed", is not worth a fraction of them, cannot be compared with them. Why, these five hundred nymphs are far more lovely, worth looking at and charming.'[117]

The Heaven of the Thirty-Three is only two *kāmaloka* sub-planes above the world of men; but regarded even from this level the loveliest human face is repulsive. The *rūpaloka* sub-planes, corresponding to the four *rūpa-dhyānas*, are higher still. Viewed from these levels the five hundred nymphs called 'dove-footed' are ugly. Thus objects are *śubha* in comparison with those of a lower plane, and *aśubha* in comparison with those of a higher plane of existence.

The type of meditation exercise that will help one to realize this personally by ascending into the *dhyānas* and actually seeing the lower ranges of conditioned existence as *aśubha* differs according to temperament. The *lobhacaritra* or 'passionate temperament', which tends to concentrate on the bright side of life ignoring the dark, and in which greed and attachment therefore predominate, will find the *aśubhabhāvanā* helpful. This method consists in contemplating the ten progressive stages of decomposition of a corpse. The *dveṣacaritra* or 'malevolent temperament', which sees the bad side of everything, and in which aversion predominates, on the contrary will be helped by concentrating on discs of pure bright beautiful colours such as those of flowers. One of passionate temperament should never begin by concentrating on attractive objects, which in his case will stimulate greed, nor one of malevolent temperament on repulsive objects, which in him will excite hatred, and greed and hatred are hindrances to meditation. On attaining the *rūpa-dhyānas*, however, both see the *rūpaloka* as beautiful and the *kāmaloka* as, in comparison, ugly.

Unfortunately, the specific function of those practices which focus attention on the repulsive and disgusting aspects of existence, as well as their special relation to one type of temperament, is not always understood even by Buddhist writers, some of whom appear to believe that according to Buddhism ugliness is real and beauty unreal and that one progresses in the spiritual life merely by seeing more and more ugliness and less and less beauty everywhere and at all levels of existence. As a well-known Sri Lankan Thera remarked to the writer once when shown an album of Tibetan religious paintings, 'I'm afraid that being a monk I'm not allowed to appreciate beauty.' Such strange misunderstandings, though current in some modern Theravādin circles, are easily refuted even from the Pāli scriptures. Addressing a non-Buddhist recluse the Buddha says:

> Now, Bhaggava,... certain recluses and brahmins have abused me with groundless, empty lies that have no truth in them, saying: 'Gotama the recluse and his brethren have gone astray. For Gotama the recluse teaches this:
>
> "When one reaches up to the Release, called the Beautiful, and having reached it abides therein, at such a time he regards the Whole (Universe) as ugly."'
>
> But I never said that, Bhaggava. This is what I do say: 'Whenever one reaches up to the Release, called the Beautiful, then he knows indeed what Beauty is.'[118]

However necessary a negative approach may be at first for those of passionate temperament, it is clear from this notable passage that, in principle, awareness of beauty, the positive factor, predominates in the Buddhist spiritual life over awareness of ugliness, the negative one. In the absence of any awareness of and delight in the 'beauty' of the Unconditioned all our efforts to convince ourselves rationally that conditioned existence is *aśubha* are likely to remain unfruitful, with the result that despite our protestations we shall continue to wallow in the mire of the *kāmaloka*. The failure to appreciate this fact is one of the reasons for the spiritually moribund condition of most parts of the Theravādin Buddhist world today.

'*Sabbe saṅkhārā aniccā*.' The characteristic of all conditioned things being impermanent, the first *lakṣana* according to the traditional order, and the second *vipariyāsa*, occupies a position as it were intermediate between the characteristics of *anātman* and *duḥkha*, the one representing a higher, the other a lower, degree of generality of the same truth. For this reason, personified Impermanence, and not Insubstantiality or Pain, is the monster shown clutching the wheel of life in murderous fangs and claws. The idea thus concretely expressed is not, of course, peculiar to Buddhism: in one form or another it is a commonplace of all higher religious and philosophical thought, as well as the oft-recurring theme of poets and mystics in every age and clime. What distinguishes the Buddhist treatment of it from that of other teachings is the relentless thoroughness with which it pursues, explores, and exhausts the topic. In traditional Christianity, only the more remarkable and catastrophic changes in human life, in history, and in nature were ever taken into consideration. Towards the end of the medieval period the crudely macabre vision of the Dance of Death, representing the transitoriness of mortal joys, haunted the imagination of the age; but however much a prey to worms sublunary things might be, for medieval thought all above the sphere of the moon rested in immutable perfection. Bodies might rot, but then, as now, the soul was a simple, incorruptible, and immortal substance.

No such exceptions to the law that all conditioned things are impermanent have ever been recognized by Buddhism, for it sees clearly that whatever has a beginning must also have an end. Whether in the physical universe without or the psychic world within, nothing is so huge or so minute that it can escape the clutches of the demon Impermanence. Already we have seen revealed as the cosmological background of Buddhism infinite space and infinite time wherein universes unnumbered rise into existence, persist, and disappear, the life period of each one covering thousands of millions of years (see p. 63). At the opposite end of the cosmic scale Buddhism shoots a penetrating glance at the tiniest conceivable unit of 'matter', the so-called atom, and sees not a microscopic billiard ball, static, homogeneous, and eternal, but a continuously changing dance of forces about a common centre.

Again, plunging into the spiritual depths of the universe, instead of everlasting abodes of eternally redeemed or eternally tormented spirits it beholds mental states objectified as perceptible worlds which, even though enduring for thousands of aeons, are still finite as the healthy or unhealthy volitions that first conjured them into being. Heaven, the ultimate goal of so many faiths, since it is a mode of contingent and hence of transitory existence is accounted no more than a pleasant interlude in a pilgrimage fundamentally of more serious import.

Deep as such insights into the impermanence of the conditioned go, and destructive as they are of cherished delusions, there is yet one which penetrates deeper still and destroys what, by reason of the natural resistance of the human mind, is the greatest delusion of all. Turning from the physical to the psychical, and focusing its gaze within, the Eye of Enlightenment pierces the depths of the human personality itself. Where common sense posits a real 'I', idealist philosophers the residual self, and theologians an immortal soul, that undeceivable Eye beholds not any such unchanging entity but, instead, an uninterrupted flow of mental events which, themselves arising in dependence on conditions, in turn function as conditions for the arising of further states.

For Buddhism, no less than for modern physics and psychology, all the apparently stable and solid material and mental objects in the universe are in reality temporary condensations of energy. Hence despite what some have assumed the use of such words as 'states' and 'elements' to mean, seeing conditioned things as impermanent does not consist in conceiving them as chopped up into bits (which would raise the artificial problem of how the bits were to be joined together again), but rather in seeing them as so many phases of one or the other of two pure, absolutely continuous, interdependent streams of energy which can be locked up in the atom, in the one case, and trapped in the individual mind, in the other. Whether the energy which is the reality of 'matter' and the energy which is the reality of 'mind' are ultimately one energy Buddhism does not at this stage of its analysis enquire. But according to some of the later developments in Buddhist thought, material is reducible to mental energy and both to the transcendental outpourings of the ineffable Void.

'*Sabbe dhammā anattā*.' From the impermanence of the conditioned to its insubstantiality is a short step; so much so that to penetrate at all deeply into the former is ultimately to find oneself in the midst of the latter. Like other doctrinal formulas, that of the three marks is by no means best understood when understood most literally, and it would be well to remind ourselves that in it we have to deal, not with three distinct properties of the conditioned, but rather with so many ways of penetrating into its true nature. One of the most convenient methods of making the transition from *anitya* to *anātman* is by considering the notion of change. We say 'the leaf changes from green to red.' In terms of the traditional grammatical-cum-logical analysis this is a sentence/proposition predicating in a certain subject/substance the succeeding of one attribute by another. Such an analysis implies that *in some sense* it is possible for a substance to exist without its attributes – that a leaf can hang on a tree without being red or green or yellow or blue or any other colour. In *what sense* this is possible has not always been clear, though. Quite a number of philosophers have treated what is evidently a purely linguistic convention, useful enough as a means of facilitating the acquisition of a language, as a real distinction between things. An extraordinarily large number of philosophical and religious doctrines are in fact based on this fallacy, including the conception of God as absolute being (that is, as being abstracted from all particular existent things), of the individual as embodying an immortal soul or changeless self independent of the sum total of psychophysical states, the dogma of the Trinity (unity of Godhead or substance distinct from plurality of persons), and the dogma of transubstantiation (change of the substances of bread and wine into the flesh and blood of Christ while their accidents remain unchanged). Other philosophers sought to evade the obvious difficulties of realism by maintaining that the distinction between a substance and its properties is conceptual; that it exists, but only in thought.

Buddhism, however, goes to the root of the matter and declares that, as modern studies in the subject have established, a phenomenon viewed dynamically is the totality of 'its' conditions and viewed statically the totality of its parts, and that over and above these conditions and parts no phenomenon exists. Abstracted from its green and red colour a leaf is not an independent entity but only a name. When it changes its colour what really happens is that, as the traditional formula would have it, in dependence on a green leaf a red leaf arises. This does not mean that the green leaf and the red are discrete, much less still that one is the 'cause' of the other, for the change from green to red is a continuous process. What it really means is that while the first *lakṣana* affirms only that all conditioned things change, the second *lakṣana*, penetrating far deeper, affirms that there is nothing which changes. To abstract the 'thing' which is changed from the process of change itself and set it up as an independent entity upon which change impinges as it were from outside is fallacious. The difference between *anitya* and *anātman* can also be expressed by saying that whereas according to the former the conditioned changes, according to the latter it *is* change – the implied distinction between subject and predicate, substance and attribute, being merely verbal. Further, since the change is continuous we are not to think of conditioned *dharmas* as entities lying as it were in a row side by side. They are in fact only so many sections marked off in the continuum of conditioned existence. In other words, the existence of the *dharmas* into which Buddhism resolves the so-called personality is in the final analysis as much nominal as that of the personality itself. This understanding receives explicit formulation in the doctrine of the twofold *nairātmya*, of *pudgalas* and of *dharmas*, advanced by the Mahāyāna[119] to counteract the pluralistic realism of the Sarvāstivāda, an influential early Hīnayāna school, which while agreeing that personality, as a congeries of conditioned *dharmas*, exists only nominally, maintained that the substance of these *dharmas* persists unchanged through the three periods of time.[120] Such a position, as its critics saw, and as from the positiveness of their denials we may infer even the Sarvāstivādins felt, logically results in a species of substantialism. Occasional deviations of this kind apart, Buddhist thought as a whole adhered faithfully throughout the long course of its development to the strict nominalism inherent in its doctrine of insubstantiality, for which reason it was able not only to root out from the minds of its true followers the last vestige of attachment to self, but also to remain free from the sort of confusions which arise from the uncritical assumption that the structure of reality must conform to linguistic usage.

The meaning of *anātman* is by no means exhausted, however. As we have seen, not only the conditioned, but also the Unconditioned, is insubstantial. But in what does its insubstantiality consist? Conditioned things are *anātman* because they are no more than the totality of their conditioned parts or functions and because, when they change, there is nothing which changes apart from the process of change itself. But the Unconditioned, the *asaṃskṛta* or uncompounded, is by definition impartite and unchanging. How, then, can it too be designated as *anātman*? On the face of it the term cannot be used in the same sense in both cases. The Unconditioned is *anātman* in the sense that it is *niḥsvabhāva* or devoid of determinate nature. It cannot be pointed out as this or that. All descriptions, such as that it is eternal and blissful, are true in the conventional sense only. In reality it is ineffable. Consequently it cannot be defined as existent, nor as non-existent, nor as both existent and non-existent, nor yet as neither existent nor non-existent. Carried to its logical conclusion, this means that it cannot be defined even as the Unconditioned, for such a definition limits it to being something other than the conditioned. Just as freedom, in order to be truly free, must liberate itself from the freedom that is opposed to bondage, so the Unconditioned, to be really such, must transcend the opposition between what is conditioned and what is not.

At this point the insubstantiality of the conditioned and the insubstantiality of the Unconditioned overlap. As we have already seen, the *dharmas* into which analysis resolves the so-called *pudgala* have themselves ultimately only a nominal, not a real, existence. Conditioned existence is in reality a pure continuum. The more deeply we fathom this continuum the more we realize that its true nature, too, is ineffable and that even as by penetrating into *anitya* we ultimately emerge in the midst of *anātman*, so by knowing the conditioned in its depth we know also the Unconditioned. Thus although at the level at which the two orders are seen as different *anātman* is used in one sense for the conditioned and in another for the Unconditioned, at the level where this difference is seen to be nominal the two kinds of insubstantiality resolve themselves, on sufficiently deep analysis, into a third, a profounder, kind. For *anātman* in this wider and deeper sense of the indescribable 'thusness' (*tathatā*) which constitutes the ultimate reality of both conditioned and unconditioned *dharmas* Mahāyāna thought generally appropriates the term *śunyatā*, literally 'voidness'. Nirvāṇa, the fourth or supplementary *lakṣana*, broadly coincides with the Unconditioned as cessation of the conditioned and hence as the goal of the aspiration of those to whom the surface of conditioned existence appears as permanent, pleasant, and real.

'*Sabbe saṅkhārā dukkhā*.' Though all the characteristics present difficulties to those who seek to understand Buddhism from a point of view other than its own, it is with regard to the statement that all conditioned things are suffering – corresponding to the second *vipariyāsa* and the first Āryan Truth – that they are apt to become most acute. On account of this characteristic do its critics complain that Buddhism is morbid, pessimistic, cynical, a lover of the shady side of the street, the enemy of harmless pleasures, an unfeeling trampler on the little innocent joys of life. At the same time they are confounded by the indisputable fact that the peoples of Buddhist lands seem happy; and often the more Buddhist the more happy. Some try to explain the anomaly as simply a case of Far Eastern cheerfulness breaking in through the Indian gloom of Buddhism; others dismiss it with irritation as a sheer perversity. In either case the critics remain uncomfortably aware of a plain contradiction between what they represent as the pessimistic principles of Buddhism and its optimistic practice. According to them, apparently, Buddhism being a pessimistic teaching its followers ought always to look sad.

In reality Buddhism is neither pessimistic nor optimistic. If compelled to label it in this way at all we should borrow a word from George Eliot and call it melioristic,[121] for though asserting that conditioned existence is suffering it also maintains, as the third *āryan* truth teaches, that suffering can be transcended. The mistake of the critics lies in assuming that according to Buddhism the conditioned is painful *under all circumstances and from all points of view*. Despite the loftiness of its thought, however, Buddhism is not so absurdly remote from ordinary human life as to deny that for the average man a glass of beer, an evening with his girlfriend, or a new car, are pleasant things. What it does is to point out that life also contains a number of undeniably unpleasant things, which nobody would ever pretend were enjoyable, such as old age, disease, death, being separated from what we like and associated with what we dislike. The latter make up the dark, painful side of existence which most of us do our best to ignore, and it is because we act in this ostrich-like fashion, not because, as sometimes alleged, it considers pain more real than pleasure, that Buddhism recommends various spiritual exercises which by bringing this dark side of life more prominently into view will give us a less one-sided picture of existence. Having done this, it goes a step further and points out that the pleasant things and the painful things, the sweet and the bitter experiences of life, are interconnected, so that it is impossible to enjoy the one without having to suffer the other.

This is not to say merely that a glass of beer may result in a headache, a girlfriend prove unfaithful, or a ride in a new car end in hospital, though of course all these things may happen. Pleasure and pain can be connected in much subtler ways than this. The repressed awareness that we are enjoying ourselves at someone else's expense, as nearly always is the case, gives rise to an unconscious sense of guilt that spoils the enjoyment. Pleasant things are tied up with worry and anxiety, because we are afraid of losing them. Enjoyable experiences, whether of body or mind, strengthen our attachment to the psychophysical personality that is the basis as much for suffering as for enjoyment. Moreover, pleasures differ not only in kind but in degree of intensity, and what was once pleasant may become less pleasant, or insipid, or even positively painful, in comparison with something more pleasant, or within the context of a wider range of experience. Vajrayāna tradition recognizes four stages of bliss: that arising from the senses (*ānanda*), from the *dhyānas* (*paramānanda*), from the attainment of Nirvāṇa (*viramānanda*), and from the realization of the non-duality of the conditioned and the Unconditioned (*sahajānanda*) – literally 'congenital', i.e. innate or natural bliss.[122] On experiencing the bliss of a higher degree one naturally loses interest in that of a lower degree of intensity. Thus although not maintaining the absurd thesis that all conditioned things are painful under all circumstances and from all points of view, Buddhism certainly does most vigorously maintain that no conditioned thing can be pleasant under all circumstances and from all points of view.

It goes even further than this. It maintains that even if one could cut out from the variegated web of life the bright parts of the pattern, leaving aside the dark, and assemble them into a single blaze of unmitigated brightness, the resultant experience would not even then be one of unmixed enjoyment. In the depths of the heart there would remain a void which no conditioned thing, but only the Unconditioned, could fill. This profound truth is echoed at a lower, theistic level of thought by St Augustine's famous apostrophe:

> Thou hast made us for Thyself, and our hearts are restless until they find rest in Thee.[123]

It is illustrated by Goethe's great and complex philosophical poem *Faust*, wherein the hero promises his soul to Mephistopheles if he can give him one permanently satisfying experience:

And heartily
When thus I hail the Moment flying:
'Ah still delay – thou art so fair!'
Then bind me in thy bonds undying.
My final ruin then declare.[124]

Knowledge, love, wealth, power, fail to pass the test. Like Māra in the Scriptures, Mephistopheles has at his disposal only conditioned things. The Unconditioned, which alone can satisfy the deepest longings of the human heart, is beyond his power, and Faust therefore never pronounces the word that would seal his doom.[125] What the third *lakṣana* really means is, in positive terms, that Nirvāṇa alone is peace, and negatively that conditioned things are painful because we seek in them that absolute bliss which only the Unconditioned can bestow and have, therefore, inevitably to experience disappointment and frustration.

To learn to see the conditioned as ugly, impermanent, insubstantial, and painful, instead of as the opposite, is not, of course, the work of a day. It can thus be seen only by means of *prajñā* or wisdom, a purely transcendental faculty that does not spring into existence all at once or by accident, but which has to be systematically nurtured, cultivated, and developed on the twofold basis of an ethical life expressive of healthy mental attitudes, and a purified, concentrated, and meditative consciousness. These categories, the first and second of which are covered by the terms *śīla* and *samādhi* respectively, together constitute the three great stages underlying all more detailed subdivisions of the Path to Enlightenment. Before we can proceed to discuss either the path in general, or the stages of which it consists, it will be necessary to make the acquaintance of the pilgrim.

12
THE HUMAN SITUATION

Except in the sense in which all things are unique, Buddhism, unlike the Semitic faiths, does not regard man as an absolutely unique being brought into existence by means of a special creative act and endowed by his divine maker with an immortal soul the possession of which constitutes an unbridgeable difference between him and all other creatures and entitles him to exploit and torture them for his own benefit and amusement. On the contrary it regards him as one manifestation of a current of psychophysical energy manifesting now as a god, now as an animal, revenant, tortured spirit, or titan, and now as a man, according to whether its constituent volitions are healthy, unhealthy, or mixed. Thus Buddhism does not think of sentient beings in terms of separate forms of life, one absolutely discrete from another, so much as in terms of separate currents of psychical energy each of which can associate itself with any form. Energy is primary, form secondary. It is not that man wills, but rather that will 'mans'. To state the position in this way should suffice to lay the dust raised by those according to whom Buddhism does not really teach that a man can be reborn as an animal, but only as a lower type of man dominated by a certain trait of which a particular animal is the generally recognized symbol, as the fox of cunning and the sparrow of lust. Putting as they do the cart before the horse, such misunderstandings are neither right enough to be wrong nor wrong enough to be right. According to Buddhism a man is not, strictly speaking, reborn as an animal; neither is he reborn as a man, nor as a god. What is 'reborn', in the sense of becoming temporarily linked to an appropriate form, is the continuously changing stream of psychical energy. If during the span of human life this stream consisted mainly of volitions connected with food and sex, or if the thought occurring at the moment of death was of the same low type, the consciousness arising in dependence thereon at the moment of rebirth (or, more properly, of reconception) will be an animal consciousness, and it will therefore arise in an animal womb. Apart from the exceptional cases of a yogi who has mastered the art of consciousness-transference or a bodhisattva who, out of compassion, chooses to be reborn on a subhuman plane, the idea of a human or spiritual consciousness imprisoned in an animal body is foreign to the Buddha's teaching. Besides failing to grasp the principle that sentient beings exist primarily as energy, and only secondarily as form, those for whom the Buddhist doctrines of karma and rebecoming involve any such idea are perhaps unconsciously motivated by the desire of somehow safeguarding the uniqueness of man. It is hardly necessary to elaborate the point that while Judaism, Christianity, and Islam, with their dogma of an irreducible difference between man and all other living things, condone and even encourage cruelty to animals, Buddhism, on account of its doctrine of psychical continuity, has ever taught that they should be treated with gentleness and compassion.

Though man is not unique in the sense of being at every level of his existence discrete from all other living things, human life does according to Buddhism possess a distinctive significance. For one thing, it is comparatively rare. For every one human being there exist perhaps thousands of mammals, millions of insects, and thousands of millions of microbes – not to speak of unnumbered gods, titans, revenants, and tormented spirits. Works of edification often ask us to reflect on this fact, realize the advantages of being born with a human body, and resolve to make the best possible use of the opportunity.[126] The weight of the advice derives from the fact that, besides being comparatively rare, the human estate occupies a position of centrality in relation to the other modalities of sentient existence. In fact it is in this centrality that the distinctive significance of human life mainly consists. Probably because of the difficulty of representing all the aspects of a truth simultaneously, the place which is allotted in the third circle of the wheel of life to the realm of men does not bring this fact out. From our present viewpoint a truer picture would be one which depicted man at the centre, with gods and titans in the north, tormented spirits in the south, animals in the west, and revenants in the east.

The centrality which such an arrangement would illustrate is twofold. Firstly, the human state is central in relation to pleasure and pain. While the tormented spirits experience pain without pleasure, the gods experience pleasure without pain. Man experiences both. Consequently he is neither so intoxicated with the one, nor so stupefied by the other, as to be incapable of directing his attention from the conditioned to the Unconditioned. He experiences enough suffering to make him discontented with the former, and enough enjoyment to generate in him a desire for the latter. Secondly, the human state is central in relation to karma and *karma-vipāka*. Karma, it will be remembered, means healthy or unhealthy volition, while *karma-vipāka* means the result thereof in the form of pleasant or painful experience. Only in the case of man is the balance between the two approximately equal; he both reaps what he sowed in past lives and sows what he must reap in future lives. All other forms of sentient existence are states of passive experience; they reap, but do not sow. The gods enjoy happiness corresponding in degree to the *dhyānas* which they had attained during their lives on earth as men; the titans suffer the results of jealousy, animals of mental indolence, tormented beings of violent hatred, and revenants of inordinate greed. Not that volition is entirely absent. In the case of the gods the uninterrupted experience of pleasure may give rise to an attachment so strong that, unless there is a balance of reproductive karma pertaining to the world of men still outstanding from the previous human birth, the next 'relinking' (*pratisandhi*, Pāli *paṭisandhi*) of the stream of consciousness concerned may take place on an appropriate subhuman plane. In the case of the *asuras*, animals, and revenants the painful experiences of frustration, oppression, and want that they respectively undergo are apt to occasion feelings of hatred so violent that, as a result, they are reborn either on an even lower sub-plane of the same state or among the tormented spirits. As for the tormented spirits, they can only sink deeper and deeper into hell. In other words in all the non-human planes of sentient existence conditions are such that unhealthy volitions are very much more likely to arise than healthy ones. Once involved in them, therefore, the stream of consciousness can only with extreme difficulty escape from the ever-accelerating process of deterioration, decline, and downfall. Animals and revenants can, indeed, be helped through contact with human beings, especially if the latter are spiritually advanced; but for tormented spirits the only hope lies in the actual descent to their own plane of a bodhisattva who, by preaching the Dharma to them, will provide a support for healthy volitions which, on the expiry of their term of life in hell, can function as conditions for rebirth on higher planes of existence. This dark picture throws into relief the greater freedom of action enjoyed by man, who, since he is provided with occasions for both healthy and unhealthy volitions, has facility of access to both the planes above and the planes below his own. Moreover, inasmuch as the state of concentrated wholesome volition called *samādhi* can function as a condition for the development of *prajñā* (wisdom), and *prajñā* for the attainment of *vimukti* (freedom), he also has access to the Unconditioned.

Basically, the twofold centrality of his position, in relation to pleasure and pain, and in relation to karma and *karma-vipāka*, consists in the fact that, one or two classes of quasi-exceptional cases apart, it is only when supported by a human body that the stream of consciousness can evolve to the point at which it is able to function as a basis for the manifestation of the absolute consciousness that constitutes Enlightenment. The distinctive significance of human life resides in the fact that by virtue of its mundane centrality in relation to the other forms of sentient existence it is analogous to the transcendental centrality of Buddhahood. A reference to our rearrangement of the six segments of the third circle of the wheel of life will bear this out. The rearrangement forms a sort of mandala. Snellgrove defines a mandala as

> A circle of symbolic forms … one symbol at the centre, which represents absolute truth itself, and other symbols arranged at the various points of the compass, which represent manifested aspects of this same truth.[127]

Thus there is not only a general correspondence, in the Hermetic sense, between the realm of conditioned and the realm of unconditioned existence, but also a particular, indeed a special, correspondence between the human condition and Buddhahood. This correspondence is the foundation of all such affirmations as 'I am the Buddha' and 'I am Vajrasattva' – or whatever other Buddha-form it is occupies the centre of the mandala. These affirmations, which occur in certain Mahāyāna *sūtras*, in many systems of Vajrayāna meditation, and in the sayings of Zen masters, may legitimately be made only in profound *samādhi*, in connection with which they can induce a state of consubstantiation between the yogi and the transcendental form on which he is meditating. Used indiscriminately, they are extremely dangerous. A purely theoretical concept of Buddhahood may, in effect, be superimposed upon the ego, with disastrous results. For this reason Buddhism generally prefers to speak the language not of identity but of analysis and change.

In the terms of this safer and in a way stricter language the so-called individual being is analysed into his constituent parts or, more accurately, his constituent events. According to the oldest and best-known analysis these events are of five types, technically known as 'groups' or 'heaps' (*skandhas*): (1) form (*rūpa*), (2) feeling (*vedanā*), (3) perception (*saṃjñā*), (4) mental phenomena (*saṃskāras*), and (5) discriminating consciousness (*vijñāna*). They are here spoken of as five types of event in order to emphasize the fact that, as most English renderings of the term fail to make clear, each of the *skandhas* (Pāli *khandhas*) represents not an unchanging 'thing' but rather a congeries of related processes, as well as to guard against creating the impression that the individual being can be analysed into the five *skandhas* much as a table, for instance, is analysed into four legs and a top.[128]

(1) *Rūpa* or form consists of the four great elementary qualities (*mahābhūta*) together with a number of derived or secondary qualities (*upādāyarūpa*). The former are enumerated as earth, water, fire, and air, by which are meant not the popular elements bearing those names but the forces of cohesion, undulation, radiation, and vibration. About the exact number of the secondary qualities there are differences of opinion between the various schools, the Theravādins enumerating twenty-three or twenty-four and the Sarvāstivādins and Vijñānavādins only eleven, but they may be said to comprise on the whole

> the objective constituents of perceptual situations (colors, sounds, etc.) and the 'sensitivities' (*rūpaprasāda*) of the sense organs which are manifested to a person himself by a mass of bodily feeling and to others through certain visual and tactual sensa.[129]

The fact that such items as masculinity (*puruṣendriya*), femininity (*strīndriya*), and gesture (*kāyavijñāpti*) are listed among the secondary qualities of *rūpa* should cause us to beware of thinking of this term as 'matter' in either the popular or the philosophic usage of the term.

(2) *Vedanā* or feeling, in the sense of the affective colouring which saturates a particular content of consciousness, is of five kinds, pleasant (*sukha*), painful (*duḥkha*), and neutral (*upekṣā*), the first and second being either bodily (*kāyika*) or mental (*caitasika*), and the third only mental. It covers, thus, not only sensation, or hedonic feeling, but also emotion, which can be not only hedonic but also ethical and even spiritual. Pleasant and unpleasant mental feeling are termed respectively *saumanasya* or joy and *daurmanasya* or sorrow. It is of interest to observe that while the latter can be hedonic only, the former possesses a positive ethical value and can be not only 'healthy' in the technical sense (see p. 70) but even karmically neutral. *Upekṣā* has an even wider connotation. It can mean not only hedonic indifference, both sensational and emotional, but also that positive state of spiritual balance or equanimity in respect of worldly things which plays so vital a part in the attainment of Supreme Enlightenment, being in fact reckoned, in this higher sense, as one of the seven *bodhyaṅgas* or 'Enlightenment-factors'.

(3) *Saṃjñā* (Pāli *saññā*) or perception is of six kinds, one for each of the five senses and one for the mind. Its function is twofold, consisting in the referring of a particular feeling to its appropriate basis, whether to one of the five physical senses or to the mind, as well as the awareness of the characteristics, real or imaginary, by which an object either of sense or thought is, or may hereafter be, recognized. It may also be either general or specific, the latter kind being that wherein a certain salient feature of perception is made the sole or at least the principal content of consciousness.

(4) By the *saṃskāras* (Pāli *saṅkhāras*) are meant, in this context, not conditioned things in general (see p. 62), nor the formative psychological factors (see pp. 68 and 75), but all mental phenomena whatsoever, with the exception of *vedanā*, *saṃjñā*, and *vijñāna*. As such the term corresponds to what are known, in the Abhidharma classification, as the *caitta-dharmas* (Pāli *cetasika-dhammas*) or 'mental concomitants' (here including *vedanā* and *saṃjñā*, separately enumerated in the five-*skandha* classification) which come or tend to come into operation with the arising of a particular type of consciousness. These mental concomitants are forty-six in number according to the Sarvāstivādins,

fifty-one according to the Vijñānavādins, and fifty-two according to the Theravādins. Despite minor differences of enumeration and classification, the list is substantially the same for all three schools. Each distributes the mental concomitants into various categories according to whether they arise in conjunction with all types of consciousness, healthy, unhealthy, and neutral, or in conjunction only with healthy and neutral, or only with unhealthy, states of consciousness. The Sarvāstivādins and Vijñānavādins reckon an additional category consisting of those mental concomitants which cannot, according to them, be included in any of the categories already mentioned.

(5) *Vijñāna* (Pāli *viññāṇa*) or discriminating consciousness is according to the Sarvāstivādins in itself only one, though sixfold in function inasmuch as it arises in dependence on the contact of the six sense-organs, including the mind, with their respective objects. The Theravādins, however, distinguish from the ethical point of view eighty-nine types of consciousness, twenty-one being karmically healthy, eleven karmically unhealthy, and fifty-five karmically neutral. The Vijñānavādins, who continue and develop the Abhidharma tradition of the Sarvāstivādins, count eight *vijñānas*. The two extra ones are the *kliṣṭa-mano-vijñāna* or 'defiled mind-consciousness' and the *ālaya-vijñāna* or 'store consciousness', which occupies an important place in the philosophy of this school. All three schools agree in regarding every 'unit' of consciousness as momentary (*kṣaṇika*) and as arising in dependence on a certain complex of conditions.[130]

From this fivefold Buddhist analysis of the individual being, of which only a sketch has here been given, it is obvious that corresponding to the term 'man' (*pudgala*), or to such terms as 'being' (*sattva*), 'living being' (*jīva*), and 'self' (*ātman*), there exists no unchanging substantial entity but only an ever-changing stream of physical and psychical (including mental and spiritual) events outside which no such entity can be discerned. Hence there can be no such thing, either, as human nature in the sense of a fixed and determinate quality or condition holding good of such an entity at all times and places and under all possible circumstances. Human nature is in reality a no-nature. Though capable of unspeakable wickedness man is not, for that reason, essentially and by very definition a miserable sinner, as some believe; neither is he 'in reality' a stainless immortal spirit, as supposed by others. Man is in fact indefinable.

This is the very conclusion reached from similar premises by the French existentialist Jean-Paul Sartre. Explaining what existentialism means by speaking of man as the being whose existence comes before its essence, he says:

> If man as the existentialist sees him is not definable, it is because to begin with he is nothing. He will not be anything until later, and then he will be what he makes of himself. Thus, there is no human nature, because there is no God to have a conception of it. Man simply is. Not that he is simply what he conceives himself to be, but he is what he wills, and as he conceives himself after already existing – as he wills to be after that leap towards existence. Man is nothing else but that which he makes of himself. That is the first principle of Existentialism.[131]

It is also the first principle of Buddhism. In Buddhism, however, the range of possibilities of conditioned existence open to man by virtue of his 'central' position in the universe is incomparably wider than that envisaged by existentialism. Moreover, in Buddhism the principle possesses an infinitely greater depth. As we have already seen, the mundane centrality of human life in respect of other forms of sentient existence is analogous to the transcendental centrality of Buddhahood. This means that man can not only make of himself whatever he wants to be but also cease altogether from making himself anything whatsoever. Existentialism goes as far as to assert that human nature is a no-nature. Buddhism, however, proclaims that this no-nature is Buddha-nature. Man realizes 'his' Buddha-nature when the energy of which 'he' is the expression no longer craves manifestation in any other form of conditioned existence.[132] Since this happens neither automatically nor instantaneously but by pursuing a regular sequence of steps with energy and determination over a certain period of time we again come back to the Path.

13
THE STAGES OF THE PATH

This subdivision of the Dharma, being the central one and pragmatically the most valuable, ought to be the clearest and simplest. In fact, however, it is often the most complex, not to say complicated. Such a state of affairs has come about due principally to two causes. Firstly, formulations of the Path as consisting of a specific set of moral and spiritual qualities or a particular sequence of steps and stages are so numerous, so rich in variety, and withal so often seemingly divergent, that what the Path is *in principle*, apart from all such formulations, is as much lost sight of as the original central trunk of the banyan tree amid the vast proliferation of supporting stems. Secondly, each school of Buddhism has tended to interpret the Path, not only in terms of the common doctrinal tradition, but also in accordance with its own distinctive tenets. In this account we shall be concerned with what the Path is in principle and with the formulation that seems to exhibit that principle with the greatest distinctness.

Man, as we have seen, is by nature indefinable. Human life represents a transformation of energy in dependence on which any other transformation of energy, mundane or transcendental, can arise. This is not to say that it is possible for any one such transformation to arise in immediate dependence on any other. As when a seed produces a flower, or when rough ore is smelted into gold and the refined metal wrought into an ornament, a number of intermediate steps connect the beginning with the end of the process. In the case of conditioned sentient existence the transformation takes place through the operation of the laws in accordance with which individualized consciousness determines being, that is to say, through karma and *karma-vipāka*, while the intermediate steps are the twelve *nidānas* depicted in the outermost circle of the wheel of life. In the case of the Higher Evolution from a mundane to a transcendental consciousness the laws governing the process are represented by the technical terms *mārga* and *phala*, 'path' and 'fruit', the intermediate steps being set forth in the negative and positive counterparts of the twelve *nidānas*.

These two sets of terms, that is to say karma and *karma-vipāka* on the one hand, and *mārga* and *phala* on the other, correspond respectively to the first two and the second two of the four noble truths. In the formula of the truths, however, the sequence is not deductive from cause to effect, but inductive from effect to cause. Thus karma corresponds to the second noble truth, the cause of suffering (*duḥkha-samudaya*), in this case craving (*tṛṣṇā*), and *karma-vipāka* to the first noble truth, namely suffering (*duḥkha*); similarly, *mārga* corresponds to the fourth noble truth, the way (*mārga*) leading to the cessation of suffering, i.e. to Nirvāṇa. More philosophically speaking, karma and *karma-vipāka*, the first two noble truths, and the arising of the twelve *nidānas* from ignorance to old age, disease, and death, represent a process of reaction in a cyclical order between two opposites, such as pleasure and pain, virtue and vice, healthy and unhealthy mental states, as a result of which what is popularly termed 'the world' or *saṃsāra* comes into existence. *Mārga* and *phala*, the second two noble truths, and the non-arising of the twelve *nidānas* from ignorance to birth, old age, disease, and death, represent not merely the counter-process of cessation, through which 'the world' or *saṃsāra* passes out of existence, disappears, or is annihilated, but also a process of reaction in a progressive order between two things of the same genus, the succeeding factor augmenting the effect of the preceding one, through or by means of which the gross, turbulent, and mutually conflicting energies inherent in *saṃsāra* are progressively refined, transmuted, and transformed into the state of harmonious and beneficent activity popularly termed Nirvāṇa.[133]

This process of reaction *in a progressive order* constitutes the basic principle of the Path taught by the Buddha as distinct from the various formulations wherein, for pedagogical reasons, the principle is given concrete expression. As the embodiment of this 'spiral' principle, moreover, and not because it represents a 'golden mediocrity' of the Aristotelian type or a half-hearted spirit of compromise, the Path receives its primary designation as the Middle Path or Way (*madhyama-mārga*). In the *Nidāna-vagga* of the *Saṃyutta Nikāya* the number of intermediate steps that connect the saṃsāric beginning with the nirvāṇic 'end' of the process whereby mundane mind is transformed into transcendental mind appear as a series of positive counterparts to the negative process of the cessation of the twelve *nidānas*.

In the canonical passage referred to the twelve factors constituting what may be termed the positive and progressive aspect of the *pratītya-samutpāda* are enumerated three times, once in descending and twice in ascending order. According to the latter mode of enumeration there is causal association of *saddhā* with *dukkha*, *pāmojja* with *saddhā*, *pīti* with *pāmojja*, *passaddhi* with *pīti*, *sukha* with *passaddhi*, *samādhi* with *sukha*, *yathābhūta-ñāṇadassana* with *samādhi*, *nibbidā* with *yathābhūta-ñāṇadassana*, *virāga* with *nibbidā*, *vimutti* with *virāga*, and *khaye ñāṇa* with *vimutti*.[134]

(1) *Dukkha* (Sanskrit *duḥkha*) or suffering. This is not only the first member of the nirvāṇic but according to our present text the last of the saṃsāric series, here replacing the more usual *jarā-maraṇa* or old age and death. As the second of the two *nidānas* which make up the result-process of the future life it corresponds to *vedanā* or feeling, the last of the five *nidānas* constituting the result-process of the present life (see p. 75). It also corresponds to the first noble truth or, more generally, to 'the world' as presented to the senses and the mind. Upon the attitude that we take up towards it depends our future fate. If we react with craving (*tṛṣṇā*), the first *nidāna* of the action-process of the present life, then we become once again caught up in the process of reaction in a cyclic order between opposites, and the wheel of life continues to revolve. If we refuse to react in this manner and respond instead with a healthy mental attitude we are carried out of *saṃsāra* into the process of reaction in a progressive order between two counterparts or complements, at the 'end' of which lies Nirvāṇa. *Vedanā* in general and *dukkha* in particular thus represent the point of intersection of the two different orders of reaction. It is the point of choice and decision, a choice, moreover, that confronts us not on two or three momentous occasions only but every instant of our lives.

Theoretically, of course, a total annihilation of craving, with a consequent instantaneous realization of Nirvāṇa, is possible at any time. In practice it is impossible. Whenever such cases seem to occur they will be found, on examination, to be the result of prolonged preparation. Nor might it be advisable to attempt a really instantaneous total destruction of craving even if this could be achieved. As with a sudden slamming on of brakes when the train is going at full speed such an achievement is likely to result in a derailment. What is needed is a smooth and gradual application of brakes. However quickly, or however slowly, they may be applied, the mechanical process of application consists of a certain number of stages. In the present series the first of these stages is represented by the second *nidāna*. In causal association with *dukkha* arises

(2) *Saddhā* (Sanskrit *śraddhā*) or faith. Though the Indian term is by no means equivalent to 'belief' in the Christian sense of accepting as literally true statements about God, the Fall of Man, the Virgin Birth, etc. for which there is no evidence, we have nevertheless rendered it by 'faith' in order to emphasize its definitely emotional character. *Saddhā* is, in fact, the healthy counterpart of *taṇhā* (Sanskrit *tṛṣṇā*), thirst or craving. It develops when, as the result of our experience of the painful, unsatisfactory, and frustrating nature of saṃsāric existence, we begin to 'place the heart' (the literal meaning of the verb with which *saddhā* is connected) not so much on the conditioned as on the Unconditioned. At first this is no more than a vague intermittent stirring of the emotions, hesitant and confused. But as it grows stronger, and as its object comes more clearly into focus, it develops into *saddhā* proper, that is to say into faith in the Buddha, the Dharma, and the Sangha, the first being primary, the other two secondary. Taken in this more definite sense *saddhā* may be defined as the heartfelt acknowledgement of the fact that the historical personality Gautama is the Buddha or Enlightened One, grounded firstly on the intuitive response that arises out of the depth of our heart by reason of the affinity existing between his actual and our potential Buddhahood, and secondly on the sensible evidence and rational proofs of his Enlightenment afforded us by the records of his life and teachings. When by following the Dharma we experience for ourselves the successive stages of the Path this faith, without losing its emotional character, becomes consolidated into confidence. At the stage with which we are now concerned *saddhā* expresses itself as

generosity (*dāna*) and ethical behaviour (*sīla*), which as we shall see later, are the first two *pāramitās*. Through the practice of these virtues the mind is purged of its feelings of guilt, repentance, and remorse, and thus a healthy mental attitude is created. In causal association with *saddhā* arises

(3) *Pāmojja* (Sanskrit *prāmodya*) or satisfaction and delight. Negatively this is the feeling experienced on becoming aware that one has nothing with which to reproach oneself as to morals. As such it is equivalent to the possession of an easy conscience. Positively it is the feeling of cheerfulness and content that arises in a man's mind out of his awareness that he is following the path of virtue. In Buddhism great importance is attached to this state. A mind that is disturbed by the recollection of a breach of moral precepts is incapable of concentration, so that the way to further progress is barred. Meditation masters such as Zhiyi, the founder of the Chinese Tiantai school, therefore recommend that before embarking on the practice of *dhyāna* one who has been guilty of any such lapse should undergo various observances, including confession, repentance, ritual worship of the Buddha, and the ceremonial recitation of *sūtras*, for a certain number of days, weeks, or months, or until such time as his mind is freed from the burden of guilt and again feels fresh, clear, and light.[135] Whether induced in the former or in the latter manner, *pāmojja* represents a blending (*modanā*) of the various elements in the emotive aspects of concentration, because the absence or resolution of the conflicts which arise whenever a man's behaviour fails to accord with his own ethical ideals inevitably promotes a sense of unity, harmony, and integration. As this develops and grows stronger, in causal association with *pāmojja* arises

(4) *Pīti* (Sanskrit *prīti*) or interest, enthusiasm, joy, rapture, ecstasy. This *nidāna*, the development of which marks the transition from the *kāmaloka* to the *rūpaloka* or in other words to a level of consciousness higher than that of the 'normal' waking state, arises naturally and spontaneously in the course of meditation practice as methodical concentration on a given object becomes more and more intense. Just as in the case of the previous *nidāna* the absence of any conflict between one's ethical ideals and one's actions produces a feeling of satisfaction and delight, so *pīti* represents the much greater sense of relief which comes about as the result of the liberation of the emotional energies which had been locked up in the deep-seated conflicts of the unconscious

mind. Guenther therefore quite rightly speaks of it as 'a driving and even overwhelming emotion'.[136] As, by a sort of psychological chain-reaction, greater and greater quantities of energy are released, *pīti* becomes more and more transporting. Tradition therefore distinguishes a number of different degrees of *pīti*. In the words of the *Aṭṭhasālinī*,

> Rapture is of five kinds: the lesser thrill, momentary rapture, flooding rapture, all-pervading rapture and transporting rapture. Of these, the lesser thrill is only able to raise the hairs of the body; the momentary rapture is like the production of lightning moment by moment; like waves breaking on the seashore, the flooding rapture descends on the body and breaks; the transporting rapture is strong, and lifts the body up to the extent of launching it in the air....[137] when all-pervading rapture arises, the whole body is completely surcharged, blown like a full bladder or like a mountain cavern pouring forth a mighty flood of water.[138]

From these descriptions it is evident that far from being only mental, *pīti* is accompanied by a variety of physical innervations. It is this that distinguishes it from *sukha*, the next *nidāna* but one. Hence before *sukha* can arise, in causal association with *pīti* arises

(5) *Passaddhi* (Sanskrit *praśrabdhi*) or calmness, repose, tranquillity, serenity. When the energies which in the process of liberation were experienced as *pīti* have been, as it were, exhausted, the accompanying physical innervations subside and in the ensuing mood of relaxation the attention is first disengaged and then wholly withdrawn from the body and its concerns. Consequently there also takes place a subsidence of feeling, in the sense of pleasurable sensation, and a subsidence of the perception and motivation derived therefrom. *Passaddhi* is therefore spoken of as twofold: that of the mind (*citta*) and that of the body (*kāya*) – here not the physical body but the mental factors of feeling (*vedanā*), perception (*saññā*), and motivation (*saṅkhāra*) collectively. It would be a mistake, though, to regard *passaddhi* as a merely passive state. Not only does it tranquillize consciousness and the mental factors but also, by easing strain and tension, bring about in them a condition of functional lightness, plasticity, adaptability, readiness, and directness. *Passaddhi* is thus a state of extreme refinement and delicacy of feeling, in causal association with which therefore arises

(6) *Sukha* (Pāli and Sanskrit) or bliss. Though the word has a very wide range of meaning, including that of pleasurable bodily sensation, it stands in this context for the apparently causeless feeling of intense happiness that wells up from the depths of his being when, the physical innervations associated with *pīti* having subsided, the meditator is no longer aware of the physical body. When discussing *vedanā* or feeling we saw that the term covers not only sensation, or hedonic feeling, but also emotion, which can be not only hedonic but ethical and spiritual. In the terms of this *sukha* may be defined as non-hedonic spiritual happiness. The author of the *Aṭṭhasālinī*, according to whom *pīti* belongs to the *saṅkhāra-khandha* and *sukha* to the *vedanā-khandha*, endeavours to exhibit the true meaning of the present *nidāna* by contrasting it with *pīti* by means of an apt similitude.

> A man who, travelling along the path through a great desert and overcome by the heat, is thirsty and desirous of drink, if he saw a man on the way, would ask, 'Where is water?' The other would say, 'Beyond the wood is a dense forest with a natural lake. Go there, and you will get some.' He hearing these words would be glad and delighted and as he went would see lotus leaves, etc., fallen on the ground and become more glad and delighted. Going onwards, he would see men with wet clothes and hair, hear the sound of wild fowl and pea-fowl, etc., see the dense forest of green like a net of jewels growing by the edge of the natural lake, he would see the water lily, the lotus, the white lily, etc., growing in the lake, he would see the clear transparent water, he would be all the more glad and delighted, would descend into the natural lake, bathe and drink at pleasure and, his oppression being allayed, he would eat the fibres and stalks of the lilies, adorn himself with the blue lotus, carry on his shoulders the roots of the mandālaka, ascend from the lake, put on his clothes, dry the bathing cloth in the sun, and in the cool shade where the breeze blew ever so gently lay himself down and say: 'O bliss! O bliss!' Thus should this illustration be applied: The time of gladness and delight from when he heard of the natural lake and the dense forest till he saw the water is like rapture [*pīti*] having the manner of gladness and delight at the object in view. The time when, after his bath and drink he laid himself down in the cool shade, saying, 'O bliss! O

> bliss!' etc., is the sense of ease [*sukha*] grown strong, established in that mode of enjoying the taste of the object.[139]

As the comparison suggests, *sukha* in this context is not something which comes and goes in a moment, or which touches one superficially. On the contrary it is an experience of so enthralling and overwhelming a character that the meditator is occupied and absorbed, even immersed, in it, at times for days on end, to the exclusion of all other interests.

Non-Buddhist mystics who reach this stage, especially those belonging to schools which, like those of the Vedānta, define reality in terms of bliss (*ānanda*), are prone to imagine that such an attainment is sufficient evidence of their having realized God, or Brahman, or whatever for them constitutes the ultimate goal of life. To the Buddhist, however, the experience of meditative bliss is only a milestone on the way, and even while most deeply immersed in it he is careful to cultivate an attitude of detachment towards it and to avoid the mistake of settling down in it as though it was a permanent and final achievement. The Scriptures more than once represent the Buddha as saying with reference to his own early practice of the *dhyānas*,

> Yet the happiness which in that way arose in me, could not obsess my mind.[140]

At the same time neither the Buddha nor his followers have ever tended to underestimate the role of happiness in the spiritual life. In a passage of striking force and beauty Lama Anagarika Govinda writes:

> Out of the 121 classes of consciousness which are discussed in [Theravādin] Buddhist psychology, sixty-three are accompanied by joy and only three are painful, while the remaining fifty-five classes are indifferent. A stronger refutation of pessimism than this statement is hardly possible. How deluded is man, that he mainly dwells in those three painful states of consciousness, though there are overwhelmingly more possibilities of happiness! But what a perspective this knowledge opens to those who strive earnestly, what an incentive even to the weak! The more man progresses, the more radiant and joyful will be his consciousness. Happiness,

> indeed, may be called a characteristic of progress. In the course of its development it becomes more and more sublime, until it grows into that serenity which radiates from the face of the Enlightened One with that subtle smile in which wisdom, compassion, and all-embracing love are mingled.[141]

What the Buddhist tradition in all its branches is concerned to emphasize is that however natural, healthy, and intense the experience of meditative bliss may be, the meditator must be careful not to allow it to overpower his mindfulness in such a way that the path to further progress is barred. The immediate nature of that progress is indicated by a number of scriptural aphorisms, such as 'The mind of the happy one becomes concentrated'.[142] Thus in causal association with *sukha* arises

(7) *Samādhi* (Pāli and Sanskrit) or 'concentration'. Like that of several other terms in the series, the meaning of *samādhi* tends to vary according to context. At its simplest it is mere one-pointedness of mind, or concentrated attention on a single object. Such one-pointedness may be associated with a morally healthy or unhealthy, or with a neutral, consciousness. The minds of the fornicator and the murderer are certainly concentrated on their respective objects, but being concentrated through lust in the one case and hatred in the other their concentration is said to be unhealthy. *Samādhi* is therefore properly not one-pointedness of mind in general but healthy one-pointedness, *kauśalya-ekāgratā-citta* (Pāli *kosalla-ekāggatā-citta*).

In connection with the systematic cultivation of this *nidāna* through the practice of definite spiritual exercises three degrees of depth and intensity of *samādhi* are distinguished: preparatory concentration – when the mind is fixed on the gross external object pertaining to the particular practice adopted, say on the process of respiration, an image of a Buddha or bodhisattva, or the sound of a mantra audibly repeated; intermediate concentration – when the mind is fixed on the subtle and frequently luminous counterpart that arises when the gross object has been attended to for a sufficient length of time; and full concentration – which is attained when the mind is absorbed in the subtle counterpart to such an extent that it becomes as it were one with it and no longer experiences it as something objective and external. Full concentration corresponds to *dhyāna* (Pāli *jhāna*). This in turn consists of eight degrees, four belonging to the 'form' (*rūpa*) and four to the 'formless' (*arūpa*) plane, each degree more refined than the one preceding.

In the first *rūpa-dhyāna* is present a residue of mental activity, besides the experience of *pīti* and *sukha*; in the second, mental activity subsides entirely, and *pīti* and *sukha* alone remain associated with *samādhi*; in the third *dhyāna* even *pīti*, comparatively the grosser factor, disappears; and in the fourth, *sukha* is replaced by *upekṣā* (Pāli *upekkha*). Despite the drily analytical manner in which some of the older texts tabulate these experiences one is not to suppose that the mental content can really be thus split up into various component factors which literally appear or disappear as concentration deepens. What the series of *rūpa-dhyānas* in fact represents is the progressive unification of consciousness, especially of its cognitive and affective aspects, on the basis of a stability which the unification itself progressively strengthens and makes more profound.

The four *arūpa-dhyānas* appear not to carry this process of unification any further but to render the fully concentrated mind subtler and as it were more transparent, as well as simultaneously broader and more universal, by confronting it with ever sublimer cosmic objects. These *dhyānas* are: that of the sphere of infinite space (*ākāśānatyāyatana*, Pāli *ākāsānañcāyatana*), of infinite consciousness (*vijñānānantyāyatana*, Pāli *viññāṇañcāyatana*), of no-thing-ness (*ākiñcanyāyatana*, Pāli *ākiñcaññāyatana*), and of neither-perception-nor-non-perception (*naivasaṃjñānāsaṃjñāyatana*, Pāli *nevasaññānāsaññāyatana*). Some scholars are of the opinion that the second set of four *dhyānas*, though known to the Buddha, was added to the first set so as to form a single continuous series only after his *parinirvāṇa*. Be that as it may, there is certainly a problem to be cleared up in connection with the Master's experience of the *dhyānas* the discussion of which will, even in the absence of a final solution, help to elucidate the true meaning of *samādhi* in the present context.

In the *Mahāsaccaka Sutta*, one of the great autobiographical discourses of the Pāli canon, the Buddha describes to the Jain ascetic Saccaka, whom he addresses by his clan name, the course of fearful asceticism to which he had subjected himself prior to the attainment of Enlightenment. After relating how the attempt had failed he continued:

> This, Aggivessana, occurred to me: 'I know that while my father, the Sakyan, was ploughing, and I was sitting in the cool shade of a rose-apple tree, aloof from pleasures of the senses, aloof from

> unskilled states of mind, entering on the first meditation, which is accompanied by initial thought and discursive thought, is born of aloofness, and is rapturous and joyful, and while abiding therein, I thought: "Now could this be a way to awakening?" Then, following on my mindfulness, Aggivessana, there was the consciousness: This is itself the Way to awakening.'[143]

He then described how, after attaining the remaining three *rūpa-dhyānas*, he had developed the three superknowledges (*abhijñās*), eradicated the three biases (*āśravas*), and finally attained *sambodhi*. From the passage quoted it is evident that during the whole course of his 'noble quest', from the time of leaving his father's mansion to the time of abandoning the path of extreme asceticism, the Buddha had not experienced even the first of the *rūpa-dhyānas*. Yet earlier in the same discourse, as well as in the *Ariyapariyesanā Sutta*, the Buddha relates his attainment of the spheres of 'no-thing-ness' and 'neither-perception-nor-non-perception', the last two *arūpa-dhyānas*, as already described (see p. 21).[144] If the two sets of *dhyānas* really constitute a single continuous series of meditative attainments how is it possible that the Buddha should have experienced the seventh and eighth members of the series before he had experienced the first? While the possibility that according to the Buddha himself the two sets of *dhyānas* are discontinuous and were arranged as a single series only later cannot be ruled out, there are other considerations relating to the true nature of *samādhi* which may help explain the discrepancy.

The distinguishing feature of the Buddha's boyhood experience of *samādhi* is its spontaneity; it came of itself, naturally and without effort. His later experience of the *dhyānas*, including that of the spheres of no-thing-ness and neither-perception-nor-non-perception, on the contrary seem to have been achieved at the cost of great exertion, as a result of a stupendous exercise of will-power involving the conscious and deliberate forcing of all his energies into a single narrow channel. What the sudden flashing of his boyhood experience into his mind probably conveyed to the Buddha was that the Way consisted not in achieving with grim determination goals fixed for itself by the conscious mind without reference to the total psyche but in the harmonious unfoldment, in and through mindfulness, of one's deepest potentialities. The way to Enlightenment was a middle way between making no effort at all and intellectually directed effort. In other words the Buddha discovered that the attainment of *samyak-samādhi*, the final stage of the Eightfold Path, as distinguished from the forcible fixation of the mind on any object however healthy or for however long a time, involves not merely the exercise of the understanding and the will but the transformation and integration of the total psyche in all its sublimest heights and most abysmal depths.

For this reason the practice of *samādhi* can never be reduced to the practice of a certain series of concentration exercises or to a special technique, much less still to a matter of professional expertise. It was their awareness of this danger which prompted the Sōtō branch of the Zen school to insist that one does not sit to meditate: one sits to sit. Not all schools of meditation, not even all Buddhist schools, have succeeded in steering so clear of the danger. Hindu yoga is exclusively a system of techniques; however efficacious as a means of physical and mental hygiene, it therefore possesses by itself no spiritual value. The so-called New Burmese Method of Satipaṭṭhāna, with its system of grades, examinations, certificates, and titles, even apart from the other objections that have been urged against it, would seem open, in the case of some at least of its exponents, to similar criticism.

Yet one need not go to the extreme of denying that techniques have any place at all in the practice of meditation, thus avoiding the Scylla of technism only at the cost of falling a prey to the Charybdis of quietism. As the whole progressive sequence of causally associated factors leading up to *samādhi*, the present factor, itself serves to illustrate, the following of the spiritual path is from stage to stage less a matter of egoistically willed achievement as of a growth, in and through awareness, of the total psyche. As Tagore says,

> No hurried path of success, forcibly cut by the greed of result, can be the true path.[145]

Energetic recourse to techniques of concentration by one who had not cultivated the preceding *nidānas* could result in complete frustration or produce, if apparently successful, either a morbid state of hypnotic fixation or a violent reaction from those parts of the psyche which had not co-operated in the attempt. In the opposite case, however, that of one who had cultivated the preceding *nidānas*, even the moderate practice of a concentration technique would be sufficient to induce profound *samādhi* experience. It might even be enough for him to see a beautiful flower, or to look at something bright and shining. For him who had cultivated the five previous *nidānas* to perfection the *samādhi*-experience would arise as soon as he seated himself and was mindful; he would not need to 'meditate'. This seems to have been the case, practically, of the Buddha.

Diseased or injured seed will produce only a deformed and stunted plant. Unless the preceding factor has been cultivated, if not to perfection, at least to an advanced degree, the factor which arises next in causal association with it will be only a caricature of what it ought to be. Though true of every factor, this is particularly true of *samādhi*. *Samādhi* is the last of the *laukika* (Pāli *lokiya*), or mundane, factors; the one immediately succeeding it will be the first of the *lokuttara* or transcendental factors which, as regress from them is impossible, constitute the Path to Enlightenment proper. Scriptural aphorism indicates this supremely important, indeed crucial, transition, in such words as 'The concentrated mind sees things as they really are.'[146] But if the *samādhi* is not true *samādhi*, but a mere forcible fixation of attention disrupting one part of the psyche from the rest there will arise in causal association with it nothing but delusions; one may imagine one has realized what one has not: in the case of a Buddhist, he may mistake purely intellectual reminiscence of the Dharma for actual penetration of its import. In any case, instead of safely traversing the point where wheel and spiral intersect one will, unknowingly, become more deeply and inextricably involved in *saṃsāra* than ever. Only in causal association with true *samādhi* arises

(8) *Yathābhūta-ñāṇadassana* (Sanskrit *yathābhūta-jñānadarśana*), 'Knowledge and Vision of Things As They Are' or 'According to Reality'. What needs above all to be emphasized in connection with this *nidāna*, with the arising of which we enter on the transcendental path, is the fact of its being essentially an experience. The preceding *nidānas* were, of course, also experiences, in their case experiences, in varying degrees, of psychic wholeness; but the knowledge and vision now attained differs from them in being also an experience of the ultimate meaning of things. As the terminal part of the compound suggests, far from resembling knowledge in the ordinary sense this experience is, rather, analogous to physical sight. The same comparison is implied in the word *vipaśyanā*

(Pāli *vipassanā*) or 'insight', which, in its more restricted sense, may be regarded as synonymous with the present *nidāna*. Both terms are moreover related in meaning to *prajñā* (Pāli *paññā*) or 'wisdom'; the difference being – though the usage is by no means rigid – that whereas they stand for the first intermittent flashings of insight *prajñā* represents its steady beam-like radiation: *bodhi* or *sambodhi* is the same faculty when it has succeeded in saturating the entire psychic contents and organizing them around itself in a harmonious system.

Apart from its intrinsic importance, the fact that *yathābhūta-ñāṇadassana* stands for a transcendental experience has been emphasized because the term itself and those which are approximately synonymous with it have been subject to so long a process of scholastic elaboration that it might otherwise be overlooked. Just as there is the danger of *samādhi* being confused with the practice of concentration exercises, so this *nidāna* might be identified with an understanding of the complex conceptual formulations of it that have been worked out over the centuries from Kātyāyana to Vasubandhu, and from Buddhaghosa and Anuruddha to Ledi Sayadaw. This does not however constitute an objection to such an elaboration, which as a means of giving the widest intellectual expression to the transcendental content of the experience is on its own level a quite legitimate activity. Though a rare orchid cannot really be valued in terms of money, the fact that a florist prices it at so many pounds sterling may stimulate the insensitive into a vague awareness of its beauty.

Historically perhaps the earliest, and 'philosophically' the most important, is that formulation according to which *vipaśyanā* or *prajñā* they are hardly differentiated at this stage consists in seeing the true nature of all conditioned things, that is, in seeing them as characterized by impermanence, pain, insubstantiality, and ugliness as already described in a previous chapter. Inasmuch as, according to the explicit teaching of the great Mahāyāna schools, the conditioned in its depth is non-different from the Unconditioned, insight into the one becomes eventually insight into the other. The fact of this ultimate non-duality finds expression in the correspondence which all schools of Buddhism, both Hīnayāna and Mahāyāna, acknowledge to exist between the three characteristics (or first three perversities) and the three *vimokṣas* (Pāli *vimokkhas*). The latter represent different approaches to, or dimensions of, Nirvāṇa, access to any of them being obtainable through the cultivation of insight into the corresponding characteristic. They will be discussed in the next chapter.

As already insisted, the present *nidāna* is of crucial importance in the series as it represents the point of transition from the mundane to the transcendental order of existence. One who reaches this stage, for whom through insight into the three characteristics there arises Knowledge and Vision of Things As They Are, ceases to be a *pṛthagjana* (Pāli *puthujjana*), or ordinary man, and becomes one of the Noble, an *ārya* (Pāli *ariya*). Insight being of varying degrees of profundity, the Noble do not all belong to one grade of attainment but make up a spiritual, or rather a transcendental, hierarchy. This hierarchy constitutes the Āryasaṅgha (see Chapter 15). At the bottom rung of the great ladder stands the *śrotāpanna* (Pāli *sotāpanna*) or Stream-Winner who, as his designation suggests, having escaped from the vortex of *saṃsāra* joyously abandons himself to the irresistible sweep of the mighty current that will infallibly bear him one day to the infinite ocean of Nirvāṇa. From the point of view from which the two are seen as a duality, the nearer one approaches Nirvāṇa the further behind he leaves *saṃsāra*. Thus in causal association with *yathābhūta-ñāṇadassana* arises

(9) *Nibbidā* (Sanskrit *nirvid, nirveda*) or disgust. As this *nidāna*, like the four other members of the transcendental series, remains associated with the state of perfect psychic wholeness termed *samādhi*, it would be a mistake to regard it as being merely a movement of recoil or withdrawal from the imperfections of the world in the ordinary psychological sense as, in fact, its translation by such words as disgust, aversion, and repulsion tends to suggest. The latter type of reaction is, of course, a common enough phenomenon in both worldly and religious life, and in the latter sphere may sometimes play a quite legitimate preliminary role; but it must never be confused with *nibbidā*, which it resembles only analogically. Disgust and aversion are generally rooted in unhealthy mental attitudes. *Nibbidā*, however, springs from an insight which, though based on healthy mental factors, is itself neither healthy nor unhealthy, but transcendental. The way in which insight into the three characteristics of conditioned things results in a 'serene withdrawal' from them as we might paraphrase the term – though in ordinary parlance serenity excludes the idea of speed – is the main point of Buddhaghosa's apt illustration of the relation between these two experiences.

> A man thought to catch a fish, it seems, so he took a fishing net and cast it in the water. He put his hand into the mouth of the net under the water and seized a snake by the neck. He was glad, thinking 'I have caught a fish.' In the belief that he had caught a big fish, he lifted it up to see. When he had seen three marks [on its head] he perceived that it was a snake, and he was terrified. He saw danger, felt revulsion for what he had seen, and desired to be delivered from it. Contriving a means of deliverance, he unwrapped [the coils from] his arm, and when he had weakened the snake by swinging it two or three times round his head, he flung it away, crying 'Go, foul snake!'[147]

Quite apart from the fact that three more *nidānas* remain to be developed, withdrawal is far from being the last word even at this stage. Though the fact was made fully explicit only by the Mahāyāna, inasmuch as *sambodhi* is not in the ultimate sense a personal acquisition, however much the structure of language may compel us to speak of it as such, concern for the temporal and spiritual welfare of others cannot be entirely excluded at any stage of the Path. Withdrawal must therefore be conjoined with compassion (*karuṇā*). In the beautiful words of Tsongkhapa:

> But since that withdrawal, too, unless controlled
> By a pure 'mind-generation' does not become the cause
> Of unsurpassed Enlightenment's consummate felicity,
> Intelligent ones should generate the excellent bodhi-mind.[148]

This *bodhicitta* or will to Supreme Enlightenment not for one's own sake only but for the benefit of all sentient beings arises out of the conjunction of the present movement of serene withdrawal from the conditioned, viewed as impermanent, painful, and insubstantial, with the paradoxical feeling of compassion for sentient beings who, from the previous stage onwards, have been recognized as in reality no-beings. According to a popular Far Eastern exegesis the Buddha is called Tathāgata because he 'thus goes' (*tathā-gata*) out of the world through wisdom and 'thus comes' (*tathā-āgata*) back into it through compassion.

Nibbidā, therefore, at its own level of attainment, is to be confused no more with spiritual individualism and escapism than with a mere psychological reaction. This clarification will help us avoid an analogous misunderstanding of the next *nidāna*, to which attention must now be directed. In causal association with *nibbidā* arises

(10) *Virāga* (Sanskrit *vairāgya*) or 'dispassion'. Having recognized the true nature of conditioned things and finally 'withdrawn' from them the mind has now reached a stage where they are no more able to disturb or move it than the soft clouds nestling on the lower slopes of the Himalayas have the power to shake to its foundations the loftiest peak. This is the mental state of unruffled tranquillity which Buddhist art strives to depict in its vision of the majestically calm figure of the Buddha seated, with eyes half closed, beneath the bodhi tree, while Māra's three daughters exhibit their charms, and the demon armies brandish their weapons, in vain. It is the attainment hymned in the eleventh verse of the *Maṅgala Sutta* as the culmination of all temporal and spiritual weal:

> He whose mind does not shake
> When touched by the [eight] worldly conditions,
> Being sorrowless, stainless and secure –
> This is the greatest blessing.[149]

Despite the poverty of our vocabulary, which forces us to apply analogically to transcendental realizations terms derived from mundane experiences, the exalted state here described is much more than an ethical state of impassibility, like the Stoic *apatheia*, or a merely psychological condition of equanimity. To an even greater extent than its predecessor *virāga* is essentially the consequence of a profound 'metaphysical' cognition. This cognition, penetrating from the emptiness of the conditioned to the Emptiness of the Unconditioned, comes to rest in the realization that all *dharmas* whatsoever, conditioned and unconditioned, are equally *śūnyatā* and that they are, therefore, in respect of their emptiness, identical. At the level of Buddhahood this type of realization is known as *samatā-jñāna*, the wisdom of sameness or equality, and is symbolized by the Buddha Ratnasambhava. The conditioned having been seen as in reality unconditionally identical with the Unconditioned there can be no question of any real movement from the one to the other. It is the absence of movement in this sense, and for this reason, that constitutes *virāga*. In causal association with *virāga* there arises, as the penultimate stage of the Path,

(11) *Vimutti* (Sanskrit *vimukti*) or liberation. This is often popularly interpreted in a dualistic sense simply as liberation from *saṃsāra*, and on its own level the interpretation is a perfectly valid one. But as we have already had occasion to point out, in order to be truly free one has to escape not only from bondage but from liberation, not only from *saṃsāra* into *nirvāṇa* but from *nirvāṇa* back into *saṃsāra* (see p. 56). If one gets as it were 'stuck' in *nirvāṇa* conceived as a totally distinct entity from *saṃsāra*, one is, indeed, in a sense free, but it is not the ultimate and absolute freedom, for in another sense one has only become subject to a still more subtle bondage. One can never be really free so long as ideas, even the most highly refined and spiritualized, are treated as corresponding to ultimately real objects instead of as operative concepts.

Reference to the four degrees, or four successively more comprehensive dimensions, of *śūnyatā*, may help make the point clearer. (a) *Saṃskṛta-śūnyatā* or Emptiness of the Conditioned. Here one recognizes that being devoid of happiness, stability, and true being conditioned things are incapable of yielding any genuine or lasting satisfaction. (b) *Asaṃskṛta-śūnyatā* or Emptiness of the Unconditioned. The Unconditioned is seen as not only devoid of pain and the other characteristics of the conditioned but as being on the contrary a blissful, unchanging, and sovereign entity. These two degrees are represented by the Hīnayāna schools. (c) *Mahāśūnyatā* or Great Emptiness. At this stage the concept of emptiness is recognized as devoid of ultimate significance. In reality there is no difference between the conditioned and the Unconditioned, an ordinary man and a Buddha. Consequently there is in the ultimate sense neither abandonment of *saṃsāra* nor attainment of *nirvāṇa*. All concepts, even the most sacred, are merely words designating no separate real entities and possessing, therefore, no absolute significance. This degree corresponds to the general standpoint of the Mahāyāna, as exemplified in particular by the *Prajñāpāramitā* or 'Perfection of Wisdom' literature. (d) *Śūnyatā-śūnyatā* or 'Emptiness of Emptiness'. Here the concept of emptiness is itself rejected. As Vimalakīrti meant to convey, when he answered Mañjuśrī's question with a 'thunderous silence', in the ultimate sense nothing can be said.[150] This degree is represented by the Vajrayāna which instead of trying to elaborate a systematic conceptual formulation of this degree concentrates all its energies on the task of actually realizing it in the present life. *Vimutti* corresponds to the third of the four degrees, Great Emptiness. Having transcended the relatively true, yet not absolutely false, distinction between *saṃsāra* and *nirvāṇa*, it moves about as freely in the one as in the other. Hence this is also the stage of absolute compassion which, from the standpoint of the conditioned, appears to 'break through' from the Unconditioned in the form of the beneficent activity of Buddhas and bodhisattvas innumerable. However, the ultimate stage of the Path, though now in sight, has still not been reached. The pilgrim must press on to 'the endless end'. In causal association with *vimutti* arises

(12) *Āsavakkhayañāṇa* (Sanskrit *āśravakṣayajñāna*) or Knowledge of the Destruction of the Biases towards sensuous desire (*kāmāsava*), desire for continued existence (*bhavāsava*), and spiritual ignorance (*avijjāsava*). Despite the negative form of the first part of the compound it is far from representing a state of unrelieved annihilation: the emphasis is on the *knowledge* (*ñāṇa*) of the destruction of the *āsavas*. The correctness of this interpretation is sufficiently borne out by the number of times that, in what appear to be very early records, the Buddha's own attainment of *sambodhi* is spoken of in just these terms. Corresponding as it does to the fourth degree of *śūnyatā* in the absolute sense, nothing can be said about it. What little can usefully be said from the relative point of view belongs to the next chapter, when the truth behind the term will appear, not as the final member in the series of twelve positive *nidānas* which we have selected as the formulation that best exhibits the true nature of the Path, but independently, in its own right, as the Goal.

14
THE GOAL

Man is a constantly changing stream of psychophysical energy capable of manifesting, under the laws of karma, as any form of sentient conditioned existence. His nature is therefore a no-nature. This no-nature is Buddha-nature. Such were the conclusions reached in the last chapter but one. Accordingly we may now assert that the goal of human life is to realize Nirvāṇa or *sambodhi.*

But what is Nirvāṇa? What is the nature of Enlightenment? Some there are who maintain that while the Buddha described the Path in copious detail he remained silent regarding the Goal. This is only partly correct. Though he strongly discouraged the very human tendency of indulging in speculations about reality to the neglect of actually implementing the means to its attainment, his references to the Goal are for practical if not for philosophical purposes sufficiently explicit. At the same time it cannot be denied that in comparison to his long, systematic, and precise descriptions of the Path such references appear, for the most part, tantalizingly meagre and fragmentary.

As the centuries rolled by, it was inevitable that, with the constant growth and development of Buddhist thought, one reference to Nirvāṇa should be compared with another, and these correlated with yet others, until eventually as many of them as possible had been organized into a more or less systematic account of their great subject. Moreover, taking advantage of the immensely enhanced linguistic and other means of expression afforded them by a now highly developed tradition, some of the more gifted of the Buddha's followers began elaborating, out of their own spiritual experience, delineations of the Goal that were infinitely more rich, subtle, bold, grand, and complex than any before known. Though full documentation is impossible, most of these sources will be taken into consideration in the following short account.

In accordance with their natural phenomenology, descriptions of the Goal may be classified as negative, positive, paradoxical, and symbolic. Before proceeding to treat them in this order, however, we must introduce a formula which, since two of its terms belong to both the Path and the Goal, logically has a prior claim on our attention.

This is the formula of the three *vimokṣa-mukhas* (Pāli *vimokkha-mukhas*) or entrances to liberation. From a point of view somewhat deeper than that of their duality, conditioned and Unconditioned are not discrete but as it were continuous. Penetrating, through insight, into the painful, impermanent, and insubstantial nature of *saṃsāra,* one eventually catches sight of Nirvāṇa. Though the three characteristics are ultimately inseparable, one may begin by concentrating on any one of them. Fathoming the impermanence of conditioned things to its depth and emerging so to speak on the other side one sees the Unconditioned as the Imageless (Sanskrit and Pāli *animitta*); penetrating their unsatisfactoriness, as the Unbiased (Sanskrit *apraṇihita*, Pāli *appaṇihita*); and plumbing their insubstantiality, as the Void (Sanskrit *śūnyatā*, Pāli *suññāta*). By *nimitta*, image or sign, is meant the whole structure of subjectively conditioned ideas and concepts which we first build up round a particular sensuous perception and then regard as constituting its true nature as the 'object' of that perception. Prominent among such concepts are 'being' and 'non-being'. Seeing conditioned things as impermanent does not mean seeing them first as actually existing and afterwards as no longer existing but rather in reducing them to an absolutely continuous flow, or pure 'becoming', in connection with which the terms 'being' and 'non-being' are meaningless. The Unconditioned is spoken of as imageless in the sense that it transcends all ideas and concepts whatsoever and in the ultimate sense can be spoken of neither as existent nor non-existent, nor yet as both, nor even as neither.

Perceiving conditioned things as *duḥkha* means realizing that even the best of them are incapable of giving full and permanent satisfaction to the human heart. In ordinary life, pleasure gives rise to greed (*lobha*), pain to hatred (*dveṣa*), neutral feeling to delusion (*moha*). Here, since the true nature of these experiences has been understood and there exists neither attraction nor aversion, nor even indifference in the worldly sense, no bias or tendency towards greed, hatred, or delusion obtains. Nirvāṇa is called the Unbiased because of its complete immunity from these three 'poisons'. The connection between the insubstantiality (*nairātmyatā*) of the conditioned and the Emptiness (*śūnyatā*) of the Unconditioned has been explained already (see pp. 89 *et seq.*).

While the 'unbiased' and the 'empty' are reckoned as belonging to the transcendental path, as well as applying to Nirvāṇa, the 'imageless' *vimokṣa* is not so reckoned. This is because in the Abhidharma the Path is defined according to the nature of its objective reference. In the case of the other *vimokṣas* this is the Unconditioned; but the 'imageless', being occupied with actually opposing and destroying such concepts as eternalism (*śāśvatavāda*, Pāli *sassatavāda*) and nihilism (*ucchedavāda*), has for its objective reference these conceptual constructions. Hence it is not reckoned as included in the transcendental path. The drawing of this distinction raises a problem which, as Guenther points out, pursued to its logical consequences leads to the acceptance of the Madhyamaka view that the Path and the Goal cannot legitimately be separated.

> For when Nirvāṇa is *śūnyatā* and *apraṇihita* as is The Path, no logical reason exists to make a distinction between path and goal.[151]

The end is the extreme of means. In the same way, there is no absolute distinction between the conditioned and the Unconditioned.

Negatively speaking the Goal consists in the complete and permanent eradication of all unhealthy mental attitudes. To cover these there are several well-known formulas, such as the three 'poisons', the three 'biases' (*āśravas*), and the ten defilements (*kleśas*). When, for example, 'the wanderer who ate rose-apples' asked Śāriputra what Nirvāṇa was, the great disciple replied,

> Whatever … is the extinction of passion [*lobha*], of aversion [*dosa*], of confusion [*moha*], this is called Nirvana.[152]

In the formula of the four *āryan* truths the third truth, that of the cessation of pain (*duḥkha-nirodha*, Pāli *dukkha-nirodha*), is equivalent to Nirvāṇa. As we saw in connection with karma and the wheel of life, it is in dependence on our unhealthy, as well as on even our mundane healthy, volitions, that there takes place in any one of the five (or six) realms of conditioned existence a renewal of sentient being, popularly called rebirth. With the eradication of these attitudes or volitions, therefore, no further rebirth can occur. When its hub is smashed the wheel is no longer able to revolve. The oil in the lamp exhausted, the flame goes out. Hence the Goal also consists in the absolute cessation, so far as the individual sentient being is concerned, of the whole process of phenomenal existence. Nirvāṇa is whatever the world is not. Language having its origin in mundane experience, words are logically powerless to describe it except by negations. Typical of this approach is the famous passage in which the Buddha, solemnly addressing his disciples, declares:

> There is, monks, that plane where there is neither extension nor ... motion nor the plane of infinite ether ... nor that of neither-perception-nor-non-perception, neither this world nor another, neither the moon nor the sun. Here, monks, I say that there is no coming or going or remaining or deceasing or uprising, for this is itself without support, without continuance (in saṃsāra), without mental object – this is itself the end of suffering.
>
> There is, monks, an unborn, not become, not made, uncompounded, and were it not, monks, for this unborn, not become, not made, uncompounded, no escape could be shown here for what is born, has become, is made, is compounded. But because there is, monks, an unborn, not become, not made, uncompounded, therefore an escape can be shown for what is born, has become, is made, is compounded.[153]

Some writers, stressing the introductory verb (*atthi*) with which each paragraph begins, classify this passage as a positive rather than as a negative description of the Goal. This is, we believe, an instance of the common error of reading metaphysical meanings into what are simply linguistic conventions. Nevertheless, taken even in this sense the quotation is not out of place, for it provides us with a means of transition to the second class of descriptions.

In the same way that negative descriptions of the Goal deny, so positive ones affirm, some aspect or feature of conditioned existence. They affirm it not in the ordinary manner, but eminently, or to a superlative degree of perfection impossible under mundane conditions. This is the well-known *via affirmativa* of mysticism as contrasted with the *via negativa*. Language arises out of man's experience of the mundane. Conditioned existence, in part the object and in part the subject of that experience, is reducible to the five *skandhas* or aggregates (see pp. 97 *et seq*). Consequently the terms by means of which a positive description of the Goal is attempted must be derived ultimately from any one of these aggregates or from two or more of them in combination. Such descriptions are therefore necessarily in terms of form, feeling and emotion, knowledge, will, and consciousness. The first of these, being applied symbolically, belongs to the fourth category of descriptions of the Goal, and will be dealt with later. This leaves us with a fourfold classification of all positive descriptions.

In terms of feeling and emotion the Goal is bliss, peace, love, and compassion. Commenting on the fact that esoteric (i.e. Vajrayāna) Buddhism speaks of the ultimate realization as 'supreme bliss', Susuma Yamaguchi remarks that this 'sounds very sensual'.[154] Yet far from being peculiar to one school, descriptions of this type are a commonplace of Buddhist literature from the earliest period. '*Nibbāṇaṃ paramaṃ sukhaṃ*. Nirvāṇa is the supreme bliss,' says the *Dhammapada*,[155] and one could hardly accuse the *Dhammapada* of displaying a tendency to sensuality. The scholastics, though, are always careful to point out that unlike its mundane counterpart nirvāṇic bliss arises not out of physical and mental contact but in the absence of any such contact. We have already seen that the Vajrayāna itself is not oblivious to such distinctions (see p. 91).

As a feeling of peace, the Goal tends to be contrasted with the turmoil and 'unrest which men miscall delight'[156] of worldly life. It is the state of *yogakkhema* (Sanskrit *yogakṣema*), defined in the Pali Text Society's dictionary as

> rest from work or exertion, or fig. in scholastic interpretation 'peace from bondage', i.e. perfect peace or 'uttermost safety'.[157]

Like the term *samyak-sambodhi*, or complete perfect Enlightenment, with which it is ultimately synonymous, *yogakkhema* is often qualified by the prefix *anuttara*, unsurpassed or unexcelled. Being a state of utter peace the Goal is also one not only of complete harmony, balance, and equilibrium, but of absolute metaphysical axiality whereof the psychic condition of equanimity (*upekṣā*), the last of the four *brahma-vihāras*, constitutes but a faint mundane reflection. Nevertheless this state, though not one of 'life' as generally understood, is emphatically not inaction or death.

This aspect of the Goal as somehow involving a release of energy, an outflow, even as it were an overflow of itself, back onto the world, is covered when it is spoken of in terms of love (*maitrī*) and compassion (*karuṇā*). As the first and second *brahma-vihāras* these two terms cover not the ordinary feelings which go by these names, but levels of meditative consciousness representing certain non-hedonic emotional aspects of the state of perfect psychic wholeness or *samādhi*. The *brahma-vihāras*, however, are mundane, not transcendental. In order to distinguish the transcendental emotion of *karuṇā* (this term now being used exclusively) from its mundane analogue the former is usually spoken of as *mahākaruṇā*, 'great compassion'. Whereas ordinary compassion has for its object living beings conceived as separate real entities, and partially enlightened compassion their constituent psychophysical phenomena, Great Compassion has for its real object their ultimate voidness. So extraordinary was the importance of *karuṇā* in this sense felt to be that the Mahāyāna eventually recognized it as equal to and co-ordinate with the *mahāprajñā* or Great Wisdom. Speaking of this virtue, which must never be confused with mere sentimental pity, the *Amitāyur-dhyāna Sūtra*, or 'Meditation on the Buddha of Infinite Life', declares with reference to those who have practised the various exercises described therein:

> Since they have meditated on Buddha's body, they will also see Buddha's mind. It is great compassion that is called Buddha's mind.[158]

The *Nirvāṇa Sūtra* says:

> Great compassion and a great pitying heart is called Buddha-nature. Compassion is Tathāgata; Tathāgata is Compassion.[159]

In the *Dharmasaṅgīti Sūtra*, quoted by Śāntideva in his *Śikṣā-samuccaya*, the bodhisattva Avalokiteśvara, himself the embodiment of compassion, is represented as thus addressing the Enlightened Lord:

> The Bodhisattva, Blessed One, should not be taught too many things. One virtue should be fully mastered and learned by him, in which are included all the virtues of the Buddha. And what is that? It is great compassion.[160]

Despite the later development of this tendency to speak of the Goal not in terms of feeling and emotion only, but above all as compassion, this is for Indian Buddhism as a whole the exception rather than the rule. Descriptions in terms of knowledge are not only commoner but more characteristic. Indeed, notwithstanding the much greater prominence given to compassion in its Far Eastern developments, especially by the highly devotional Jōdo Shinshū of Japan, Buddhism is generally recognized as a religion of knowledge. For the Goal as a state of transcendental cognition there is naturally, therefore, a plethora of practically synonymous terms. Of these *bodhi*, awakening (often prefixed by *sam-*, full or complete) is perhaps the best known, if only because therefrom derives one of the most ancient and popular appellatives of the Master, as well as the modern coinage under which his teaching is now most widely current. The traditional pre-eminence of this term is indicated by the fact that it forms part of a number of important doctrinal compounds. One self-dedicated to the attainment of Supreme Enlightenment for the benefit of all beings is known as a bodhisattva. The thought of, or aspiration to, that same Enlightenment is called the *bodhicitta*, by the arising of which an ordinary person is transformed into a bodhisattva much as a beggar, on finding a jewel in a dunghill, instantly becomes rich. *Anubodhi*, 'after-Enlightenment', is a state of attainment subsequent to, though identical with, that of the Buddha which the disciple gains by following his instructions. Mindfulness, investigation of the Doctrine, energy, rapture, serenity, concentration, and equanimity,[161] a well-known canonical series, are collectively termed the seven *bodhyaṅgas* (Pāli *bojjhaṅgas*), the 'factors', 'links', or 'limbs' of Enlightenment. Even more important is the list of thirty-seven items, distributed over seven sets of practices and qualities, which according to the *Mahāparinibbāna Sutta* the Buddha, three months before his great decease, reminded his disciples he had taught them.[162] These subsequently became known as the *bodhipakṣyā-dharmas* (Pāli *bodhipakkhiya-dhammas*) or 'principles conducive to Enlightenment'.

Among the other terms for transcendental cognition are *vidyā* (Pāli *vijjā*), 'knowledge', as when the Buddha, in the canonical recital of his attributes, is styled *vijjā-caraṇa-sampaññā*, 'The One Fully Endowed with Knowledge and Practice';[163] *yathābhūta-jñānadarśana*, 'Knowledge and Vision of Things As They Really Are', as in the eighth positive *nidāna*; *vipaśyanā* (Pāli *vipassanā*) or insight; *prajñā* (Pāli *paññā*), most inadequately rendered as wisdom; *jñāna* (Pāli *ñāṇa*), also from the root *jñā* 'to know', and *ārya-jñāna* (Pāli *ariya-ñāṇa*), cognition and noble cognition respectively; *samyak-dṛṣṭi* (Pāli *samma-diṭṭhi*) or Axial Vision, commonly translated by such feeble equivalents as 'right understanding' and 'perfect view'; and *dhīḥ* (Pāli *dhi*), knowledge, best known as the last syllable of the mantra of Mañjughoṣa, 'The Sweet-Voiced One', the bodhisattva who *par excellence* embodies transcendental wisdom.

Despite their varying shades of meaning, every one of these descriptions of the Goal in terms of knowledge fundamentally denotes a cognition of the ultimate reality of things, a realization of the true meaning of life, the directness and immediacy of which is hinted at by such of them as either wholly or in part compare it with the act of seeing. On the conceptual side, the content of this cognition, ineffable in itself, is conterminous with the whole Dharma, hence with the entire contents of this Part.

Bondage is essentially a state of impeded volition. Freedom is unimpeded volition. In terms of will, therefore, the Goal is a state of absolute freedom from all restrictions. As *vimutti* (Sanskrit *vimukti*), the eleventh positive *nidāna*, this aspect has already been covered. All that need be added is that the restrictions meant are those imposed not by external circumstances but by the unhealthy affectivity and 'primitive beliefs about reality' (*kleśāvaraṇa* and *jñeyāvaraṇa*) of our own minds. In a spiritual sense bondage is subjection to oneself. True freedom, therefore, consists in freedom from oneself.

Though the Goal has now been described positively in terms of emotion, knowledge, and will, the descriptions remain somehow inadequate. For as we know them, these faculties go to make up a concrete living person. Prescinded from him and as it were suspended in mid-air they are apt to seem unreal, and a description of the Goal in terms of such bloodless abstractions does not always carry conviction. The Mahāyāna therefore describes it not only in terms of emotion *et cetera* taken separately but also as an absolute person in whom wisdom, compassion, and power in the highest conceivable degree of purity and perfection are found inseparably united. From this point of view the Buddha himself is the Goal and the Goal is the Buddha. Here by the Buddha is meant not simply the historical Śākyamuni, but that Eternal Buddha who, in the fifteenth chapter of the *Saddharma Puṇḍarīka Sūtra* (the sixteenth chapter of the Chinese translation) brings the whole discourse to a climax by revealing that his transcendental compassionate activity is unlimited by space and time and eternally embraces the whole universe.[164] Concrete doctrinal expression to this sublime conception is given in the teaching of the *trikāya*, or 'triple body' of the Buddha, an outline of which was attempted in Chapter 5.

As an absolute person, the Goal now becomes more and more the object of worship and devotion. One cannot adore an abstraction. Except metaphorically, one cannot love wisdom and compassion. The object of love is invariably a person. Parallel with the tendency to describe the Goal doctrinally in terms of an eternally Enlightened absolute person there naturally developed, therefore, a popular movement which Conze has named the Buddhism of Faith and Devotion.[165] For the adherents of this movement, which attained its apogee in China and Japan, faith (*śraddhā*, Pāli *saddhā*) occupies the position traditionally assigned to wisdom.

Both the doctrinal tendency and the popular movement associated with it are sometimes objected to as aberrations. How is it possible to describe the Goal in terms of personality when the Buddhist tradition invariably speaks of it as involving the complete eradication of the false view that things and persons are in themselves ultimately real? Does it not amount, as some scholars have maintained, to the deification of the Buddha, to the surreptitious introduction into non-theistic Buddhism of the incongruous notion of a God? In reply to the first objection it may be pointed out that if descriptions of the Goal as the absolute person are inadmissible, so will be those in terms of emotion and knowledge. Thus all attempts at positive delineation would have to be abandoned. In point of fact, however, the absolute person is no more a person as we understand the word than wisdom and compassion are the intelligence and pity of our ordinary experience. As we made clear at the beginning, positive qualities are affirmed of the Goal eminently, or to a superlative degree. Moreover, after realizing the Goal the historical Śākyamuni himself did not cease to function recognizably as a person. Personality and the Goal are not, it would therefore seem, incompatible. In any case, the inadequacy of all positive descriptions being fully admitted, it is not a question of *defining* the Goal as *being*, in the ultimate sense, personal, but of describing it *as though* it was such for practical purposes. After all, personality, even of the 'normal' human type, is the highest category available to ordinary consciousness, and premature renunciation of the use of it might involve the risk of the Goal being conceived not as transcendent to personality so much as infra-personal. As for the charge of deification, no Buddhist text, of any school, attributes to the Buddha the creation of the universe. God as Creator the Buddha therefore most certainly is not, either in the Hīnayāna or the Mahāyāna. Murti, however, in a penetrating discussion of 'Absolute and Tathāgata', has not hesitated to assert:

> Buddha is Bhagavān, God, endowed as he is with power and perfection. He possesses, in entirety, all power, splendour, fame, wealth, knowledge, and act.[166]

Though not overlooking the difference between the two in respect of their cosmic functions, as God he therefore speaks of the Tathāgata throughout the chapter. The difficulty is at bottom one of definition. A Christian missionary, finding no word for God in the Thai language, is said to have coined a neologism meaning 'the-Buddha-who-created-the-universe'. The Buddha of the Mahāyāna might be described as the God who did not create the universe. Whether the latter term will be able to bear so profound a modification of its traditional meaning cannot now be predicted.

The description of the Goal in positive terms as consciousness, the fifth *skandha*, seems to have been a tradition from early times. A few scattered references are found even in the Pāli *Nikāyas*. In the *Kevaddha Sutta*, for example, a monk asks what that place is where distinctions such as water and earth, fire and air, disappear absolutely. Correcting and expanding his question, the Buddha in part replies:

> It is consciousness [which is] invisible, infinite, radiant on all sides (*viññāṇam anidassanaṃ anantaṃ sabbato pahaṃ*).[167]

Elsewhere he is represented as declaring:

> This consciousness (*citta*) is luminous, but it is defiled by adventitious defilements.[168]

Whether all such descriptions refer to Nirvāṇa or to a state somewhat short of it is a moot point. According to Buddhaghosa's commentary the infinite radiant consciousness of the first quotation is identical with Nirvāṇa.[169] About the *citta* of the second quotation we cannot be so sure. In the absence of clear contextual indication, uncertainty is created with regard to the correct meaning of this and the few other similar passages by the fact that throughout the *Nikāyas citta* and *viññāṇa* denote empirical mind, or mundane consciousness: their use in a higher, transcendental sense would be in any case exceptional for this literature.

Despite these difficulties, it is clear that there existed in Buddhism from the beginning a definite, though undeveloped, tradition of idealism. This tradition eventually found vigorous expression in a group of idealist *sūtras* in which the Goal was the realization, by the bodhisattva, of the truth that the three worlds were 'Mind-Only' (*citta-mātra*).[170] From this point of view Nirvāṇa became the state of absolutely pure, blissful, and radiant consciousness. This state was sharply distinguished from the *paramātman* or 'Supreme Self' of certain non-Buddhist schools. Whereas the latter was static, the former was dynamic. Being dynamic it was void (*śūnya*). The fact that in order to prevent serious misunderstanding it is necessary to speak of absolute mind as empty shows that for Buddhism idealism cannot be the last word. In view of its close connection with meditation, however, it remains even at the penultimate stage of the Path an indispensable stepping-stone.

The paradox is a figure of speech widely current in mystical literature. In this context it may be defined as the attempt to describe an ineffable state or experience by the forcible juxtaposition of contradictory attributes. Thus for Dionysius the Deity is 'a deep but dazzling darkness';[171] Jesus declares that we must lose our life in order to find it;[172] Kabir urges us to listen to 'the unstruck sound'.[173] Despite its universal currency in this semi-poetic form, deliberate and systematic recourse to paradox as the best means of describing the spiritual life in all its aspects and at every stage is a development that tends to come late in the evolution of spiritual traditions, if at all. It flourishes as the 'chrysanthemum of autumn' rather than as the 'orchid of spring'.[174]

Early Buddhist literature seems entirely innocent of this sophistication. Positive and negative descriptions of the Goal, as well as of the successive steps of the Path, are the rule; paradoxical ones not even the exception. But with passage of time, as one generation of teachers succeeded another, the categories of Buddhist thought tended to become fixed and rigid, description hardened into definition, while teachings that had originally been suggestive rather than definitive were interpreted with ever-increasing literal-mindedness. This naturally led to the movement of reaction, and of restatement of fundamentals, known to us as the Mahāyāna.[175]

The literary spearhead of the movement was the continually-expanding *Prajñāpāramitā* or 'Perfection of Wisdom' corpus. Herein the fact that in emptiness the logical principle of contradiction is abrogated is explicitly affirmed: A is A because it is not-A. Out of this affirmation arises the need for having exclusive recourse to paradox, as the one type of description compatible with a logic of contradiction. In terms of paradox, therefore, the *Prajñāpāramitā* describes not only all possible objects of cognition but also the time-honoured categories of Buddhist thought. The *dharmas*, in the Abhidharma sense of ultimate elements of existence, are non-*dharmas*; therefore they are *dharmas*. In reality there are no sentient beings to be delivered; therefore the bodhisattva should vow to deliver them. One should abide in a state of non-abiding. That which is supported has no support. Nirvāṇa should be attained by means of a non-attainment.

Besides serving to counteract the Hīnayāna tendency to think of the Goal as actually existing 'out there' with a real path leading up to it as though to the door of a house, this devastatingly radical procedure created a new awareness of the fact that reality was in truth ineffable, that all attempts to divide and classify it were futile, and that in the end the only way of reaching the Goal was by realizing that there was in the ultimate sense no Goal to be reached. Though enjoying a considerable vogue wherever the *Prajñāpāramitā* literature circulated, the method of description by paradox did not come fully into its own, perhaps, until the rise of the Chan or Dhyāna school in China and its continuation in Japan as Zen. Brought very much down to earth, it lived on in the *kung an* (Chinese) or *kōan* (Japanese).

For descriptions of the fourth class symbolical is perhaps not the best word. Poetical might have been better. Though resembling the paradox in being a figurative rather than a scientific statement of truth, it differs from it by speaking the language not of abstractions but of concrete images. Twentieth-century work in psychology, especially that of Jung and his disciples, has helped to rehabilitate the image as an independent vehicle of psychological and spiritual truth, and no more than the 'legends' of the Buddha's life need we dismiss as worthless the symbolical descriptions of the Goal found in Buddhist literature. Pāli texts speak in symbolical terms of the Goal only by way of an occasional simile or metaphor: Nirvāṇa is the Cool Cave, the Island in the Floods, the Further Shore, the Holy City.[176]

The Sanskrit scriptures are more expansive. Whole *sūtras*, such as the *Larger* and *Smaller Sukhāvatī-vyūha* or 'Array of the Happy Land', are taken up by lengthy and elaborate accounts of the glories and beauties of a realm which, though apparently a 'heaven' located within the phenomenal universe, is really the transcendental state of Nirvāṇa as expressed not abstractly but in terms of a harmonious disposition of images aglow with supernatural life and movement. Though music and perfumes are not absent, the impression is predominantly one of light and colour. Against a background of radiance millions of rays and beams spring up, intersect, and weave themselves into incredibly beautiful patterns. Rainbows appear and disappear. There is a shining forth as of silver and gold and everything flashes as though with strings and nets of multicoloured gems. Flowers fall like rain. At the centre of this blaze of splendour, its focal point and its crown, sits as Lord of the Happy Land the Buddha of the Mahāyāna, the rays converging into a canopy above his head, the flowers at his feet, and his unnumbered auditors ranged in attitudes of expectancy and devotion on all sides.[177]

A more formal and geometrically organized version of this exalted scene, which is the usual setting for the revelation of a Mahāyāna *sūtra*, is found in the mandala, a definition of which was given on page 96. What Lama Anagarika Govinda writes of the latter is relevant to the whole question of description in terms of images:

> In order to understand the qualities of sunlight or the nature of the sun, we have to separate its rays in the spectrum. Likewise, if we want to understand the nature of an Enlightened One or of the consciousness of Enlightenment, we have to spread out before our inner eye the various qualities of such a state. Because

> an unenlightened being cannot grasp an Enlightened mind in its totality, but only in separate aspects, which – according to the plane on which they are experienced and the range of their manifold relations and mental associations – lead to an ever wider and deeper understanding.[178]

While negative descriptions of absolute whiteness tell us it is not black, positive ones that it is like milk or snow only whiter, and paradoxical ones that it is in reality a non-whiteness, symbolical or poetical descriptions exhibit before us all the magic colours of the rainbow. Vajrayāna tradition in fact speaks of reality in terms of divine images appearing and disappearing in the Void like rainbows in a clear blue sky or like reflections coming and going in a spotless mirror.[179] As the *Prajñāpāramitā-hṛdaya Sūtra* or 'Heart of the Perfection of Wisdom' reminds us:

> Form is not separate from voidness; voidness is not separate from form.[180]

Open though it may be to popular misunderstanding, the symbolical description of the Goal in terms of concrete sensuous images at least possesses the merit of protecting us against the more insidious error of thinking of it in merely abstract terms as a featureless and inert Absolute.

PART III
THE SANGHA

15
THE ASSEMBLY OF THE NOBLE

Without a centre, a radius, and a circumference a circle cannot exist. Of the circle of Buddhism the Buddha is the radiant centre, the Dharma, as the shortest distance from potential to actual Enlightenment, the radius, and the Sangha the perfect unbroken circumference. Each of these terms is multidimensional, possessing sphere within sphere of spiritual significance which no one rendition can exhaust. The Buddha is, simultaneously, a unique historical figure, the supreme object of the religious consciousness, and reality itself; his Dharma is the sum total of conceptual formulations of the Teaching as well as the spiritual principle which both transcends all formulations and, running at the same time through every one of them, communicates to them vitality and meaning. Even so does the Sangha, literally 'assembly', meet not at one level of existence only but at several. The term stands, according to context, for a spiritual élite, an ecclesiastical corporation, and the whole community of the faithful, monk and lay, as well as covering various intermediate shades of significance. Of the three principal meanings, that of the spiritual élite is the primary one; all the rest are secondary. Whether one is in spiritual relation with the Buddha, through the Dharma, and therefore whether one is truly a segment of the circumference of the circle, is determined not by the assumption of external differentiae, nor by verbal professions, but by whether one actually practises the Dharma or not.

In a well-known episode the Buddha declares that he who walked step by step behind the Master, holding fast to the hem of his robe, but who did not follow his instructions, was far from him. But one who, on the contrary, though living a thousand miles away, yet realized the import of the Teaching, dwelt in his very presence.[181] The true criterion of the relation between the Buddha and his followers is not physical, not spatio-temporal, but spiritual. Whether now or in what we call, from the historical point of view, his 'own' times, or whether in the future even, we are nearest to him when we most perfectly follow his example. The Sangha is primarily the community of those who, by virtue of their immediate or remote approximation to Enlightenment, stand in spiritual relation to the Buddha and dwell spiritually in his presence. It is the community of those who, through their relationship with him, are also all spiritually related to one another. The Sangha is the Buddha's spiritual family. In the *Nikāyas* he is indeed represented as telling his disciples:

> Ye are mine own true sons, born of my mouth; heirs of the Dhamma, not heirs of worldly things.[182]

Centuries later the same theme finds beautiful expression as a trinity consisting of the Buddha as Father, the Dharma as Mother, and the Sangha as Son.[183]

As the spiritual élite the Sangha is known as the Āryasaṅgha or 'Assembly of the Noble', the word *ārya* here connoting an aristocracy not of race but of transcendental attainment. As an ecclesiastical corporation it is known as the *bhikṣu* sangha or 'assembly of monks', and as the whole community of the faithful as the *Mahāsaṅgha* or 'great assembly' and the *caturvarga* or 'four classes'.[184] Like many other doctrinal categories, the term 'Āryasaṅgha' underwent a certain narrowing at the hands of the Hīnayānists and had to be reinterpreted by the Mahāyānists who, while not rejecting the earlier formulations, did their best to incorporate them within the broader framework of their own ampler version of the Buddha's teaching. Though precise demarcation is impossible, the earlier and the later interpretations are best dealt with separately.

Intelligent sentient beings are either *āryas* or *anāryas*. In the Scriptures the latter are generally referred to as *pṛthagjanas* (Pāli *puthujjanas*) or average men. As they outnumber the *āryas* by many millions to one the term *bahujana* or 'manyfolk' may also be applied to them.

An average man is one who, dominated by the delusion of 'I' and 'mine', identifies himself with, or imagines he possesses, form, feeling, conception, volition, and consciousness. He is the fool (*bāla*) described in the *Dhammapada*:

> Sons are mine, wealth is mine,' thus the fool torments [himself]. Indeed, he does not belong to himself. Whence sons? Whence wealth?[185]

Not knowing the true Dharma, he develops attachments to things which should be avoided, thereby creating and strengthening the biases towards thirst for sensuous experience, prolonged mundane existence, and spiritual ignorance. Hence he continues to revolve with the wheel of life, occupying now one and now another of its segments.

Not only most men, but most gods too, are *pṛthagjanas*. For this reason the Buddhist expects no spiritual help or guidance from them. In Tibet they are known as the Gods of the Round. The exceptions are those who, either during the Buddha's earthly lifetime or later, had an opportunity of hearing the Teaching and developing transcendental insight. These together with the bodhisattvas, whom they resemble in certain respects, make up the Deities of the Path, and from them inspiration and spiritual guidance can be received.

Āryas are in the first place of two kinds: *arhants* and *śrotāpannas* (Pāli *sotāpannas*). An *arhant* is literally a 'worthy one', the term being (according to the Pali Text Society's dictionary),

> before Buddhism used as honorific title of high officials like the English 'His Worship'; at the rise of Buddhism applied popularly to all ascetics.[186]

It is interpreted scholastically as meaning one who, by virtue of his supreme attainment, is worthy of the respectful offerings of the whole world. There are several stock descriptions of such beings. In the Pāli scriptures they are frequently represented as declaring, upon attainment:

> Destroyed is (re-)birth; lived is the higher life; done is what had to be done; after this present life there is [for me] no beyond.[187]

The *Large Prajñāpāramitā Sūtra*, probably following Sarvāstivādin sources, exclaims of a gathering of them:

> Their outflows dried up, undefiled, fully controlled, quite freed in their hearts, well freed and wise, thorough-breds, great Serpents, their work done, their task accomplished, their burden laid down, their own weal accomplished, with the fetters that bound them to becoming extinguished, their hearts well freed by right understanding, in perfect control of their whole minds.[188]

In later Hīnayāna, as well as earlier Mahāyāna literature, the *arhant* is represented as having gained Nirvāṇa for himself alone; in the latter he therefore stands for spiritual individualism.

A *śrotāpanna* or 'Stream Entrant' occupies a position midway between the average man and the *arhant*, at the point of intersection between the vicious circle of mundane existence and the spirals of the transcendental path. Having died to the grosser aspects of worldly life he is now reborn into the spiritual family of the Buddha. He is no longer liable to be reborn in the three lowest spheres of sentient existence, that is to say the world of animals, of revenants, or of tormented spirits. Henceforward, he is incapable of relapse; though further progress may be delayed, the attainment of Nirvāṇa within not more than seven human or heavenly births is assured. At its own much higher level entering the Stream corresponds to the psychological phenomenon of religious conversion. It marks not only the beginning of the end of mundane existence, but a transvaluation of values more radical than any envisaged by Nietzsche.[189] Consequently the texts are loud in its praises. Says the *Dhammapada*:

> Better is the fruit of entering the Stream than sole sovereignty over the earth, than going to heaven, than rule supreme over the entire universe.[190]

This decisive and far-reaching reorientation, this spiritual revolution, takes place upon the initial flashing forth of transcendental insight into the true nature of existence, upon the first overwhelming glimpse of Nirvāṇa. Thus it coincides with the eighth positive *nidāna*, that of Knowledge and Vision of Things As They Are, as well as with Axial

Vision (*samyak-dṛṣṭi*), the first step of the transcendental – as distinct from the mundane – Eightfold Path. For this reason the path of Stream Entry (*śrotāpatti-mārga*) is also known as the Path of Seeing (*darśana-mārga*).

But tremendous though the impact of this experience is – for it represents the first triumphant irruption of the transcendental order into a particular psychophysical continuum – and shaking though it does the individuality almost to its foundations, the irruption is not a taking of complete possession, the shaking not a demolition of the entire superstructure. To accomplish this is the work of the stage intermediate between that of the Stream Entrant and the *arhant* which, on account of the extreme difficulty with which it is traversed, is divided, as will be seen below, into various sub-stages. It is known as the path of practice or path of development (*bhāvanā-mārga*). What is developed is of course the whole individuality, not merely in its sublimest heights, as in the Path of Seeing, but also in its murkiest depths. The term is perhaps best translated as Path of Transformation. Since *bhāvanā* is widely used in the sense of meditation there is the implication that the transformation is to be effected principally by this means. It coincides with the last four positive *nidānas* and with the transcendental Eightfold Path from Axial Emotion (*samyak-saṅkalpa*), the second member, to Axial Absorption (*samyak-samādhi*), the eighth – the latter here representing not merely 'right concentration', as in the mundane Eightfold Path, but the state of purity and pellucidity consequent upon the complete saturation of the entire psychic contents with the light of transcendental realization.

The *bhāvanā-mārga* is subdivided into the stages of the *sakṛdāgāmin* (Pāli *sakadāgāmin*), or 'once-returner', the *anāgāmin* or 'non-returner', and the *arhant*. By including the Stream Entrant, and combining this subdivision with other principles of classification – such as temperament, the number of fetters destroyed, and the number of rebirths remaining to be undergone – the Hīnayāna arrived at a total of seven, or eight, or nine *ārya-pudgalas* (Pāli *ariya-puggalas*) or holy persons who, from different points of view, collectively make up the Āryasaṅgha or Assembly of the Noble.

The seven holy persons are:

(1 and 2) The *śraddhānusārin* or 'faith-follower' and the *dharmā-anusārin* or 'doctrine-follower'. This distinction calls attention to the vital role temperament plays in the religious life. According to some

authorities differences of temperament exist even in the Buddhas, who respectively exhibit a predominance of knowledge, or love, or activity. This would seem to indicate that such differences are innate, hence not to be ignored by any truly practical scheme of spiritual self-culture. The faith-follower, as the name itself indicates, is one of predominantly devotional temperament. Emotions of love, worship, admiration, and surrender are apt to well up in him uncontrollably, and he is highly susceptible to suggestions of religious exaltation in the surrounding atmosphere. In the spiritual life of such a person the guru occupies an absolutely central place. Scriptures and studies count for nothing. Drawn only by the grace of the guru, and solely out of faith in him, a person of this type takes up the systematic practice of mindfulness, or any other spiritual exercise, without developing at the same time, or even caring to develop, an intellectual appreciation of the Doctrine. Provided the guru in whom he has taken refuge is himself Enlightened, a faith-follower will make good progress; otherwise he may become emotionally unbalanced, or a fanatic, or even a religious hysteric.

The doctrine-follower typifies the predominantly intellectual approach. He takes up the practice of the whole body of spiritual exercises after an extensive and painstaking course of scriptural study. Relying on the guru much less than the faith-follower does, or even not at all, he abides by the Buddha's dying injunction that his disciples should be 'islands unto themselves, refuges unto themselves',[191] and makes his own understanding of the sacred tradition his guide to the attainment of Nirvāṇa. Though in no danger of emotional extravagance, the doctrine-follower, unless upheld by an exceptionally strong desire for Enlightenment, may sink into sterile scholasticism or even scepticism; misled by his learning, he may also be tempted to deviate from the norm of doctrinal orthodoxy. A doctrine-follower who succeeds in avoiding the pitfalls peculiar to his type, however, is capable of making to the elucidation and development of the Doctrine contributions of profound and far-reaching significance.

According to some sources not all *śraddhānusārins* and *dharmānusārins* are members of the Āryasaṅgha, but only those who have attained to the path of Stream Entry (*śrotāpatti-mārga*). The discrepancy is due to the fact that between the average man and the Stream Entrant there is the 'lightning-like transitional stage'[192] of the *gotrabhū*, literally 'one who has entered the lineage [of the *āryas*]'. A *gotrabhū* in this sense (there are higher senses) is sometimes reckoned as an *ārya*, sometimes as an *anārya*. It seems agreed, though, that whether *āryas* or not, all such *gotrabhūs* are either faith-followers or doctrine-followers.

Such differences of religious temperament are well known to all students of comparative religion. In Hinduism a distinction is made between the *bhakta* or devotee, who follows the path of devotion (*bhakti-mārga*), and the *jñānin* or knower, who follows the path of knowledge (*jñāna-mārga*). A similar difference can be traced between the intellectual mysticism of Eckhart and the devotional mysticism of St Teresa of Ávila – to take no more extreme examples.[193] In Theravādin terminology the *śraddhānusārin* is said to follow the way of contemplative insight (*vipassanā-dhura*) and the *dharmānusārin* the way of study (*ganthadhura*). Drawing on the Tibetan tradition it may be said that Milarepa provides a good example of the first, Tsongkhapa of the second.[194] Types in whom devotion and understanding are almost, if not quite, perfectly balanced do of course exist; but when present at the beginning difference of temperament may persist, as we shall see, up to the very farthest reaches of the transcendental path.

(3 and 4) The *śraddhādhimukta* (Pāli *saddhāvimutta*) or 'faith-liberated one' and the *dṛṣṭiprāpta* (Pāli *diṭṭhipatta*) or 'vision-attained one'. These are respectively the designations of the faith-follower at all the remaining stages of the transcendental path and of the doctrine-follower at all of them save the last one.

(5) The *kāyasākṣin* (Pāli *kāyasakkhī*) or 'body-witness'. This would seem to be the name of an independent type of holy person distinct from both the faith-follower and the doctrine-follower, though more closely allied to the latter, for according to the texts such a one receives the same designation at all stages of his career. It corresponds to what may be called the psychic type. The body-witness is the yogi *par excellence*. All the sources, canonical and extra-canonical, Theravādin and Sarvāstivādin, speak of him as practising a set of concentrations known as the eight *vimokṣas* (Pāli *vimokkhas*) or 'releases' from thought-constructions. As one has not met, nor even heard of, anyone with a personal experience of these states, the elucidation of the cryptic formulas with which the Scriptures are content to describe them is a matter of some difficulty. Nalinaksha Dutt, following the *Abhidharmakośa-vyākhyā*, says of the first four:

(i) In the first Release, a meditator introspects his own body, its colour and contents as also those of others and realises only that the colour and other characteristics of his own body is undesirable (*aśubha*) and substanceless (*suññā*). He controls his visual perception and therefore he does not perceive the colour of his body and regards it as unattractive (*amanojñam*).

(ii) In the second Release, the meditator thinks no longer of his own body but his attention is still diverted to others' body and its characteristics, internal and external, which he then tries to regard as undesirable (*aśubha*) and substanceless (*suññā*).

(iii) In the third Release, the meditator derives a feeling of satisfaction, which pervades his whole body on account of his success in removing his mental obsessions caused by his previous notions about his own and other's body.

(iv) In the fourth Release, the meditator frees his mind from the notion of material objects (*rūpa*) and their repercussive nature (*paṭigha*) and dismisses from his mind the sense of distinction, which exists among beings and objects, and regards the world as just infinite space free from all obstructions.[195]

The remaining four *vimokṣas* are identical with the four formless *dhyānas* (see p. 110). The body-witness is so designated because he not only experiences personally (*kāyika*) ever higher levels of concentration, but with the detachment of a mere observer (*sākṣin*) realizes their true nature. Though perhaps extinct as an independent practice, the eight *vimokṣas* would seem to have been incorporated into the Vajrayāna tradition; the Thai *sammā arahaṃ* method of meditation may also owe something to their influence.

According to the canonical definitions of these terms the faith-follower is one who, at the beginning of his spiritual career, being filled with resolution, considers the aggregates as impermanent (*anitya*); similarly, the doctrine-follower, filled with wisdom, considers them as insubstantial (*anātman*). the body-witness is one who, filled with tranquillity, considers them as painful (*duḥkha*). By making the painfulness, rather than the impermanence, of conditioned things his object, a faith-follower who has attained the path of Stream Entry (*śrotāpatti-mārga*) may as it were change his type and become a body-witness.

(6 and 7) *Prajñāvimukta* (Pāli *paññāvimutta*) or 'wisdom-liberated one' and *ubhayatobhāgavimukta* (Pāli *ubhatobhāgavimutta*) or 'doubly-liberated one'. Both these types are *arhants*. The distinction between them is based not on any difference in the actual content of their realization but in the mode of its attainment. A doctrine-follower on becoming an *arhant* is known as a wisdom-liberated one, while the faith-follower and the body-witness alike receive the designation of doubly-liberated one. Despite the misunderstandings at present current in some parts of the Buddhist world, the former does not attain arhantship by means of wisdom (*prajñā*) alone; for to the development of wisdom itself, in the sense of transcendental insight into the true nature of existence, concentration (*samādhi*) is accessory. In the spiritual life of the doctrine-follower, the one does not exclude, but only predominates over, the other. Speaking in terms of the eight *dhyānas*, it is therefore said that such a one attains Nirvāṇa by means of wisdom having experienced the four lower, but not the four higher, of these superconscious states. Similarly the predominantly devotional and contemplative career of the other types does not altogether exclude wisdom. Nirvāṇa is simultaneously a state of perfect knowledge and absolute mental purity. What the distinction between the two types of *arhant* on the whole means is that whereas one type perfects first wisdom and then concentration, the other proceeds in the reverse order. The traditional Theravādin distinction between *cetovimutti*, emancipation of mind, and *j778*, emancipation of wisdom, refers not so much to two mutually exclusive attainments as to this difference of procedure. Consequently the Buddha is time and again represented in the Scriptures as saying that a monk, after destroying the biases, himself realizes, in this life, through his higher attainments, emancipation of both mind and wisdom.[196]

Nevertheless, the fact that perfect knowledge necessarily involves absolute mental purity, but not *vice versa*, is explicitly recognized at least by the Sarvāstivādins. Consequently they recognize what is termed *samayavimukti*, temporary emancipation, that is to say the possibility, in the case of an *arhant* who had been a faith-follower, of a fall from arhantship if after perfecting concentration he did not make a special effort to perfect wisdom.[197] Though the subject has been much debated,[198] whether in the interval between perfecting concentration and perfecting wisdom one can properly be called an *arhant*, or not – which is all the controversy really amounts to – would seem to be largely a matter of definition.

The eight holy persons are:

(1 and 2) The Stream Entrant counted twice over, as two persons, in respect of his attainment of the path of Stream Entry (*śrotāpatti-mārga*) and of the fruit of that path (*śrotāpatti-phala*). By *mārga*, according to the Abhidharma, is meant – both here and in the case of the remaining holy persons – the moment of entering upon one or another of the stages of the transcendental path, while by *phala* is meant those moments of consciousness which follow immediately after the moment of entry and which may, under certain conditions, go on repeating themselves an indefinite number of times.[199] Thus the former represents the actual process of breaking through from the mundane into the transcendental, and the latter the continuing resultant state of having broken through. At what level the breakthrough takes place depends on how many of the *daśa-saṃyojana* or 'ten fetters' of mundane existence one is able to break.

In the case of the Stream Entrant, besides being endowed with unshakeable faith in the Three Jewels, perfect observance of the five precepts, and other spiritual qualities, he is required, in order to reach his own stage of the transcendental path, to break the first, second, and third of them. These are *satkāyadṛṣṭi* (Pāli *sakkāya-diṭṭhi*) or 'personality-view', *vicikitsā* (Pāli *vicikicchā*) or doubt, and *śīlavrata-parāmarśa* (Pāli *sīlabbata-parāmāsa*) or 'dependence on moral codes and religious observances'. All of them represent various aspects not of greed or aversion but of spiritual blindness or ignorance. This is because the path of Stream Entry is also the Path of Seeing, the attainment of which depends less on the eradication of unhealthy emotions than on the removal of the intellectual obstacles to clear vision. Together they embody the irreducible minimum of wrong ideology of which an average man must rid himself before he can become one of the Noble.

Personality-view is of two kinds: one posits the survival, after death, of a separate, immortal, unchanging soul or self (*ātman*) eternally distinct from the body; the other, identifying the personality either with the body or the body plus the mind, maintains that at death it perishes. The first is a form of *śāśvatavāda* (Pāli *sassatavāda*) or eternalism, the second of *ucchedavāda* or annihilationism. The next fetter, only most approximately rendered as doubt and scepticism, represents not that honest doubt in which, so the poet assures us, 'there lives more faith than half the creeds',[200] but rather a culpable state of uncertainty and indecision; a reluctance, even a refusal, finally to make up one's mind about the Buddha, Dharma, and Sangha and *commit* oneself – in the existentialist sense – wholeheartedly to the logical consequences of having taken refuge in them.

Dependence on moral codes and religious observances, the third fetter, is often mistranslated and misunderstood. Protestantizing English writers of the nineteenth century, with the great Ritualist controversy fresh in mind,[201] understood it as belief in the efficacy of rites and ceremonies. *Śīla*, however, means behaviour, especially ethical behaviour; *vrata* covers the sacrificial and other observances of the Vedic tradition as well as the more eccentric types of ascetic practice. What this fetter in fact consists of is the wrong belief that any external observance, whether one's own or another's on one's behalf, is in and by itself sufficient for, or even conducive to, the attainment of salvation. Not by *śīla*, or even by *samādhi*, can the transcendental path be gained, but only by *prajñā* based upon *śīla* and *samādhi*.

Ritual, in the sense of symbolical or spiritually significant acts, far from being condemned in Buddhism in fact forms part of the heritage of all schools, not excluding even the Theravāda. In the Vajrayāna especially it plays an important part. Ceremonies of course are inseparable from organized religious life and though its estimate of their value may be a comparatively low one Buddhism no more excludes them on principle than does any other religion.

(3 and 4) The *sakṛdāgāmin* (Pāli *sakadāgāmin*) or 'once-returner'. Whereas the Stream Entrant is sure to attain Nirvāṇa in not more than seven human and heavenly births, the second type of holy person, as his name reveals, will attain it after returning once more only to the world of men. Having broken already the first three fetters, he achieves the path of once-return (*sakṛdāgāma-mārga*) by weakening the fourth and fifth. These are *kāma-rāga* or sensuous craving and *vyāpāda* or aversion. The fact that at this stage these fetters are merely weakened, not broken, reminds us that we have now left the Path of Seeing and arrived at the Path of Transformation. Guenther's remarks on the importance of the distinction are worth quoting in this connection:

> It shows that it is a fairly simple task to get rid of intellectual fetters. It is easy to accept the findings of science, to use modern examples,

> to discard the 'ghost-in-a-machine' theory of the relation between body and soul, to attend to a problem seriously instead of talking hazily about it and in order to conceal one's ignorance about it, resorting to sophistry and misapplied scepticism, to discard mere ritualism because in all honesty in most cases it has turned into a meaningless formalism; but it is a gigantic task to tame or to sublimate our deep-rooted emotions. I may believe anything about myself, whether it makes sense or not, but anything that attempts to encroach upon my precious ego will meet with undisguised hostility. Emotions are not sublimated by recognizing the validity of a proposition or by seeing things by themselves, but only by paying the closest attention to that which is the nature of any living process, by working hard on ourselves. Hence the emotions are refined by a path of practice (*bhāvanāmārga*). When, therefore, the texts speak of three paths that have to be walked to the end, viz., the Second, Third and Fourth Path, they imply the difficulty of refining our emotional nature.[202]

(5 and 6) The *anāgāmin* or non-returner. In his case sensuous craving and aversion are not merely weakened but wholly eradicated. Thus up to and including this stage of the transcendental path five fetters in all have been broken. These are the five lower fetters, so called because they bind one to repeated birth in the world of sensuous experience (*kāmaloka*), the lowest of the three into which conditioned existence is stratified. Only five fetters now remain. These are known as the five higher fetters, as through them one is bound to continued existence in the world of pure form (*rūpaloka*) and the formless world (*arupaloka*). Not having broken them the non-returner, though exempt from human birth, on death passes to the *śuddhāvāsa* (Pāli *suddhāvāsa*) or Pure Abodes, a group of celestial sub-planes located at the summit of the world of pure form. They are five in number: the worlds known respectively as the *avṛhā* (Pāli *aviha*) or Not-Great, the *atapa* (Pāli *atappā*) or Unscorched, the *sudṛśa* (Pāli *sudassā*) or Clearly-Visible, the *sudarśana* (Pāli *sudassī*) or Clear-Visioned, and the *akaniṣṭha* (Pāli *akaṇiṭṭhā*), Greatest or Highest. From one or another of these sub-planes the non-returner, now a divine being, traverses the remaining stages of the transcendental path and attains Nirvāṇa. According to whether this takes place within the first or second half of the celestial life-term, with or without exertion, or after

he has been in each of the Pure Abodes successively, five sub-types of non-returner are distinguished. By enumerating the *anāgāmin* as one of the eight holy persons and describing him as above, the Hīnayāna bears witness to the fact that the possibility of post-mortem emancipation has been recognized in Buddhism from the earliest times. One has no reason to feel astonished, therefore, if later on similar ideas crop up, albeit within a modified doctrinal framework, in the Nyingma and the Jōdo Shinshū traditions.

(7 and 8) The *arhant* (Pāli *arahant*) or worthy one. As this type of holy person has been discussed already we now need concern ourselves only with the fetters he must break in order to achieve his exalted station. The five higher fetters are: *rūpa-raga* and *arūpa-raga*, or craving for existence in the world of pure form and in the formless world, *māna* or conceit; *auddhatya* (Pāli *uddhacca*), restlessness; and *avidyā* (Pāli *avijjā*) or lack of a clear understanding of reality. From the point of view whence they appear as a duality – a duality that for the Hīnayāna is final – mundane and transcendental experience, Nirvāṇa and *saṃsāra*, are sharply distinguished. The true, the ultimate goal of the spiritual life is not any state of conditioned existence, however sublime, but solely the Unconditioned. However subtle, however 'spiritualized' it may be, the craving for personal immortality, for eternal life in heaven, leads not to emancipation but only to continued rebirth. Here, as invariably in the spiritual life, the good is the enemy of the best. That which for the average man would be an achievement the Noble regard as a failure. Broadly speaking, the first and second of the higher fetters stand for the danger of theism.

By the third higher fetter is signified not conceit in the ordinary worldly sense, but its spiritual counterpart. The average man is dominated by the awareness of 'I' and 'mine' in its grossest form. But subtler forms persist and linger on up to the very threshold of Enlightenment. The Stream Entrant is subtly aware of himself as such; this awareness vanishes upon his becoming a once-returner. At each stage of the transcendental path there is a conceit which can be eradicated only by the attainment of the next succeeding stage. *Māna* is the subtlest conceit of all, that of the non-returner, which is destroyed only in the *arhant*. According to the Mahāyāna, however, because he strives only for his own individual emancipation there is present in the *arhant* himself a still more subtle self-awareness which he must overcome by having recourse to the highest stage of all, that of the bodhisattva who aspires to perfect Buddhahood for the sake of all sentient beings. *Auddhatya* is far from being restlessness in the ordinary physical or mental sense; it is not even the much subtler psychic instability which may occur at the various levels of concentration. Rather it is the last, faintest tremor or vibration of consciousness between the most rarefied heights of the conditioned, on the one hand, and the Unconditioned, on the other, before it achieves that state of immovable tranquillity, of transcendental axiality, whereof *upekṣā* or ordinary meditative equanimity is a remote mundane analogue. Similarly *avidyā*, the fifth of the higher fetters, is the last faintest shadow of non-understanding of reality to disappear when in the fullness of its undimmed glory Nirvāṇa dawns at last in one indistinguishable blaze of light.

Finally, the nine holy persons are the seven holy persons plus:

(8) The *pratyekabuddha* (Pāli *paccekabuddha*) or 'solitary', 'independent', or 'private' Buddha. What type of spiritual ideal this personage was originally intended to stand for is still a mystery. Traditionally he occupies a position intermediate between the *arhant* and the perfect Buddha. Whereas an *arhant* neither himself discovers the Path nor, after reaching the Goal, declares it to others, and the perfect Buddha discovers, realizes, and reveals it by his own efforts, the Solitary Buddha, though able to discover the Path independently, fails to reveal and teach it to the world. If wisdom and compassion are really co-ordinate, a defect in the latter – and failure to preach argues such a defect – surely implies a corresponding defect in the former. Theravādin sources indeed seem to suggest as much. The *Puggala-Paññātti* or 'Designation of Human Types', probably the first Abhidharma work to be compiled by this school, defining the private Buddha says:

> Here a certain person who, in regard to doctrines he has not heard of before, himself thoroughly understands the truths but attains neither the omniscience nor the mastery over the fruition thereof.[203]

Even this, however, does not altogether suffice to explain the enigmatic silence of the Solitary Buddha. Leaving aside the case of the *arhants*, whom the Buddha himself exhorted to go about preaching the Dharma out of compassion,[204] even *āryas* of lesser attainments feel impelled to share the fruit of their experiences with others. For the Mahāyāna tradition the *pratyekabuddha*, like the *arhant*, represents spiritual selfishness. This may not be the whole story. Some Theosophists assert that his function in the spiritual world is not pedagogic but administrative. The entire subject awaits further investigation.

(9) The *samyak-sambuddha* (Pāli *sammā-sambuddha*), the fully or perfectly Enlightened One. This foremost of all holy persons has already been systematically dealt with in Part 1. With the exception of Chapter 5, therefore, on the *trikāya* – a doctrine not accepted by the Hīnayānists, though the germs of it are discernible in their canons – whatever was said there should be understood as being repeated here. The sole difference is that we are now concerned, not merely with the historical Śākyamuni, but with the particular type of holy person which he alone has exemplified in historical times.

Of the sets of seven, eight, or nine holy persons constituting the Āryasaṅgha the second came to be regarded by the Hīnayāna as the definitive one. This is significant, for with its formalistic pattern of four main types, each subdivided according to path and fruit, its enumeration of the fetters broken at each stage, and the number of rebirths remaining, this was the most unimaginative, schematic, and rigid of them all. References to the more complex and spiritually vital sets of seven and nine do, indeed, occur from time to time in scholastic literature, but they are rarely if ever met with in modern manuals and never made the basis of popular expositions of the subject. Such a whittling down of the Assembly of the Noble is symptomatic of the general movement, not merely of conservatism, but of contraction, rigidity, and, eventually, of progressive spiritual petrifaction which set in within a century or two of the Buddha's *parinirvāṇa*. In particular it is symptomatic of the stunting of spiritual ideals that then took place. According to the Hīnayāna one should aim not at perfect Buddhahood but at arhantship, or emancipation for oneself alone. In the light of such a development as this its marked preference for the set of eight holy persons becomes intelligible, for by diverting attention from the set of nine, ending with the perfect Buddha, it is able virtually to exclude the latter from the Āryasaṅgha, thus implying that for the whole body of the faithful there is no higher goal than arhantship. The exclusion of the Buddha automatically leads to the exclusion of the Bodhisattva, who, according to the majority of Hīnayāna schools, is simply the

Śākyamuni in his pre-Enlightenment days, and not, as maintained by the Mahāyāna, a universally valid ideal.

This lowering of spiritual standards was paralleled by movements of contraction in other fields. Though their own scriptures contained evidence to the contrary, the Hīnayāna schools tended more and more to regard the higher spiritual attainments as prerogatives of the monk. Thus the Āryasaṅgha became in effect a subdivision of the *bhikṣu* sangha or monastic order. For the laity it was sufficient to make offerings to the monks and on the strength of the merit thus accumulated to aspire to a happy heavenly birth. 'Keeping up the faith of the laity' in this sense is still a major preoccupation of the Sangha in Theravādin lands. Since the quantity of merit accruing from an offering depends on the virtue of the recipient, and since the appearance of virtue is more easily achieved than the reality, the growth of ethical formalism, and eventually of conscious or unconscious hypocrisy, is inevitably encouraged.[205] Moreover, the absence of a more inspiring ideal soon affected the Hīnayāna monks themselves, and after the rise of the Mahāyāna such religious activity as there was among them increasingly tended to take the form of scholasticism in the sense of a purely formal elaboration of existing doctrinal patterns. The Sarvāstivādins succeeded in counting 147,825 kinds of faith-followers and 29,565 kinds of doctrine-followers.[206] The Uttarapāthakas, alone even among the Hīnayāna schools, distinguished themselves by eliminating compassion from their conception of Buddhahood.[207] Fortunately, long before these extreme developments took place the Mahāyāna had already outlined its own revivified and greatly enlarged conception of the Buddha's spiritual family.

16
THE GLORIOUS COMPANY OF BODHISATTVAS

The Buddha of the Mahāyāna is not merely a historical figure but the embodiment of the highest and most universal ideal of spiritual life. Consequently the Mahāyāna conception of his spiritual family is universal too. Essentially it comprises all those who, moved by the sufferings of others, dedicate themselves to the attainment of the highest spiritual good not for the sake of their own salvation only but in order that they may be able to benefit all sentient beings. A great soul of this type is technically called a bodhisattva and the spiritual community to which he belongs is known as the bodhisattva sangha. It is to the flower of this 'ocean-wide' assembly that the Buddha, in his *sambhogakāya*, principally addresses the teachings recorded in the Mahāyāna *sūtras*. Many of these *sūtras* open with a vivid description of the vast and brilliant concourse then in attendance upon him, the description being idealized and emotionally heightened in such a way as to raise the mind to an exalted spiritual plane and prepare it for the apocalyptic revelations that are to follow. Thus after describing 1,250 *arhants* in the terms already quoted (see p. 140), and noticing 500 liberated nuns, laymen, and laywomen, the 'Large Perfection of Wisdom' speaks of

> hundreds of thousands of niyutas of kotis of Bodhisattvas – (1) all of whom had acquired the dhāraṇīs; (2) dwellers in emptiness, their sphere in the signless, who had not fashioned any desire for the future; (3) who had acquired sameness and patience; (4)

who had acquired the dhāraṇī of non-attachment; (5) who had imperishable superknowledges; (6) were of acceptable speech; (7) not tricksters; (8) not chatterers; (9) with thoughts that had left behind all desire for reputation and gain; (10) disinterested demonstrators of the spiritual dharma; (11) ready to accept deep dharmas without reserve; (12) who had obtained the grounds of self-confidence; (13) had transcended Mara's deeds; (14) were free from obstacles caused by their (past) deeds; (15) and skilful in expounding the analysis of investigations into dharma; (16) who had formed their vows incalculable aeons ago; (17) who address others with smiling countenances; (18) without a frown on their faces; (19) skilful in songs, chants and benedictions; (20) with thoughts free from sluggishness; (21) with their flashes of ideas uninterrupted; (22) endowed with self-confidence when engaged in overpowering endless assemblies; (23) skilled in going forth during endless kotis of aeons; (24) resolutely intent on dharmas which they held to be like an illusion, a mirage, a reflection of the moon in water, a dream, an echo, an apparition, an image in the mirror, a magical creation; (25) skilful in understanding the destiny of beings, their subtle thoughts, their conduct and intentions; (26) with unobstructed thoughts; (27) endowed with extreme patience; (28) skilful in teaching others how to penetrate to the true character of reality; (29) acquiring through their vows and their setting-out the endless harmonies of all the Buddha-fields; (30) always face to face with the concentrated recollection of the Buddhas of countless world systems; (31) skilful in soliciting innumerable Buddhas; (32) skilful in appeasing the various views, biases, prepossessions, and defilements; (33) and in producing a hundred thousand concentrations and in playing with them.[208]

Some of the more distinguished bodhisattvas, ending with Maitreya, are then enumerated. Iconographically the 1,250 *arhants* are depicted as elderly shaven-headed monks clad in yellow robes, each holding a begging-bowl or a staff; they stand stiffly, with compressed lips, and their attitude seems not altogether free from strain. The bodhisattvas, by way of contrast, are all beautiful young princes. Gem-studded tiaras sparkle on their brows, while their nobly proportioned limbs are clad in light diaphanous garments of coloured silk. They wear gold bracelets and strings of jewels, and round their necks hang garlands of fragrant flowers. Their expression is smiling, their poses graceful and easy. These splendours do not indicate that the bodhisattvas are laymen; they symbolize their status as heirs of the Buddha, the King of the Dharma, and the untold spiritual riches to which they will one day succeed when, in the final stages of their career, they are themselves consecrated to Buddhahood. Despite the difference between their respective ideals, it is noteworthy that the Mahāyāna does not exclude the *arhants* from membership of the Buddha's spiritual family. In the second chapter of the *Saddharma Puṇḍarīka Sūtra*, or 'White Lotus of the Good Law', some members of the assembly, who apparently believe themselves to be *arhants*, are so scandalized by the Buddha's announcement that they have something further to learn that they stage a walkout by way of protest[209] – an episode that is not without its humbler parallels in the Buddhist world today.

As in the case of their Hīnayāna brethren, those making up the Glorious Company of Bodhisattvas are not all equal in attainment but distributed into a spiritual hierarchy consisting of various grades: some stand nearer to the throne of the Buddha, others further away. An account of this hierarchy, in brief but luminous outline, as well as of the various types of bodhisattva, is essential for a full understanding of the present subject. At the same time, here much more than when dealing with the Assembly of the Noble, must we be on our guard against the ever-recurrent danger of treating what is above all an ideal – according to the Mahāyāna the supreme ideal – of spiritual life, in so drily analytical a fashion, subdividing stages of progress and cataloguing their respective attributes, that the ideal as such is lost sight of. The anatomist may know every bone, and be able to trace every vein and sinew, of a dead human body, but he does not thereby know the living spirit of man. A mere enumeration of virtues and stages will never reveal to us the secret of bodhisattvahood. Such a warning is all the more necessary because much of the enormous quantity of canonical and commentarial literature dealing with the subject contains a strongly analytical element. In a truly Mahāyāna environment this is no disadvantage, for the living spiritual tradition, continued down to the present day by those who exemplify the bodhisattva ideal in their own persons, is powerful enough to correct the doctrinal tradition and prevent it from degenerating into scholasticism. But in the case of a purely theoretical account such as the present one awareness of the existence of such a possibility is not out of place. Before describing the different degrees and types of bodhisattva let us therefore contemplate the bodhisattva ideal itself in all its grandeur so that some reflection of the unique spiritual glory thereof may irradiate the details that follow.

The best picture of the bodhisattva is of course given in the Mahāyāna *sūtras*. Answering its own question as to how 'a son or daughter of good family' first aspires to become a bodhisattva, the *Aṣṭasāhasrikā* or *Perfection of Wisdom* 'in Eight Thousand Lines' says:

> He becomes endowed with that kind of wise insight which allows him to see all beings as on the way to their slaughter. Great compassion on that occasion takes hold of him. He surveys countless beings with his heavenly eye, and what he sees fills him with great agitation: so many carry the burden of a karma which leads to immediate retribution in the hells, others have acquired unfortunate rebirths (which keep them away from the Buddha and his teachings), others are doomed to be killed, or they are enveloped in the net of false views, or fail to find the path, while others who had gained a fortunate rebirth have lost it again. And he attends to them with the thought that: 'I shall become a saviour to all those beings, I shall release them from all their sufferings!'[210]

Despite the emphasis on compassion the bodhisattva is no mere sentimentalist. Nor, for all his tenderness, is he an effeminate weakling. He is the Great Hero, the embodiment not only of wisdom and compassion, but also of *vīrya* or vigour, a word which like the etymologically equivalent 'virility' signifies both energy and masculine potency. This aspect of the bodhisattva's personality is prominent in the well-known Ahicchatra image of Maitreya, with its powerful torso, massive yet graceful limbs, and clinging nether garment that covers without concealing his evident masculinity. The right hand is raised palm facing outwards and fingers slightly curved in the symbolical gesture of bestowing fearlessness (*abhaya-mudrā*).[211] Literary expression to the conception of the bodhisattva as Great Hero is given in another chapter of the *sūtra* already quoted.

> Suppose [says the Lord to Subhūti] that there were a most excellent hero, very vigorous, of high social position, handsome, attractive and most fair to behold, of many virtues, in possession of all the finest virtues, of those virtues which spring from the very height of sovereignty, morality, learning, renunciation and so on.

A whole catalogue of virtues and accomplishments then follows. After demanding of Subhūti whether such a person would not feel 'ever-increasing joy and zest' and receiving a reply in the affirmative, the Lord continues:

> Now suppose, further, that this person, so greatly accomplished, should have taken his family with him on a journey, his mother and father, his sons and daughters. By some circumstances they find themselves in a great, wild forest. The foolish ones among them would feel fright, terror and hair-raising fear. He, however, would fearlessly say to his family: 'Do not be afraid! I shall soon take you safely and securely out of this terrible and frightening forest. I shall soon set you free!' If then more and more hostile and inimical forces should rise up against him in that forest, would this heroic man decide to abandon his family, and to take himself alone out of that terrible and frightening forest – he who is not one to draw back, who is endowed with all the force of firmness and vigour, who is wise, exceedingly tender and compassionate, courageous and a master of many resources?
>
> Subhuti: No, O Lord. For that person, who does not abandon his family, has at his disposal powerful resources, both within and without.... He is competent to deal with the situation, and is able, unhurt and uninjured, soon to take out of that forest both his family and himself, and securely and safely they will reach a village, city or market-town.
>
> The Lord: Just so, Subhuti, is it with a Bodhisattva who is full of pity and concerned with the welfare of all beings, who dwells in friendliness, compassion, sympathetic joy and impartiality.[212]

These two quotations depict the bodhisattva from without, as he appears to others. Is it not possible to have a glimpse of his mind? Śāntideva, who was himself a bodhisattva, quotes from the *Vajra-dhvaja* or 'Diamond

Banner' *Sūtra* a passage wherein the Great Being resolves and reflects as follows:

> I take upon myself the burden of all suffering, I am resolved to do so, I will endure it. I do not turn or run away, do not tremble, am not terrified, nor afraid, do not turn back or despond.
>
> And why? At all costs I must bear the burdens of all beings. In that I do not follow my own inclinations. I have made the vow to save all beings. All beings I must set free. The whole world of living beings I must rescue, from the terrors of birth, of old age, of sickness, of death and rebirth, of all kinds of moral offence, of all states of woe, of the whole cycle of birth-and-death, of the jungle of false views, of the loss of wholesome dharmas, of the concomitants of ignorance, – from all these terrors I must rescue all beings.... I walk so that the kingdom of unsurpassed cognition is built up for all beings. My endeavours do not merely aim at my own deliverance. For with the help of the boat of the thought of all-knowledge, I must rescue all these beings from the stream of Samsara, which is so difficult to cross, I must pull them back from the great precipice, I must free them from all calamities, I must ferry them across the stream of Samsara. I myself must grapple with the whole mass of suffering of all beings. To the limit of my endurance I will experience in all the states of woe, found in any world system, all the abodes of suffering. And I must not cheat all beings out of my store of merit. I am resolved to abide in each single state of woe for numberless aeons; and so I will help all beings to freedom, in all the states of woe that may be found in any world system whatsoever.
>
> And why? Because it is surely better that I alone should be in pain than that all these beings should fall into the states of woe. There I must give myself away as a pawn through which the whole world is redeemed from the terrors of the hells, of animal birth, of the world of Yama, and with this my own body I must experience, for the sake of all beings, the whole mass of all painful feelings. And on behalf of all beings I give surety for all beings, and in doing so I speak truthfully, am trustworthy, and do not go back on my word. I must not abandon all beings.

And why? There has arisen in me the will to win all-knowledge, with all beings for its object, that is to say, for the purpose of setting free the entire world of beings.[213]

Even more fervent are Śāntideva's own outpourings in the *Bodhicaryāvatāra* or 'Introduction to the Way of Enlightenment'; but they are well known and need not be quoted here. What needs to be borne in mind is that the spirit of unprecedented altruism breathed by all these passages is the outcome not simply of mundane pity, nor even of spiritual compassion alone, but of compassion conjoined with wisdom. Self and non-self are equally real empirically and equally unreal metaphysically. To dedicate oneself to the salvation of others with the conviction that there in reality exist others who need saving is as much a source of bondage as to devote oneself to the task of one's own liberation under the impression that one has a real self to be liberated. The bodhisattva lives simultaneously in two worlds, the world of appearances and the world of reality, *saṃsāra* and *nirvāṇa*, wisdom and compassion, though not because he commutes back and forth between them, but because of his realization that in the absolute sense they are not two. This dual – even paradoxical and contradictory – attitude of the bodhisattva, as it must seem from the standpoint of the rational mind, is the subject of endless repetition in the 'Perfection of Wisdom' literature. Thus at the very outset of the *Vajracchedikā* or 'Diamond-Cutter' *Sūtra* the Lord declares:

Here, Subhuti, someone who has set out in the vehicle of a Bodhisattva should produce a thought in this manner: 'As many beings as there are in the universe of beings, comprehended under the term "beings" – egg-born, born from a womb, moisture-born, or miraculously born; with or without form; with perception, without perception, and with neither perception nor non-perception, – as far as any conceivable form of beings is conceived: all these I must lead to Nirvana, into that Realm of Nirvana which leaves nothing behind. And yet, although innumerable beings have thus been led to Nirvana, no being at all has been led to Nirvana.' And why? If in a Bodhisattva the notion of 'being' should take place, he could not be called a 'Bodhi-being'. And why? He is not to be called a Bodhi-being, in whom the notion of a self or of a being should take place, or the notion of a living soul or of a person.[214]

Unless we keep steadily in view the transcendental insight and experience against which the glorious figure of the bodhisattva stands as against a background of gold, the exalted ideal that he embodies will inevitably degenerate into one of secular humanitarianism devoid of all higher spiritual content and value.

In the career of the bodhisattva, as he progresses from stage to stage of attainment, there occur three events of outstanding importance: the generation of the will to Enlightenment (*bodhicittotpāda*), the becoming irreversible from perfect Buddhahood, and the realization of the three bodies. The second is analogous to Stream Entry, the third to arhantship. The first has no parallel, unless it be the taking of the Three Jewels (in the Hīnayāna sense) as one's sole Refuge and undertaking to observe the five fundamental precepts of ethical behaviour.

In preferring to render *bodhicitta* as the will to rather than as the Thought of Enlightenment, we emphasize its essentially dynamic character. Though a cognitive element is not excluded, it is definitely a conative and emotional experience rather than an intellectual one. Suzuki in fact enthusiastically contends that *citta* in this context means desire and that the sense of *bodhicittotpāda* is really 'cherishing the desire for Enlightenment':

> It is a sort of conversion, the turning towards enlightenment of the mind which was formerly engaged in something worldly, or the awakening of a new spiritual aspiration which has been dormant, or a new orientation of one's mental activities in a way hitherto undreamed of, or the finding of a new centre of energy which opens up an entirely fresh spiritual vista.[215]

Such being the case it is evident that the *bodhicitta* comes into being only after considerable preparation has been made. One must possess a stock of merit, be of good conduct, have equipped oneself with virtues, have respectfully served the Buddhas, have accomplished works of purity, enjoy the ministrations of spiritual friends, be thoroughly cleansed in heart, possess a firmly secured broadmindedness, have established a deep sincere faith and, above all, one's heart must be full of compassion.[216] Other lists of factors, all of which must be present before the desire for Enlightenment can arise, are also given.[217] Some of these obviously refer to external, others to internal, conditions.

In keeping with the more social character of the Mahāyāna, the importance of the spiritual friend (*kalyāṇa mitra*) is everywhere insisted upon. As the bodhisattva Mañjuśrī exhorts the youth Sudhana in the *Gaṇḍavyūha* or 'Flower-Array' *Sūtra*,

> If thou wishest to attain the knowledge which is possessed by the All-knowing One, be ever assiduous to get associated with good friends.[218]

So vital does Gampopa consider the part played in the life of the would-be bodhisattva by the meeting with such persons that he devotes to this topic the whole of the third chapter of *The Jewel Ornament of Liberation*. One of the canonical definitions of the *kalyāṇa mitra* quoted by him reads:

> A Bodhisattva is known as a spiritual friend perfect in every way if he is endowed with eight qualities: (i) to possess a Bodhisattva's discipline in ethics and manners, (ii) to be well versed in the Bodhisattvapiṭaka, (iii) fully to comprehend the ultimately real, (iv) to be full of compassion and love, (v) to possess the four intrepidities, (vi) to have patience, (vii) to have an indefatigable mind and (viii) to use right words.[219]

The essence of this and two other definitions Gampopa understands as being well versed in the message of the Mahāyāna and following the precepts of a bodhisattva.[220]

In reality the factors necessary for the production of the will to Enlightenment consist of two quite distinct, even as it might seem at first sight contrary, series, which meet for the first time when that production takes place. The first series represents simple longing for the Unconditioned. In other words it stands for the religious impulse as understood by the Hīnayāna and, in forms of varying purity, by all the more highly-developed religions. It is the urge to get out, to escape, to withdraw; to find in the stillness of the Eternal that peace and rest one can never enjoy on earth. The second series represents a movement in the opposite direction. Living beings suffer. How can one forsake them? In the course of hundreds of thousands, even millions, of human births, has not every man and woman alive been at some time or other one's own father, one's own mother? The bonds of solidarity with all that breathe, with all that suffer, are surely too strong to be broken. In the being of the would-be bodhisattva both these tendencies struggle for fulfilment. As now one, now the other becomes uppermost, he is torn between the rival claims of Nirvāṇa and the world, self-realization and social service, the cloister and the hearth. Unless he is more richly endowed than the average, and unless he meets spiritual friends, he may break down under the strain and eventually try to solve the problem by suppressing one tendency and devoting himself exclusively to the cultivation of the other. Should this happen, he may well achieve success in whichever line he pursues; but he will not have exhausted the highest potentialities of human nature. The Mahāyāna advises the simultaneous cultivation of both tendencies. If this is done the would-be bodhisattva will ultimately reach a point of tension at which his dualistic notions snap and the two 'contradictory' tendencies coalesce to produce 'not a third note but a star'. This star is the *bodhicitta*. In it the tendency towards Nirvāṇa is represented by the wisdom-component, the tendency towards living beings by the compassion-component, the one being distinguishable but no longer separable from the other.[221]

The *bodhicitta* is of two kinds, the absolute (*paramārtha*) and the relative (*saṃvṛti*). Gampopa, following the *Sandhinirmocana Sūtra*, most beautifully describes the former.

> It is Śūnyatā endowed with the essence of Compassion, radiant, unshakable and impossible to formulate by concepts or speech.[222]

The latter, with which we are at present more concerned, is twofold, consisting of simple aspiration (*bodhipraṇidhicitta*) and actual 'establishment' or practice (*bodhiprasthānacitta*). Shorn of doctrinal elaborations, the first of these consists in desiring single-mindedly, wholeheartedly, and from the very depths of one's being, to attain Supreme Enlightenment for the benefit of all. Any intense desire tends to express itself spontaneously in verbal form as a definite resolution. In the case of the *praṇidhicitta* this is technically known as the *praṇidhāna*, or vow, *mahāpraṇidhāna*, or great vow, and *pūrvapraṇidhāna*, or original vow, which every bodhisattva makes at the outset of his career. There are many versions of the vow, some of them being associated with the name of a particular bodhisattva. One of the shortest and best known is that which, according to Suzuki, is chanted in all Zen monasteries after a service, lecture, meal, or reading from the Scriptures:

> However innumerable beings are, I vow to save them;
> However inexhaustible the passions are, I vow to extinguish them;
> However immeasurable the Dharmas are, I vow to master them;
> However incomparable the Buddha-truth is, I vow to attain it.[223]

Other versions are much longer, consisting of a great number of clauses wherein the full implications of the vow are set forth in such detail as to provide almost a complete picture of the Mahāyāna religious ideal. In the *Sukhāvatī-vyūha* or 'Array of the Happy Land' *Sūtra*, Dharmākara the bodhisattva, who after his Enlightenment became known as the Buddha Amitābha, is described as making a series of (according to the Chinese translation) forty-eight vows, of which the eighteenth – known as 'The King of the Vows' – is regarded by the Jōdo Shinshū of Japan as constituting one of the main foundations of their faith.

> When I have obtained Buddhahood [resolves Dharmākara] if those beings who are in the ten quarters should believe in me with serene thoughts, and should wish to be born in my [Buddha-] country, and should have, say, ten times thought of me (or repeated my name), – if they should not be born there, may I not obtain the perfect knowledge; – barring only those beings who have committed the five deadly sins, and who have spoken evil of the good Law.[224]

However long or however short the bodhisattva's vow may be, he makes it publicly in the presence of a Buddha who thereupon predicts his attainment of Enlightenment after such-and-such number of aeons have passed and tells him the name by which, as a Buddha, he will then be known, together with the name of his Buddha-field. The inner meaning of these details is not difficult to interpret. The presence of the Buddha symbolizes the great truth that Enlightenment is a permanent possibility in the universe and the prediction (*vyākaraṇa*) the fact that its having been attained already by one human being guarantees its attainment by another possessing the same qualifications.[225]

While the *praṇidhicitta* is compared to the decision to walk, the *prasthānacitta* is said to resemble the actual process of walking. It embodies all the practices whereby a bodhisattva gradually becomes a Buddha. Prominent among these are the *pāramitās* or 'perfections', a set of six transcendental virtues associated especially with the bodhisattva ideal. They are *dāna* or giving, which is threefold, in respect of material things, education and culture, and spiritual knowledge; *śīla* or morality; *kṣānti* or patient acceptance, whether of abuse, physical suffering, or the more paradoxical and profound teachings of the Mahāyāna; *vīrya* or exertion, mental, physical, and spiritual, for the benefit of all beings; *dhyāna* or absorption in states of superconsciousness without allowing them to become the basis for future celestial rebirth; and *prajñā*, or wisdom, in the distinctively Mahāyāna sense of insight into the emptiness of persons and things and an understanding of the fundamental non-duality, in the absolute sense, of *saṃsāra* and *nirvāṇa*. Strictly speaking *prajñā* is the sole *pāramitā*, for only in association with it are the other *pāramitās* reckoned as such. When cultivated for the sake of mundane benefits, including rebirth in heaven, or in order to gain individual emancipation, they may be very great and noble qualities but they are not *pāramitās*. A *pāramitā*, in fact, is essentially any virtue practised by the bodhisattva in association with *prajñā* in order to gain Supreme Enlightenment for the benefit of all beings. Four more *pāramitās* were subsequently added to the original list of six: *upāya-kauśalya*, or skilful means; *praṇidhāna* or vow; *bala* or power, and *jñāna* or knowledge. The first of these is equivalent to compassion as spontaneously expressing itself in innumerable ways and means of leading sentient beings on the path of deliverance. The reappearance of *praṇidhāna* reminds us that the *bodhicitta* is not a phenomenon which arises once at the beginning of a bodhisattva's career and then subsides: like a tiny spark that develops from a flame into a world-engulfing conflagration it grows as he progresses. At his present level of attainment (for as we shall see later the *pāramitās* are correlated with a series of stages of spiritual progress known as the *bhūmis*) that which was once a simple aspiration has become a cosmic force showering grace and blessing on all within the sphere of its influence. *Bala* or power, the third of the additional *pāramitās*, represents this force raised to the highest possible degree and universalized. *Jñāna* or knowledge stands for the subtlest type of *prajñā*, that which sees not only the non-duality of the conditioned and the Unconditioned but also that this non-duality does not stand in the way of the one being the spontaneous outpouring of the other.[226]

With the arising of the relative twofold *bodhicitta* one passes beyond the stage of an ordinary being (says the *Gaṇḍavyūha Sūtra*), enters into the rank of bodhisattvahood, is born into the family of the Tathāgatas, is irreproachable and faultless in his (Buddha-) family honour, stands away from all worldly courses, enters into a super-worldly life, is established in things belonging to bodhisattvahood, abides in the abode of the bodhisattva, is impartially ushered into the Tathāgata-groups of the past, present, and future, and is ultimately destined for Supreme Enlightenment.[227] It is natural, therefore, that the Mahāyāna should attach great importance to this experience and be loud in its praises. Maitreya tells the youth Sudhana:

> The Bodhicitta is like a seed because from it grows all the truths of Buddhism. It is like a farm because here are produced all things of purity for the world.
>
> The Bodhicitta is like the earth because all the worlds are supported by it. It is like water because all the dirt of the passions is thereby cleansed. It is like the wind because it blows all over the world with nothing obstructing its course. It is like fire because it consumes all the fuel of bad logic.
>
> The Bodhicitta is like the sun because it leaves nothing unenlightened on earth. It is like the moon because it fills to perfection all things of purity. It is like a lamp because it brings things out in the light. It is like an eye because it perceives where the road is even and where it is uneven.
>
> The Bodhicitta is like a highway because it leads one to the city of knowledge. It is like a sacred ford because it keeps away all that is not proper. It is like a carriage because it carries all the Bodhisattvas. It is like a door because it opens to all the doings of the Bodhisattva.
>
> The Bodhicitta is like a mansion because it is the retreat where Samādhi and meditation are practised. It is like a park because it is where the enjoyment of truth (*dharmarati*) is experienced. It is like a dwelling-house because it is where all the world is comfortably sheltered. It is like a refuge because it gives a salutary abode to all

beings. It is like an asylum because it is where all the Bodhisattvas walk.

The Bodhicitta is like a father because it protects all the Bodhisattvas. It is like a mother because it brings up all the Bodhisattvas. It is like a nurse because it takes care of all the Bodhisattvas. It is like a good friend because it gives good advice to all the Bodhisattvas. It is like a king because it overpowers the minds of all the Śrāvakas and the Pratyekabuddhas. It is like a great sovereign because it fulfils all the excellent vows.

The Bodhicitta is like a great ocean because it harbours all the gems of virtues. It is like Mount Sumeru because it towers impartially above all things. It is like Mount Cakravāḍa because it supports all the world. It is like Mount Himālaya because it produces all sorts of knowledge-herbs. It is like Mount Gandhamādana because it harbours all kinds of virtue-fragrance. It is like space because it infinitely spreads out the merit of goodness....[228]

And so on for scores of pages.

The next great event that occurs in the bodhisattva's career is the attainment of what is technically called *avaivartika* or 'irreversibility'. On his first setting out he may not have realized fully how long and difficult would be the path to Supreme Buddhahood. For some time after the *bodhicitta* has arisen, therefore, the possibility exists that as the magnitude of the task he has undertaken gradually dawns on him the bodhisattva may become depressed, dispirited, and afraid, so that, overwhelmed by a sense of his own inadequacy, he may even decide to renounce his aim and fall back to the comparatively short and easy path of the *arhant* or the private Buddha. Only when he is so far advanced on the path to Supreme Buddhahood that such a possibility no longer exists is he said to be irreversible. According to some sources, this takes place when he fully realizes the meaning of wisdom in the Mahāyāna sense, that is, when he knows that *nirvāṇa* and *saṃsāra* are equally void and that between them there is as it were nothing to choose. For one bent on arhantship *saṃsāra* is a positive process of origination, *nirvāṇa* the negative counter-process of cessation, each process being different from the other and both real. As soon as the bodhisattva realizes that these two terms are discriminations of the mind, and that there is in the highest sense no difference between them, abandonment of the former in order to achieve the latter for him ceases to be even a possibility. Like a traveller on whom it dawns that what he took for a city is a mirage, so that he feels no further inclination to go there, the irreversible bodhisattva cannot be tempted by the Nirvāṇa of the Hīnayāna because for him it does not exist. Such a bodhisattva has reached a very lofty state. He is no longer an individual in the ordinary sense. Consequently it is very difficult to describe him, or to explain at length in what his irreversibility consists. The seventeenth and (in part) twentieth chapter of the *Aṣṭasāhasrikā* do, however, enumerate some of the attributes, tokens, and signs by which an irreversible bodhisattva can be recognized. In any case, the question of recognition is one which concerns only those who are not of this category, for one of the tokens is that to the irreversible bodhisattva himself it does not occur to ask whether he is irreversible or not.[229]

As listed in this *sūtra*, the attributes are very miscellaneous in character, ranging from the profound to the trivial. Haribhadra, the author of the *Abhisamayālaṅkāra*, does his best to schematize them by distributing them among various stages of progress.[230] Many are simply moral qualities of the true monk, and have no doctrinal or higher spiritual significance; others make more explicit one or another aspect of the bodhisattva ideal itself. Only a few are really relevant and striking. Thus when at the beginning of the seventeenth chapter the subject is first raised, and Subhūti asks what are the attributes, tokens, and signs of an irreversible bodhisattva, and how he can be known as such, the Lord replies:

> The level of the common people, the level of the Disciples, the level of the Pratyekabuddhas, the level of the Buddhas – they are all called the 'Level of Suchness'. With the thought that all these are, through Suchness, not two, nor divided, not discriminated, undiscriminate, he enters on this Suchness, this nature of Dharma. After he has stood firmly in Suchness, he neither imagines nor discriminates it. In that sense does he enter into it. When he has thus entered on it, even when he has gone away from the assembly where he has heard about Suchness, he does not hesitate, does not become perplexed, does not doubt, and he is not stupefied by the thought (concerning form, etc.) that 'it is not thus'. On the contrary, he firmly believes that 'it is just this, just Suchness,' and like that he plunges into it.[231]

Suchness is a more 'positive' synonym for the Void. The irreversible bodhisattva realizes that in the absolute sense there is no difference between the path of arhantship and the path of bodhisattvahood. On the relative plane this realization finds expression in the teaching that it is possible for an *arhant* who has become aware of the limitations of his attainment to develop the *bodhicitta* and traverse the remaining stages up to perfect Buddhahood. In other words the irreversible bodhisattva is not attached to his own *yāna* as to an independent reality: he knows that, as the *Saddharma Puṇḍarīka Sūtra* teaches in the Parable of the Burning House, the distinction of paths is due to differences of individual temperament and ability, and that the *yānas* of the disciple, the *pratyekabuddha*, and the bodhisattva all ultimately converge into the Buddhayāna.[232] Further tokens are that he does not pander to *śramaṇas* and *brāhmaṇas* of other schools and pays no homage to strange gods. He is not liable to be reborn as a result of karma on the planes of the animals, the revenants, and the tormented spirits, nor as a woman, though in pursuit of his mission he may, out of compassion, voluntarily assume any of these forms. Probably by way of checking any tendency to antinomianism, always a danger in India, the immaculate purity of his moral conduct is strongly insisted upon, and he is described as being ever mindful and vigilant. Formidable temptations may assail him. A monk may tell the bodhisattva:

> What you have heard just now, that is not the word of the Buddha. It is poetry, the work of poets. But what I here teach to you, that is the teaching of the Buddha, that is the word of the Buddha.[233]

Similarly he may be urged to put an end to all suffering in this very life, or it may be suggested that since even those who have been following the path of bodhisattvahood for aeons have not yet reached full Enlightenment his own case is hopeless. Such temptations are all the work of Māra, the Evil One. If a bodhisattva succeeds in overcoming them it is yet another sign of irreversibility. The twentieth chapter confines its attention to three signs, all of great interest. Suppose one bodhisattva is asked by another who wants to win full Enlightenment what kind of aspiration one should form in one's mind. If he speaks merely about Nirvāṇa, without including in his reply any reference to compassion, he is not irreversible. But if on the other hand, whether he has heard of the

Perfection of Wisdom teachings or not, he hits upon the correct answer, then he is to be known as an irreversible bodhisattva. Another mark of irreversibility relates to dream experiences. A bodhisattva may, for instance, behold in his dreams that all *dharmas* are like a dream, yet not realize the experience regarding it as final; he may see himself as a Buddha, surrounded by monks and bodhisattvas, and preaching the Doctrine; or, again, he may have the experience of remaining quite unafraid even when his head is about to be struck off. Such experiences indicate that in the case of the irreversible bodhisattva the bodhisattva ideal has sunk so deep as to influence and transform even his unconscious mind. The last mark concerns irreversibility and the magical power of veracity. As for Indian thought in general, it is axiomatic for Buddhism that truthfulness is a power capable of producing tangible results. A bodhisattva may, therefore, make a solemn asseveration of his irreversibility and on the strength thereof conjure a ghost to depart from a person of whom it had taken possession. Should the ghost depart, it could be inferred that the bodhisattva was irreversible.[234] The twenty-first chapter, however, hastens to add that the ghost might be driven out by Māra in order to make the bodhisattva think himself irreversible when in fact he was not. This possibility introduces a whole new series of temptations not directly connected with the topic of irreversibility.

About the bodhisattva's third and crowning experience, the transmutation of his body, speech, and mind into the triple body of perfect Enlightenment, even less can be said than about his attainment of irreversibility, for the further he progresses along his chosen path the less accessible he becomes even to the most highly refined categories of human thought. The *sūtras* themselves prefer to depict this experience symbolically in terms of a solemn ceremony of consecration (*abhiṣeka*, literally 'sprinkling'), or coronation as it would be in the West, at which, in the same way that the heir to an Indian throne was formally invested with the royal dignity, an assembly of all the Buddhas raised the bodhisattva to the rank of a fully Enlightened one and endowed him with all the powers of his new position. The literal enactment of this ceremony between an enlightened human guru and his disciple came later on to occupy a place of central importance in the Vajrayāna tradition. Historically speaking, the bodhisattva's Enlightenment occurs under conditions much the same as those obtaining in the case of Gautama the Buddha, within the period of whose dispensation we still live. As for the content of the experience, and the nature of the Goal realized therein, all that has been said before on these topics in this book is no less relevant to the present context. One additional word only need be said. Though what are termed the 'early' Mahāyāna *sūtras*, including the bulk of the *Prajñāpāramitā* corpus, do not teach explicitly in so many words the doctrine of the three bodies (*trikāya*), the later and more fully developed tradition is positive that on his consecration to Buddhahood the bodhisattva obtains not only the *dharmakāya*, but also the *sambhogakāya* and *nirmāṇakāya*, and that through the perfect instrumentality of these two bodies, the first of which is in a sense common to all Buddhas, he continues for endless time and throughout boundless space his work of universal salvation.

The arising of the *bodhicitta*, the attainment of irreversibility, and consecration, as well as other lesser experiences, are strung out like landmarks along a series of stages of progress generally known as *bhūmis* (literally 'grounds'). Different canonical sources give of these stages descriptions which do not tally in all particulars, not even with regard to the total number of them or their respective names. Eventually, however, the enormously detailed and systematic account given in the *Daśabhūmika Sūtra* won acceptance as the standard one. As the name of this *sūtra* reveals, it reckons the *bhūmis* as ten in number. Their names are the Joyful (*pramuditā*), the Immaculate (*vimalā*), the Illuminating or Radiant (*prabhākarī*), the Blazing (*arciṣmatī*), the Very Difficult to Conquer (*sudurjayā*), the Face-to-Face (*abhimukhī*), the Far-Going (*dūraṅgamā*), the Immovable (*acalā*), Good Thoughts (*sādhumatī*), and the Cloud of the Doctrine (*dharmameghā*). Most of these terms are obviously symbolic and poetic rather than scientific. This reminds us of the fact that divisions and subdivisions are not to be taken too literally, and that essentially the bodhisattva path is not an affair of steps and stages but of continuous progressive growth in wisdom and compassion. Nevertheless, a special feature of the *Daśabhūmika Sūtra* is that it distributes among the ten *bhūmis* all the more important doctrinal categories and spiritual practices of Buddhism. Thus in the third *bhūmi* the bodhisattva cultivates the four *brahma-vihāras*, in the fifth he understands the four noble truths. Perhaps the most valuable instance of this procedure, which constitutes the *Sūtra* a veritable encyclopedia of Buddhism, is that which correlates the ten *pāramitās* or transcendental virtues with the ten *bhūmis*, the practice of giving predominating in the first *bhūmi*, that of morality in the second, and so on. Why a teaching should be assigned to one stage rather than to another is not always clear, however. Moreover, every one of the stages is packed so full of doctrines and practices, and they are all highly praised in such identical terms, that a number of them are in danger of losing their individuality. Yet despite the presence of all these trees, the wood is not quite lost to sight. Thanks to the ten *pāramitās*, and to the placing of the three crucial experiences of his career, which provide the most important points of reference, the outlines of the bodhisattva's progress stand out with sufficient sharpness. With the arising of the *bodhicitta* he enters upon the first *bhūmi*, where he makes his great vow and receives his prediction. Having stood face to face with the common reality of *nirvāṇa* and *saṃsāra* in the sixth, and reached the seventh by going far from the possibility of gaining arhantship, he attains the immovable state of irreversibility in the eighth *bhūmi*. In the tenth *bhūmi* he receives his consecration.

Taking these three great events, and the stages in which they occur, as lines of demarcation, we find that as regards their degree of attainment bodhisattvas may be classified as belonging to four groups. First there is the novice bodhisattva, or aspirant to bodhisattvahood, who accepts intellectually the bodhisattva ideal, and does his best to live up to it, while at the same time making efforts for the generation of the *bodhicitta*. He may or may not have received the formal bodhisattva initiation described in the following chapter. To this group belong the vast majority of professing Mahāyāna Buddhists, whether monks, nuns, or lay devotees. The second group consists of all who have attained any of the first six *bhūmis*, and who may, therefore, be called bodhisattvas of the Path. In this group are also included the so-called Hīnayāna bodhisattvas, from the Stream Entrant up to the *arhant*, for if they so desire these can, according to the most liberal Mahāyāna teaching on the subject, at any time renounce the idea of individual emancipation and follow instead the bodhisattva ideal. Because of its correspondence with this group the Assembly of the Noble is regarded as comprised in the Glorious Company of Bodhisattvas. The third group is made up of the irreversible bodhisattvas, who are the bodhisattvas *par excellence*. They have already been separately dealt with. The fourth and highest group is that of the bodhisattvas of the *dharmakāya*. This includes those who, after perfect Enlightenment, retain their bodhisattva form, as well as all who are the direct emanations of the *dharmakāya* and have no human history. Between such bodhisattvas and the Buddhas there is no real difference. Broadly speaking, the former embody the static, the latter the dynamic aspect of the *dharmakāya.*

So far we have dealt with the bodhisattvas collectively. Individual bodhisattvas are, however, well known in the Mahāyāna, thousands of them being in fact mentioned in the Scriptures by name. The greatest, who are comparatively few in number, occupy in the religious life of the Mahāyāna a place not second to that of the historical founder of Buddhism himself, being regarded as supreme objects of devotion and sources of the highest spiritual inspiration, illumination, and guidance. Uninformed or unsympathetic writers on Buddhism often refer to them as gods, a misleading usage which, for those belonging to a different religious *milieu*, at once equates the worship of bodhisattvas with polytheism, and reduces Buddhism to the level of a pagan cult.

The most popular bodhisattvas constitute two well-known groups, one consisting of five and the other of eight members. The five *dhyāni* bodhisattvas (as they have been styled by Western writers) are associated with the five so-called *dhyāni* Buddhas, iconographically as their attendants, but in reality as their dynamic counterparts or emanations. The relation is also envisaged as one of spiritual sonship. Thus Samantabhadra is associated with Vairocana, Vajrapāṇi with Akṣobhya, Ratnapāṇi with Ratnasambhava, Avalokiteśvara with Amitābha, and Viśvapāṇi with Amoghasiddhi. Together with their respective *ḍākinīs* or *prajñās*, or feminine counterparts, and a host of minor emanations, these make up the five spiritual families (*pañca-kula*), on the complex symbolism of which is based much Vajrayana practice, especially in the realms of art and meditation, and to one or another of which, by reason of individual temperament and line of spiritual practice, every follower of the Vajrayāna is normally affiliated. The eight bodhisattvas are Samantabhadra, Vajrapāṇi, Avalokiteśvara, Mañjuśrī, Maitreya, Ākāśagarbha, Kṣitigarbha, and Sarvanivaraṇaviṣkambhin. Two more, Mahāsthāmaprāpta and Trailokyavijaya, are sometimes added, raising the number to ten. Some writers make a sharp distinction between the two groups, designating the latter as that of the human, and the former that of the divine bodhisattvas; but though a difference undoubtedly exists, the fact that several bodhisattvas belong to both groups shows it is not an absolute one.

After making deductions on account of the three duplicated names, we are left with a total of twelve bodhisattvas, some better known than others. The best known, whether in China, Japan, or Tibet, are Mañjuśrī, Avalokiteśvara, Vajrapāṇi, Maitreya, Samantabhadra, Mahāsthāmaprāpta, and Kṣitigarbha. For the devotee, each of these great beings possesses a distinctive spiritual personality, and is as much a reality to him as Christ and the saints to a devout Christian, or the deified heroes Rāma and Kṛṣṇa to a pious Hindu.

This is especially true of the first three, who as a triad are worshipped throughout Tibet and Nepal as the three family protectors (Tibetan *rig-sum-gon-po*), the families being those of their respective Buddhas – Vairocana, Amitābha, and Akṣobhya – who form the original nucleus out of which was developed the well-known scheme of five '*dhyāni*' Buddhas. Since there is a correspondence between the transcendental axiality of Buddhahood and the mundane axiality of the human state, it is natural that the three chief bodhisattvas, as embodiments of main aspects of the *dharmakāya*, should correspond to the three principal functions of the mind. Thus Mañjuśrī represents wisdom, or transmuted intellect, Avalokiteśvara compassion, or purified emotion, and Vajrapāṇi power, or sublimated volition. This distribution of attributes is the principal factor determining the characters and types of spiritual activity of these great beings.

Mañjuśrī-Kumārabhūta, 'Gently Auspicious One, Who Became a Prince', is known by many other names and titles. He is Mañjughoṣa, 'Gentle-Voiced One', Mañjunātha, 'Gentle Saviour', and Vagīśvara, 'Lord of Speech'. In China he is known by the transliteration Man-shu-shi-li, as well as by the epithet Wénshū, 'He of the Five [Mountain] Peaks' (a misunderstanding of Pañcaśikha, 'He of the Five [Hair-] Crests'). The Buddhists of Tibet, translating 'Gentle-Voiced One' into their own tongue, call him Jambeyang; those of Japan simply Monju. His appearance in the oldest Mahāyāna literature testifies to his pre-eminence from an early date. Besides being the main object of minor works devoted specially to his cult, he plays a leading role in the *Saddharma Puṇḍarīka* and figures prominently in the *Prajñāpāramitā*. In the *Vimalakīrti-nirdeśa*, or 'Exposition of Vimalakīrti', he alone among the bodhisattvas ventures to call on that formidable old debater.[235] As Mahāmati, 'The Greatly Intelligent One', he is the principal interlocutor of the *Laṅkāvatāra*; in the *Gaṇḍavyūha* he ranks as one of the two leaders of the 500 bodhisattvas of that *sūtra*, as well as first teacher of the youth Sudhana, whom he instructs and sends forth on his long quest; and he is honourably mentioned in the *Smaller Sukhāvatī-vyūha*. His place in Vajrayāna literature is no less distinguished, for he gives his name to the *Mañjuśrī-mūla-kalpa*, or 'Basic Rite',

> a voluminous text which represents the transitional stage from *sūtra* to *tantra*.[236]

Iconographically he is depicted in a bewildering variety of forms: Bhattacharyya lists thirteen principal ones according to Indian tradition.[237] Usually, however, he manifests as a beautiful youth, sixteen years old, golden in hue, richly clad in the silks and ornaments of a bodhisattva, and wearing at the parting of his hair and over his ears three blue lotuses. His special emblems are the lotus, book, and flaming sword; his animal, the lion. One of his most popular forms is Arapacana, so called from the first five letters of the mystic alphabet, as whom he sits cross-legged on a moon-mat and lotus brandishing the fiery sword of knowledge above his head with the right hand, while with the left he presses to his heart the book, understood to represent the *Prajñāpāramitā*, the scripture of wisdom *par excellence*, with which he is specially associated. As the patron of arts and sciences, inspirer of literature, and supreme master of sacred eloquence, he is invoked, worshipped, and meditated upon, and his mantra repeated, particularly for a retentive memory, knowledge of the Scriptures, understanding of the Doctrine, and power of exposition. With what attitude his devotees approach him is best illustrated by the following *stuti* or hymn of praise, wherein the author, *siddhācarya* Vajrayudha, lauds by turns his mind, composed of wisdom and compassion, his speech, and his body.

> To thee, whose understanding, purifying like a cloud-free sun the two obscurations (*āvaraṇa*), and very clear,
> Sees all matters whatsoever (as they are), wherefore thou dost hold the volume (of *Prajñāpāramitā*) to thy heart;
> [To thee who] in kindness, as though to an only son, to living beings – covered as they are in the prison of temporal existence
> With the darkness of *avidyā* and afflicted by *duḥkha* – [dost utter] Thy Speech, with a sixty-(four-)fold voice,

Resounding loud as thunder, waking the sleep of the *kleśas*,
unfastening the iron fetters of karma,
Dispersing the darkness of ignorance, and [who,] cutting off
every sprout of *duḥkha*, [dost] grasp the sword:
To the body of the chief among Jinas and their sons, his body-of-virtues perfected,
Pure from the start and arrived at the end of the ten *bhūmis*,
Adorned with the ten tens of ornaments and twelve, dispersing
the darkness of our mind – to [thee] Mañjughoṣa we bow.[238]

The meaning of the name Avalokiteśvara has been the subject of much scholarly debate. Iśvara indisputably means Lord. According to whether it is understood as a passive or as an active participle Avalokita may mean either one who is gazed at or one who gazes. In the latter case the name would mean, being interpreted, the Lord who looks down in pity on the miseries of the world, a popular etymology. Sometimes the last part of Avalokiteśvara is identified not with *iśvara* but with *svara*, meaning sound. The usual Chinese translation is based on this interpretation. Whatever its dictionary meaning, the sacred name undoubtedly combines, most appropriately, the ideas of spiritual sovereignty and compassion. Among the hundreds of other names of this bodhisattva are Padmapāṇi, or 'Lotus-in-hand'; Lokanātha, 'Saviour of the World'; and Mahākārunika, 'Greatly Compassionate One'. In Tibet he is known as Chenrezig, 'He Who Sees With Bright Eyes'; in China (where he underwent transformation into a female bodhisattva) as Guanyin or Guanshiyin, 'Regarder of the Cries of the World'; and in Japan as Kwannon. As simply Nātha, the saviour, he continues to be worshipped in Theravādin Sri Lanka, having temples and servitors of his own at Kandy and elsewhere. Literary references to Avalokiteśvara are fewer than to Mañjuśrī. The *Mahāvastu*, which belongs to the third century BCE, contains two *Avalokita Sūtras*, but these consist mainly of accounts of Gautama Buddha's Enlightenment, and have nothing to do with the bodhisattva. He is mentioned in the *Larger Sukhāvatī-vyūha*, and in the *Amitāyur-dhyāna*, where as an attendant of the Buddha of Infinite Life he is described in the tenth series of sixteen meditations on the glories of the Happy Land. Though having no special connection with the *Prajñāpāramitā*, he appears at the opening of the famous *Heart Sūtra*, the contents of which are presented as a revelation of his spiritual experience as he courses in transcendental wisdom. The main canonical sources of his cult are the *Saddharma Puṇḍarīka* and the *Kāraṇḍa-vyūha Sūtra*. In the twenty-fourth chapter of the former (the twenty-fifth of the Chinese translation) – which often circulates as an independent work and may have been composed separately and afterwards inserted into the *sūtra* – he appears as Samantamukha, 'The One Facing Everywhere', and is praised for the benefits he confers on all his worshippers. This chapter also contains the bodhisattva Akṣayamati's 'Hymn to Avalokiteśvara', one of the jewels of Mahāyāna literature. The *Kāraṇḍa-vyūha*, reputedly the first Buddhist text translated into Tibetan, is a composite work displaying marked Hindu features that departs so far from doctrinal orthodoxy as to describe, among the exploits of the bodhisattva, how he created the world in the time of Vipaśvin Buddha, producing the sun and moon from his eyes and the gods of Hinduism from different parts of his body. It also relates how Avalokiteśvara obtained the great six-syllabled mantra *oṃ maṇi padme hūṃ*, perhaps the most famous of all Buddhist invocations. Both these *sūtras* reflect the Mahāyāna conviction that the bodhisattva is concerned with the temporal as well as the spiritual welfare of his devotees. According to the *Saddharma Puṇḍarīka* Avalokiteśvara delivers those who call on his name from such dangers as fire, flood, shipwreck, execution by the sword, attacks of wicked demons, imprisonment, and robbery. Those possessed by craving, hatred, and delusion have only to remember and revere him and they will be set free. A woman who desires a child should pray to him.[239] Endowed as he is with such amiable qualities it is small wonder that his cult should have flourished above that of any other bodhisattva. As depicted in art his figure is hardly less attractive than that of the Buddha. Iconographically speaking he possesses at least fifteen major forms,[240] but one of the best known, even as it is among the most beautiful, is that of a slenderly built young prince in a high jewelled headdress who, with body gracefully bent, stands bearing a lotus in his left hand and making the gesture of bestowing alms with the right, while his beautiful face is alive with tenderness and compassion. More bizarre, though equally expressive, is the form in which he appears with eleven heads and a thousand arms, signifying the omnipresence and omnipotence of his compassion. In the palm of each hand is an eye, suggesting that even in its remotest operations compassion is never divorced from wisdom. His universality does not however exclude a specific cosmic function. As the spiritual son of Amitābha, of whom Gautama is the earthly reflex, he is responsible for the spiritual evolution of the human race during the interregnum between the withdrawal of the last human Buddha and the advent of the next.

Vajrapāṇi, or 'The Thunderbolt-Handed One', despite his enormous popularity throughout Tibet, Mongolia, and China, figures hardly at all in the great canonical texts of the Mahāyāna. As from his name one might expect, his distinctive emblem is the *vajra*, originally meaning thunderbolt, and sculptures and paintings invariably depict him with it. Sometimes it rests at shoulder level upon an open lotus, the stalk of which he holds; or he may press it against his chest with his right hand, or balance it upon its point on his palm. Indeed, the bodhisattva's later rise to fame may be due partly to his association with this emblem, which after its transformation into the chief symbol for wisdom and the Void, gave its name to the Vajrayāna. As befits his position as the embodiment of transcendental power, Vajrapāṇi, unlike Mañjuśrī and Avalokiteśvara, is venerated less under his peaceful (*śānta*) than his wrathful (*krodha*) aspect as destroyer of the darkness of spiritual ignorance. In Tibet, where he is known as Dorje-lek-pa and Chagna Dorje, both of which translate the Indian name, he is depicted in religious art with tremendous zest. There are many forms, but he is usually dark blue in colour, with a stout body, protuberant belly, and thick, short limbs. His heads, which may be one or many, are crowned with skulls, and his facial expression is one of terrific anger. He may be naked save for ornaments of human bone, or draped in a tiger-skin. According to the number of his arms, he carries the *vajra*, a snake, a small drum, a chopper, and a human skull filled with blood, while the disengaged hands assume various *mudrās*. Generally he moves to the right, one foot uplifted to trample upon prostrate figures representing the forces of mundane existence. Around him swirls an aureole of flames. For those brought up in, or familiar with, the Tibetan tradition, the contemplation of this awe-inspiring figure is productive of heroic emotions of fearlessness and an intense spiritual exaltation.

Like other great bodhisattvas the three family protectors project or emanate from themselves various other bodhisattvas who thereafter assume an independent or quasi-independent existence. No hard and fast line of demarcation can however be drawn between their forms and their emanations, the difference being one of degree rather than of kind.

A bodhisattva's emanations, which may themselves be polymorphous, are often of that wrathful type, the most important representatives of which are known as *dharmapālas*, or 'defenders of the faith', it being their duty to guard the Doctrine against all hostile forces. Thus Mañjuśrī emanates Yamāntaka, 'The Destroyer of Death', who in his black naked form as Vajrabhairava, 'The Fearful Thunderbolt', with nine heads, the centre one that of a bull, and thirty-four arms, two of which clasp his feminine counterpart, is the tutelary deity of the Gelugpas. Avalokiteśvara emanates Padmanarteśvara, 'The Lotus Lord of Dance'. He is generally represented in a dancing attitude, with one head and eighteen hands, all of which hold double lotuses, and he is the Tutelary Deity of the Nyingmapas. The most attractive emanation is undoubtedly the female bodhisattva Tārā, meaning both 'Saviouress' and 'Star', who appears in a multiplicity of peaceful and wrathful forms. A beautiful legend tells how she was born from the tears of Avalokiteśvara as he wept over the miseries of the world. As such she embodies the very quintessence of compassion. Her two best-known forms are the White Tārā and the Green Tārā. As the former she holds a white lotus, as the latter a blue lotus. Both depict her as a benign and beautiful woman, neither young nor old, wearing the customary silks and jewels of a bodhisattva. Besides being worshipped throughout Tibet and Mongolia, where she is known as Jetsun Dolma, 'The Faithful Dolma', she is adored in Nepal and in parts of China, and has even managed to survive under her own and other names in Hindu India. On account of her maternal qualities she is related to her devotees in a particularly affectionate and intimate manner.

Maitreya (Pāli Metteyya), 'The Friendly One', also known as Ajita, 'The Unconquered', is without question the most prominent of the remaining bodhisattvas. As the one destined to become the next human Buddha, he enjoys the unique distinction of being the only bodhisattva recognized throughout the entire Buddhist world, in Theravādin as well as in Mahāyāna lands, for which reason it has been suggested that his worship might constitute a means of unification among Buddhists. Though his name occurs only once in the *Nikāyas*, when the Buddha prophesies his advent,[241] he is frequently alluded to in Pāli exegetical literature: Buddhaghosa concludes the *Visuddhimagga* (according to the Sinhalese texts) with a fervent poetical aspiration to attain arhantship in his presence. He is also mentioned in the earlier Sanskrit and Mixed

Sanskrit works such as the *Lalitavistara*, the *Divyāvadāna*, and the *Mahāvastu*. In the *Saddharma Puṇḍarīka* he plays a prominent part, but still is subordinate to Mañjuśrī, who acts as his instructor. Minor works such as the *Maitreya-vyākaraṇa* or 'Prediction Concerning Maitreya' relate in detail the circumstances of his coming. Strictly speaking, he is at present a bodhisattva of the ninth *bhūmi*, but tradition often speaks of him, by anticipation, as a Buddha, and as such he is frequently depicted in art. Of brilliant golden hue, he bears for emblems the wheel, the stupa, and the sacred vase (*kalaśa*). The last of these, now closed, contains ambrosia, representing the truth with which he will one day besprinkle mankind. Both as Buddha and as bodhisattva he often sits not in the more usual cross-legged posture, but as though upon a chair, in European fashion, thus indicating his readiness to descend from the Tuṣita Heaven, where he now resides, to the Earth, in order to fulfil his original vow by traversing the tenth and last *bhūmi* and gaining Supreme Buddhahood for the benefit of all. Various attempts have been made by non-Buddhists to identify Maitreya with their own spiritual heroes. Christian missionaries, in an attempt to undermine the loyalties of the faithful, have been known to argue that the Buddha's predictions about Maitreya really refer to Christ. J. Krishnamurti has been similarly acclaimed.[242] For the Buddhist world, however, the messianic hopes which centre on the person of Maitreya are as yet unfulfilled. According to widespread beliefs, his advent will be preceded by the reappearance of Nāgārjuna and other ancient sages, and by the unification of the whole world under the rule of a righteous Buddhist king. Meanwhile, throughout Central Asia and the Himalayan borderlands, where his cult is strongest, the presence of numerous gigantic images, mountain rocks carved with the imploring inscription 'Come, Maitreya, come!' and even the horse races held in his honour during the Tibetan New Year, testify to the faith with which his devotees expect and the fervour with which they seek to hasten his coming.

Samantabhadra, 'The All-Good', and Mahāsthāmaprāpta, 'Attained to Great Strength', are both mentioned in the *Saddharma Puṇḍarīka*, the twenty-eighth chapter (of the Chinese version) being dedicated to the one and the twentieth to the other. Together with Mañjuśrī, Samantabhadra figures prominently in the *Gaṇḍavyūha*, which according to Suzuki is 'in a sense the history of the inner religious consciousness of Samantabhadra',[243] while Mahāsthāmaprāpta is described at length in the *Amitāyur-dhyāna*, together with Avalokiteśvara, as attending upon the Buddha of Infinite Light and Life in the Happy Land. As embodiments respectively of compassion and of power they resemble and in a way duplicate Avalokiteśvara and Vajrapāṇi; but by virtue of his association with an outstandingly popular group of *sūtras* Mahāsthāmaprāpta was able largely to supersede Vajrapāṇi throughout the Far East. In Indian iconography they are depicted in the same princely form as other bodhisattvas: Samantabhadra, white in colour, bears on a lotus his family emblem, the wheel; Mahāsthāmaprāpta is white or yellow and holds either a bunch of six full-blown lotuses or a sword. In China and Japan, where his cult flourished and he became more recognizably an individual, Samantabhadra (Chinese: Puxian, Japanese: Fugen) is green in colour and rides a white elephant. He is depicted thus when, in a popular group known as the Śākya Trinity, he and Mañjuśrī, who rides a lion, appear on either side of a larger central figure of the Buddha.

Kṣitigarbha or 'Earth-Womb' is also more popular in the Far East than he ever was in India. From a bare mention in the roll of the eight bodhisattvas he has risen, in China and Japan, to a popularity second only to that of Avalokiteśvara. The reasons for this development are obscure, though it is clear it began in Turkestan. As his name suggests, Kṣitigarbha is connected with the depths. Like all bodhisattvas, he aspires to deliver sentient beings wandering astray in the five (or six) paths of mundane existence; but he specializes, as it were, in delivering them from hell. This expresses exoterically an extremely profound and esoteric aspect of the bodhisattva's compassionate activity: he takes upon himself the fearful task not merely of plumbing the depths of existence, and bringing relief and consolation to those in torment, but of personally transforming and uplifting the vast inchoate mass of fear, hatred, and despair swarming and pullulating in the pitch darkness of the Abyss. He is that loving condescension of the highest to the lowest which, abandoning its own bright seats, does not shrink from working under conditions the most difficult and appalling – amidst scenes of horror, madness, and desolation – at the seemingly hopeless task of reclaiming what is irrecoverably lost. Kṣitigarbha is the principle of spiritual sublimation in its most radical aspect, powerful enough to transform not merely hell into heaven but the foulest dregs of *saṃsāra*, even, into the pure radiance of Nirvāṇa. He is the supreme embodiment of spiritual optimism, the extremest development of Mahāyāna universalism, which wills that not so much as a grain of dust should be left outside the scheme of salvation. This seems to have been imperfectly understood in the Far East. In China, where he was known as Ti-tsang (Japanese: Jizō), he became 'not so much a Saviour [from hell] as the kindly superintendent of a prison who preaches to the inmates and willingly procures their release'.[244] In Japan he underwent changes even more surprising. As his popularity grew, besides greatly expanding the scope of his bodhisattva activities, he became not only a sort of god of the roads, and the special protector of children, but also the patron saint of warriors. Indian iconography generally depicts him as yellow or green in colour, showing the *bhūmisparśa* or 'earth-touching' gesture with his right hand and bearing in his left a lotus with the *kalpa-vṛkṣa* or wish-fulfilling tree. Chinese and Japanese art represent him in monastic dress grasping the *khakkhara* or ringed staff of the Sarvāstivādin monk with his right hand and holding in his left the *cintāmaṇi*, or wish-granting gem, which is properly the emblem of his celestial counterpart Ākāśagarbha.

Though the majority of them are human, in the sense of having once lived on the earth as men, the bodhisattvas described above are hardly historical figures in the scientific sense: their reality is not of the mundane but primarily of the spiritual order. The Mahāyāna does however recognize another important type of bodhisattva who is both human and historical. This category consists of the most outstanding of those spiritual heroes who, as inspirers of movements and founders of schools, have been makers of Buddhist history and moulders of Buddhist thought and who, by example and precept, have in times of stagnation and decay given a fresh impetus to the practice and dissemination of the Doctrine. Prominent among them towers the mighty figure of Nāgārjuna, founder of the Madhyamaka school, whose vindication of the *Prajñāpāramitā* teaching and dialectical demonstration of the futility of all one-sided views stands as a watershed separating the Hīnayāna and the Mahāyāna. Numerous other names, the brightest in Buddhist history, could be mentioned. They would include dauntless pilgrims like Xuanzang who, in quest of the Dharma, traversed waterless deserts and pathless jungles;[245] scholars like Kumārajīva whose lives were devoted to translating the Scriptures;[246] saintly ascetics such as Milarepa who, in forest or in mountain cave, passed their days deep in *samādhi*;[247] zealous reformers of the type of Tsongkhapa[248] who 'waged contention with their time's decay';[249] and lastly, royal supporters like Shōtoku Taishi under whose patronage the Buddha's precepts were translated into principles of national life.[250] Many of these were undoubtedly bodhisattvas of the Path; a few, irreversible bodhisattvas. Among the greatest of the last, again, some are traditionally revered not as men become bodhisattvas but as bodhisattvas become men. Such are Tsongkhapa, the father of the Gelug school, who on account of his wisdom and kindred virtues is regarded as a manifestation of Mañjuśrī, and a number of other personages prominent in the history of Tibetan Buddhism. Such also, if we can take his word for it, is Nichiren, founder of the most militant Japanese sect, who identified himself with the bodhisattva Viśiṣṭacāritra of the *Saddharma Puṇḍarīka*.[251] Some bodhisattvas, indeed, are for all practical purposes identical with their manifestations. The so-called 'Laughing Buddha', for example, is Maitreya in the form of a medieval Chinese monk.

Bodhisattvas may also appear not only singly, as one more or less well-known historical figure, but as a recognizably continuous series of personalities dedicated to Enlightenment for the good of all throughout a succession of human lives. In Tibet and the adjoining regions, from Ladakh to Mongolia, where Tibetan spiritual traditions prevail, bodhisattvas of this type are known as *tulkus*. Uninformed Western writers generally refer to them as incarnate lamas and living Buddhas. *Tulku* in Tibetan corresponds to the Sanskrit *nirmāṇakāya* or 'created body' – *kāya* here standing not for 'body' as opposed to 'mind' but for the whole psychophysical aggregate – a term which also designates the third of the three bodies of the Buddha. More elaborate classifications are possible, but broadly speaking *tulkus* are of two kinds. There is the series that starts from a historical figure such as Sarahapāda or Tāranātha,[252] and the series that starts from a great bodhisattva such as Avalokiteśvara or Mañjuśrī. In the first case the succeeding human personality does not arise in dependence on the preceding one by virtue of the law of karma, but is voluntarily created by it out of compassion as a means of carrying on its mission. Here, as elsewhere in the Doctrine, though concessions may sometimes be made to conventional modes of speech, there is no question of the 'reincarnation' of an unchanging ego-entity. As was shown in Part 2, the law of conditioned co-production is universal, comprising both the Round and the Path. In terms of this law one might say of this kind of *tulku* that he arises in dependence on the wisdom, compassion, and vow of a deceased human bodhisattva. Thus the series to which he belongs is a horizontal one. In the case of the second kind of *tulku* we are concerned with the direct emanation or manifestation – the word *avatāra* or 'descent' can also be used – of a non-human bodhisattva. Hence the series to which this kind belongs, though apparently horizontal, is in reality vertical, the human personalities of which it consists being not so much a series of 'rebirths' as a succession of descents from a common transcendental source. As the *nirmāṇakāyas* of an irreversible bodhisattva or a bodhisattva of the Path possess, once emanated, a spiritual life of their own, the possibility of an initial vertical descent followed by a horizontal series of 'rebirths' cannot be ruled out. In neither case, though, does there ever occur a descent of divine soul into human body, such as the expression 'incarnate lama' implies; for according to the Mahāyāna the difference between mind and matter is not absolute: each *nirmāṇakāya* is projected as an indivisible psychophysical whole. The best known example of this kind of *tulku* is, of course, the series consisting of the four religious kings of Tibet and the line of Dalai Lamas, the present one being the fourteenth, all of whom are regarded as manifestations of Avalokiteśvara. Altogether, including those of both human and of non-human origin, there are – or were – distributed throughout Tibet and its cultural-religious dependencies about a thousand *tulkus*. The way in which they are discovered and identified has often been described. An interesting and authentic account of the present supreme spiritual head and temporal ruler of Tibet is given by Lobsang Phuntsok Lhalungpa, and the sequence of events described by him is typical of the discovery of most *tulkus*.[253]

Numerous other types of bodhisattva might also be mentioned, for as the reality of Supreme Enlightenment transcends space and time the possibilities of compassionate activity are infinite. This is not the place to discuss the significance of the fact that bodhisattvas may be either male or female, professed *réligieux* or lay devotees. Notice ought however to be taken before we conclude of the fact that in modern times liberal Mahāyānists, especially those of Japan, have begun to wonder whether the spiritual masters of other religions whose teachings in some points coincide with the Buddha's might not be bodhisattvas. The names of Laozi, Christ, Eckhart, St John of the Cross, and Guru Nanak have been proposed in this connection. Some advocates of universalism go indeed so far as to contend that all benefactors of humanity, including poets, artists, scientists, statesmen, philanthropists, and social reformers are as much bodhisattvas as those engaged in specifically religious activities. To interpret the ideal as liberally as this might be to obscure its real meaning. In any case, a distinction would have to be drawn between those who on account of their altruistic and dedicated lives approximate to the conduct expected of a human bodhisattva and those who are manifestations of one or another of the great bodhisattvas for the fulfilment of a specific purpose. Evidence would moreover be required in any given case, whether of the one kind or the other, that the career of the alleged bodhisattva was motivated by compassion, that he actually worked for the good of others, that the means adopted by him were in accordance with the ends proposed, and that he was free from wrong views. Such as pass these tests are the most distant members of the Buddha's spiritual family, the outermost of those vast concentric circles of compassionate activity whereof the Glorious Company of Bodhisattvas is the radiant nucleus and the Buddha himself the dazzling heart and centre.

17
THE MONASTIC ORDER

Corresponding to, and in the best periods largely coinciding with, the Sangha as a spiritual élite, is the Sangha as a community of men and women treading the Path and striving to realize the Goal by following either the *arhant* or the bodhisattva ideal. As in one form or another is the case in most organized religions, this community consists of two kinds of members: those whose experience of the Path is sufficient to modify the course of their lives without radically changing it and those who, to adopt the language of William James's definition of the religious man, though not necessarily having the most 'religious experience' make their experiences their *centre of gravity*.[254] While for the first kind religion is only one among a multiplicity of interests, for the second it is the supreme, even the sole, interest to which all others must be subordinated and, if necessary, sacrificed. Thus Buddhism as an institutional religion comprises both a larger body of lay followers known as *upāsakas* (fem. *upāsikās*), whose practice of the Dharma is occasional and partial, and a very much smaller body of *bhikṣus* (fem. *bhikṣuṇīs*) who dedicate to its realization their whole life and the sum total of their energies. The latter form the *bhikṣu* (Pāli *bhikkhu*) sangha, the order of monks, or the monastic order, which is the primary ecclesiastical sense in which the word 'sangha' is now used.

This order did not come into existence all at once. Like other living things, whether organisms, empires, or ideas, it has in the course of its history passed through various stages of development. This fact, obvious though it is from a careful study of the records, is generally ignored by writers on Buddhism. Some, indeed, would have us believe that the Sangha sprang fully formed from the brain of the Buddha even as Pallas Athene leapt complete with shield and spear from the forehead of Zeus. Did it not command wide acceptance, a view so astonishingly naive would not be worth mentioning. In reality the Sangha passed, during the first few generations of its existence, through three well-marked stages of development, each with certain distinctive features.

(1) According to the 'legend' of the four sights (see p. 35), and as other canonical sources abundantly testify, the Buddha – or the Bodhisattva, as he then was – decided to seek a solution to the problem of suffering by adopting the life of the *parivrājaka* (Pāli *paribbājaka*) or one who had 'gone forth' (the literal meaning of the word) from life at home to be a homeless wanderer. Whether, as Sukumar Dutt suggests, and as seems probable, the *parivrājakas* were originally the north-east Indian counterparts of the *brāhmaṇas* of the Āryan society to the north-west, does not concern us.[255] It is sufficient that the Buddha, both before and after his Enlightenment, was a *parivrājaka*, and that nearly all his closest associates were either recruited from this class or joined it in order to be with him and follow his teaching. Like Mahāvīra, the restorer of Jainism, and other teachers whose names are preserved in early Buddhist literature, the Buddha appeared to the general public of his times as the founder and head of one of the various sodalities into which the *parivrājaka* community was divided. Like other heads of sodalities, moreover, he professed and taught a special Dharma, and it was this, rather than their mode of life, which distinguished him and his adherents from the rest.

At this stage of its development the Sangha was therefore simply that section of the *parivrājaka* community which acknowledged the Buddha as master and accepted his doctrine. As yet there was no question of any code of 'monastic' discipline peculiar to the followers of the Buddha. The term *vinaya* – later appropriated as the collective designation of the monastic regula – which appears frequently in the well-known compound *Dharma-Vinaya*, bore at this time the more general import of the way of life conducive to the realization of the Master's teaching. The Buddha and his homeless disciples observed the unwritten traditional code of the *parivrājakas* and acted according to what public opinion considered proper in those who had 'gone forth'. They, too, spent the greater part of the year roaming from place to place, lived on alms, and abstained from sexual intercourse, from theft, from the taking of life, and from making false claims to supernormal attainments (the four *pārājikas* or 'defeats' of the later monastic code).[256] Except during the three months of the rains, when they took shelter in a hut or cave, they too were without fixed abode. Like the members of other sects, they held a fortnightly congregational service, known as the *poṣadha* (Vedic *upavastha*, Pāli *uposatha*), on the full-moon and new-moon days, at which they recited a *prātimokṣa* (Pāli *pāṭimokkha*) or verse summary of the special Dharma to which they adhered. One such *prātimokṣa* has been preserved in the *Dhammapada*, as well as in the *Mahāpadāna Suttanta* of the *Dīgha Nikāya*;[257] the latter attests its extreme antiquity by attributing it not to Gotama Buddha, but to Vipassin, one of his remote 'legendary' predecessors. According to the *Dhammapada*, which reverses the order of the first and second stanzas, it runs:

> Abstention from all evil,
> Cultivation of the wholesome,
> Purification of the heart:
> This is the Message of the Buddhas.
>
> Forbearance is the highest ascetic practice;
> 'Nirvāṇa is supreme,' say the Buddhas.
> He is not a 'gone forth' one who harms another;
> He is not a recluse (*samaṇa*) who molests another.
>
> Not to speak ill, not to injure,
> To observe the *pāṭimokkha*,
> To be moderate in eating,
> To live alone in a secluded abode,
> To devote oneself to meditation:
> This is the Message of the Buddhas.

In the Buddha's day it was the Dharma as embodied in such stanzas as these, and *not* a code of rules, that constituted the bond of union (probably the original meaning of *prātimokṣa*) between his followers. Similarly, the rite of *upasampadā* meant at that time not initiation into a monastic order fully equipped with rules and regulations but simply the formal recognition of the Buddha as teacher and the 'acceptance' (the literal meaning of the word) of his teaching. At first, this was considered as taking place when the Buddha uttered the words 'Come, *bhikṣu*'.[258] Later on, applications for admission having greatly increased, he permitted the senior disciples to receive candidates on his behalf by causing them to repeat the formula of taking refuge in the Buddha, the Dharma, and the Sangha. The body of adherents which thus grew up around him and often accompanied him as he walked from place to place was known as the *bhikṣu* sangha of the four quarters. An invaluable glimpse of the sangha at this stage of its existence, termed by G. F. Allen 'The Pristine, Ascetic Stage',[259] is provided by the oldest portions of the *Sutta-Nipāta*, especially the *Aṭṭhaka-* and *Pārāyana-vaggas*, and by the *Bhikkhu-vagga* of the *Dhammapada*.

(2) After the *parinirvāṇa* of the Buddha his disciples found themselves confronted by a number of problems, not the least of them being that of the preservation of the *Dharma-Vinaya*. For some, perhaps most, the proper fulfilment of this great responsibility involved not only creating from their individual recollections of what the Buddha had said and done a common stock of oral tradition but also adopting a code of discipline the observance of which might further differentiate them from the rest of the *parivrājaka* community. The drawing up of the rudiments of such a code was perhaps the principal item on the agenda of the First Council, which the Pāli canonical texts describe as a *Vinaya-saṅgīti*.[260] Ancient *parivrājaka* conventions which had received the stamp of the Buddha's approval, directives which he had himself issued from time to time, either on his own initiative or in response to public opinion, together with – in all likelihood – a few regulations thought necessary by the Council itself, were collected and classified. The resultant body of rules, which was made binding on every individual *bhikṣu*, eventually became fixed at 550 items.[261] Since it was recited at the fortnightly congregational meetings, displacing the original Dharma-stanzas, it gradually took over the designation *prātimokṣa*. In other words, during the second stage of its existence the Sangha besides continuing to possess a spiritual bond of union in the Dharma in addition acquired an external bond of union in the form of the monastic code.

This development had far-reaching consequences. From being socially indistinguishable from the other *parivrājaka* groups the Sangha became an independent ecclesiastical corporation recognizable as such to the general public. *Upasampadā* was no longer a simple acceptance of the Buddha and his teaching; it became the ceremony of ordination into a monastic order. From a common declaration of faith the *poṣadha* was transformed into a service of confession of individual failures to observe the Code. The difference between monk and layman was accentuated, being no longer merely that between those who had left and those who had not left home but between the ordained, who observed the Code, and the unordained, who did not. Yet though much was altered, much remained the same. The *bhikṣus* were still largely eremitical, still lived on alms, and still remained in one spot during the rains.

(3) The third stage of development arose out of a change more radical than any that had previously taken place. During the Buddha's lifetime, even, parks and gardens had been donated to the Sangha with provision for accommodation during the rains.[262] These were certainly not monasteries in the modern sense, and whether in art or in literature, or merely in one's own imagination, it is a grave anachronism to depict Anāthapiṇḍada or Bimbisāra as putting up large and complex structures of brick and stone. Scattered up and down the donated area, known as the *āvāsa*, were a number of lodgings or *vihāras* in the form of wattle-and-daub huts such as can be seen all over India even today. A *bhikṣu* had the right of occupying one of these lodgings during the rains. When the rains were over he continued his wanderings. Later on it became possible to reserve the lodging one had just vacated and thus to spend a number of rainy seasons consecutively in one *vihāra*, as the Buddha himself had done at Śrāvastī.

In the stage of development that had now been reached the Sangha took the revolutionary step of abandoning the *parivrājaka* tradition of a wandering life in favour of permanent residence at an *āvāsa*. The reasons for this transition from the eremitic to the cenobitic type of religious life are obscure; they are probably bound up with the growth of the monastic code and with the need for collating the floating mass of oral tradition existing in the memories of hundreds of reciters. Be the reasons for it what they may, the change modified the constitution of the Sangha to an unprecedented degree. The Sangha of the Four Quarters was replaced, for all practical purposes, by the local Sangha resident at a particular *āvāsa*. As the *prātimokṣa*, or monastic code, was unable to cover all the exigencies of the more complex type of communal life that now rapidly developed it was in practice supplemented and to some extent superseded by the *Skandhakas* (Pāli *Khandhakas*) or *Chapters*, a series of elaborate treatises on such subjects as medicine, robes, ordination, and schism. This led to another change in the *poṣadha*; from a confessional it became a liturgical service at which the *prātimokṣa* was solemnly recited not, as before, in order that erring monks might confess and atone for their transgressions, but simply as a formal expression of the unity and solidarity of the local, cenobitical, sangha. Similarly *upasampadā* now meant ordination not so much into the Sangha of the Four Quarters governed by the *prātimokṣa* as into the resident sangha of a particular *āvāsa* living in accordance with what, by yet another appropriation of an ancient term, came to be known as the *Vinaya*. Moreover, as it settled down in the *āvāsas*, the sangha naturally became more accessible to the laity. Donations therefore poured in and endowments multiplied. Eventually, though some remained faithful to the old tradition, it was no longer necessary for the monks to go out and beg their food from door to door.

Exactly how long it took for the characteristic features of each of these stages to emerge is not clear. The sangha of the third stage, which was responsible for compiling the extant biographical-cum-disciplinary traditions into a Vinaya Piṭaka (or Piṭakas: there were several versions), being anxious to father its distinctive innovations upon the Master himself, telescoped them into a period coeval with that of his pastoral activity and manufactured, as part of his biography, incidents and episodes out of which they were supposed to have arisen. These legends (in the sense of fictions), which were incorporated into the Vinaya Piṭaka, cannot stand up to critical examination. The entire process of development from primitive eremitical to sophisticated cenobitical 'monasticism' must in fact have taken at least a century, so that we may safely conclude that probably by the time of the Second Council, the Council of Vaiśālī, and certainly that of Aśoka's accession to the throne of Magadha, it was complete.[263] Whether earlier by a few decades or later, though, the fact that such a process had taken place does not mean, nor in the history of Buddhism ever meant, that a later stage of development supplanted, in the sense of ousting and wholly superseding, an earlier one. As with the Doctrine, so with the Discipline (in the widest sense of the term Vinaya), development almost invariably took place by way of a process of gradual accretion and elaboration rather than by one of summary rejection and reform. The second stage of the process overlaid, without being able entirely to conceal, the first, and was in its turn overlaid but not concealed by the third. Thus from the beginning of the third period the individual *bhikṣu*, or member of the sangha, grew up under the influence of, and was confronted by, three different, not to say contradictory, ideals of 'monastic' life. He was simultaneously exhorted to

> wander alone, even as the horn of the rhinoceros is single',[264]

the refrain of an early ballad, without caring for rules and regulations;[265] to observe scrupulously the 150 clauses of the individualistic monastic code; and to participate in, even identify himself with, the complex corporate life of a permanently resident monastic community.

These discrepancies did not escape the notice of the Indo-Bactrian king Milinda, or Menander, who, with a critical acumen quite modern, quoted verses pertaining respectively to the earlier eremitical and the later cenobitical stage and propounded the obvious contrast of ideals to Nāgasena as his forty-first dilemma.[266] In the life of the sangha their conflicting demands naturally generated a certain amount of tension. However, as it was believed that the Buddha himself had, at different periods, sanctioned both ideals, the latter admittedly by way of concession to the weaker brethren, the tension between them never became a disruptive influence. The doctrine of concessions finds classic expression in that part of the *upasampadā* ceremony where, having been exhorted to subsist on alms, wear robes made from cast-off rags, live at the foot of a tree, and use cow's urine for medicine (the four *niśraya* (Pāli *nissayas*) or 'supports'), the newly ordained *bhikṣu* was informed that accepting invitations from the laity, wearing robes offered by them, dwelling in *vihāras*, and having recourse to ordinary medical treatment, were also permissible.[267] This in effect meant that he was free to follow the eremitical or the cenobitical ideal, or a compromise between the two, according to his individual temperament and convictions. Nevertheless, owing not only to human weakness but to the necessity of preserving and transmitting enormous bodies of traditionary lore, as well as to the fact that much of this was compiled and edited under cenobitical auspices, it was the cenobitical type of monasticism that triumphed. In its fully developed form it eventually reached its apogee in such great institutions as the Mahāvihāra, Nālandā, and Drepung, and even today constitutes, in most parts of the Buddhist world, the normal working basis, though not necessarily the sole theoretic ideal, of the monastic order.

Before describing the life of a *bhikṣu* under the dominant cenobitical system we shall have to guard against a possible grave misunderstanding. We have already seen that the whole course of development of the sangha, with its three clearly marked stages, was probably complete by the time of the Second Council, the Council of Vaiśālī. Now it was in connection with this Council, held 100 or 110 years after the *parinirvāṇa*, that there occurred the first great schism in the sangha, that between the conservative minority known as the Sthaviravādins, and the progressive majority, known as the Mahāsāṃghikas. This means that the development of cenobitical monasticism preceded the rise of the Mahāyāna, which as a distinct historical movement originated among the Mahāsāṃghikas. The point is important and significant because, in recent times, certain uninformed followers of the Theravāda (an offshoot of the original Sthaviravāda) have accused the Mahāyānists of having no Vinaya, no *upasampadā* lineage, and therefore no *bhikṣus* or *bhikṣuṇīs* and no real monastic order. In the case of the Chinese, Tibetan, Korean, and Vietnamese adherents of the Mahāyāna the accusation is completely unfounded. Far from rejecting any of them, the Mahāyāna took up and incorporated in its own movement the whole stock of primitive traditions, including the monastic code and *upasampadā* lineage as transmitted by the Mahāsāṃghika, the Sarvāstivāda, and other early schools. For historical reasons there have survived in the Buddhist world only two of the ancient traditions of cenobitical monasticism, the Theravāda and the Sarvāstivāda. The former is transmitted with Pāli for its literary medium in the Theravādin countries of South-east Asia; the latter, the medium of which was originally Sanskrit, in China, Japan, Tibet, Korea, and Vietnam and other parts of the 'Mahāyāna' world in the languages of those countries. Despite minor discrepancies between these two great traditions in regard to both material included and the manner of its arrangement, there can be no doubt that their respective versions of the monastic code and the *Chapters*, at least, represent different recensions of one and the same basic material.[268] Both the Theravādin monks of Sri Lanka, and the 'Mahāyāna' (strictly Sarvāstivādin) monks of Tibet, for example, are the true lineal descendants of the original cenobitical monastic order which came into existence during the third stage of development of the early sangha.

As it has the same spiritual orientation, and is based upon what are, substantially, the same Vinaya traditions, the pattern of monasticism naturally varies little from one part of the Buddhist world to another. This fact makes possible an account of the monastic life which, ignoring variations due to differences of national culture, directs attention to its main features.

The *bhikṣu*'s life begins with ordination. This is of two kinds, known respectively as *pravrajyā* and *upasampadā*. The former, which may be taken as soon as one is old enough to earn a living by scaring crows, that is to say, at any time after the age of seven or eight, consists in shaving hair and beard, donning the saffron robes, and taking from an *upādhyāya* (Pāli *upajjhāya*) or preceptor the Three Refuges (*tri-śarana*): in the Buddha, the Dharma, and the Sangha, and the ten precepts (*daśa-śikṣāpada*): to abstain from injury to living beings, from taking what has not been given, from unchastity, from wrong speech, from intoxicating drinks and drugs (the five precepts of the *upāsaka*, except that unchastity here replaces sexual misconduct), from untimely meals, from dance, song, music, and unseemly shows, from the use of garlands, perfumes, unguents, and things that tend to beautify and adorn the person, from lofty and luxurious seats, and from handling gold and silver. The latter may be conferred on any virile male human being who has attained the age of twenty (reckoning from conception, not birth), whose begging-bowl and three monastic robes are complete, who has obtained the permission of his parents, if living, and who moreover is free from serious disease, from civil obligations, and from various other disqualifications. Unlike its orthodox Hindu counterparts, known as *saṃnyāsa*, which traditionally is open only to those who are brahmins by birth, the *upasampadā* is given without any restriction of caste, nationality, race, or social position – an attitude of typical Buddhist universality to which the practice of the Siyama *nikāya* of Sri Lanka constitutes a unique and most regrettable exception.[269]

The actual ordination is effected by means of what is known as a *saṅgha-karma* (Pāli *-kamma*) or corporate official act of the sangha consisting, in this case, in the unanimous passing of a formal resolution (*jñapti*, Pāli *ñatti*) by the entire sangha resident at a particular *āvāsa*, and assembled for the purpose, the number of such *bhikṣus* being not less than five (ten in the 'Middle Country'), all of whom must be exempt from certain technical disabilities. Having been interrogated regarding his freedom from the disqualifications by one of the *bhikṣus*, known in the Sanskrit tradition as the *raho'nuśāsaka-bhikṣu* or privy admonisher (*not* 'monk who imparts the esoteric teaching'),[270] the candidate for ordination is brought within the circle of the sangha where, after saluting the *bhikṣus* one by one in order of seniority, he petitions the sangha for ordination with a certain elder, whom he names, and who, generally, is the seniormost *bhikṣu* present, as his preceptor (*upādhyāya*). Then, in the presence of the sangha, he is formally interrogated regarding the disabilities by the *karmakāraka-bhikṣu* or 'master of ceremonies'. Finally the subject matter of the proceedings, namely that the candidate, being a virile male and so on, desires ordination from the sangha with the elder named as his preceptor, is embodied in a formal resolution (*jñapti*), which, after being proposed to the assembly by the master of ceremonies, is repeated three times in the form of a declaration (*karmavācanā*, Pāli *kammavācā*). If the *bhikṣus* remain silent the resolution is taken as passed, and the master of ceremonies announces that the *upasampadā* has been granted.

After the date and exact time of the candidate's formal admission to the sangha have been ascertained, various monastic obligations are taught and explained. In particular he is informed of the four *niśrayas* (Pāli *nissayas*) or 'supports' and the various concessions allowed with regard to them (see p. 191) and of the four *patanīya-dharmas* or things bringing about downfall. The latter are identical with the four *pārājikas* or 'defeats' (see p. 187). The remaining sets of obligations need not be taught immediately after the formal ceremony. They comprise the four *śramaṇakāraka-dharmas*, or duties of an ascetic, the 150 prohibitions of the monastic code, and various duties which the newly ordained monk has to perform towards his *upādhyāya*. The first set embodies the principle of non-retaliation. Even when others revile, or become angry with, or beat, or upbraid him, the *śramaṇa* must refrain from acting in like manner. The 150 *śīlas* of the *prātimokṣa* or monastic code are divided according to the nature of the penalties incurred by their descending order, from the graver to the lighter offences. These all concern the conduct of the individual *bhikṣu*. A seventh category, which is binding upon the sangha collectively, consists of rules for the settlement of internal disputes at an *āvāsa*.

According to the nature of the penalties involved the seven categories of offences are known as (1) *pārājika* or 'defeat', permanent expulsion from the sangha without the possibility of readmission in the present lifetime; (2) *saṅghāvaśeṣa* (Pāli *saṅghādisesa*) or temporary suspension from full membership of the sangha; (3) *aniyata* or undetermined, an offence of one or another type having been committed or not committed according to circumstances; (4) *naiḥsargika-pātayantika* (Pāli *nissaggiya-pācittiya*) or forfeiture and expiation, when the possession of a prohibited article is acknowledged as a fault and the article surrendered; (5) *pātayantika* or *prāyaścittika* (Pāli *pācittiya*) or expiation by simple acknowledgement; (6) *pratideśanīya* (Pāli *pāṭi-desanīya*) or confession; and (7) *adhikaranaśamatha* (Pāli *adhikaraṇasamatha*) or rules of procedure for the settlement of disputes within the sangha. As might be anticipated, the four 'defeats' are identical in all Vinaya traditions. The seven categories are also common to the Theravāda and the various branches of the Sarvāstivāda. Excluding the *aniyata* and *adhikaranaśamatha*, many differences do however exist with regard to the number of offences included in a category, the nature and wording of the offences, and the order of their arrangement.[271] The Sarvāstivāda, for instance, gives the number of the *pātayantika* rules as 90 whereas according to the Theravāda there are 92. Nevertheless such differences, though not to be overlooked, are so much less numerous and striking than the resemblances that the predominant impression remains one of uniformity. Nalinaksha Dutt, the editor of the Gilgit Manuscripts, indeed states categorically that

> substantially the Pāli and Sanskrit versions agree not only in the main contents but also in details and sometimes one version appears to be based on the other.[272]

It is curious, though, that while the Sarvāstivādins and their branch the Mūlasarvāstivādins both managed to preserve 150 *prātimokṣa* rules the Theravāda, while retaining the traditional number for the total, has actually transmitted 152 – a fact for which there appears to be no explanation. All Vinaya traditions also transmit, in addition to the monastic code proper, a list of *śaikṣa* (Pāli *sekhiya*) rules which differ from the *prātimokṣa* in being binding on both *bhikṣu* and *śrāmaṇera*. As they are concerned with matters of etiquette, decorum, and good manners rather than with ethics or discipline, no penalties attach to their infringement. The Sarvāstivādins transmit 113 such rules, the

Mūlasarvāstivādins 108, and the Theravādins 75. Adding the 150 prohibitions of the *prātimokṣa* (152 for the Theravāda) to their respective lists of *saikṣa* rules we arrive at the grand total of rules transmitted by each of these schools in their individual versions of the full monastic code for *bhikṣus* – namely 263, 258, and 227 respectively. *Bhikṣuṇīs* observe a much larger number of rules, 371 in the Mūlasarvāstivāda and 311 in the Theravāda.[273] Except that there are no *aniyata* or undetermined rules these are distributed into the same categories as those governing the *bhikṣu*. The Theravādin *bhikkhunī*-lineage, though extinct in the Theravādin countries,[274] is said to have survived in China.

The relation between the *upādhyāya* and his *saddhivihārika* or 'co-resident', as the newly ordained monk is called, is essentially that of father and son transposed to the spiritual plane. Besides learning from him, the *saddhivihārika* is expected to render the *upādhyāya* all manner of personal service, and upon each is incumbent for life the duty of nursing the other when sick. Without the permission of the *upādhyāya* the *saddhivihārika* may do nothing. This condition of spiritual tutelage is known as *niśraya* (Pāli *nissaya*), literally 'dependence' (on a teacher) and it lasts for a minimum of five, usually for ten, years, during which period the *saddhivihārika* resides permanently with the preceptor: a dull or undisciplined *bhikṣu* may be kept under such tutelage all his life. Probably because the seniormost elder of an *āvāsa* is often obliged to ordain more disciples than one person can train, an *ācārya* (Pāli *ācariya*) or instructor also is appointed. The relation between the *ācārya* and his *antevasika*, as the young monk is termed in relation to him, is identical with that between *upādhyāya* and *saddhivihārika*. Nevertheless the *upadhyaya* enjoys a certain precedence, for whenever all three happen to be together *niśraya* towards the *ācārya* automatically ceases. It is, though, the *ācārya* who, under the *upādhyāya*, is responsible for the day-to-day teaching and training of the newly ordained monk. Only those monks who are richly endowed with various ethical and spiritual qualities, and who have completed ten years in the sangha, are considered fit to ordain and teach others. They should be deeply learned, with a natural understanding of educational psychology, and capable not only of instructing the disciple but skilled in resolving his doubts and dispelling the moods of depression to which he may be subject during the training. They must be able to nurse him should he fall ill. The relation between master and disciple is the axle upon which turns the entire monastic system. Some *bhikṣus*, out of devotion and a desire to learn, remain with their tutor for some years after the cessation of formal *niśraya* or even attend permanently upon him until his death.

In the early days of Buddhism, when the *Dharma-Vinaya* was transmitted orally, much time was spent in learning the words of the sacred tradition by heart and reciting them in unison. As it was of vast extent, and constantly expanding, the tradition soon transcended the powers of all save a few prodigies of mnemonic capacity. Specialization therefore became the rule; individual monk-reciters learned, and in turn passed on to their own disciples, not the whole *Dharma-Vinaya* as handed down at a particular *āvāsa* or group of *āvāsas* but only a section of it. *Sūtrāntikas* transmitted the *sūtras*, *vinayadharas* the Vinaya, and so on. They also explained and commented upon what was transmitted, thus building up a secondary tradition of exegesis which could easily become confused with the primary one. This is particularly the case with the Abhidharma, which was elaborated out of the *mātṛkās* or 'matrices' transmitted by the *mātṛkadharas* and finally came to be regarded, in some circles at least, as canonical. When the sacred tradition was committed to writing, probably in the fourth century after the *parinirvāṇa*, all this was changed. Though learning by heart continued to be a highly respectable occupation for a monk, and enjoyed great prestige long after its utility had been exhausted, the emphasis eventually shifted from reciting to reading: the oral became a literary tradition. At the same time the curriculum of monastic studies broadened. Time was devoted not only to the scriptures, commentaries, and independent expository texts, but ancillary subjects such as grammar, rhetoric, and prosody. Quasi-religious subjects, ranging from ecclesiastical history to logic and dialectics, and from medicine to various branches of the fine and applied arts, were also introduced. Secular literature was cultivated and non-Buddhist religious and philosophical texts critically studied. Like their later European counterparts, the monasteries came to be not only centres of spiritual life and religious activity but repositories of all the learning and culture of the age. This naturally encouraged further specialization. Each *ācārya*, on the basis of a sound knowledge of the Scriptures, took up a single subject or group of subjects. Once this stage had been reached there was nothing left for the cenobitical monastic system to do but to evolve, out of the very perfection of its development, its own antithesis. The best *ācāryas* were not always available all under the same roof. In some parts of the Buddhist world, therefore, part of the novitiate became a kind of *Wanderjahr*, with the young monk begging his way from one monastic centre to another and sitting for a season at the feet now of one, now of another, great specialist in Buddhistic lore until his monastic education was complete. Xuanzang's 'pilgrimage' to India partly conforms to this pattern, which in China itself seems to have been a popular one.[275]

Every member of the sangha possessed as such certain inherent rights. These the young monk learned to exercise not only by studying the Vinaya but by participating in the communal religious life of the *āvāsa* to which he belonged. For instance his personal property was limited to certain articles, known as the *aṣṭapariṣkāra* (Pāli *aṭṭhaparikkhāra*) or 'eight requisites': the three robes, the begging-bowl, a razor, a needle, the girdle, and a water-strainer. All other property, whether lands, buildings, or furniture, was vested in the sangha; that is to say it belonged, even when nominally dedicated to the *bhikṣu* sangha 'of the four quarters', to the monks resident at an *āvāsa* in their collective capacity. This property the individual *bhikṣu* was entitled to utilize. The most important right he possessed, however, was that of participating in all corporate official acts of the sangha. Without his presence, or his formal consent to the proceedings if unable to attend, no such act was valid. As Sukumar Dutt insists,

> The right of direct participation in the Sanghakamma inheres in each duly qualified member of an āvāsa and is very jealously guarded.[276]

This right conferred upon the sangha a strictly republican character. Though the minimum number of *bhikṣus* required for a particular type of corporate official act varied from four to twenty, an act would not be valid if carried out by them alone without the participation of all the other *bhikṣus* who, at the time, happened to be resident at the *āvāsa*. In other words, every assembly of the sangha had to be complete in respect of the *āvāsa* concerned.

Among the more important corporate acts of the sangha, apart from the *upasampadā*, were the *poṣadha*, the *varṣāvāsa*, the *pravāraṇā*, and the *kaṭhina*, all of which occurred, or recurred, at fixed points in the ecclesiastical year. In its original form, the *poṣadha* was a full-moon and new-moon day observance common to all the *parivrājaka* communities, its introduction into Buddhism being due to the suggestion of certain lay devotees. As an institution of cenobitic monasticism, it consisted in the solemn ceremonial recitation of the monastic code. Sometimes the entire code was recited, sometimes only the more serious offences. In either case, at this stage in the development of the sangha, infringements were no longer confessed in the course of the actual recital; instead, the participating *bhikṣus* made mutual confession in pairs beforehand. This preliminary ceremony, known as *pariśuddhi*, purification, ultimately became as much a formality as the ceremony it preceded. The three remaining *saṅgha-karmas* occurred only once a year. In the rhythm of the old eremitic monastic life the *varṣāvāsa* (Pāli *vassāvāsa*) or 'rains residence' naturally occupied a place of the highest importance. But as the sangha gradually settled down into permanent residence at the *āvāsas* that had served, in the earliest days of its existence, merely as temporary shelters from the torrential monsoon rains, the institution lost much of its original significance. For the majority of *bhikṣus* the only difference between this period and the remaining eight or nine months of the year was that during the one they might not and did not travel, while during the other they might but did not. Nevertheless, formal observance of the institution continued, and a monk's seniority was still reckoned according to the number of rains residences he had observed since ordination. Countries where there were no seasonal rains could not observe the rains residence even as a formality. In some parts of the Buddhist world, such as China, it therefore became a summer residence. Eventually the 'residence' developed into a kind of spiritual retreat, for the duration of which the monks observed the Vinaya more strictly than usual and devoted themselves to intensive study, teaching, and meditation. In this form the institution lives on in almost all Buddhist lands and possesses enormous value.

The *pravāraṇā* (Pāli *pavāraṇā*), which marked the conclusion of the *varṣāvāsa*, was generally held on the fourteenth or fifteenth day of Kartika (October-November), that is to say, on the full-moon day of that month or the day after. On this occasion the *bhikṣus*, having observed the rains residence together, assembled to give 'satisfaction' (the literal meaning of the term) to one another by inviting inquiry as to their conduct during this period, confessing their transgressions, and mutually asking forgiveness for any fault committed. The *kaṭhina* or 'difficult' ceremony was that of the distribution, among the monks who had completed the *varṣāvāsa*, of the robes or robe material offered on the occasion by the laity. It received its designation from the hardship originally suffered by the eremitic monks who, at the official conclusion of the residence – which did not always coincide with the end of the actual monsoon – had to resume their travels without sufficient protection from the weather. In addition to these the sangha performed, as circumstances required, a variety of other acts. It might have to try a case of alleged breach of the monastic code and, if the accused was found guilty, impose on him the prescribed penalty; or appoint the various officers necessary for the running of a large cenobitic establishment; dedicate a building or part of a building for any special purpose; settle the boundary of an *āvāsa*; or determine the succession to the personal belongings of a deceased *bhikṣu*. In all these proceedings every monk of good standing had the right and the duty of full participation.

The practice of meditation also was not forgotten. In the earliest days of the sangha, during the lifetime of the Buddha and immediately after, the best part of a monk's time was spent in this manner. Such portions of the Scriptures as reflect the life of this period describe how, having returned from the almsround and rested a while after eating, the monk passed the remainder of the day under a tree absorbed in *dhyāna*, sometimes practising until far into the night. According to the Tibetan version of the *Vinayavastu* of the Mūlasarvāstivādins the Buddha introduced the practice of meditation and the observance of the *poṣadha* simultaneously, which suggests a special connection between them.[277] The prologue to the Pāli *Sāmaññaphala Sutta* relates that when, one beautiful full-moon night in autumn, Jīvaka the physician escorted Ajātasattu on a visit to the Blessed One, they found him and 1,200 disciples sitting together in absolute silence.[278] On another *uposatha* day, when the monks had been meditating half the night, the Buddha held up the proceedings for several hours until an impure monk, who had failed to leave of his own accord, had been ejected by Moggallāna. Only when the assembly was pure did he allow the *pāṭimokkha* to be recited.[279] If it represents the general practice of the sangha at that time, this incident shows the *poṣadha* observance originally consisted of two parts, group meditation and the recitation of the Dharma-stanzas. As the cenobitic system developed, however, the practice of meditation declined. The necessity of transmitting the *Dharma-Vinaya* took precedence, for the time being, over all other duties. The *Chapters*, in its several versions, draws a picture of monastic life devoted almost exclusively to study, recitation, and doctrinal discussion. The first part of the *poṣadha* observance, namely the group meditation, was abolished, possibly at the same time that the second part became a recitation of the monastic code. Xuanzang, describing the glories of seventh-century Nālandā, has much to say about lectures, studies, and general academic routine; but he is strangely silent regarding meditation.[280] We are not to infer, of course, that so vitally important a subject was ever totally neglected. Every monk certainly learned the theory of meditation and acquired the rudiments of the practice of one or another of the various methods in vogue. All the same, there prevailed from an early period the feeling that study and meditation were incompatible, and that one could be wholeheartedly prosecuted only at the expense of the other. Buddhaghosa, in the *Visuddhimagga*, says of books that 'for one who is constantly busy with recitations, etc.' they are an impediment to *samādhi*.[281] Having students to instruct is another impediment. The same author's enumeration of the eighteen faults of a monastery indeed suggests that the busy life of any large cenobitic establishment is in itself unfavourable to meditation.[282] A division of labour, as it were, therefore became the rule; one group of *bhikṣus* devoted itself to study, the other to meditation. In India the first group seems to have predominated, though the evidence on which an impression is based, being itself literary, is not really conclusive. In any case, a movement known as the Yogācāra, devoted – as its name suggests – to the practice of meditation, eventually sprang up and gained many adherents. China and Japan, and to a lesser extent Tibet, where the meditative tradition flourished in the form of independent schools, saw the rise of a new type of cenobitical monasticism, organized in accordance with the special requirements not of the life of study but the life of meditation. And all over the Buddhist world, in every age, a few meditating monks remained aloof from every form of organized monasticism, preferring to dwell alone, like their predecessors of old, in dense forests and remote mountain caves.

18
THE PLACE OF THE LAITY

With the exception of the eventful weeks succeeding the Enlightenment (see p. 23), when Buddhahood made its first tremendous impact on mankind, only a small percentage of the faithful ever belonged to the spiritual élite, whether of *āryas* or bodhisattvas, or even to the monastic order. Everywhere and at all times the great majority were common people for whom the Dharma was an important but not the predominant interest of their lives. In the broadest sense of the term the sangha therefore coincided with the entire Buddhist community, consisting of what became known as the *caturvarga* or 'four companies', namely *bhikṣus, bhikṣuṇīs, upāsakas,* and *upāsikās*. As such it was called the *Mahāsaṅgha* or 'great assembly'.

During the lifetime of the Master relations between the eremitical monks who had 'gone forth' and the householders at whose doors they daily stood for alms, and in whose outhouses and gardens they lodged during the rains, were close and cordial, and a spirit of camaraderie prevailed. The latter could, if necessary, bring to the notice of the Master public complaints against the *parivrājakas*, and suggest changes in their mode of living. Such equalitarianism was natural. Their common devotion to the Buddha, and the extent to which his attainments transcended theirs, tended to reduce all distinctions among his followers, including that between monks and laymen, to a position of comparative insignificance. His impatience with the formalistic element in religion, and his uncompromising insistence on the necessity of personal realization of Nirvāṇa, moreover ensured that they should be distinguished, if at all, according to their intrinsic merits rather than their socio-ecclesiastical status.

> Even though a man be richly attired, if he develops tranquillity, is quiet, subdued and restrained, leading a holy life and abstaining from injury to all living beings – he is a *brāhmaṇa*, he is a *samaṇa*, he is a *bhikkhu*.[283]

That the homeless wandering monk, totally free from all worldly concerns, had a far better chance of reaching the Goal, was admitted, even emphasized; but that a householder, if sufficiently resolved, might sometimes reach it too, and that in the last resort it was transcendental attainment that mattered, not the wearing of yellow robes, more than one such saying of the Buddha testifies. In a passage tucked away in the *Aṅguttara Nikāya* he indeed speaks of the righteous of all four *vargas* as illuminating the sangha:

> Brethren, these four persons, who are full of wisdom and insight, are well-disciplined, learned [in the Dharma] and have reached complete righteousness, shed lustre upon the Sangha. Which are the four? Brethren, the bhikkhu, the bhikkhuṇī, the upāsaka, the upāsikā, who are full of wisdom and insight, well-disciplined, and learned, and have reached complete righteousness, shed lustre upon the Sangha. Brethren, these four beings do indeed shed lustre upon the Sangha.[284]

Here the *vargas* are clearly placed on a footing of complete spiritual equality.

With the growth of the cenobium, and the consequent tendency of religious life towards claustration in the *āvāsas*, a change took place. Dharma developed into Abhidharma, and Vinaya, originally signifying the practical side of a universal spiritual ideal, into Abhivinaya, in the sense of a body of rules and regulations for ordained monks only. Spiritual life was identified with monastic life. Though the Pali scriptures, even after having passed through the hands of generations of monk redactors, preserve the names of twenty-one lay disciples who had attained Release, it was now generally agreed that a layman was incapable of the higher transcendental attainments. Arhantship, in the narrower, more individualistic Hīnayāna sense which the term now assumed, was regarded not as the common goal of the entire Buddhist community, irrespective of socio-ecclesiastical status, but as the prerogative of monks and nuns. The laity could aspire only to the inferior goal of rebirth, after death, in a happy heavenly abode. To the two different goals there appertained two different paths. The monk traversed the stages of *śīla, samādhi*, and *prajñā*, culminating in *vimukti*; the layman or laywoman cultivated *dāna, śīla*, and (*śamatha-*) *bhāvanā*. In practice, the latter were expected simply to give alms to the monks and to observe the five or, on *poṣadha* days at least, the eight precepts; *bhāvanā*, in the sense of 'cultivation' (the literal meaning of the term) of the mundane *dhyānas*, though it could not be forbidden, was hardly encouraged. As the Buddha apparently had taught them, the two paths overlapped, the first and second stages of the one coincided with the second and third stages of the other, thus in effect forming between them a single path of five stages from *dāna* to *vimukti* which could be traversed, according to their capacity, by any member of the Buddhist community. During the period of which we are speaking, however, the first path was interpreted so exclusively in terms of the current type of monastic spiritual culture, and the second so exclusively in terms of ordinary lay ethics, that inevitably they assumed the appearance of independent 'careers'. The laity not being personally concerned with the higher spiritual life, it was held unnecessary for them to know much about the Buddha's teaching. Restrictions were therefore imposed. It became an offence for a monk to make one who was not ordained recite the *suttas* line by line.[285] Śāriputra was represented as consoling Anāthapiṇḍada on his deathbed with a religious talk and telling him, when he had shed tears of emotion, that such teachings were not communicated to the white-robed householders, but only to those who had gone forth.[286]

This virtual exclusion of the laity from spiritual life, resulting in the identification of the sangha with the monastic order, did not pass unchallenged. The Buddha had, incontestably, exhorted his first sixty disciples to wander about 'for the good of the many, for the happiness of the many (*bahujana hitāya, bahujana sukhāya*)'[287] (see pp. 23 and 58). Śāriputra's alleged remark was, as a generalization, even untrue, being contradicted by the Buddha's own practice as recorded in, for example, the *Aṭṭhaka-vagga* and the *Pārāyana-vagga* – the oldest portions of the *Sutta-Nipāta* – wherein various brahmins ask him, and he answers, questions on the profoundest of themes.[288] In any case, far from being wholly dependent on the monks for their knowledge of the Dharma, the laity possessed certain unsystematized traditions of their own regarding the Buddha's life and teachings, handed down not from master to disciple but from father to son. They were therefore unwilling to accept the position of second-class Buddhists, or to participate in the spiritual life of the community merely to the extent of acquiring *puṇya* (Pāli *puññā*) or merit by patronizing and supporting the monks. Even though it might be for them a remoter possibility, to be consummated only after innumerable lives, they persisted in regarding Supreme Enlightenment as their proper goal, not rebirth as a *deva* or even the attainment of arhantship in the current monastic sense. In this aspiration they enjoyed the sympathy of a section of the monks themselves, many of whom felt that an exclusively monastic interpretation of Buddhism, in terms of Abhidharma and Abhivinaya, besides failing to do full justice to the depth and universality of the Master's teachings, suffered from the further defect of ignoring the splendid lessons of his personal example.

Between 100 and 200 years after the *parinirvāṇa* these tensions in the Buddhist community resulted in a schism. Despite its crucial importance, the traditions regarding this event are late, unreliable, and far from unanimous, there being no concurrence of testimony as to the initiators of the break, its immediate cause, its venue, and the age in which it took place. Fortunately the identity of the parties involved, and the general nature of the grounds of difference between them, as disclosed partly by their subsequent development as independent schools, is perfectly clear, and this is all that concerns us now. The Sthaviravāda, or 'School of the Elders' (i.e. of the senior monks), who are represented as *arhants*, was the extreme monastic party, according to whom Buddhism was primarily, if not exclusively, a religion for monks, and who not only insisted that they alone had the right of determining what was Buddhism and what was not but sought to impose their own one-sided version of the Master's teaching on the entire Buddhist community. On the other side stood the Mahāsāṃghikas, 'Those of the Great Order' or 'The Great Assemblists'. They were the liberal party. Unlike their opponents, they did not represent only the more conservative elderly cenobites but, as their name suggests, all the four *vargas*. They maintained that the Dharma having been preached for the benefit of everyman and everywoman, irrespective of socio-ecclesiastical status, the right of determining the true nature of the religion inhered in the whole Buddhist community, not in any one section of it exclusively, and that in compiling a standard version of the Master's teaching all surviving traditions should be taken into account, including those current among the laity. They also felt that there should be a common spiritual ideal, not a higher one for monks and nuns and a lower one for lay people. As the Mahāsāṃghikas were, by all accounts, the larger party, they probably represented contemporary Buddhist thought more faithfully than the Sthaviravādins, who consisted, not even of all monks, but only of some of the senior members belonging to a particular group of *āvāsas*.

Once begun, the process of division could not be checked. Out of the Sthaviravāda arose, in the course of the next century or two, a succession of schools afterwards known collectively to their opponents as the Hīnayāna or 'Little Way'. Similarly among the Mahāsāṃghikas there sprang up various schools which gave rise to, and partly merged with, a movement terming itself the Mahāyāna or 'Great Way' which, taking its stand on the more liberal and catholic aspects of the tradition, aimed at not less than a complete restatement of the Buddha's message in terms more in keeping with its original spirit. Whether conservative or liberal, however, none of the schools could afford to ignore the fact that the monastic order was economically dependent on the laity, whether in the form of the general public, a few wealthy burgesses and merchants, or the king. A complete separation, even in the religious sphere, between the two monastic and the two lay *vargas* was, therefore, as unthinkable as a complete identification. A place for the aspirations of the laity had to be found. Eventually, owing to both the necessities of their common economic situation and the interactions which took place between them, the Hīnayāna and the Mahāyāna worked out solutions to the problem which, certainly in India and to a large extent in the rest of Asia too, in practice coincided to a greater extent than the difference between their respective attitudes might have led one to expect.

The Mahāyāna solution was the more radical. Impelled by the universalism and optimism that had given it birth, it evolved for all followers of the Buddha a common spiritual ideal which, integrating devotion and understanding, derived inspiration as much from the living personal example of the Buddha as from the records of his teaching. This was the bodhisattva ideal (see Chapter 2). At the same time it worked out a common path, the path of the six (or ten) *pāramitās* (see p. 164), which was in fact a revised and enlarged edition of the old series of stages from *dāna* to *prajñā*. By restoring this ideal and this path to their proper place at the very centre of the Buddha's teaching whence, as from a heart, flowed the lifeblood of the religion, as well as by stressing the fact that all, whether monks or laymen, were bodhisattvas, and thus potential Buddhas, the Mahāyāna was able to lessen the tensions between the *vargas*, which were now united through the pursuit of a common spiritual objective by means of the same, or similar, spiritual methods. This meant that for the Mahāyāna the *Mahāsaṅgha* coincided with the bodhisattva sangha in the widest sense of the latter term. The lay Buddhist ideal was no longer embodied in a figure such as Anāthapiṇḍada, patron and supporter of the Order in the Buddha's day, but in Vimalakīrti, the wealthy householder of Vaiśālī, the profundity of whose spiritual understanding was such that he could give a lesson in wisdom even to the bodhisattva Mañjuśrī.[289]

As time went on, a common Vinaya for all bodhisattvas, whether monks or laymen, was also evolved. Though much less systematized than its Hīnayāna counterpart – as from the very nature of the Mahāyāna had to be the case – it included both an ordination ceremony and a code of discipline. The first of these, known as the *bodhisattva-saṃvara*, could be conferred by any spiritually qualified bodhisattva on any person in whom the will to Enlightenment had arisen (see p. 160). Though longer than the *upasampadā-saṃvara* it was concerned, as the following short extract reveals, less with the punctilious observance of ceremonial minutiae than with the promotion of a certain type of spiritual attitude:

> I (person's name), who have thus caused the thought of enlightenment to arise, accept the infinite world of living beings as my mother, father, sister, brother, son, daughter, and any other blood-relations, and having accepted them as far as is in my power, strength, and knowledge, I cause the roots of goodness to grow in them. From now on, whatever gift I shall give or moral rule I shall keep, or act of patience I shall perform, acting vigorously, or whatever meditation I shall attain, or acting with wisdom shall learn skill in means, all that shall be for the profit and welfare of living beings.

> And having undertaken to win supreme, perfect enlightenment, and having done homage to those Bodhisattvas of great mercy who have entered the Great Stage, I go forth after them. Having gone forth, a Bodhisattva am I, a Bodhisattva. From now on may my teacher support me.[290]

If no teacher was available, self-ordination was, as an exceptional measure, permitted. The code of discipline, known as the *bodhisattva-śīla*, seems to have been derived partly from its Hīnayāna counterpart, the *prātimokṣa*, and partly from passages in the Mahāyāna *sūtras*, dealing with the life and duties of the bodhisattva, of the type which Śāntideva collected and arranged in his *Śikṣā-samuccaya* or 'Compendium of Instruction'. The possibility that the *bodhisattva-śīla* is based on an early, precenobitical form of the Hīnayāna *prātimokṣa* current among the Mahāsāṃghikas and their offshoots should not be overlooked. According to the *Brahmajāla-bodhisattva-śīla Sūtra*, or 'Grand Net of the Bodhisattva's Precepts', a work of great influence and authority in China and Japan, one who has received the bodhisattva ordination should observe ten major and forty-eight minor rules of conduct. The first four major rules are identical with the four *pārājikas*. The additional six are:

(1) trading in intoxicating drinks or inducing others to do the same;

(2) divulging the offences committed, or the way in which they were committed, by a householder, *bhikṣu*-bodhisattva, monk, or nun;

(3) vaunting one's own qualities and disparaging others;

(4) giving nothing to the destitute, and even ignoring them;

(5) not forgiving a person who has injured the bodhisattva but asked for pardon; and

(6) speaking ill of the Triratna.

The minor rules are even more Mahāyānic in emphasis, and cover a wide range of topics, ranging from abstention from garlic to the development of the *bodhicitta*; they are applicable, some to monks and nuns, some to householders, and some to all four *vargas*.[291] As extant in Tibet the *bodhisattva-śīla* consists of a rather different set of sixty-four rules, eighteen major and forty-six minor, the major rules being available in two recensions. All these versions of the *bodhisattva-śīla* breathe the same spirit of unbounded altruism.[292]

The evolution of the Mahāyāna Vinaya, as it may be called, did not result in the supersession of its Hīnayāna counterpart. After receiving the bodhisattva ordination a follower of the Mahāyāna remained faithful to, and continued to observe, either the five or eight precepts, in the case of a householder-bodhisattva, or the monastic code, in that of a *bhikṣu-* or *bhikṣuṇī*-bodhisattva; *but they observed them in the spirit of the Mahāyāna*. Such, at least, was the Sino-Indian and Central Asian tradition. In China the bodhisattva ordination, though also conferred on lay people, invariably followed within a few days of monastic ordination, with which it comprised as it were an extended Hīnayāna-cum-Mahāyāna ceremony. Developments in Japan were less fortunate. The *upasampadā* lineage having become practically extinct, so that, except in the Ritsu Shū, or Vinaya school, there were really no *bhikṣus* and *bhikṣuṇīs* in the country, the bodhisattva ordination in effect took its place. As in most schools of Japanese Buddhism the latter now came to be conferred only on those engaged in pastoral activities, it became to this extent a dividing rather than a uniting factor in the Buddhist community.

The measures taken by the offshoots of the Sthaviravādins to accommodate the spiritual aspirations of the laity were less thoroughgoing. They were in fact a compromise. Unwilling to recognize a common spiritual ideal for all *vargas*, and unable either to ignore the growing popularity, or resist the influence, of the bodhisattva ideal, these schools eventually conceded that the laity as such might aim not merely at heavenly rebirth but at being a bodhisattva and becoming, after three whole aeons of striving, a Supreme Buddha. A list of ten *pāramitās*, less systematic than their Mahāyāna original, was drawn up in time to be included in some of the later, more obviously apocryphal, books of their respective canons. In the case of the Pāli Tipiṭaka, the only one of these collections to survive complete, the fact that the bodhisattva ideal finds admission only to such books has unfortunately helped confirm an impression that the ideal is a late and spurious one, whereas, on the contrary, it is as ancient as Buddhism itself, and late only in respect of its recognition by the Hīnayāna schools and its belated partial incorporation in their canonical literature. Arhantship remained, however, for these schools the monastic ideal. Thus a curious situation developed in which the more spiritually-minded Hīnayāna laymen could model themselves upon an ideal which, in theory, was recognized as superior to that followed by the monks and nuns. Doctrinal expression to this plurality of religious ideals was given in the formula of the three *yānas* or spiritual careers, a distinction the Mahāyāna rejected as merely provisional on the grounds that ultimately there was but one *yāna* for all sentient beings, that of the bodhisattva. As the Hīnayāna tradition, both doctrinal and disciplinary, had already been worked out in purely monastic terms and systematically oriented towards the attainment of arhantship, its attempt to 'contain' – rather than really to incorporate – the bodhisattva ideal by recognizing it as suitable for lay people failed to result in any deep or lasting modification of its basic attitude. The *Jātaka* stories were treated as matter for edification rather than for exemplification and the style of bodhisattva was appropriated, not to pious lay folk, but more often to rulers who, being obviously unfitted for arhantship in the present life, might be regarded as aiming at Buddhahood in the distant future.

The Theravādin countries of South-east Asia, unable to formulate a common spiritual ideal without violating the basic assumptions of the Hīnayāna, have tended to rely on a social rather than on a purely religious solution to the problem. Recourse to such an expedient was facilitated by the fact that, practically the entire population of these countries being Buddhist, national and religious loyalties have tended if not to coincide then at least strongly to reinforce each other. With the exception of Sri Lanka, which might have inherited Indian prejudices in the matter, they all introduced a system of temporary monastic ordination which, though hardly in keeping with the spirit of the Vinaya, nevertheless contributed to the solidarity of the community to an extent that more than compensated for any shortcomings. On the completion of the more secular side of his education (which might in any case have been received under monastic auspices), and before assuming the responsibility of marrying and bringing up a family, a young man would, and often still does, enter the sangha and devote a few months to the acquisition of spiritual knowledge. An *upāsaka* moreover enjoyed the privilege of repeating this invaluable experience at any time during his life, as often as he wished, and for however long or short a period. Wherever the ancient traditions are honoured a male Buddhist who has not been a monk for at least three days is even now regarded as scarcely human, and certainly not fully educated. The *bhikṣuṇī* ordination having died out in the Theravādin countries[293] the system does not extend to women. Its popularity even among the male section of the community has, however, sufficed to ensure a general understanding of and sympathy with the monastic vocation, and an appreciation of its special requirements, which are of immense value in creating among the laity a feeling of participation in the spiritual life of the religion. The system has also been largely responsible for the wide diffusion of elementary religious knowledge in those parts of the Theravādin world where it obtains.

Just as it was impossible for the Hīnayāna, even at its most rigid, entirely to ignore the higher aspirations of the laity, so the Mahāyāna, even in its most liberal form, could not overlook the fact that it was easier for a monk to be a bodhisattva than a layman and that there existed, in consequence, a real difference between the monastic order and the community of lay devotees. According to the Mahāyāna, this difference was socio-ecclesiastical rather than spiritual; or, if spiritual, one of degree only, not of kind. For the classical Hīnayāna the danger consisted in making too absolute a distinction between *bhikṣus* and *upāsakas* and interpreting Buddhism too exclusively in terms of monasticism; for the Mahāyāna it lay rather in confounding the spiritual with the socio-ecclesiastical order of things in such a way that the sangha was submerged in the laity. Albeit from opposite extremes each of these two great traditions in practice tended, when dealing with the laity, to converge upon a common mean position. This in combination with the facts previously mentioned was responsible for the creation of a common pattern of sangha–laity relations throughout practically the entire Buddhist world. Though the sangha in Mahāyāna lands may be characterized more by compassionate participation in the affairs of secular life, and the sangha in Theravādin lands more by cool aloofness from them, such a difference of emphasis by no means obscures the fact that whether in Sri Lanka or Tibet, Burma or Vietnam, Buddhist laymen and laywomen everywhere look up to the members of the sangha as to their elder brothers in religion, reverencing them as (1) and (2) their teachers, both spiritual and secular, as (3) objects of devotion, as (4) sources of merit, as (5) a means of magical protection and blessing, and as (6) their trusted advisers in worldly affairs.

(1) Since they devote not a part but the whole of their time to the study and practice of the Dharma the standard of religious knowledge and spiritual experience is naturally higher among monks than laymen. Consequently, though a *bhikṣu* sometimes has a spiritually advanced *upāsaka* for his guru, especially in the Mahāyāna countries, the lay

community as a whole stands in a relation of discipleship to the sangha, the members of which function primarily as *spiritual teachers* and are honoured as such.

Instruction in the Dharma is imparted in various ways. One of the most ancient and popular is the religious discourse, which the preacher delivers sitting cross-legged on a special raised seat, and which may consist of an exposition of the Scriptures, of edifying stories and moral exhortations, of hints on the practice of meditation, or of an original presentation of the Doctrine. Whatever its theme, such a discourse is distinguished from an ordinary lecture by an ethical and spiritual emphasis powerful enough to inspire the congregation with a distaste for worldly things and an ardent desire for the realization of Nirvāṇa. Religious discourses are generally delivered in that integral part of any large monastery, the preaching hall. Sometimes they are delivered in the homes of the laity. On such occasions they often follow a ceremonial food-offering (*bhojana-dāna*) to one or more monks, a practice symbolic of the system of mutual dependence wherein *upāsakas* support *bhikṣus* with the gift of material things (*āmisa-dāna*) and *bhikṣus*, in return, sustain *upāsakas* with that greatest of all gifts, the gift of the Dharma (*dhamma-dāna*).

The monks are not only preachers but writers. For the benefit of the laity they translate the Scriptures into the vernacular, compose religious songs, stories, and dramas, compile tracts and manuals, and engage in a variety of other literary undertakings. Nor is the importance of visual aids to religious education unknown. Through sculptured images of the Buddhas and bodhisattvas and mural paintings such as those of Ajanta, where incidents from the Scriptures are vividly depicted, generations of monk-artists have sought to impress the facts of the Master's life and the truths of his teaching upon the minds even of the illiterate. Religious instruction is also imparted through special classes and courses, the 'meditation week' being particularly popular in some areas. Being endowed with a greater mobility and freedom of action than the laity, the monks are moreover able not only to consolidate the Dharma at home but to propagate it abroad. Apart from the intermittent patronage of kings, the story of the spread of Buddhism throughout Asia is largely that of the missionary enterprise of individual members of the sangha.

(2) As the most literate section of the community, the monks tended to function not only as spiritual but as secular teachers. Once the

Scriptures had been committed to writing, an event that occurred about four centuries after the *parinirvāṇa*, literacy became almost a Buddhist virtue. Many Mahāyāna *sūtras* contain colophons detailing the merit to be derived from copying them.

> Peeling your own skin for paper [says Locana Buddha in the *Brahmajāla-bodhisattva-śīla Sūtra*] with blood for your inkstick and using spinal fluid for the water to mix it, using your own bones for a pen, you should copy out the precepts of the Buddha.[294]

With exhortations such as these ringing in its ears, it is hardly astonishing that wherever the sangha penetrated literacy was encouraged and education became more widespread. The monasteries, both large and small, were simultaneously centres of spiritual life, of cultural activity, and of learning. If the standard of popular education is even today higher in the Buddhist than in the non-Buddhist regions of Asia it is due mainly to the fact that, in the former, the village temple has been for centuries the village school. Individual monks often ranked as poets and artists with the most celebrated. Siri Rāhula, the best classical Sinhalese poet, was Sangharaja of Ceylon, while Milarepa enjoys the double distinction of being both the greatest poet and the greatest yogi of Tibet.[295] The earliest and at least the second best epic and dramatic poet to have written in Sanskrit was Aśvaghoṣa, a Buddhist monk.[296] In China and Japan, among hundreds hardly less illustrious, there was Wu Daozi, the poet-painter, whose dragon flew away as soon as he had painted in its eyes, and Kōbō Daishi, the founder of the Shingon Shū, a man of many-sided religious and artistic genius who is traditionally credited with the invention of the Japanese system of syllabic writing.[297] Apart from educational and cultural activities, the monks also engaged in social work. Some, inspired by the bodhisattva ideal, and desirous of alleviating suffering, studied medicine and gave free treatment to the sick. Others built roads and bridges, introduced useful arts and crafts, and popularized improved methods of agriculture.

(3) Inasmuch as the monks not only preach the Dharma but practise it more intensively than anybody else, they become *objects of devotion* to the laity. This is natural. The impulse to admire, to revere and worship, is deep-rooted in the human psyche, and requires for its full satisfaction

as concrete an embodiment of one's ideals as possible. The Buddhas, in their golden aureoles, tend to appear remote, perhaps a little unreal, to the average man and woman. Entangled in doctrinal formulas, and submerged beneath layers of scholastic commentary, the Dharma seems abstruse. The members of the Āryasaṅgha, and even the Bodhisattvas, recede into the sunset glow of the legendary past. Only the *bhikṣus*, the members of the monastic order, fall within range of the layman's experience. From them he hears the Dharma. In their lives he sees more intelligence, more kindness, more self-control – in short a fuller realization of the Buddhist ideal – than in his own. Thus seeing, his faith in the Three Jewels is confirmed and strengthened. Throughout the Buddhist world, therefore, the laity treats the sangha with a respect and devotion that at times astonishes the outsider. In a thoroughly orthodox community the most junior *bhikṣu* takes precedence over kings. No one sits on a higher level than a *bhikṣu*, or sits while he stands. Particularly on formal occasions, the members of the sangha are commonly saluted with a threefold prostration. In several Buddhist lands special honorific speech-forms are used in addressing monks or referring to them.

(4) *Dāna* or giving, the first *pāramitā*, was a virtue to be practised, in one form or another, by the whole Buddhist community. From ancient times the belief prevailed that the amount of merit accruing to the donor was, in part, determined by the worthiness of the recipient. On account of the holiness of its members, the sangha was the *puṇya-kṣetra* (Pāli *puññā-khetta*) or field of merit *par excellence*; for, as seed planted in fertile soil yielded more abundantly than that planted in barren, any offering made to the sangha was productive of greater *puṇya* than one bestowed elsewhere. With a sufficient quantity of *puṇya* to his credit one could pass, at death, to rebirth in a happy heavenly abode. The latter, as we saw above (p. 204), was according to the Hīnayāna the proper goal of the lay devotee. In Theravādin countries, therefore, the religious life of the devout laity consists largely of making offerings to the monks in the hope of getting to heaven. This is no more spiritual than a shrewd investment in stocks and shares. Carried to extremes, it can even prove dangerous. A layman preoccupied with the accumulation of a private stock of merit may, unintentionally, do harm to the sangha by thrusting upon the *bhikṣus* articles for which they have no need, or which are forbidden by the Vinaya, or which are so luxurious as to be obviously unsuitable for anyone intent on the higher life. Undue emphasis on the

doctrine of *puṇya*, and on the sangha as the most worthy recipient of gifts, also leads to a channelling of public generosity so exclusive that other deserving objects of charity, such as the sick, the poor, and the aged, are neglected. Burmese 'nuns' who are not technically *bhikṣuṇīs*, being considered barren soil in respect of the harvest of merit to be obtained from them, are often left to fend for themselves. In Mahāyāna countries, where the altruistic emphasis is more pronounced and where *bhikṣus* are not so exclusively the object of devotion, such abuses are rare. Even in Theravādin countries they are not without their corresponding compensations. Throughout almost the entire Buddhist world, in fact, the practice of regarding the sangha as *puṇya-kṣetra*, to whatever degree, has for centuries past ensured for it the steady, continuous, and most lavishly generous support of the faithful.

(5) By virtue of their austerities, particularly the practice of *dhyāna*, the monks were able to exercise control over not only their own mental states but the objective correlates of those states in the external world. They were thus *a means of magical protection and blessing*. The laity, though devout, was generally interested more in material gains than in spiritual attainments; they wanted long life, health, riches, progeny, success in all their undertakings, and a host of other mundane things. Sometimes what they wanted could not be obtained, or obtained only with great difficulty, by the ordinary methods. The sangha was therefore called upon to invoke the hidden powers on their behalf.

It is wrong to view this aspect of Buddhism as a regrettable lapse from the purity of a strictly rational, 'scientific' original teaching. As far back as literary evidence goes, even to what are apparently the oldest portions of the Scriptures, belief in the existence of occult forces which the monk, through a high degree of concentration, can manipulate for the benefit of humanity, is present; the life of the Buddha himself, as it has come down to us, cannot be wholly dissociated from such elements. Neither is the magical aspect of Buddhism the prerogative of any particular school. Though the Vajrayāna may be richer in specifically magical expressions, which are for this school symbolic of higher, even transcendental, forces and values, magical practices are equally characteristic of the Mahāyāna and the Hīnayāna, and constitute an important aspect of Buddhist life in every age and clime.

The occult forces are invoked through repetition of the Sacred Word. The more intrinsically sacred the Word, as well as the holier and more numerous the reciters, the more powerful will be the effect produced. Consequently it is the Tripiṭaka, or a selection of texts from it, which, as the Word of the Buddha, the most sacred of all utterances, is commonly employed. This sometimes results in curious situations. The grosser the object desired, the stronger the desire for it is likely to be, and the more powerful, therefore, the forces that must be conjured up for its acquisition. In Thailand the *upasampadā-kammavācā* is recited as a love charm.[298] The diary of the Japanese monk Jojin describes how, when on pilgrimage to Wutaishan in 1073 CE, he was commanded by the Chinese emperor to make rain; which he did by setting up a lotus altar and reciting the *Saddharma Puṇḍarīka*.[299] No portion of the Scriptures excels in sublimity as the discourses on the 'Perfection of Wisdom', yet in one of the most famous of them the Lord says, addressing Śakra:

> If a follower of perfect wisdom were to go into battle, to the very front of it, he could not possibly lose his life in it. It is impossible that he should lose his life from the attack of somebody else. If someone strikes at him, – with sword, or stick, or clod of earth, or anything else – his body cannot be hit.[300]

Here an exalted teaching is clearly made to function as a lucky charm or talisman. Sometimes the magical potency of a *sūtra* is condensed into a *dhāraṇī*, a 'meaningless' combination of syllables the repetition of which produces the same results as the recitation of the *sūtra*.[301]

However strange such a view may seem today, the ceremonial recitation of the sacred texts by the monks, for magical purposes, has ever been regarded in all Buddhist countries as an important public service, for performing which the sangha was entitled to the gratitude of the laity. Indeed the mere presence of a body of austere and saintly monks exerted, it was believed, a beneficial influence on the entire national economy, and acted as an insurance against such calamities as fire, flood, epidemics, earthquakes, and invasion. Monks were therefore regarded as a national asset.

(6) On the principle that the spectator sees more of the game than the players, the monks, with their more detached attitude towards life, often had a clearer and more balanced understanding even of worldly affairs than the laity. They were therefore greatly in demand as *advisers*. In a traditional Buddhist community, no matter is too trivial or too important

to be brought to them for their consideration, from the settlement of a dispute to the choice of a new site for the village. Especially when sought in connection with those matters with which it is improper for a monk to concern himself, such as marriage, the advice given may be couched not in categorical but in hypothetical terms, the monk doing no more than indicate the probable consequences of certain lines of action. Whatever the advice given, it would tend to promote the best interests of the community, both material and spiritual. In times of sickness and bereavement, and at the hour of death, the monk administers spiritual consolation. According to some traditions, his care for the laity extends even beyond this life, continuing in the form of instructions which can be heard and acted upon, in the 'intermediate state' (*antarābhava*), by a stream of consciousness newly dissociated from the physical body. At a time of national emergency the government may call upon the sangha, or upon prominent individual monks, not only for magical protection and blessing but for counsel.[302] Monks are also sometimes employed as ambassadors to negotiate terms of peace. Though invested thereby with the power of doing a great deal of good, the sangha is simultaneously exposed to the corrupting influence of politics. Examples of politically ambitious ecclesiastics are, of course, not lacking in Buddhist history, but on the whole the political record of the sangha is not only far cleaner but incomparably more tolerant and pacific than that of its counterparts in other religions.

19
POPULAR BUDDHISM

Between the purely spiritual exercises pertaining to the Path, and the predominantly mundane activities of lay society, there intervenes an aspect of the religion which may be termed Popular Buddhism. Like Diotima's Eros, who was neither divine nor human but daimonic,[303] it is neither wholly sacred nor wholly profane in character, but of a mixed or intermediate nature. As such it constitutes an important link between the intenser but more confined religious life of the monasteries and temples, with their monks and nuns, and their small bands of more seriously-minded lay devotees, and the more widely diffused but lukewarm and fitful piety of the vast mass of more or less nominal adherents of the Teaching. Both in the past and now, being a Buddhist always consisted, for the average person, in participation in this popular aspect of the religion rather than the systematic cultivation of the Eightfold Path or the six perfections. This is no more than may be expected. Few strive for Enlightenment; the majority are concerned with other things. What is required, under such circumstances, is not recriminations and regrets, but provision for at least a peripheral contact with, or a partial and occasional participation in, the life of the religion, on the part of those who for the time being demand nothing more. This is the function of Popular Buddhism. Ideally it is an *upāya*, a skilful means, perpetuating the flame of popular awareness of spiritual values, however dimly, and keeping open the channels of communication between the spiritual and secular worlds.

In practice this aspect of Buddhism is an extremely rich and composite one, consisting of an immense number of elements that do not easily lend themselves to generalization. Apart from the recitation of the Three Refuges and Five Precepts, without which one is not even nominally a Buddhist, it comprises elements evolved out of the Teaching itself by a natural process of development and adaptation, elements assimilated from non-Buddhist cultures, and, at the lowest level, foreign elements that may, in extreme cases, even be incompatible with Buddhism. Popular devotional observances, as an expression of faith in, and adoration of, either the Enlightened and compassionate master or his teaching, generally belong to the first category. Likewise observances connected with the sangha. The celebration of the New Year, and other seasonal festivities, belong to the second, having been carried over from pre-Buddhist times and given a Buddhistic colouring. The Tibetan New Year, for example, is now connected with the advent of Maitreya. Sometimes it is not definitely known whether a particular element was developed from within the religion or assimilated from without. Such is the case with regard to one of the main focal points of Popular Buddhism, the Buddha image. Astrology and divination, though widespread in all Buddhist lands, both Theravāda and Mahāyāna, belong to the third category, that of the foreign elements.[304] So too does the caste system which, though prevalent among the Buddhists of Sri Lanka, is incompatible with the Buddha's teaching even as handed down in that country.[305]

Among the varied elements making up Popular Buddhism there exists, also, a relative distribution of emphasis, which varies from one age and one part of the Buddhist world to another, and even, perhaps, from school to school. Ideally, if Popular Buddhism is really to function as an *upāya*, not only should it be counterbalanced, in the community as a whole, by a sufficiency of activities pertaining directly to the Path, but within this aspect of Buddhism itself the first and second categories should take precedence over the third. With regard to any form of Popular Buddhism, from the adoration of relics to the wearing of amulets, what falls to be considered, in the present context, is not so much its intrinsic value in comparison with the activities connected with the Path, so much as the degree of prominence assigned to it within the whole system of popular observance. The worship of the bodhi tree, beneath which the Bodhisattva gained Supreme Enlightenment, is an integral part of traditional practice; but a Buddhism, even a Popular Buddhism, that consisted exclusively in the veneration of such trees, would not be deserving of the name. The 'corruptions' in Buddhism of which some observers complain are generally found to consist, whenever the complaints are well founded, either in an imbalance between the Dharma proper and Popular Buddhism or in a wrong distribution of emphasis among the latter's various constituent elements. As a historical phenomenon Buddhism has carried tolerance of what did not belong to it and sometimes of what was bad in itself – to adapt Sir Charles Eliot's language in respect of Indian religions generally – to an extreme that constituted almost a betrayal of its own principles. It has therefore perpetually stood in danger of forfeiting its distinctive character. Eliot points out that

> The weakness comes from the absence of any command against superstitious rites and beliefs. When the cardinal principles of Buddhism are held strongly these accessories do not matter, but the time comes when the creeper that was once an ornament grows into the walls of the shrine and splits the masonry.[306]

The present account deals with some of the more truly Buddhistic components of Popular Buddhism, and presupposes them to occupy no more than their rightful place in the total tradition.

Lay Buddhists have always tended to be more emotionally than intellectually inclined. They are faith-followers rather than doctrine-followers. In fact, the development of the devotional element in the Teaching was originally due to their influence rather than to the efforts of the monks, the more conservative minority of whom indeed admitted it with reluctance as the result of popular pressure. Being more the creation of the laity than of the sangha, whose function is generally limited to supplying doctrinal connections, Popular Buddhism is therefore strongly emotional, consisting largely of fervent expressions of faith in and devotion to the Three Jewels, or, more correctly, to their various symbols and representatives.

Among symbols of the Buddha, one of the most ancient and best known is the *caitya* (Pāli *cetiya*) or stupa (Pāli *thūpa*), a tumulus or artificial mound consisting, originally, of a cube surmounted by a hemisphere on which rested an honorific umbrella. One kind of stupa, the *dhātugarbha* (Sinhalese *dagoba*) or reliquary, enshrines a portion of the bone-relics of the Buddha, worship of which tended to be assimilated to the cult of the stupa. Besides being connected with his *rūpakāya*, the stupa as an assemblage of architectural elements symbolic of the Doctrine is also an embodiment of the Lord's *dharmakāya*. As might have been expected, the *Mahāvastu Avadāna* of the Lokottaravāda, an offshoot of the Mahāsāṃghika, supports the worship of stupas much more enthusiastically than does the Theravāda Tipiṭaka. Speaking of the events immediately following the *parinirvāṇa*, the latter merely says

> At the four cross-roads a Thūpa should be erected to the Tathāgata: And whoever shall there place garlands or perfumes or paint, or make salutation there or become in its presence calm in heart, that shall long be to them for a profit and a joy.[307]

The former is more explicit. It represents the Buddha himself as declaring

> He who, having turned his thoughts to enlightenment for the sake of all living things, reverentially salutes the tope of the Saviour of the world, becomes everywhere in all his lives as he fares on the way to enlightenment, mindful, thoughtful, virtuous and assured.[308]

The text then eulogizes stupa worship at length in the most extravagant terms, attributing to it all possible merits. Despite the initial lack of enthusiasm, in certain quarters, for this expression of popular devotion to the Buddha, it was firmly established by the time of Aśoka, whom later traditions indeed represent as being himself a great builder of stupas. Today, as in the past, the veneration of stupas of various shapes, sizes, and materials is as striking a feature of Asian Buddhism as the whitewashed, gaily tiled, gilded, or moss-grown structures themselves are of the landscapes of Buddhist countries.

A slightly less ancient symbol of the Buddha, but a no less popular one, is the image. So much is image worship a part of Buddhist devotion, and so highly characteristic of popular practice, that its comparatively late introduction into the religion is sometimes overlooked. It has, in fact, no canonical sanction. The commentarial literature does, however, incorporate late traditions about the carving of a wooden likeness of the

Master during his lifetime. Though its time and place of origin were long a matter of scholarly dispute, it now seems probable that the Buddha image was first introduced among the Sarvāstivādins of Mathura during the first century CE. Despite its late appearance, so admirably did it meet the requirements of the masses that as an object of devotion its popularity soon rivalled even that of the stupa. Artistically it is the most beautiful expression of the spirit of Buddhism. Images of bodhisattvas, *arhants*, guardian deities, and saintly teachers are also widely venerated. Theravādin worship usually consists of offering only flowers, lights, and incense, and chanting verses in praise of the Three Jewels and passages from the Scriptures. In the Mahāyāna, and even more so in the Vajrayāna, the ritual is not only more complex and artistic but symbolical of psychological processes and spiritual experiences.

Other popular ancient objects of devotion are the bodhi tree and the Buddha's footprint. According to tradition, the Bodhisattva attained Supreme Enlightenment while meditating at the foot of an *aśvattha* or *pīpal* (*ficus religiosa*). What appear to be the oldest canonical accounts of this event make no mention of this circumstance, but by the time of Aśoka the cult of the bodhi tree, as it came to be known, was evidently well established, for one of the gates of the Great Stupa at Sanchi depicts that monarch himself in the act of adoration before it. According to the *Mahāvaṃsa*, which devotes two whole chapters to the incident, Aśoka's daughter Sanghamittā brought with her to Sri Lanka a cutting from the original tree which the king and people of that country received with tremendous jubilation.[309] The worship of the bodhi tree seems to represent an incorporation into Buddhism of primitive tree-worship and its associated solar cosmic symbolism. Due to climatic reasons the cult is confined to India and the Theravādin countries of South-east Asia, though it is said that in China the *pīpal* is commonly identified with a sacred tree connected with Taoism. Bodhi trees are worshipped by decorating their branches with flower-garlands and coloured flags, by lighting rows of lamps, and by sprinkling their roots with milk and perfumed water. The worship of the *śrīpāda* (Pāli *siripāda*) or sacred footprint may owe something to the Indian custom, referred to in the Tipiṭaka, of touching, stroking, and even kissing the feet of a religious teacher as a mark of the profoundest devotion. Such footprints are of two kinds, those believed to have been left by the Buddha himself in the course of his legendary visits to different parts of the Buddhist world, and facsimiles in gold, silver, and other substances. According to Sinhalese tradition, the Buddha impressed his footprint on the bank of the Narmada River and on Mount Elumalai near Tirūpati, both in South India, on 'Adam's Peak' in Sri Lanka, and in Yonaka-pura, which is probably Gāndhāra.[310] Another, over which stands an imposing pinnacled shrine, is found in the Sarapuri province of Thailand. The footprint at Gayā, in Bihar, having been appropriated by Hinduism after the virtual disappearance of Buddhism from India, is now popularly venerated as that of the god Vishnu.

Associated as they are with the chief events of his life, the four great centres of pilgrimage – Lumbinī, Bodh Gaya, Sārnāth, and Kusinārā – are also in a way symbolical of the Master. One might even claim that involving as it does the worship of stupas and images, and of the bodhi tree, as well as a certain amount of hardship, pilgrimage is the most comprehensive of all popular devotional practices. A passage in the *Mahāparinibbāna Sutta* attests the antiquity of the custom. Addressing Ānanda, the Buddha declares that there are four places upon which the believer should look with emotion: the Tathāgata's birthplace, the place of his Supreme Enlightenment, the place where he set in motion the wheel of the Dharma, and the place of his *parinirvāṇa*. He continues

> And whosoever, Ānanda, shall make an end with peaceful heart, while wandering in pilgrimage to (such) shrines, upon the breaking up of the body all such shall be reborn beyond death in the blissful heaven-world.[311]

These words have over the centuries inspired millions of monks, nuns, and lay people to brave all dangers and take the long road that from a remote corner of the Buddhist world led, through desert and jungle, and over mountains and seas, to the peaceful shrines of the 'Middle Country'. It was regarded as particularly meritorious to go all the way on foot and to beg one's food. Even now, when the journey is more often made by rail or air, Tibetan devotees can (or could until recently) be seen prostrating themselves the whole distance from Lhasa to Bodh Gaya. As the practice increased in popularity, the pilgrim's itinerary came to include not only numerous additional places connected with events in the Buddha's life, but also others associated with his lives as a bodhisattva and with previous accounts of many of these places, not all of which fall within the present political boundaries of India. Eventually, as Buddhism overspread Asia, and became consolidated in one country after another, historic local shrines also developed into centres of pilgrimage. In China this was the case with the sacred mountains of Wutaishan, Emeishan, and Putuoshan, which were the seats of special manifestations of the spiritual power of the bodhisattvas Mañjuśrī, Samantabhadra, and Avalokiteśvara respectively. In *The Wheel of Life* John Blofeld describes a modern pilgrimage to the gilded and lacquered shrines of Wutaishan.[312]

Though popular devotion tends to centre upon the Buddha, the two other Jewels are not neglected. If we except the stupa, which to the masses is commemorative of the Buddha rather than symbolic of spiritual truths, the Dharma is embodied principally in the written or printed volumes of the Scriptures. In contrast to the traditionally theistic West, where the true worship that can be offered to God alone is sharply distinguished from all other acts of homage, the Buddhist East tends to regard religious worship – including ritual worship – reverence, and respect as the various manifestations, in differing degrees, of a single devotional attitude. Veneration for the Scriptures, which sprang up immediately the Dharma was committed to writing, could therefore express itself in Buddhism with the greatest freedom. Apart from the fact that the Theravādins refuse to recognize the Mahāyāna *sūtras*, respect is of course shown for the whole body of the Scriptures, extending by association even to commentaries and exegetical works. Popular devotion has, though, tended to crystallize round individual texts. Mahāyāna Buddhists have a special regard for the *Prajñāpāramitā* and *Saddharma Puṇḍarīka Sūtras*. The *Perfection of Wisdom* 'in Eight Thousand Lines' describes how the bodhisattva Dharmodgata created for the former:

> a pointed tower, made of the seven precious substances, adorned with red sandalwood, and encircled by an ornament of pearls. Gems were placed into the four corners of the pointed tower, and performed the functions of lamps. Four incense jars made of silver were suspended on its four sides, and pure black aloe wood was burning in them, as a token of worship for the perfection of wisdom. And in the middle of that pointed tower a couch made of the seven precious things was put up, and on it a box made of four large gems. Into that the perfection of wisdom was placed, written

> with melted vaidurya on golden tablets. And that pointed tower was adorned with brightly coloured garlands which hung down in strips.[313]

The *sūtra* further relates how the bodhisattva Sadaprarudita and the merchant's daughter, with her 500 maidens, who had come to hear Dharmodgata preach,

> all paid worship to the perfection of wisdom – with the flowers which they had brought along, and with garlands, wreaths, raiment, jewels, incense, flags and golden and silvery flowers.[314]

This brilliantly colourful scene, representing a highly idealized version of what must have been a common feature of Indian Buddhism, was partly responsible for the more gorgeous and extravagant aspects of Far Eastern bibliolatry. In Japan the *Saddharma Puṇḍarīka* is the object of special, indeed exclusive, devotion for the adherents of the Nichiren sect, in the sanctuaries of whose temples it occupies a position of honour. Theravādin Buddhists often exhibit a corresponding veneration for the Abhidharma Piṭaka and the *Mahāsatipaṭṭhāna Sutta*. Narrating the meritorious deeds of Kassapa V of Lanka, the *Cūḷavaṃsa* says:

> He had the Abhidhamma-piṭaka written on tablets of gold, the book Dhammasaṅgaṇī, adorned with all kinds of jewels, and having built a splendid temple in the midst of the town he placed the book in it and caused festival processions to be held for it.[315]

Even when it stopped short of actual worship, popular devotion to the Dharma as symbolized by the Scriptures was responsible not only for the production of an immense number of beautifully written, lavishly illustrated, and magnificently ornamented copies of the canonical texts, but also for their preservation over a long period, in some cases down to the present day.

Though the sangha is symbolized – sometimes represented – broadly speaking by the monastic order, this is naturally not quite so much the case for the Mahāyāna as for the Theravāda. In Tibet, for example, it is the *tulkus* or *nirmāṇakāyas*, rather than monks as such, who are the great objects of popular devotion; but as these are, more often than not, themselves members of the monastic order, the difference does not – in William James's phrase – really make a difference. Throughout the Buddhist world, in fact, except in Japan and Nepal, 'sangha' and '*bhikṣu* sangha' are for the bulk of the faithful practically synonymous terms. Devotion to the sangha expresses itself principally by external acts of reverence and by the giving of material support. In Sri Lanka, Burma, and Thailand, where climatic conditions do not greatly differ from those in India, saffron-robed figures still flit at dawn with their begging-bowls from house to house, standing in silence for a few minutes at each door to receive alms which the laity, with joyous faces, offer them not as beggars but as honoured guests.[316] Besides food, the laity also supplies the members of the sangha with clothing, shelter, medical treatment, and other requisites. The scale on which this is done naturally varies from one part of the Buddhist world to another; sometimes, as in Tibet until recently and in Thailand, the responsibility is shared by the government. Though devotion to the sangha is a regular feature of Buddhist life, it reveals itself with particular exuberance at the time of the *kaṭhina* ceremony (see p. 199). In some countries the lavish, indeed spectacular, generosity of the lay people on this occasion has succeeded in transforming a purely monastic function not only into a great popular festival but also, for the monks, into the veritable highlight of the ecclesiastical year.

Festivals and celebrations, which often incorporate practically all the expressions of devotion to the Three Jewels just described, are perhaps the most direct, spontaneous, and colourful manifestations of popular religious sentiment. The most ancient and most important are, of course, those commemorating events in the Buddha's life, particularly his birth, his attainment of Supreme Enlightenment, and his *parinirvāṇa*. Unfortunately there is no unanimity regarding the dates of these events. According to the *Mahāvaṃsa*, the kings of Ceylon sponsored elaborate celebrations on the full-moon day of the Indian lunar month Vaiśākha (Pāli Vesākha, Sinhalese Wesak) corresponding to the months April–May of the Roman calendar, as far back as the reign of Duṭṭhagāmini in the first century CE.[317] These celebrations were apparently in honour of the Buddha's attainment of Enlightenment, which according to the first chapter of the same work had occurred on that day. Modern Sinhalese tradition assigns his birth and *parinirvāṇa* also to the same full-moon day, so that Vaiśākha is now celebrated throughout the Theravādin world as a threefold festival. Japanese Buddhists celebrate the three events separately, on 8 April, 8 December, and 15 February respectively. In Tibet the Shaga Dawa (= *Śākya-pūrṇimā*) day, commemorating the Enlightenment only, falls in the fifth month of the Tibetan calendar corresponding normally to the full-moon day of the Indian month Jeyṣṭha (Pāli *jeṭṭha*), the month after Vaiśākha. Despite differences of national culture, there are, in the words of a Sinhalese Buddhist,

> two features which are very characteristic of Vesak, namely Colour and Serene Joy.[318]

Both are certainly conspicuous in the same writer's description of Vaiśākha in Sri Lanka, which may be taken as typical of the way in which the day is celebrated by Buddhists everywhere. Houses are swept and garnished, streets decorated with lanterns and festooned with six-hued Buddhist flags and coloured streamers. At the entrances of the temples and other public buildings, and across the roadways, stand huge bamboo arches covered with greenstuff. While older devotees prefer spotless white, young people love to go clad in the gayest colours. Having worshipped at the local temple or monastery, where offerings are made and devotional stanzas chanted, many take the eight precepts, involving abstention from food after midday, and spend the remainder of the day meditating and listening to religious discourses. At every street corner stand free refreshment stalls, the contents of which are practically forced upon passers-by. Roads are thronged with people, some on foot and others riding in every type of vehicle from a bullock cart to a car, while at intervals elephants, dancers, drummers, and long lines of yellow-robed monks sweep past in procession bearing, amidst a glitter of gold and jewels, and with royal pomp, a sacred image or relic from one shrine to another. When night falls both town and countryside are transformed into a fairyland of lights. The temples, redolent of flowers and incense, are packed with devotees, and such is the spiritual fervour generated by the events of the day that worship continues until long past midnight.[319]

In Japan the Buddha's birthday is the most popular of the three great festivals connected with his life.

> In temples [writes Beatrice Lane Suzuki] a miniature canopy, 12 to 16 inches high, is erected over the statue of the Buddha in the

form of a child, the shrine with its flower decoration representing the grove of Lumbini where the Buddha was born.[320]

On account of its floral decorations this anniversary is popularly known as the Flower Festival. The image of the infant Bodhisattva is also ceremonially bathed in tea, to represent the bath which, according to tradition, he was given immediately after birth by the four *lokapālas* or 'world protectors'. Several other anniversaries of events in the life of the Buddha are celebrated in different parts of the Buddhist world. They include the anniversaries of the First Sermon, sometimes known as Dharmacakra Day, and his descent from the Trayastriṃśa Heaven where, some years after his Enlightenment, he had spent the rains residence preaching (according to the Hīnayāna) the Abhidharma or (according to the Mahāyāna tradition) the 'Perfection of Wisdom' to his deceased mother, who had been reborn as a goddess there.

Besides those which are, in principle, common to the entire Buddhist world, each Buddhist country has national festivals commemorating events and personalities connected with its own religious history. Thus Sri Lanka celebrates the arrival of the *arhant* Mahinda, who according to tradition was responsible for the introduction of Buddhism to the island, while Japanese Buddhists observe the death anniversary of Shōtoku Taishi, who on 1 February, 594 CE, promulgated an imperial ordinance supporting and urging the worship of the Three Jewels. The foundation days of monasteries and temples, as well as the anniversaries of the consecration of an image or stupa, are also celebrated with more or less pomp by the devotees of the area over which their influence extends. Among Mahāyāna Buddhists, individual Buddhas and bodhisattvas are honoured on particular days and special services are held on the death anniversaries of founders of schools and sects, initiators of new spiritual movements, and other prominent religious personages. In Japan, where for historical reasons sectarianism is much stronger than is usually the case in Buddhism, the death anniversaries of Dōgen, Kōbō Daishi, Shinran Shonin, Nichiren, and other founders of sects are said to be celebrated, by their respective adherents, in an even more gorgeously elaborate manner than the Buddha's birthday.[321] New Year's Days and national days, though non-Buddhist in origin, as well as the birthdays of kings, presidents, and party chairmen, are often observed as semi-religious festivals and made occasions for a display of traditional Buddhist piety and pageantry. With the exception of Sri Lanka, the Theravādin countries of South-east Asia celebrate New Year's Day principally as a water-throwing festival which, though not devoid of religious significance, in Burma at least sometimes results in ugly scenes of vulgarity and violence.

In addition to these more public manifestations Popular Buddhism also possesses a domestic aspect which, since it touches them more nearly, in the eyes of the lay followers is of no less importance. This aspect relates, not to the powerful upward surge of emotion towards the Transcendental represented by the various devotional observances connected with the Three Jewels, but rather in the desire for a descent of the Transcendental into ordinary human affairs in such a way as to bless and sanctify them on their own level. This desire finds typical expression in the practice of maintaining a household shrine and performing various religious ceremonies at the time of birth, marriage, and death. A miniature shrine, consisting of a representation of the Buddha and accessories, is found in most Buddhist homes, and may range from a separate richly-appointed chapel, complete with image or images, to a scroll-painting hung in an alcove or a framed lithograph on a shelf. In Theravādin countries the Buddha is sometimes accompanied by the *arhant* Sīvali who, according to tradition, was distinguished among the disciples of the Master by the fact that his begging-bowl was never empty.[322] Mahāyāna household shrines often contain images or pictures of the more approachable bodhisattvas, such as Avalokiteśvara and Tārā, from whom, on account of their compassionate nature, help in worldly affairs might be expected. Representations of teachers and initiators of traditions such as Tsongkhapa and Padmasambhava fulfil a similar function. In the Far East, instead of an icon, there may be a column of ideograms, in beautiful calligraphy, or a flower or landscape painting instinct with wordless meaning. From the spiritual point of view the household shrine, with its symbol of Enlightenment, stands for the presence of the Unconditioned in the midst of the conditioned, Nirvāṇa in *saṃsāra*, as well as for the presence of the Enlightened mind behind the dust and dirt of mundane consciousness. Ultimately it stands for the unconditioned non-duality of these pairs of opposites. Yet despite the fact that lamps may be lit, incense burned, and flowers and other offerings presented, if not daily, at least on special occasions, the Buddha image or other symbol of Enlightenment is popularly conceived not even as an object of actual worship – much less still metaphysically – but rather as a talismanic source of blessing and magical protection. All the same, obscured by secondary considerations though its real signification may be, the practice of maintaining a household shrine is of value to the laity as providing a constant unobtrusive reminder of the existence of a higher world of spiritual values to the realization of which they ought, as followers of the Buddha, to direct themselves.

Buddhism being concerned primarily, if not exclusively, with the path to Enlightenment, no provision was originally made in it for the performance of domestic ceremonies. In all communities, however, from the most primitive to the most highly developed, the great turning-points of human life, especially birth, puberty, marriage, and death, are marked by observances which, by linking them with the vaster social and cosmic order around, simultaneously invest them with a deeper significance and invoke upon them the blessing and protection of higher powers. The domestic ceremonies now current in Buddhist countries consist, broadly speaking, of a substratum of local, more or less secular, pre-Buddhist practices upon which have been superimposed religious observances of Buddhist origin. While the local element naturally varies enormously from one part of the Buddhist world to another, the religious part follows a fairly constant pattern, of which inviting monks to the house for the recitation of sacred texts is the commonest feature. The Thai tonsure ceremony, as described by Ananda Maitreya, is a good example of this type of observance:

> On the first day, Buddhist monks are invited to the home and seated on a raised platform. The child then enters dressed in his best clothes and accompanied by appropriate music and, after saluting the monks, places his head upon a cushion while the leading monk ties a cotton cord around the topknot. Then all the people repeat the Triple Refuge and the Five Precepts. After that religious ceremony, all the guests are entertained for the rest of the day. On the second day the Bhikkhus return and chant Parittas, the sayings of the Buddha which have been selected because they create in the hearers a suitable psychic condition. On the third day, again, the monks chant passages from the Canon, and the topknot is cut off by the guest of highest rank.... The long hairs severed from the head are saved until the child makes his first pilgrimage

> to the shrine of the Buddha's footprint at Prabat, and then they are offered to the footprint to be used as a brush for sweeping the holy shrine; the short hairs are put in a tiny boat made from banana leaves and cast into the nearest stream to float to the sea.[323]

It is significant that the actual cutting off of the topknot is done not by a monk, but by the guest of highest rank, that is to say by a layman. The initiation ceremonies which, in many communities, take place at the time of puberty, are represented, in some Theravādin countries at least, by the practice of temporary ordination (see p. 210). The marriage ceremony is almost entirely a secular affair. Not only is it performed by an elderly *upāsaka*, never by a *bhikṣu*, but normally monks are not even present on the occasion. Instead, they are invited to bless the newly married couple shortly afterwards, or, alternatively, the latter go themselves to the nearest monastery or temple and there, after worshipping the Buddha, receive the blessings of the sangha.

On the other hand monks take a prominent part in the performance of the death ceremony, which throughout the Buddhist world is not only the most elaborate of the domestic ceremonies but the one most closely associated with Buddhism. So elaborate are these rites, indeed, and so greatly do they vary from one country to another, that generalization is out of the question. Travellers have in any case often described them, though descriptions as well informed and sympathetic as Evans-Wentz's account of the Sikkimese death ceremony are rare.[324] Only a very few of the most salient features can be touched upon. As rebirth takes place in accordance mainly with the nature of the last thought, great importance is attached to making 'a good death'. Buddhists are expected to pass away peacefully, either reciting the name of the Buddha or remembering their past good deeds. Spiritually advanced persons die in the *dhyāna* state, as the Buddha himself is reported to have done. Both the Nyingmapas of Tibet and the Japanese Jōdo Shinshū have, in fact, sought to give effect to an ancient tradition of liberation at time of death, the former by addressing to the dying or 'dead' person instructions which will enable him to recognize the various visions he then experiences as the creations of his own mind.[325] Noisy deathbed scenes, with women beating their breasts, tearing their hair, and wailing, are regarded with disapproval, since by disturbing the mind of the dying person they jeopardize his chances of a happy rebirth. The actual funeral, in the sense of the ceremonies connected with the immediate disposal of the dead body, is usually short and simple, compared with the post-mortem observances. Cremation is general, though burial, and dismemberment and exposure to birds of prey and wild beasts are also practised. The most elaborate funerals are those of famous monks or other outstandingly holy persons. In Burma, China, and Tibet the embalmed and gilded body is the centre of ceremonies and festivities that may last for a year or two, even before it is finally cremated or, as sometimes happens, either enclosed in a stupa or enshrined image-wise in a temple for the veneration of the faithful. In Theravādin countries the post-mortem observances consist mainly in the performance of meritorious acts, such as the making of a ceremonial food-offering to the sangha in the name of the deceased person and transferring to him the merit accruing therefrom. Throughout the Far East, where they have tended to amalgamate with the deeply-rooted indigenous ancestor-worship, the corresponding Mahāyāna observances though identical in principle are much more elaborate in form. Chinese monks are in fact traditionally concerned mainly with the performance of such rites. In Japan, according to Beatrice Lane Suzuki, the O-Bon

> is perhaps the most striking, most important and most observed [of all the religious observances of that country]. It is a ... three day reunion of the living with the spirits of the dead.... Graveyards are visited, incense burned, flowers offered, and lanterns lighted.... Throughout the ceremony temple priests are busy holding services and reciting *sūtras*.[326]

Apart from devotional and ceremonial expressions, Popular Buddhism pervades the domestic and social life of the entire Buddhist community in the form of hospitality and good manners. Both are, in fact, esteemed as religious virtues, one being classified under *dāna* or giving, the first perfection, the other under *śīla* or morality, the second. Despite the disturbing effects of modern civilization, the impact of which has now been felt almost universally, they continue to impart a grace and charm to life wherever the Three Jewels are revered.

The Meaning of Conversion in Buddhism

INTRODUCTORY NOTE

In the summer of 1965 Sangharakshita delivered a lecture series with the title 'The Meaning of Conversion in Buddhism'. The lectures were given at the Hampstead Buddhist Vihara where he had arrived in the summer of 1964 at the invitation of the English Sangha Trust. During his stay there he delivered upwards of two hundred lectures, but these four were of especial significance dealing, as they do, with the central topic of what it really means to convert to Buddhism. Many of those who came to the lectures did not consider themselves to be Buddhist but were interested – at least to some extent. Those who did consider themselves to be Buddhist had usually converted from Christianity, often with a rather vague idea of what being a Buddhist actually meant. In his four lectures Sangharakshita sought to make clear the unequivocally radical nature of Buddhist commitment pointing as it does to a profound transformation of mind. The lectures were transcribed, edited, and published as a small book by Windhorse Publications in 1994.

'The Meaning of Conversion in Buddhism' lectures are referred to in Moving Against the Stream, *Windhorse Publications, Birmingham 2003, p. 67 (*Complete Works, *vol. 23) and in* The History of My Going for Refuge, *section 15, in this volume, p. 460.*

I
INTRODUCTION

What is conversion? For many of us in the West, the word immediately conjures up the image of a missionary going forth armed with a Bible and a bottle of medicine to convert the heathen in the depths of some Eastern jungle. This is, of course, very much a stereotype, although one does come across rather alarming examples of it from time to time. I remember that when I was living in the Himalayan town of Kalimpong some fourteen years ago,[327] someone showed me a copy of a Christmas card which was being sent out by a four-year-old girl, the daughter of a couple of missionaries who lived in Ghoom.[328] This remarkable child was asking her little friends back in England to pray for the conversion of the 'heathen' – the heathen being, of course, all the Buddhists and Hindus in Ghoom and the surrounding area. In particular she asked the recipients of her cards to pray to Jesus that these heathens should stop doing their pujas. And for the benefit of those who might have been unfamiliar with this term for devotional practice, she added (in brackets) 'devil worship'.

This is obviously a very primitive conception of conversion; to be fair, Christian conversion is often misunderstood. It may popularly be thought to be the turning of the heathen from their heathenish ways to the light of the 'true faith' but it also has a much higher and more valuable meaning. The general meaning of the word conversion is clear enough; any dictionary will tell us that it means simply 'turning around'. And when one turns around, this involves a double movement:

a movement away from something and also a movement towards something. So what is one turning away from, and what is one turning towards? For many people, both Christians and adherents of other faiths, 'conversion' means a turning from a lower to a higher way of life, from a worldly to a spiritual life. Conversion in this sense is often spoken of as a change of heart – a change of heart which leads you to stop running after the transitory things of this world and to direct your attention and energy to the sublime, everlasting things of the spirit.

Put in this way, conversion is common to all religions in one form or another. The classic case is that of St Paul on the road to Damascus,[329] but such sudden and dramatic conversions also occur in the Buddhist scriptures. One of the most notable examples is the case of the robber Aṅgulimāla, who changed in the course of a few days, perhaps even a few hours, into an emancipated being, if not an Enlightened one.[330] Indeed, conversion can happen even faster than that, according to an epitaph written in the sixteenth century by William Camden 'for a man killed by falling from his horse'. The epitaph goes:

> Betwixt the stirrup and the ground
> Mercy I asked, mercy I found.[331]

This would suggest that, even for someone whose friends might have thought him spiritually speaking a no-hoper, conversion can come at the very last minute – 'betwixt the stirrup and the ground'. More conventionally, of course, it occurs as what we call a 'deathbed conversion'. But while some people have these apparently genuinely instantaneous experiences, conversion can come about in a much more gradual way. There may be a 'moment of conversion', the experience may be sudden, even catastrophic, but then it dawns on you that actually your whole life, your whole being, has been building up to that moment over many years.

But however it comes to us, over a period of years or in a matter of seconds, the experience of conversion is of the greatest possible importance, because it marks the beginning of our spiritual life. The meaning of conversion therefore deserves our closest attention. However, although there have been many studies of the nature of conversion in Christianity, there has as far as I know been no systematic study of Buddhist conversion.[332] Perhaps, indeed, one might consider the meaning of conversion in Buddhism to be a simple matter, hardly worth studying. People tend to think, 'Once upon a time I was a Christian. Then I read a book about Buddhism, and I changed my faith. Now I'm a Buddhist and that's that.' But it is not really that simple. If we look at what the phenomenon of conversion means in Buddhism, we find that it occurs on several different levels and presents several different aspects.

In this book, four of these aspects are explored: Going for Refuge (or the transition from the wheel of life to the spiral path); Stream Entry; the arising of the will to Enlightenment; and what the *Laṅkāvatāra Sūtra* calls the 'turning about' (the term is *parāvṛtti*, which can be translated quite literally as 'conversion'). This list, which includes some of the most fundamental of Buddhist terms, is by no means exhaustive, but it is sufficient to illustrate, or at least throw some light upon, what conversion means, not just to the aspiring Buddhist but to practising Buddhists at all levels of spiritual attainment, right up to Buddhahood itself.

2
GOING FOR REFUGE

In a sense, Going for Refuge is the simplest, almost the most elementary, aspect of conversion in Buddhism; but in a wider, more comprehensive sense, it includes and informs all the other types and levels of conversion. So first, what is Going for Refuge? Although the term is so widely used in Buddhism, it can be rather mystifying when you first come across it. What does one mean by 'Refuge'? And who or what does one 'go for Refuge' to? The short answer is that as a practising Buddhist one goes for Refuge to the Buddha, the Enlightened teacher, to the Dharma, or his teaching of the way or path leading to Enlightenment, and to the Sangha, the community or Order of those progressing along that path in the direction of Enlightenment.[333] These three Refuges are also commonly known as the Three Jewels.

In many traditional Buddhist cultures, Going for Refuge has become – it has to be said – little more than a formality. Just as if you want to be formally admitted into a Christian church you have to undergo the rite of baptism, in the same way, if you wish formally to signalize the fact that you consider yourself to be a Buddhist, you receive the Refuges and Precepts from an accredited representative of the Buddhist tradition, a *bhikṣu*, and by doing this you formally join the Buddhist community. Some people therefore consider that Going for Refuge is just a matter of recitation. By saying, 'To the Buddha for Refuge I go, to the Dharma for Refuge I go, to the Sangha for Refuge I go,' in Pāli or Sanskrit, and repeating it three times, one is considered to have gone for Refuge. Sometimes people even speak of 'taking Refuge', although the Pāli word *gacchami* means 'I go', not 'I take'.[334] In many parts of the Buddhist world, Going for Refuge is understood in no deeper sense than this verbal repetition of a formula. People go along to the temple, or to a Buddhist meeting, recite these sentences, then go home and forget all about it. So far as they are concerned, they have gone for Refuge, conversion has taken place. They see no need to ponder the meaning deeply or try to explore its significance, much less still put it into practice.

This degeneration of Going for Refuge into a formality is a very unfortunate development. Nothing in the Buddha's teaching is meant to be practised mechanically or as a matter of mere tradition, without an understanding of its inner meaning and its relevance to one's own life. It behoves us, therefore, to take a closer look at the phrase 'Going for Refuge' and try to see what its significance really is. To begin with, what is meant by 'Refuge'? Refuge from what? The traditional explanations are quite clear on this point: the Three Jewels are a refuge from suffering. It is the existence of the Buddha, the Dharma, and the Sangha that makes it possible for us to escape from the unsatisfactoriness, the transitoriness, the conditionedness, the 'unreality' of the world as we experience it. In a well-known passage in the *Udāna*, one of the earliest Buddhist scriptures, the Buddha tells the monks that there exists an unborn, unmade, unoriginated, uncompounded reality, and that it is this which makes it possible to escape from the born, the made, the put-together – in other words, from the world as we experience it.[335]

The Buddha, the Dharma, and the Sangha are called the Three Jewels because they represent the world of the highest spiritual values. Just as in the ordinary world jewels are the most precious of all material things, so in the spiritual world – in fact in the whole of existence – the Buddha, Dharma, and Sangha are those values which are the most sought after, which are ultimately the most desired and the most worthwhile, and from which all other values derive by way of direct or indirect reflection. When we call the Buddha, Dharma, and Sangha the Three Jewels, we are considering them in the abstract, as it were. We are considering their value – their ultimate or supreme value – as compared with all other things. When we speak of them as the Three Refuges, however, we are considering the practical implications of that evaluation. The fact that those values exist gives us the possibility of development, evolution, and progress far beyond our present comparatively low level. Considered as refuges, the Three Jewels represent the possibility of complete liberation from suffering.

It is no linguistic accident that we speak of *Going* for Refuge. You don't just *accept* the Three Refuges; you *go* for Refuge. This action is a total, unqualified reorientation of your life, your existence, your striving, in the direction of the Three Jewels or Refuges. When you say 'I go for Refuge' you are not only acknowledging that the Three Jewels are the most supremely valuable things in existence; you are also acting upon that acknowledgement. You see that the Three Jewels provide a possibility of escape into a higher spiritual dimension, and so you *go* – you completely redirect and reorganize your life in the light of that realization. Bearing in mind the definition 'turning around', if this is not conversion it would be difficult to say what is.

It is all very well, of course, to say, 'Reorganize your life around the Three Jewels'; obviously this is something which is not easily done. We need to explore how it works out in concrete terms, and this we can do by looking at each of the Three Refuges in turn.

In practice, Going for Refuge to the Buddha means taking the Buddha (the historical Buddha Śākyamuni) as the living embodiment of the highest conceivable spiritual ideal. It means that after surveying and comparing all the great spiritual teachers, while fully appreciating each and every one of them, you nevertheless come to the conclusion that all their spiritual values and attainments are, as it were, summed up in the person of the Buddha. To your knowledge there is no attainment higher than his. If you regard any other being, any other teacher, as having gained a spiritual level or knowledge higher than that of the Buddha, then there is no Buddha Refuge for you. You may be an admirer of the Buddha, but you are not a Buddhist unless you see in the Buddha the highest embodiment of the highest spiritual ideal.

One might object, especially if one was universalistically inclined, that this is a rather narrow attitude. Why does one need to consider the Buddha to be supreme? Why not regard all great spiritual teachers as equal and have the same appreciation for them all – even go for refuge to them all? In fact, the Buddhist attitude is not narrow so much as pragmatic. We are concerned here not with matters of abstract theory, but with authentic, heartfelt, living spiritual practice. And in the spiritual life one of the most important elements, if not in a sense *the* most important element, is devotion. It is devotion which provides the driving power. The intellect, we might say, is like a motor car: the machinery is all there, but without the fuel, without the igniting spark, it just won't move. We may know all the philosophies and systems of religion, we may even be able to write and speak about them, but if our knowledge is just cold, intellectual, and abstract, if that living spark of inspiration, devotion, and faith is not there, we shall never make any progress.

Devotion flows most easily towards a person, or at least towards a personified embodiment of the ideal we want to reach. Because it is directed in this way, it is by its very nature exclusive. We cannot be deeply devoted to a number of spiritual ideals simultaneously. If we are going to develop devotion to an intensity which is capable of propelling us along the spiritual path in the direction of the Goal, it must be fixed on just one figure, the one which we consider to be the highest. The Sanskrit term for faith or devotion, *śraddhā*, comes from a root which means 'to place the heart'; devotion is necessarily to some degree exclusive because the heart can truly be placed only on one object.

At the same time, intolerance has no place in Buddhism. In regarding the Buddha as pre-eminent, as the supremely Enlightened One above all other religious teachers, Buddhism does not dismiss, much less still condemn, any other religious teacher. Indeed, while Buddhists honestly and straightforwardly regard the Buddha as the greatest of all spiritual teachers that have ever lived, they are at the same time quite prepared to respect and even admire other spiritual leaders. Many Chinese Buddhists, for instance, entertain deep admiration and respect for Confucius and Laozi (Lao-tzu). It is one of the great beauties of Buddhism that while Buddhists have a faith which is exclusive in the sense of being concentrated – they direct their whole heart's devotion to the Buddha – this faith is not exclusive in the sense of being intolerant or fanatical.

The word *dharma* has many meanings; as the second Refuge, the Dharma, it has two principal ones. Firstly it refers to the teaching of the Buddha, the *buddhavacana* or word of the Buddha; secondly it means the spiritual law, truth, or ultimate reality. These two meanings are obviously interconnected. The Buddha had a certain spiritual experience of reality, and out of that experience he gave his teachings; so the formulated Dharma is the external expression, in terms of human thought, conception, and speech, of the Buddha's experience of the

Dharma as ultimate reality.

On the intellectual plane, Going for Refuge to the Dharma means being convinced of the essential truth of the Buddha's teaching. One must be convinced that it exhibits clearly and unambiguously, above all other teachings, the way leading to Enlightenment. Obviously Going for Refuge to the Dharma in this sense involves knowledge of it, and in order to know the Dharma you have to study it. This, I am afraid, is where many of us fall down. However many Buddhist lectures we attend, however many books we read, if we cannot answer a simple factual question about the four noble truths or the Eightfold Path or the twelve *nidānas*, what has been the point? Without any lasting knowledge of the Dharma, we can hardly be said to be Going for Refuge to it.

I once attended a talk by Krishnamurti in Bombay.[336] It was a beautiful talk, absolutely crystal clear; but at the end a woman got up, almost tearing her hair out in frustration, and said in a voice quivering with emotion (as people's voices tended to in Krishnamurti's meetings): 'Sir, we have been following you and listening to you for forty years, but we do not seem to have got anywhere.' If as Buddhists we have not got anywhere, at least on the intellectual level, after forty years, or even after four years, even four months, it may well be because we have not got down to the study of Buddhism. If we were taking up engineering or medicine, or even pig-keeping, we would expect to have to study it; similarly, knowledge of Buddhism does not just come automatically when we say '*dhammaṃ saraṇaṃ gacchāmi*' ('To the Dharma for Refuge I go'). Even the most devout Buddhist cannot bypass an intellectual acquaintance with the Buddha's teaching.

In one of his essays T. S. Eliot makes a caustic little remark which goes right to the point:

> People talk of transcending the intellect, but of course first one must have an intellect.[337]

While we have to go beyond an intellectual understanding of the Dharma, we cannot afford to look down upon that understanding until we possess it. It is no good being 'deep and mystical', and thinking that we can skip the hard intellectual study of Buddhism. Study has its limitations, of course – we have to bear in mind that we are studying the expression of spiritual truths which ultimately have to be realized – but it is important to know the basic doctrinal principles thoroughly and be convinced of their truth. So in order to go for Refuge to the Dharma, you have to read books about it, talk about it, hear lectures about it, and develop a clear intellectual understanding of it – without in the end being confined or limited by that understanding.

This clear understanding is necessary but not, of course, sufficient. Going for Refuge to the Dharma means not just understanding the doctrines but realizing for oneself the principle or reality which the doctrinal formulations represent. To put it more simply, Going for Refuge to the Dharma means the actual practice of the Dharma, through observance of Buddhist ethics, through meditation, and through the cultivation of transcendental wisdom.

Just as Going for Refuge to the Buddha does not preclude intelligent receptivity to teachers from other traditions, so Going for Refuge to the Dharma need not exclude appreciation of other spiritual teachings, whether Hindu, Christian, Taoist, Confucian, or whatever. Indeed, after leaving behind some other religion and penetrating deeply into Buddhism, we may be surprised to discover that we now understand our former religion better. As we begin to make sense of Buddhism we begin to find that all the other religions also make sense. The Buddhist would say that this is because the part cannot really be understood apart from the whole. Buddhism, as well as being a sublime and noble teaching, is comprehensive, neither rejecting nor repudiating any truth however humble, any spiritual discovery wheresoever made, but weaving them all into one great system, as it were, in which they all find the appropriate place. It is not, of course, that Buddhists take all other religions on their own valuation – if they did that they could not be Buddhists – but from a Buddhist perspective many teachings make sense at a level even deeper than their own estimation, and what is imperfect in them finds its fulfilment, its culmination, in the Buddha's teaching.

While having this comprehensive approach, however, Buddhism is not simply prepared to embrace all so-called religious teachings willy-nilly, and there are many teachings which it explicitly rejects. For instance, as far as Buddhism is concerned, the idea of a supreme being, a personal God who created the universe, is a wrong view which hinders the attainment of Enlightenment.[338] A belief in God may be widely believed to be practically synonymous with religious faith, but it completely contradicts Buddhism's vision of reality. If one accepts a doctrine which

Buddhism regards as untrue then obviously one is no longer Going for Refuge to the Dharma. Here, as elsewhere, Buddhism follows a middle path, neither indiscriminately accepting all the teachings of other faiths, nor rejecting them wholesale. Like the pioneer in search of gold, Buddhism sifts and sorts out, rotating the pan so that all the dirt and water falls out, to reveal whatever grains of shining gold are there.

In all the cultures to which Buddhism has spread it has never totally rejected the existing religious traditions, but at the same time it has always gone beyond them, and jettisoned elements in those traditions which are incompatible with its own vision. That is why we find Buddhism having a purifying and refining influence on Hinduism in India, on Taoism in China, and on Shinto in Japan. Even in the West there are many Christians whose conception of Christianity has been elevated by their acquaintance with Buddhism, even though they have not chosen actually to become Buddhists.

In the West we tend to put up barricades and station ourselves either on one side or the other, as if to say, 'Either take a religion or leave it. Either you are of it or you are not of it.' But Buddhism does not see things quite like that. It is more objective, more balanced. It does not hesitate to discard doctrines it considers to be immature, false, or untrue, even if they are sanctified by the name of religion. A teaching may be time-honoured, it may have been believed by millions of people for thousands of years, but this does not matter. If it is untrue, Buddhism rejects it. At the same time, if there is reality, if there is beauty, in any other tradition, Buddhism is ready, willing, and even eager to accept and make use of it. This is what we find it doing in all ages and in all countries, and there is every reason to hope that the same process will continue in the West.

In the context of Going for Refuge, the third Jewel, the Sangha, is to be understood in three principal ways. Firstly, it means the transcendental hierarchy of Enlightened and partly-Enlightened persons existing on a purely spiritual plane. Things get rather complicated here, because this is not to say that these beings do not exist simultaneously here on earth. They are not necessarily organized into one spiritual community on a worldly level, however, because the unity of these beings is on a transcendental level. In Buddhist terminology, they are the Buddhas, *arhants*, bodhisattvas, and other great Enlightened and partly Enlightened beings who have reached a level far above that of ordinary mundane life and consciousness. Secondly, Sangha means all those who have been ordained as Buddhists – traditionally this refers to the monastic order of *bhikṣus* or monks and of *bhikṣuṇīs* or nuns. And thirdly, there is the *Mahāsaṅgha*. *Mahā* is Sanskrit for 'great', so this is the whole Buddhist community – all those who, to whatever degree, go for Refuge to the Three Jewels.[339]

We can go for Refuge to the Sangha in all these three senses. We go for Refuge to the Sangha as the spiritual or transcendental hierarchy when by our own spiritual attainments we become members of that hierarchy. We go for Refuge to the Sangha in the second sense either by being ordained into a Buddhist order or by supporting the order and relying on its members for spiritual advice and instruction. And we go for Refuge to the *Mahāsaṅgha*, the whole Buddhist community, simply by our fellowship with that community on whatever level, even simply on the ordinary social plane.

Of course, the Sangha Refuge cannot really be understood in isolation from the context of the Three Jewels as a whole. Those who go for Refuge to the Sangha also necessarily go for Refuge to the Buddha and the Dharma. In other words, before you can effectively go for Refuge to the Sangha, you and all the people who form that Sangha need to have a common spiritual teacher or ideal and a common spiritual teaching or principle. It is this which makes it possible for people to come together into the spiritual community or sangha. The fact that they go for Refuge to the Buddha and the Dharma naturally draws people together.

But is this all? What do we mean by 'together'? It does not mean just physical proximity. Coming together to sit in a kind of congregation is not enough to form a sangha. We may all quite sincerely take the Buddha for our spiritual teacher, and we may all be sincerely trying to practise, follow, and realize the Dharma. We may all agree on doctrinal questions, and even have the same meditation experiences. But these things do not in themselves mean that we constitute a sangha. Going for Refuge to the Sangha is rather more subtle than that. It is essentially a matter of communication. When there is communication among those who go for Refuge to the Buddha and the Dharma, then there is Going for Refuge to the Sangha.

The communication which characterizes the sangha is not merely an exchange of ideas and information. If I say to someone, 'Last week I was in Norwich,' they will no doubt understand that statement perfectly

– a successful exchange of ideas will have taken place – but there has not necessarily been any communication. If we find our contacts with others, even our friendships, frustrating and disappointing, if we find the exchanges we have with people at work or at parties a bit meaningless, it is because we are not using them as a medium for communication. So what is communication? It isn't very easy to say. For the purpose of exploring the Sangha refuge, a working definition might be: 'a vital mutual responsiveness on the basis of a common ideal and a common principle'. This is communication in the context of Going for Refuge: a shared exploration of the spiritual world between people who are in a relationship of complete honesty and harmony. The communication is the exploration and the exploration is the communication; in this way spiritual progress takes place. It may not be clear exactly how it happens, but happen it certainly does.

The most common, or the most generally accepted, mode of this kind of communication is the relationship between spiritual teacher and disciple. When in this relationship there is a mutual responsiveness on the basis of a common allegiance to the Buddha and the Dharma, there is also a common refuge in the Sangha. Such depth of communication is, however, not limited to that between teacher and disciple. It may also take place between those who are simply friends, or *kalyāṇa mitras* – 'good friends' in the spiritual sense – to each other. Going for Refuge to the Sangha takes place when, on the basis of a common devotion to the Buddha and the Dharma, people explore together a spiritual dimension which neither could have explored on their own. Of course, beyond a certain point there is no question really of any sort of mutual relationship at all. In the process of communication and Going for Refuge to the Sangha, a dimension is eventually reached in which distinctions between the people involved no longer have any meaning – such distinctions have been transcended.

From all this we can begin to understand what Going for Refuge means, and in what sense it constitutes conversion. It is clearly not just a question of conversion from, say, Christianity to Buddhism, or of exchanging one set of ideas for another, even wrong ideas for right ones. It is infinitely more profound than that. Fundamentally it is a question of conversion from an ordinary mundane way of life to a spiritual, even a transcendental, way of life. More specifically, it consists of three distinct processes of turning around: firstly from limited ideals to an absolute, transcendental ideal; secondly from what Tennyson calls our 'little systems' that 'have their day'[340] to a path based on unchanging spiritual principles and truths; and thirdly from meaningless worldly contact to meaningful communication. All these things are involved when we say:

Buddhaṃ saraṇaṃ gacchāmi
Dhammaṃ saraṇaṃ gacchāmi
Saṅgham saraṇaṃ gacchāmi

To the Buddha for Refuge I go
To the Dharma for Refuge I go
To the Sangha for Refuge I go.

3
ENTERING THE STREAM

Going for Refuge may seem radical enough, involving as it does a total reorientation of our lives towards the spiritual values symbolized by the Three Jewels. This, however, is by no means all that is implied by conversion in Buddhism; indeed, it is only the beginning. We may start off by Going for Refuge to the Three Jewels, but in the end we must ourselves *become* the Three Jewels. There must be a permanent shift of the centre of gravity of our being from the conditioned to the Unconditioned, from *saṃsāra* to Nirvāṇa. That is to say, conversion in Buddhism means not just a turning around *to* Buddhism, which happens when we go for Refuge to the Three Jewels, but a turning around *within* the context of our Buddhist practice itself.

I have chosen here to describe this essential shift in terms of gravity, but this particular point in one's spiritual career seems to lend itself to all kinds of metaphors. One of the most traditional, for example, is 'Stream Entry'. The 'Stream' is the current which flows to Enlightenment, and the point of Stream Entry is the stage of spiritual practice at which your momentum towards Enlightenment is so strong that no obstacle can hinder your progress. Until this point, spiritual life is bound to be a struggle – you are going 'against the flow' of your own mundane nature – but when you enter the Stream, all the struggling is over.

In this chapter, we shall be looking more closely at the crucial experience expressed by metaphors such as 'Stream Entry', a 'shift in gravity', and several more. But first we will focus on another aspect of conversion, one which comes earlier in the spiritual life, and which in fact corresponds to Going for Refuge to the Three Jewels. This experience can also be described in terms of a metaphor: the metaphor of the wheel and the spiral. And to understand the metaphor of the wheel and the spiral, to get just a glimmer of what it means, we have to go back 2,500 years to the foot of the bodhi tree, back to the night of the Buddha's realization of supreme and perfect Enlightenment.

What was attained on that night, only a Buddha can say – indeed, not even a Buddha can really describe it. The *Laṅkāvatāra Sūtra* goes so far as to say that from the night of his Enlightenment to the night of his final passing away, the Buddha uttered not one word.[341] In other words, the secret of his Enlightenment, the nature of the great transforming experience that he underwent, is incommunicable, and that is all that we can really say about it. We cannot say that it is this, or it is that, or even that it is not this or not that, because that would be to limit it. Nor can we say that it is this *and* that. According to the Buddha himself, we cannot even say that it is neither this nor that. All ways of speaking, all ways of telling, are transcended.

The Enlightenment experience is inexpressible, but we can get some hint of what it is by taking a more indirect view of it – by looking at it in terms of the difference which that experience made to the Buddha's outlook on existence as a whole. The scriptures tell us that when the Buddha surveyed the universe in the light of his supreme spiritual experience, he saw one prevailing principle or truth at work. He saw that the whole vast range and sweep of existence, from the lowest to the highest, in all its depth and breadth, was subject to what he subsequently called the law of conditionality. He saw that whatever arises anywhere in the universe, from the grossest material level up to the most subtle spiritual level, arises in dependence on conditions, and that when those conditions cease, the arisen phenomena also cease. He further saw that there are no exceptions to this principle. All things whatsoever within the sphere of phenomenal existence, from tiny cells to empires and great galactic systems, even feelings and thoughts, are governed by this law of conditionality.[342] Expressed in conceptual terms, this great truth or law of 'conditioned co-production' (*pratītya-samutpāda* in Sanskrit) became the basis of Buddhist thought.

There is a lot that could be said about conditionality, but there is one point in particular which we must understand, not only to enable us to grasp Buddhist thought but, even more importantly, to enable us to practise Buddhism effectively. This crucial fact is that conditionality is of two kinds: the 'cyclical' and the 'progressive' or 'spiral'.

In the cyclical mode of conditionality, there is a process of action and reaction between pairs of opposites: pleasure and pain, virtue and vice, birth and death and rebirth. What usually happens is that we swing back and forth between these pairs of opposites. We experience pleasure, for example, but sooner or later the pleasure goes and we experience pain; then, after some time, the pain swings back again into pleasure. In the spiral mode of conditionality, on the other hand, the succeeding factor increases the effect of the preceding one rather than negating it. When you are experiencing pleasure, instead of reacting in the cyclical order – with pain – you go from pleasure to happiness, and then from happiness to joy, from joy to rapture, and so on. The cyclical mode of conditionality, in which you go round and round, governs the *saṃsāra*, the round of conditioned existence, but the spiral mode, in which you go up and up, governs the spiritual life, especially as embodied in the path or way laid down by the Buddha, and the goal of that path, Enlightenment.[343]

In the Tibetan Buddhist tradition, the round of conditioned or mundane existence is commonly represented in pictorial form. If you walked into a Tibetan temple or monastery you would see on the right-hand side of the entrance, inside the vestibule, an enormous painting of the wheel of life. In the hub of the wheel, you would see three animals: a pig, a cock, and a snake, each biting the tail of the one in front. These symbolize the three basic human passions. The pig represents ignorance, in the sense of basic spiritual confusion, lack of an appreciation of spiritual values, and mental bewilderment of the deepest and darkest kind; the snake stands for anger, aversion, or irritation; and the cock symbolizes desire, craving, and lust in all their forms. These three animals are at the centre of the wheel to indicate that it is our basic spiritual ignorance, together with the craving and aversion connected with it, that keeps us within the round of existence, undergoing birth and death and rebirth. The animals are depicted biting each other's tails because ignorance, craving, and hatred are all interconnected. If you have one, then you will have the other two. They cannot be separated, being different manifestations of the same primordial alienation from reality.

Round the hub of the wheel of life you would see another circle, divided into two segments, one side black and the other white. In the white half there are people moving upwards, happy and smiling; in the black half people are tumbling down in a very wretched and terrible condition. The white side represents the path of virtue; the dark one the path of vice. So this circle represents, on one hand, the possibility of attaining to higher states within the round of existence, and on the other, the possibility of sinking to lower ones. The white and black paths do not refer to spiritual progress – or lack of it – towards the Unconditioned, but only to higher or lower levels of being (determined by ethical or unethical actions) within conditioned existence itself.

Moving outwards from the hub, the third circle – which takes up the most space in the wheel – is divided into six segments, each vividly depicting one of the spheres of sentient conditioned existence. At the top we see the world of the gods; next to that, working clockwise, the world of the *asuras* or anti-gods; then the world of the hungry ghosts; then the lower realm of torment and suffering; above that, on the other side, that of the animals; and then the human world. These are the six spheres of sentient existence within which we may be reborn, according to whether the deeds we have performed and the thoughts we have entertained have been predominantly ethical or unethical.

So the meaning of the wheel, as far as these three circles are concerned, is that sentient beings – and that means us – dominated by greed, anger, and ignorance, perform either skilful or unskilful actions and are reborn accordingly in an appropriate realm of conditioned existence. But there is also a fourth circle, right on the rim, divided into twelve segments; this represents the twelve *nidānas* or links of the chain of conditioned co-production, the chain which explains in detail how the whole process of life comes about. In the wheel of life's depiction of this chain, each segment contains an illustration of a particular *nidāna*, and these illustrations proceed clockwise round the wheel.

At the top we see a blind man with a stick, an illustration of *avidyā*, which means ignorance in the spiritual sense of ignorance of the truth, ignorance of reality. Next comes a potter with a wheel and pots, representing the *saṃskāras* or karma formations – volitional activities which issue from that ignorance. In other words, because of our primordial spiritual ignorance, and the things we have done in previous existences based on that ignorance, we have been reborn into our present life. Together, these two links make up what is called the 'cause process' of the past life, due to which we have arisen in this new existence.

The third image is a monkey climbing a flowering tree. This represents *vijñāna*, consciousness, which here means the first moment – almost, we might say, the first throb – of consciousness of the new being (or more accurately, the neither old nor new being) which arises in the womb of the mother at the time of conception. Fourth, arising in dependence on that, there is *nāma-rūpa*, the whole psychophysical organism (the image for this is a boat with four passengers, one of them steering). In dependence upon that arises *ṣaḍāyatana*, the six sense organs (in Buddhism, the mind is counted as a sixth sense) symbolized by a house with five windows and a door. Then, as the six sense organs come into contact with the external world, *sparśa*, touch or sensation, arises; the wheel of life's image for this is a man and woman embracing. And in dependence upon touch arises *vedanā* or feeling (pleasant, painful, or neutral), represented by a man with an arrow in his eye. This group of five *nidānas* together makes up the 'effect process' of the present life; they are the effects of actions based on ignorance performed in the previous life.

Next, there is a picture of a woman offering a drink to a man. This stands for the link of *tṛṣṇa* or thirst – craving or desire in the widest sense. Then comes *upādāna*, clinging or attachment, represented by a man gathering fruit from a tree; then *bhāva* or becoming, the image for which is a pregnant woman. These three constitute the 'cause process' of the present life, because they set up actions which must bear fruit in the future, either in this life or in some future existence. Lastly *jāti* or birth and then *jarā-maraṇa*, old age and death, bring us full circle and constitute the 'effect process' of the future life. These last two cast imagery aside; the pictures simply show the truth in its starkness – a woman giving birth and a corpse being carried to the cremation ground.

So what does all this signify? It is a graphic illustration of the whole of human life. Due to our ignorance, and activities based on that ignorance, the seed of consciousness arises again in a new existence, which develops into a new psychophysical organism endowed with six senses. This inevitably comes into contact with the corresponding six sense-objects, as a result of which feelings and sensations arise. We start craving for the pleasant feelings and rejecting the unpleasant ones, while we remain indifferent to the neutral ones – and we therefore start clinging to what is pleasant and avoiding what is unpleasant. Habitually reacting in this way, grasping at pleasure and shrinking from pain, we eventually precipitate ourselves into another life, a life which is again subject to old age, disease, and death.

In this way, the twelve links explain how the whole process of life comes about. For explanatory purposes they are spread over three lives (past, present, and future), and in particular they show the alternation of cause and effect. First you get the cause process of the previous life; second, the effect process of the present life; third, the cause process of the present life; and fourth, the effect process of the future life. In this way there is an alternation between the two processes, cause and effect, a cyclical movement between pairs of opposites. This is all getting rather complicated, but it is leading us to a crucial point. Within the context of the three lives there are three points, known as the three *sandhis* or junctures, at which the cause process changes into the effect process or vice versa. *Sandhi* is an evocative term, being the Pāli and Sanskrit word for dawn and twilight, the time when night passes over into day, or day into night.

The first *sandhi* occurs at the point where the volitional activities, the last link in the cause process of the past life, are followed by the arising of consciousness in the womb, the first link of the effect process of the present life. Another *sandhi* occurs at the juncture where in dependence upon feeling, the last link in the effect process of the present life, arises craving, the first link in the cause process of the present life. And the third juncture is where becoming, the last link in the cause process of the present life, gives rise to birth, the first link in the effect process of the future life.

The first and third of these *sandhis* are 'non-volitional' – that is, effect follows cause without our being able to do anything about it. But the second *sandhi*, between feeling and craving, is of crucial importance for us because it is a juncture at which we can make a choice. In fact, it is the point of intersection between the two kinds of conditionality, the cyclical and the progressive. This is where we either make a mess of things and as a result revolve once again in the wheel, or start to progress and enter the spiral. So we need to understand exactly what happens at this point.

All the time, whatever we are doing, even when we are just sitting reading a book, various sensations are impinging upon us – sensations of cold, heat, sound, light, and so on. All these sensations, whether we are aware of them or not, are either pleasant, painful, or neutral. Now, as these feelings arise, how do we react? To pleasant sensations we react most of the time with craving. We want them to continue, we don't want to lose them, so we try to cling on to them. Our natural tendency is to try to repeat pleasant experiences. This is the fatal mistake we are only too apt to make. We are not content to let the experience come and go; we want to perpetuate it, and so we react with craving. If, on the other hand, the sensation is unpleasant, painful, or at least unsatisfactory, we instinctively, even compulsively, try to thrust it away from us. We don't want it. We don't want anything to do with it. We try to escape from it. In short, we react with aversion. And if we feel a sensation which is neither pleasant nor painful, we just remain confused. Not knowing whether to grasp it or reject it, we react with bewilderment.

This is how we react all the time to the sensations and experiences that are continually impinging upon our consciousness through all the senses, including the mind. In this way an effect process is followed by a cause process, and we circle once more in the round of existence. The wheel of life makes one more revolution, and all the conditions are created or recreated for a fresh rebirth. This is where it all happens, at the point where in dependence upon feeling there arises craving.

But suppose we do not react in this way. Suppose, when sensations and feelings befall us, we do not react with craving or aversion or confusion. Suppose we can stop the process, suppose we can stop the wheel turning – then what happens? Quite simply, what happens then is that mundane, conditioned existence comes to an end, and only the transcendental is left. We attain Enlightenment, Nirvāṇa, or whatever else we like to call it.

The next question is how to stop the process. It is easy to say, but how do we do it? Broadly speaking, there are two ways of ensuring that feeling is not succeeded by craving, two ways of ensuring that the wheel does not make another revolution. The first is a sudden way which shatters the wheel at a single blow; the second is a gradual way which progressively slows the wheel down, gently applying a brake to bring the whole thing slowly to a halt.

The sudden way may sound rather Zen-like, Zen being famous for its abrupt methods, but we can illustrate it with a story not from the Zen tradition but from the *Udāna* of the Pāli canon, the story of Bāhiya. Bāhiya was a monk who had been admitted to the order in some distant part of the country, which meant that he had never had the chance to meet the Buddha or ask him any questions. He wanted to put this right as soon as possible, so he made the long journey to the place where the Buddha was staying. When he arrived, however, the Buddha was out on his daily almsround, going from house to house for food. Having come so far, Bāhiya wasn't going to hang around waiting for the Buddha to come back, so he asked someone which direction the Buddha had taken and eagerly went after him.

It wasn't long before he caught up with the Buddha, still walking mindfully from door to door. Bāhiya had no thought of waiting for a suitable moment to speak with his teacher for the first time. Almost treading on the Buddha's heels, he called out, no doubt rather breathlessly, 'Please give me a teaching.' But it was the Buddha's custom never to speak during his almsround, so he ignored Bāhiya's request and kept on walking. A second time Bāhiya asked, even more urgently this time, 'Please give me a teaching.' But again the Buddha ignored him and kept walking. Refusing to give up, Bāhiya made his request for a third time. And this time he got a response. It was apparently a rule with the Buddha that if anyone asked him something three times, he would answer the question, whatever it was and however serious the consequences might be for the questioner. So, stopping in his tracks, he turned round, gave Bāhiya a very direct look, and said, 'In the seen, only the seen. In the heard, only the heard. In the touched, only the touched. In the tasted, only the tasted. In the smelt, only the smelt. In the thought, only the thought.' He then turned round and went on with his almsround – and Bāhiya became Enlightened on the spot.[344]

The Buddha was saying, in effect, 'Don't react.' If a sound impinges on your eardrums, it's just a sound – you don't have to react to it. You don't have to like it or dislike it. You don't have to want it to continue or want it to stop. 'In the heard, only the heard.' The same goes for the seen, the touched, the tasted, the smelt, and even the thought. Don't react. Let the bare experience be there, but don't make that experience the basis for any action or reaction in the cyclical order. If you can do that, you abruptly stop the wheel revolving and realize Nirvāṇa here and now, on the spot – as Bāhiya, it seems, actually did.

The sudden way is obviously very, very difficult. In fact, it may even sound impossible. The example of Bāhiya, and many similar cases, shows that it *is* possible, but for most people it is a much more reliable and sound procedure to try to follow not this sudden path but the gradual path (which of course does not mean the 'never-never path'!). The gradual path can be laid out in terms of the Noble Eightfold Path, the seven stages of purification, the ten *bhūmis*, and many other formulations, but in this context it is perhaps best explained in terms of the twelve positive links which constitute, psychologically and spiritually, the successive stages of the progressive movement of conditionality as it spirals away from the wheel. For our present purposes we shall ignore the last four of these, as they take us beyond Stream Entry. Here we shall be concerned only with the first eight links, and particularly with the first and second and with the seventh and eighth.[345]

The first and second links leading up and away from the cyclical mode of action and reaction are *duḥkha*, suffering or unsatisfactoriness, and *śraddhā*, faith or confidence. In the twelve links of the wheel of life, suffering corresponds to feeling, the last link in the effect process of the present life, and faith corresponds to craving, the first link in the cause process of the present life. What this means is that when sensations and experiences impinge upon us we do not have to react with craving and thus perpetuate the cyclical movement of existence. We can react instead in a positive way. As we experience pleasant, unpleasant, and neutral feelings, we can begin to see, to feel, that none of them are really very satisfactory, not even the pleasant ones. Even they are not enough. Even if we could perpetuate pleasant experiences and eliminate painful ones, there would still be some hidden lack, something unsatisfied and frustrated. So we begin to see, we begin to feel, we begin to realize, that this whole conditioned existence – our life, our ordinary experience – is not enough. It cannot give us permanent, true satisfaction or happiness. If we analyse it deeply, in the long run it is unsatisfactory.

As we start to see that this is so, we begin to sit loose to mundane existence. We begin to detach ourselves from it. We don't care about it so much. We start thinking that there must be something higher, something beyond, something which can give satisfaction of a more permanent, deeper, and truer nature – in a word, something spiritual, even something transcendental. So we begin to shift the focus of our interest, and eventually we develop faith. We 'place the heart' less and less on our everyday experience, and more and more on the Unconditioned, the Transcendental. At first our faith may be confused, vague, and inchoate, but gradually it clears, it settles down, it strengthens, and eventually it becomes faith or confidence in the Three Jewels. We begin to see the Buddha, the Dharma, and the Sangha as the embodiments of those higher spiritual values which both stand above and beyond the world yet at the same time give meaning and significance to the world. We place our heart more and more on them, and when that faith waxes strong enough we are galvanized into action and we go for Refuge.

In this way, faith is the positive, spiritual counterpart of craving. Instead of craving arising in dependence upon feeling, we find that faith in the Unconditioned (as represented by the Three Jewels) arises in dependence upon the experience of the unsatisfactoriness of conditioned existence. At this juncture we have left the wheel and entered the spiral; we have begun to move not in a cyclical order, but in a progressive, spiral order. We have, in fact, entered upon the path leading to Nirvāṇa. This transition from the wheel to the spiral is a moment of conversion. In fact, although it is expressed in different terms, it corresponds to conversion in the sense of Going for Refuge, and there is the same sense of movement – away from the endless round of conditioned existence, towards the infinite spiral of the Transcendental. The transition from the wheel to the spiral still leaves us a long way short of Stream Entry, but we could say – mixing our metaphors – that at this stage we begin to enter the tributary which leads, by way of the next six positive progressive links of the spiral, to the Stream.

In dependence upon faith there arises *prāmodya*, usually translated as satisfaction or delight. This is the feeling which arises when you see that you have no cause for self-reproach because you have not done anything, so far as you can recollect, which makes you feel guilty. You have a perfectly clear conscience. In Buddhism, great importance is attached to this state. If you have anything on your mind that you regret or are ashamed of, anything unatoned for, anything you have not come to terms with, it is difficult, if not impossible, to make any further progress, certainly not progress in meditation. Buddhists therefore carry out various practices of confession of faults and self-purification which eliminate remorse or guilt and replace it with this state of satisfaction and delight, this state in which you are on good terms with yourself.[346]

It is important, of course, to distinguish clearly between genuine remorse for unskilful actions of body, speech, and mind, and the irrational sense of guilt which dogs so many people, often because it has been instilled into them from early childhood, whether through the pervasive Christian doctrine of original sin or by some other means. In Buddhism, confession of faults is a straightforward acknowledgement of whatever one has done out of craving, hatred, or delusion. To be able to confess in this way requires not an abject submission to some external power but an awareness that one is responsible for one's own actions and a confidence that one is capable of developing skilful mental states. As the terms skilful and unskilful indicate, in the Buddhist way of looking at things there is no question of irredeemable evil.

On the basis of this mental state of delight there arises *prīti*, which is usually translated as interest, enthusiasm, rapture, or even ecstasy. It represents an upsurge of joy from your very depths as a consequence of the liberation of all the emotional energies which have previously been blocked up, in the form of various mental conflicts, in the subconscious or even unconscious mind. Something lifts from your mind, freed energy comes bubbling up from within, and you feel much lighter. When all these submerged emotional energies are released, there is an experience not only of release but also of intense joy, enthusiasm, and rapture. It is psychophysical – an experience of the body as well as of the mind – so that your hair may stand on end and you may shed tears.

In dependence upon this experience of rapture, which can reach a very great degree of intensity, there arises *praśrabdhi* – repose or tranquillity. This represents the calming, the dying away, of the purely bodily manifestations of *prīti*. And once *prīti* has died away, what is left is a state of happiness, *sukha*, in which there is no sense consciousness. *Sukha*, which arises in dependence upon *praśrabdhi*, is a purely mental – or rather spiritual – feeling of bliss; this pervades the entire being with a concentrating and integrating effect which harmonizes it and makes it whole. Then, in dependence on this experience of bliss, there arises a state called *samādhi*. The usual translation is 'concentration', but this is clearly far from adequate. *Samādhi* is really an experience of perfect wholeness at a very high level of awareness.

At this point – and we have come quite a long way – we need to acknowledge two important facts. In the first place, *samādhi* is not something which can be acquired forcibly or artificially by means of exercises or techniques. They may be of incidental help, but fundamentally *samādhi* represents a spiritual growth or evolution of the whole being. It is not enough just to concentrate your mind on an object for half an hour at a time if the rest of your life is pulling in the opposite direction. If ninety-nine per cent of your life is oriented in the direction of the mundane, it is no use just spending half an hour a day trying to orient it in a spiritual direction. That would be like taking an elastic band and pulling it taut – as soon as you release it, it snaps back. Unfortunately, this is how meditation is most commonly practised. Meditation proper, however, represents the spearhead of a basic reorientation of one's whole being. Mere forcible fixation of the mind for a period of time on a certain point or object is certainly not true meditation in the sense of the total growth or spiritual evolution of the whole being.

The second fact is that it is possible for us to fall back from these first seven stages on the spiral. Although they are part of the spiral, although they do not constitute a cyclical reaction, although they are part of the path to Nirvāṇa, regression from them is possible. Even when you have gone up to *samādhi*, you can descend into bliss. From that you can lapse into tranquillity, from that into rapture, from that down into faith – and in that way you re-enter the wheel. And this, of course, is what usually happens. Even if we really succeed in getting up the spiral so far, up all those seven stages, it is only for a while. Even if it is a real experience, a real development – even if we are not just pulling the elastic – the experience is only temporary and we still fall back. We can balance ourselves at that level for a few minutes, but then we sink down and down until we are once again going round the wheel. This happens because this section of the spiral, these seven stages from the experience of unsatisfactoriness up to *samādhi*, are still subject to what we could call the 'gravitational pull' of the round of existence, the wheel of life.

So what is the point of it all? Is there any more sense in the spiritual life than in the endless chore given to Sisyphus in Hades, of pushing a great stone up a mountainside just so that it can roll all the way down again?[347] Or can we get so far up the spiral that there is no possibility of regression? Is it possible to reach a vantage point from which there is no falling back to the wheel, or are we bound to go up and down like a yo-yo for all eternity?

The eighth positive *nidāna* provides the way out of this dismal predicament. In dependence upon *samādhi* arises *yathābhūta-jñānadarśana* – 'knowledge and vision of things as they really are'. In other words, in dependence upon the pure, concentrated, integrated, totally balanced mundane mind, at the highest pitch of its development, there arises transcendental wisdom. So how does this come about? What is really involved in this development?

Knowledge and vision of things as they really are arises when, in the state of *samādhi*, we get our first glimpse of reality itself, free from all veils and obscurations. It's like the moment when you get up to the top of a high mountain and the clouds roll aside to reveal the vast expanse of the horizon. *Samādhi* represents getting to the peak, the vantage point from which you can see reality itself.

But how, in practice, do we glimpse reality? Does it just arise spontaneously, or can we consciously work towards the experience? Well, the answer is that both are possible. For some people, Insight does come quite spontaneously. We don't know why a vision of reality is just 'given' to some people – perhaps the reasons are hidden within the depths of their past lives. But one need not wait around for the experience to arise spontaneously. It can be developed on the basis of *samādhi* or, to put it more accurately, the conditions for the possibility of its arising can be created. It is not that you do this, that, and the other, and then you get knowledge and vision of things as they are, like getting a bar of chocolate out of a slot machine. The arising of Insight is not within the sphere of causality at all. We are dealing, after all, with the Unconditioned.

According to the Buddhist tradition, we can induce this experience (without of course implying anything artificial or even causative by such an expression) through the contemplation, in a state of *samādhi*, of the three marks or characteristics (*lakṣaṇas* in Sanskrit) of all conditioned things. These characteristics are that conditioned things are unsatisfactory, impermanent, and, in the depths of their being, devoid of self – devoid, that is, of any separate, unchanging individuality which might mark them off from all other things.

Another way of approaching this experience is to contemplate the idea of Nirvāṇa. I say *idea* because we have not yet got Nirvāṇa itself into view; but in the state of *samādhi* we can bring to mind the idea of Nirvāṇa, in whatever way appeals to us. As we are doing this, a flash of Insight may illuminate what Nirvāṇa *really* is, and at that instant we enter upon the transcendental Path of Vision, the *darśana mārga*; or, to bring in another of the metaphors which describe this moment, we enter the Stream.

Another way to put it, of course, is the one mentioned at the beginning of the chapter. At this point one's personal centre of gravity has permanently shifted from the conditioned to the Unconditioned, so that from now onwards one is not just oriented in the direction of Nirvāṇa, but actually moving irrevocably towards it. From this point on progress is assured, because one has reached that part of the spiral which is not subject to any gravitational pull from the mundane, from the wheel of life.

To develop the metaphor of gravity a little, we may say that one's progress is rather like that of a space probe launched from the Earth. After a certain distance – so many thousand miles – it is no longer so affected by the Earth's field of gravity and begins to be influenced instead by the gravitational pull of the Moon, Mars, or whichever body it is heading for. So at a certain point the gravitational pull of the wheel of life ceases to have an influence, and one begins to feel more and more powerfully and decisively the gravitational pull of the unconditioned, of Nirvāṇa. This is the moment of conversion *within* Buddhist practice, the beginning of the transformation from a conditioned to an unconditioned mode of being. According to Buddhist tradition, if we reach up this far, if we undergo conversion in this sense, we are assured of Enlightenment within no more than seven further rebirths in the wheel of conditioned existence.[348]

All this is to look at the experience subjectively – from within, as it were. It can be described more objectively as consisting in the bursting asunder of three fetters. This is, of course, to bring in another metaphor – and again it is a traditional one. The Pāli canon enumerates ten fetters that bind us to the wheel of life.[349] When all ten have been broken, Enlightenment is attained; the Stream Entrant is said to have broken the first three of them. The first of these three fetters is *satkāya-dṛṣṭi*, usually translated as 'self-view' (*satkāya* means 'personal' or 'individual', and *dṛṣṭi* means 'view' or 'doctrine'). *Satkāya-dṛṣṭi* is the view that 'I' constitute something ultimate; that I, as I know myself here and now, with this particular body and mind, this particular history, represent a sort of unchanging, fixed entity. In other words it is the belief that 'I' am real.

This 'fixed self-view' is the biggest mistake of all, according to Buddhism, and it is the first fetter to be broken; you cannot enter the Stream unless you overcome it. Indeed, *you* do not enter the Stream at all. The whole point is that you cannot enter the Stream until you have detached yourself from name and form, from personal existence, from all the things that you think of as being 'you' – in short, until you have realized that you are not ultimately real. This is not to say, of course, that there is no such thing as the 'self', though this is how the Buddhist doctrine of *anātman* (literally 'no-self') is often misunderstood. The point is that we do not have an *unchanging* self. There is nothing fixed, 'underneath it all', about us; every single aspect of our being is subject to change. We have an empirical reality, it could be said, but not an ultimate reality. So this fixed self-view is a tremendous fetter, and one which is not easily broken.

The second fetter is *vicikitsā*, which is usually translated as 'doubt', although it is not really so much doubt as doubtfulness. It is a sort of wavering or hesitation. You hear about the Buddha, you listen to his teachings, you meet people who are trying to put those teachings into practice, but you hesitate. You say, 'Yes, well, it sounds good, but…', 'I'd like to give it a try, but…', 'I have nothing against it, but…'. That 'but' which is always coming in indicates that you are bound by the fetter of doubt. You don't quite believe, but you don't quite disbelieve either; you are wavering and hesitating between the two, which is a horrible state to be in. Unfortunately it is also a very common state. So many people go along to Buddhist groups and hear a few lectures, or read a few books, but never actually do anything about it. *Vicikitsā* is this kind of refusal to commit oneself unreservedly to the spiritual life; you hear about it, talk about it, but you keep holding back. How can you become a Stream Entrant if you persist in dithering on the bank? If you want to swim, it is no use hesitating on the edge wondering how warm or cold or deep the water is – you just have to jump in. *Vicikitsā* is that fear of jumping in, that refusal to commit oneself, that viewing from a distance without participating.

The third fetter is *śīlavrata-parāmarśa*. This always used to be translated as 'dependence upon rites and ceremonies', a translation which has given rise to a great deal of misunderstanding. *Śīla* means a moral observance or precept, *vrata* means a religious practice or observance (an example given in the scriptures is the Brahminical practice of tending the sacred fire),[350] and *parāmarśa* means attachment or clinging. This fetter therefore represents dependence upon moral rules and religious practices *as ends in themselves*. This does not mean that practices such as observing the precepts and engaging in religious ceremonies are a fetter *in themselves*; such practices are of course very beneficial. It only means that if we cling on to these practices, forgetting that they are only means to an end, they will become a fetter that holds us back and prevents us from entering the Stream.

Precepts and practices become fetters when you carry them out almost as if you were hypnotized, without thinking, 'What does this mean?' 'Where is this getting me?' 'Is this actually doing any good?' So this fetter is really – roughly speaking – about conventional morals and religion. Conventional attachment to morality and religion, though not bad in a way, doesn't get you very far along the spiritual path, and it can even prevent you from entering the Stream. You can meet people who seem very ethical and noble, who observe all the precepts, but who are a bit obsessed with their own virtue, a bit 'holier than thou'. They make a whip of their own virtue – as the saying goes – with which to beat other people. It is not that we should discard such things as precepts and devotional practices; that would be to go to the opposite extreme, which would be even more damaging. We need to make full and exhaustive use of them, but always remembering that they serve a purpose that lies beyond them.

As long as these three fetters – belief in one's 'self' as ultimately real, refusal to commit oneself unreservedly to the spiritual life, and dependence on moral rules and religious practices as ends in themselves – remain unbroken, no Stream Entry is possible. No escape from the gravitational pull of the conditioned is possible. One is bound to fall back down the spiral and continue circling round the wheel of life. In other words, only with the breaking of these fetters is real conversion within Buddhism possible – conversion, that is, in the sense of a permanent transition from the conditioned to the unconditioned mode of awareness and being.[351]

4
THE ARISING OF THE *BODHICITTA*

Having looked at conversion *to* Buddhism, and conversion *within* Buddhism, one might think that it is hardly possible to go any further, and in a sense – though only in a sense – this is true. But conversion in Buddhism not only has different levels; it can also be approached from different aspects and points of view. This brings us to conversion understood in terms of what is known in Mahāyāna Buddhism as the *bodhicitta utpāda* (*bodhicittotpāda*).

We can provisionally render this term *bodhicitta utpāda* as 'the arising (*utpāda*) of the will (*citta*) to Enlightenment (*bodhi*)', but the term *bodhi* in particular needs a little more elucidation. It derives from a Sanskrit root meaning 'to know' or 'to understand', so it comes to mean 'understanding', 'wisdom', or even 'Enlightenment'. Traditional Buddhism distinguishes three kinds of bodhi: *śrāvaka-bodhi*, 'Enlightenment of the disciple'; *pratyeka-bodhi*, 'private' or 'individual' Enlightenment; and *anuttara-samyak-sambodhi*, 'unsurpassed, perfect Enlightenment'.[352] Until we have grasped what is meant by these three kinds of Enlightenment, there is much in the development of the history of Buddhist thought, especially in India, which we are not really in a position to understand.

Śrāvaka literally means 'one who hears'; it is the Indian word for a disciple. However, a disciple not only hears with the ear, but also hears within; that is, he or she is receptive to the word of the teacher. *Śrāvakabodhi*, the Enlightenment of the disciple or hearer, therefore means the illumination which is gained not only by one's own effort but also on the basis of having been taught the method and discipline by someone else. Having been shown the path, one makes an effort and gains Enlightenment. However, one makes no attempt to communicate that experience to anyone else; one has a teacher but no disciples.

Pratyeka-bodhi differs from *śrāvaka-bodhi* in that it is gained without the benefit of a teacher's instruction; one discovers the path for oneself. This is, of course, very difficult to achieve, and it is therefore very rare. And having attained Enlightenment in this way, one makes no attempt to communicate one's knowledge and experience to anyone else: hence 'private' or 'individual' Enlightenment.

Thirdly, there is *anuttara-samyak-sambodhi*: unsurpassed, perfect Enlightenment. This too is gained without a teacher, but having been gained it is not kept to oneself but communicated to other beings so that they may have the opportunity of sharing the experience of Enlightenment. Gaining Enlightenment 'without a teacher' is to be understood in quite a narrow sense, of course, because it refers only to the present existence. Having been shown the way by others in previous lives, one has accumulated sufficient momentum to be carried through the present existence without a teacher, and to make the ultimate discovery by oneself.

At this stage a very important question arises, a question with far-reaching implications. What is the real, basic difference between these three kinds of *bodhi*? Are we concerned here with three different types of spiritual experience, or is it one and the same Enlightenment in each case? Is the difference between these three kinds of *bodhi* essential or merely accidental? When we first come across them, we might naturally conclude that the difference is circumstantial, or even adventitious, but in fact it is much more fundamental than that. Provisionally, the three *bodhis* may be said to represent three grades of Enlightenment within a hierarchical structure, the third of which is the highest, the consummation as it were, of the whole series.

If we want to identify the single essential distinction between these 'grades', we can simplify things by amalgamating the first and second of them and setting them apart from the third, *anuttara-samyak-sambodhi*. The basic difference between these two categories obviously lies in the relation of the Enlightened being to other, unenlightened, people. The first group, whether they gain Enlightenment with or without a teacher, do not communicate their experience, whereas the second group do. This difference between the two is neither accidental nor merely external, because the communication, the 'giving away', of spiritual experience is not at all the same as the giving of material things. If we happen to acquire a precious stone, the jewel itself remains the same whether we keep it or give it away. But with spiritual experiences it is not like that in the least, because something far more subtle, delicate, and complex is involved. A spiritual experience which can be kept to oneself, we can say, is not the same as one which is communicated – which indeed *has* to be communicated, in the sense that the very nature of the experience *demands* that it should be communicated.

The fundamental difference between these two kinds of spiritual experience lies in whether or not the experience includes a feeling of selfhood. The feeling of selfhood has various forms, some gross and easily detected, others infinitely subtle and extremely difficult to detect. The subtlest of all the forms of this feeling is the form which arises in connection with the gaining of Enlightenment itself. We have a certain experience which we take as tending in the direction of Enlightenment, but then we attach to that experience a feeling that this is *my* experience, *my* Enlightenment, this is what *I* have gained. It is because this subtle feeling of selfhood arises that we may consider it possible not to communicate our experience to others. From the mundane point of view it may be a very high and sublime experience, but it is not the experience of unsurpassed, perfect Enlightenment; it is not the Enlightenment of the Buddha himself. So long as that feeling of 'my' can be attached to it, it is not the ultimate experience.

When we speak of conversion in Buddhism in terms of the arising of the *bodhicitta* – the will to Enlightenment – it is the second of these two kinds of Enlightenment which is meant: the unsurpassed, perfect Enlightenment, Enlightenment for the benefit of all sentient beings. So the will to Enlightenment is the aspiration to that Enlightenment wherein there is not a shadow of selfhood and which, paradoxically, cannot therefore be called 'mine'. There is no question of keeping it to oneself; by definition, it *has* to be communicated.

Having arrived at a sense of the meaning of *bodhi*, we need to find out a bit more about *citta*. *Citta* is usually translated as 'thought', and therefore *bodhicitta* is often translated as 'the Thought of Enlightenment' as though it were a concept or idea about Enlightenment.

But this is exactly what it is not. It has nothing to do with thought in that discursive or abstract conceptual sense at all. *Citta* represents an immensely powerful drive, a drive which is not unconscious but perfectly aware, a drive which has one's whole being behind it. It is better, therefore, to speak not of the Thought of Enlightenment but of the *will to* Enlightenment, although even this is not quite accurate because this 'will' is infinitely more powerful than determination in the ordinary sense.

Finally, *utpāda* literally means 'arising': hence our working translation of *bodhicittotpāda* as 'the arising of the will to Enlightenment'. The arising of the *bodhicitta* is the initial process of orienting all one's energies and all one's strength, at all levels of one's being and personality, in the direction of Enlightenment understood as unsurpassed, perfect Enlightenment, Enlightenment for the benefit and welfare of all sentient beings.

Having worked out an appropriate translation, we can now turn to consider what light the arising of the will to Enlightenment sheds on the meaning of conversion in Buddhism. It can be said to represent conversion from an individualistic conception of Enlightenment to a non-individualistic ideal of Enlightenment, from the kind of Enlightenment which can be kept to oneself to the kind of Enlightenment which cannot possibly be kept to oneself. In other words, it represents a transition, a breakthrough, from that last most subtle sense of spiritual selfhood to an experience of complete and total selflessness.

Obviously this aspect of conversion is very important indeed, but it is not so easy to put your finger on it and say 'It is like this' or 'It occurs at a certain point' in the way that you can with Going for Refuge and Stream Entry. One might even say that this type of conversion can occur at any stage of spiritual development, or in connection with any spiritual experience. This is why in Mahāyāna Buddhism there is the practice of 'turning over' – that is to say, turning over one's merits to the cause of perfect Enlightenment. Although it is often neglected, this is one of the most important teachings in the whole of Buddhism. In the Perfection of Wisdom scriptures the bodhisattva (the Mahāyāna's idea of the Buddhist *par excellence*) is advised. 'Whenever you perform any good action, whenever you practise morality, or meditate, or help anybody, or give anything, turn over the merit – dedicate it to the cause of perfect Enlightenment.'[353] In other words, don't think, 'This skilful action is going to help *me* attain liberation.' Instead, reflect or resolve: 'Whatever merit derives from my good deeds, I dedicate it to Enlightenment not just for my own benefit but for the benefit of all.' By practising regularly and systematically in this way, we ensure that in the course of our spiritual lives we do not build up a subtle spiritual selfhood which would eventually rise up and bar our way to the ultimate spiritual attainment, unsurpassed perfect Enlightenment.

The bodhisattva is further told that this transference of merit in the direction of Enlightenment for the benefit of all beings is possible only on the basis of some insight into the doctrine of *śūnyāta* (which is often translated 'voidness' but really means 'non-dual reality'), according to which there is no substantial distinction between self and other. However, this practice of turning over the merits accruing from good deeds should accompany us all along the spiritual path; we need not – cannot – leave it until Insight arises. On the other hand, it is not something you do once and for all – nor is it the case that if you did it last week you can forget about it until next year. It is something you have to do all the time, as a constant accompaniment to every practice, throughout your spiritual life.

Actually, this is not the only way to guard against spiritual individualism. You can, if you so wish – and some people do so wish – pursue spiritual individualism to its limits. You can think grimly in terms of '*my* Enlightenment', disregarding everything else, and get quite a long way. Then, when you have attained your own 'individual Enlightenment' and are, as it were, resting on it, as if upon a celestial pinnacle, you can lift up your eyes to the even loftier peak of unsurpassed, perfect Enlightenment. This can be done, but there is a danger that you may get stuck, perhaps stuck indefinitely, in spiritual individualism. Even at this very high level you can end up in a sort of spiritual cul-de-sac.

It is better, therefore, if conversion in the sense of the arising of the *bodhicitta* occurs early on in one's spiritual life in the form of a decisive experience. It is not enough just to practise transference of merits with regard to one's everyday spiritual life and practice. One aims to precipitate the arising of the will to Enlightenment right from the start of one's spiritual career, without settling down, even for a short period, in the path of spiritual individualism. The question is, as usual, how to do it. To understand this, we need to look at the conditions on the basis of which the *bodhicitta* arises.

The will to Enlightenment is said to arise as a result of the coalescence of two trends of experience which are generally considered to be contradictory, since in ordinary experience they cannot both be pursued simultaneously. We might call these the trend of withdrawal from the world and the trend of involvement in the world.

The first of these trends represents renunciation in the extreme sense, a withdrawal from worldly activities, worldly thoughts, and secular associations. This withdrawal is aided by a particular practice, that of reflection on the faults or imperfections of conditioned existence. You reflect that life in this world, whirling round and round in the wheel of life, is profoundly unsatisfactory, involving as it does all sorts of disagreeable experiences. You experience physical pain and discomfort, you don't get what you want, you're separated from people you like, you have to do things you don't want to do. There's the whole wretched business of having to earn a living, doing your daily chores, taking care of your body – feeding it, clothing it, housing it, looking after it when it gets sick – not to mention taking responsibility for looking after your dependants. It all seems too much. All you want to do is get away from it all, away from the fluctuations, vicissitudes, and distractions of mundane life into the peace of the perfection of the Unconditioned, the unchanging rest of Nirvāṇa.

The second trend in our experience – involvement – represents concern for living beings. You reflect, 'Well, it would be all right for me to opt out and withdraw from it all – I'd like that – but what about other people? What will happen to *them*? There are people who have a much harder time in this world than I do, who can stand it even less than I can. How will they ever get free if I abandon them?' This trend of involvement is aided by the practice of reflection on the sufferings of sentient beings. In the trend of withdrawal, you reflect on the sufferings and imperfections of conditioned existence only in so far as they affect you, but here you reflect on them as they affect other living beings. You just look around at all the people you know, your friends and acquaintances, all the people you meet, and you reflect on all their troubles and difficulties. Perhaps one or two have lost their jobs, another's marriage has broken up, yet another may have had a nervous breakdown, and there may well be someone who has recently been bereaved. If you think it over, there is not a single person you know who is not suffering in some way. Even if they seem comparatively happy in the ordinary sense, there are still things that they have to bear: separation or illness, the weakness and tiredness of old age, and finally death, which they almost certainly don't want.

Then, when you cast your gaze further afield, there is so much suffering in so many parts of the world: wars, catastrophes of various kinds, floods and famines, people dying in horrible ways. You can even think of animals and how they suffer, not only at the teeth and claws of other animals but at the hands of human beings. The whole world of living beings is involved in suffering. And when you reflect on this, you ask yourself, 'How can I possibly think simply in terms of getting out of it all on my own? How can I possibly think of getting away by myself to some private Nirvāṇa, some private spiritual experience, which may be very satisfactory to me but is of no help to others?'

So there is a conflict, if you are big enough and rich enough in your nature to embrace the possibilities of such a conflict. On one hand you want to get out; on the other you want to stay here. Of course, the easy solution is simply to choose between them. There are some people who withdraw into spiritual individualism, private spiritual experience, while others remain in the world without much of a spiritual outlook at all. But although these trends are contradictory, both of them must be developed in the course of the spiritual life. The trend of withdrawal may be said to embody the wisdom aspect of the spiritual life, while the trend of involvement embodies the compassion aspect.

These two practices – reflecting on the faults of conditioned existence and reflecting on the sufferings of sentient beings – form part of a traditional method of creating the conditions in dependence upon which the *bodhicitta* can arise. This is the method taught by a great Indian master of the Mahāyāna, Vasubandhu, who lived, so the Mahāyāna tradition says, in the latter half of the fifth century CE. Vasubandhu enumerated four practices which would provide a basis for the arising of the *bodhicitta*; they are known as Vasubandhu's four factors.[354] We have already identified two of these factors. The other two are 'the recollection of the Buddhas' and 'the contemplation of the virtues of the Tathāgatas' (Tathāgata being another word for Buddha).

In recollecting the Buddhas, one brings to mind the historical Buddha Śākyamuni, who lived in India about 2,500 years ago, and the lineage of his great predecessors of which the Buddhist tradition speaks. In particular, one reflects that these Buddhas started their spiritual careers as human beings, with their weaknesses and limitations, just as we do. Just as they managed to transcend all limitations to become Enlightened, so can we, if only we make the effort.

There are several ways of approaching the fourth practice, the contemplation of the virtues of the Tathāgatas. One can dwell on the life of an Enlightened One – the spiritual biography of the Buddha or Milarepa, for example. One can perform pujas in front of a shrine, or perhaps just sit and look at a Buddha image, really trying to get a feeling for what the image represents. Then again, one can do a visualization practice in which – to be very brief indeed – one conjures up a vivid mental picture of a particular Buddha or bodhisattva, an embodiment of an aspect of Enlightenment such as wisdom, compassion, energy, or purity.

We can think of these four factors as forming a kind of sequence. First, through recollecting the Buddhas, we become convinced that Enlightenment is possible for us. Then, on seeing the faults of conditioned existence, we become detached from it, and the trend of our being is set in the direction of the Unconditioned. Thirdly, through observing the suffering of sentient beings – whether in imagination or close at hand – compassion arises, and we want to rescue not only ourselves but other beings from suffering. Then, as we contemplate the virtues of the Tathāgatas, we gradually become assimilated to them, and approach Enlightenment itself.

However, although we can think of the four factors sequentially in this way, the *bodhicitta* in fact arises in dependence on all four simultaneously. This means – returning to the tension between withdrawal and involvement – that we must not allow the tension between these two trends to relax. If we do that, we are lost. Even though they are contradictory, we have to follow both trends simultaneously, seeing the faults of conditioned existence and at the same time feeling the sufferings of sentient beings, developing both wisdom and compassion. As we develop and pursue both of these, the tension – and this tension is not psychological but spiritual – builds up and up until we simply can't go any further.

At that point, something happens. It is very difficult to describe exactly what does happen, but we can think of it provisionally as an explosion. The tension which has been generated through following simultaneously these two contradictory trends results in a breakthrough into a higher dimension of spiritual consciousness. Withdrawal and involvement are no longer two separate trends, not because they have been artificially amalgamated into one, but because the plane or level on which their duality existed, or on which it was possible for them to be two things, has been transcended. When that explosion occurs, one has the experience of being simultaneously withdrawn and involved, simultaneously out of the world and in the world. Wisdom and compassion become non-dual, not separate, not-two – without, at the same time, being simply numerically one. When this breakthrough occurs, when for the first time one is both withdrawn and involved, when wisdom and compassion are not two things side by side but one thing, then the *bodhicitta* has arisen. There has occurred a conversion from spiritual individualism to a life of complete selflessness – or at least such a life has been initiated.

According to the Mahāyāna, when that happens one gives expression to the experience which one has gained, to the new dimension of spiritual consciousness into which one has broken through, by taking four great vows, the vows of the bodhisattva:

> However innumerable beings are,
> I vow to save them;
> However inexhaustible the passions are,
> I vow to extinguish them;
> However immeasurable the Dharmas are,
> I vow to master them;
> However incomparable the Buddha-truth is,
> I vow to attain it.

So the bodhisattva vows in the first place to deliver all beings from difficulties, both spiritual and mundane. The second vow is to destroy all spiritual defilements within one's own mind, and – through one's advice – in the minds of other living beings. The third vow is to learn the Dharma, to practise and realize it in all its aspects, and to communicate it to others. And the fourth and final vow is that in all possible ways one will help to lead all beings in the direction of Buddhahood, that is, towards unsurpassed perfect Enlightenment. When these four vows of the bodhisattva are made, then one's conversion, in the sense of the arising of the will to Enlightenment, is complete.[355]

5
THE TURNING ABOUT IN THE DEEPEST SEAT OF CONSCIOUSNESS

So far we have certainly thought of conversion in Buddhism in very radical terms. It is not enough to convert *to* Buddhism; we need to experience conversion within the context of our Buddhist practice, at ever deeper levels. It is not enough to think in terms of our own spiritual development; we need to think in terms of the spiritual welfare of all living beings. And we can think of conversion in more radical terms still. We can think of it in terms of a shift in the very nature of our experience of the world.

The ordinary experience which we have almost all the time is firmly and securely based on subject–object dualism. All our knowledge, all our thinking, takes place within the framework of this dualism – subject and object, me and you, 'me in here' and 'the world out there'. But the Enlightened mind is completely free of such dualism. It's an experience of just One Mind – *citta-mātra*, 'mind only' to use the terminology of the Yogācāra, one of the two main schools of Mahāyāna Buddhism in medieval India. The experience of the one mind is like a great expanse of water, absolutely pure, absolutely transparent, with nothing in it, not a single speck, other than the water itself.

Between the experience of One Mind and our ordinary, everyday consciousness, based as it is on subject–object dualism, there is obviously a great gulf. To go from one to the other requires a tremendous change, a complete and absolute reversal of all our usual attitudes. The Yogācāra insists on this very strongly. The spiritual life doesn't consist in a little chipping away here, a little chipping away there, a slight improvement here, a slight improvement there. It involves a complete turning about, even a complete turning upside-down. Before we can make the leap from ordinary mind, empirical mind, to the One Mind, all our established values and attitudes and ways of looking at things have to be turned topsy-turvy.

This reversal, this great change, this great death and rebirth, is what the Yogācāra terms the *parāvṛtti*, and this technical term gives us an entirely different angle on the meaning of conversion in Buddhism from those we have so far examined. Some scholars translate *parāvṛtti* as 'revulsion', but this is not really satisfactory because it implies a psychological process rather than a spiritual and metaphysical one. It is much better to use the literal translation of *parāvṛtti* – 'turning about'.

The *parāvṛtti*, the turning about, is synonymous with conversion in the very deepest and most radical sense of the term. It is the central theme of the *Laṅkāvatāra Sūtra*,[356] and indeed we may say that it is the central theme, the central concern, of the spiritual life itself. If the spiritual life doesn't turn you upside-down, if you don't feel as though you're hanging head downwards in a void, then it isn't the spiritual life. If you feel all safe and secure and firm and nicely going ahead, step by step, you haven't yet begun to live the spiritual life in earnest.

Before going into the nature of this turning about, let's have a brief look at its scriptural source, the *Laṅkāvatāra Sūtra*. In Nepal, continuing an originally Indian tradition, they have a list of ten canonical scriptures which they regard as constituting the fundamental Mahāyāna canon, and the *Laṅkāvatāra* is one of them, so we can say that it is one of the ten most important *sūtras* in the Mahāyāna tradition. In fact, it was not only the Nepalis who had a high regard for this particular *sūtra*. It was a seminal work for the Yogācāra, and it was also central to the development of Chan (or Zen), having been taken from India to China (so it is said) by Bodhidharma, the founder of Chan Buddhism. According to the legends, Bodhidharma went wafting over the ocean from India to China on a reed, and didn't take anything with him but his robe, his bowl, – and a palm-leaf copy of the *Laṅkāvatāra Sūtra*. It was no doubt by reason of its tremendous emphasis on personal experience and inner realization that the *sūtra* exerted such a strong influence on Zen. Indeed, whole schools of Buddhism have devoted themselves to the study of just this one text;

it is certainly one of the most exhaustive and profound *sūtras* in the Buddhist canon.

The full title of the work is the *Saddharma-laṅkāvatāra Sūtra*. *Sūtra* means a discourse of the Buddha, *saddharma* means 'the good law', or 'the real truth', and *laṅkāvatāra* means 'entry into Lanka', so we can render the whole title as 'The Buddha's discourse on the entry of the real truth into Lanka'. Lanka is a city or castle situated on a mountain-top in the ocean somewhere off the Indian coast. In Indian literature, of course, Lanka usually stands for what we call Sri Lanka, but here no such specific identification can be inferred; in this *sūtra* we are in the realm of myth rather than geography.

The *sūtra* is a fairly lengthy work of nine chapters, the English translation by D. T. Suzuki running to about 300 pages. It contains a large number of extremely profound and valuable teachings, though in a rather scattered form, the text being an anthology of extracts or excerpts in no systematic order. But of the immense number of topics with which the *sūtra* deals, we are here concerned with only one: the *parāvṛtti*, the turning about.

The first chapter of the *Laṅkāvatāra* is called 'The Invitation of Rāvaṇa', Rāvaṇa being the king of the Rākṣasas, the beings who inhabit the island of Lanka. In Buddhist texts Rāvaṇa appears as a wise sage, a great disciple of the Buddha, but it is interesting to note that in Hindu texts such as the *Rāmāyaṇa* he is the villain of the piece; this only goes to show that there is always more than one way of looking at not only a particular religious doctrine but even a particular individual. According to the introduction to the *sūtra*, Rāvaṇa invites the Buddha to preach (a conventional Buddhist procedure – one is generally invited to preach rather than taking the initiative oneself). In response the Buddha delivers a succinct and profound discourse, as a result of which Rāvaṇa experiences the *parāvṛtti*.

It seems to him that the whole universe vanishes and all that is left is an expanse of absolute consciousness, or absolute mind, within which there is no differentiation of subject and object. Furthermore, he hears a voice proclaiming that this is the state which has to be realized. It is this experience, this change in Rāvaṇa's consciousness from awareness of the ordinary external universe in all its discreteness and diversity to awareness of absolute mind, free from all distinction between universe and void, which constitutes what is called the *parāvṛtti*.

To understand how this process of turning about happens, we need to refer to a rather technical but absolutely fundamental aspect of the Yogācāra teaching called the system of the eight *vijñānas*.[357] *Vijñāna* is usually translated as 'consciousness', but that is not exactly accurate. The prefix *vi-* means 'to divide' or 'to discriminate', and *jñāna* means 'knowledge' or 'awareness', so we can translate *vijñāna* as 'discriminating awareness'. *Vijñāna* therefore refers to awareness of an object not just in a pure mirror-like way but in a way which discriminates the object as being of a particular type and belonging to a particular class, species, or whatever. In the Yogācāra teaching there are eight of these *vijñānas*, eight forms of discriminating awareness or consciousness. The first five are the five 'sense *vijñānas*', the modes of discriminating awareness which operate through the five senses – through the eye with respect to form, the ear with respect to sound, and so on.

The sixth consciousness is called the *mano-vijñāna*. *Mano* means simply 'mind', so this is discriminating awareness functioning through mind. Mind, by the way, is usually classified in Buddhism as a sort of sixth sense, so it doesn't have a special, elevated position above the five sense consciousnesses. According to Yogācāra psychology, there are two aspects of *mano-vijñāna*. The first of these is awareness of what we might describe as 'ideas of sense' – in other words, the mind's awareness of impressions presented to it by the five senses. And the second aspect is awareness of ideas which arise independently of sense-perception, out of the mind itself. This latter aspect of *mano-vijñāna* is of three kinds. First of all, there are the ideas and impressions which arise in the course of meditation, as when one experiences light which doesn't have its origin in any sense impression but comes from the mind itself. Then secondly there are functions such as imagination, comparison, and reflection. And thirdly there are the images perceived in dreams, which again come not from sense impressions but directly from the mind itself. All this is the *mano-vijñāna*.

Seventhly, there is the *kliṣṭa-mano-vijñāna*. *Kliṣṭa* means 'afflicted', or 'suffering', and it also means 'defiled', because defilement is a source of suffering. This mode of awareness, therefore, is afflicted or defiled by a dualistic outlook. Whatever it experiences, it interprets dualistically in terms of a subject and an object – subject as self, and object as world or universe. So everything is seen in terms of pairs of opposites: good and bad, true and false, right and wrong, existence and non-existence, and so on. This dualistic mode of discriminative awareness or consciousness is, of course, what characterizes the way we usually live and work.

The eighth consciousness is called the *ālaya-vijñāna*. Strictly speaking, however, this is not a *vijñāna* at all, because in it there is no discrimination, but just awareness. *Ālaya* literally means a repository or store, or even treasury; we are all familiar with the word in the compound 'Himalaya', which means 'the abode of snow' or 'the repository of snow'. This 'store consciousness' has two aspects: the 'relative *ālaya*' and the 'absolute *ālaya*'. The relative *ālaya* consists of, or contains, the impressions left deep in the mind by all our previous experiences. Whatever we have done or said or thought or experienced, a trace or residue of it remains there; nothing is absolutely lost. The relative *ālaya*, in fact, is not unlike Jung's collective unconscious, although this is a very approximate analogy which cannot be pushed too far.[358] The Yogācāra school conceives of the impressions which are deposited in the *ālaya-vijñāna*, the consequences of our various thoughts and deeds, as 'seeds' (*bījas*). In other words, these impressions are not passive; they are not just like the impression left by a seal in a piece of wax. They are *active* impressions, left like seeds in the soil, and when conditions are favourable they sprout up and produce fruits.

Ālaya in its absolute aspect is reality itself, conceived of in terms of pure awareness free from all trace of subjectivity and objectivity. It is a pure, continuous, and non-dimensional – or even multidimensional – awareness in which there is nothing of which anyone is aware, nor anyone who is aware. It is awareness without subject and without object, something which is very difficult for us to apprehend.

It is at the level of the *ālaya* – the 'deepest seat of consciousness' as Suzuki calls it[359] – that the turning about with which we are concerned takes place. We can say (although the *Laṅkāvatāra* itself does not actually say this explicitly) that the turning about takes place at the borderline separating the relative *ālaya* (that is, *ālaya* as a sort of collective unconscious) from the *ālaya* as reality, as pure awareness.

How this actually takes place is not at all easy to describe, but the texts give us some hints. What we can say is that as we go through our lives, we have all sorts of experiences of one kind or another, all the time, every day, every hour, every minute; and as a result more and more impressions accumulate in the relative *ālaya*. These impressions are known as 'impure seeds', because the thoughts, words, and deeds which deposited or sowed them are defiled by our dualistic outlook, especially – to put it in more ethico-psychological terms – by our craving, our aversion, and our fundamental spiritual ignorance. However, just as, in consequence of our ordinary actions, we can deposit impure seeds, so we can also deposit and accumulate 'pure seeds'. These are pure impressions or traces, produced by our more spiritual thoughts, words, and deeds. The more we devote ourselves to the spiritual life, the more we accumulate spiritual impressions or traces – or pure seeds – in the relative *ālaya*.

There comes a point when so many of these pure seeds are amassed in the relative *ālaya* that the absolute *ālaya* (which 'borders' on the relative *ālaya*) starts to push on them. And as the absolute *ālaya* presses on the pure seeds, they in turn bring their weight to bear upon the impure seeds, and in the end they push them right out. It is this pushing out of the impure seeds that constitutes the turning about within the *ālaya*, within the deepest seat of consciousness. Once this has taken place, a complete transformation is set up within the entire *vijñāna* system, and the eight *vijñānas* are transformed into what are called the five *jñānas*, usually translated as the five knowledges or wisdoms. The eight modes of discriminating awareness are transformed into five modes of pure – that is, non-discriminating – awareness or wisdom. Hence the term *jñāna*. *Vijñāna* means discriminating awareness, but *jñāna* means simply awareness.

These five *jñānas* or wisdoms represent the five aspects of Enlightenment, and they are personified in Buddhist iconography as five Buddhas of various colours. The first five *vijñānas*, the sense-consciousnesses, are collectively transformed into what is called the all-performing wisdom. This wisdom, which is capable of doing anything, is personified by the green Buddha, Amoghasiddhi, whose name means 'Infallible Success'. So the five ordinary sense consciousnesses start functioning as the all-performing wisdom, or the all-performing awareness. The next one, the *mano-vijñāna*, the mind consciousness, is transformed into distinguishing wisdom, the wisdom which appreciates the infinite variety of existence down to even the minutest differences. This is personified by the red Buddha, Amitābha – 'Infinite Light'.

As for the *kliṣṭa-mano-vijñāna*, the defiled mind consciousness, this is transformed into the wisdom of equality. It is a characteristic of the defiled mind consciousness to see things in terms of subject–object duality, in terms of opposition or conflict, but once the turning about has taken place, this is transformed into an awareness which sees everything as equal, sees everything with complete objectivity, and has the same attitude of compassion towards all. It is not that differences are obliterated, but one becomes aware that running through the differences – and even not different from the differences – is a thread of unity, of sameness. All things are equally void, equally one pure mind. This is personified by the yellow Buddha, Ratnasambhava, whose name means 'Jewel-born One'.

The relative *ālaya* is transformed into what is called the mirror-like wisdom, which reflects everything impartially and without distortion, which does not stick or cling to anything, but sees things just as they are. This wisdom is personified by the dark blue Buddha, Akṣobhya, 'the Imperturbable'.

The absolute *ālaya*, of course, is not transformed at all, because it does not need to be transformed. It is equivalent to the fifth wisdom, the wisdom of the *dharmadhātu*, the wisdom of the universe perceived as fully pervaded by reality, the absolute wisdom. This is personified by the white Buddha, Vairocana, whose name means 'the Illuminator'. Just as white is composed of all the colours of the rainbow, so this is the basic wisdom of which the other four are aspects.

In this way, after the turning about at the *ālaya* level has taken place, the eight consciousnesses become the five wisdoms, and one is utterly transformed – transformed into an Enlightened being, a Buddha, functioning in these five different ways, with these five modes of awareness. In other words, as a result of the *parāvṛtti*, as a result of this turning about, this conversion, one's whole being and one's whole consciousness is transformed, translated, from an unenlightened level to an Enlightened level.

There still remains unanswered, of course, the usual practical question. How do we bring about the *parāvṛtti*? It can hardly come about by accident. According to the Yogācāra, although we have eight modes of consciousness, we normally function only on the basis of the first seven. Our five sense consciousnesses function vigorously all the time we are awake, the mind consciousness keeps on functioning whether we are awake or asleep, and the defiled mind consciousness is of course very active indeed. But the *ālaya* – the relative *ālaya* and especially the absolute *ālaya* – is normally hidden from us. The highest level of consciousness to which we normally have access is the *kliṣṭa-mano-vijñāna*, the level of the mind defiled by duality, by seeing things in terms of opposites, especially subject and object, self and other. So this is the level on which we have to operate. We have to work with the tools that lie to hand.

It is at this level, therefore, with this dualistic outlook, that we take up various spiritual practices. For instance, when we take up meditation our ultimate goal is non-dualistic, but our practice is necessarily dualistic. Here we are sitting meditating, while the object of our meditation – our breathing, or maybe a mantra – is, as it were, over there. The basis is dualistic because that is how we are constituted, that is the level on which we are functioning. All our various religious practices and spiritual exercises, especially meditation, are taken up on the level of the defiled mind consciousness. But by means of these practices on that level, impressions of a better type are left; pure seeds, as the Yogācārins call them, are accumulated. And eventually, as we practise day by day, week by week, year by year, enough pure seeds are deposited in the relative *ālaya* for the turning about to take place.

We should not feel discouraged at the thought of all the time and effort this will take. It's rather like dropping a depth charge. If you are out at sea in a boat and you want to cause an explosion right down in the depths, you may have to spend hours or even days assembling the various component parts of the depth charge, and priming and adjusting the mechanism. And you do all that on the deck, even though you want to produce an effect many fathoms below. It's no use getting impatient and thinking, 'Why waste all this time putting it all together here on deck? Why not just throw the stuff overboard and hope for the best?' Spiritual practice is rather like that. It is easy to get discouraged, and think, 'I've been meditating (or doing some other practice) for all these weeks and months and years, but I'm still not Enlightened. I haven't even entered the Stream. What's going on?' Even when we feel we're not getting anywhere, though, the important thing is to carry on, because all this work has to be done at the level of the defiled mind consciousness in order to produce the required result at the level of the *ālaya*.

This reminds me of a story I heard when I was in southern India many years ago, visiting the ashram of Ramana Maharshi, one of the most famous Hindu teachers of this century.[360] Someone had apparently asked him how it is that our spiritual practice sometimes seems to have so little effect. We do all this meditation, we read all these scriptures, we give all these gifts, but nothing seems to happen. We're just the same, apparently. So the questioner wanted to know why this was – why was there no change, no improvement? In reply, Ramana Maharshi told a little story. He said:

> Once upon a time there was a man who wanted to split into two an enormous rock. So he went up to the rock with a great sledge-hammer, and swinging it with all his might he delivered a terrific blow, right in the centre of the rock. Nothing happened. So he drew a deep breath, flexed his muscles, and delivered another great blow in the same spot. Nothing happened. The rock stayed perfectly intact, just as it had been before. So, in the same way, sweating more and more, struggling more and more, panting for breath, the man delivered blow after blow, until he had struck the rock nineteen times. Still nothing happened. There was not a mark, not a dent. The man thought, "All right, now or never," collected all his strength, and gave one last tremendous blow. And with that twentieth blow, the rock split neatly, cleanly, quietly, into two halves.

So were the first nineteen blows completely useless? Was it just that last one that did the trick? No. Although no result could be seen, with each blow the rock was weakened along the line where the hammer struck. The twentieth blow just gave the last touch that was needed to split the rock. Though the results could not be seen, they were there all the time.

It is just like that when we work at the level of the defiled mind consciousness, hammering away at the rock of the empirical self. It may seem that our spiritual practices aren't producing any results. We may think: 'I'm the same person that I always was. I get angry just as easily. I'm just as greedy, just as interested in worldly things. Nothing has happened.' But all the time, at a deeper level, something *is* happening: blows are being struck, pure seeds are accumulating, the depth charge is being prepared. The important thing is to keep going, not to get discouraged by apparent failures or temporary setbacks, not to give up.

There are just two more crucial points to be stressed. The teaching of *parāvṛtti* draws attention to the fact that in the religious life an intellectual understanding is not enough. People who have read many books on the subject might think they have a good understanding of Buddhism, but according to the *Laṅkāvatāra* this is not enough. 'No dependence on words and letters' is the Zen way of putting it.[361] Through its doctrine of *parāvṛtti*, the *Laṅkāvatāra* is saying that there must also be a definite spiritual experience. There must be a conversion, a tremendous change in our mode of awareness, our way of looking at things, and our way of behaving, for there to be any real spiritual life at all. This is the first basic point that this doctrine is making. Most of the time we are just acquiring intellectual information from external sources; there is no fundamental modification of the quality of consciousness itself. But it is this radical transformation in the mode of our consciousness – as the Buddha says in the *Laṅkāvatāra* – which is the point of the whole exercise. There must be this turning about, even turning upside-down – or, as Nietzsche says, 'a transvaluation of all values'[362] – in which we see things not just in a slightly different way, but in a totally different way, with all our previous values reversed. We must be prepared even for that.

The other significant point implied by this doctrine is that the turning about, this conversion, is sudden – that it takes place in an instant. Here we can see at once the connection with the Zen idea of 'sudden Enlightenment', and it should now be clear what is really meant by this idea. Unfortunately it is still commonly taken to mean that you can get Enlightened easily and quickly, without any trouble at all. You just go along to the library, take out one or two books on Zen, read them, and hey presto! There you are! – Conveniently forgetting that the books themselves say, 'No dependence on words and letters'. Indeed, 'a book on Zen' is really an absolute contradiction in terms. Where there are books, there is no Zen – or one might say, where there is Zen, there are no books. At least, there is in Zen no dependence on books, no reliance upon them. Conversion, Enlightenment, or *satori*, is sudden only in the sense that the splitting of the rock is sudden. All the other nineteen blows had to be made. In truth, then, the splitting is not sudden at all. It only appears to be so because its coming about has been taking place at a different, deeper level, hidden from view.

So it is true that the *parāvṛtti*, the conversion, is sudden, that it takes place in the twinkling of an eye, but the preparation for it takes a very long time. There are no short cuts; a very great deal of discipline, training, and meditation is necessary. This is true not only with regard to Zen, not only with regard to the Yogācāra school or the teaching of the *Laṅkāvatāra*. It holds good for all forms of Buddhism. Whether you take up the Theravāda, or Zen, or Tibetan Buddhism, the culminating experience may come suddenly in a flash, but the process of building up to that experience takes a very long time. It may take the whole of your life. But if you believe that the experience itself is worthwhile – is indeed the only truly meaningful aim of human life – then of course you will not begrudge the time spent.

In this overview of the meaning of conversion in Buddhism, I hope that we have clearly established at least one fact. This is that conversion in Buddhism is a complex and arduous task. It is all too easy to say *Buddhaṃ saraṇaṃ gacchāmi* and consider oneself to be converted to Buddhism, but it is really not so simple. Conversion to Buddhism or conversion within Buddhism, whether in terms of Going for Refuge, Stream Entry, the arising of the will to Enlightenment, or the turning about of the mind in the deepest seat of consciousness, is by no means easy. We have to build up to it over a period of days, weeks, months, and even years, because it takes place on a very high level indeed, a level on which we do not usually function.

This is, however, the level on which we have to function eventually if we take our Buddhism seriously, if it is to mean more to us than an intellectual pastime – if, in short, we are really to experience conversion. And our conversion is complete only when the aim of the Buddhist path is fulfilled, when our practice of Buddhism has taken us through these levels of conversion right to the turning about in the deepest seat of consciousness, to Enlightenment itself.

Going for Refuge

INTRODUCTORY NOTE

Going for Refuge was originally a talk delivered on 31 December 1981 during a three-month tour Sangharakshita made in India. The talk was given at Theosophy Hall, Bombay (Mumbai), the headquarters of the Bombay branch of the United Lodge of Theosophists founded by B. P. Wadia. In the audience were people from very diverse backgrounds. As well as theosophists there were local Buddhists, Parsis, liberal Hindus, and Christians. The talk was introduced by Sangharakshita's old friend Mme Wadia, widow of B. P. Wadia to whom his *Survey of Buddhism* had been dedicated (see *Complete Works*, vol. 1). The talk was transcribed, edited, and published by Triratna Grantha Mala (Poona 1983); and translated into Marathi for inclusion in the July–September 1983 edition of *Buddhayan*, a quarterly publication of TBMSG (as the Indian wing of Triratna was then known). It was revised and published as a booklet by Windhorse Publications in 1986 and it is this version that is included here.

A version of the talk complete with Sangharakshita's introductory remarks to his Indian audience appears in volume 9 of the Complete Works *alongside all thirty-three talks and three question-and-answer sessions from his 1981–2 India tour.*

After his Enlightenment the Buddha spent a great deal of time wandering from place to place making known the Dharma or Truth he had discovered, and the way leading to its realization. Much of what he said is preserved in the Pāli scriptures, but although in some cases we have what may well be the Buddha's actual words, we probably do not appreciate the powerful effect of those words on the listener when spoken by the Enlightened One himself. What we usually find happening is that in the course of his wanderings the Buddha meets someone, whether a wealthy brahmin, a fellow-wanderer, or a young prince, and the two of them get into conversation.[363] As the conversation deepens, the Buddha begins to speak from the depths of his spiritual experience. In other words, the Buddha expounds the Dharma: the Dharma *emerges*.

Sometimes, when reading the Buddhist scriptures, we get the impression that the Dharma is a matter of *lists*, the five of this and the six of that and so on – an excessively schematized and tabulated thing. But it certainly wasn't like that at the beginning. It was all fresh, original, and creative. The Buddha would speak from the depths of his spiritual experience. He would expound the truth and show the way leading to Enlightenment, and the person to whom he was speaking would be absolutely astounded and overwhelmed. In some cases he might not be able to speak or do more than stammer a few incoherent words. Something had been revealed to him. Something had burst upon him that was above and beyond his ordinary understanding. For an instant, at least, he had glimpsed the truth, and the experience had staggered him. Time and again, on occasions of this sort, the scriptures tell us that the person concerned exclaimed,

> 'Excellent, lord, excellent! As if one should set up again that which had been overthrown or reveal that which had been hidden, or should disclose the road to one that was astray, or should carry a lamp into darkness, saying, "They that have eyes will see!" even so hath the Truth been manifested by the Exalted One in many ways.'[364]

In this manner would he express himself. Then, out of the depth of his gratitude, such a person would fervently declare,

> *Buddhaṃ saraṇaṃ gacchāmi!*
> *Dhammaṃ saraṇaṃ gacchāmi!*
> *Saṅghaṃ saraṇaṃ gacchāmi!*
>
> To the Buddha for refuge I go
> To the Dharma for refuge I go
> To the Sangha for refuge I go![365]

These words from the ancient past reveal to us the origin of an act which lies at the heart of Buddhist life: Going for Refuge. They also tell us something of the tremendous spiritual significance of this act. Going for Refuge represents your positive emotional response – in fact your total response – to the spiritual ideal when that ideal is revealed to your spiritual vision. Such is its appeal that you cannot but give yourself to it. As Tennyson says, 'We needs must love the Highest when we see it.'[366] Going for Refuge is a bit like that. You've seen the 'Highest' – it has been shown to you – so you needs must love it, needs must give yourself to it, needs must commit yourself to it. That commitment of yourself to the 'Highest' is Going for Refuge. It is this topic, which has been close to my heart for many years, that I want to address here.

As the words of the Buddha's followers suggest, the object of Going for Refuge is threefold. One goes for Refuge to the Buddha, the Dharma, and the Sangha – known in Buddhism as the Three Jewels. But what does it mean in practice to 'go for Refuge' to each of these Three Jewels?

GOING FOR REFUGE TO THE BUDDHA

The Buddha is an Enlightened human being. He is not God or a messenger of God, but a human being who, by his own efforts, has reached the summit of human perfection. He has gained the ineffable state which we call Enlightenment, Nirvāṇa, or Buddhahood. He is, indeed, not only a Buddha but a *samyak-sambuddha*, a fully and perfectly Enlightened One. When we go for Refuge to the Buddha, we go for Refuge to him in this sense. Not that we just admire him from a distance. We admire him indeed, and certainly he is very distant at present, but great as the gap between the Buddha and ourselves may be, that gap can be closed. We can close it by practising the Dharma. We too can become as the Buddha. We too can become Enlightened. *That* is the great message of Buddhism. Each and every human being who makes the effort can become what the Buddha became. When, therefore, we go for Refuge to the Buddha, we go for Refuge to him as the living embodiment of a spiritual ideal which is a spiritual ideal *for us*, a spiritual ideal we can actually realize. When we go for Refuge to the Buddha it is as though we say, 'That is what I want to be. That is what I want to attain. I want to be Enlightened and develop the fullness of wisdom and compassion.' Going for Refuge to the Buddha means taking the Buddha – taking Buddhahood – as our personal spiritual ideal, as something we ourselves can achieve.

GOING FOR REFUGE TO THE DHARMA

The Dharma is the Path or Way. It is the path of what I have sometimes called the Higher Evolution of man, a stage of purely spiritual development above and beyond biological evolution.[367] As a path, the Dharma exists in a number of different formulations. We speak of the threefold path: of morality (*śīla*), meditation (*samādhi*), and wisdom (*prajñā*). There is the path of the bodhisattva, otherwise known as the path of the six perfections (*pāramitās*): giving (*dāna*), morality (*śīla*), patience and forbearance (*kśānti*), vigour (*vīrya*), higher consciousness (*samādhi*), and wisdom (*prajñā*).[368] These are just two among many other formulations, but the basic principle of the path is always the same. The path is essentially the path of the Higher Evolution.

The Dharma is not to be identified with this or that particular teaching. According to the Buddha's own express declaration the

Dharma is whatever contributes to the spiritual development of the individual. When his maternal aunt and foster mother, Mahāprajāpatī the Gotamid, asked him for a criterion by means of which she could distinguish between what was his teaching, his *Dharma-Vinaya*, and what was not, he replied,

> Of whatsoever teachings Gotamid, thou canst assure thyself thus: 'These doctrines conduce to passions, not to dispassion; to bondage, not to detachment; to increase of (worldly) gains, not to decrease of them; to covetousness, not to frugality; to discontent, and not content; to company, not solitude; to sluggishness, not energy; to delight in evil, not delight in good': of such teachings thou mayest with certainty affirm, Gotamid, 'This is not the Dharma. This is not the Vinaya. This is not the Master's Message.' But of whatsoever teachings thou canst assure thyself (that they are the opposite of those things I have told you), of such teachings thou mayest with certainty affirm: 'This is the Dharma. This is the Vinaya. This is the Master's Message.'[369]

When we go for Refuge to the Dharma we commit ourselves to the path of the Higher Evolution. We commit ourselves to whatever helps us to develop spiritually – to whatever helps us to grow towards Enlightenment.

GOING FOR REFUGE TO THE SANGHA

Sangha means 'spiritual community'. Primarily this is the community of all those who are spiritually more advanced than we are: the great bodhisattvas, the *arhants*, the Stream Entrants, and so on. (I will have a little to say about each of these later on.) Together they form the Āryasaṅgha, the 'noble sangha', the spiritual community in the highest sense. Secondarily, it is the community of all Buddhists, all those who go for Refuge to the Buddha, Dharma, and Sangha. In the case of the Āryasaṅgha, Going for Refuge to the Sangha means opening ourselves to the spiritual influence of the sublime beings of whom it consists. It means learning from them, being inspired by them, reverencing them. In the case of the Sangha in the more ordinary sense, that of the community of all Buddhists, it means enjoying spiritual fellowship with one another and helping one another on the path. Sometimes you may not need a highly advanced bodhisattva to help you. All you need is an ordinary human being who is a little more developed spiritually than you are, or even just a little more sensible. Only too often people are on the lookout for a great, highly developed guru, but that is not what they really need, even if such a person was available. What they need is a helping hand *where they are now*, on the particular stage of the path which at present they occupy, and this kind of help can generally be given by an ordinary fellow Buddhist.[370]

This, then, is what it means to go for Refuge to the Buddha, the Dharma, and the Sangha; and it is this threefold Going for Refuge – in the way that I have described – that makes one a Buddhist. Going for Refuge is therefore of crucial importance in the Buddhist life. But having said that one must sound a note of regret. Unfortunately, Going for Refuge, despite its crucial importance, is often undervalued in the Buddhist countries of Asia, about which I shall say something below. In the Friends of the Western Buddhist Order (FWBO)[371] it is certainly not undervalued and some people might think we overvalue it, but I would say that is not possible. You *cannot* overvalue the Going for Refuge because the Going for Refuge is the basis of everything else. When in the FWBO we emphasize the importance of the Going for Refuge we are trying to get back to the way things were in the Buddha's own time. We are trying to restore the original significance of the Going for Refuge.

THE EYE OF THE DHARMA

Returning once more to the Buddha's own time we find something else of great interest happening. Not only may someone be so impressed and thrilled by the Buddha's exposition of the truth that he goes for Refuge but, even as he listens, actual insight into that truth may arise in his mind. In the language of the Buddhist scriptures, there arises for that person the pure and stainless Eye of Truth (*dharma-cakṣus*) – a profound spiritual experience.[372] This 'Eye of Truth' is one of five 'eyes' distinguished by the Buddhist tradition. Firstly, there is the 'Eye of Flesh' (*māṃsa-cakṣus*), which is what we usually mean by an eye, the organ of physical sight, by means of which material objects are perceived. Secondly, there is the 'Divine Eye' (*divya-cakṣus*). If you were able to see what was happening on the other side of the city, or even in another country, it would be this eye you would be using. This is known as the faculty of clairvoyance and it is one of the supernormal powers that may arise spontaneously in the course of meditation practice. Thirdly, there is the 'Eye of Truth' (*dharma-cakṣus*), the inner spiritual eye, or inner spiritual vision, with which you 'see' the truth of things. Fourthly, there is the 'Eye of Wisdom' (*prajñā-cakṣus*) which 'sees' even further than the Eye of Truth, and arises only when one becomes an *arhant* (an *arhant* being one in whom transcendental insight has arisen). Fifthly and lastly, there is the 'Universal Eye' (*samanta-cakṣus*), also known as the 'Buddha Eye', which arises when one is fully Enlightened, when one's spiritual vision is total and absolute.[373]

So let us look more closely, as it were, into this 'Eye of Truth', this Dharma Eye or Dharma vision. There is a formula in the Buddhist scriptures which gives succinct expression to the particular insight which is seen through this 'eye'. This formula simply states that whatever arises – whatever comes into existence – must pass away.[374] This is so simple and straightforward that you might think you knew it already. But the opening of the Eye of Truth represents not a theoretical knowledge of the fact of universal impermanence or transitoriness but a deep spiritual insight into it, a real understanding. The fact that all things are impermanent – that you have to give up everything and lose everything in the end – may seem to some people a very terrible message indeed. Yet this is not really so. Impermanence implies not only change but also development and transformation. If things were *not* impermanent and did *not* change – if you were the same today as you were yesterday, and the same yesterday as you were the day before – that would be terrible indeed, for then you would not grow and develop. The law of impermanence guarantees the possibility of development.

And this is what you see when your Dharma Eye opens. You see not only the fact of impermanence, the fact that everything changes, but also the possibility of human growth and development, the possibility of the transformation of ordinary humanity into Enlightened humanity or Buddhahood.

When that kind of insight is developed, and your Dharma Eye opens, something tremendous happens. To use another traditional Buddhist image, you 'enter the Stream' – the Stream that leads directly to Nirvāṇa. Your whole being now flows irreversibly in the direction of Enlightenment. This is the 'real' Going for Refuge, the 'transcendental'

Going for Refuge. By entering the Stream, by Going for Refuge in this higher, transcendental way, you at once break three of the ten fetters binding you to mundane existence.[375] It is, indeed, by breaking these three fetters that you enter the Stream, thus becoming a Stream Entrant (*śrotāpanna*). Since they occupy an important place in Buddhist teaching, let me say a few words about each of the three fetters in turn.

THREE FETTERS

The first fetter is that of 'self-view' (*satkāya-dṛṣṭi*). When you are the victim of self-view your attitude is that what you experience as the self or ego is something fixed, irreducible, and ultimate. You think there is a core of selfhood in you which is never going to change, and which is the real 'you'. Such an attitude blocks change and inhibits growth, because you think that as you are now so you will be for ever. It is very difficult to break this fetter, and imagine oneself as different from what one is now. But it can be done. If you are genuinely committed to the spiritual path the time will come when you will be able to look back and see that great changes *have* taken place. You will see that you *have* grown, even that you have been transformed. But so long as the fetter of self-view remains unbroken there is no real spiritual development.

The second fetter is that of 'doubt' (*vicikitsā*). This is not doubt in the intellectual sense so much as indecision – deliberate, culpable indecision. You actually *refuse* to make up your mind and commit yourself. Rather than give yourself wholeheartedly to something you prefer to keep all your options open. You make excuses, you wobble, you shilly-shally, you delay, you hesitate, you temporize, you rationalize. This is the fetter of doubt. It is doubt that prevents you from throwing yourself into the spiritual life – from plunging in at the deep end. Consequently you get nowhere with the spiritual life: you fail to make real spiritual progress.

The third fetter is that of 'dependence on moral rules and religious observances' (*śīlavrata-parāmarśa*), which could be paraphrased as the belief that 'going through the motions' will do. You go through the motions when your heart is not really in what you are doing. You think that if you keep up appearances externally, if you observe the moral rules because that is what society requires, and maintain the religious observances because that is what your co-religionists require, then everything will be all right. There is a split between the external observances and your inward state of being. Although the things you are doing may be good in themselves, your heart is not in them and therefore your performance of them is empty, mechanical, rigid, and artificial. Hence they don't really help you to develop: they don't get you anywhere spiritually.[376]

Such are the three fetters. All these different images – breaking the three fetters, entering the Stream, opening the Dharma Eye – correspond. When you enter the Stream, the three fetters are broken; when the fetters are broken, you enter the Stream. When your Dharma Eye is opened you see the truth of impermanence, including the truth of the possibility of total transformation, and it is that insight, or higher spiritual vision, that causes the three fetters to break. Thus we have two things happening together. We have the (transcendental) Going for Refuge to the Buddha, the Dharma, and the Sangha and, at the same time, we have the opening of the Dharma Eye, or higher spiritual vision, leading to the breaking of the three fetters and to entering the Stream. Indeed, these two things – (transcendental) Going for Refuge and Stream Entry – do not just happen together; they are different aspects of one and the same spiritual experience or spiritual process.

GOING FORTH

Still remaining in the Buddha's own time, we can go a little further. Suppose someone hears the Buddha expound the Dharma. Suppose he is impressed and thrilled and goes for Refuge; suppose, even, he gains Stream Entry. There is still something else that may happen at this point. He may leave home and become a monk or *bhikṣu*.[377] Not that this was invariably the case. Sometimes people went for Refuge and, at the same time, their Dharma Eye opened, but they did not leave home.[378] But sometimes, in fact very often, they did. In such cases we have not two but three things happening at the same time: Going for Refuge, Stream Entry, and what subsequently became known as 'ordination' – 'Going Forth' into homelessness and becoming a *bhikṣu* or monk. This was the situation during the Buddha's lifetime.

After the Buddha's death, or what we call his *parinirvāṇa*, many changes took place. Perhaps inevitably, a certain spiritual deterioration set in. Stream Entry became rarer and rarer. As centuries went by, the emphasis came increasingly to be placed on becoming a monk in the more formal sense, and Going for Refuge gradually lost its significance as the central act of the Buddhist life. This happened especially in the Theravādin countries of South-east Asia. Today, if you visit these countries or talk to Theravādin Buddhists, they will not say very much to you about the importance of Going for Refuge. They will be much more likely to speak in terms of becoming a monk in the more formal sense: shaving one's head and donning the yellow robe. For the Theravādins there are two kinds of people: the monks and the lay people. On *this* side there are the monks, who are the 'real' Buddhists; on *that* side the lay people, who are the 'not-so-real' Buddhists. One could even say that the distinction made seems to be between first-class Buddhists and second-class Buddhists.

Looking at things from a different point of view, however, and seeing them more as they were in the Buddha's day, one might say that though there certainly is a difference, it is of a different kind. The real difference is not between monks and lay people but between those who go for Refuge and those who do not go for Refuge. Whether you are a monk who goes for Refuge or a layman who goes for Refuge, a man who goes for Refuge or a woman who goes for Refuge, is of secondary importance. That you live in a certain kind of way, or follow a certain discipline, is of secondary importance. What is of overriding importance is your spiritual commitment, your Going for Refuge. This is why in the FWBO we have a sort of saying, or slogan: 'Going for Refuge – or commitment – is primary; lifestyle is secondary.'

THE WAY OF THE BODHISATTVA

Now although in the Theravādin countries the distinction between monk and layman was unnecessarily insisted upon, and the significance of the Going for Refuge lost sight of, this did not happen in the Mahāyāna countries to nearly so great an extent. As their designation itself suggests, the Mahāyāna countries followed the Mahāyāna – the Great Way. They followed the bodhisattva ideal, the ideal of attaining Enlightenment not just for one's own individual sake but for the sake of all.[379] Ultimately, of course, the distinction between the two ideals falls to the ground. You cannot really gain Enlightenment for the benefit of others unless you are a person of considerable spiritual development yourself, and you cannot develop spiritually yourself unless you are at the same time mindful of the needs of other people. In the long run spiritual individualism and spiritual altruism coincide. But as a necessary corrective to the earlier, more individualistic approach of the Theravāda, and of the Hīnayāna generally, the Mahāyāna stressed the bodhisattva ideal. The attitude of the bodhisattva is: 'I don't want Enlightenment only for myself. If it's to be only for myself, in a sense I'm not interested. I want Enlightenment for all. I am therefore working for Enlightenment for all – including myself.' Not that the bodhisattva leaves himself out. He includes himself, but only as one among many. His or her mission is to work for the spiritual progress, the ultimate Enlightenment, of all living beings.

Since the Mahāyāna adopted, or developed, the bodhisattva ideal, all lesser distinctions lost their significance. The Mahāyāna insisted that *everybody* should aim to be a bodhisattva, *everybody* should follow the bodhisattva ideal. Be they monk or lay person, literate or illiterate, rich or poor, spiritually developed or spiritually not so developed, all should aspire to Enlightenment for the sake of all living beings. On account of the presence of the bodhisattva ideal, therefore, we find that in the Mahāyāna there is less of a difference between monk and layman, or at least that the difference is less insisted upon.

But what is a bodhisattva, and what does it mean to aim for Enlightenment for the sake of all? According to Mahāyāna tradition a bodhisattva, in the real sense, is one in whom the *bodhicitta* or 'will to Enlightenment' (as I translate the term) has arisen as a vital spiritual experience.[380] The *bodhicitta* is not a mere pious aspiration, nor a concept, nor an abstract ideal. When, within the depths of your being, there arises an immensely powerful impulse towards Enlightenment for the benefit of all, and when that impulse dominates your whole life and becomes the master-current of your being, *that* is the arising of the *bodhicitta*.

DIMENSIONS OF ONE SPIRITUAL EXPERIENCE

Here an interesting question arises concerning the nature of the relation between on the one hand the *bodhicitta*, or the arising of the *bodhicitta*, and on the other hand the Going for Refuge, the opening of the Dharma Eye, Stream Entry, and even Going Forth into homelessness and becoming a monk. The *bodhicitta*, or the arising of the *bodhicitta*, represents, we may say, the more altruistic dimension of these four other experiences.

Or rather, all five of them, including the *bodhicitta* itself, represent the five different aspects of a single basic, crucial, and unique spiritual experience. The Going for Refuge draws attention to the emotional and volitional aspect of this experience, the opening of the Dharma Eye to the unconditioned depth of its cognitive content, Stream Entry to the permanent and far-reaching nature of its effects, while Going Forth into homelessness draws attention to the extent of the reorganization which, regardless of whether or not one becomes a monk in the formal sense, the experience inevitably brings about in the pattern of one's daily life. As for the *bodhicitta*, it represents, as I have said, the other-regarding aspect of the experience.

This perhaps gives some idea of the broad conception of Going for Refuge. Much more is implied by it than people usually think. Incidentally, the use of the word 'refuge' sometimes creates confusion, because it is associated in people's minds with 'refugee'. Expressions like 'taking refuge' or 'going for refuge' have, in fact, distinct connotations of running away from difficulties, taking the easy way out, and so on. From what I have already said it should be clear that Going for Refuge in the Buddhist sense has nothing to do with running away. However, to avoid the possibility of misunderstanding, I often speak not of 'Going for Refuge' but of 'commitment'. Commitment is rather a favourite word in the West at the moment; an 'in' word, as we say. So I often speak not of Going for Refuge to the Buddha, Dharma, and Sangha but of committing oneself to the Buddha, committing oneself to the Dharma, committing oneself to the Sangha. Nor is that all. In the course of years I have come to distinguish four levels of Going for Refuge, four levels of commitment.[381]

LEVELS OF GOING FOR REFUGE

First of all there is 'provisional' Going for Refuge, sometimes called 'ethnic' Going for Refuge.[382] This consists in simply reciting the Refuge-going formula in Pāli, or some other language, just because it is part of your national culture. In Buddhist countries like Sri Lanka, Thailand, and Burma, one often finds people reciting the Refuge-going formula, *Buddhaṃ saraṇaṃ gacchāmi* and so on, without understanding its meaning. It is just part of their culture; it has no real spiritual significance for them. That one should recite the Refuge-going formula, even though without understanding it, is by no means a bad thing, but it is certainly not sufficient.

In much the same way, one sometimes finds people in the Buddhist countries of Asia describing themselves as 'born Buddhists'. But how can you be a born Buddhist? Do you issue from your mother's womb reciting '*Buddhaṃ saraṇaṃ gacchāmi*'? A 'born Buddhist' is a contradiction in terms. You can become a Buddhist only consciously and deliberately, as a result of personal choice. You cannot possibly be *born* a Buddhist. The Buddha himself criticized 'brahmins' of his day for thinking that one could be born a brahmin. You were a brahmin, he insisted, only to the extent that you acted like one. If truth and righteousness were in you, then you could be called a brahmin; not otherwise.[383] Similarly you cannot be a Buddhist by birth. People in Buddhist countries who say they are Buddhists by birth are no better than the ancient brahmins who said that they were brahmins by birth. What it really means is that Buddhism, so called, has simply become Brahminism. This is a very important point. The Going for Refuge must be a true Going for Refuge. If you are a Buddhist it must be on account of your own, individual, independent volition, your own understanding. Thus you cannot be born a Buddhist. If you think you can, you are still on the level of 'provisional' Going for Refuge, the significance of which is cultural rather than genuinely spiritual.

Secondly, there is 'effective' Going for Refuge. This is a wholehearted, conscious commitment to the Buddha, Dharma, and Sangha. Though such commitment is sincere and genuine, it is not powerful enough to break the three fetters and does not amount to Stream Entry. From 'effective' Going for Refuge you can fall away.

Thirdly, there is 'real' Going for Refuge. This coincides with Stream Entry, which occurs with the breaking of the three fetters. From this Going for Refuge you cannot fall away.

Fourthly and lastly, there is 'absolute' Going for Refuge. On this level there is, in a sense, no Going for Refuge. Though you indeed go for Refuge to the Buddha, now that Enlightenment has been attained you are yourself the Buddha. Here, the goal of your quest having been reached, the subject of Going for Refuge and the object of Going for Refuge are one and the same. Buddha goes for Refuge to Buddha.

In the Mahāyāna it is sometimes said that ultimately there is only one Refuge: the Buddha. In a sense there is a Dharma Refuge, and a

Sangha Refuge, but again in a sense there is not. After all, the Dharma comes from the Buddha. It is the product, the creation, of the Buddha's Enlightenment experience – the means by which that experience is communicated to other human beings in such a way as to help them. Similarly, the Sangha is the Spiritual Community of those who practise the Dharma. Just as the Dharma is dependent on the Buddha, the Sangha is dependent on the Dharma, so that the Sangha is also dependent on the Buddha. Thus there is only the Buddha: only the Buddha Refuge. Though we speak of three Refuges, ultimately the three Refuges are one Refuge. For the time being, however, it is no doubt helpful for us to think in terms of the Three Refuges, or the Threefold Refuge.

A NEW BUDDHIST MOVEMENT

On the basis of these Three Refuges a whole Buddhist movement has grown up in the West. It began in 1967, when I returned from India to set up the first centre of what has become a network of urban centres in many countries, known as the Friends of the Western Buddhist Order. At these centres we conduct a wide range of activities including lectures and study courses on Buddhism, meditation classes, hatha yoga classes, and arts events. From time to time retreats are held which involve spending the whole day at the centre – or sometimes a weekend in the countryside – engaged in meditation, study, discussion, and communication.

People come to hear about our activities in various ways – sometimes through our publicity, but more often simply by word of mouth. One friend tells another that there is a place where you can meditate, or where you can learn about Buddhism, or practise hatha yoga. Anyway, by one means or another people make contact with their local FWBO centre. At first they may be interested simply in meditation or Buddhist philosophy, and come to us just for that. In most Western countries, there are thousands of people who are engaged in sampling all kinds of spiritual groups. They go along to one group for a while, then to another, and so on, and in this way they sample quite a number of groups. Some of the people who come to us are of this type. They come to us for a time, then leave to continue their search elsewhere.

In the FWBO we have no membership in the ordinary sense. You cannot 'join' by filling in a form and paying a subscription; we have a different system. Anybody who comes along and participates in any of our activities to however small an extent is regarded as a Friend (with a capital F). You don't have to join in any formal sense; you are free to derive whatever benefit you can from our activities without incurring any obligation or responsibility. We are quite happy for you to do this.

But some people, when they have been coming to the centre for a while, decide to stay with us because they like our approach and feel at home. They become more deeply involved in our activities and one day it dawns on them that they would like to identify themselves with us and, in a word, 'belong'. When they reach that point they can become what we call a Mitra (*mitra* being simply the Sanskrit word for friend). If you decide that you want to become a Mitra, you make your wishes known and, if your desire is genuine and you have a real interest in the work of the FWBO, a simple public ceremony is held at which you offer flowers, a lighted candle, and a stick of incense before an image of the Buddha. In this way you become a Mitra.

The fact that you have become a Mitra means that your search for a spiritual group to which you can belong has now ended, and that henceforth your time, energy, and interest will be devoted exclusively to the FWBO. A Mitra is expected: (1) to attend their local FWBO centre regularly and participate in its activities, (2) to keep up a daily meditation practice, (3) to maintain contact with local Order members and develop *kalyāṇa mitratā* ('spiritual fellowship') with them, and (4) to help the centre, and the Movement generally, in any practical way he or she can.[384]

As a Mitra you will probably find yourself becoming increasingly involved with the Movement and increasingly attracted by the beauty of the Buddhist spiritual ideal, the ideal of human Enlightenment. You may find that your experience of meditation is becoming deeper, that your communication with other people is expanding, and that psychological problems are being overcome. Eventually, you may find that the centre of gravity of your whole existence has subtly shifted, and that you now want to give up your old interests and activities and commit yourself wholly to Buddhism, to the Dharma, to the spiritual life. When that point is reached you start thinking in terms of 'joining the Order' or, to put it more traditionally, in terms of Going for Refuge to the Buddha, the Dharma, and the Sangha.

If the existing Order members are convinced that your aspiration is genuine, and that you truly are able to go for Refuge – by no means an easy thing to do – then your 'application' is accepted and in due course the very beautiful ordination ceremony is held. You become a *dharmacārī* (masc.) or *dharmacāriṇī* (fem.), one who goes for Refuge to the Buddha, the Dharma, and the Sangha and who, in addition, takes upon himself or herself the ten *śīlas* or moral precepts by means of which body, speech, and mind are progressively and systematically purified.[385]

The Order is at the heart of the FWBO. It is a spiritual community of people who have gone for Refuge – that is to say, who have 'effectively' gone for Refuge. Few of them, perhaps, if indeed any, have got so far as the 'real' Going for Refuge, but at least they have transcended the 'provisional' Going for Refuge, to make the act of Going for Refuge central in their lives, and place the emphasis there. Some of them live at home with their wives or husbands and families. Some live in communities. (There are communities for men and communities for women.) A few of them are *angārikas* who have taken a vow of celibacy.[386] As I mentioned, all members of the Order observe the ten precepts: abstention from injury to living beings; from taking what is not given; from sexual misconduct (in the case of the *anagārikas*, from non-celibacy); from false speech; from frivolous, idle, and useless speech; from speech which divides and disunites people; from craving; from hatred; and from wrong views. According to Buddhist tradition, *bhikṣus* or monks observe 227 (or 250) precepts,[387] but in the course of ages quite a few of these have been lost on the way, so to speak, and are nowadays honoured more in the breach than in the observance. We therefore decided to have a short list of precepts that people would take and actually observe.

Thus we have this order, this sangha or spiritual community, of people who have gone for Refuge to the Buddha, Dharma, and Sangha: people who actually practise the Dharma; who observe the ten precepts. Some of them have been members of the Order for a number of years, and are gathering experience all the time – taking meditation classes, giving talks, and running our team-based right livelihood businesses. It is, in fact, this dedicated, committed core of people at the heart of the Movement which is responsible for running everything.

I hope that I have said enough to show the vital importance, both for each of us individually and for the society to which we belong, of the Going for Refuge. It is my hope that we will be able to create a sangha, a spiritual community, of people who have gone for Refuge not just in the West but in many countries throughout the world. If we are to do this, however, it can be only on the basis of the Buddha, the Dharma, and the Sangha. It can be only on the basis of the Going for Refuge.

The Ten Pillars of Buddhism

INTRODUCTORY NOTE

The Ten Pillars of Buddhism is the first of several communications from Sangharakshita on essential topics that originally took the form of a paper read aloud to Order members at the annual celebrations marking the founding of the Order. This paper was delivered on 7 April 1984 when over half the Order had gathered at York Hall, Bethnal Green, near the London Buddhist Centre, to celebrate the Order's sixteenth birthday. Sangharakshita read the first part of the text, after which there was a break. Owing to a sore throat which was making it difficult for him to speak, he then handed the paper to Dharmachari Devamitra, formerly a professional actor, who read out the rest of the paper 'from sight'. According to the report in the newsletter *Golden Drum*, no. 62, the whole presentation lasted some four hours. *The Ten Pillars of Buddhism* was published by Windhorse Publications that same year. Three further editions were published in 1985, 1989 and 1996.

THE TEN PRECEPTS IN PĀLI

pāṇātipātā veramaṇī-sikkhāpadaṃ samādiyāmi
adinnādānā veramaṇī-sikkhāpadaṃ samādiyāmi
kāmesu micchācārā veramaṇī-sikkhāpadaṃ samādiyāmi
musāvādā veramaṇī-sikkhāpadaṃ samādiyāmi
pharusavācāya veramaṇī-sikkhāpadaṃ samādiyāmi
samphappalāpā veramaṇī-sikkhāpadaṃ samādiyāmi
pisuṇavācāya veramaṇī-sikkhāpadaṃ samādiyāmi
abhijjhāya veramaṇī-sikkhāpadaṃ samādiyāmi
byāpādā veramaṇī-sikkhāpadaṃ samādiyāmi
micchādiṭṭhiyā veramaṇī-sikkhāpadaṃ samādiyāmi

THE TEN PRECEPTS IN ENGLISH

I undertake the item of training which consists in abstention from killing living beings.

I undertake the item of training which consists in abstention from taking the not-given.

I undertake the item of training which consists in abstention from sexual misconduct.

I undertake the item of training which consists in abstention from false speech.

I undertake the item of training which consists in abstention from harsh speech.

I undertake the item of training which consists in abstention from frivolous speech.

I undertake the item of training which consists in abstention from slanderous speech.

I undertake the item of training which consists in abstention from covetousness.

I undertake the item of training which consists in abstention from hatred.

I undertake the item of training which consists in abstention from false views.

THE TEN POSITIVE PRECEPTS

With deeds of loving-kindness I purify my body.
With open-handed generosity I purify my body.
With stillness, simplicity, and contentment I purify my body.
With truthful communication I purify my speech.
With kindly communication I purify my speech.
With helpful communication I purify my speech.
With harmonious communication I purify my speech.
Abandoning covetousness for tranquillity I purify my mind.
Changing hatred into compassion I purify my mind.
Transforming ignorance into wisdom I purify my mind.

INTRODUCTION

The Western Buddhist Order (known in India as the Trailokya Bauddha Mahasangha) was founded in London in 1968.[388] Today we meet to celebrate its sixteenth anniversary – or sixteenth birthday, as one might say. Without being over fanciful one might, perhaps, attach a special significance to the fact that the Order has now attained this particular number of years. Sixteen is twice eight, or four times four, and both four and eight are traditionally regarded as numbers indicative of 'squareness' and stability. It is also the sum of ten and six, both of which numbers have their own symbolical associations. In pre-Buddhist Indian tradition groups of sixteen, or sixteenfold divisions of things, are extremely common. One of the commonest is that of the sixteen 'digits' of the moon. Sixteenth parts are also referred to in Buddhist literature. Thus in the *Itivuttaka* the Buddha declares:

> Monks, whatsoever grounds there be for good works undertaken with a view to rebirth, all of them are not worth one sixteenth part of that goodwill [i.e. *mettā*] which is the heart's release; goodwill alone, which is the heart's release, shines and burns and flashes forth in surpassing them. Just as, monks, the radiance of all the starry bodies is not worth one sixteenth part of the moon's radiance, but the moon's radiance shines and burns and flashes forth in surpassing them, even so, monks, goodwill … flashes forth in surpassing good works undertaken with a view to rebirth.[389]

Perhaps the best-known group of sixteen in Buddhism is that of the sixteen *arhants* – mysterious personages who exist from age to age and periodically reinvigorate the *sāsana*.[390]

For many people in the FWBO, however, whether Order members, Mitras, or Friends,[391] the most familiar association of the figure sixteen – the one that springs most readily to mind – is with the 'archetypal' bodhisattvas. Mañjuśrī, Avalokiteśvara, and the rest, are all described in the literature, and depicted in the visual arts of Buddhism, as appearing in the surpassingly beautiful form of Indian princes, clad in rich silks and adorned with jewels, and *sixteen years old*. They are sixteen because sixteen is the age at which a youth is considered in India to have attained to the full development of his faculties, both physical and mental, to be in the full bloom of masculine strength and beauty, and to be ready for the duties and responsibilities of adult life. In Western terms, at sixteen one reaches the years of discretion, one grows up, one passes from immaturity to maturity. The sixteenth birthday therefore has, for Indian tradition, something of the significance that the twenty-first birthday has in the West, the five-year difference between them no doubt being attributable to the fact that in Europe and North America human beings mature later than they do in warmer climes.[392]

In celebrating its sixteenth birthday the Order is therefore celebrating, i.e. we as Order members are celebrating, the attainment of our 'collective' majority as a spiritual community. We have reached the age of discretion. We have grown up. We have passed – collectively, at least – from immaturity to maturity. We now have our own front door key, and are free to come and go as we please. In celebrating the attainment of our majority, however, we must not forget that although we are Buddhists we are, most of us, also Westerners, and that it *may* take us a few more years to achieve, as an Order, the kind of spiritual maturity that is symbolized by the physical and mental maturity of the sixteen-year-old Indian youth. It may not be until our twenty-first birthday that the Order will, in fact, be a recognizable reflection, on the mundane level, of the thousand-armed and thousand-eyed *sixteen-year-old* Avalokiteśvara.[393]

None the less, today *is* our sixteenth birthday, and therefore the day on which we celebrate the attainment of our 'official' majority, even though we may be a bit backward in our development. It was for this reason, partly, that I decided not only that as many of us should meet together on this occasion as possible but also that I should, as part of the proceedings, deliver a lecture or read a paper. It is not often that we are able to come together in this way. Most Order members are very busy, and there are problems of travel and accommodation, but it is at least some consolation that so large a section of the Order should have been able to gather here today – the more especially since we are not able to hold our biennial convention this year as planned.[394] The first of the seven times seven, minus one, conditions of the stability of the Order laid down by the Buddha shortly before his *parinirvāṇa*, i.e. that the brethren should assemble repeatedly and in large numbers, is being fulfilled at least to a limited extent![395] Moreover, in gathering here today we do not forget those members of the Order who are unable to be with us and who, no doubt, are also celebrating our sixteenth birthday. We know that we are united with them, as they with us, through our common commitment to the Three Jewels, and through the all-pervading spirit of *mettā* which, transcending time and space, links mind to mind and heart to heart in world-wide spiritual fellowship.

Now as soon as I had decided that I would give a lecture or read a paper to you today, I let it be known that I was open to suggestions as to what the subject of the lecture or paper should be. Various suggestions have, in fact, been made. They range from a suggestion that I should speak on whether there was a philosophical term or phrase that would summarize the nature of Buddhism, much as the term 'monotheism' summarizes the nature of Christianity and Islam, to the suggestion that I should speak on *prajñā* in the sense of 'not settling down' – a sense which, according to the Order member making the suggestion, runs through the *Heart Sūtra*. However, I shall not be speaking on any of the topics suggested, though I hope to be able to say something about all of them, in one context or another, sooner or later. Since I do not often have the opportunity of personally addressing so many of you at the same time, I wanted to speak, on this our sixteenth birthday, on a topic of fundamental importance to the whole Order. After giving the matter some thought I therefore decided to speak on the ten precepts, i.e. the ten *akuśala-dharmas* from which one undertakes to refrain, and the ten *kuśala-dharmas* which one undertakes to observe, on the occasion of one's 'ordination' into the Western Buddhist Order or Trailokya Bauddha Mahasangha.[396]

I have chosen this topic mainly for three reasons. Firstly, because despite the importance of the subject I have not – to the best of my recollection – ever devoted a whole lecture to it. Secondly, because as the years go by I see, more and more clearly, how profound is the significance, and how far-reaching the implications – both theoretical and practical – of each apparently simple precept. Thirdly, because I want to emphasize yet again our principle of 'more and more of less and less', i.e. our principle of trying to go more and more deeply into the so-called basic teachings of Buddhism rather than trying to hurry on to teachings which are allegedly more advanced. This emphasis is perhaps all the more necessary now that we are celebrating our sixteenth birthday. As I mentioned earlier, now that we are sixteen we have attained the years of discretion. We are grown up. But as I also mentioned, we may not, in fact, as an order, be quite so mature as our sixteen years might lead us to suppose. One of the signs of immaturity – whether individual or collective – is that one thinks that now one is out of leading-strings, so to speak, one can safely forget the lessons learned in one's childhood. Translated into more specifically Buddhist terms, it means that one thinks one can afford to neglect the 'elementary' teachings of Buddhism – and by elementary one of course usually means the ethical teachings as embodied in, for example, the five or the eight or the ten precepts. It is in order to forestall any such development, rather than because I see any sign of it actually happening, that I want to speak on the ten precepts on this occasion.

I hope no one feels disappointed. I hope no one was expecting me to speak on some very advanced, or very esoteric, subject. If this was the case, and especially if anyone still harbours the idea that ethics is a dull and uninteresting topic, you will at least be glad to know that I am entitling this paper not simply 'The Ten Precepts', which admittedly does not sound very colourful or very inspiring, but 'The Ten Pillars of Buddhism'. The ten precepts are, indeed, the massy supports of the entire majestic edifice of the Dharma. Without the ten precepts the Dharma could not, in fact, exist. Continuing the architectural metaphor, one might say that the Three Jewels are the three-stepped plinth and foundation of the Dharma, the ten precepts the double row of pillars supporting the spacious dome, meditation the dome itself, and wisdom the lofty spire that surmounts the dome. Elaborating, one might say that each of the ten pillars was made of a precious stone or precious metal, so that there was a pillar of diamond, a pillar of gold, a pillar of crystal, and so on. In this way we would be able to gain not only an understanding of the importance of the ten precepts but also, perhaps, an appreciation of their splendour and beauty. Having exclaimed, 'How charming is divine Philosophy' Milton, in a well-known passage, goes on to assert that it is

> Not harsh and crabbéd as dull fools suppose
> But musical as is Apollo's lute.[397]

In similar vein one could assert that, like Buddhism itself, the subject of Buddhist ethics – particularly as represented by the ten precepts – was not dull and uninteresting, as to the superficial observer it might appear, but on the contrary full of light, life, warmth, and colour. Paraphrasing the paradoxical words of another poet, one might also say of Buddhist ethics – might say of the ten precepts – that you must love them before they will seem to you worthy of your love.[398]

Though I may not have devoted a whole lecture to the subject of the ten precepts, I have certainly both spoken and written on Buddhist ethics, particularly as a constituent of the Noble Eightfold Path and of the path of the ten *pāramitās* or perfections.[399] I have also dealt with the subject in an article entitled 'Aspects of Buddhist Morality', in which I discuss (1) the nature of morality, (2) morality and the spiritual ideal, (3) morality mundane and transcendental, (4) patterns of morality, (5) the benefits of morality, and (6) determinants of morality.[400] In the present paper I shall try to avoid covering ground I have already covered elsewhere, or dealing with matters that have been adequately dealt with by other writers on Buddhism, whether ancient or modern. In particular I shall try to avoid losing myself in the details of scholastic analysis in the sort of way that has become traditional for some forms of Buddhism.

Even limiting myself in this way there is still, however, a good deal of ground to be covered, and if I am to cover it even cursorily the subject matter of this paper will have to be tightly organized. In speaking on 'The Ten Pillars of Buddhism' I shall therefore divide the paper into two parts. In the first part I shall deal with the ten precepts collectively, so to speak. In the second part I shall deal with them individually, i.e. I shall deal with each of the ten precepts separately. For the sake of further convenience, the discussion of the ten precepts collectively will be broken down into a discussion of eight distinct topics, between which there will of course be various interrelations and even a certain amount of overlapping. The eight topics are (1) the relation between refuges and precepts, (2) the canonical sources of the ten precepts, (3) the ten precepts and total transformation, (4) the ten precepts as principles of ethics, (5) the ten precepts as rules of training, (6) the ten precepts as '*mūla-prātimokṣa*', (7) the ten precepts and other ethical formulas, and (8) the ten precepts and lifestyle. The division of the first part of the paper in this way will, I hope, enable us to obtain a more comprehensive view of the ten pillars of Buddhism in their collective majesty.

PART I

THE TEN PRECEPTS COLLECTIVELY

I

THE RELATION BETWEEN REFUGES AND PRECEPTS

The Three Refuges (or the Three Jewels) are, of course, the Buddha or Enlightened One, the Dharma or teaching of the way to Enlightenment, and the Sangha or spiritual community of those following the way to Enlightenment, especially those who have attained to the higher, transcendental stages of spiritual progress from which recession is not possible. One goes for Refuge to the Buddha, the Dharma, and the Sangha – or, in more contemporary idiom, commits oneself to them – when one decides that to attain Enlightenment is the most important thing in human life, and when one acts – or does one's best to act – in accordance with that decision. This means organizing one's entire life, in all its different aspects, in such a way as to subserve the attainment of Enlightenment. It means placing the ideal of Enlightenment, i.e. placing the Buddha (which Buddha one can oneself become), at the centre of one's personal mandala, and arranging one's different interests and activities in such a way that they are placed nearer to, or further away from, the centre of that mandala in accordance with the degree to which they help or hinder the attainment of Enlightenment. Interests and activities which are opposed to the ideal of Enlightenment should, of course, be banished from the mandala. Going for Refuge is the fundamental Buddhist act. It is what makes one a Buddhist, a follower of the Dharma, or a *dharmacārī/dharmacāriṇī*.[401] It is what makes one a member of the Sangha. The Going for Refuge is what, above all else, one has in common with other Buddhists. In other words, the Going for Refuge is the highest common factor of Buddhism.

Unfortunately, in many parts of the Buddhist world the Going for Refuge has long been regarded as the lowest common denominator of Buddhism rather than as the highest common factor – an undervaluation which was one of the main reasons behind the formation of the Western Buddhist Order. If there is any lowest common denominator in Buddhism it is, one might say, the five, or the eight, or the ten precepts which, on ceremonial occasions, one 'takes' from one's preceptor immediately after Going for Refuge. Again unfortunately, it is the observance of these five, or eight, or ten precepts, rather than the threefold Going for Refuge, that has come to be regarded as the highest common factor – instead of as the lowest common denominator – of Buddhism, with the result that the Buddhist community has tended to be divided by the fact that some of its members observed a lesser, and some a greater, number of precepts (generally five in the case of the 'laity' and a total of 227 or 250 in the case of the 'monks'),[402] rather than united by the fact that they all went for Refuge to the same Buddha, Dharma, and Sangha.[403]

Without understanding the supreme importance of the Going for Refuge as the central act of the Buddhist life it is quite impossible to understand the true nature of the relation between the Refuges and the Precepts. This principle holds good regardless of the actual number of precepts one undertakes to observe. The relation between refuges and precepts is not merely external. It is not that having gone for Refuge to the Buddha, the Dharma, and the Sangha, one now undertakes, in addition to that, to observe the five, or the eight, or the ten, or any other particular number of precepts. It is not that when, on ceremonial occasions, one recites first the Going for Refuge formula and then, immediately afterwards, the precept acceptance formula, one recites them in this order for purely historical reasons, so to speak, and that had things turned out differently one might just as well have been reciting them in the reverse order. The relation between one's Going for Refuge and one's observance of the precepts is an organic one, observance of the precepts being as much an expression of Going for Refuge as the flower is an expression of the seed or his *œuvre* an expression of the writer or artist. In a sense, the Going for Refuge and the observance of the precepts are part of a single process of spiritual life and growth.

When one places the Buddha, that is to say places the spiritual ideal, at the centre of one's personal mandala, a radical reorganization of the contents of that mandala naturally follows. If no such reorganization follows, then one's placing of the Buddha at the centre of one's mandala has been purely nominal, or perhaps what one has placed there is not really the Buddha at all. The placing of the Buddha at the centre of one's personal mandala corresponds to Going for Refuge. The radical reorganization of the contents of that mandala corresponds to the observance of the precepts as its natural consequence, that is to say, as the prolongation of the act of Going for Refuge itself into every aspect of one's existence.

Going for Refuge, or commitment to the Three Jewels, is one's lifeblood as a Buddhist. Observance of the precepts represents the circulation of that blood through every fibre of one's being. By its very nature blood must circulate. If it does not circulate this means that the organism to which it belongs is dead, and that the blood itself, stagnating, will soon cease to be blood. Similarly, by its very nature the Going for Refuge must find expression in the observance of the precepts. If it does not find such expression this means that as a Buddhist one is virtually dead and that the Going for Refuge itself, becoming more and more mechanical, will soon cease to be effectively such.

It is because the Going for Refuge must find expression in the total transformation of the individual, both in himself and in his relations with other people, and because this total transformation is represented more adequately by the ten precepts than by any other set of precepts, that in the Western Buddhist Order we not only go for Refuge to the Buddha, the Dharma, and the Sangha, but also undertake to observe the *ten* precepts rather than the five, or the eight, or any other specific number of precepts. To the topic of the ten precepts and total transformation we must now therefore turn. Before we do so, however, let me briefly remind you of what I have called the canonical sources of the ten precepts. Buddhist friends outside the FWBO have been known to doubt whether the ten precepts observed by members of the Western Buddhist Order were actually taught by the Buddha, and whether they are anywhere to be found in the Buddhist scriptures, and it therefore behoves us to be sure of our ground.

2

THE CANONICAL SOURCES OF THE TEN PRECEPTS

It is well known that the Buddha wrote nothing, and that for several generations his teachings were preserved by purely oral means. Only when the orally transmitted traditions were finally written down did there come into existence what we call the Buddhist scriptures or the canonical literature of Buddhism. Following the classification adopted during the period of oral transmission, this vast body of material was traditionally known as the Tripiṭaka or 'three collections', the three being the Vinaya Piṭaka or Collection of Monastic Discipline, the Sūtra Piṭaka or Collection of Discourses, and the Abhidharma Piṭaka or Collection of Further Doctrine. Both spiritually and historically speaking, the most important of the three is the Sūtra Piṭaka, and references to the ten precepts, in one form or another, are to be found in each of the four (or in the case of the Pāli Tipiṭaka five) *āgamas* or *nikāyas* of which this *piṭaka* consists.

In the case of the Pāli recension of the Tripiṭaka, the first reference to the ten precepts is to be found in the *Kūṭadanta Sutta*, the fifth *sutta* of the *Dīgha Nikāya* or 'Collection of Long Discourses'. This *sutta* deals with the subject of sacrifice, and is concerned to establish the superiority of the purely moral and spiritual 'sacrifice' taught by the Buddha over the bloody sacrifices of the old Brahminical religion. The brahmin Kūṭadanta, who gives his name to the title of the *sutta*, has assembled many hundreds of animals in readiness for a great sacrifice, but not knowing how to perform it, with its threefold method and its *sixteen* accessory instruments (another important instance of this numerical group), he decides to go and ask the Buddha, who knows all about such things. In response to Kūṭadanta's enquiry the Buddha relates the story of a great king of former times called Mahāvijita. This king, too, had wanted to offer a great sacrifice, and had asked the royal chaplain to instruct him how the sacrifice should be performed. The royal chaplain (who, it turns out, was the Buddha himself in a previous existence) had thereupon given what was, in effect, a systematic allegorization of the entire sacrificial procedure. Among other things he told the king – and it is with this part of the *sutta* that we are at present concerned – about the different kinds of men who would come to his sacrifice.

> Now there will come to your sacrifice, Sire, men who destroy the life of living things, and men who refrain therefrom – men who take what has not been given, and men who refrain therefrom – men who act evilly in respect of lusts, and men who refrain therefrom – men who speak lies, and men who do not – men who slander, and men who do not – men who speak rudely, and men who do not – men who chatter vain things, and men who refrain therefrom – men who covet, and men who covet not – men who harbour ill-will, and men who harbour it not – men whose views are wrong, and men whose views are right.[404]

Here the ten precepts, in their positive and negative forms, are clearly referred to. After being given further instruction by the Buddha, who sets forth for his benefit the successive stages of spiritual progress, Kūṭadanta realizes what is the best sacrifice of all and obtains the pure and spotless Eye of Truth, thus becoming a Stream Entrant. The fact that the ten precepts should be referred to, in this *sutta*, in the context of a story of former times is interesting, suggesting as it does that for the compilers of the Collection of Long Discourses this particular ethical formula was of great antiquity, or that it belonged, as we would say, to the earliest days of Buddhism.

Passing from the *Dīgha Nikāya* to the *Majjhima Nikāya* or 'Collection of Middle Length Discourses', we find a detailed exposition of the ten precepts in the important *Sevitabbāsevitabba Sutta,* or 'Discourse on What is to be Followed and What is Not to be Followed'.[405] The exposition is given not by the Buddha but by Sāriputta, who explains to the monks what he understands to be the meaning in full of what has just been spoken by the Buddha in brief. There are two kinds of bodily conduct, the Buddha has told them, two kinds of vocal conduct, and two kinds of mental conduct, as well as two kinds of arising of thoughts, two kinds of assumption of perception, two kinds of assumption of views, and two kinds of assumption of individuality, and in the case of each dyad there is one kind which should be followed and one which should not be followed. Sāriputta explains this by distinguishing between that kind of bodily conduct etc. as a result of which unskilled (*akusala*) states of mind grow much and skilled (*kusala*) states decrease and that kind as a result of which unskilled states of mind decrease and skilled states of mind grow much. The first kind should not be followed, the second kind should be followed. Applying this to bodily conduct, vocal conduct, and mental conduct (the four other dyads appear to be treated as subdivisions of mental conduct), he describes in each case what kind of conduct makes unskilled states of mind grow and skilled states decrease and vice versa. In this way he describes, in some detail, the ten *akusala-dhammas* from which a man should abstain and the ten *kusala-dhammas* which he should observe and cultivate, i.e. he describes the ten precepts. (Significantly, it is only *bhikkhus* or 'monks' who are present throughout the *sutta*.)

As an example of Sāriputta's exposition, all of which is approved and in fact repeated verbatim by the Buddha, let me quote part of his explanation of the content of the eighth and ninth precepts, i.e. abstention from covetousness and from malevolence and the cultivation of their opposites. First he is careful to make clear what it is he is explaining. In expositions of this sort we can, perhaps, see the beginnings of the Abhidharma, with which the name of Sāriputta is, of course, associated.

> 'I, monks, say that mental conduct is of two kinds, one of which is to be followed and the other which is not to be followed; and there is this disparity in mental conduct.' This was said by the Lord. In reference to what was it said? Revered sir, if a certain kind of mental conduct is followed and unskilled states of mind grow much, skilled states of mind decrease, this kind of mental conduct is not to be followed. Revered sir, if a certain kind of mental conduct is followed and unskilled states of mind decrease,

skilled states of mind grow much, this kind of mental conduct is to be followed.

And what kind of mental conduct, revered sir, does a man follow that unskilled states of mind grow much in him, skilled states of mind decrease? As to this, revered sir, someone is covetous; he covets that which is the property of another, thinking: 'O might that which is the other's be mine'; he is malevolent in thought, corrupt in mind and purpose, and thinks: 'Let these beings be killed or slaughtered or annihilated or destroyed, or may they not exist at all.' If this kind of mental conduct is followed, revered sir, unskilled states of mind grow much, skilled states of mind decrease.

And what kind of mental conduct, revered sir, does a man follow that unskilled states of mind decrease in him, skilled states of mind grow much? As to this, revered sir, someone is not covetous; he does not covet that which is the property of another, thinking: 'O might that which is the other's be mine'; he is not malevolent in thought, not corrupt in mind and purpose, but thinks: 'Let these beings, free from enmity, peaceable, secure and happy, look after self.' If this kind of mental conduct is followed, revered sir, unskilled states of mind decrease, skilled states of mind grow much. When the Lord said: 'I, monks, say that mental conduct is of two kinds, one of which is to be followed and the other which is not to be followed; and there is this disparity in mental conduct,' it was said in reference to this.[406]

Though the *Sevitabbāsevitabba Sutta* is perhaps the most important of the Pāli canonical sources of the ten precepts, there are a number of others also. In particular there is an important group of about fifty short *suttas* in the *Aṅguttara Nikāya* or 'Collection of Gradual (or Numerical) Sayings', i.e. sayings on the ones, the twos, the threes, and so on up to the elevens. Many of these *suttas* differ only in respect of the place at which they were delivered, and the person to whom the teaching was addressed, the speaker being in all cases the Buddha himself. Some *suttas* resemble the *Kūṭadanta Sutta* in that the observance of the ten precepts is represented as being a better way of offering a sacrifice, or performing rites of purification, or making offerings to the dead. Among the *suttas* of this type there is one (untitled) *sutta* which is characteristic of the whole group. In this *sutta* the Buddha explains to Cunda the silversmith, who finds satisfaction in the purifying rites of 'the brahmins of the west who carry waterpots', in what real purification consists. After describing how the ten precepts are observed in their negative form, he proceeds to describe how they are observed in their positive form.

> But, Cunda, threefold is cleansing by body, fourfold is cleansing by speech, threefold is cleansing by mind. And how is cleansing by body threefold?
>
> Herein, Cunda, a certain one abandons taking life, abstains therefrom; he has laid aside the rod, has laid aside the knife; he dwells modest, charitable, feeling compassion towards every living creature.
>
> He abandons taking what is not given, abstains therefrom; the property of another, situated in jungle or in village, if not given, he takes not with thievish intent.
>
> In sexual desires he abandons wrong action, abstains therefrom. He has no intercourse with girls in ward of mother or father, of brother, sister or relatives (or clan), with girls lawfully guarded, already plighted to a husband and protected by the rod, even with girls crowned with the flower-garlands (of betrothal). Thus, Cunda, threefold is cleansing by body.
>
> And how is cleansing by speech fourfold? Herein, Cunda, a certain one abandons lying, abstains therefrom. When cited to appear before the council or a company or amid his relatives or guild-men or before the royal family and asked to bear witness with the words: 'Come, good fellow! Say what you know,' not knowing, he says, 'I know not'; knowing, he says 'I know'; not having seen, he says, 'I saw not'; having seen, he says, 'I saw'. Thus for his own sake or for the sake of others or to get some carnal profit or other he does not utter any deliberate falsehood.
>
> Abandoning slanderous speech he abstains therefrom. When he hears something at one place he does not proclaim it elsewhere to bring about a quarrel between the parties; what he has heard here he does not report there to bring about a quarrel between the parties; thus he brings together the discordant, restores harmony, harmony is his delight, he exults in, is passionately fond of harmony; he utters speech that makes for harmony. Also he

> abandons harsh speech, abstains therefrom. Whatsoever speech is blameless, pleasant to the ear, affectionate, going to the heart, urbane, agreeable to many folk, delightful to many folk, of such speech he is a speaker. Also abandoning idle babble he abstains therefrom; he speaks in season, of facts, of the aim, of dhamma, of discipline; he utters speech worth treasuring up, speech seasonable and worth listening to, discriminating and concerned with the aim.
>
> Thus, Cunda, fourfold is cleansing by speech. And how is cleansing by mind threefold?
>
> Herein a certain one is not covetous; he covets not the property of another, thinking: O that what is another's were mine! He is not malevolent of heart, the thoughts of his heart are not corrupt. He wishes: Let these beings carry about the self in peace, free from enmity, free from sorrow and in happiness.
>
> Also he has right view; he is reasonable in outlook, holding that there are such things as gift, offering, oblation, fruit and ripening of deeds done well or ill; that this world is, that the world beyond is; that mother, father and beings of supernatural birth (in other worlds) do exist; that there are in the world recluses and brāhmins who have gone rightly, who fare rightly, men who of their own comprehension have realized this world and the world beyond and thus declare it.
>
> Thus, Cunda, threefold is the cleansing by the mind. So these are the ten ways of right doing.[407]

In other *suttas* the Buddha speaks of the observance and the non-observance of the ten precepts (usually in their negative form only) in terms of the hither and the further shore, Dhamma and not-Dhamma, the bright and the dark way, and so on, thus making it clear that the ten precepts represent a pattern of ethical behaviour that can be looked at in a number of different ways, and from a number of different points of view.[408] In several *suttas*, moreover, the Buddha speaks in terms of one's possessing or not possessing ten, or twenty, or thirty, or forty meritorious or demeritorious qualities. The ten qualities are equivalent to one's observing (or not observing) the ten precepts, the twenty qualities to one's not only observing (or not observing) them oneself, but also encouraging (or not encouraging) another to observe them too. Similarly, the thirty qualities consist in one's observing the ten precepts oneself, encouraging another to do likewise, and giving one's approval thereto (as well as the opposites of these), while the forty qualities are the thirty qualities plus speaking in praise, or not speaking in praise, of the ten precepts.[409] Here the self-regarding and other-regarding aspects of the ethical and spiritual life are given equal prominence.

The canonical sources of the ten precepts are also to be found in the Sanskrit recension of the Tripiṭaka, including the Mahāyāna *sūtras*. Since the fact that the ten precepts were actually taught by the Buddha, and are indeed to be found in the Buddhist scriptures, has already been sufficiently established, I shall deal with the Sanskrit canonical sources of the ten precepts even more summarily than with their Pāli counterparts. The Sanskrit recension of the Tripiṭaka does not, of course, survive complete in the original language. Of the portions that do survive, one of the most interesting and important is the *Mahāvastu*, a work which purports to belong to the Vinaya Piṭaka of the Lokottaravādins, a sub-school of the Mahāsāṃghikas, though it does not deal with Vinaya or monastic discipline in the ordinary sense of the term at all. The *Mahāvastu* is, in fact, a highly devotional 'legendary biography' of the Buddha, interspersed with numerous *Jātakas* or Birth Stories. It is in one of the *Jātakas* that the reference to the ten precepts occurs.

The *Jātaka* in question is the *Kinnarī Jātaka*, a charming tale of love, adventure, and magic that recalls the Arthurian romances and the stories of the *Arabian Nights Entertainments* rather than the sort of material normally found in the Buddhist scriptures, especially the Vinaya Piṭaka. There is no time even to summarize the *Kinnarī Jātaka*, but at one point Prince Sudhanu, who is the hero of the tale and, therefore, the Buddha himself in a previous existence, attends the great Brahminical sacrifice which King Sucandrima is about to perform 'with every kind of animal', including Manoharā, the *kinnarī* or 'elf maiden', the heroine of the tale, who has just been captured. When Prince Sudhanu asks the king why so many living beings (including the unfortunate *kinnarī*) are enclosed in the sacrificial enclosure, and what profit there is in the sacrifice, the king replies that the living beings who will be slain in the sacrifice will go to heaven, while he himself will be reborn in heaven a number of times equal to the number of beings he will slay in the sacrifice.

The prince is deeply shocked, and tells the king that this is a wrong view, since the highest rule of *dharma* (*paramaṃ dharmaṃ*) is not to cause harm (*ahiṃsa*). To take life is not *dharma*, he declares; to abstain from taking life is *dharma*. Similarly, to steal is not *dharma*; not to steal is *dharma*. In this way Sudhanu enunciates the ten precepts. Indeed, he does more than that. Between the third and fourth precepts he inserts an extra precept, relating to the drinking of intoxicating liquor and spirits. It is interesting, though, that after enunciating the precepts he concludes by saying that the path of the *ten* right actions is *dharma*. Those who follow the path of the ten wrong actions, he tells the king, are reborn in hell. Those who follow the path of the ten right actions are reborn in heaven. In the present instance the path taken by the king is not the path to heaven; it is the path that leads to hell.

So impressed is King Sucandrima by this exposition of the Dharma that he releases all the living things he had brought together for the sacrifice, including the *kinnarī*, whereupon Sudhanu and Manoharā, who have of course fallen in love, leave for the prince's own city – but this is only the beginning of the tale.[410]

Few of the Mahāyāna *sūtras* survive in the original Sanskrit, most of them being extant only in Chinese and/or Tibetan translation. Among those still available in Sanskrit is the *Aṣṭasāhaṣrikā-prajñāpāramitā* or 'Perfection of Wisdom in Eight Thousand Lines', in which the Buddha, addressing the *arhant* Subhūti, speaks of the signs of an irreversible bodhisattva, i.e. a bodhisattva who, having renounced the possibility of Nirvāṇa for himself alone, is irreversible from supreme perfect Enlightenment for the benefit of all living beings. Such an irreversible bodhisattva, the Buddha says, undertakes to observe the ten avenues or ways of wholesome action. He himself observes, and instigates others to observe, abstention from taking life and so on, down to abstention from wrong views.

> It is quite certain that an irreversible Bodhisattva observes the ten ways of wholesome action, and instigates others to observe them, incites and encourages them to do so, establishes and confirms others in them. Even in his dreams he never commits offences against those ten precepts, and he does not nurse such offences in his mind. Even in his dreams an irreversible Bodhisattva keeps the ten wholesome paths of action present in his mind.[411]

One of the most important of the Mahāyāna *sūtras* that do *not* survive in the original Sanskrit, but only in Chinese and Tibetan translation, is the *Vimalakīrti-nirdeśa* or 'Exposition of Vimalakīrti'. Here the purity of the *kuśala-karma-pathas* or ten ways of skilful action, as the ten precepts are termed in this context, is said to be the *buddha-kṣetra* or Buddha-field of the bodhisattva.[412] It is from the ten paths of skilful action, moreover, that the Tathāgata's body (*kāya*) is born.[413] The ten ways of skilful action are one of the ways in which, according to Vimalakīrti, the Blessed Lord Śākyamuni expounds the Dharma here in the Sahā-world, and so on.[414] Finally, the ten precepts are mentioned in the celebrated third chapter of the *Suvarṇa-prabhāsa Sūtra* or 'Sūtra of Golden Light', the chapter on Confession, which probably forms the original nucleus of the entire work,[415] and they are the principal subject matter of the *Discourse on the Ten Wholesome Ways of Action*, a short work said to have been translated into Chinese from the Sanskrit.[416]

Having shown that the ten precepts observed by members of the Western Buddhist Order actually were taught by the Buddha, and that references to them are found throughout the Tripiṭaka, we are now in a position to turn to the question of why the total transformation of the individual in which the act of Going for Refuge finds, and must find, expression, is represented more adequately by the ten precepts than by another set of precepts.

3
THE TEN PRECEPTS AND TOTAL TRANSFORMATION

The human individual in his or her concrete reality is not simple but composite, consisting of various elements which can be distinguished even if not actually divided. These elements are variously enumerated. Pauline Christianity has its body, soul, and spirit, Upanishadic Hinduism its five *kośas* consisting, respectively, of food, breath, mind, intelligence, and bliss, Neoplatonism its soma, psyche, and pneuma, and so on. In Buddhism the human individual is traditionally analysed into two, three, or five principal elements, each one of which is, of course, susceptible of further analysis. The twofold analysis resolves man into *nāma* or 'name', by which is meant his subjective mental existence, and *rūpa* or form, by which is meant his objective material existence. The threefold analysis resolves him into body (*kāya* in Sanskrit and Pāli), speech (Sanskrit *vāc,* Pāli *vācā*), and mind (*citta,* Sanskrit and Pāli). In the more elaborate fivefold analysis the human individual is resolved into body (*rūpa* in Sanskrit and Pāli), feeling (*vedanā,* Sanskrit and Pāli), perception (Sanskrit *saṃjñā*, Pāli *saññā*), volition (Sanskrit *saṃskāra,* Pāli *saṅkhāra*), and consciousness (Sanskrit *vijñāna,* Pāli *viññāṇa*), collectively known as the five 'heaps' (Sanskrit *skandhas,* Pāli *khandas*).

Each set of elements, whether of a twofold, threefold, or fivefold nature, forms the centre of a vast and complex network of doctrinal, ethical, and symbolical correlations and associations which, in the course of centuries of development, grew more and more elaborate.

What in the case of an ordinary unenlightened human being is simply name and form, in the case of a Buddha is *dharmakāya* and *rūpakāya*, i.e. the 'body' in which he realizes the ultimate truth of things and the 'body' in which he continues to function in the world of appearances. Similarly, there is a correlation between the threefold composition of man, as consisting of body, speech, and mind, and the threefold composition of the Buddha, as consisting (according to the Yogācāra systematization subsequently adopted by all the Mahāyāna schools) not only of a *dharmakāya* and a *rūpakāya* (in this scheme termed the *nirmāṇakāya* or 'created body') but also of a *sambhogakāya* or 'body of glory' (literally 'body of mutual enjoyment') in which he functions on the higher spiritual planes and by means of which, in particular, he communicates with the Buddhas of other world-systems and with advanced bodhisattvas.[417] In the case of the fivefold analysis of man, the five heaps are correlated with various other sets of five, both microcosmic and macrocosmic. There are the five Buddha families, the five knowledges (*jñāna*), the five passions (*kleśa*), the five elements, the five colours, and so on.[418]

In addition, inasmuch as they are all analyses of the same 'object', i.e. the concrete reality of the human individual, the twofold, threefold, and fivefold analyses are naturally interrelated. 'Name' in the twofold analysis corresponds to speech and mind in the threefold analysis (and vice versa), while mind in the threefold analysis corresponds to feeling, perception, volition, and consciousness in the fivefold analysis (and vice versa). In other words, each analysis is an analysis of the total human being and it is, of course, of the transformation of the total human being that we speak when we speak of the ten precepts and total transformation. Total transformation represents the complete transformation of the total individual in accordance with the highest imaginable ideal, the ideal of human Enlightenment.

But how is it that the *ten* precepts, in particular, should be associated with this process of total transformation, rather than the five or the eight, for instance? The answer to the question is implicit in what has already been said. The precepts represent, in principle, the prolongation of the act of Going for Refuge into every aspect of one's existence. They represent, in other words, the total transformation of the individual who goes for Refuge, in accordance with the ideal which that Going for Refuge implies. The precepts which such an individual undertakes to observe, as the natural extension of his Going for Refuge, should therefore correspond to the principal elements of his existence. This means, in effect, that the division of the precepts should correspond to the 'division' of the individual human being as represented by one or another of the traditional Buddhist analyses.

The only set of precepts which fulfils this requirement is that of the ten precepts, which inasmuch as it comprises three precepts governing the body, four governing the speech, and three governing the mind, corresponds to the threefold analysis of man into body, speech, and mind. It is only the ten precepts, therefore, that bring out with sufficient clarity the fact that the precepts represent the total transformation of the individual as the consequence of his Going for Refuge, and it is the ten precepts, therefore, that members of the Western Buddhist Order undertake to observe.

Before we conclude our consideration of this topic let me draw your attention to an interesting and significant fact. As we have seen, Buddhism analyses man into body, speech, and mind, and it is this triad which provides the framework for the ten precepts. References to 'body, speech, and mind' are, in fact, found throughout the Tripiṭaka, and it would appear that the triad goes back to the earliest period of Buddhism and formed part of the Buddha's own 'language'. As we know, that language was adopted, and in part adapted, from the existing Indian religious tradition or traditions, some terms and concepts indeed being subjected to radical redefinition and reinterpretation. The triad of body, speech, and mind did not form part of this already existing 'language'. Indeed, according to sources which I have not, as yet, had the opportunity of checking, the concept of man as consisting of body, speech, and mind is not to be found in the Vedas. If the Buddha did not think of it himself, and it seems unlikely that he did, then where did he get it from? He could only have got it – and this is the interesting and possibly significant fact to which I wanted to draw your attention – from the Zoroastrian tradition, in which the same triad occupies an extremely important place and where, as in Buddhism, there is a strong emphasis on a corresponding threefold purification.

This raises all sorts of fascinating questions concerning the relations between India and the Persian Empire, and between India and Central Asia, as well as concerning the extent to which Zoroastrianism may have influenced Buddhism, and Buddhism, in its turn, may have influenced Sufism. Fascinating as they are, however, these are questions which must be pursued on some future occasion. Meanwhile, we must proceed to our next topic.

4
THE TEN PRECEPTS AS PRINCIPLES OF ETHICS

First a few definitions. By 'principle' is meant, in this connection, (a) 'a fundamental truth; a comprehensive law or doctrine, from which others are derived, or on which others are founded', and (b) 'a settled rule of action; a governing law of conduct; an opinion, attitude, or belief which exercises a directing influence on the life and behaviour; a rule (usually a right rule) of conduct consistently directing one's actions'. From this it is evident that the English word 'principle' (deriving ultimately from the Latin *principium, princeps*) has much in common with the Sanskrit word *dharma* (Pāli *dhamma*, Chinese *fa*, Tibetan *chös*). The Dharma taught by the Buddha, and to which as the second of the Three Jewels we go for Refuge, represents not only the fundamental truth or reality of things, as revealed in the Enlightened consciousness of the Buddha, but also that truth or reality as communicated to mankind in the form of a comprehensive law or doctrine from which there proceeds a governing law of conduct that exercises a directing influence on the life and behaviour of the individual '*dharmacārī* or *dharmacāriṇī*', i.e. the one who 'courses' (*carati*) in the Dharma-as-truth and the Dharma-as-righteousness. Thus the terms principle and *dharma* have a double significance, a significance that relates to both thought and action, theory and practice. Ethics is generally defined as 'the science of moral duty' or, more broadly, as 'the science of the ideal human character and the ideal ends of human action'. For the purpose of this discussion, it could be defined as that branch of knowledge which is concerned with human behaviour in so far as that behaviour is considered with regard to notions of right and wrong.

The expression 'the ten precepts' is, of course, English, and I have been using it as the equivalent of a number of different terms in Sanskrit and Pāli. What we call the ten precepts is referred to, in the canonical sources, as the ten *śīlas* (a term which is applied, as we shall see later on, to more than one set of precepts), as the ten *śikṣāpadas*, as the ten *kuśala-karma-pathas*, and so on. (It must be emphasized that although the terms for them vary, the number of items comprised in the set remains unchanged, as does the actual content of each item.) Indeed, as we saw when referring to the fifty *suttas* of the *Aṅguttara Nikāya* which are canonical sources of the ten precepts, what we call the ten precepts are in fact known by a wide variety of designations, their actual content however always remaining the same. Perhaps the best-known term for the ten precepts is that which speaks of them as consisting of abstention from the ten *akuśala-dharmas* (Pāli *akusala-dhammas*) as they are called, and in the observance, practice, or cultivation of the ten *kuśala-dharmas* (Pāli *kusala-dhammas*).

Kuśala is a very important term. In its broader significance it means clever, skilful, or expert in the sense of knowing how to act in a way that is beneficial rather than otherwise. *Kuśala-karma* or skilful action thus is action that is directed towards securing, both for oneself and others, the best possible results in terms of happiness, knowledge, and freedom, i.e. it is action which is constantly mindful of the law of *karma*, as well as of the painful, impermanent, and insubstantial nature of conditioned existence, and of the blissful, permanent, and 'empty' nature of the Unconditioned. *Kuśala* thus is an ethical term, since it is a term which is applied, in the words of our definition of ethics, to 'human behaviour in so far as that behaviour is considered with regard to the notions of right and wrong.' Nor is that all. The term *kuśala* is not applied to human behaviour considered with regard to notions of right or wrong in any merely abstract or 'comparative' sense. It is applied to it as considered with regard to a very definite and specific notion which the term *kuśala* itself implies, and which it even embodies, i.e. the notion that 'right' is what conduces to the attainment of Enlightenment and 'wrong' what does not. The meaning of 'ethics' and the meaning of '*kuśala*' therefore coincide. *Kuśala* is not simply an ethical term. *Kuśala* is itself the ethical.

But we can go further than that. The topic with which we are at present concerned is 'the ten precepts as principles of ethics'. We have seen that the best-known term for the ten precepts is the ten *kuśala-dharmas*. We have also seen that the word 'principle' has much in common with the word '*dharma*', even to the extent of their sharing the double connotation of relating to both thinking and doing, the theoretical and the practical, and that the word *kuśala* coincides in meaning with 'ethical' and even with 'ethics'. Such being the case it should be clear, without further explanation, that what the ten precepts really represent are principles of ethics, or ethical principles. They are not rules, in the narrow, pettifogging sense of the term. They are not directly concerned with the minutiae of conduct, though they of course may be concerned with them indirectly.

The fact that, as we have seen, the observance of the precepts represents the prolongation of the act of Going for Refuge into every aspect of one's existence, i.e. represents the total transformation of the individual who goes for Refuge in accordance with the ideal which the Going for Refuge implies, means that one's behaviour comes to be increasingly governed by ten great ethical principles, the principles of non-violence or love, of non-appropriation or generosity, and so on. Thus the ten precepts are not rules, though rules may be founded on them, or derived from them. If we could think of the precepts as being what in fact they are, ethical principles in accordance with which, as a result of our commitment to the ideal of Enlightenment, we are doing our best to live, a good deal of confusion would be avoided. We would also find the precepts themselves more inspiring.

Though the precepts are most decidedly principles and not rules, yet rules in the sense of rules of training may, as I have said, be founded on them or derived from them. Moreover, both as principles and as rules the precepts may be transmitted, within the appropriate ceremonial context, from teacher to disciple. To the topic of the ten precepts as rules of training we must now therefore turn.

5
THE TEN PRECEPTS AS RULES OF TRAINING

The expression 'rules of training' is being used in this connection simply as the working equivalent of the Sanskrit *śikṣāpadas* (Pāli *sikkhāpada*), otherwise rendered as 'moral commandments' or even as 'set of precepts'. In speaking of the ten precepts as rules of training we are, therefore, really speaking of the ten precepts as *śikṣāpadas*, and for this reason it is necessary for us to inquire into the meaning of the term. *Pada* means 'step, footstep', and thus, in its applied meaning, 'case, lot, principle, part, constituent, characteristic, ingredient, item, thing, element'. In the present context it is best rendered as 'item', so that if *śikṣa* is 'training', *śikṣāpada* is 'item of training'. *Śikṣā* is an interesting word, and one that forms part of a number of compounds. It derives from the desiderative of a verbal root meaning 'to be able', and therefore means 'learning, study, art, skill in', as well as 'teaching, training'. Thus it is approximately equivalent to the English word 'education', though since this derives from a Latin root meaning 'to draw out', whereas *śikṣā* derives from a Sanskrit root meaning 'to be able', there must be subtle differences in connotation between the two terms which educationists and *śikṣāvādins* alike might find it useful to study. In speaking of the ten precepts as *śikṣāpadas* we are, therefore, speaking of them as something to be learned, which means that we are speaking of them as *capable* of being learned. Indeed, in speaking of the precepts as *śikṣāpadas*, and therefore as capable of being learned (and one speaks of them in this way when 'taking' them from a teacher), one is at the same time speaking of oneself as one who is capable of learning them, i.e. capable of observing, or putting into practice, those ethical principles which, as we have already seen, are what the ten precepts primarily represent.

This emphasis on capability, learning, and training is, of course, very much in accordance with the spirit of Buddhism. Indeed, a well-known canonical formula declares the Buddha to be *purisadamma-sārathi*, 'the charioteer for the training of persons',[419] and in more than one passage of the Tripiṭaka the Buddha himself describes the course of the spiritual life in terms of the gradual taming and training of a mettlesome young horse (cf. the Zen 'ox-herding pictures').[420]

Now learning implies its correlate, which is teaching; that one person learns implies that another teaches. In other words, just as education implies the existence of an educator, as well as the existence of one who is being educated, so a trainee implies the existence of a trainer, and the precepts the existence of a preceptor. The fact that the ten precepts, i.e. the ten great ethical principles, are *śikṣāpadas*, therefore means that the ten precepts are not only something to be learned (and, therefore, something one considers oneself capable of learning) but also something to be learned personally from a teacher. It is for this reason that the ten precepts are 'taken', at the time of 'ordination', from a teacher or preceptor, and the fact that in this context the ten precepts are termed *śikṣāpadas* or things one is able and willing to learn means that they are taken not simply as ethical principles – ethical principles which henceforth will govern one's entire life – but also as principles which have to be learned, i.e. learned from a teacher.

Learning the ten precepts or ten great ethical principles in this way involves a number of things. It involves learning – in the sense of genuinely imbibing – the spirit as distinct from the letter of the ten precepts, learning how to apply the ten precepts to the affairs of everyday life, and learning how to confess breaches of the ten precepts and how to make any such breaches good. It also involves learning how to make and keep vows, in the sense of solemn promises to do something (e.g. to perform the Sevenfold Puja every day) or not to do something (e.g. not engage in sexual activity) for a certain specified period.[421] Obviously there is a great deal that could be said on all these things, but time is short, there is still a good deal of ground to be covered, and we must pass on to the next topic.

6
THE TEN PRECEPTS AS 'MŪLA-PRĀTIMOKṢA'

The term *prātimokṣa* (Pāli *pāṭimokkha*) is one of the most interesting and important terms in Early Buddhism or, more precisely, in what some scholars have called Early Monastic Buddhism. Despite the importance of the term, however, its real meaning, and even the nature of its original significance for the Buddhist community, are still matters of debate. With Childers, most modern scholars seem to regard it as being the same word as *praṭimokṣa* in the sense of 'binding, obligatory, obligation',[422] so that *prātimokṣa* (with a long ā) means 'that which should be made binding'. A popular traditional explanation is that it means 'release from', the release in question being the release (*mokṣa*) from (*praṭi*) a breach of the precepts obtained by a monk when he confesses his offence at the fortnightly meeting of the chapter of the monastic community. According to a Tibetan tradition, possibly deriving from Indian sources, *prātimokṣa* is to be understood as 'individual liberation' (*so sor thar pa*) in the sense of the discipline that supports the individual liberation of the monk or nun.[423] Whatever the literal meaning of the term, and whatever the nature of its original significance for the Buddhist community may have been, there is no doubt that it very early came to be applied to the set of 150 rules[424] binding on the individual monk – rules that formed the backbone, so to speak, of the code of between 227 and 263 rules (the traditions differ) governing the system of fully-developed cenobitical monasticism.[425] By an extension of its meaning, the term also came to be applied, eventually, to the respective codes of all seven of the different socio-religious classes of persons comprising the Buddhist community. Besides the *bhikṣu-prātimokṣa* there was a *bhikṣuṇī-prātimokṣa* or code of rules for the nuns, a *prātimokṣa* for the *śikṣamānā* or female probationer, a *prātimokṣa* for the *śrāmaṇera* or male novice, a *prātimokṣa* for the *śrāmaṇerikā* or female novice, a *prātimokṣa* for the *upāsaka* or male lay devotee, and a *prātimokṣa* for the *upāsikā* or female lay devotee. Thus there were seven different *prātimokṣas* or seven different sets of rules or sets of precepts which, though they were different *as prātimokṣas*, were not always different in respect of the actual rules or precepts of which they consisted.[426]

In those parts of the Buddhist world where the precepts, i.e. the *prātimokṣa*, took the place of the Going for Refuge as the highest common factor of Buddhism, the fact that the monks observed a much bigger number of precepts (the nuns, who were neither numerous nor influential, do not come into the picture), and the male and female lay devotees a very much smaller number, meant that the difference between the monks and the laity was exaggerated to such an extent that the unity of the Buddhist community was virtually disrupted. When we compare the different sets of precepts, however, from the 227 to 263 observed by the monk to the five (occasionally eight) observed by the lay devotee, we find that the precepts they observe in common are of far greater importance than the precepts observed only by the monks. Indeed, we find that some of the precepts observed only by the monks represent, in fact, not *additional* precepts so much as either (a) a more thoroughgoing application of the precepts observed by the laity, i.e. the precepts that the monks and laity observe in common, or (b) an application of those precepts to certain more specific conditions, especially the conditions of cenobitical monastic life.

We also find that some of the precepts observed only by the monks are of no real ethical significance, being in some cases concerned with matters of a quite trivial nature and demonstrably the product of social conditions prevailing at the time of the Buddha or shortly after.[427] Unfortunately, it is 'precepts' of this sort which, only too often, have been emphasized at the expense of that part of the *bhikṣu* code of rules which is of a genuinely ethical character, i.e. at the expense of what I am calling the '*mūla-prātimokṣa*', with the result that the division between the monks and the laity has widened, in some Buddhist countries, to so great an extent that one is justified in speaking of there being, in the religious or spiritual sense, first-class Buddhists and second-class Buddhists.

If the spiritual unity of the Buddhist community is to be preserved from disruption, therefore, what is needed is (a) an uncompromising assertion of the primacy of the Going for Refuge as the fundamental Buddhist act, and (b) a drastic reduction of the rules comprising the seven different *prātimokṣas* to those precepts of genuinely ethical significance which they have in common, together with a firm insistence on the necessity of one's actually observing those precepts. If the different *prātimokṣas* are 'reduced' in this way what one will have left will be, in effect, the ten precepts – though inasmuch as they include three purely 'mental' precepts the ten precepts are, in fact, more comprehensive in scope than are all the seven *prātimokṣas* combined.

The ten precepts therefore constitute the *'mūla-prātimokṣa'* or 'fundamental *prātimokṣa*', as I have called it, the term being not a traditional one – though it might well have been – but one of my own devising. It is the ten precepts in the sense of the ten great ethical principles which, in reality, all practising Buddhists – and there is really no other kind – have in common. When one has refined the crude ore of popular Buddhist ethical and pseudo-ethical observance, whether 'monastic' or 'lay', when one has removed the accretions and excrescences, and picked out the foreign bodies, one finds that one then has left the scintillating diamond, the gleaming gold, and the pure crystal, and so on, of the ten precepts, i.e. one has left those ten great ethical principles which, as prolongations of the act of Going for Refuge into every aspect of one's existence, govern and eventually transform one's life.

It is for this reason that the ten precepts have been adopted by the Western Buddhist Order in preference to any of the other traditional sets of precepts, whether they are merely mentioned in the Buddhist scriptures or actually transmitted by the various Buddhist schools. For the Western Buddhist Order the ten precepts, as *mūla-prātimokṣa*, are in fact the discipline that supports the 'individual liberation' not only of the monk and the nun, but of all members of the Buddhist community irrespective of lifestyle.

Since there is only one set of precepts, i.e. the ten precepts, so far as the Western Buddhist Order is concerned there is only one 'ordination', i.e. the *dharmacārī/dharmacāriṇī* ordination, which means that in the

Western Buddhist Order one is not ordained as a monk, or as a nun, or as a female probationer, or as a male novice, or as a female novice, or as a male lay devotee, or as a female lay devotee, but simply and solely as a full, practising member of the sangha or Buddhist spiritual community, though it is of course open to one to observe, as personal vows, any of the rules traditionally observed by the monk, or the nun, and so on. Strictly speaking, these rules are not observed *in addition to* the ten precepts but as representing the more intensive practice of one or more of the precepts within a certain specific situation or for a certain purpose.[428]

Not being a *bhikṣu*, a member of the Western Buddhist Order does not wear the stitched yellow garment of the *bhikṣu*, and not being an *upāsaka* he does not wear the white garments of the *upāsaka*. He wears the ordinary 'lay' dress of the society to which he belongs, though without the implication that because he is not a monk he must therefore be a layman in the traditional Buddhist sense.

Thus from the reduction of the rules comprising the seven different *prātimokṣas* to the ten precepts or *mūla-prātimokṣa*, there follows a reduction – or rather an elevation – of the various socio-religious groups within the Buddhist community to one great spiritual community or *Mahāsaṅgha*. Such a reduction represents a return to, and a renewed emphasis upon, the basics of Buddhism. It can be regarded as innovative only by adopting a standpoint from which those basics are ignored or from which they cannot be seen for the accretions and excrescences by which they have become overlaid.

As we saw when considering the sources of the ten precepts in the *Majjhima Nikāya*, Sāriputta and the Buddha are represented in the *Sevitabbāsevitabba Sutta* as in turn expounding the ten precepts in front of an assembly of *bhikkhus* or monks, though we may be sure that they were not 'monks' in the full cenobitical sense of later times. Among the fifty *suttas* of the *Aṅguttara Nikāya*, another canonical source of the ten precepts, there are three *suttas* in which the ten precepts are referred to as being observed (or not observed) by womenfolk (*mātugāma*), by a female lay devotee, and by a female lay devotee who dwells at home with (or without) confidence, respectively.[429] The ten precepts are thus shown to have been the common observance of persons of different socio-religious classes. Moreover, the *Sevitabbāsevitabba Sutta* concludes with the Buddha saying, with regard to all the teachings given in the *sutta*, including that of the ten precepts:

> And, Sāriputta, if all nobles … all brahmans … all merchants … all workers could thus understand the meaning in full of this that was spoken of by me in brief, for a long time it would be for their welfare and happiness. And, Sāriputta, if the world with the *devas*, with the Māras and Brahmās, and if the generations of recluses and brahmans, *devas* and men could thus understand the meaning in full of this that was spoken of by me in brief, for a long time it would be for their welfare and happiness.[430]

This would suggest that the ten precepts represent the norm of ethical behaviour not only for all Buddhists but for all human beings – indeed, for all forms of self-conscious sentient existence.

Such being the case it is the ten precepts which, together with the Three Jewels or Three Refuges, constitute the surest possible basis for unity among Buddhists. The time has come for Buddhists to give greater emphasis to what is common and fundamental rather than to what is distinctive and superficial, and in this respect the Western Buddhist Order has, perhaps, given a lead to the rest of the Buddhist world. In the ten precepts we have a set of ethical principles that is both clear and comprehensive. There is no point whatever in taking a large number of precepts in the knowledge that one will not, in fact, be observing some of them. Such a proceeding, unfortunately so common in many parts of the Buddhist world, is extremely demoralizing in its effects, and in fact undermines the whole basis of the ethical and spiritual life. In the Western Buddhist Order, therefore, the ten precepts are not only seen as *mūla-prātimokṣa*, but also taken with the intention that they should be observed. Indeed, they are taken with the intention that they should be observed more and more perfectly, as an expression of an ever deepening commitment to the Three Jewels.

7
THE TEN PRECEPTS AND OTHER ETHICAL FORMULAS

The ten precepts have already been spoken of as *kuśala-dharmas*, which as we have seen really means ethical principles, as *śikṣāpadas* or rules of training, and as avenues or ways of skilful (or wholesome) action, as well as in terms of their being the *mūla-prātimokṣa*, implicitly for all Buddhists and explicitly for the members of the Western Buddhist Order. It now remains for us to relate the ten precepts to certain of the other ethical formulas which are found figuring so prominently in Buddhist literature and Buddhist life.

One of the most important of these is, of course, the formula of the Eightfold Path, to which the ten precepts can be related through the formula of the three *skandhas* or 'groups' or, for that matter, through one or the other of the two broadly equivalent formulas of the three *saṃpādas* or 'attainments' and the three *śikṣās* or 'trainings', as well as through the formula of the three ways of skilful action.[431] The three groups are the noble group of *śīla* or ethics, *samādhi* or concentration and meditation, and *prajñā* or wisdom. Since the first seven precepts are concerned with bodily and vocal conduct they comprise the noble group of *śīla* or ethics, and since in terms of the Noble Eightfold Path ethics consists of right (or perfect) speech, action, and livelihood, it is clear that the first seven precepts correspond to the third, fourth, and fifth stages of the Noble Eightfold Path. Similarly, since the eighth and ninth precepts are concerned with that part of mental conduct which comprises the noble group of *samādhi* or concentration and meditation, and since in terms of the Noble Eightfold Path concentration and meditation consists of right (or perfect) effort, mindfulness, and concentration, the eighth and ninth precepts must correspond to the sixth, seventh, and eighth steps of the Noble Eightfold Path. Finally, since the tenth precept is concerned with that part of mental conduct which comprises the noble group of wisdom, and since in terms of the Noble Eightfold Path wisdom consists of right (or perfect) emotion and understanding (or vision), the tenth precept must correspond to the first and second steps of the Noble Eightfold Path.

In any case, it will be noticed that although I have spoken of all ten precepts as ethical principles, in the present connection it is only the first seven precepts that are said to comprise the noble group of *śīla* or ethics. The contradiction is more apparent than real. The term ethics can be used in two senses, a broader and a narrower. Ethics in the broad sense is the art or science of human conduct and character as possessing value in relation to a standard or ideal, and it is in this sense of the term that the ten precepts are ethical principles. As such, ethics is more or less identical with religion in its more practical aspect. Ethics in the narrow sense is concerned with external, bodily and vocal behaviour, and it is in this sense of the term that the first seven precepts are said to comprise the noble group of ethics.

Besides relating the ten precepts to certain other ethical formulas, it is also necessary to distinguish it from another formula similarly termed. This is the formula of the ten precepts observed by the *śrāmaṇera* or novice monk, a set of rules which comprises, in addition to the five precepts ('abstention from sexual misconduct' being in this context replaced by 'abstention from non-celibacy'), the precepts of abstaining from untimely meals, from song, dance, music, and indecent shows, from the use of flower-garlands, scents, unguents, and ornaments, from the use of luxurious beds and seats, and from handling gold and silver.[432] It will be readily seen that these precepts are of a very different character from the precepts making up the second half of the *mūla-prātimokṣa*, since however useful and even necessary they may be to certain people, or in certain circumstances, they are hardly of fundamental importance.

8

THE TEN PRECEPTS AND LIFESTYLE

Most Order members will be familiar with the aphorism 'Commitment is primary, lifestyle secondary'. What its original source was, and how it came to be introduced into the FWBO, is a matter of some uncertainty. I may even have introduced it myself, in which case I have quite a lot to answer for, since from the day of its introduction the aphorism seems to have been the innocent cause of a good deal of confusion and misunderstanding. In the first place it has sometimes been assumed that 'secondary' meant 'unimportant', or even 'irrelevant', with the result that the aphorism was understood to mean that provided you were committed, i.e. committed to the Three Jewels, it was a matter of indifference what lifestyle you followed and that, indeed, no lifestyle was intrinsically better – or worse – than any other, and that to try to make it out to be so was a sign of intolerance. However, 'secondary' most certainly does not mean 'unimportant', and when it is said that commitment is primary and lifestyle secondary what this means is that the lifestyle of a Buddhist, i.e. of one committed to the Three Jewels, is dependent on, or follows from, or is an expression of, the fact that he is thus committed or, in more traditional language, that he goes for Refuge.

Reference to the dictionary definition of 'lifestyle' will help to make this clearer. According to *Collins English Dictionary* (1979), lifestyle is 'the particular attitudes, beliefs, habits, or behaviour associated with an individual or group.' Since things like attitudes, beliefs, habits, and behaviour can be either skilful or unskilful it follows that the lifestyle that they collectively represent can be either skilful or unskilful too. Not all lifestyles, therefore, can be expressions of one's commitment to the Three Jewels. Similarly with the ten precepts and lifestyle. Just as the ten precepts themselves are an expression of one's Going for Refuge, so one's lifestyle is an expression of one's observance of the ten precepts. One could therefore say that the ten precepts are primary and lifestyle secondary, though perhaps it would be better for the sake of consistency to say that commitment was primary, the observance of the ten precepts secondary, and lifestyle tertiary, by which one would mean that although all three were of importance, the second was important as an expression of the first, and the third important as an expression of the second. 'Lifestyle' does not, therefore, represent some ethically neutral way of life which can be combined, without modification, with the pursuit of Enlightenment. For this reason one's lifestyle is something that is open to criticism, so that one cannot, as a Buddhist, rebut criticism of such things as one's particular attitudes, beliefs, habits, or behaviour with the indignant rejoinder, 'Oh, but that's my lifestyle', as though this at once placed the matter not only beyond criticism but beyond discussion.

One of the main sources of the confusion and misunderstanding to which I referred is, no doubt, the word 'style'. In the context of the visual arts one can speak of the baroque style and the rococo style without necessarily implying that one is better than the other. Similarly, in the context of literary criticism one can speak of a plain style and an artificial style, and in the context of book production of the distinctive house styles of different publishers, without thereby implying the absolute superiority of one style over another. But one can speak of lifestyles in this way only to a very limited extent. In other words, very few lifestyles are truly neutral in character. One can, indeed, speak of a rural lifestyle and an urban lifestyle without necessarily implying an ethical judgement, but one can hardly speak of the lifestyle of a slaughterman or of a prostitute – to take two quite extreme examples – without, as a Buddhist, thereby implying a very definite ethical judgement indeed.

With this brief discussion of the ten precepts and lifestyle – a topic of perhaps more limited interest than the seven topics preceding it – we conclude our discussion of the ten precepts collectively and, therewith, the first part of this paper. The discussion of the eight topics into which the whole discussion of the ten precepts was broken down has, I hope, helped us to achieve a more comprehensive view of the ten pillars of

Buddhism in their collective majesty. In the second part of the paper we shall be dealing with each of the ten precepts separately. This will enable us, I trust, to see each pillar in its individual splendour. As before, I shall try to avoid losing myself in details, and instead concentrate on the spiritual significance of the great principles involved, and on some of their more practical consequences. I shall, also, seek to enhance our appreciation of the splendour and beauty of the ten precepts, not only by speaking of one pillar as a pillar of diamond, one as a pillar of gold, one as a pillar of crystal, and so on, but also by explaining why a particular pillar is associated with a particular precious stone or precious metal.

PART II

THE TEN PRECEPTS INDIVIDUALLY

I

THE FIRST PRECEPT: THE PRINCIPLE OF ABSTENTION FROM KILLING LIVING BEINGS; OR LOVE

The more important an ethical principle is, the more likely it is that it will be so obvious as to be overlooked or neglected. This is certainly true of the principle with which we are at present concerned. *Of course* one should not kill human beings, or even animals (though important exceptions are often made when the human being happens to be of a different race, religion, or nationality, or when the animal is wanted for food or sport, or when it is more valuable dead than alive)! *Of course* murder is wrong! Murder is a crime, a sin! But this acknowledgement once made, most people assume that since they have never personally killed a living being, and are unlikely to do so in the future, the matter does not really concern them and they can get on with their lives without giving it a further thought. Even Buddhists tend to think that because they are observing the first precept anyway there is no need for them to think about it. After all, there are much more interesting and important aspects of the Dharma for one to concern oneself with, and simple and obvious things like the first precept can be safely left to the dull and unintelligent while one explores the secrets of Tantra or the mysteries of Zen.

But the truth is that the first precept is not to be disposed of in this way. The principle of abstention from killing living beings, or love, in fact runs very deep in life, both social and spiritual, and its ramifications are not only very extensive but enormously significant. Within the specifically Buddhist context of the ten precepts it is the most direct and most important manifestation of the spiritual and existential act of Going for Refuge. Moreover, it is a principle that finds expression, in one way or another, and to a greater or lesser degree, not only in the first precept itself, but in all the other precepts as well. For this reason it merits our serious consideration.

Let us begin by considering the precise significance of 'abstention from killing living beings' or, in terms of the positive formulation of the precepts, the precise significance of 'love'. (If each precept is a pillar of diamond, or gold, or crystal, and so on, its negative and positive formulations are the dark and bright sides of the pillar as it stands fronting the sun.) Though the literal meaning of *atipāta* is 'striking down', the word *pāṇātipāta* – for the sake of convenience I shall use the simpler and more familiar Pāli forms – actually means destruction of life, slaying, killing, murder. But why should killing be wrong? One explanation, of course, is that as the expression of a mental state rooted in greed, hatred, and delusion (or at least two of these), killing is an unskilful act in the sense that it brings suffering upon the doer and prevents him from attaining Enlightenment. But we can go deeper than that. Generally speaking, to kill a living being means to inflict upon him the greatest of all sufferings or evils, for inasmuch as life itself is the greatest good, so the greatest suffering, or greatest evil, that can befall one, is to be deprived of life.

Now one cannot do to a man what he regards as evil except against his will, that is to say, one cannot do it except by force or violence (*hiṃsā*), by which is meant not only physical force but also such things as emotional blackmail and fraud. Violence indeed consists in our doing to another person, by whatever means, what he does not want us to do to him. Since what he least wants us to do to him is to deprive him of life, which being the greatest good is what he most values, to kill him is to commit the greatest violence against him that it is possible to commit. We ourselves, of course, do not want to be deprived of life, any more than he does, so that to kill him is not only the extreme of violence; it is also, at the same time, the absolute negation of the solidarity of one living being *qua* living being with another and, in the case of human beings, of the solidarity of one human being *qua* human being with another. Non-violence (*ahiṃsā*) is said to be the highest rule of religion (*paramaṃ dharmaṃ*), because violence (*hiṃsā*) is the basest rule of irreligion and – barring certain refinements introduced by the perverted imagination of certain monsters of iniquity – the most extreme form that unethical behaviour can take. Violence and killing are, in fact, closely connected, killing being the most extreme form of violence and, in a sense, its logical consequence. The first precept is, therefore, often spoken of in terms of abstention from violence, though since killing in any case presupposes violence, and since (as we have seen) the Pāli word *pāṇātipāta* means destruction of life, the precept is probably best spoken of as abstention from killing.

Be that as it may, the deeper significance of the first precept consists in the fact that killing is wrong because it represents the extremest form that the negation of one ego by another, or the assertion of one ego at the expense of another, can possibly take – though, paradoxically, the negation of another's ego is, at the same time, in principle the negation of one's own. Killing is tantamount to a complete rejection of the golden rule, and without the golden rule there can be no human society, no culture, and no spiritual life. In its Buddhist form the golden rule finds expression in two well-known verses of the *Dhammapada*.

> All (living beings) are terrified of punishment (*daṇḍa*); all fear death. Making comparison (of others) with oneself one should neither kill nor cause to kill.
>
> All (living beings) are terrified of punishment (*daṇḍa*); to all, life is dear. Making comparison (of others) with oneself, one should neither kill nor cause to kill.[433]

Here the golden rule is stated in negative terms: you should *not* do unto others what you would *not* that others should do unto you. It can also be stated positively: you should *do* unto others as you would they should *do* unto you. (George Bernard Shaw does, of course, say, 'Do not do unto others as you would that they should do unto you. Their tastes may not be the same',[434] but this is only to draw attention to the fact that it is the spirit of the golden rule that matters, not the letter.) Just as abstention from killing represents the golden rule in its negative form, so the cultivation of love represents the golden rule in its positive form. As Shelley so finely says:

> The great secret of morals is love; or a going out of our own nature, and an identification of ourselves with the beautiful which exists in thought, action, or person, not our own. A man, to be greatly good, must imagine intensely and comprehensively; he must put himself in the place of another and of many others; the pains and pleasures of his species must become his own.[435]

This putting oneself in the place of another amounts to the same thing as the 'making comparison (of others) with oneself' of which the *Dhammapada* speaks. In the *Bodhicaryāvatāra* or 'Entry into the Way of Enlightenment' Śāntideva gives to this same principle what is probably its sublimest expression in Buddhist literature. After describing how by pondering upon the excellencies of solitude a man stills vain imaginations and strengthens his Thought of (or will to) Enlightenment (*bodhicitta*), he proceeds:

> First he will diligently foster the thought that his fellow-creatures are the same as himself. 'All have the same sorrows, the same joys as I, and I must guard them like myself. The body, manifold of parts in its division of members, must be preserved as a whole; and so likewise this manifold universe has its sorrow and its joy in common. Although my pain may bring no hurt to other bodies, nevertheless it is a pain to me, which I cannot bear because of the love of self; and though I cannot in myself feel the pain of another, it is a pain to him which he cannot bear because of the love of self. I must destroy the pain of another as though it were my own, because it is a pain; I must show kindness to others, for they are creatures as I am myself.... Then, as I would guard myself from evil repute, so I will frame a spirit of helpfulness and tenderness towards others.'
>
> By constant use the idea of an 'I' attaches itself to foreign drops of seed and blood, although the thing exists not. Then why should I not conceive my fellow's body as my own self? That my body is foreign to me is not hard to see. I will think of myself as a sinner, of others as oceans of virtue; I will cease to live as self, and will take as myself my fellow-creatures. We love our hands and other limbs, as members of the body; then why not love other living beings, as members of the universe? By constant use man comes to imagine

> that his body, which has no self-being, is a 'self'; why then should he not conceive his 'self' to lie in his fellows also? Thus in doing service to others pride, admiration, and desire of reward find no place, for thereby we satisfy the wants of our own self. Then, as thou wouldst guard thyself against suffering and sorrow, so exercise the spirit of helpfulness and tenderness towards the world.[436]

This is what is known as the practice of equality of self and others (*parātmasamatā*) and substitution of self and others (*parātmaparivartana*). Blake gives succinct expression to much the same principle when he declares, 'The most sublime act is to set another before you.'[437] Whether described in terms of making comparison of others with oneself, however, or in terms of the substitution of self and others, or in any other way, the love which is the positive form of the first precept is no mere flabby sentiment but the vigorous expression of an imaginative identification with other living beings. 'Love' is in fact far too weak a word for the positive counterpart of non-killing or non-violence, and even *maitrī* (Pāli *mettā*) is not altogether satisfactory. Just as killing represents the absolute negation of another person's being, 'love' as we must perforce call it represents its absolute affirmation. As such it is not erotic love, or parental love, or even friendly love. If it is love at all, it is a cherishing, protecting, maturing love which has the same kind of effect on the spiritual being of others as the light and heat of the sun have on their physical being.

Such 'love' is, of course, quite rare. Violence is much more common, even though it only exceptionally takes the form of actual killing. Putting things in another way, it may be said that human beings operate much more frequently in accordance with the power mode than in accordance with the love mode. But what is power? In this context power means simply the capacity to use force, violence being the actual use of that capacity to negate the being of another person, whether wholly or in part. To operate in accordance with the power mode means, therefore, to relate to other living beings in terms of violence, or in such a way as to negate rather than affirm their being. To operate in accordance with the love mode is the opposite of this. Since every living being, including every human being, has the capacity to use force, to however limited an extent, every living being possesses power, in however limited a degree. Human beings possess more power, both material and mental, than any other living beings, both in relation to their own species and in relation to other species.

From this point of view observance of the first precept means that, as a result of our imaginative identification with others, we not only abstain from actually killing living beings but operate more and more in accordance with the love mode and less and less in accordance with the power mode. In this way there takes place within us a change so great as to amount to a change in our centre of gravity, so to speak, and this change manifests both as observance of the first precept and, to the extent that their individual natures permit, as observance of all the other precepts as well.

It will not, of course, be possible for even the most faithful observer of the first precept to operate, all at once, in terms of the love mode, eschewing the power mode completely. We live in a world dominated by the power mode. The love mode comes into operation only in the case of exceptional individuals, and even they may not always find it possible, or even desirable, to act in accordance with the love mode. In this connection two principles may be laid down: (a) Whenever one has to operate in accordance with the power mode, the power mode must always be subordinated to the love mode. A simple, everyday example of such subordination is when the parent, out of love for the child, forcibly restrains him from doing something that will harm him. (b) Within the spiritual community it is impossible to act in accordance with the power mode, for by its very nature as a voluntary association of free individuals sharing certain common goals the spiritual community is based on the love mode. This means that should an Order member so far forget himself as to relate to another Order member in terms of force or violence, he to that extent places himself outside the spiritual community and ceases, in fact, to be an Order member. Acts of violence between Order members are, therefore, the most serious breach of the unity and solidarity of the Order that can possibly be imagined, even as the best conceivable means of strengthening that unity and solidarity are thoughts, words, and deeds of love.

Besides operating in accordance with the power mode only to the extent that the power mode is subordinated to the love mode, Order members should do their best to switch from the power mode to the love mode in as many different ways as possible, and to extend the principle of abstention from killing living beings, or principle of love, into as many different areas of life as possible, both individual and collective. Observance of the first precept will, in fact, naturally result in one's being a vegetarian, in one's refusing to have oneself, or to assist or encourage others in having, an abortion, in one's feeling concern for the environment, and in one's being opposed not only to the production and deployment of nuclear weapons but to the manufacture of all armaments whatsoever, as well as in many other things.

Not that the observance of the first precept consists simply in one's doing, or not doing, a certain stated number of things of this sort. Non-violence, or love, is a principle, and being a principle there is no limit to the number of ways in which it can be applied. No one is so unskilful in his conduct that his practice of non-violence, or love, could not be worse, and no one is so skilful in his conduct that his practice of it could not be better. As the most direct manifestation of one's Going for Refuge, the potentialities of non-violence, or love, are infinite.

In terms of the precious stone of which it consists, the first precept is a pillar of diamond. It is a pillar of diamond because the diamond is the most valuable of all precious stones, and capable of being cut into facets so as to make a brilliant. It is also the hardest substance known, even as the love mode is 'stronger' than the power mode and capable of 'overcoming' it in all its forms.

2

THE SECOND PRECEPT: THE PRINCIPLE OF ABSTENTION FROM TAKING THE NOT-GIVEN; OR GENEROSITY

Just as the first precept is not simply a matter of not killing, even though the negative form of the precept is couched in those terms, so the second precept is not simply a matter of not stealing; and in this case the negative form of the precept does in fact make this quite clear. *Adinnādāna veramaṇī* means, literally, abstention (*veramaṇī*) from seizing or grasping (*ādāna*) that which is not given (*adinna*). In other words it means not taking or appropriating that which another is not willing to give. Since violence consists in our doing to another what he does not want us to do to him, taking the not-given is therefore a form of violence. It is a violence committed not in respect of the actual person of the other, as in the case of physical attack, but in respect of his property; though it is arguable that violence in respect of property is indirectly violence in respect of the person inasmuch as property by very definition belongs to someone, in this case the other, and is *his* property. (This of course raises the whole question of ownership, about which I shall have something to say in a minute.)

Since taking the not-given is a form of violence, all that has been said about force and violence in connection with the first precept – including what has been said about the golden rule, and about the power mode and the love mode – can be taken as also said about the second precept, and applied accordingly. For this reason it will not be necessary for us to deal with the second precept at quite the same length as the first. After dealing with generosity, the positive form of the second precept,

I shall make a few remarks on three points arising in connection with its observance, and then conclude by dealing, very briefly, with the subject of ownership.

In 'Song of Myself', one of the earliest sections of *Leaves of Grass* to be composed, Walt Whitman announces:

> Behold, I do not give lectures or a little charity,
> When I give I give myself.[438]

These lines illustrate the difference between love, in the sense that the term was used in connection with the first precept, and generosity, in the sense that the word was used in connection with the second. Love gives itself, i.e. love is a self-giving of person to person or, if you like, a surrender of person to person ('surrender' here meaning the complete abandonment of any advantage derived from the power mode). Generosity is a giving of property to person, and is an expression of love. Indeed, where love exists in its fullness there is no question even of generosity, because love is, in the last resort, incompatible with the sense of ownership and, therefore, with property, and thinks not so much in terms of generosity as in terms of common 'ownership' or sharing.

Shakespeare gives matchless expression to the paradoxical implications of this mutual 'generosity' in one of his poems. (When I started preparing this paper I did not know that I would be quoting the poets so much, or that the poets would have so much to say on the subject of ethics.) Speaking of the mutual love of the Phoenix and the Turtle, he assures us:

> So between them love did shine,
> That the Turtle saw his right
> Flaming in the Phoenix' sight;
> Either was the other's mine.
>
> Property was thus appalled,
> That the self was not the same;
> Single nature's double name
> Neither two nor one was called.

Reason, in itself confounded,
Saw division grow together,
To themselves yet either neither,
Simple were so well compounded,

That it cried, 'How true a twain
Seemeth this concordant one!
Love hath reason, reason none,
If what parts can so remain.'[439]

For Buddhism it is not so much a question of a twain seeming 'a concordant one' as of the whole spiritual community being such. Ultimately, as in the case of the bodhisattva, generosity reaches a point where the giver, the gift, and the recipient of the gift, cease to be distinguishable. It is this kind of generosity that constitutes the positive form of the second precept, as well as the true counterpart, within the context of so-called property relations, of the positive form of the first precept, i.e. love.

The three points that arise in connection with the observance of the second precept concern ways of taking the not-given not specifically mentioned in the Buddhist tradition, gratitude, and indebtedness.

Since the second precept is, like all the other precepts, primarily an ethical principle, it follows that we should not be content to confine ourselves to such applications of this principle as are specifically mentioned in the Buddhist scriptures. To confine ourselves in this way is to be guilty of ethical formalism, and ethical or pseudo-ethical formalism is one of the greatest enemies of Buddhism and of the spiritual life generally.

Among the various forms of taking the not-given which are not, to the best of my knowledge, known to Buddhist tradition (at least in the sense that abstention from them is not explicitly enjoined in connection with the second precept) are taking the time or taking the energy of another person against his or her wishes. We take time from another person when we force ourselves upon them when they have work to do, or when we force them to listen to talk that they have no wish to hear. This form of *adinnādāna* or seizing or grasping the not-given is very common in modern social life (and not entirely unknown in ancient social life either, if we can believe Horace).[440] Buddhists should do their best to avoid it, both inside and outside the spiritual community.

Taking the energy or vitality of another person against his or her wishes, which is closely connected with taking their time, is even more pernicious. Here one forces oneself upon another to such an extent, and compels them to listen to one's complaints, or appeals or tirades, for so long, that one eventually reduces them to a state of physical prostration, emotional exhaustion, and even nervous collapse. Having drained another of their energy in this way, one may sometimes be heard to remark, either to one's victim or to some third party, 'I really enjoyed our little chat.' Human vampires of this sort are sometimes quite oblivious to the damage they do and fail to realize, if they are Buddhists, that they are breaking the second precept – and probably the first as well.

This is not to say that one may not take the time and energy of another, and even drain them, if one really needs to do so and if they are themselves willing to give their time and energy to this extent – which brings us to the subject of gratitude.

When you are given something you need, and especially when you are given it freely and willingly, the natural human response is to feel grateful. If you do not feel grateful something is wrong. Either the need itself is an unhealthy and even neurotic need, and hence not really capable of satisfaction (and one can hardly feel gratitude for a satisfaction that has not been experienced), or else your attitude is one of seizing and grasping regardless of whether the other person wants to give you what you need or not. Real gratitude can be felt only when you take from another both what you genuinely need and what they are willing to give. Gratitude can be felt, therefore, only by the mature and integrated, i.e. by true individuals, and true individuals not only feel but express gratitude. It is perhaps significant that within the Western Buddhist Order and the Friends of the Western Buddhist Order expressions of gratitude have become increasingly common in recent years. This is a very positive development indeed. Formerly one hardly heard an expression of gratitude from one year's end to the other. Now, I am glad to say, expressions of gratitude are to be heard if not every day then at least two or three times a week.

The connection between indebtedness and the second precept is not always appreciated. Wilfully to withhold from another the money, for example, that one owes him – money which he wishes one to repay, and of which he may be in need – is to be guilty of taking that which is not given and, therefore, of violence. It also means that so long as a debt is undischarged one cannot, in fact, give *dāna*, i.e. cannot practise generosity, for one's so-called *dāna* will be no more than a robbing of Peter to give to Paul and Paul himself, if he knows what the situation is, will be virtually a receiver of stolen goods. Indebtedness in this context does not, of course, include being in debt to a bank for a loan which must be repaid by a certain date, and on which one is in the meantime paying interest. But it certainly does include being in debt to friends and relations, whether in respect of money, goods, or services, as well as being in debt to tradesmen, professional advisers, and the state. This is the reason why prospective Order members are asked, before ordination, to discharge all debts, since otherwise their observance of one, at least, of the precepts taken at the time of ordination will be seriously vitiated from the very outset.

Within the Order itself, that is to say, between Order members themselves, whether individually or 'collectively', there can be no question of taking that which is not given, and therefore no question of indebtedness in the ordinary sense, since although members of the Order do not hold their property in common it is widely accepted that, within the spiritual community, common ownership is the ideal. In any case, by virtue of their observance of the second precept, all members of the Order are deeply imbued with the principle of generosity, or sharing, and do their best to practise it in their relations with one another.

This brings us to the question of ownership in general. According to Proudhon, 'property is theft',[441] but this does not help us very much. If property is theft there is no one who is not a thief, since there is no one of legal age who does not own property, and the question of ownership – whether common or otherwise – can hardly be decided by a community of thieves. We shall therefore have to start all over again. There is no doubt that property is inequitably distributed, in the sense of not being distributed in accordance with the genuine needs of people, but what can we do about it? For a Buddhist the answer is to be found in the combined operation of the power mode and the love mode, the power mode of course operating in subordination to the love mode. In a democratic country, a more equitable distribution of property or wealth can be achieved through legislation, which means in effect the forcible expropriation of the minority by the majority, as well as by the encouragement of a deeper understanding, and a more effective practice, on the grandest possible scale, of the principle of generosity, or sharing. The latter, as I need hardly remind you, is particularly the responsibility of a body like the Western Buddhist Order. More than that it is not possible for me to say on this occasion. The subject of ownership is a vast one, but we shall surely not go far wrong if we adhere, and encourage others to adhere, to the principle of generosity, or sharing.

Since gold is the most precious of all metals, and a common medium of commercial exchange, the second precept is a pillar of gold. 'Yellow, glistering gold', as Shakespeare calls it,[442] is the most malleable and ductile of all metals, and therefore well represents the infinite adaptability to the needs of living beings which generosity, the positive form of the second precept, represents. Gold is quite unalterable by heat, moisture, and most corrosive agents. In the same way, generosity is not affected by the conditions under which it has to function, or by such things as ingratitude in the recipient.

3

THE THIRD PRECEPT: THE PRINCIPLE OF ABSTENTION FROM SEXUAL MISCONDUCT; OR CONTENTMENT

It will help us to understand the third precept, especially in its positive form as contentment, if we can see it within the context of traditional Buddhist cosmology. That cosmology reveals to us what may be described as a three-tiered universe. Mundane existence is divided into three horizontal layers, as it were, the second of which is higher than the first, in the sense of being more refined, positive, blissful, and luminous, and the third higher than the second. These three 'layers' are the planes, worlds, or spheres – the terminology varies – of sensuous desire (*kāma*), of archetypal form (*rūpa*), and of no archetypal form (*arūpa*). The plane of sensuous desire comprises (in ascending order) the hell world, the world of hungry ghosts, the world of *asuras* or anti-gods, the animal world, the human world, and the world of the (lower) gods, from the four great kings (or gods of the four directions of space, as they are also called) up to the gods who control the creations of others. The plane of archetypal form comprises altogether sixteen sub-planes, from the heaven of the gods belonging to the company of Brahmā, up to and including the five 'pure abodes', which are inhabited by non-returners, i.e. those great spiritual beings who have developed transcendental insight to such an extent as to break the five fetters binding them to the plane of sensuous desire, so that they will no more be reborn there. The third plane, the plane of no archetypal form, comprises four sub-planes, all of which are inhabited by Brahmās, a class of spiritual beings superior even to the gods (though sometimes spoken of as such).[443]

Much could be said about these three planes of conditioned existence. All that concerns us at the moment is the fact that on the planes of archetypal form there is no such thing as sexual dimorphism, i.e. no separation into male and female, the inhabitants of these planes all being what we would call, from the human point of view, androgynous. Sexual dimorphism, or separation into male and female, is found only on the plane of sensuous desire, including, of course, the human world. Since spiritual life consists, in objective or cosmological terms, in a progression from lower to higher planes and worlds, spiritual life also consists in a progression from a state of biological and psychological sexual dimorphism to a state of spiritual androgyny. Moreover, since a state of sexual dimorphism is a state of polarization, tension, and projection, it is also a state of discontent. The state of spiritual androgyny, on the contrary, is a state of harmony, relaxation, and content. Observance of the third precept, therefore, does not consist simply in abstention from the various well-known forms of sexual misconduct, but also, and more importantly, in the experience of contentment, the 'vertical' as distinct from the 'horizontal' counterpart of such abstention.

In meditation the state of sexual dimorphism is transcended. In meditation one ceases, for the time being, to be either male or female. This is because in meditation, in the sense of *śamatha bhāvanā* or 'development of calm', one progresses through the *dhyānas* or states of higher consciousness, as they may be called, and these states of higher consciousness are the subjective, psychological counterparts of the different sub-planes of the planes of archetypal form and no archetypal form. While meditating, in the sense of actually experiencing the *dhyānas*, one is therefore a *deva* or Brahmā. In terms of the Western spiritual tradition, one is an angel and leading an angelic life – angels of course being by nature androgynous. It is thus no accident of language that the Sanskrit word for what we call celibacy or, more correctly, chastity, is *brahmacarya* (Pāli *brahmacariya*), which literally means faring, practising, or living like Brahmā, i.e. not merely abstaining from sexual activity but transcending the sexual dimorphism on which sexual activity and sexual desire are based.[444]

This is why Vajraloka, our meditation and retreat centre in North Wales, is dedicated not only to meditation (*dhyāna*) but also to celibacy (*brahmacarya*). Meditation and celibacy go together: they mutually reinforce each other. For the same reason, we encourage single-sex situations of every kind. This is not simply in order to curtail the opportunities for sexual misconduct, but also, more positively, to give both men and women some respite from the tensions of sexual polarization and to provide them with an opportunity of transcending, for a few moments, the state of sexual polarization and being simply a human being and – to some extent – a true individual. For those who wish to develop as individuals, and to progress on the path to Enlightenment, meditation and all kinds of single-sex situations are, in the absence of transcendental insight, absolutely indispensable.[445]

From all this it also follows not only that abstention from sexual misconduct is not enough, not only that one must experience contentment, but that one should not think of oneself as being either a man or a woman in any absolute or exclusive sense. After all, according to traditional Buddhist teaching, in the course of the beginningless series of one's existences one has been both a man and a woman many times. One has even, perhaps, been a god – an androgynous being. Within a perspective of this kind it would seem quite ridiculous to think and to feel that, just because one happened to be a man or a woman in this existence, one was a man or a woman for ever and ever, world without end, amen.

To the extent that one ceases to think of oneself as being a man or a woman in any absolute and exclusive sense, to that extent one will cease to speak and act as though one was a man and nothing but a man or a woman and nothing but a woman, i.e. one will cease to behave in that sexually ultra-polarized fashion which for Buddhism is exemplified by the figures of the male and female *asuras*. Male *asuras* are fierce, aggressive and very ugly, rather like the orcs in *The Lord of the Rings*.[446] The female *asuras* are voluptuous, seductive, and very beautiful, and eat any human males who are so unfortunate as to fall into their clutches. What the male *asuras* do to human females we are not told, though no doubt it can be imagined. Members of the Western Buddhist Order have no wish to resemble *asuras* of either sex.

This does not mean that sexual differences can be simply 'ironed out' or ignored, or that it is possible to pretend that they do not exist. A feeble and colourless unisexuality, which merely seeks to negate sexual differences on their own level, is not to be confused with the ideal of spiritual androgyny. A castrate is not an angel, certain representations of angels in Christian art notwithstanding. Here as elsewhere in the spiritual life what is needed is not negation but transformation, not evasion but progression. So far as the third precept is concerned, especially in its positive formulation as contentment, this progression is from an absolute identification with one psycho-physical sex to a relative and provisional identification with it, and from a relative and provisional identification with it to no identification at all. If we can only see this, whether with or without the help of traditional Buddhist cosmology, we shall understand the third precept more deeply, and because we understand it more deeply we shall observe it with greater confidence. Theory and practice will both be clear.

They will be clear as crystal, for the third precept is a pillar of crystal. It is a pillar of crystal because crystal is pure, transparent, and brilliant, and either colourless or only slightly tinged with pink or blue.

4
THE FOURTH PRECEPT: THE PRINCIPLE OF ABSTENTION FROM FALSE SPEECH; OR TRUTHFULNESS

Before we deal with this precept let me make a few general remarks about the four speech precepts collectively. The first thing that strikes us is that there should be four of them at all. Even though speech is a 'door' or 'avenue' in its own right, and as such of equal importance with body and mind, it is rather as though there should be four separate precepts for four different kinds of killing, or four separate precepts for as many different ways of taking what is not given. Obviously, speech is of great importance. As the principal vehicle of communication between man and man it plays a social role in human development, while as the principal medium for that system of expression which we call language it is, with language itself, one of the distinguishing characteristics of man as compared with other animals.

For Buddhism speech is important because it occupies an intermediate position between body and mind, or between action and thought, being neither so gross as the one nor so subtle as the other. It is because it occupies this intermediate position that it is so important to control speech – and also why it is so difficult to control it. It is important to control speech because speech is, in a sense, a form of action, i.e. a form of overt action, and as such takes its place in the external world and has consequences there both for oneself and for others. As the *Dhammapada* says with regard to one particular form of unskilful speech:

> Do not speak roughly to anyone: those thus spoken to will answer back. Painful indeed is angry talk, (as a result of which) one will experience retribution.[447]

It is difficult to control speech because speech is, in a sense, not just thought indeed but, for the speaker himself, so close to thought (after all, speech is only vocalized thought) that he often has difficulty in realizing that what he says is capable of producing tangible effects in the outside world and that speech ought, therefore, to be controlled. No doubt it is for this reason that in the formula of the ten precepts no fewer than four precepts out of ten are concerned with speech, whereas in the formula of the Noble Eightfold Path only one 'member' out of eight is so concerned (though that member is, of course, divided into four).

Buddhist tradition also points out that speech can be controlled by paying systematic attention to what comes out of this 'door', as well as by observing periods of complete silence from time to time. (Vows of perpetual silence are not permitted in Buddhism, as hindering the propagation of the Dharma.)

For the vast majority of people the stream of speech is so constant and so uninterrupted, and so much under the influence of unskilful mental factors, many of them unconscious, that all four speech precepts are likely to be broken many times a day, every day of the week. Speech is therefore something about which all Buddhists are expected to be particularly careful.

'Abstention from false speech' can be practised without practising 'truthfulness' only by abstaining from speech itself altogether. But abstention from false speech is by no means enough. Like all the other precepts, the fourth precept must be observed in its positive form as well as in its negative form. When one says that speech is important because it is the principal vehicle of communication between man and man one is really speaking of truthful speech, and of truthful speech only.

Untruthful speech cannot be a vehicle of communication, so that in any human society in which untruthful speech predominates communication will break down. Without truthful speech there can be no civilization and culture; indeed, there can be no spiritual life and no spiritual community. Without truthfulness society itself cannot exist, so that whoever is guilty of false speech in fact undermines the foundations of society.[448] A liar is an anti-social element – especially in a court of justice.

This is why telling lies in a court of justice when one has been called upon to speak the truth, is for Buddhism the paradigmatic form of false speech, just as speaking the truth in those circumstances is the paradigmatic form of truthfulness – as we saw in the case of the Buddha's teaching to Cunda the silversmith about the threefold cleansing. The bearing of false witness is such a terrible offence because it renders the administration of justice impossible, and if justice cannot be administered society ceases to be a moral order, the rule of right being replaced by the rule of might.

Bearing false witness is not the only form of false speech that undermines the foundations of society. George Orwell's Newspeak – indeed, any kind of insincere jargon – can have the same devastating effect.[449] Confucius, when asked what he would put first if entrusted with the administration of a state, replied, 'The rectification of terms.'[450] In similar vein, what Nietzsche appreciated most about Zarathustra (i.e. the real Zarathustra, not the product of his own philosophico-poetic imagination) was that his teaching upheld truthfulness as the supreme virtue. 'To tell the truth and *to shoot well with arrows*: that is Persian virtue',[451] he tells us, as though these two things comprised both the law and the prophets. The *Dhammapada* says much the same thing, though in negative rather than positive terms, when it declares:

> There is no wrong that cannot be committed by a lying person who has transgressed one (good) principle (i.e., that of truthfulness), and who has given up (all thought of) the other world.[452]

As if to say that a man who tells lies, and who does not recognize the existence of a higher world of moral and spiritual values, is capable of breaking every other precept.

One of the simplest yet most important forms of abstention from false speech and cultivation of truthfulness is that of factual accuracy. This consists in telling what one has seen, for example, or what one has heard, with scrupulous fidelity to the facts as they actually occurred, neither adding nor subtracting anything, nor exaggerating or minimizing anything, and without failing to recount any relevant circumstances. The observance of the fourth precept even in this limited sense is extremely difficult, and there is no doubt that we need to school ourselves in factual accuracy much more rigorously if we are to have any hope of observing this precept in its subtle, refined, and advanced forms. On numerous occasions I have been both astonished and dismayed at the careless manner in which some of my own remarks have been reported, or verbal messages delivered, even by those from whom I had reason to expect greater scrupulousness in this regard.

Such carelessness can be not only a source of general uncertainty and confusion but also of serious misunderstanding between one person and another. In repeating to one person what has been said by another one cannot, therefore, take too much trouble to ensure that one repeats what was said, and repeats it in such a way as to convey both the spirit and the letter of the other person's utterance, since otherwise a breach of the fourth precept will very likely become a breach of the seventh as well.

There are many other points that could be made in connection with the fourth precept, but most of them are points I have already made on other occasions.[453] Before telling you of which precious stone or precious metal the pillar of the fourth precept is made I shall, therefore, make a point which I have never made before. Though it does not concern one's personal observance of the fourth precept it is, nonetheless, a point of very great importance.

When we speak the truth we do, of course, expect to be believed, since otherwise no communication can take place. Similarly, *we* should believe others when *they* speak the truth. Next to killing a man, perhaps the worst possible thing you can do to him – and this is the point I want to make – is not to believe him when he is speaking the truth. Not to believe him when he is speaking the truth negates his identity as a social being and disrupts human solidarity. Such disbelief is, in fact, an act of violence.

It is not enough, therefore, that we should speak the truth: we should also believe others when they speak it – especially within the spiritual community. This means that we shall have to develop sufficient awareness and sensitivity to tell when another person really is speaking the truth, since otherwise we may unintentionally do them a great wrong.

The fourth precept is a pillar of pearl, if you can imagine such a thing. It is a pillar of pearl because in order to find pearls one must dive into the depths of the ocean. Similarly, one has to dive very deep to discover the truth, even in the most obvious factual sense, and until one has discovered it one can hardly speak it.

5
THE FIFTH PRECEPT: THE PRINCIPLE OF ABSTENTION FROM HARSH SPEECH; OR KINDLY SPEECH

Much of what has been said with regard to the deeper significance of the four previous precepts, especially the last one, can be applied, *mutatis mutandis,* to the remaining three speech precepts. Hence it will not be necessary for us to deal with these precepts at anything like the same length as the fourth precept. I shall confine myself to making a few points which, though minor in relation to the great themes already discussed, are nevertheless of some practical importance.

With regard to the negative form of the fifth precept, it is necessary to abstain not only from harsh speech in its cruder and more obvious forms, but also from indulgence in coarse, indecent, and obscene language of every kind. Such language has become extremely common in recent decades, the use of four-letter words in particular now being variously regarded as a sign of rugged masculinity, of freedom from convention, and of artistic integrity, instead of what in truth it is, a sign of emotional immaturity, impoverished imagination, and limited vocabulary. Speaking personally, I think I can say that with the possible exception of two or three occasions on which I quoted remarks made by other people, I have not used bad language even once in my life. Even as a boy, the few mild expletives I heard within the family circle pained and disgusted me, and when I was still quite young I realized that for me the use of such language was, in fact, an impossibility. Coarse, indecent, and obscene language, it seemed to me, even then, was the expression of strongly negative emotional states and quite literally poisoned the atmosphere.

Perhaps I should make it clear that I regard as being included in language of this sort all those unpleasant and offensive expressions by which women are reduced, in the mouths of some men, to their lowest common sexual denominator. Such expressions are a form of harsh speech, and Buddhists are expected to eschew them no less than their various unlovely brethren.

Just as harsh speech poisons the atmosphere, so kindly speech, the positive counterpart of abstention from harsh speech, purifies and invigorates it. Kindly speech is like the warm rays of the rising sun, that cause leaves to expand and flowers to open. People often do not realize how positive an effect can be produced by a few friendly words. Kindly speech, or affectionate speech, as we can also call it, should be habitual to us, not just something we keep for use in emergencies, or for special occasions, or special people.

One of the principal forms of kindly speech is what is known in Buddhism as rejoicing in merits, and I am glad to say that within the FWBO this particular expression of emotional positivity has become more and more popular in recent years. Among the subordinate forms of kindly speech are gentle speech, courteous speech, and even polite speech, which although of minor importance are not so unimportant that we can afford to neglect them. Whether inside or outside the FWBO, they all help to create an atmosphere of positivity within which spiritual friendship can develop and the spiritual life be led.

The fifth precept is a pillar of amber, which is neither a precious stone nor a precious metal, but a translucent organic substance that takes a fine polish. In colour amber is a deep, warm, reddish yellow, rather like honey, and has a kind of fiery gleam in its depths. Moreover, by friction amber becomes strongly electric, and capable of attracting other bodies.

6
THE SIXTH PRECEPT: THE PRINCIPLE OF ABSTENTION FROM FRIVOLOUS SPEECH; OR MEANINGFUL SPEECH

In a passage that occurs more than once in the Pāli scriptures the Buddha lists thirty-two kinds of frivolous, idle, useless, or meaningless talk in which his followers should not indulge.[454] 2,500 years later there are – thanks to radio, television, and the press – at least thirty-two thousand kinds of such talk, and it is more important than ever that we should not lose sight of the principle that underlies lists of this sort, i.e. the principle of abstention from frivolous speech or, in terms of its positive formulation, of meaningful speech.[455]

Speech can be truly meaningful only when life is meaningful, and life can be meaningful only when we have a definite purpose and a definite goal. For a Buddhist, this goal is Enlightenment, which means that for a Buddhist meaningful speech is speech about the Dharma, for it is the Dharma that is the means to Enlightenment. Indeed, it is not so much that the Dharma is the means to Enlightenment, in its own right as it were, as that 'the Dharma' is the collective designation for all those doctrines and methods, insights and observances, that actually help us to move in the direction of the Transcendental. The Dharma is whatever helps us to develop as individuals, though not individualistically, since true individual development comprises an other-regarding as well as a self-regarding aspect.

Meaningful speech is therefore not speech about the Dharma in any merely formal sense, much less still a matter of 'pious talk' (as more than one eminent translator has rendered the Pāli term '*dhamma-kathā*'), but talk about the means to Enlightenment, or whatever helps us to develop as individuals. One can say more than that. Meaningful speech is itself a means to Enlightenment inasmuch as it is a communication in depth between two or more people who are committed to the ideal of Enlightenment, or who have gone for Refuge.

That one should engage in meaningful speech to the entire exclusion of frivolous speech does not, however, mean that one should drag in the subject of Buddhism on each and every occasion, in season and out, like the man in one of G. K. Chesterton's stories who, regardless of what the other person started talking about, always contrived to bring the conversation round to the subject of the Roman Catholic Church.[456] If one is oneself committed to the ideal of Enlightenment the fact of that commitment will emerge quite naturally in the course of conversation, and one's speech will become meaningful speech without any special effort. This will happen, though, only if one remains constantly aware of one's commitment, or of the overall purpose of one's existence, and constantly aware of the direction in which the conversation is moving, as well as of the atmosphere of the gathering. Frivolous speech is liable to erupt whenever two or three people meet, and unless one is unremittingly vigilant the pure silver of meaningful speech will soon be tarnished by the breath of one or more of its thirty-two – or thirty-two thousand – noxious forms.

Thus meaningful speech is a pillar of silver. It is a pillar of silver not only because it is liable to tarnish unless burnished by insight, but because, like gold, it is malleable and ductile, and capable of taking on as many different forms as the Dharma. Like gold too, it is a common medium of exchange, the exchange in this case being the spiritual and existential exchange that takes place in the course of genuinely human communication.

7

THE SEVENTH PRECEPT: THE PRINCIPLE OF ABSTENTION FROM SLANDEROUS SPEECH; OR HARMONIOUS SPEECH

The malicious speech from which the seventh precept requires us to abstain is malicious in a special way, so that the harmonious speech which constitutes the positive counterpart of such abstention is harmonious in a special way. Malice is, of course, enmity of heart, hatred, or ill will, and malicious speech in the most general sense is speech that proceeds from, or is dictated by, unskilful mental states of that kind. In the context of the seventh precept, however, the object of the enmity, hatred, or ill will from which malicious speech proceeds, or by which it is dictated, is the state of unity, concord, or amity existing between two or more people. Thus malicious speech is speech which brings about – and is intended to bring about – disunity, discord, and enmity. For this reason *pisuṇavācā* is sometimes translated not as malicious speech but as 'slanderous speech' or 'backbiting'.

The real nature of the principle of abstention from malicious speech, or harmonious speech, is well brought out in the Buddha's teaching to Cunda the silversmith, reference to which has already been made. Abandoning slanderous speech and abstaining therefrom, the Buddha says of one who observes this precept:

> When he hears something at one place he does not proclaim it elsewhere to bring about a quarrel between the parties; what he has heard here he does not report there to bring about a quarrel between the parties.[457]

Quarrels, and hence disunity, often begin with a third party deliberately stirring up trouble by telling two people, or two groups of people, what each is supposed to have said about the other in their absence. Sometimes this is a pure invention, but more often it is something which actually was said but which has been taken out of context, or garbled in the telling. The person observing the seventh precept abstains from all such crooked behaviour. 'Thus he brings together the discordant, restores harmony.' In other words, even when people have fallen out of their own accord, so to speak, harmony can be restored if others do not make matters worse with their tale-bearing. Harmony is 'his delight, he exults in harmony, he is passionately fond of harmony.' (See note 457.)

The Buddha's language here is very strong. One who observes the seventh precept does not merely abstain from malicious speech: he takes a positive delight in harmony, and it is because of this that 'he utters speech which makes for harmony', as when one tells somebody what good things a friend has said about him, or how he has defended him against criticism. From this it is evident that the positive counterpart of abstention from malicious speech is not so much harmonious speech as harmonizing speech, i.e. speech which transforms discord into harmony and raises the harmony that already exists between people to an even higher level. The applicability of this to the spiritual community should be obvious.

The seventh precept is a pillar of opal. It is a pillar of opal, or of what is called precious or noble opal, because opal brings all the different colours of the rainbow together in a single gem, just as the principle of abstention from malicious speech, or of harmonious – or harmonizing – speech brings people of many different kinds together in a single society or community.

8

THE EIGHTH PRECEPT: THE PRINCIPLE OF ABSTENTION FROM COVETOUSNESS; OR TRANQUILLITY

With the eighth precept we pass from the precepts governing speech to the precepts governing mind. We also pass from the seven precepts that make up *śīla* or ethics in the narrower sense to the three precepts that, together with the seven previous precepts, make up *śīla* or ethics in the broader sense. Since the three precepts governing mind are concerned not so much with bodily and vocal behaviour as with the inner attitudes of which that behaviour is the outward expression they are obviously of the utmost importance. Unfortunately, however, we shall have to deal with the first two of them, at least, no less briefly than with the last three speech precepts. The reason for this is that, as we shall see (and as we indeed saw in connection with the ten precepts and other ethical formulas), the eighth and ninth precepts are concerned with that part of mental conduct which comprises the noble group of *samādhi* or concentration and meditation, even as the tenth precept is that part of it which is concerned with the noble group of wisdom, and with a subject as vast as that of concentration and meditation it is not possible for us to deal on this occasion. It will be enough if I can establish a few connections.

In its negative form the eighth precept consists in abstention from covetousness, the Pāli word here rendered as 'covetousness' being *abhijjhā*. We can arrive at some understanding of the deeper significance of this term not only by analysing the meaning of the term itself but also by examining three other important terms with which it is approximately synonymous. Strange as it may seem at first sight, the second part of the word *abhijjhā* is from *jhāyati* (Sanskrit *dhyāyati*), meaning 'to meditate, contemplate, think upon, brood over, search for, hunt after', from which the word *jhāna* (Sanskrit *dhyāna*) is also derived. *Abhi* is a prefix meaning 'very much, greatly'. *Abhijjhā* thus signifies a mental state of intense thinking upon, or brooding over, something by which we are attracted, or which we desire, i.e. signifies a mental state of covetousness. The three terms that are approximately synonymous with *abhijjhā* are *lobha* (equal in Sanskrit), *taṇhā* (Sanskrit *tṛṣṇa*), and *rāga* (equal in Sanskrit). *Lobha* means greed, lust, longing, desire, and is cognate with the Latin *libido*, as well as with the German *Lieb* and English love. *Taṇhā* means 'thirst', and like the English words thirst and drought is ultimately from a root meaning dryness, while *rāga* (literally colour, hue, dye), has the meaning of 'excitement, passion'.

From the nature of these terms we can see, in a general way, what kind of mental state it is with which the principle of abstention from covetousness is concerned. It is a state, essentially, in which the self or ego reaches out towards the non-self or non-ego with a view to appropriating and even incorporating it, thus filling the yawning pit of its own inner poverty and emptiness. Since it is not really possible to appropriate an external object in this way the state of covetousness is, therefore, also a state of perpetual frustration. For this reason the term *abhijjhā* is often combined, in the Pāli scriptures, with the term *domanassa* or 'distress, dejectedness, melancholy, grief'. In other words, the principle of abstention from covetousness is concerned with that state of general, existential polarization between coveting subject and coveted object of which the sexual polarization referred to in connection with the third precept is only a particular – though perhaps the most conspicuous – example.

For the positive counterpart of abstention from covetousness there is no wholly suitable term. In the context of the ten positive precepts we speak of 'abandoning covetousness for generosity', but besides being the positive counterpart of abstention from taking the not-given the term generosity is not really radical enough. Just as covetousness represents the mental state on account of which one takes what is not given, so the positive counterpart of abstention from covetousness should represent the mental state on account of which one practises generosity. Such a state could, of course, be spoken of as a state of depolarization, except that the expression is rather abstract, and in any case negative in form. It could also be spoken of as a state of detachment, except that that too is negative, or as one of contentment, had that term not already been used as the positive counterpart of abstention from sexual misconduct. Perhaps it will be best to speak of the positive counterpart of abstention from covetousness as tranquillity.

The connection between the eighth precept and meditation – indeed, between all the three mind precepts and meditation – should be obvious. Meditation is the subjective or direct method of raising the level of consciousness, as distinct from right livelihood, or hatha yoga, or *kalyāṇa mitratā*, which are objective or indirect ways of raising it. Since consciousness is made up of various mental states, the fact that meditation is the direct means of raising the level of consciousness does not mean that there is a single, as it were generic form of meditation which does this. Meditation has a number of specific forms, each one of which raises the general level of consciousness by working on a particular unskilful mental state. Covetousness being a reaching out of the self or ego towards the non-self or non-ego, that form of meditation will be able to eradicate covetousness which has the effect of checking this tendency and enabling one to realize its futility.

There are several meditations of this kind. Among them are the recollection of death, the recollection of impurity (i.e. the ten 'corpse meditations'), and the recollection of the six elements, with all of which practices most Order members are well acquainted.[458] Indeed, in recent years it has become a tradition for Mitras to engage in an intensive practice of the recollection of the six elements during the weeks immediately preceding 'ordination' or Going for Refuge. In this way they not only experience the 'death' that precedes spiritual 'rebirth' as an Order member, but also lay the foundation for a thoroughgoing practice of the principle of abstention from covetousness, or tranquillity.

The eighth precept is a pillar of emerald. It is a pillar of emerald because the deep rich green of the emerald is a 'cool' rather than a 'hot' colour and as such fittingly stands for a state in which the fever of covetousness has cooled down. Green is also the colour of vegetation, the calming and soothing effect of which on the mind is well known.

9
THE NINTH PRECEPT: THE PRINCIPLE OF ABSTENTION FROM HATRED; OR COMPASSION

As in the case of *abhijjhā*, we can arrive at a deeper understanding of the term rendered by 'hatred' not only by analysing the meaning of the term itself but also by examining other terms with which it is approximately synonymous. *Vyāpāda* (or *byāpāda*) means 'making bad, doing harm; desire to injure, malevolence, ill will', and it is cognate with *vyādhi* meaning 'sickness, malady, illness, disease', as well as with *vyādha* or huntsman. Thus it is clear that the general sense of the word is that of wishing evil. The terms which are closest to *vyāpāda* in meaning are *dosa* (Sanskrit *dveṣa*), *kodha* (Sanskrit *krodha*), and *vera* (Sanskrit *vaira*). *Dosa* is 'anger, ill will, evil intention, wickedness, corruption, malice, hatred', while *kodha* is simply 'anger' and *vera* 'enmity'.

The real nature of the unskilful mental state with which the ninth precept is concerned emerges, however, only when we are able to see the connection between 'hatred' and 'covetousness'. If covetousness is the state in which the self or ego reaches out towards the non-self or non-ego with a view to appropriating or even incorporating it, hatred is the state that arises when that movement of reaching out is checked, hindered, or obstructed either by the non-self or non-ego itself or by some other factor or party. Thus if covetousness is the primary psychological formation, hatred is the secondary one. It is the murderous wish to do the utmost possible harm and damage to whatever interposes itself between coveting subject and coveted object.

As for the positive counterpart of the principle of abstention from hatred, this is not love, as one might have thought, but compassion. The term love has, of course, already been used as the positive counterpart of abstention from killing; but the real reason why it is compassion rather than love is that the positive counterpart of abstention from hatred is to be found in the bodhisattva ideal. According to the *Upāli-paripṛcchā* or 'Questions of (the Arhant) Upāli', a Mahāyāna *sūtra* of the Ratnakūṭa class, for a bodhisattva to break precepts out of desire (= covetousness) is a minor offence, even if he does so for innumerable *kalpas*, whereas for him to break precepts out of anger (= hatred) even once is a very serious offence. The reason for this is that

> A Bodhisattva who breaks precepts out of desire [still] holds sentient beings in his embrace, whereas a Bodhisattva who breaks precepts out of hatred forsakes sentient beings altogether.[459]

Here as elsewhere, of course, the Mahāyāna is not saying that the breaking of precepts out of desire doesn't matter, but saying – in its own hyperbolical way – that for the bodhisattva it is of supreme importance that he should not, under any circumstances, forsake sentient beings, which of course he does do when he breaks precepts out of hatred. Hatred and compassion are mutually exclusive. Thus 'compassion' rather than 'love' is the positive counterpart of abstention from hatred.

The forms of meditation which have the effect of checking the hatred which arises when covetousness is hindered or obstructed are the four *brahma vihāras*, i.e. the systematic cultivation (*bhāvanā*) of the positive mental states of love, compassion, sympathetic joy, and equanimity, as well as such practices as rejoicing in merits and the Sevenfold Puja. Once hatred has been eradicated one can then proceed to deal with the underlying state of covetousness that makes hatred possible.

The ninth precept is a pillar of ruby. It is a pillar of ruby because the typical ruby is a deep clear red, and red is not only the colour of love and compassion but also, more literally, the colour of blood – of that blood which the bodhisattva is willing to shed, throughout hundreds of lives, for the benefit of all living beings.

10
THE TENTH PRECEPT: THE PRINCIPLE OF ABSTENTION FROM FALSE VIEWS; OR WISDOM

In relation to the importance of its subject matter, the length at which we shall be dealing with the tenth precept will mean that even less justice will be done to the principle of abstention from false views, or wisdom, than was done to the subject matter of the last two precepts. It will be possible to do little more, in fact, than indicate what is meant by false views and how they are to be abandoned, though for the purposes of this paper that will be enough. The Pāli term for which 'false views' is the generally accepted rendering is *micchā-diṭṭhi* (Sanskrit *mithyā-dṛṣṭi*). *Micchā* means simply 'wrong or false', while *diṭṭhi* means 'view, belief, dogma, theory, esp. false theory, groundless or unfounded opinion.' Thus *micchā-diṭṭhi* means in the first place a wrong or false view, in the sense of a wrong or false way of seeing things, and in the second place a wrong or false view as expressed more or less systematically in intellectual terms in the form of a doctrine.

What makes the view, or the doctrine, wrong or false is the fact that it is an expression, not to say a rationalization, of a mental state contaminated by covetousness and hatred, as well as by delusion (*moha*), the cognitive counterpart of covetousness. Only that view is *samyak* (Pāli *sammā*) or right, true, or perfect, which is the expression of a mental state uncontaminated by covetousness, hatred, and delusion, i.e. which is the expression of an Enlightened consciousness which sees things as they really are, though it is not right simply in the sense of being the opposite of wrong or false view.

Right view is also a non-view. It is a non-view in the sense that it is not held with the same pertinacity, or the same conviction of its absolute rightness, with which false views are usually held (such pertinacity and conviction are themselves unskilful mental states), but as it were provisionally and tentatively as a means to the attainment of Enlightenment and not as an end in itself. The Buddha indeed once declared: 'The Tathāgata has no views.'[460] Though seeing things as they really are, he has a 'critical' awareness of the impossibility of giving full and final expression to his vision in fixed conceptual terms. It is for this reason that, although he teaches the Dharma, he teaches it 'as a raft', i.e. as something to be left behind once the Other Shore has been reached.

In his teaching to Cunda the silversmith the Buddha enumerates some four or five false views of a very simple and basic kind. (The corresponding right views, which are enumerated later in the *sutta*, form part of the passage quoted in connection with the canonical sources of the ten precepts.) Speaking of the one whose mind is defiled, the Buddha says:

> Also he has wrong view, he is perverse in outlook, holding: There is no gift, no offering, no sacrifice; there is no fruit or ripening of deeds well done or ill done; this world is not, the world beyond is not; there is no mother, no father, no beings supernaturally born; there are no recluses and brāhmins in the world who have gone right, who fare rightly, men who by their own comprehension have realized this world and the world beyond and thus declare.[461]

In other words, such a person holds, in effect, that actions do not have consequences and that there is no difference, therefore, between skilful and unskilful actions; that there are no higher spiritual values, and no such thing as a distinctively human, morally-based social order; that in the scale of existence there are no living beings higher than sexually dimorphous man, as we at present know him, and no such thing as the spiritual life and no possibility of anyone personally realizing the ultimate truth of things. These false views are simple and basic in the sense that they deny, in the crudest and bluntest fashion, the possibility of even the most rudimentary form of moral and spiritual life and render the observance of the ten precepts unnecessary.

False views of a more subtle and sophisticated kind, which preclude the possibility of more advanced forms of spiritual life and experience by absolutizing, rather than denying, its more elementary forms, are to be found in the *Brahmajāla Sutta*, the first of the thirty-two discourses of the *Dīgha Nikāya*. That the *Brahmajāla Sutta* or 'Perfect Net' discourse should be the first discourse of the *Dīgha Nikāya*, and thus the first discourse of the entire Tripiṭaka, is no less significant than that the Book of Genesis should be the first book of the Bible. In this *sutta* the Buddha enumerates and systematically analyses a total of sixty-four false views, some of which are very subtle and sophisticated indeed. These views between them comprehend all possible false views, and are thus the 'Perfect Net' in which all these 'recluses and brāhmins' (i.e. philosophers and theologians) who adhere to false views are caught. Whether subtle and sophisticated, however, or simple and basic, all false views must be abandoned before Enlightenment can be attained.

Since false views are the precipitates and crystallizations of unskilful mental states, the most effective way of abandoning false views is by eradicating the unskilful mental states by which they are produced. This is best done with the help of meditation. It is, indeed, by preventing and eradicating unskilful mental states, and originating and developing skilful ones, that meditation raises the level of consciousness, the *dhyānas* or so-called 'states of higher consciousness' being in fact nothing but an uninterrupted flow of skilful mental states of increasing purity and intensity.

As we have already seen, covetousness can be eradicated with the help of the recollection of death, the recollection of impurity, and the recollection of the six elements, and hatred with the help of the four *brahma vihāras*, as well as by such practices as rejoicing in merits and the Sevenfold Puja. Similarly, delusion, which is in a sense the ultimate source not only of all false views but also of covetousness and hatred themselves, can be eradicated with the help of such practices as the mindfulness of breathing, the recollection of the six elements, and the contemplation of the twelve (or the twenty-four) *nidānas*, as well as by concentrated reflection on such doctrinal formulas as the three characteristics of conditioned existence and the four kinds of *śūnyatā* or voidness.[462]

False views can also be abandoned with the help of Dharma study of the traditional type, and by open-hearted discussion with those members of the spiritual community whose emotional positivity and intellectual clarity are superior to one's own.

Whatever the means employed, the more that false views are genuinely and radically abandoned, the more there shines forth what is variously termed Insight, or Perfect Vision, or Wisdom; and conversely the more Insight, or Perfect Vision, or Wisdom shines forth, the more false views are abandoned. When false views have been entirely abandoned, what shines forth in all its glory is wisdom in its fullness, and it is this wisdom which is the positive counterpart of abstention from false views. That it is the positive counterpart of abstention from false views does not mean that it consists simply in holding right views rather than wrong views. Wisdom holds no views, not even right views, though it may make use of right views for the communication of the Dharma.

In the world of today wisdom is a rare and precious thing, and much could be said about the false views that assail us from every side, particularly as a result of the dominance of the media of so called mass-communication. But it is time for us to see of what kind of precious stone the tenth and last pillar is made. Before we do this I would like to make it clear that if we want even to begin to observe the tenth precept, under the present very difficult circumstances, we must do at least three things. (1) We must become more acutely aware of the extent to which our thinking, and the expression we give our thinking, is influenced by the false views by which we have been surrounded since birth. (2) We must realize not only that false views are the product of unskilful mental states but that, so long as they are not definitely abandoned, they actually reinforce the unskilful mental states which produce them, thus doubly obstructing the path to Enlightenment. (3) We must resolve that whenever we discuss personal spiritual difficulties, or issues concerning the Order and the Movement as a whole, and above all when we discuss the Dharma itself, we should do so in terms of right views – if possible in terms of wisdom – and *not* in terms of any of the false views which are currently fashionable in the outside world. We should discuss Buddhism in the language of Buddhism. If after careful study we come to the conclusion that the language of Blake, or of Heidegger, or of William Morris,[463] to some extent coincides with the language of Buddhism, then that is a different matter, and we can feel free to communicate the Dharma in their language too if that seems the skilful and appropriate thing to do. But to try to communicate the Dharma in terms of a view, or a language, which explicitly or implicitly negates the very possibility of wisdom can only result in confusion.

The tenth precept is a pillar of sapphire. It is a pillar of sapphire because sapphire is a deep, intense blue, and blue is the colour of the unclouded sky, with which wisdom, the positive counterpart of abstention from false views, is often compared.

CONCLUSION

Now that we have seen of which precious stone the last pillar is made, we can see the ten precepts both in their collective majesty and their individual beauty and splendour. We can see that the ten precepts are indeed the ten pillars of Buddhism, and that they comprise a pillar of diamond, a pillar of gold, a pillar of crystal, a pillar of pearl, a pillar of amber, a pillar of silver, a pillar of opal, a pillar of emerald, a pillar of ruby, and a pillar of sapphire. These ten pillars are the massy supports of the entire majestic edifice of the Dharma, and if some of you are disappointed that some of your favourite precious stone or precious metal does not enter into the composition of any of the pillars, let me remind you that although no mention has been made of them the pillars themselves all have bases and capitals, arches and archivolts, and that these too are made of precious substances of various kinds.

Indeed, though at the beginning of this paper I spoke not only of the ten precepts as the double row of pillars supporting the spacious dome of the Dharma edifice, but also of meditation as the dome itself, and of wisdom as the lofty spire that surmounts the dome, we have not seen of which precious substances the dome and the spire are made. From what has been said about the last three precepts, however, it will be obvious that the dome – a double dome – must be made of something not unlike emerald and ruby, and the spire of something not unlike sapphire.

There has also been no mention of the people who resort to the majestic edifice of the Dharma, wandering among the precious pillars and gazing up through the precious dome into the precious spire – and beyond. As it should hardly be necessary for me to tell you, we are the people who resort to the edifice of the Dharma, and in fact we are standing in the midst of it at this very moment, together with all those who have gone, and do now go, and will in future go, for Refuge to the Buddha, the Dharma, and the Sangha. But once here, surrounded by the precious pillars, and surmounted by the precious dome and the precious spire, what use of the majestic edifice do we make? And here our architectural metaphor breaks down. It breaks down because we are ourselves the pillars, the dome, and the spire, at least potentially. The architectural metaphor has to be replaced by a biological metaphor, in fact by a botanical metaphor.

The ten precepts are not only ten pillars; they are ten petals, the ten petals of a magnificent flower, of which meditation is the stamen, and wisdom the seed or fruit. We ourselves are that flower, both individually and 'collectively', and we grow and we bloom not for our own sake only, but for the sake of all living beings. In other words, dropping all metaphors, we observe the ten precepts because – apart from Going for Refuge itself – there is hardly anything that would be of greater importance and hardly anything that would be of greater benefit to ourselves and others. For this reason there could hardly be a better way for us to celebrate the sixteenth anniversary of the Western Buddhist Order than by trying to see more clearly how profound is the significance, and how far-reaching the implications, of the ten precepts. The more faithfully we observe the ten precepts the greater will be the likelihood of the Western Buddhist Order truly attaining its 'collective' majority as a spiritual community – whether this year itself or in five years' time.

Let us therefore resolve that in the days that lie ahead we shall do all we can to strengthen and sustain the ten pillars of Buddhism.

The History of My Going for Refuge

REFLECTIONS ON THE OCCASION OF THE TWENTIETH ANNIVERSARY OF THE WESTERN BUDDHIST ORDER

INTRODUCTORY NOTE

The History of My Going for Refuge was originally a paper delivered to members of the Western Buddhist Order at York Hall, Bethnal Green, London on 11 April 1988. As reported in the editorial of *Golden Drum,* no. 9, 'more than a hundred Dharmacharis and Dharmacharinis' – a large number in those days – had gathered together to celebrate the twentieth anniversary of the founding of the Order. Owing to the length of the paper the reading was divided into four parts with short breaks. Sangharakshita read sections 1–5 and 16–22, Dharmacharini Srimala sections 6–10, and Dharmachari Ratnaprabha sections 11–15. *The History of My Going for Refuge* was published by Windhorse Publications that same year.

To discover that within myself which I *must* obey, to gain some awareness of the law which operates in the organic whole of the internal world, to feel this internal world as an organic whole working out its own destiny according to some secret vital principle, to know which acts and utterances are a liberation from obstacles and an accession of strength, to acknowledge secret loyalties which one cannot deny without impoverishment and starvation, – this is to possess one's soul indeed, and it is not easy either to do or to explain.[464]

John Middleton Murry (1889–1957)

I

INTRODUCTION

Today marks the twentieth anniversary of the Western Buddhist Order, which came into existence on Sunday, 7 April 1968, when in the course of a ceremony held at Centre House, London, nine men and three women committed themselves to the path of the Buddha by publicly 'taking' the Three Refuges and Ten Precepts from me in the traditional manner. In the terse phrases of the diary which I kept for the first three and a half months of that year, and which has only recently come to light:

> Arrived at Centre House at 10.15. Found nothing ready. Cleared and arranged room, set up shrine etc. People started coming, including bhikkhus. Started at 11.15. Welcome by Jack [Austin]. Had lunch with bhikkhus and Jack while Mike Rogers conducted first meditation. Emile [Boin] very worried, as Indians who had undertaken to provide lunch did not turn up until very late. At 12 o'clock spoke on 'The Idea of the Western Buddhist Order and the Upasaka Ordination'. Then, while others were having lunch, spoke to the press. Many photographs taken. Guided group discussion. Meditation. Tea. More press people and more photographs. At 5.30 spoke on 'The Bodhisattva Vow'. At 7 o'clock conducted ordination ceremony, which lasted till 8.15. Mike Ricketts, Mike Rogers, Sara [Boin], Emile [Boin], Terry O'Regan, Stephen [Parr], Marghareta [Kahn], Geoffrey [Webster], John Hipkin, Roy Brewer, Penny [Neild-Smith], and David Waddell received their [public]

ordinations. Everything went off very smoothly and successfully. All most pleased.

A further (visual) record of the occasion is provided by four colour slides taken by my friend Terry Delamare.[465] The first slide is a close up of the shrine, the centre of which is occupied by a sedent bronze image of Amitayus, the Buddha of Infinite Life, flanked by slightly smaller images of Avalokiteśvara, the Bodhisattva of Compassion, and Mañjughoṣa, the Bodhisattva of Wisdom. Behind the images is a miniature Japanese screen of white silk brocade; in front, an arrangement of white carnations, irises, lilies, and narcissi. The second and third slides show me giving one or other of my lectures, while in the fourth and last I am about to place the white *kesa* of the Order round the neck of Sara Boin (Sujata), who kneels on a cushion before me with joined hands. Since the seven other members of the Order who appear in the slide are not wearing *kesas*, Sara may well have been the first person to be ordained.[466]

Immediately after the ceremony I hurriedly dismantled the shrine and with Stephen (Ananda)[467] caught the 9.50 train to Haslemere, where we spent four tranquil days at a semi-derelict cottage in the extensive grounds of Quartermaine[468] and where I worked on my memoirs and wrote a few 'Chinese' poems. One of these poems read:

Beyond the deserted paddock, a dark wood;
Before our secluded cottage, wet strips of green and brown.
Watching the incense burn in this quiet room
We have forgotten the passing of days and hours.[469]

We were not allowed to forget them for long, however. On the afternoon of the fourth day Ananda had to return to London and to his work as a recording engineer at Bush House,[470] while I had to go over to Keffolds, the Ockenden Venture's other property in Haslemere, and lead the FWBO Easter retreat.[471] This retreat was attended by several of the new Order members, some of whom indeed made themselves useful in various ways. The Western Buddhist Order had not only come into existence but had started functioning.

But what was this Western Buddhist Order – or Trailokya Bauddha Mahasangha, as it was subsequently known in India – that after a year or more of preliminary work had suddenly blossomed lotus-like from the mud of the metropolis? Essentially it was a body of people who had gone for Refuge to the Buddha, the Dharma, and the Sangha and who, by virtue of that common spiritual commitment, now constituted a spiritual community – a spiritual community that symbolized, on the mundane level, the same transcendental spiritual community or Sangha which was the third of those same Three Jewels to which they had gone for Refuge. Moreover, the twelve people who made up the Western Buddhist Order had not only gone for Refuge to the Three Jewels: they had 'taken' the Refuges and Precepts from me or had, in other words, been ordained by me. Their understanding of what was meant by Going for Refuge must therefore have coincided with mine, at least to some extent. In what sense, then, did I myself go for Refuge? How did I understand that central and definitive act of the Buddhist life and how had I arrived at that understanding? On an occasion like this, when we have assembled in (relatively) large numbers to celebrate the twentieth anniversary of the spiritual community that forms the heart of the new Buddhist movement we have inaugurated, it is no doubt appropriate that I should cast a backward glance over the various stages by which the meaning, the significance, and the importance of Going for Refuge became clear to me. It is no doubt appropriate that I should endeavour to trace the history of my Going for Refuge, and that, having done this, I should share with you some of my current thinking as regards my own relation to the Order and the relation of the Order itself to the rest of the Buddhist world.

In tracing the history of my Going for Refuge I shall not simply be tracing a series of logical deductions from – or even of more and more extensive practical applications of – a concept or principle comprehended in its fullness, and in all its bearings, from the very beginning. My progression here has resembled that of Yeats' butterfly rather than that of his gloomy bird of prey.[472] Indeed in order to make clear what follows, or at least avoid misunderstandings, at this point it becomes necessary for me to say a few words about my personal psychology. Some years ago an astrologer friend drew my birth chart, and according to this chart I had most of my planets below the horizon, which apparently meant that the influences these planets represented were operating not in the field of consciousness but below it.[473] Though I have never taken astrology very seriously, or indeed had any real interest in the subject, reflecting on this fact I nonetheless came to the conclusion that the course of my life had been determined by impulse and intuition rather than by reason and logic and that, for me, there could be no question of first clarifying an idea or concept and then acting upon it, i.e. acting upon it in its clarified form. An idea or concept was clarified in the process of its being acted upon. This was certainly what happened in the case of my Going for Refuge. The full significance of that supremely important act became apparent to me only gradually as, over the years, I acted upon the imperfect idea of Going for Refuge which I already had and as, my idea of it being clarified to some extent, I again acted upon it and it was again clarified – the act becoming more adequate to the idea as the idea itself became clearer, and the idea becoming clearer as the act became more adequate. In tracing the history of my Going for Refuge, therefore, I shall be tracing the history of a process of discovery which follows a rather erratic course and which consists, besides, of a series of slow, sometimes virtually imperceptible developments wherein are no dramatic breakthroughs except, perhaps, at the very beginning. So slow and so little perceptible, indeed, were some of those developments, that they can be discerned only with difficulty, so that it is fortunate that some of them found expression – either at the time or shortly afterwards – in certain of my writings, lectures, and seminars. In the case of the first of the various stages by which the meaning, the significance, and the importance of Going for Refuge became clear to me no such *aides mémoire* are necessary. After more than forty-five years the experience retains its original freshness for me, at least when I call it to mind and dwell upon it.

2

THE *DIAMOND SŪTRA* AND THE *SŪTRA OF WEI LANG*

The experience with which the history of my Going for Refuge begins took place in the late summer or early autumn of 1942, when I was sixteen or seventeen, and it took place as a result of my reading the *Diamond Sūtra* and the *Sūtra of Wei Lang* (*Huineng*), especially the former. I have described this crucial experience in my (unpublished) memoirs of the period, written in the late fifties,[474] and since I am unable to improve upon the account I then gave I shall simply quote from the first part of it. Speaking of my initial response to the *Diamond Sūtra*, I wrote,

> Though this book epitomizes a teaching of such rarefied sublimity that even *arahants*, saints who have attained individual Nirvāṇa, are said to become confused and afraid when they hear of it for the first time, I at once joyfully embraced it with an unqualified acceptance and assent. To me (the truth taught by the Buddha in) the *Diamond Sūtra* was not new. I had known it and believed it and realized it ages before and the reading of the *Sūtra* as it were awoke me to the existence of something I had forgotten. Once I realized that I was a Buddhist it seemed that I had always been one, that it was the most natural thing in the world to be, and that I had never been anything else.[475]

After offering two possible explanations for my feeling that I had always been a Buddhist I went on to describe my experience of the *Sūtra of*

Wei Lang which, I wrote, threw me into 'a kind of ecstasy' whenever I read it. The truth taught by the Buddha in the *Diamond Sūtra* and to a more limited extent by the Sixth Patriarch in the *Sūtra of Wei Lang* was, of course, the highest truth of Buddhism (so far as that truth can be expressed in words), the truth of *śūnyatā* or 'Voidness' – the truth, that is to say, that the phenomena of existence are ultimately non-different from absolute reality and absolute reality ultimately non-different from the phenomena of existence. Such being the case, the fact that I had responded so positively and unreservedly to this teaching meant that my Dharma Eye had been opened, at least to some extent, and that as a result of my reading of the *Diamond Sūtra* and the *Sūtra of Wei Lang* I had in fact gone for Refuge to the Dharma, the second of the Three Jewels.[476]

Whether I also went for Refuge to the first and third of the Three Jewels as a result of my reading the two *sūtras*, and, if so, whether I went for Refuge to them in the same way that I did to the second, is another question. I was certainly aware that the truth taught in the *Diamond Sūtra* had been taught by the Buddha and that, although its immediate recipient was the *arhant* Subhūti, it had in fact been addressed to an assembly of monks and bodhisattvas representing the spiritual community or sangha. I was even aware that in the *Sūtra of Wei Lang* the Sixth Patriarch had exhorted his listeners to take refuge in the Three Jewels of their 'essence of mind' (as Wong Mou-lam translated the expression).[477] Nevertheless, so overwhelmed was I by what the *Diamond Sūtra* itself calls 'the impact of the Dharma' that for the time being I was virtually oblivious to the existence of the Buddha and the Sangha.[478] Indeed, were it not for the fact that both the Buddha and the Sangha are ultimately non-different from *śūnyatā* it might be said that, so far as I was concerned, the first and third of the Three Jewels had both been swallowed up by the Void!

But though for the time being I was oblivious to the existence of the first and third Jewels, I had long been fascinated by the life and personality of the Buddha. Three or four years before my encounter with the *Diamond Sūtra* and the *Sūtra of Wei Lang* I had, in fact, written a 'Life of Siddhartha Gautama the Buddha', as I called it. This little work I compiled mainly from the *Children's Encyclopaedia* and H. G. Wells' *A Short History of the World* and it is perhaps significant that, apart from school essays, it was my first completed piece of writing.[479]

At about the same time I bought, at a curio shop in Brighton, a small brass Kamakura Buddha in which – the top of its head being perforated for the purpose – I regularly burned joss sticks.[480] This act of devotion did not in itself amount to Going for Refuge, of course, any more than did the writing of my 'Life of Siddhartha Gautama the Buddha', but at least it showed that I had a feeling for the Buddha that I certainly did not have for the Sangha or spiritual community. After my realization that I was a Buddhist nearly two years, in fact, were to pass before I made personal contact with other Buddhists and two years and a few months before I formally went for Refuge to all Three Jewels.

3
U THITTILA AND *PANSIL*

These other Buddhists with whom I made personal contact, in the winter of 1943-44, were the members of the Buddhist Society, founded in London in 1924 by Christmas Humphreys as the Buddhist Lodge of the Theosophical Society.[481] By the time I made contact with them, I had been conscripted into the army, but I attended meetings whenever I could and struck up acquaintance with a few people. At one of these meetings (it may have been a Wesak meeting, but I cannot be sure) I found myself 'taking *pansil*', as it was called, from an orange-robed figure seated behind a table at the far end of the room. '*Pansil*' was the Sinhalese corruption of the Pāli *pañcasīla* or 'five precepts', and one 'took *pansil*' by repeating the five precepts, preceded by the Three Refuges, after whoever happened to be conducting the ceremony. Though many of the circumstances of that meeting have long faded from my mind, I have vivid recollections of myself and some fifteen or twenty other people standing in our places with our *pansil* cards in our hands as, with varying degrees of uncertainty with regard to the pronunciation of the unfamiliar Pāli words, we followed a clear-voiced and confident Christmas Humphreys as he led us in the chanting of the responses. Most vivid of all is the recollection of looking down at the *pansil* card I held in my own two hands. Even now I can see the oblong of shining white card, on which the Refuges and Precepts were printed in both Pāli and English. Even now I can hear the voice of Christmas Humphreys pronouncing the *dutiyampis* and *tatiyampis* of the Refuge-going formula in a way that, to my unaccustomed ear, seemed to bear little relation to the words as printed.[482]

The orange-robed figure from whom I had 'taken *pansil*', and whose gutteral tones had been too low for me to catch, was the Burmese monk U Thittila.[483] He was the first Buddhist monk I had seen, and in view of some of the developments which, many years later, took place in my own life and thought as a Buddhist, it was significant that it was he, rather than a more 'orthodox' representative of Eastern Buddhism, who conducted the ceremony whereat I recited for the first time the formula which, publicly repeated after a leading Buddhist, constitutes 'conversion' to Buddhism and formal acceptance into the Buddhist community. It was significant that it was U Thittila who conducted the ceremony because, though on this occasion he wore the robes of the branch of the Theravāda monastic order to which he belonged, he did not always wear them. On less formal occasions, as when he was out with the ARP,[484] he wore whatever form of Western dress was appropriate. Years later, when I was myself 'in the robes', I learned that this 'unorthodox' behaviour had not met with universal approval. As I wrote in my unpublished memoirs:

> Narrowly-formalistic Burmese Buddhists had severely criticized him for his supposed misconduct in wearing ordinary European clothes when not actually performing his religious duties. English Buddhists saw the matter in quite a different light. Throughout the Blitz U Thittila had worked as a stretcher-bearer, on several occasions risking his life to rescue people trapped beneath fallen masonry. Finding that the voluminous drapery of his robes hampered his movements he sensibly exchanged them for more practical garments. People who knew him said he practised what he preached.[485]

For my own part, I have always been glad that I first took the Refuges and Precepts from this quiet and unassuming man for whom, as we now say, commitment was primary and lifestyle secondary – a man who, whether wearing orange robes or a blue boiler-suit, was at heart neither monk nor layman but simply a Buddhist.

4
GOING FORTH

Between my 'taking *pansil*' from U Thittila and my 'Going Forth' there was an interval of more than three years. During that period the signals unit to which I belonged had been ordered overseas, I had been stationed in Delhi, Colombo, Calcutta, and Singapore, had made contact with Chinese and Sinhalese Buddhists, had returned to India (for good, as I then thought), had been associated with various religious organizations and groups, both Buddhist and Hindu, and had taken up the regular practice of meditation.[486] Now I was ready to enter upon the next of the various stages by which the meaning, the significance, and the importance of Going for Refuge became clear to me and accordingly, on 18 August 1947 (three days after the Union Jack ceased to flutter over the Indian subcontinent and eight days before my twenty-second birthday), in Kasauli in East Punjab, I renounced the household life and went forth into the life of homelessness.[487] The immediate cause of my taking this drastic step was disillusionment with worldly life, especially with worldly life as represented by organized religion. Together with the Bengali friend with whom, on my return to India, I had joined forces, I had worked for the Ramakrishna Mission Institute of Culture and for the Maha Bodhi Society.[488] More recently, I had been involved in a project for the revival of the Dharma Vijaya Vahini, an organization for the propagation of Buddhism in India that had been started, many years earlier, by an old scholar whom I happened to meet at an inter-religious gathering in Ahmedabad. With all these organizations, as well as with the group that had formed round a well-known female ascetic, I had been deeply disappointed, as had my friend.[489] Working with such bodies was, it seemed, a hindrance rather than a help to spiritual development. They had a natural tendency to degenerate and the only course open to us was to sever our connection not just with them but with the world. As related in that portion of my memoirs which was published in 1976 as *The Thousand-Petalled Lotus*, we therefore dyed our clothes the traditional ochre, disposed of our worldly possessions, said goodbye to our friends, and the following morning – the morning of the 18th – set out on foot down the road that led from Kasauli to the plains.

In 'Going Forth' in this way we were of course following an ancient Indian tradition, a tradition which the Buddha himself had followed some twenty-five centuries earlier. Indeed, both before and after my companion and I took our plunge into the ocean of the spiritual life instead of sitting hesitating on the shore (to vary the metaphor), I was very conscious that in exchanging the household life for the life of homelessness we were following the personal example of the Buddha, as well as that of many of his closest followers, and the consciousness that we were so doing inspired and uplifted me.[490] The Buddha's own 'Going Forth' had terminated at the foot of the bodhi tree, when he attained the Supreme Enlightenment that, for the last six years, had been the object of his 'noble quest'.[491] So far as his followers were concerned (i.e. those of them whom had 'Gone Forth' either before meeting him or after Going for Refuge to the Three Jewels as a result of hearing his teaching), some attained Enlightenment while others did not, depending on how faithfully they had followed the path he had shown.[492] As time went on, and especially after the Buddha's *parinirvāṇa* or 'great decease', Going for Refuge, 'Going Forth', and even 'becoming a monk' in the later narrow, more formalistic sense, came to be more and more closely identified (just as the sangha or spiritual community and the monastic order came to be more and more closely identified). The story of how this happened is a long one, and I have no time to tell it now. I mention the matter at all only because I want to make the point that at this stage in the history of my Going for Refuge I had not sorted these things out. Despite having taken *pansil* from U Thittila I had not realized that Going for Refuge was the central and decisive, indeed the definitive, act of the Buddhist life (one did not go for Refuge because one was a Buddhist but was a Buddhist because one went for Refuge), and that 'Going Forth' and 'becoming a monk', were spiritually of significance and value only to the extent that they were expressions of one's Going for Refuge. I had not realized that 'Going Forth', far from being simply a matter of renouncing the household life, in fact consisted in the emergence of the individual – in the sense of the self-aware, emotionally positive, and responsible human being (to name only a few of his or her characteristic qualities) – from the matrix of group or merely-collective existence.[493]

Because I did not realize this latter point, for me, as for many Eastern Buddhists, the next step after 'Going Forth' (which in any case had been formalized as *śrāmaṇera* or 'novice' ordination) consisted not, as it should really have done, in finding and being accepted into a (spiritual) community of those who had both gone for Refuge and 'Gone Forth', so much as in taking *bhikṣu* ordination and, in this way, entering into full membership of the monastic order. Thus it was not surprising that my companion and I, having 'Gone Forth', should not only want to study Buddhism but should also want to take ordination as *bhikṣus*. Our original plan had been to study and, if possible, to take ordination, in Ceylon, and on reaching Delhi we had accordingly lost no time in heading south. On our arrival in Colombo, however, we were refused entry into Ceylon[494] and were forced to return to South India where, after some interesting adventures, we eventually settled in a deserted ashram on the outskirts of the town of Muvattupuzha, in the state of Travancore, where we stayed for fifteen months.[495]

Looking back over the years, it is difficult not to feel that the failure of our original plan was in fact an instance of the proverbial blessing in disguise, since it is extremely unlikely that we should have found in Ceylon the right conditions for our spiritual development. During the period of our stay in Muvattupuzha the greater part of my time was spent in study, meditation, and reflection, and in this way I came to have a clearer understanding of the Dharma, especially of the Dharma as represented by the teachings of dependent origination (conditioned co-production), the four noble truths, and the three characteristics of conditioned existence, as well as a keener awareness of the fact that I was a Buddhist.[496] This keener awareness of my spiritual identity, as it may be termed, was due in part at least to the fact that throughout our stay in South India I was surrounded by Hindus of various castes and sects (the few Indian Christians did not really count) and had no contact with Buddhists whatever, for my companion, though in some respects appreciative of Buddhism, was by birth a Brahmin and had not yet completely freed himself from his Hindu conditioning. Indeed, I had had no contact with Buddhists of any kind since my departure from the Maha Bodhi Society nearly two years earlier. Despite this prolonged spiritual isolation, however, my allegiance to Buddhism remained unshaken. If anything it was more firmly and deeply rooted than ever, so that by the time our stay in Muvattupuzha came to an end I was again thinking of ordination and thinking of it more seriously than ever, as indeed was my companion. Nevertheless, though I was again thinking of ordination, I still thought of it not in terms of finding and being accepted into a spiritual community but in terms of taking *bhikṣu* ordination and joining the monastic order. In other words, I had not understood that for the Buddhist, at least, the act of 'Going Forth' was a transition from group or merely-collective existence as represented by the household life to supra-collective but associated existence as represented by the spiritual community. I had not understood this because I did not, at this stage, have a clear understanding of the difference between the group, consisting of those who are merely group-members, and the spiritual community, consisting of those who are individuals in the sense I have indicated. Because I did not have a clear understanding of this vitally important difference, I was unable to envisage the possibility that in becoming a monk and joining the monastic order I might become, not a 'member' of a spiritual community, but only a member of *another kind of group* – not a secular group but a religious or even an ecclesiastical group.

For my failure to understand the difference between the group and the spiritual community, the group-member and the individual, I was not altogether to blame, for, as I came to appreciate only years later, it was a failure common to virtually the whole Buddhist world, many parts of which were sunk in monastic or pseudo-monastic formalism of an extreme kind. As I trace the early stages of this history of my Going for Refuge, therefore, I must be careful not to be too hard on my younger and less experienced self and careful not to expect too much of him. More important still, I must be careful lest I forget, or lose touch with, or even start underestimating, the mood of spiritual exaltation with which I renounced the household life and went forth into the homeless life. Our past selves underlie our present self, even as the catacombs underlie modern Rome, or rather, they live on in our present self and in a sense actually form part of it. This is certainly the case with my 'Going Forth' in Kasauli and the period of seclusion at Muvattupuzha that followed. Indeed, despite the fact that I did not, at the time, understand the full significance of the step I was taking, I regard my 'Going Forth' as being not only one of the most important stages in the history of my Going for Refuge but one of the principal turning-points in my life. For this reason, when I realized last year that the fortieth anniversary of my 'Going Forth' was approaching, I could not help feeling that I would like to commemorate the occasion in some way, if only by preparing a paper in which I would recall my 'Going Forth' and reflect on its significance. This did not prove practicable. I was still recovering from the effects of the operations I had undergone earlier in the year,[497] besides being busy with the women's ordination retreat and the various order conventions. When 18 August came I found myself – most appropriately – at Guhyaloka, where I quietly celebrated the day on my own account.[498] As I sat on the veranda of my bungalow, looking out over the bright green pine trees of our magical valley at the wall of grey rock immediately opposite, there flashed on my 'inward eye' the small hill station in distant India and my saffron-clad, twenty-two year old self 'Going Forth' on that fateful morning all those years ago, and I mused on the step I had taken and on the consequences it had had for myself and others.

One of the thoughts that occurred to me, as I sat there in the sunshine, was that experiences like taking *pansil* and 'Going Forth' were more than just stages in the long process of discovery whereby the meaning and significance of Going for Refuge had gradually become clear to me; each stage also possessed, quite apart from that process, an independent value and significance that ought to be appreciated for its own sake. But I have no time to pursue the implications of this idea, or to consider its bearing on the actual discovery-process, to the next stage of which I must now turn.

5
ŚRĀMAṆERA ORDINATION

The scene of this next stage was Kusinara, the site of the Buddha's *parinirvāṇa* or great decease, where my companion and I arrived a few days before Wesak, having walked all the way from Benares at the hottest time of year. As related at length in *The Thousand-Petalled Lotus*, we had left Muvattupuzha four or five months earlier and had gradually made our way north with the intention of visiting the Buddhist sacred places and, if possible, taking formal ordination as Buddhist monks.[499] During this period my desire for contact with other Buddhists, already quite strong by the time of our departure from Muvattupuzha, had become unbearably intense. It had also become centred on Sarnath, where the Buddha had delivered his first discourse and where, as I knew, there was a centre of the Maha Bodhi Society and a small monastic community. Here, then, we had presented ourselves, and here, to our bitter disappointment, we had been received with hostility and suspicion and had had our request for ordination turned down with flimsy excuses which were, we later discovered, little better than lies.[500] On the advice of a scholar-monk in Benares whose disciple I subsequently became,[501] we had therefore decided to seek ordination in Kusinara and, being entirely without money, had proceeded to make the hundred-mile journey on foot – an arduous and at that time of year a positively dangerous undertaking.

In Kusinara we fared better than we had done at Sarnath (we could hardly have fared worse). U Chandramani Maha Thera, the seventy-two year old Burmese monk who had devoted his life to the restoration of the place,[502] listened to our request for ordination sympathetically, asked a number of questions, promised to consider our request, and a few days later informed us that provided it was clearly understood that he could accept no responsibility for our future training, and that it would not be possible for us to stay with him at Kusinara, he was ready to ordain us. On Wesak morning, 12 May 1949, my companion and I therefore took ordination as *śrāmaṇeras* or novice monks by repeating after U Chandramani the Three Refuges and Ten *śrāmaṇera* Precepts.[503] For me the principal significance of the occasion was to be found in the re-establishment of my contact with other Buddhists (it had hardly been re-established at Sarnath), as well as in the formalization of my 'freelance' Going Forth of nearly two years ago and the consequent regularization of my hitherto ambiguous position within the (monastic) community – a regularization that would, I hoped, pave the way to my becoming a *bhikṣu*. Thus although my desire for contact with other Buddhists was intense it lacked clarity, being in effect a desire, not so much to find and be accepted into the spiritual community as to join the monastic order as such. The reason for this was that I was thinking, basically, in terms of 'becoming a monk' rather than in terms of Going for Refuge, having not yet realized that the act of Going for Refuge was the central and definitive act of the Buddhist life and that becoming a monk (including formal Going Forth) was of spiritual significance and value only to the extent that it was an actual expression of one's Going for Refuge.

This is not to say that the formal taking of the Three Refuges did not feature prominently in the ordination ceremony. It featured very prominently indeed, but in such a way that its real significance tended to be obscured rather than revealed. Taking the Three Refuges (and Ten *śrāmaṇera* Precepts) was simply one of the things one did when one became a novice monk. It was not seen as constituting the very essence of true monkhood, in comparison with which such things as shaving hair and beard, donning saffron robes of the prescribed cut, exhibiting the alms bowl (as well as the belt, water-strainer, needle, and razor), saluting the feet of the preceptor, having one's own feet saluted by the laity, and sharing in the ceremonial food-offering were, in themselves,

> Worthless as withered weeds,
> Or idlest froth amid the boundless main.[504]

Thus while U Chandramani was much concerned that I should pronounce the words of the Refuge-going formula with perfect correctness, both in Pāli and in Sanskrit, and took a great deal of trouble to ensure this, he had absolutely nothing to say about the *meaning* of those words or about the significance of the act of Going for Refuge itself, so that in one respect, at least, I was no wiser after my *śrāmaṇera* ordination than I had been after taking *pansil* from U Thittila. At our first meeting U Chandramani had, however, been gratified to learn that I had not only taken *pansil* five years earlier but taken it from a *Burmese* monk, and this fact probably had something to do with his deciding to grant our – or at least my – request for ordination. Be that as it may, even though I had not yet realized the position Going for Refuge occupied in the Buddhist life – or rather, had not yet realized that being a Buddhist and Going for Refuge were in fact one and the same thing – I was conscious that between my taking *pansil* in London and my becoming a monk in Kusinara there was a definite continuity, a continuity that had less to do with the nationality of my two preceptors than with the Three Jewels or Three Refuges themselves.

Since I have emphasized the lack of clarity with which I took *śrāmaṇera* ordination, I would not like to conclude this section without redressing the balance a little and emphasizing what an extremely positive occasion the ordination was for me. I felt delighted, thrilled, exhilarated, and inspired, as well as intensely grateful for all the kindness I had received at the hands of U Chandramani and his little band of followers. Like my taking *pansil* and my Going Forth, my *śrāmaṇera* ordination was not just part of a process but was of value and significance on its own account.

6
BHIKṢU ORDINATION

In many parts of the Buddhist world *bhikṣu* ordination follows directly after *śrāmaṇera* ordination, provided the candidate is twenty or more years of age. In my own case a year and a half elapsed before I could take higher ordination, as it was also called, the principal reason for the delay being that in a non-Buddhist country like India it was no easy matter to bring together the minimum of ten *bhikṣus* needed for the correct performance of the ceremony. Usually they could be brought together only on the occasion of major festivals, when *bhikṣus* from many parts of the Buddhist world would be among the thousands of pilgrims flocking to the sacred places of north-east India. Thus it was that I received my *bhikṣu* ordination at Sarnath on 24 November 1950 (a full moon day), on the occasion of the nineteenth anniversary of the opening of the Mulagandhakuti Vihara, having come down from Kalimpong for the purpose.[505]

The ceremony took place in the Burmese temple, in the presence of four or five dozen people, and lasted about an hour. U Chandramani being unavoidably absent, his place as preceptor (*upādhyāya*) was taken by a well-known preacher from Rangoon,[506] so that my *bhikṣu* ordination, like my taking *pansil* and my *śrāmaṇera* ordination, took place under the auspices of the Burmese branch of the Theravāda monastic order. Since I have given a fairly detailed account of the ceremony in the as yet unfinished continuation of *The Thousand-Petalled Lotus*,[507] in this paper I shall mention only those aspects of it that are relevant within the present context, that is, the tracing of the history of my Going for Refuge. What struck me most forcibly, both at the time and afterwards, was the fact that nowhere in the ceremony was there any provision for Going for Refuge, in the sense of repeating the Refuge-going formula after the preceptor. True, I had to repeat it after my teacher (*ācārya*) as part of the re-ordination as a *śrāmaṇera* which, in accordance with tradition, preceded my ordination as a *bhikṣu*, but in the *bhikṣu* ordination ceremony itself Going for Refuge did not feature in any way, nor was it so much as mentioned afterwards. This was all the more remarkable in that – as I discovered only much later – *bhikṣu* ordination had in the early days of Buddhism consisted simply in the threefold repetition of the Refuge-going formula.[508] Mention was, however, made of the four reliances (*nissaya*) of the monk, which my preceptor in fact explained to me after the ceremony proper. Ideally a monk should rely on alms for food, on dust-heap rags for robes, on the roots of trees for lodging, and on cow's urine for medicine; but should he find this too difficult he might accept invitations to meals, wear robes made of various materials, live in a house or cave, and take ghee, butter, oil, honey, and sugar when sick.[509] Thus full allowance was made for human weakness, though I could not help wondering whether a monk would not be more likely to adhere to the four reliances if he was not given the impression, so soon after his ordination, that he was not really expected to take them seriously.

During the ordination itself, however, I was troubled by no such doubts or reservations. Indeed, I was troubled by very few thoughts of any kind, the reason for this being that proceedings were for the most part conducted in 'Burmese Pāli', so that for much of the time I was free simply to immerse myself in the positive atmosphere generated by the occasion. With me in the consecrated area, and completely surrounding me, were monks of four different nationalities, including the same Maha Bodhi Society *bhikṣus* who had turned down my request for ordination eighteen months earlier. Surrounding the monks, but outside the consecrated area, were laymen and laywomen of at least six different nationalities, while immediately behind the monks and in front of the laity was a Tibetan incarnate lama,[510] who, since he was an upholder of the bodhisattva ideal, could be regarded as transcending the dichotomy between monk and layman. It was therefore not surprising that despite the lack of provision for Going for Refuge – indeed, despite my own lack of clarity on this all-important subject – I should have been conscious of the third Jewel, at least, in a way that I had not been conscious of it before. Whether this consciousness amounted to Going for Refuge to the spiritual community in the strict sense is doubtful, but at least it gave me my first intimation of what such Going for Refuge was really like.

7
'TAKING REFUGE IN THE BUDDHA'

In the introduction to this paper I spoke of the 'Chinese' poems I wrote at Quartermaine shortly after the first ordinations into the Western Buddhist Order. These were by no means my first poems nor were they to be my last. I have in fact been writing poetry, of a sort, since I was eleven or twelve and probably have not finished writing it even yet. Quite a few of my poems give expression to thoughts and feelings which, for one reason or another, could find an outlet in no other way. Thus whatever their deficiencies as poetry, they may be of interest and value as an indication of my state of mind at the time of writing.[511] As I have commented in the Preface to *The Enchanted Heart*, with regard to the poems selected from my poetic output for the years 1946–1976 for inclusion in that volume:

> Many of them, if not the majority, have only a biographical – even a sentimental – interest. They give expression to passing moods and fancies as well as to deeper experiences and insights. They also reflect my response to my surroundings. As such they constitute a sort of spiritual autobiography, sketchy indeed, but perhaps revealing, or at least suggesting, aspects of my life that would not otherwise be known.[512]

This is certainly true of a poem entitled 'Taking Refuge in the Buddha', which I wrote when I had been a *bhikṣu* for just over two years.[513]

The poem was written in Kalimpong, where for the last three years I had been doing my best to obey my teacher Kashyapji's injunction to 'stay there and work for the good of Buddhism'.[514] Neither in my work for Buddhism nor in my personal life had I received the help and co-operation to which, I felt, I was entitled, and the poem gave expression to my deep disappointment and frustration. The circumstances which led to its production are briefly described in the diary I was then keeping. The entry for Monday 26 January reads:

> Puja and meditation. The remarks Joe made yesterday caused me to feel that I had no earthly refuge, that none understood me or sympathized with the aim I was striving to achieve. In this mood a line which I had composed some months ago as the refrain of a poem came into my mind, and during breakfast I composed the first one and a half verses of 'Taking Refuge in the Buddha'. Then came Sachin, and we read seven of Shakespeare's sonnets, and studied a chapter of logic, on which I dictated him seven pages of notes. After he had gone I completed the poem.

The 'Joe' referred to in this extract was an elderly and extremely cantankerous Canadian Buddhist who had settled in Kalimpong with the intention of helping me in my work; 'Sachin' was a talented Nepalese college student to whom I gave tuition in English and logic and for whose benefit I subsequently wrote my essay 'Advice to a Young Poet'.[515]

'Taking Refuge in the Buddha' is too long to be quoted in full, but its seven eight-line stanzas constituted a resounding declaration of my heartfelt conviction that for me there could be no refuge in the beauties of nature, no refuge in the world of literature and the arts, no refuge in politics, no refuge in professional or commercial activity, no refuge in Christianity, Islam, or Hinduism, no refuge in the observances of conventional Buddhism, no refuge anywhere in conditioned existence, and no refuge, even, in a Nirvāṇa conceived simply as the opposite of *saṃsāra*. For me there could be refuge only at the feet of the Buddha, above the dualism of subject and object. The fact that in this poem I spoke only of taking refuge in the Buddha did not, of course, mean that I did not likewise take refuge in the Dharma and the Sangha; it simply meant that my taking refuge in the Dharma and the Sangha was contained within my taking refuge in the Buddha, even as the

Dharma-Jewel and the Sangha-Jewel were themselves contained within the Buddha-Jewel. As Gampopa points out in his *Jewel Ornament of Liberation*, the English translation of which I read eagerly on its appearance five years later, the ultimate refuge is the Buddha alone.

> He is the ultimate refuge because He possesses the Dharmakāya and the devotees of the three paths, [i.e. the *śrāvakas*, the *pratyekabuddhas*, and the bodhisattvas] also find their fulfilment in Him by obtaining the final pure Dharmakāya.

If one asks whether the Dharma and the Sangha are not the ultimate refuge the answer is in the negative for, as Gampopa goes on to explain, basing himself on the *Mahāyāna-uttaratantra*:

> The Dharma that is taught is only a collection of words and letters and has to be discarded like a raft when we have reached the other shore. The Dharma that is understood has two aspects, the Truth of the Path and the Truth of the Cessation of Misery. The former is a product and not eternal, hence is deceptive and no refuge, while the latter has no real existence being compared by the Śrāvakas to the extinction of a lamp. The Sangha itself also has taken refuge in the Buddha, because it was afraid of Saṃsāra and so is no ultimate refuge.[516]

In short, 'refuge is only one, the means is threefold,'[517] the refuges having been split up into three simply as a way of attracting people of different spiritual capacities. Thus even though I did not know it at the time, the conviction to which 'Taking Refuge in the Buddha' gave expression – the conviction, namely, that for me there could be refuge only in the Buddha – was fully in accordance with the best Buddhist tradition.

When I came to transcribe the poem into my 'poetry notebook' I placed at its head, by way of a motto, the words *Naṭṭhi me saraṇaṃ aññaṃ, Buddho me saraṇaṃ varaṃ*, 'For me there is no other refuge, the Buddha is the supreme refuge.' These words were a quotation from the *Tiratana Vandanā* or 'Salutation to the Three Jewels', which I had recited as part of my daily office ever since becoming a *śrāmaṇera*. Shortly after my *bhikṣu* ordination I had, in fact, rendered the *Vandanā* itself into English verse:

To all the Buddhas [or Dharmas or Sanghas] of the past,
To all the Buddhas yet to be,
And all the Buddhas that now are,
My worship flows unceasingly.
No other refuge than the Wake [or the Law, or the Brotherhood] –
Refuge Supreme – there is for me!
Oh by the virtue of this truth
May grace abound, and victory![518]

Though I recited the *Vandanā* in Pāli and not in English, the words 'Oh by the virtue of this truth/May grace abound, and victory!' haunted me in a way that the corresponding words in Pāli never did. With their distant echoes of Bunyan, and still more distant echoes of St Paul,[519] the words 'May grace abound, and victory!' were not quite a literal translation of the words *hotu me jayamaṅgalaṃ*, but I thought they captured their spirit very well indeed. Whether or not this was the case, there is no doubt that the fact that I was reciting the *Tiratana Vandanā* every day, and repeating 'May grace abound, and victory!' under my breath on all sorts of occasions, contributed to the growth of the feeling and the conviction which, at a time of disappointment and frustration, found expression in 'Taking Refuge in the Buddha'.

8
A SURVEY OF BUDDHISM

A Survey of Buddhism was written between the end of 1954 and the beginning of 1956, on the basis of lectures delivered in Bangalore in the summer of 1954, and was published in 1957.[520] It is sometimes referred to as my *magnum opus*, and such indeed it is in the sense that it is the most comprehensive and systematic of all my writings on Buddhism. It is, however, quite an early work. When I gave the lectures on which it is based I had been a Buddhist for thirteen years and a monk for five and, as I wrote in the preface to the fifth edition of the *Survey*, the giving of the lectures, and the subsequent preparation of them for publication in book form,

> gave me the opportunity of standing back and taking a look at the great spiritual tradition to which I had committed myself, and of trying to sum up, for my own benefit as much as for that of other people, what I had learned about Buddhism in the course of my thirteen years as a Buddhist and how, at the end of that time, I saw the Buddha's teaching. It gave me the opportunity, in other words, of finding out what I really thought of Buddhism – what Buddhism really meant to me.'[521]

More than thirty years have passed. I have now been a Buddhist not for thirteen years but for forty-seven and it would be strange if today I saw the Buddha's teaching in exactly the same way as I saw it then. It would be strange if there had been no change, or rather no development, in my thinking about Buddhism – strange if Buddhism did not mean even more to me now than it did when I wrote the *Survey*. This is not to say that I have found anything wrong with the fundamental principles on which the book is based, or any reason to change my approach to Buddhism or my method of treatment, even though the work admittedly has its limitations – limitations which I have tried to make good in some of my subsequent writings and lectures.[522] Such changes as have taken place in my thinking about Buddhism during the last thirty years have taken place entirely as a result of the further application of some of the principles enunciated in the *Survey* itself. As I have explained in my preface to the fifth edition, in taking my look at Buddhism I was concerned principally to do two things. I was concerned to see Buddhism in its full *breadth* and in its ultimate *depth*, by which I meant that I was concerned firstly to see Buddhism as a whole and secondly to see it in its deeper interconnections both within itself and in relation to the spiritual life of the individual Buddhist. Seeing Buddhism as a whole meant doing justice to all its principal teachings and major historical forms, as well as showing that these were interconnected by virtue of their common basic principles and their bearing on the spiritual life of the individual. Seeing it in its depth meant trying to understand why the Buddha had taught this or that doctrine or what relation it had to the needs of the individual as he wrestled with the problems of existence.[523]

Breadth and depth were, however, inseparable. As the years went by I increasingly found that the more I related Buddhism to the spiritual life of the individual Buddhist the more I saw it in its deeper interconnections within itself, and the more I saw it in its deeper interconnections within itself the more I saw it not as a collection of miscellaneous parts but as an organic whole. This was nowhere more apparent than in the case of Going for Refuge, which I eventually came to see as the central and definitive act of the Buddhist life and as the unifying principle, therefore, of Buddhism itself. At the stage in the history of my Going for Refuge which we have now reached – the stage represented by *A Survey of Buddhism* – I did not, however, realize the absolute centrality of the act of Going for Refuge, or rather, though I realized it in principle to some extent, I had not yet worked out its implications, which were in fact very far-reaching indeed.

If the (new) index to the sixth edition of the *Survey* can be relied on, in the body of the work (as distinct from the Introduction, which was added later)[524] the Three Jewels are mentioned as a triad three times and the Three Refuges once, while Going for Refuge is mentioned six times. Interestingly enough, the most extended treatment of the subject is to be found in chapter 4, 'The Bodhisattva Ideal', in the section dealing with the preliminary devotional practices undertaken by the would-be bodhisattva. These preliminary devotional practices are collectively known as supreme worship (*anuttara-pūjā*) or – as we generally say in the FWBO – the Sevenfold Puja, the third 'practice' (or the second, if one follows Śantideva in conflating the first and second practices and counting six altogether instead of seven) being that of Going for Refuge (*śaraṇa-gamana*).[525] The key passage in the two pages dealing with Going for Refuge as one of the preliminary devotional practices occurs at the very beginning and reads as follows:

> Going for Refuge (*śaraṇa-gamana*) means, of course, going for refuge to the Buddha, the Dharma, and the Sangha. While even a non-Buddhist can, in a sense, respect and honour the Triple Gem, to take refuge in them is the prerogative of the professing and practising Buddhist alone. Formal refuge, which is held to constitute one a member of the Buddhist community, can be taken simply by repeating after any ordained monk the refuge formulas and the five precepts. But effective refuge, of which the formal refuge is at once the expression and the symbol, can be taken only by one who has an understanding of the true nature of the Triple Gem. The deeper this understanding goes, the more effective will be his refuge. Taking refuge in the Triple Gem is not, therefore, an act to be done once and for all time, but something which grows with one's understanding of Buddhism. The refuge is complete when one's understanding of Buddhism is complete, that is to say, when one attains Enlightenment. Then, paradoxically enough, there is no going for refuge: the Enlightened One is his own refuge.[526]

I then go on to discuss the minimum degree of understanding needed for taking effective refuge in the Three Jewels, and in this connection point out that inasmuch as the Mahāyāna has a deeper understanding of the

Triple Gem than the Hīnayāna the significance that it attaches to the act of taking refuge is naturally more profound. Nevertheless, I am at pains to make it clear that, doctrinal differences notwithstanding,

> all schools of Buddhism, whether of the Great or Little Vehicle, agree in recognizing the decisive importance in the Buddhist life of the act of taking refuge.[527]

– a statement which to some extent anticipates my present general position. In the 'key passage' itself I distinguish between formal refuge and effective refuge in much the same way that I was later to distinguish between provisional (or ethnic) refuge, and between effective refuge and real refuge.[528] More important still, I insist that taking refuge in the Triple Gem is not an act to be done once and for all time but something that grows with one's understanding of Buddhism – an insight that made the development of my thinking about Buddhism possible and which underlies much of my current thinking, except that I would now add that one's understanding of Buddhism grows as one's Going for Refuge becomes more effective and more real.

Yet despite such anticipations and semi-anticipations the key passage in my discussion of Going for Refuge, considered as one of the preliminary devotional practices undertaken by the would-be bodhisattva, cannot really be regarded as foreshadowing either the deeper understanding of the significance of the act of Going for Refuge at which I eventually arrived or my realization of the implications of that act, properly understood, for the whole theory and practice of Buddhism. I am not referring to the comparatively unimportant fact that, speaking of formal refuge in the Triple Gem, I say that it can be taken 'simply by repeating after any ordained monk the refuge-formula and the five precepts'. This statement is in any case modified towards the end of my discussion of Going for Refuge as one of the preliminary devotional practices of the would-be bodhisattva, where I say that the Refuges are 'generally taken from a *bhikṣu*' and that, in the absence of a *bhikṣu*, 'a Buddhist assembly may be "led" in the taking of the Three Refuges by any senior lay devotee'[529] – though even this does not go nearly far enough and begs all sorts of questions. In insisting that the key passage in the *Survey*'s most extended treatment of Going for Refuge cannot really be regarded as foreshadowing my later views on the subject I am referring to something much more subtle and profound. Though in the purely formal or abstract sense my understanding of the meaning of Going for Refuge was not incorrect, and though I even realized in principle, to some extent, the absolute centrality of the act of Going for Refuge, I did not actually place that act, as I then understood it, at the very heart and centre of Buddhism, with all the momentous consequences that would have then followed. I did not accord it that absolute priority over all other acts which, by its very nature, it demands.

Thus at the beginning of the 'key passage' already quoted, after defining Going for Refuge as going for refuge to the Buddha, the Dharma, and the Sangha, I continue:

> While even a non-Buddhist can, in a sense, respect and honour the Triple Gem, to take refuge in them is the prerogative of the professing and practising Buddhist alone.

This is really to put the cart before the horse, for, as I observed in section 4, in connection with my Going Forth, one does not go for Refuge because one is a Buddhist but is a Buddhist because one goes for Refuge. Similarly, Going for Refuge is not simply one of the preliminary devotional practices which one undertakes in order to develop the *bodhicitta* or 'will to Enlightenment', thus becoming a bodhisattva; it is because one goes for Refuge that one is a bodhisattva. As I came to realize only at a subsequent stage in the history of my Going for Refuge, the bodhisattva's aspiration to attain Supreme Enlightenment for the benefit of all sentient beings is in fact the altruistic dimension of the act of Going for Refuge itself, which by its very nature cannot be regarded as having implications for oneself alone.[530] Provisional Going for Refuge can, of course, be regarded as a means to the arising of the real *bodhicitta*; but equally, the provisional *bodhicitta* can be regarded as a means to real Going for Refuge. We must be careful not to make the mistake of thinking that what is, in fact, only a 'revised version' of a certain stage of spiritual development is actually a higher stage. The Mahāyāna came to see the (real) *bodhicitta* as superior to the (provisional) Going for Refuge for much the same reason that it came to see the bodhisattva ideal as superior to the *arhant* ideal, i.e. because in the hands of the Hīnayāna the concept of Going for Refuge had lost much of its original significance, so that a fresh formulation of what it had been intended to convey had to be found. Earlier on in chapter 4, 'The Bodhisattva Ideal', in the section entitled 'The Unifying Factor', I describe the bodhisattva ideal as 'the principal unifying factor' not only for the Mahāyāna schools but for the entire Buddhist tradition.[531] But inasmuch as the bodhisattva is one in whom the *bodhicitta* has arisen, and inasmuch as the arising of the *bodhicitta* is the altruistic dimension of Going for Refuge, it is in fact the act of Going for Refuge that is the principal unifying factor in Buddhism. What I say about the bodhisattva ideal in chapter 4 of the *Survey* has to be read, where necessary, in the light of this realization.

In much the same way, those passages in chapters 1–3 of the *Survey* which intend to identify the sangha or spiritual community with the monastic order must be read in the light of the realization that, as I have explained in section 5 of this paper, becoming a monk is of significance and value only to the extent that it is an expression of one's Going for Refuge. Indeed, in chapter 2 of the *Survey*, 'Hīnayāna and Mahāyāna', in the section entitled 'What is Mahāyāna Buddhism?', having commented on the Mahāyāna *bhikṣus*' healthier and more truly orthodox attitude to the formal aspects of monasticism, I not only point out that, once it has been admitted that a bodhisattva may be either a monk or a layman, 'it becomes impossible to identify the spiritual life exclusively with a life of monasticism', but also make it clear that the Buddha himself did not identify commitment to the spiritual life with adoption of the monastic lifestyle by quoting *Dhammapada* verse 142 to this effect.[532]

In this connection I have one more point to make before concluding this section. In various parts of the *Survey*, but particularly in chapter 2, section 4, 'Factors in the Emergence of the Mahāyāna', I severely criticize the Hīnayāna in general and the Theravāda sangha (i.e. the Theravāda monastic order) in particular for what I term 'over-attachment to the merely formal aspects of monasticism', which I in fact enumerate as one of the five factors which were responsible, on the negative side, for the emergence of the Mahāyāna as a historical phenomenon. Rereading my strictures twenty-one years later I found them milder than I had thought and, though severe enough, fully justified, and therefore wrote in the Preface to the fifth (1980) edition of the *Survey*:

> In the light of subsequent experience I am convinced that my criticisms of the modern Theravāda were – and still are – not only fully justified but absolutely necessary, and I do not retract a word of what I wrote. I would only like to add that, far from being confined to the modern Theravāda, the canker of formalism can sometimes be found in other forms of Buddhism too, not least in contemporary Zen.[533]

Ten years further on I would like to add that although my criticisms of the Theravāda were 'harsh' (as one of my friends called them), and although that 'harshness' was fully justified, they were in reality not harsh enough, in the sense that they were not sufficiently radical. Though I speak in unfavourable terms of 'that identification of the religious life exclusively with the formal aspects of monasticism which is so prominent a feature of the Hīnayāna' I do so only incidentally, and in giving my various colourful examples of formalism and hypocrisy within the modern Theravāda (monastic) sangha do not sufficiently bring out the fact that what is really wrong with it is its confusion of Going for Refuge with becoming a monk, commitment with lifestyle. Members of the Theravāda (monastic) sangha are not so much bad monks as bad Buddhists. Indeed, it is possible to be a good monk, in the formalistic sense, and at the same time a bad Buddhist. One might even go so far as to say that it is possible to be a bad monk and a good Buddhist.

If one bears this in mind, and bears in mind that the arising of the *bodhicitta* or 'will to Enlightenment' represents the altruistic dimension of Going for Refuge, one will have gone a long way towards placing the act of Going for Refuge at the very heart and centre of Buddhism, and a long way, therefore, towards seeing the extent to which my later thinking about Buddhism is implicit in my earlier.

9

DHARDO RIMPOCHE AND *THE PATH OF THE BUDDHA*

When I was in the midst of writing the *Survey* a Tibetan friend asked me to help him with the English of an article on 'Buddhism in Tibet' that he had agreed to write for an American publication. The friend was Lobsang Phuntsok Lhalungpa, an official of the Tibetan government who had grown up in Lhasa and now lived in Kalimpong, and the publication was *The Path of the Buddha*, a book aiming to present Buddhism 'from the Buddhist point of view'. Helping Lobsang with the English of his article actually involved the complete rewriting of some three-hundred foolscap pages of manuscript, my friend's command of the 'tongue/ That Shakespeare spake' being then quite rudimentary.[534] Though the work was onerous, and could hardly have come at a more inconvenient time, I did it willingly, the more especially when I discovered that in writing his article Lobsang Phuntsok was drawing not so much on his own knowledge of Tibetan Buddhism as on the knowledge of an eminent incarnate lama who afterwards became one of my most revered teachers. This was Dhardo Rimpoche, the Greatly Precious One of Dhartsendo.

For a period of several months, therefore, I not only carried on writing the *Survey* but wrestled with Lobsang Phuntsok's grammar and syntax, not to mention his spelling and handwriting. Sometimes what he had written was so confused as to be unintelligible. When that was the case I was obliged to call on him for verbal explanations of what he was trying to say, and these explanations often led to our becoming involved in prolonged doctrinal discussion. Such discussion did not always succeed in making his account of *śūnyatā*, or of the *trikāya* doctrine, seem any the less confused, with the result that he had to refer back to Dhardo Rimpoche, the original source of his material, for further clarification. Having done this, he could be sure that whatever explanations he now gave me were correct and I, for my part, could be sure that in rewriting his pages in accordance with them I was not misinterpreting Tibetan Buddhism. All this naturally took time, but eventually the work was done and the article dispatched to the United States where, after being edited and drastically shortened, it appeared as chapter 6 of *The Path of the Buddha* in 1956.

As so often happens, a benefit conferred turned out to be a benefit received. As a result of rewriting Lobsang Phuntsok Lhalungpa's article, and especially as a result of the prolonged doctrinal discussion to which this frequently led, in the space of three or four months I received from him and, through him, from Dhardo Rimpoche, a comprehensive grounding in the history, the schools, the doctrines, and the practices of Tibetan Buddhism – a grounding that often went far beyond the topics actually dealt with in the article. At a time when reliable books on Tibetan Buddhism could be counted on the fingers of one hand the experience was of immense value to me, and laying down my pen after rewriting the last sentence of Lobsang's manuscript I felt as though I had been given an intensive course in the subject. Nevertheless, owing to my preoccupation with the writing of the *Survey* I was not in a position to absorb what I had learned to the extent that I might otherwise have done, though traces of my newly acquired knowledge of Tibetan Buddhism are discernible here and there in my *magnum opus*. Among the topics with regard to which I was unable to absorb what I had learnt was the topic of Going for Refuge, which was dealt with in a short section of the article entitled 'The Three Precious Ones' (i.e. the Three Jewels). According to Lobsang Phuntsok/Dhardo Rimpoche, Tibetan Buddhists took heartfelt refuge in the Buddha, the Dharma, and the Sangha, and this taking refuge in the Triple Gem was 'the most fundamental belief and most widely accepted practice in Buddhism', preceding all other religious acts such as reading of scriptures, making of solemn vows, receiving ordination, performance of ceremonies, and practice of meditation.[535] Moreover, Tibetan Buddhists placed great emphasis on the good intention preceding the taking of the Three Refuges.

> The intention must be of a sincere and benevolent nature, supported by a strong resolve, and the vow itself [i.e. one's Going for Refuge] must be constantly borne in mind while performing any religious practices.[536]

Most important of all:

> The taking of the Three Refuges includes within its scope the taking of all the principles of Buddhism; one who does not take the Triple Gem is not a Buddhist'.[537]

The full significance of these statements, especially of the last, dawned on me only later, as I became more closely acquainted with the Tibetan Buddhist tradition through the study of books and through personal contact with Dhardo Rimpoche and other incarnate lamas. But before proceeding to deal with this stage in the history of my Going for Refuge, which in a sense constitutes a continuation of the stage dealt with in the present section, I must say something about my contact with Buddhists of a very different type – a contact which, in its own way, also contributed to the process whereby the meaning and significance of Going for Refuge became clear to me.

10
AMBEDKAR AND THE EX-UNTOUCHABLES

Bhimrao Ramji Ambedkar was an Untouchable from Bombay state who, overcoming enormous obstacles, became an economist, a lawyer, an educationalist, a politician and, finally, free India's first Law Minister and the chief architect of her Constitution. Throughout his life he fought for the amelioration of the lot of India's tens of millions of Untouchables and for the removal of the age-old social, religious, economic, political, and educational disabilities imposed on them by the caste Hindus – disabilities which reduced them to a state of virtual, even of actual, slavery. However, his efforts met with little or no success, and after thirty years of struggle Ambedkar came to the conclusion that the caste Hindus were not going to mend their ways, that there was no salvation for the Untouchables within Hinduism, and that they would have to change their religion. On 14 October 1956, when he had been out of office for six years, he therefore not only embraced Buddhism himself by publicly taking the Three Refuges and Five Precepts from U Chandramani Maha Thera, from whom I had received my *śrāmaṇera* ordination, but also inaugurated the historic movement of mass conversion to Buddhism by administering those same Refuges and Precepts, together with twenty-two vows of his own devising, to the 380,000 Untouchable men, women, and children who had assembled for the occasion. Six weeks later he died.

As related in *Ambedkar and Buddhism*,[538] I had known Ambedkar since 1952, when we met after an earlier exchange of letters, and during the critical period immediately following his death I did whatever I could to ensure that the movement of mass conversion to Buddhism continued. This involved the making of a whole series of lecture tours in the course of which I visited cities, towns, and villages all over central and western India and came into contact with tens upon tens of thousands of ex-Untouchable Buddhists, some of whom I indeed received into Buddhism myself. But whether received into Buddhism by me, by a fellow monk, or by one of their own leaders, like their great emancipator they all became Buddhists simply by taking the Three Refuges and Five Precepts. Taking the Refuges and Precepts by reciting them after a monk or other leading Buddhist was, of course, a standard procedure among lay Buddhists, especially in south-east Asia. I had witnessed the ceremony at centres of the Maha Bodhi Society and elsewhere on numerous occasions and had myself conducted it scores of times. But never before had I seen the Three Refuges and Five Precepts taken with the sincerity, zeal, and fervour that I saw them taken by the largely illiterate and wretchedly poor ex-Untouchables, many of whom had travelled a hundred miles or more on foot for the purpose. For the 'born Buddhists' of Ceylon and Burma, 'taking *pansil*', as the Sinhalese called it, was little more than a pious formality, the sort of thing that a good Buddhist did, and not so much an expression of commitment to the Three Jewels as an affirmation of one's cultural and ethnic identity. In the case of the ex-Untouchables it was very different. For them taking the Refuges and Precepts, or becoming Buddhists, meant conversion in the true sense of the term. It meant not only the repudiation of Hinduism, not only deliverance from what Ambedkar called 'the hell of caste',[539] but also being spiritually reborn in the sense of becoming free to develop in every aspect of their lives, whether social, economic, cultural, or religious. Indeed, as I could see from the light in their eyes and the rapturous look on their faces, in repeating the words of the ancient Pāli formula the ex-Untouchables, far from just 'taking *pansil*', were in fact giving expression to their heartfelt conviction that Buddhism was their only hope, their only salvation. They were *Going for Refuge* to the Three Jewels.

In the course of my tours I had many opportunities of seeing Ambedkar's followers take the Three Refuges and Five Precepts, sometimes in very large numbers, and the sight of their sincerity, zeal, and fervour never failed to move me deeply. Moreover, I felt that they were taking the Refuges and Precepts, and becoming Buddhists, out of feelings very similar to those which, in my own case, had found an outlet in the poem 'Taking Refuge in the Buddha'. There was one big difference. Whereas I had written my poem after a single experience of disappointment and frustration, they had all gone for Refuge as a result of a lifetime of systematic harassment and humiliation. But though the difference was a big one, it was quantitative rather than qualitative, so to speak, and in spite of it I felt very close to my ex-Untouchable brothers and sisters. It did not matter that I was English and they were Indian, or that I was a monk and they were laymen and laywomen. For them as for me there could be refuge only at the feet of the Buddha, even though their conception of that refuge was less metaphysical than mine.

Thus as a result of my contact with the ex-Untouchable Buddhists I came closer to seeing that monasticism and the spiritual life were not identical, and that Going for Refuge was the principal unifying factor in Buddhism. I came closer to seeing that Going for Refuge was the central and definitive act of the Buddhist life.

11
MORE LIGHT FROM TIBETAN BUDDHISM

The English Translation of Gampopa's *Jewel Ornament of Liberation* appeared in 1959, by which time my personal contact with Dhardo Rimpoche had deepened and I had received Tantric initiation from Jamyang Khyentse Rimpoche. As Dr Herbert V. Guenther, the scholarly translator of the work, explained in his Preface:

> The work belongs to the group of texts which are known as 'Stages on the Path' (*lam.rim*). They are manuals which guide the student from the elementary tenets of Buddhism to the profoundest realization of Buddhahood. sGam.po.pa's work seems to have been the first Tibetan text of this kind and it has remained famous to the present day. It deals with the whole of Buddhism in such a lucid manner that it can be studied and understood without constantly looking up long-winded and often rather obscure commentaries and sub-commentaries. It is therefore a real 'Jewel Ornament', a title which is an allusion to a particular type of literature known as 'adornments' (*alaṃkāra*) in Buddhist Sanskrit, because they give the choicest and most important subjects in a highly polished and rather concise form. Another outstanding feature of sGam.po.pa's work is that it is addressed to all people who are, or may become, spiritually inclined. It appeals to the layman as well as the monk and the philosopher who unceasingly pursues man's perennial quest for the meaning of life.[540]

On going through the work thus described I found it to consist of twenty-one chapters, one of which was headed 'Taking Refuge'. Though the manner in which Gampopa dealt with this supremely important step was certainly lucid, the fact that he explained it by way of 'nine topics of taking refuge', most of which were divided and subdivided and even sub-sub-subdivided, gave his whole treatment of Going for Refuge an air of pedantry and scholasticism that was hardly in keeping with the spirit of the subject. This did not bother me, however, though it has bothered others ('laymen' studying the *Jewel Ornament* have found it less appealing than Guenther thought they would mainly on account of its scholasticism), and when I read Gampopa's chapter on 'Taking Refuge' for the first time it was with a sense of light being shed upon the topic. Besides pointing out that the Buddha was the only refuge, as I mentioned in section 7 in connection with my poem, he explained why powerful deities like Brahmā, Vishnu, and Mahādeva are unable to provide us with a refuge; singled out 'not hurting other beings' as the consequence of taking refuge in the noble Dharma; distinguished between the different levels of taking refuge even more radically than I had done in the *Survey*; enumerated the eight benefits of taking refuge; and made it clear that the difference between the *prātimokṣa* and the bodhisattva-discipline was primarily one of attitude. But what really shed light on the topic of Going for Refuge was the fact that Gampopa had devoted a whole chapter to it. The medium was the message, the message being that 'taking Refuge' (as Guenther unfortunately called it) was not just a formality, not something one did to show that one was a Buddhist, but actually one of the stages of the spiritual path – the *Jewel Ornament* itself being a guide to the Path, as Guenther had explained in his Preface.

But though light was shed on Going for Refuge both by Gampopa's treatment of the topic and by the fact that he had devoted a whole chapter of his book to it, that light was by no means sufficient to illuminate the subject completely. For Gampopa the Hīnayāna represented a lower and the Mahāyāna a higher stage of the Path, and since Going for Refuge epitomized the Hīnayāna, just as the arising of the *bodhicitta* or will to Enlightenment epitomized the Mahāyāna, it was in effect the arising of the *bodhicitta* that was the central and definitive act of the (Mahāyāna) Buddhist life rather than Going for Refuge. Going for Refuge, together with the observance of the *prātimokṣa*, was a means to the arising of the *bodhicitta*, just as the *bodhicitta* itself was a means of entering upon the Vajrayāna through the receiving of *abhiṣeka* or 'Tantric initiation'. In Gampopa's own words, those taking refuge in the Three Jewels were the 'working basis' for the arising, or as Guenther called it the development, of the *bodhicitta*.

The reason why Gampopa was unable to see the *bodhicitta* as the altruistic dimension of Going for Refuge was, of course, his lack of a sufficiently broad historical perspective. For him both the Hīnayāna and the Mahāyāna had been taught by the Buddha. He was therefore unable to see them as representing successive developments from the Buddha's original teaching, and because he was unable to see them in this way he was unable to appreciate (1) that historically speaking the Mahāyāna was to a great extent a restatement of the original teaching in terms more in accordance with the spirit, as distinct from the letter, of that teaching than were those of the Hīnayāna, and (2) that in the Mahāyāna restatement of the original teaching the place of Going for Refuge was occupied by the arising of the *bodhicitta*. Thus he had no alternative but to treat Going for Refuge as a means to the arising of the *bodhicitta*, which meant that Going for Refuge was at least recognized as constituting a definite stage of the Path, as indeed it had been since the time of Atīśa[541] and as it was to continue to be right down to the present day – not just in Gampopa's own Kagyu school but throughout the whole Tibetan Buddhist tradition. Nor was that all. While in theory Going for Refuge remained a means to the arising of the *bodhicitta*, in the course of centuries it became, in the hands of certain teachers, something very much more. It was transformed, in fact, into a virtually independent spiritual practice wherein the entire personality of the practitioner was involved in a particularly moving and significant manner, and it was the discovery of this practice that, some three years after the appearance of the English translation of Gampopa's *Jewel Ornament of Liberation*, provided me with further illumination on the topic of Going for Refuge.

The discovery in question took place in Kalimpong, shortly after I had received the *abhiṣeka* of the Greatly Precious Guru, Padmasambhava, from Kachu Rimpoche, a leading disciple of Jamyang Khyentse Rimpoche.[542] I received the *abhiṣeka* on 24 October 1962. The following morning I went into town and on my way through the bazaar happened to see a Tibetan monk squatting at the roadside. In his lap was a small bundle of rather grubby xylograph texts that he was offering for sale. Since the monk was obviously in need of money, and since the texts were very cheap (so cheap that even I could afford to buy them), I at once bought them and returned with them to the Vihara, where I showed them to Kachu Rimpoche. His response was one of surprise and delight. They were Nyingma texts, he exclaimed joyfully, as he thumbed his way through them. Most of them had to do with the Greatly Precious Guru, and the fact that I had come across them so soon after receiving the *abhiṣeka*, and in such a totally unexpected manner, was extremely auspicious. It showed that I had a special connection with the Greatly Precious Guru,[543] and with the Nyingma tradition, and that my efforts to realize the import of the teachings which the *abhiṣeka* had empowered me to practise would prove successful. Whether or not Kachu Rimpoche's 'reading of the signs' was correct is not for me to say. In any case, what I am concerned with at this juncture is the fact that among the texts I had bought, and which Kachu Rimpoche had greeted with such enthusiasm, was one entitled *Tharpe Delam* or 'The Easy Path to Emancipation'. This little work dealt with the general and special preliminaries to the practice of *ati-yoga*, the highest teaching of the Nyingmapas, and the main general preliminaries consisted of the four *mūla* or 'foundation' *yogas*, in the first of which Kachu Rimpoche had already given me some instruction. The first *mūla yoga* was, of course, the Going for Refuge and Prostration practice, the remaining three being the arising of the *bodhicitta*, the meditation and mantra recitation of Vajrasattva, and the offering of the mandala, after which followed the Guru Yoga. Having received further instruction from Kachu Rimpoche, I therefore took up the Going for Refuge and Prostration practice, as well as the other *mūla yogas*, and continued to do it regularly until my departure for England two years later. With the help of Dhardo Rimpoche, I moreover made a rough translation of the entire *Tharpe Delam*. Though I was able to do the Going for Refuge and Prostration practice for only two years, which by Tibetan standards was not very long, during this period I had a more intense and more sustained experience of Going for Refuge than ever before. I also arrived at a clearer understanding of the fact that 'the taking of the Three Refuges includes within its scope the taking of all the principles of Buddhism,' and a clearer understanding, therefore, of the meaning and value of the act of Going for Refuge itself.

Those members of the Order who have done the Going for Refuge and Prostration practice will hardly need to be told why this should have been so.[544] At the beginning of the practice one visualizes the Greatly Precious Guru, Padmasambhava, the founder and patron of the Nyingma tradition, seated on the calyx of a lotus which itself rests on a multicoloured cloud floating in the midst of a brilliantly blue sky; and one sees Padmasambhava as the embodiment of all the Buddhas. Below Padmasambhava, seated on the petals of the lotus, are one's various gurus, below them the four orders of Tantric divinities, and lower still the *dharmapālas* and *ḍākinīs*. On the four sides of the lotus, i.e. the central lotus on the calyx of which sits Padmasambhava, are four more lotuses. On the front lotus stands Śākyamuni and the other human Buddhas; on the lotus to the right (i.e. to the right of Padmasambhava) the principle bodhisattvas, and on the lotus to the left the leading *arhants*, while on the rear lotus are piled the volumes of the sacred scriptures. In front of the Refuge Tree, as it is called (for the five lotuses all spring from a single stem), is oneself, together with all sentient beings. Having visualized Padmasambhava and the other objects of Refuge in this way, one repeats not the usual Refuge-going formula but a slightly more elaborate 'Tantric' version, saying aloud '*oṃ āḥ hūṃ*, to the best of all refuges I go. To the Lama the Buddha, the Lama the Dharma, the Lama the Sangha; to the Lama the Sri Maha Heruka; to the Lama the All-Performing King; to the Three Jewels in one, Guru Rimpoche, for Refuge I go.'[545] With each repetition one prostrates oneself before the visualized Refuge Tree (which one carries on visualizing throughout the session), or before its iconic counterpart. Thus in doing the Going for Refuge and Prostration practice one goes for Refuge with body, speech, and mind, that is, with the whole of one's being. One goes for Refuge with one's mind by visualizing Padmasambhava and the other objects of Refuge on their respective lotuses, one goes for Refuge with one's speech by repeating the words of the 'Tantric' Refuge-going formula, and one goes for Refuge with one's body by making a full length prostration. At the conclusion of the practice white light issues from the objects of Refuge and, falling upon oneself, one's father and all men, and one's mother and all women, takes away all their sins, which are dissolved into light. This light returns to the objects of Refuge, whereupon the *gurus, devas, dharmapālas*, and so on are dissolved into the body of Padmasambhava and Padmasambhava himself into the Void.

As those who have done the Going for Refuge and Prostration practice will be aware, in the course of each session of practice one not only visualizes the Refuge Tree throughout; one also repeats the words of the ('Tantric') Refuge-going formula, and prostrates oneself, as many times as one can, the sessions being kept up until such time as one has completed at least 100,000 repetitions and 100,000 prostrations, as some members of the Order have actually done.[546] It is therefore not surprising that the practice should have a very powerful effect, even to the extent of bringing about a radical change in one's mental and spiritual outlook. Indeed, as the months and the years go by the practitioner may well find himself becoming so deeply absorbed in the experience of Going for Refuge that it is no longer possible for him to think of the Going for Refuge and Prostration practice simply as one of the four *mūla yogas*, or of the act of Going for Refuge itself simply as a means to the arising of the *bodhicitta*. If he continues to think in such terms at all, he thinks of the Going for Refuge and Prostration practice as being virtually a spiritual practice in its own right. Thus it may be said that the practice which I discovered shortly after receiving the *abhiṣeka* of the Greatly Precious Guru, and which provided me with further illumination on the topic of Going for Refuge, in fact represented a transposition of the act of Going for Refuge into the rich and colourful mode of the Indo-Tibetan Tantric tradition. As such, it also represented a restoration of Going for Refuge to something like its original place in Buddhism and in the Buddhist life.

But it was not only through Gampopa's *Jewel Ornament of Liberation* and my discovery of the Going for Refuge and Prostration practice that light on the topic of Going for Refuge came to me from Tibetan Buddhism. Albeit less directly, light also came through personal contact with Tibetan Buddhists, especially through personal contact with certain eminent Nyingmapa incarnate lamas. Kachu Rimpoche, from whom I had received the Padmasambhava initiation, was a monk (as was Dhardo Rimpoche, who had been educated in the Gelug tradition); but other Nyingmapa lamas were married. Indeed, among the married lamas were some of the most eminent of all Nyingmapa lamas – towering spiritual personalities whom Kachu Rimpoche himself regarded with the utmost veneration and from whom he was proud to receive initiation and instruction.[547] As I came to know these lamas myself I could not but recognize that in respect of learning and spiritual attainment there was, so far as I could see, no real difference between them and their celibate counterparts either in the Nyingma tradition itself or in the other Tibetan Buddhist traditions – though it could always be argued that had they not been married their spiritual attainment, at least, would have been even greater. Moreover, I could not but recognize that among the disciples by whom each of these lamas was surrounded there existed a strong feeling of spiritual fellowship and that in consequence of this feeling differences of lifestyle, particularly as between the monk and the lay disciples, were regarded as being of very little account. This gave me food for thought. Not all Buddhists, it seemed, identified the spiritual life with a life of strict monasticism in the way that the Theravādins of south-east Asia did, or as some Gelugpas tended to do, despite the unifying influence of the bodhisattva ideal. Thus my contact with the married Nyingmapa lamas and their disciples had much the same result as my very different contact with the ex-Untouchable Buddhists. I came closer to seeing that monasticism and the spiritual life were not identical and closer, therefore, to realizing that what really mattered was not whether one was a monk or a layman but the depth and intensity of one's Going for Refuge.

12

THE THREE JEWELS AND OTHER WRITINGS

Between 1959 and 1964, when I returned to England, much of my time was devoted to literary work, and since it was during this same period that light on the topic of Going for Refuge came to me from Tibetan Buddhism it was only natural that a portion of that light should be reflected in some of the books and articles I was then engaged in producing.

The first of these, chronologically speaking, was an article on 'Ordination and Initiation in the Three Yanas' which appeared in the November 1959 issue of *The Middle Way*.[548] As its title suggested, the purpose of the article was to clear up some of the confusion that, for many people, surrounded the whole subject of ordination and initiation by explaining what the different ordinations and initiations actually were and how they corresponded to the three *yānas* and to the particular spiritual ideals in which those *yānas* found expression. The three *yānas* were, of course, the Hīnayāna, the Mahāyāna, and the Vajrayāna, representing the three successive phases of development through which Buddhism passed in India as well as the three progressive stages of spiritual ascent in the life of the individual Buddhist.[549] But though Going for Refuge was mentioned in the article only once, in connection with ordination in the Hīnayāna, 'Ordination and Initiation in the Three Yanas' is far from being devoid of significance for the process whose history I am now tracing. Speaking of the difference between ordination or *saṃvara* on the one hand and (Tantric) initiation or *abhiṣeka* on the other I pointed out that:

according to the fully developed Indo-Tibetan tradition the rite of admission to *upāsaka, śrāmaṇera, bhikṣu*, or *bodhisattva* status is in each case termed a *saṃvara*, literally 'restraint', 'control', 'obligation', or 'vow'.[550]

This was an important discovery. The fact that admission to *upāsaka, śrāmaṇera, bhikṣu*, and *bodhisattva* status was in each case termed a *saṃvara* or 'ordination' meant that the differences between the various grades of religious persons were of far less significance than they were sometimes thought to be. In particular it meant that the difference between the monk and the layman was not a difference between the ordained and the unordained. Both monks and laymen were ordained persons and both monks and laymen were, therefore, full members of the Buddhist spiritual community. This came very close to saying that *saṃvara* or ordination was a unifying rather than a dividing factor in Buddhism, and therefore very close to saying, as I afterwards did say, that ordination and Going for Refuge were in fact synonymous and that Going for Refuge was a unifying factor in Buddhism – indeed, that it was *the* unifying factor. Moreover, speaking of the three successive phases of Buddhist historical development, I pointed out that the Hīnayāna, Mahāyāna, and Vajrayāna were not to be thought of as lying end to end like so many sections of railway track, but that

the earlier phase not only passes over into the latter, but is taken up into, and incorporated by it, and lives on in it'.[551]

This meant, in effect, that Going for Refuge was taken up in the *bodhicitta*, so that the way was now clear for my later realization that the *bodhicitta* was the altruistic dimension of Going for Refuge.

In 1961, by way of contributing to the debate that followed the publication, in Ceylon, of the report of the Buddha Sasana Commission, I wrote an article to which I gave the controversial title 'Wanted: A New Type of Bhikkhu'. A year later, encouraged by the letters of appreciation I had received, I wrote a second article, to which I gave the hardly less controversial title 'Wanted: A New Type of Upāsaka'. Both articles took the form of a series of aphorisms (fifty-four in the case of the first article and sixty-three in the case of the second) and both were reproduced in virtually all the English language Buddhist journals.[552] Since they were written mainly for a south-east Asian Buddhist readership, the articles were reformist rather than revolutionary in tendency. As the concluding aphorism of the first article expressly stated, the 'new *bhikkhu*' was the old one adapted to modern conditions. Nevertheless, since both articles were concerned to stress the importance of moral and spiritual qualifications they both attempted, in effect, to bridge the gap between the monks and the laity. In the case of 'Wanted: A New Type of Bhikkhu' the attempt took the form of a strong attack on monastic formalism, which I continued to see as the besetting sin of the whole Theravāda branch of the monastic order.

> The new type of *bhikkhu* will never commit the mistake of thinking that the wearing of the yellow robe makes him a monk.[553]

declared the opening aphorism, and in many of the succeeding aphorisms this principle was applied to specific areas of the monk's life. In the case of 'Wanted: A New Type of Upāsaka' the attempt to bridge the gap between monks and laity took the form of a strong insistence that the *upāsaka*, too, was a Buddhist and that it was incumbent on him to act accordingly. In the words of the first three aphorisms of the article:

> The new type of *upāsaka* will never commit the mistake of thinking that it is really possible for anyone to be 'a born Buddhist'.
>
> He will not recite the *triśaraṇa* and *pañcaśīla* mechanically on Uposatha days without making any effort to embody them in his daily life.
>
> He will not think the practice of the Dharma is the duty of the *bhikkhu*, but not of the *upāsaka*.[554]

Clearly my new type of *bhikkhu* and new type of *upāsaka* would have a lot in common. So much in common would they have, indeed, that one might be forgiven for thinking that together they heralded the emergence of the *dharmacārī* and *dharmacāriṇī*; for, as I was shortly to realize, what Buddhists above all had in common – and what therefore constituted the fundamental basis of unity among them – was the fact that they all went for Refuge to the Buddha, Dharma, and Sangha and that such Going for Refuge was of central importance in their lives.

As far as I know, this realization found its first unambiguous expression in the Preface to *The Three Jewels*, where I spoke of Going for Refuge as:

> the central act of the Buddhist life, from which all other [Buddhist] acts derive their significance, and without reference to which Buddhism itself is unintelligible.[555]

Since the Preface is addressed from the Hampstead Buddhist Vihara, London, it must have been written in either 1965 or 1966, probably the latter. *The Three Jewels* itself, which was not published until 1967, had been written during the second half of 1961 and together with *The Eternal Legacy* constituted my major literary undertaking during the period covered by this section of my *History*.[556] Like the latter work, it started life as a series of articles for the *Oriya Encyclopaedia* that, in the process of writing, considerably outgrew the purpose for which they had been commissioned. Though in it I did not speak of Going for Refuge in the terms in which, three or four years later, I spoke of it in the Preface, some of my remarks on the subject of spiritual community showed how close I was to realizing the absolute centrality of that unique act both for the individual Buddhist and for Buddhism. Thus having insisted that the true criterion of the relation between the Buddha and his followers was not physical, not spatio-temporal, but spiritual, and that we were nearest to him when we most perfectly followed his example, I went on:

> The Sangha is primarily the community of those who, by virtue of their immediate or remote approximation to Enlightenment, stand in spiritual relation to the Buddha and dwell spiritually in his presence. It is the community of those who, through their relationship with him, are also all spiritually related to one another.[557]

In other words, the Sangha is primarily the community of those who go for Refuge, for it is Going for Refuge that enables us to achieve the stages of the path and 'approximate' to Enlightenment and Going for Refuge that forms the ultimate basis of our relationship with the Buddha and, therefore, the ultimate basis of our relationship with other members of the sangha. Again, enlarging on the fact that in the broadest sense of the term the sangha coincided with the entire Buddhist community, monastic and lay, male and female, I wrote:

> During the lifetime of the Master relations between the eremitical monks who had 'gone forth' and the householders at whose doors they daily stood for alms, and in whose outhouses and gardens they lodged during the rains, were close and cordial, and a spirit of camaraderie prevailed. The latter could, if necessary, bring to the notice of the Master public complaints against the *parivrājakas*, and suggest changes in their mode of living. Such equalitarianism was natural. Their common devotion to the Buddha, and the extent to which his attainments transcended theirs, tended to reduce all distinctions among his followers, including that between monks and laymen, to a position of comparative insignificance. His impatience with the formalistic element in religion, and his uncompromising insistence on the necessity of personal realization of Nirvāṇa, moreover ensured that they should be distinguished, if at all, according to their intrinsic merits rather than their socio-ecclesiastical status.
>
>> Even though a man be richly attired, if he develops tranquillity, is quiet, subdued and restrained, leading a holy life and abstaining from injury to all living beings – he is a *brāhmaṇa*, he is a *samaṇa*, he is a *bhikkhu*.[558]
>
> That the homeless wandering monk, totally free from all worldly concerns, had a far better chance of reaching the Goal, was admitted, even emphasized; but that a householder, if sufficiently resolved, might sometimes reach it too, and that in the last resort it was transcendental attainment that mattered, not the wearing of yellow robes, more than one such saying of the Buddha testifies.[559]

Here the fact that it is their common devotion to the Buddha that tends to reduce all distinctions among his followers, including that between monks and laymen, to a position of comparative insignificance, implies that it is their common devotion to the Buddha that constitutes the fundamental basis of unity among Buddhists. But devotion to the

Buddha finds its fulfilment in Going for Refuge to the Buddha, as well as to the Dharma and the Sangha. In saying that their common devotion to the Buddha tended to reduce all distinctions among his followers to comparative insignificance I was therefore in effect saying that it was their common Going for Refuge that constituted the fundamental basis of unity among them. Moreover, having referred to the schism that took place in the Buddhist community between a hundred and two hundred years after the Buddha's *parinirvāṇa*, I pointed out that the Mahāyāna had 'evolved for all followers of the Buddha a common spiritual ideal,' i.e. the bodhisattva ideal, and worked out a common path, the path of the six (or ten) *pāramitās*, thus lessening the tensions between the monastic and lay wings of the (Mahā-) sangha,

> which were now united through the pursuit of a common spiritual objective [i.e. Supreme Buddhahood] by means of the same, or similar, spiritual methods.[560]

A common Vinaya for all bodhisattvas, whether monks or laymen, was also evolved. Thus I had seen that the Mahāyāna had already made the bodhisattva ideal the unifying factor of Buddhism, and having seen this I had only to realize that the *bodhicitta* was the altruistic dimension of Going for Refuge in order to see that it was in reality Going for Refuge that was the unifying factor and, therefore, 'the central act of the Buddhist life.'

'A Bird's-Eye View of Indian Buddhism', as I called it at one stage, was a lengthy article produced on the eve of my departure from India in 1964.[561] Editorials for the *Maha Bodhi* journal excepted, it was therefore the last of my writings to be produced during the period covered by the present section of this *History*. It had been commissioned by the Syndics of the Oxford University Press for the second edition of *The Legacy of India*, but having heard nothing from them for a long time and having assumed (wrongly, as it turned out) that they had decided not to use the article, in 1980 I included it in the fifth edition of *A Survey of Buddhism* as the Introduction to that work.[562] Originally, very little of the light that had come to me from Tibetan Buddhism on the subject of Going for Refuge was reflected in its pages. Having dealt with the Āryasaṅgha and the *bhikṣu* sangha or order of monks I wrote:

In a more general sense the sangha comprises the entire Buddhist community, sanctified and unsanctified, the professional religieux and the lay devotees, men and women. As such it is sometimes known as the *Mahāsaṅgha*, or 'great assembly'. Lay devotees (*upāsakas* and *upāsikās*) are those who go for refuge to the Three Jewels, worship the relics of the Buddha, observe the five precepts of ethical behaviour, and support the monks.[563]

This did not go nearly far enough. In 1978, when revising the article for inclusion in the fifth edition of the *Survey*, I therefore made the following addition to the passage:

Although as time went on the life of the monks diverged more and more sharply from that of the laity the fact that all alike went for refuge to the Buddha, the Dharma, and the Sangha remained a common, potentially uniting, factor – a factor that, in the case of the Mahāyāna, was strengthened by the development of the bodhisattva ideal, which was an ideal equally for the monk and the layman, the nun and the laywoman.[564]

This had the effect of bringing the article of 1964 more into line with my current thinking.

Mention of the Preface to *The Three Jewels* and the inclusion of 'A Bird's-Eye View of Indian Buddhism' in the fifth edition of the *Survey* has, however, taken us rather too far ahead. Before leaving India I went through one more stage in the process by which the meaning, significance, and importance of Going for Refuge became clear to me.

13
BODHISATTVA ORDINATION

The bodhisattva ideal has attracted me from quite an early period of my Buddhist life. Indeed, it had attracted me from the time when, shortly after reading the *Diamond Sūtra* and the *Sūtra of Wei Lang*, I came across a copy of *The Two Buddhist Books in Mahāyāna*. The second of these books, which had been translated and compiled by Upasika Chihmann, Bodhisattva in Precepts (Miss P. C. Lee of China), was 'The Vows of the Bodhisattva Samantabhadra', which formed part of the *Avataṃsaka* (or 'Flower Ornament') *Sūtra*. This work I read repeatedly, and its picture of the infinitely wise and boundlessly compassionate bodhisattva must have made a deep impression on me for the words

> Thought following upon thought without interruption, and in bodily, oral, and mental deeds without weariness[565]

kept going through my head for days together. It was as though they embodied Samantabhadra's – or any other bodhisattva's – constant, unflagging fulfilment of his great vows through infinite time and infinite space. Seven or eight years later, shortly after my arrival in Kalimpong, I came across Śāntideva's *Śikṣā-samuccaya* or 'Compendium of Instruction [for Novice Bodhisattvas]'[566] and as a result was more strongly attracted to the bodhisattva ideal than ever – so strongly, in fact, that attraction is far too weak a word for what I then felt. The truth was that I was thrilled, exhilarated, uplifted, and inspired by the bodhisattva ideal, and my feeling for it found expression in some of the poems and articles I wrote during this period, as well as in chapter 4 of *A Survey of Buddhism*.[567] There were two reasons for my being so strongly affected. In the first place, there was the sheer unrivalled sublimity of the bodhisattva ideal – the ideal of dedicating oneself, for innumerable lifetimes, to the attainment of Supreme Enlightenment for the benefit of all living beings. In the second, there was the fact that, as enjoined by my teacher Kashyapji, I was 'working for the good of Buddhism',[568] and that I could not do this without strong spiritual support, the more especially since I received very little real help or co-operation from those who were supposedly working with me. This spiritual support I found in the bodhisattva ideal, which provided me with an example, on the grandest possible scale, of what I was myself trying to do within my own infinitely smaller sphere and on an infinitely lower level.

It was therefore not surprising that on 12 October 1962 – nine days before receiving the Padmasambhava initiation – I should have received the bodhisattva ordination.[569] By that time I had been a Buddhist for more than twenty years, and a monk for thirteen, and I had been working for the good of Buddhism for twelve years. For the last five years I had, indeed, been working for it not only in Kalimpong and the neighbouring hill towns, as originally enjoined, but among the ex-Untouchable Buddhists of central and western India. I therefore felt ready to take the bodhisattva ordination and, in this way, give formal expression to my acceptance of the bodhisattva ideal. Moreover, I had found a preceptor from whom I could take the ordination. This was Dhardo Rimpoche, the Greatly Precious One of Dhartsendo, whom I had known since 1953 and whom I had come to revere as being himself a living bodhisattva. On the occasion of my *śrāmaṇera* ordination U Chandramani had been concerned that I should pronounce the words of the Refuge-going formula correctly, but he had said nothing about the meaning of those words or about the significance of the act of Going for Refuge itself. Similarly, at my *bhikṣu* ordination my Burmese preceptor had explained to me only the four reliances of the monk. Dhardo Rimpoche, however, not only gave me the bodhisattva ordination but subsequently explained the sixty-four bodhisattva precepts to me in considerable detail, so that I was able to translate them from Tibetan into English.[570] What was no less important, whereas I had had no further contact with my two previous preceptors after receiving ordination at their hands, in the case of Dhardo Rimpoche I was able to remain in regular personal contact with him for the rest of my stay in India.[571]

But what effect did the taking of the bodhisattva ordination have on me? At the time it gave me a definite sense of spiritual progression, for I still thought of the Hīnayāna, Mahāyāna, and Vajrayāna as representing successive phases or stages of development and still, therefore, thought of the bodhisattva ordination as being 'superior' to the *bhikṣu* ordination, just as the *bhikṣu* ordination was 'superior' to the *upāsaka* ordination. In the long run, however, the taking of the bodhisattva ordination had the effect of making me think of myself not as a monk who happened to accept the bodhisattva ideal but rather as a (*triyāna*) Buddhist who happened to be a monk. Since the arising of the *bodhicitta* – and becoming a bodhisattva – was in fact the altruistic dimension of Going for Refuge, this in turn had the effect of making me think of myself simply as a monk who went for Refuge, or even as a human being who went for Refuge and who happened to live in monastic or semi-monastic fashion. Commitment was primary, lifestyle secondary.

14
LIGHT FROM VATICAN II

In August 1964, in response to an invitation from the English Sangha Trust, I returned to England and took up residence at the Hampstead Buddhist Vihara.[572] My original intention was to stay for only four months, or at the most six, since I considered myself to be permanently domiciled in India;[573] but in the end, after two years at the Hampstead Buddhist Vihara, I decided to stay in England indefinitely. I therefore paid a farewell visit to India and in March 1967 returned to England for good.[574]

During the two years that I spent at the Hampstead Buddhist Vihara I was extremely busy, my time being occupied mainly with giving lectures and holding meditation classes, both at the Vihara itself and at the Buddhist Society, as well as with visiting the various provincial Buddhist groups. I was also available for personal interviews. Though there was no question of my being able to engage in literary work, I did however manage to find time for a certain amount of reading, being then particularly interested in informing myself about current developments in Christianity. One day I came across a book on the Second Vatican Council, and plunged into it immediately. Later I read other books on the subject with no less avidity. In one of these books the Roman Catholic Church was said to be characterized by authoritarianism, centralism, and triumphalism. Whether the characterization represented the Church's own verdict, via the Council, on its pre-conciliar Tridentine self, or whether it represented simply the verdict of the author, I do not remember, but it was a characterization that at once arrested my attention. I had heard of authoritarianism and centralism before, but I had not heard of triumphalism, which apparently meant exulting in the purely secular victories and achievements of the Church in general, and of the hierarchy and the clergy in particular, as though they were spiritual victories and spiritual achievements. It meant, in fact, mistaking the worldly power and glory of the Church for its spiritual power and glory, and thinking that in working for the former one was working for the latter.

This certainly shed light on the Roman Catholic Church, and explained much that was regrettable in the history of Christianity itself. But suddenly there struck me, with the force of a thunderbolt, the thought that the Theravāda monastic order, too, was characterized by triumphalism. I recalled occasions on which Sinhalese monks had arrogantly insisted on taking precedence over everyone else and on being treated, in effect, like VIPs, in the belief that they were thereby upholding the supremacy of the Dharma. Similarly, I recalled the way in which visiting Thai *bhikṣus* had confined themselves to teaching the newly converted ex-Untouchable Buddhists such things as how to prostrate themselves before members of the monastic order and how to make offerings to them, as though in so doing they were propagating Buddhism among the ex-Untouchables with a vengeance. In fact, the more I reflected on the insidious nature of triumphalism the more instances of it among Theravāda monks I could recall, and the more instances I recalled, the more convinced I became that the Theravāda monastic order was indeed characterized by triumphalism. Nor was that all. I had myself been ordained into the Theravāda monastic order, and I realized with horror that I may well have been unconsciously influenced by its triumphalist attitude, if only to a limited extent. An element of triumphalism may even have crept into some of my writings, especially my editorials in the *Maha Bodhi* journal.[575] Having realized this, I resolved that in future I would be on my guard against triumphalism, both in myself and in others, and that I would discourage it by all possible means. Whether it characterized the Roman Catholic Church or not, there was no place for it in Buddhism and no place for it in the spiritual life.

Strange to say, at about the same time that I became aware that the Theravāda monastic order was characterized by triumphalism I became more aware of the fact that there was a good deal of triumphalism in my immediate surroundings, as well as a good deal of formalism. Four or five Sinhalese and Thai monks were then staying with me at the Hampstead Buddhist Vihara, and all of them manifested a degree of triumphalism in their dealings with British Buddhists. So much was this the case, indeed, that I was reminded of the way in which the visiting Thai monks had taught the ex-Untouchable Buddhists, for though the monks who were staying with me at the Vihara certainly did not confine themselves to teaching their British disciples how to prostrate themselves before members of the monastic order and how to make offerings to them there was the same disproportionate emphasis on these things that I had witnessed in India. Such an emphasis was by no means a new thing to British Buddhists, however. Whether in the person of its Eastern or its Western representatives, the triumphalism of the Theravāda monastic order had been a dominant factor in a section of the British Buddhist movement for more than a decade, as I quickly discovered when, a few days after my arrival in England, I shocked some participants in the Buddhist Society's annual summer school (and surprised and delighted others) by actually eating at the same table as everyone else.[576] It was on account of incidents like this that I eventually concluded that while there was a potential for the Dharma in the West the existing British Buddhist movement had already strayed from the right path in certain respects and that a new Buddhist movement was badly needed.

15
'THE MEANING OF CONVERSION IN BUDDHISM'

In the course of my two years at the Hampstead Buddhist Vihara I must have given upwards of two hundred lectures. Some of the people attending these lectures considered themselves to be Buddhists while others – no doubt the majority – did not. Among those who considered themselves Buddhists there were many who also considered themselves to have been *converted* to Buddhism, usually from Christianity, and this led to my giving more thought to what was meant by conversion, especially within the context of Buddhism, than I had done before. It also led to my delivering, under the title 'The Meaning of Conversion in Buddhism', a series of four lectures in which I dealt with conversion to (and within) Buddhism in terms of Going for Refuge, Stream Entry, the arising of the will to Enlightenment, and turning about in the deepest seat of consciousness.[577]

These lectures were delivered in the summer of 1965, and in them I was able to give expression to some of the new ideas that had come to me as a result of my realization of the central importance of Going for Refuge in the Buddhist life. This is not to say that such ideas did not find their way into some of the other lectures I gave during my two years at the Hampstead Buddhist Vihara. Looking through my lecture notes of the period, in preparation for writing about this stage in the history of my Going for Refuge, I was indeed surprised at the extent to which later developments in my thinking had been anticipated. But though some of my new ideas (or rather, my new interpretations of old ideas) may have found their way into other lectures, it was only in the four lectures on 'The Meaning of Conversion in Buddhism' that certain of them found more or less systematic expression within the context of traditional Buddhist thought. Conversion itself I defined as a 'turning around' from a lower to a higher way of life or, more specifically, from a worldly life to a spiritual life. Sometimes it was a slow and gradual process, lasting many years; sometimes it was almost instantaneous, in which case one could speak of 'sudden conversion'. However it took place, it was of the greatest importance, as marking the beginning of the spiritual life, and hence was deserving of serious consideration. If the meaning of conversion was studied in connection with Buddhism, it would be found that it was not such a simple matter as had been supposed. In Buddhism conversion was of several kinds, and took place on different levels.

In terms of Going for Refuge, conversion meant the orientation of one's life in the direction of the Buddha, Dharma, and Sangha, which as the 'Three Jewels' represented the world of the highest spiritual values, or what was attractive and desirable above all else. It meant organizing one's life around the Three Jewels, and the greater part of the first lecture was devoted to an explanation of how this worked out in the case of each individual Jewel. In the case of the Buddha, Going for Refuge meant taking him as the living embodiment of the highest spiritual ideal. If anybody else was regarded as such there was no Refuge, and though one might be an admirer of the Buddha and Buddhism one would not be a Buddhist. This might seem narrow but was not really so. Devotion was by its very nature exclusive, for the heart could be fixed only on what was perceived as the highest. In the case of the Dharma, which was both 'teaching' and 'spiritual principle', Going for Refuge was of two kinds: intellectual and spiritual. Intellectually, it meant studying the doctrinal formulations in which the Dharma, as a spiritual principle, found expression; spiritually, it meant the personal realization of that principle. In the case of the Sangha, which at one and the same time denoted the spiritual hierarchy, the monastic order, and the whole Buddhist community, Going for Refuge was threefold in that one could go for Refuge to the Sangha in all these senses. But there was a deeper meaning. Those who went for Refuge to the Sangha also went for Refuge to the Buddha and the Dharma, that is, they had a common spiritual teacher (or spiritual ideal) and a common teaching (or spiritual principle), and this tended to draw them together, even on the social plane. But what did one mean by 'together'? One did not mean physical proximity, or agreement on doctrinal questions, or even the attainment of the same stages of the spiritual path. It was rather more subtle than that. The 'together' lay in communication, which was not just an exchange of ideas but a vital mutual responsiveness, on the basis of a common spiritual ideal and a common spiritual principle. It was a common exploration, in complete harmony and complete honesty, of the spiritual world. In this way spiritual progress took place. The exploration might be between guru and disciple, or it might be between friends (this anticipated the 'vertical' and 'horizontal' communication/spiritual friendship of later expositions) – though in the course of communication such distinctions might have lost their significance. In any case, in Going for Refuge to the Sangha one would be Going for Refuge to spiritual communication from mere contact, which was in most cases meaningless and superficial.

In this way did I draw attention, in the first of my lectures on 'The Meaning of Conversion in Buddhism', to the fact that sangha or spiritual community meant communication – a theme that, in later years, was to resound throughout the WBO and FWBO. Having done this, I reminded my listeners that Going for Refuge to the Three Jewels constituted conversion not merely in the sense of conversion from Christianity, or any other religion, to Buddhism, but in the sense of conversion from mundane life to spiritual life. It meant conversion from limited human ideals to an absolute spiritual ideal, for 'little systems' that 'have their day' to a path based on spiritual principles, and from meaningless worldly contact to meaningful spiritual communication. All this was involved when one repeated the words '*Buddhaṃ saraṇaṃ gacchāmi*' and so on. But even more than that, conversion meant 'changing into'. Going for Refuge was not just 'turning to' the Three Jewels but being transformed into them. Thus one aspect of the meaning of conversion in Buddhism was transformation into the Three Jewels. One's mind became Enlightened – became 'Buddha'; one's thoughts became in conformity with that Enlightenment – became 'Dharma'; and one's actions, especially one's communication, became spiritually meaningful – became 'Sangha'.[578]

This brought me from conversion *to* Buddhism, as represented by Going for Refuge, to conversion *within* Buddhism, as represented by

Stream Entry and the arising of the will to Enlightenment. It was not enough to orient one's life in the direction of the Three Jewels, or to organize one's life around them, in a general sort of way. It was not even enough to be transformed into them. The transformation had to be made permanent. There had to be a permanent shift of the centre of one's being, a shift from conditioned existence to the Unconditioned; there had to be a permanent switch over from the round to the spiral – and this was what was meant by Stream Entry. The greater part of my second lecture on 'The Meaning of Conversion in Buddhism' was therefore devoted to explaining what was meant by the round and the spiral, which involved dealing with such topics as the principle of conditionality, the two kinds of conditionality, i.e. the cyclical and the progressive, the Tibetan wheel of life, the twelve *nidānas*, the cause process and the effect process, the three junctures, the twelve positive *nidānas*, the Path of Vision, the three characteristics of mundane existence, and the three fetters. Similarly, the greater part of my third lecture, on the arising of the will to Enlightenment, was devoted to explaining what was meant by Enlightenment (*bodhi*), by will (*citta*), and by arising (*utpāda*). According to tradition, there were three kinds (or grades) of *bodhi* or Enlightenment, and these I reduced to two: Enlightenment which was gained but not communicated, and Enlightenment which was both gained and communicated. The arising of the will to Enlightenment referred to the second of these, and represented the transition, within the transcendental order, from an individualistic to an altruistic attitude. It represented conversion from subtle spiritual selfhood to a life of complete selflessness.

Since one could hardly go further than that, in my fourth and last lecture I approached the subject of conversion in Buddhism from an entirely fresh point of view and dealt with it in terms of turning about in the deepest seat of consciousness. *Parāvṛtti* or turning about consisted in turning from a superficial to a profound mode of awareness. According to the *Laṅkāvatāra Sūtra*, one of the key texts of the Yogācāra school, there were eight consciousnesses (*vijñāna*) or, more literally, discriminative awarenesses. These were the five sense-consciousnesses, the mind-consciousness, the afflicted, or defiled, mind-consciousness (afflicted by a dualistic outlook, so that it interpreted experience in terms of subject and object, self and world), and the *ālaya-* or store-consciousness. The *ālaya-* or store-consciousness had two aspects, the relative and the absolute. The relative *ālaya* consisted of the impressions left by our past experiences, both those of the present life and those of previous lives. These impressions were thought of as seeds: they were not passive but (potentially) active, and could sprout again whenever conditions permitted. The absolute *ālaya* was reality itself, conceived as pure awareness, free from all trace of subject-object duality. Turning about took place on the borderline between the relative *ālaya* and the absolute *ālaya*. As a result of our performing religious actions pure seeds, as they were called, were deposited in the relative *ālaya* and when enough of these had been accumulated the absolute *ālaya* acted upon them in such a way that they pushed out the impure seeds deposited by our mundane actions. This pushing out constituted the turning about in the deepest seat of consciousness (i.e. in the *ālaya*) and brought about the transformation of the entire *vijñāna* system, the five sense consciousnesses being collectively transformed into the all-performing wisdom, the mind-consciousness into the distinguishing wisdom, the afflicted mind-consciousness into the wisdom of equality, and the relative *ālaya* into the mirror-like wisdom. The absolute *ālaya* did not need to be transformed and was equated with the wisdom of the *dharmadhātu*. Thus in terms of turning about in the deepest seat of consciousness conversion in Buddhism consisted in turning from a dualistic to a non-dualistic mode of awareness and bringing about a radical transformation of one's entire being.

By dealing with conversion to (and within) Buddhism in terms of Going for Refuge, Stream Entry, the arising of the will to Enlightenment, and turning about in the deepest seat of consciousness I made it clear that all were aspects of a single process. This process was, of course, the process of conversion. Since Going for Refuge was an aspect of conversion, and since Stream Entry was also an aspect of conversion, Going for Refuge and Stream Entry could therefore in principle be equated, as could Going for Refuge and the arising of the will to Enlightenment. Though in my lectures on 'The Meaning of Conversion in Buddhism' I did not explicitly make the equation, and was not to do so for a few more years, in the lecture on the arising of the will to Enlightenment I came close to doing so. Having reduced the three kinds (or grades) of Enlightenment to two, i.e. Enlightenment which was gained but not communicated and Enlightenment which was both gained and communicated, I went on to lay it down as an axiom (and in my notes the words are italicized) that

> A spiritual experience which can be kept to oneself is not the same as one which is communicated – which indeed *has* to be communicated, in the sense that the very nature of the experience *demands* that it should be communicated.[579]

This meant, in effect, the abolition of the distinction between the two kinds (or grades) of Enlightenment (keeping a spiritual or transcendental experience to oneself was in fact a contradiction in terms), which meant the abolition of the distinction between Going for Refuge and the arising of the will to Enlightenment, for the Enlightenment in respect of which the will to Enlightenment arose was none other than the Enlightenment that was the ultimate object of Going for Refuge. The arising of the will to Enlightenment did not carry on from where Going for Refuge left off, so to speak (for Going for Refuge did not 'leave off' at all) but was what I subsequently called the altruistic dimension of Going for Refuge. Similarly with Going for Refuge and Stream Entry. Stream Entry, too, did not carry on from where Going for Refuge left off, but was Going for Refuge itself on a higher, transcendental plane: it was what I subsequently called *real* Going for Refuge, as distinct from the *provisional* Going for Refuge which was merely cultural and formal and the *effective* Going for Refuge from which one could still fall away. Thus with the help of the conception of conversion I paved the way, in my four lectures on 'The Meaning of Conversion in Buddhism', for that radical reduction of Stream Entry and the arising of the will to Enlightenment – and even of turning about in the deepest seat of consciousness – to Going for Refuge which characterized my later Buddhist thinking and constituted one of the principle foundations of the WBO and the FWBO.

16
FOUNDING THE WESTERN BUDDHIST ORDER

In the last section but one I related how, at the end of my first two years in England, I came to the conclusion that a new Buddhist movement was badly needed in Britain. Having paid my farewell visit to India and having returned to England for good in March 1967 (this time not at the invitation of the English Sangha Trust) I therefore set about creating that new Buddhist movement and after a year of preliminary work founded the Western Buddhist Order which, in the opening words of this paper,

> came into existence on Sunday 7 April 1968, when in the course of a ceremony held at Centre House, London, nine men and three women committed themselves to the Path of the Buddha by publicly 'taking' the Three Refuges and Ten Precepts from me in the traditional manner.[580]

Thus we have now come full circle, so to speak. We have returned to the point from which we set out, the point, that is to say, at which twelve people's understanding of what was meant by Going for Refuge coincided, at least to some extent, with the understanding at which I myself had arrived after traversing the stages in the history of my Going for Refuge so far described.

But why did my – why did *our* – new Buddhist movement take precisely the form that it did? Why did I found an *order* rather than the more usual society, with its general membership, annual subscriptions, democratically elected office-bearers, and so on? In order to answer this question I shall have to go back a little.

During my long stay in India I had observed that the Buddhist movement there for the most part consisted, organizationally speaking, of a number of Buddhist societies, and that these societies did not always live up to their name. On looking into the matter more closely I discovered that this was due not so much to ordinary human weakness as to the fact that some of the office-bearers and other influential members of the societies in question were not even nominally Buddhists and had joined their respective organizations for reasons that had little or nothing to do with Buddhism.[581] This was not to say that they were necessarily bad people: some of them were very good people; but the fact that they were not committed Buddhists, and made no serious effort to understand and practise the Dharma, meant that the Buddhist societies of which they were a part could not be run with the energy and inspiration that alone could make them worthy of their name. The basic reason for this unsatisfactory state of affairs was that membership of these societies, as of others similarly constituted, was open to anyone who cared to fill in a form and pay the membership fee. During my long stay in India I had therefore become convinced that it was not really possible for a Buddhist movement to consist, organizationally speaking, of a society or societies (the expression 'Buddhist society' was in fact virtually a contradiction in terms), but that it had to consist, essentially, of a group or groups of committed Buddhists, and my recent experiences in England had left me more convinced of this than ever. It was therefore an order, in the sense of a sangha or spiritual community, that I founded on Sunday 7 April 1968.

As must have been obvious to those who were present, though they may not have realized the significance of the fact at the time, this order of ours – the Western Buddhist Order – was what I subsequently termed a unified order.[582] It was a unified order in that it consisted of both men and women, who went for Refuge to the same Three Jewels, observed the same ten precepts, practised the same meditations and other spiritual disciplines, and who, where qualified, performed the same administrative and 'ministerial' functions.[583] The Western Buddhist Order was also a unified order in that it was envisaged as consisting of people of different lifestyles and different degrees of commitment to the Three Jewels. Since it was a unified order, and especially since it consisted of both men and women, the Western Buddhist Order represented something of a departure from Eastern Buddhist tradition, at least as that tradition was understood in some parts of the Buddhist world.[584] In all other respects, however, it was fully traditional in structure, and as I was careful to point out towards the end of my lecture on 'The Idea of the Western Buddhist Order and of Upāsaka Ordination', the first of the two lectures I gave on that historic day, when after summarizing the history of Buddhism in Britain and explaining the meaning of Going for Refuge I dealt with the four grades of ordination of which the Western Buddhist Order was to consist.

These four grades of ordination, representing four increasing degrees of commitment to the Three Jewels, were those of (1) the *upāsaka/upāsikā*, the lay brother or lay sister, (2) the *mahā-upāsaka/upāsikā*, the senior lay brother or lay sister, (3) the (novice) bodhisattva, and (4) the *bhikṣu* or monk. Since it was the *upāsaka/upāsikā* ordination that the twelve ordinands were to receive that evening I naturally had more to say about this grade of ordination than about the three others, which in any case soon fell into desuetude. An *upāsaka* (or *upāsikā*) was one who engaged in *upāsana* or religious practice; literally, he was one who 'sat near' (a teacher), that is, who was a disciple. Thus an *upāsaka* was not just a 'lay Buddhist' in the sense of a purely nominal follower of the Buddha's teaching. Though continuing to lead a secular life he at the same time tried to purify himself with the help of ten vows, three for body, four for speech, and three for mind. These vows were: (1–3) Abstention from taking life, from taking the not-given, and from sexual misconduct – by which body was purified; (4–7) abstention from false, harsh, and frivolous speech, as well as from slander and backbiting – by which speech was purified; and (8–10) abstention from covetousness, animosity, and false views – by which mind was purified. *Upāsaka* ordination consisted, essentially, in taking these ten vows preceded by the Three Refuges or, as I had called them earlier in the lecture, the three commitments. An *upāsaka* member of the Western Buddhist Order was also expected to be a vegetarian, or at least to make an effort to be one, to practise right livelihood (the fifth constituent of the Buddha's Noble Eightfold Path), and to lead a simple life, as well as to meditate every day, attend a class every week, and go on retreat every year. On a more 'mundane' level, he (or she) was expected to give whatever practical help he could, whether financial or otherwise, to the new Buddhist movement of which the Western Buddhist Order was now the heart and centre. These additional requirements were not embodied in any rule but were left to the discretion of the individual *upāsaka*.

Having dealt with the *upāsaka/upāsikā* ordination in this way, I emphasized that it represented a very definite degree of commitment indeed. Though the *upāsaka* grade was in one sense the lowest of the Order's four grades of ordination in another sense it was the most important, for it was the basis on which the whole structure rested – an insight that may well have foreshadowed the later absorption of the second, third, and fourth grades of ordination into the first, and the renaming of that as the *dharmacārī/dharmacārinī* ordination. Foreshadowing or not foreshadowing, it was to the three remaining grades of ordination that I now turned.

The *mahā-upāsaka/upāsikā*, the senior (literally 'great') lay brother or lay sister, was an *upāsaka* of several years standing. He (or she) had a certain amount of understanding and experience of the Dharma and was able to help out with the giving of lectures and taking of classes. He was, however, still a householder in the sense of still having a family and a full-time job. The bodhisattva in the full traditional sense was one who aimed at the attainment of Enlightenment for the benefit of all sentient beings. He (or she) was one who took the bodhisattva vow, and in the Mahāyāna the taking of this vow was associated with a definite ordination. In the context of the Western Buddhist Order, the bodhisattva was one who showed signs of possessing exceptional spiritual gifts and who was only technically a layman. Though he might have a part-time job, he would function in a 'ministerial' capacity. The *bhikṣu* or monk was the (celibate) full-timer. He might devote himself to teaching the Dharma, to study and literary work, or to meditation, or to a combination of two or three of these. In any case, his material needs would be supplied by other members of the order and by the general – that is, the general Buddhist – public. (I spoke of the *bhikṣu* or monk, and not of the *bhikṣu* or monk *and* the *bhikṣuṇī* or nun, because it was widely believed in the Buddhist world that the tradition of *bhikṣuṇī* ordination had died out many centuries ago and could not be renewed.[585] With the absorption of the three higher grades of ordination in the first and the emergence within the Western Buddhist Order of *anagārikas* or (celibate) 'homeless ones' of both sexes[586] this ceased to be a problem for our new Buddhist movement, if indeed it had ever been one.)

Though the greater part of my lecture was devoted to explaining the meaning of Going for Refuge and dealing with the four grades of ordination, I also touched on a number of other topics. Apart from issues of a more general nature such as the connection between Western Buddhism and the events of the age in which my audience and I were living, these included the difference between the academic study of Buddhism and actual commitment to the Three Jewels, the importance of spiritual fellowship and spiritual community, and the inability of Buddhist societies to meet the growing needs of Western Buddhists, as well as the reasons that had led to the establishment of the Western Buddhist Order. It had been established, I declared, to enable people to commit themselves more fully to the Buddhist way of life, to provide opportunities for spiritual fellowship, and to provide an 'organizational' base for the propagation of Buddhism in the United Kingdom. I also took note, before describing the structure of the Western Buddhist Order, of a difference of opinion on the subject of sangha or spiritual community. There were, I said, two extreme views. According to one view, the sangha consisted only of monks; the rest were not really Buddhists at all, their duty being merely to support the monks. Buddhism was in fact a purely monastic religion, and a 'Buddhist laity' a contradiction in terms. According to the other view, the sangha consisted of the entire population of a Buddhist country. Thieves, prostitutes, drunkards, and policemen – all were Buddhists. They were 'born Buddhists', and in my experience 'born Buddhists' knew nothing of Buddhism. These, then, were the two extreme views, one too narrow, the other too broad. So far as the Western Buddhist Order was concerned, it was proposed to follow a middle way between them, as would be evident from its very structure. Having described this structure, and having said a few words about the 'Friends' of the Western Buddhist Order, I concluded the lecture by saying that I had explained the idea of the Western Buddhist Order and of *upāsaka* ordination in some detail because of its extreme importance and because it was probably the biggest step yet taken by British Buddhism.

In the second of my two lectures of the day, on 'The Bodhisattva Vow', I dealt with the bodhisattva ideal, and particularly the bodhisattva vow itself, as exemplifying the way in which we rose above the pairs of opposites, and in this connection gave a straightforward exposition of the arising of the will to Enlightenment, the Sevenfold Puja, the four great vows, and the six *pāramitās*.[587] Thus my second lecture was less closely connected with the actual ordination ceremony than was my first. Towards the end of it I did, however, say a few words about the bodhisattva ordination, which was of course the third grade of ordination in the Western Buddhist Order. I also referred to the fact that I had myself taken the bodhisattva ordination from Dhardo Rimpoche, whom I described as perhaps embodying the bodhisattva ideal to a greater extent than any other person I had known. It was my hope, I concluded, that in the course of time a few people in Britain would be ready to take the bodhisattva ordination, in which case our Western Buddhist Order would be well under way. But whether they took the bodhisattva ordination or not, everybody present should try to imbibe the bodhisattva spirit and echo the bodhisattva vow in their own hearts.

So far as I remember, the main reason for my speaking on the bodhisattva vow that day, apart from the fact that the bodhisattva ordination formed part of the structure of the Western Buddhist Order, was that I wanted to emphasize the altruistic and other-regarding aspect of Buddhism and the Buddhist spiritual life. Though I had not yet explicitly identified the arising of the will to Enlightenment as the altruistic dimension of Going for Refuge, I was well aware that in the individualistic and self-regarding atmosphere of British Buddhism the act of Going for Refuge, and therewith the *upāsaka/upāsikā* ordination, was likely to be understood as possessing significance only for the person immediately concerned, and that it was therefore necessary to introduce a 'Mahāyāna' element into the proceedings. It was almost as if, having not as yet established a direct connection between the arising of the will to Enlightenment and Going for Refuge, I at least wanted the bodhisattva ideal to 'be around' and ready to enter into the situation as soon as conditions permitted.

The founding of the Western Buddhist Order was not only an important stage in the process whereby the significance and value of Going for Refuge became clear to me. It also marked the beginning of a new phase in that process. Though I had realized that Going for Refuge was the central act of the Buddhist life, and that it meant organizing one's existence round the Three Jewels, that realization had so far found expression only in my personal life and in my writings and lectures, and even then only to a very limited extent. But now the situation was entirely changed. The twelve people who made up the

Western Buddhist Order had 'taken' the Three Refuges and Ten Precepts from me, – had been ordained as *upāsakas* and *upāsikās* by me – and their understanding of the meaning of Going for Refuge coincided with mine, at least partly. Like one lamp lighting a dozen others, I had been able to share with them my realization of the absolute centrality of the act of Going for Refuge and henceforth that realization would find expression not in my life only but also in theirs. Not that the realization in question was something fixed and final. It could continue to grow and develop, and find expression in a hundred ways as yet unthought of. Unfortunately, some founder members of the Western Buddhist Order found it difficult to appreciate this fact, or even to sustain their original commitment, and before long either resigned from the Order or withdrew from active participation in its affairs. Their places were, however, soon filled and more than filled, and I had the satisfaction of lighting first scores, and then hundreds of lamps, and the still greater satisfaction of seeing them, together with those lamps that had burned undimmed from the beginning, grow brighter as my own lamp grew brighter. In other words I had the satisfaction of knowing that in founding the Western Buddhist Order I had founded a sangha or spiritual community that not only shared my realization that Going for Refuge was the central and definitive act of the Buddhist life but also shared, in the person of at least some of its members, my conviction that that realization itself was capable of continued growth and development.

With the founding of the Western Buddhist Order my own Going for Refuge thus became bound up with the Going for Refuge of a number of other people, so that from this time onwards my *History* will be covering ground with which many Order members are already familiar. In the sections that follow I shall, therefore, be more selective and more succinct.

17
THE WIDER CONTEXT

The act of Going for Refuge is an individual act, that is, it is an act of the individual. But it is not only an act of the individual. It is also an act that can be performed by a number of people and these people may have the same (individual) understanding of its meaning, the same (individual) realization of its significance, in which case they together form a sangha or spiritual community, as in the case of the Western Buddhist Order. Where there is a sangha or spiritual community, therefore, the individual's act of Going for Refuge is one of a number of such acts, all of which take place within a common framework – a framework of which the individual who goes for Refuge is himself a part. Thus although the act of Going for Refuge is an individual act it is, at the same time, an act that takes place within a wider context, that is, a context wider than the individual's own personal life. Indeed it is from that wider context that the act of Going for Refuge derives part of its significance or, as one might also say, it is because it takes place in this wider context that the act of Going for Refuge is able to reveal itself more fully. About the time that I founded the WBO and FWBO I started giving serious thought to the question of the nature of this wider context. Though my thinking was not very systematic, I soon realized that Going for Refuge in fact took place within a threefold context, or rather, within three quite different contexts, all of which were interconnected. These three contexts may be termed, very provisionally, the social or communal, the higher-evolutionary, and the cosmic.

The social or communal context of Going for Refuge is, of course, the sangha or spiritual community as I have already indicated. Between a spiritual community and what I term a group there is a world of difference. Whereas a group consists of 'group members', or those who are self-conscious (i.e. self-aware) only in a very rudimentary way, and whose attitudes and behaviour are determined entirely by those of the group, a spiritual community consists of (true) individuals, or those who are self-conscious, independent, sensitive, emotionally positive, responsible, and creative.[588] Unfortunately, the English language has no proper term for individuals of this sort and consequently no proper term for the kind of 'group' to which they 'belong', so that it is extremely difficult to explain the nature of the difference between a group and a spiritual community and extremely difficult, therefore, to explain the nature of the spiritual community itself. It is also extremely difficult to explain the nature of the consciousness or awareness that characterizes the spiritual community as such. This consciousness is not the sum total of the individual consciousnesses concerned, nor even a kind of collective consciousness, but a consciousness of an entirely different order for which we have no word in English but to which the Russian word *sobornost* perhaps gives a clue. At the stage of this *History* with which I am now concerned I started thinking of this 'third' order of consciousness in terms of the transcendental *bodhicitta* or will to Enlightenment. I saw the *bodhicitta* as arising within the sangha or spiritual community as a whole rather than as being an individual's personal possession, so to speak. Similarly, I saw the sangha or spiritual community as being the reflection of the ideal figure of the bodhisattva or 'personified' *bodhicitta*. By the time of my 1973 'sabbatical'[589] I had come to see our new Buddhist movement, particularly the Western Buddhist Order, as constituting a tiny reflection of the bodhisattva Avalokiteśvara, the Bodhisattva of Compassion, in his eleven-headed and thousand-armed form. Each member of the Order was, in fact, one of Avalokiteśvara's arms (or hands), for each Order member went for Refuge, and the *bodhicitta* – whose various beneficent activities those arms symbolized – was the altruistic dimension of Going for Refuge. Thus in the same way that each of Avalokiteśvara's arms formed part of his body, so the act of Going for Refuge took place within the wider context of the sangha or spiritual community, which was the bodhisattva's reflection – even, in a sense, his embodiment – or within the wider context of the 'third' order of consciousness. Strictly speaking, I should have thought of this 'third' order of consciousness not so much in terms of the transcendental *bodhicitta* as in terms of transcendental Going for Refuge, just as I should have thought of the sangha or spiritual community as being the reflection not so much of the 'personified' *bodhicitta* as of the 'personified' Going for Refuge; but since Buddhist tradition had not 'personified' Going for Refuge in an ideal figure, and surrounded that figure with myth and symbol, in the way that it had done with the *bodhicitta*, it was not really possible for me to do so – nor, in the last analysis, was it really necessary. Inasmuch as the *bodhicitta* was the altruistic dimension of Going for Refuge whatever was said of the *bodhicitta* could also be said – *mutatis mutandis* – of Going for Refuge.

The higher-evolutionary context of Going for Refuge, as I have termed it, is Buddhism conceived of as corresponding to – even as coinciding with – the upper reaches of the total evolutionary process. Towards the end of 1969 I gave a series of eight lectures entitled 'The Higher Evolution of Man'.[590] In these lectures, which were in part based on lectures given three years earlier, I divided the evolutionary process into two main sections, one of which I termed the Lower Evolution and the other the Higher Evolution. Man, in the sense of the self-conscious or self-aware human being, occupied a point midway between the two. The Lower Evolution represented what he had developed out of, the Higher Evolution what he could develop into. The Lower Evolution was the process of development from amoeba to man, and was covered by the sciences, especially biology; the Higher Evolution was the process of development from man to Buddha, and was covered by psychology, by the fine arts, and by religion. The Lower Evolution was collective, the Higher Evolution individual. Buddhism, as a universal religion, that is a religion that addressed itself to the individual and affirmed individual rather than collective values, belonged to the Higher Evolution. In the fifth lecture in this series I indeed spoke of Buddhism as the path of the Higher Evolution, that is, I spoke of it as representing a continuation, on increasingly higher levels, of the evolutionary process itself. It was the evolutionary process become, in the person of the individual, self-conscious or self-aware. This was not the way in which we usually thought of Buddhism, but it was what Buddhism essentially was. In Buddhism there were many doctrines and disciplines, many moral rules and devotional observances, but they were all secondary. Even meditation was secondary. What was important, for Buddhism, was that man should grow and develop – that he should evolve. Buddhism was not a matter of thinking and knowing, or even of doing, but of being and becoming. In other words Buddhism was a matter of following the path of the Higher Evolution.[591]

As I was careful to point out, such a way of looking at Buddhism was fully in accordance with the Buddha's own teaching, and in this connection I referred to the Mahāprajāpatī incident (the Dharma was 'whatever conduced to one's spiritual growth and development'),[592] as well as to the simile of the lotus flowers in various stages of unfoldment and to the Parable of the Herbs and Plants, otherwise known as the Parable of the Rain Cloud.[593] With so much emphasis on growth and development it was not surprising that the image of the path should have been at the very centre of the Buddha's teaching, or that Buddhism itself should have been a path – the path to Enlightenment or Nirvāṇa. There were many different formulations of this path, but the one that brought out most clearly the fact that Buddhism was essentially a path, and that this path was the path of the Higher Evolution, was that of the twelve positive *nidānas*, and it was with this particular formulation of the path that I wanted to deal on that occasion. The last third of the lecture therefore consisted of a detailed exposition of the twelve positive *nidānas* or links, from suffering/faith to freedom/knowledge of the destruction of the *āśravas*.[594]

The reason why this particular formulation is able to bring out so clearly the fact that Buddhism is essentially a path, and that this path is the path of the Higher Evolution, is that it consists of a progressive series of mental and spiritual states or experiences – a series wherein each state or experience arises in dependence on the one immediately preceding. Since the Higher Evolution consists in the development of progressively higher states of consciousness, just as the Lower Evolution consists in the development of progressively more complex material forms, it is obvious that there is a correspondence between the twelve positive *nidānas* and the process of the Higher Evolution. Indeed, it is obvious that in principle the twelve positive *nidānas* and the process of the Higher Evolution actually coincide, so that in causing the mental and spiritual states or experiences represented by the *nidānas* to arise within oneself – or rather, in causing oneself to become them – one is at the same time participating in the higher-evolutionary process. Now the first two positive *nidānas* are suffering (*dukkha*, Sanskrit *duḥkha*) and faith (*saddhā*, Sanskrit *śraddhā*), for in dependence on suffering there arises 'faith', and this faith – as I made clear in the lecture itself – is faith in the Three Jewels, as representing the highest values of existence. It is our *total* response to those values, and as such manifests as actual commitment to them, that is, manifests as Going for Refuge. Thus the act of Going for Refuge is identical with the arising of faith in dependence on suffering, the more especially since one goes for Refuge *from* those very things on account of the painful and unsatisfactory nature of which one goes in quest of higher values. This means that the act of Going for Refuge takes place within the series of mental and spiritual states or experiences represented by the twelve positive *nidānas* and, therefore, within the wider context of the higher-evolutionary process. Not that the act of Going for Refuge is limited to the second positive *nidāna*. The series of the twelve positive *nidānas* is not only a progressive but a cumulative series, so that the subsequent positive *nidānas* arise in proximate or remote dependence on faith in the Three Jewels and, therefore, on the act of Going for Refuge.

Just as the social or communal context of Going for Refuge is connected with the *bodhicitta*, and the higher-evolutionary context with the path, so what I have termed the cosmic context of Going for Refuge is connected with the bodhisattva ideal in the broadest sense. Originally, there was only one Bodhisattva, who was the Buddha himself during the pre-Enlightenment phase of his career, that phase being first understood as comprising the first thirty-five years of his life and then understood as comprising the whole series of his previous existences as recorded in the *Jātaka* or 'Birth' Stories. Later, after the bodhisattva ideal had come to be regarded as the ultimate spiritual ideal for all Buddhists, even for all human beings, the bodhisattvas multiplied and their unwearied activities were seen as extending through infinite time and infinite space, as we saw in section 13, when I spoke of *The Two Buddhist Books in Mahāyāna* and of 'The Vows of the Bodhisattva Samantabhadra'. Eventually, the figure of the bodhisattva was seen as transcending history altogether and he, she, they, or it became the 'personification(s)' of a cosmic principle. Some years later I termed this principle the bodhisattva principle, or principle of perpetual self-transcendence,[595] but at this stage of my *History* I more often spoke of it as the cosmic *bodhicitta* or cosmic will to Enlightenment, as I did in my 1969 lecture 'The Awakening of the Bodhi Heart'.[596] It is the reflection of this same cosmic *bodhicitta* that, appearing in the psyche-continuum of the individual, is the *bodhicitta* in the more usual sense of the term. Since this latter *bodhicitta* is the altruistic dimension of Going for Refuge, as I have more than once observed, the reflection of the cosmic *bodhicitta* also appears as the act of Going for Refuge (the two reflections are in fact one), so that the individual's act of Going for Refuge takes place within the cosmic *bodhicitta* and, therefore, within the wider context of the bodhisattva ideal in the broadest sense.

In speaking of the act of Going for Refuge as taking place within a wider context, whether that of the sangha or spiritual community, the path, or the bodhisattva ideal in the broadest sense, I do not mean to suggest that it takes place within it as a high dive might take place within the four walls of an indoor swimming pool. Between the act of Going for Refuge and the context within which it takes place there is an organic connection – a connection which I tried to express, at the beginning of this section, by speaking of the individual who goes for Refuge as being himself a part of the common framework within which he and others go for Refuge. Because there is this organic connection the act of Going for Refuge is able to reveal itself – that is, reveal its nature and significance – more fully. Because there is this organic connection the act of Going for Refuge is also able, as the reflection, in the individual, of the wider context within which that act takes place, to reveal something of the nature and significance of the wider context itself.

18

LEVELS OF GOING FOR REFUGE

In *A Survey of Buddhism* I drew attention to the fact that Going for Refuge is not an act to be done once and for all time, but that it is something which grows with one's understanding of Buddhism.[597] Thus not only does the act of Going for Refuge take place within a wider context; it also takes place on different levels, passage from one to another of which constitutes one's spiritual life as a Buddhist. According to tradition there are two levels of Going for Refuge, the mundane and the transcendental,[598] but in a talk on 'Levels of Going for Refuge' which I gave in 1978, at the Western Buddhist Order's tenth anniversary convention, I distinguished altogether six.[599] This talk was given on 3 April, which means that it was given almost exactly ten years ago, and my six levels of Going for Refuge were the cultural, the provisional, the effective, the real, the ultimate, and the cosmic.

Before describing these levels I reminisced for a few minutes about my own experience of 'formal' Going for Refuge, that is, my own experience of reciting the words of the Three Refuges and the Five (or Ten) precepts, prior to the founding of the Western Buddhist Order, and in this connection described six different incidents, some of which I have dealt with in the first half of this paper. These incidents, like many others I could have mentioned, showed that appreciation of the real significance of Going for Refuge was rather lacking in Buddhist circles in the East, and even in Buddhist circles in the West. The Refuges were simply something one recited, or something that showed one was a Buddhist, in the merely social sense. They were a sort of flag which was waved on special occasions. If one went to the temple on Wesak day – one recited the Refuges, as one also did when there was a wedding, or a name-giving ceremony, or a memorial service, or a public meeting. Not that there was anything wrong with reciting the Refuges, I hastened to add. The trouble was that people generally recited them without thinking about their meaning. In my experience it was only the Tibetans who had any appreciation of what Going for Refuge really meant or any realization of its tremendous – indeed its central – importance in and for the Buddhist life. Elsewhere in the Buddhist world people seemed to have forgotten its importance. True, they recited the Refuges often enough (and it was good that they recited them), but hardly ever did they actually *go for Refuge*. This was really surprising. The significance of Going for Refuge was clear enough from the Buddhist scriptures, especially from the Pāli scriptures. Time and again in those scriptures did one find the Buddha giving a teaching, and time and again did one find the recipient of that teaching responding to his words with exclamations of amazement and wonder and with the heartfelt declaration 'I go for Refuge to the Buddha, to his Dharma, and to his Sangha!'[600] This was no mere recitation of a formula. It was the response of one's total being to the Truth. One committed oneself to the Truth, surrendered to the Truth, wanted to devote one's whole life to the Truth, and this effect could be produced not only by the hearing of the Dharma but also by the sight of the Buddha or the sight of the Sangha – or even by the sight of a team of Order members and Mitras at work.

Thus the importance of Going for Refuge was clear from the Buddhist scriptures, even though the greater part of the Buddhist world might have forgotten it, and having shown this I turned to my six levels of Going for Refuge. Cultural Going for Refuge, which could also be called formal or ethnic Going for Refuge, was the Going for Refuge of those Eastern Buddhists who did not actually follow Buddhism as a spiritual teaching (though they might be positively influenced by it on the social level), and who made no effort to evolve spiritually, but who were nonetheless very proud of Buddhism as part of their cultural heritage and who definitely considered themselves (ethnic) Buddhists. Such people recited the Refuges as an affirmation of their cultural and national identity and even went so far as to claim that they were 'born Buddhists', though in truth one could no more be a born Buddhist than one could (according to the Buddha) be a born Brahmin. In our own Movement there was no cultural Going for Refuge because no one was a 'born Buddhist' but there was, perhaps, something like it when someone was attracted to the Movement as a 'positive group' and happily joined in everything we did, including chanting the Refuges. Provisional Going for Refuge went beyond cultural Going for Refuge but fell short of effective Going for Refuge. Here someone who was a 'born Buddhist', in the sense of having been born into Buddhist surroundings, started taking Buddhism seriously to some extent, even started practising it to some extent, but did not really commit himself (or herself) either to Buddhism or to his (or her) own spiritual development. He (or she) might, however, be aware of the possibility, even the desirability, of committing oneself, and might be thinking of doing so later on. In our own Movement this level of Going for Refuge was represented by the Mitra, who regarded himself (or herself) as 'belonging' to the FWBO, who meditated regularly, who helped out in various practical ways, and who might be thinking of ordination.

Effective Going for Refuge consisted of actually committing oneself to the Three Jewels. Since I was addressing a gathering of Order members there was no need for me to elaborate, as I indeed remarked at the time, for they all knew very well what effective Going for Refuge meant and that it corresponded to *upāsaka/upāsikā* ordination in the Western Buddhist Order. I therefore confined myself to saying a few words about the esoteric Refuges, that is, the *guru*, the *deva*, and the *ḍākinī* – particularly about the *ḍākinī*.[601] Before so doing, however, I pointed out that while effective Going for Refuge corresponded to *upāsaka/upāsikā* ordination in the Western Buddhist Order the traditional Buddhist socio-religious categories were, in fact, becoming less and less relevant to us. Perhaps it would be better if we spoke not in terms of *upāsaka/upāsikā* ordination but simply of 'ordination' or even of 'threefold commitment' (i.e. commitment with body, speech, and mind) – a speculation that no doubt foreshadowed the development with which I shall be dealing in section 20. Real Going for Refuge took place when one developed insight and wisdom and thus entered upon the transcendental path or, in other words, became a Stream Entrant. In traditional terms real Going for Refuge was transcendental Going for Refuge, all the previous Refuges – even effective Going for Refuge – being mundane, which was quite a sobering thought. Until one had entered the Stream one could fall back: could leave the spiritual community – resign from the Order. For this reason a positive, spiritually supportive environment was of the utmost importance – at least until such time as one entered the Stream. Ultimate Going for Refuge occurred when one attained Enlightenment. On this level one did not go to any outside Refuge but was one's own Refuge. In fact, on this level there was neither inside nor outside, neither self nor other.

Cosmic Going for Refuge was not exactly another level of Going for Refuge but referred to the evolutionary process, that is, referred to the Lower Evolution and the Higher Evolution. First came the amoeba, then the mollusc, then the fish, the reptile, the bird, and the mammal. Finally there came man – *homo sapiens*. Looking at this process, what one in fact saw was a Going for Refuge. Each form of life aspired to develop into a higher form or, so to speak, went for Refuge to that higher form. This might sound impossibly poetic, but it was what one in fact saw. In man the evolutionary process became conscious of itself; this was the Higher Evolution. When the Higher Evolution became conscious of itself (and it became conscious of itself in and through the spiritually committed individual) this was Going for Refuge in the sense of effective Going for Refuge. Through our Going for Refuge we are united, as it were, with all living beings, who in their own way, and on their own level, in a sense also went for Refuge. Thus Going for Refuge was not simply a particular devotional practice or even a threefold act of individual commitment, but the key to the mystery of existence.

Three or four years later I gave another talk on 'Going for Refuge'.[602] The talk was given in Bombay, to a mixed audience of Theosophists and ex-Untouchable Buddhists, and in it I approached the subject via my experience of our new Buddhist movement in the West, involvement with which culminated in 'joining the Order' or, in more traditional terms, Going for Refuge to the Buddha, the Dharma, and the Sangha. In the course of this talk I distinguished only four levels of Going for Refuge, the provisional, the effective, the real, and the absolute (= the ultimate), ethnic Going for Refuge being subsumed under provisional Going for Refuge and cosmic Going for Refuge being omitted. Real Going for Refuge was, however, correlated with the opening of the Dharma Eye, or Eye of Truth, the third of the five eyes of Buddhist tradition, and this in turn with (transcendental) Going for Refuge and with Stream Entry. Indeed, having discussed the three fetters (i.e. self-view, doubt, and dependence on moral rules and religious observances), the breaking of which was equivalent to Stream Entry, and distinguished between commitment and lifestyle, I raised the question of the nature of the relation between the arising of the *bodhicitta*, Going for Refuge, the opening of the Dharma Eye, Stream Entry, and Going Forth, and explained it as follows:

> The *bodhicitta*, or the arising of the *bodhicitta*, represents, we may say, the more altruistic dimension of these four other experiences. Or rather, all five of them, including the *bodhicitta* itself, represent the five different aspects of a single basic, crucial, and unique spiritual experience. The Going for Refuge draws attention to the emotional and volitional aspect of this experience, the opening of the Dharma Eye to the unconditioned depth of its cognitive content, Stream Entry to the permanent and far-reaching nature of its effects, while Going Forth into homelessness draws attention to the extent of the reorganization which, regardless of whether or not one becomes a monk in the formal sense, the experience inevitably brings about in the pattern of one's daily life. As for the *bodhicitta* it represents, as I have said, the other-regarding aspect of the experience.[603]

19
GOING FOR REFUGE OLD AND NEW

In December 1973 I held the first of what was to be a long series of FWBO study retreats, as they came to be called. On these retreats I would take a group of Order members and others through a Buddhist text, discussing it line by line and word by word and trying to relate it to our own understanding and practice of the Dharma. Most of the texts we studied were classics of Buddhist literature, canonical and non-canonical, but a few were modern works. Among the latter were Nyanaponika Thera's essay *The Threefold Refuge*, a study retreat on which I held at Padmaloka in the autumn of 1978.[604] Nyanaponika Thera was a Theravādin monk of German extraction who had resided in Kandy since 1952 and who had been largely responsible for founding and running the Buddhist Publication Society. His essay dated from 1948. In it he not only explored the meaning of Going for Refuge from the standpoint of a liberal Theravādin but also tried, as it seemed, to find a way of reviving the practice of Going for Refuge as an act of individual commitment to the Three Jewels, and it was mainly for this reason that I decided to hold a study retreat on this work.[605]

The Threefold Refuge was divided into two parts. Part 1 consisted of an abridged translation of Buddhaghosa's exposition of a passage in the *Majjhima Nikāya* dealing with the Refuges, part 2 of Nyanaponika's own thoughts and comments. The latter fell into two sections. In the first section Nyanaponika made some general comments on the subject of Going for Refuge, while in the second he commented on

Buddhaghosa's exposition of the *sutta* passage. Instead of going through the work in regular order, which would have meant plunging straight into Buddhaghosa's rather scholastic exposition, we studied first Nyanaponika's general comments on Going for Refuge, then Buddhaghosa's exposition, and finally Nyanaponika's comments on that exposition, which in any case seemed a more logical way of proceeding. In the course of our study a number of topics arose and were discussed. While these did not always relate directly to the subject of Going for Refuge, they invariably had a definite bearing on one or another aspect of the spiritual life. Among the topics discussed were the difference between passivity and receptivity, the beauty of 'the spiritual', emotional self-indulgence, love and power, authority, (irrational) guilt, immanence, 'making merit', magic and technology, and the difficulty of reforming a religion that has become corrupt.

For the most part, however, our discussion revolved around Nyanaponika's exploration of the meaning of Going for Refuge, both in his own terms and as expounded by Buddhaghosa. With some of his thoughts and comments we found ourselves very much in agreement, as we certainly were when he pointed out that Going for Refuge was, or should be,

> a conscious act, and not the mere profession of a theoretical belief, still less the habitual rite of traditional piety.[606]

Indeed, there were times when the scholarly German monk seemed to be giving expression to our innermost convictions and, what was more, giving expression to them not only with precision but with eloquence. Nonetheless, the more we went through *The Threefold Refuge* the more we became aware that, despite the author's evident sincerity, there was something seriously wrong with his whole approach to Going for Refuge. Though he defined Going for Refuge briefly as 'a conscious act of determination, understanding and devotion' adding that those aspects of taking Refuge '[had] their counterparts in the volitional, rational and emotional sides of the human mind' and that 'for a harmonious development of character the cultivation of all three [was] required',[607] the fact was that in the last analysis Nyanaponika's approach to Going for Refuge tended to be one-sidedly intellectual. He was more aware that devotion needed the support of understanding than aware that understanding needed the support of devotion, and more concerned to emphasize the difference between devotion and blind faith than the difference between understanding and merely theoretical appreciation. Faith might be explained in terms of reason, but understanding could not, it seemed, be explained in terms of emotion. As I observed in the course of our discussion, Nyanaponika's onesidedness (and his apparent fear of emotion) may have been due to the fact that, living and working as he did in Buddhist Ceylon, surrounded by devout lay Buddhists who were accustomed to recite the Refuges and Precepts without thinking about their meaning, he felt it important to emphasize the aspect of understanding. Alternatively, he may have thought of his paper as being addressed to Westerners, or at least to the Western-educated, and therefore assumed that for such people an intellectual approach to Going for Refuge was the most appropriate. Whatever the reason for his onesidedness may have been, Nyanaponika's tendency to play down the importance of emotion was characteristic of his whole attitude towards Buddhism and the spiritual life, at least so far as that attitude could be inferred from his paper. He made no mention of spiritual friendship, and in fact appeared to see the spiritual life exclusively in terms of a progressive disillusionment with the imperfections of conditioned existence instead of seeing it, equally, in terms of an increasing attraction to and fascination with the beauty of the Unconditioned.

Perhaps the most interesting part of Nyanaponika's paper was that in which he dealt with the four kinds of mundane Going for Refuge described in the expository passage translated in part 1. These four modes of Refuge, as he also called them, were the surrender of self, the acceptance of the guiding ideal, the acceptance of discipleship, and homage by prostration, and Buddhaghosa explained the last three of these by reference to scriptural passages in which a particular disciple, having heard the Dharma from the Buddha, went for Refuge using a formula other than the customary *Buddhaṃ saraṇaṃ gacchāmi* etc.[608] In Nyanaponika's view the scriptural passages in which reference was made were not very enlightening, and indeed the connection between these passages and the modes of Refuge which they supposedly illustrated was not always clear. The first kind of mundane Going for Refuge, the surrender of self, Buddhaghosa did not explain by reference to any scriptural passage, though he gave the Refuge-going formula, with which it was traditionally associated. Thus there were not only four kinds of mundane Going for Refuge but also four alternative Refuge-going formulas, which served to emphasize the fact that it is Going for Refuge that matters rather than the particular form of words in which that act finds expression. According to Nyanaponika the four modes of Refuge were given in *descending* order (though he was not completely sure of this),

> beginning from the highest form, the complete self-surrender, and ending with the lowest, the Homage by Prostration,[609]

so that it was possible for him to correlate the three lowest modes with the three aspects of Going for Refuge, that is, the emotional, the rational, and the volitional. Homage by prostration represented the emotional side of taking Refuge, acceptance of discipleship the rational, and acceptance of the Three Jewels as one's guiding ideal the volitional. Once again emotion was devalued in relation to reason. As for surrender to self, it represented the highest form of Going for Refuge, and Nyanaponika cited from Buddhaghosa's *Visuddhimagga* or 'Path of Purity' a passage that seemed to indicate that in what he called 'the early days of the Dhamma' it was customary to go for Refuge in this way, employing the appropriate formula, before asking the *guru* for a subject of meditation.

This appears to have led Nyanaponika to wonder whether it might not be possible for the formula of self-surrender to be used by those who, like the meditators of old, wanted to take Buddhism more seriously than did the majority of their co-religionists. Indeed, his conception of surrender of self seemed to correspond to Going for Refuge as understood in the Western Buddhist Order – that is, to our *upāsaka/upāsikā* ordination. In other words, it corresponded to what I called effective Going for Refuge as distinct from cultural or ethnic Going for Refuge; for, as he was at pains to point out, though taking Refuge by way of self-surrender was still far from the complete abolishing of egotism and self-delusion it was a powerful means to that end and

> [might] mark the transition from the worldly or mundane Refuge to which it still belong[ed], to the Supermundane Refuge at which it aim[ed].[610]

However, the correspondence between Nyanaponika's conception of surrender of self and Going for Refuge, in the sense of *upāsaka/upāsikā* ordination, as understood in the Western Buddhist Order, was by no means perfect. In the case of the Western Buddhist Order one not only went for Refuge as an individual but also found that one was, by virtue of one's Going for Refuge, one of a number of people who had also gone for Refuge: one found that one was a 'member' of a sangha or spiritual community, with all that that implied in the way of spiritual friendship and co-operation. In Nyanaponika's conception of Buddhism and the spiritual life there was, seemingly, no place for spiritual community, so that for him Going for Refuge by way of self-surrender was an essentially individual affair and 'the greatest of all vows', as he called the formula of self-surrender, was to be taken 'in the secrecy of one's heart', the presence of any witness to the taking of the vow being dismissed as 'publicity'. Thus although Nyanaponika saw that Going for Refuge had become 'the mere profession of a theoretical belief' and 'the habitual rite of traditional piety', and though he saw in surrender of self the possibility of making Going for Refuge 'a conscious act', the fact that he was a Theravādin and living in Ceylon meant that he was not really able to do very much towards replacing the 'old' (cultural and ethnic) Going for Refuge by a 'new' (more conscious and individual) Going for Refuge.

20
UPĀSAKA INTO *DHARMACĀRĪ*

As I had explained on the day the Western Buddhist Order was founded, *upāsaka/upāsikā* ordination consisted in taking the Three Refuges and Ten precepts, and the *upāsaka/upāsikā* was expected to be a vegetarian, to practise right livelihood, and to lead a simple life. In addition, he or she was expected to meditate daily, to attend classes and go on retreat, and to give practical help to our new Buddhist movement. This was far, far more than was expected of an *upāsaka* or 'lay Buddhist' in most parts of the Buddhist world, as I well knew, but as the years went by, and as Order members increasingly organized their lives round the Three Jewels, the difference between them and the *upāsaka* of the East grew more and more pronounced. So long as the Order was confined to Britain this did not really matter, though the occasional visiting *bhikkhu* might express his astonishment that 'mere *upāsakas*' should be so devoted to the Dharma and wonder why they were not all in yellow robes. When our new Buddhist movement spread to India, however, and when *upāsaka/upāsikā* ordinations started being given on Indian soil, the difference between an ordinary 'lay Buddhist' and a member of the Western Buddhist Order – or Trailokya Bauddha Mahasangha, as it was known in India – became more striking than ever. Indeed, the fact that ordinary 'lay Buddhists' and members of the Trailokya Bauddha Mahasangha were called *upāsakas* tended to confuse people and, therefore, to make our work more difficult, so that it soon became obvious that we would have to consider a change of nomenclature.

The Western Buddhist Order was established in India in February and June 1979, in the course of my first two visits to the subcontinent since the founding of our new Buddhist movement in Britain. By the time of my third visit, which took place during the winter of 1981–2 and lasted four months, the Order there had grown in strength and maturity and already the ex-Untouchable Buddhists of central and western India were beginning to look to it for guidance. Indeed the Indian members of the Trailokya Bauddha Mahasangha were themselves ex-Untouchables, several of them being old friends and disciples of mine with whom Lokamitra had made contact on his arrival on the scene in 1977.[611] Since my final departure from India in 1967 the followers of Dr Ambedkar had had few opportunities of hearing the Dharma, and though much of the fervour with which they had originally embraced Buddhism remained the vast majority of them were, unfortunately, Buddhists only in a very nominal sense. Thus their Going for Refuge was, at best, a cultural or ethnic Going for Refuge, so that the difference between them and the *upāsakas* and *upāsikās* of the Western Buddhist Order/ Trailokya Bauddha Mahasangha who were by this time working among them was truly enormous. At an Order meeting held in New Bombay in March 1982, and attended by twenty-one Order members (including six of non-Indian origin) I therefore proposed that the terms *upāsaka* and *upāsikā* should be dropped and that in future members of the Order should be known as *dharmacārīs* and *dharmacāriṇīs*. Such a change of nomenclature would have several advantages. Besides distinguishing Order members from ordinary 'lay Buddhists', it would serve to underline the difference between cultural or ethnic Going for Refuge and effective Going for Refuge. It would also make it easier for Order members to deal with *bhikṣus*, some of whom were inclined to adopt an arrogant and overbearing attitude towards 'mere *upāsakas*', even when they themselves were making no effort to practise the Dharma. After a short discussion the meeting accepted my proposal,[612] and in the course of the next few months Order members elsewhere in the world followed suit. Thus took place the transformation of *upāsaka* into *dharmacārī* and *upāsikā* into *dharmacāriṇī*.

Whether in its masculine or feminine form, the term by which members of the Western Buddhist Order were henceforth known was not in general use among Buddhists, and it was partly for this reason that we had selected it. At the same time, it was a thoroughly traditional term, being found in several places in the scriptures, notably in two successive verses of the *Dhammapada*, in each of which the Buddha declares

> The *dhammacāri* lives happily, (both) in this world and in the world beyond.[613]

Literally, *dharmacārī* (Sanskrit) or *dhammacārī* (Pāli) meant 'Dharma-farer' or 'practitioner of the Dharma' (from Dharma *car*, 'one who walks or lives') and was therefore an exact description of what a member of the Order was or tried to be. It was also analogous in form to such terms as *brahmacārī*, *bhadracārī*, and *khecārī*,[614] just as *dharmacarya* or 'Dharma-faring' was analogous to *bodhicarya*.[615] Moreover, by a fortunate coincidence the second of the two *Dhammapada* verses in which the term *dharmacārī* occurred was one of the three verses from the *Dhammapada* included in the 'Last Vandanā', as it was called, a set of Pāli verses which the ex-Untouchable Buddhists were in the habit of singing to a solemn and deeply moving melody at the conclusion of meetings and which we ourselves had already adopted, both in India and elsewhere.[616]

But though *upāsakas* were now known as *dharmacārīs* and *upāsikās* as *dharmacāriṇīs* this was not just a change of nomenclature. It was very much more than that. During the fourteen or more years that had elapsed since the founding of the Western Buddhist Order many changes had taken place. Not only had Order members increasingly organized their lives round the Three Jewels so that they less and less resembled the *upāsakas* or 'lay Buddhists' of the East; they had, also, organized their lives round the Three Jewels in such a way that, in the majority of cases, it was not really possible to regard them as belonging to any of the seven different socio-religious classes of persons into which the Buddhist community was traditionally divided.[617] *Dharmacārīs* and *dharmacāriṇīs* were simply Buddhists. They were individuals who had gone for Refuge to the Buddha, Dharma, and Sangha and who, as a means of giving expression to that act in terms of their everyday lives, undertook to observe the ten precepts. Thus the ten precepts were not the *prātimokṣa* – to use the technical term – of any particular socio-religious class of persons but represented the ten great ethical principles which all seven classes of such persons had in common. They were what

I called the *mūla-prātimokṣa* or 'fundamental moral code' and as such constituted, together with Going for Refuge itself, the fundamental basis of unity among Buddhists.

Two years after the transformation of *upāsaka* into *dharmacārī* and *upāsikā* into *dharmacāriṇī* I sought to make this clear in section 6 of *The Ten Pillars of Buddhism*, the paper I read to you when we celebrated the Order's sixteenth anniversary. Towards the end of that section I said:

> For the Western Buddhist Order the ten precepts, as '*mūla-prātimokṣa*', are in fact the discipline that supports the 'individual liberation' not only of the monk and nun, but of all members of the Buddhist community irrespective of socio-religious status or, in contemporary idiom, irrespective of lifestyle.
>
> Since there is only one set of precepts, i.e. the ten precepts, so far as the Western Buddhist Order is concerned there is only one 'ordination', i.e. the *dharmacārī(iṇī)* ordination, which means that in the Western Buddhist Order one is not ordained as a monk, or as a nun, or as a female probationer, or as a male novice, or as a female novice, or as a male lay devotee, or as a female lay devotee, but simply and solely as a full, practising member of the sangha or Buddhist spiritual community, though it is of course open to one to observe, as personal vows, any of the rules traditionally observed by the monk, or the nun, and so on. Strictly speaking, these rules are not observed *in addition* to the ten precepts but as representing the more intensive practice of one or more of the precepts within a certain specific situation or for a certain purpose.
>
> Not being a *bhikṣu*, a member of the Western Buddhist Order does not wear the stitched yellow garment of the *bhikṣu*, and not being an *upāsaka* he does not wear the white garments of the *upāsaka*. He wears the ordinary 'lay' dress of the society to which he belongs, though without the implication that because he is not a monk he must therefore be a layman in the traditional Buddhist sense.
>
> Thus from the reduction of the rules comprising the seven different *prātimokṣas* to the ten precepts or '*mūla-prātimokṣa*' there follows a reduction – or rather an elevation – of the various socio-religious groups within the Buddhist community to one great spiritual community or *Mahāsaṅgha*. Such a reduction represents

a return to, and a renewed emphasis upon, the basics of Buddhism. It can be regarded as innovative only by adopting a standpoint from which those basics are ignored or from which they cannot be seen for the accretions and excrescences by which they have become overlaid.[618]

21
AMBEDKAR AND GOING FOR REFUGE

From 1981 to 1986 I spent the autumn of each year in Tuscany, taking part in the annual men's pre-ordination retreat.[619] In the middle of the 1985 retreat, during the eight days devoted to the private ordinations, I found the thought of Dr Ambedkar constantly impressing itself on my mind in a very powerful fashion and refusing, as it were, to go away. What could be the reason for this, I wondered. Eventually I realized that those were the very days when the ex-Untouchable Indian Buddhists would be commemorating the original mass conversion, which had taken place on 14 October 1956. This realization brought to a head a number of things about which I had been thinking for some time. In particular, I felt I really did want to write the booklet on Ambedkar and Buddhism to which I had been giving thought – on and off – for two or three years. I could now see how it should be done, and towards the end of the month actually wrote to Lokamitra giving details of the nine chapters into which it would be divided. Though I had hoped to start work on the booklet soon after my return to Padmaloka, in the event I was not able to do so before mid-February and it was not until early September that this latest product of my pen was ready for the press, having grown in the course of writing from a booklet into a small book.[620]

Ambedkar and Buddhism was published on 12 December 1986, six days after the thirtieth anniversary of Ambedkar's death, and launched at a public meeting in London at which tribute was paid to the memory of the great Untouchable leader. In the book I drew attention to the real significance of Ambedkar and the nature of his achievement, looked at the diabolical system from which he had sought to deliver the Untouchables, and traced the successive steps of the road by which he – and his followers – travelled from Hinduism to Buddhism. I also studied the way in which Ambedkar discovered his spiritual roots, explored his thoughts on the subject of the Buddha and the future of his religion, surveyed the historic occasion on which he and 380,000 Untouchables were spiritually reborn, studied his posthumously published *magnum opus*, and saw what happened after his death. In addition, I gave my personal recollections of Ambedkar. Though the subject of conversion to Buddhism cropped up in most chapters of the book, and though conversion to Buddhism meant Going for Refuge to the Three Jewels, only in one chapter did Going for Refuge feature at all prominently. This was, of course, chapter 7, 'The Great Mass Conversion', which in a way constituted the central chapter of the whole book. In this chapter I not only described the colourful and moving ceremony at which first Ambedkar and his wife and then his followers went for Refuge to the Buddha, Dharma, and Sangha but also attempted to explain the implications of certain aspects of that ceremony.

Ambedkar and his wife took the Three Refuges and Five precepts from U Chandramani, the oldest and seniormost monk in India, repeating the Pāli formulas after him thrice, in the usual manner. Having taken the Three Refuges and Five precepts from U Chandramani, however, Ambedkar proceeded to *administer them to his followers himself.* This constituted a definite break with tradition – or with what had come to be regarded as tradition. In Theravādin South-east Asia, at least, where pseudo-monastic triumphalism was rife, and where monks invariably took the lead on ceremonial occasions, it was unthinkable that a mere layman should presume to administer the Refuges and Precepts in the presence of his socio-religious superiors. Such a proceeding would have been considered as showing gross disrespect not only to those monks who were actually present but to the whole monastic order and would not have been tolerated for an instant. Ambedkar's action in administering the Refuges and Precepts to his followers himself, instead of allowing U Chandramani to administer them, therefore represented a bold and dramatic departure from existing Theravādin praxis and, indirectly, a return to something more in accordance with the spirit of the Buddha's teaching. Indeed, it represented even more than that; for, as I also explained:

> By [thus] demonstrating that an *upāsaka* no less than a *bhikṣu* could administer the Refuges and Precepts Ambedkar was reminding both the old Buddhists and the new that the difference between those who lived as *bhikṣus* and those who lived as *upāsakas* and *upāsikās* was only a difference, not a division, since all alike went for Refuge to the Buddha, the Dharma and the Sangha. Thus he was, in effect, asserting the fundamental unity of the whole Buddhist spiritual community, male and female, monastic and lay.[621]

That same unity was also asserted in Ambedkar's other break with tradition. Having converted his followers to Buddhism, he was determined to make sure that they would remain Buddhists and not revert to their old ways and be reabsorbed into Hinduism, as had happened once before in Indian history.[622] After repeating them himself, therefore, he also administered to his followers a series of twenty-two vows which he had drawn up specially for the occasion. These vows spelled out the implications of being a Buddhist – as distinct from a Hindu – in some detail. Indeed, in making the vows an integral part of the conversion ceremony Ambedkar made it clear that a lay Buddhist was a full member of the Buddhist spiritual community (thereby asserting the fundamental unity of that community), and that the lay Buddhist, no less than the monk, was expected actually to practise Buddhism. His followers could hardly be expected to practise Buddhism, however, unless they *felt* that they were full members of the Buddhist spiritual community – and, therefore, real Buddhists. This meant that they had to be formally received into that community, just as the monk was formally received into the monastic order, and undertake to live as lay followers of the Buddha with the same seriousness as the monk undertook to live as a monk follower. They had, in other words, to take the Refuges and Precepts *plus* the twenty-two vows.[623]

As I worked on my description of that historic ceremony, and tried to bring out the significance of some of the things Ambedkar had done, I became more than ever aware how much there was in common between his approach to Buddhism and mine. Though the saying itself may not have been current in his day, for him, too, commitment was primary, lifestyle secondary, as his contemptuous dismissal of pseudo-monasticism in 'The Buddha and the Future of His Religion' abundantly testified.[624] His assertion, in effect, of the fundamental unity of the Buddhist spiritual community, corresponded to my own insistence on the central importance of Going for Refuge, for did not that unity consist in the fact that *all* members of the Buddhist spiritual community went for Refuge to the Buddha, Dharma, and Sangha, and had not Ambedkar shown that in respect of giving, no less than in respect of taking, those Refuges, monks and laymen were on an equal footing? Moreover, in the course of a press conference held on the eve of his conversion Ambedkar made it clear, in response to a question as to which form of Buddhism he would be adopting when he embraced Buddhism, that his Buddhism

> would adhere to the tenets of the faith as taught by the Buddha himself, without involving his people in differences which had arisen on account of Hīnayāna and Mahāyāna.[625]

This corresponded to my own 'ecumenical' attitude, as well as to the fact that in the Western Buddhist Order or Trailokya Bauddha Mahasangha we consider ourselves to be simply Buddhists, in the sense of individuals who have gone – and continue to go – for Refuge to the Three Jewels, and who look for guidance and inspiration to the scriptures and teachings of all the different schools of Buddhism. Thus it was not surprising that on the completion of my chapter on 'The Great Mass Conversion', and indeed on the completion of *Ambedkar and Buddhism* itself, I should have been more than ever convinced that my approach to Buddhism was in line with that of the great Untouchable leader and that the new Buddhist movement with which so many of Ambedkar's followers were now in contact was a direct continuation of his own work for the Dharma.

22
CONCLUSION

Such, then, is the history of my Going for Refuge. These are the various stages by which the meaning and significance of Going for Refuge became clear to me, as well as those by which, since the founding of the Western Buddhist Order, that meaning and significance has become still more clear, both to me and to others. As I warned you at the very beginning would be the case, in tracing the history of my Going for Refuge I have been tracing the history of a process of discovery which followed, and perhaps continues to follow, a rather erratic course. Indeed, I confessed that my progression here had resembled that of the butterfly, which flutters zigzag fashion from flower to flower, and symbolizes the psyche or soul, rather than that of the hawk, which hurls itself straight on its prey, and symbolizes the logical mind. For this reason some of you may have found this *History* of mine confusing and difficult to follow. You may even have found it, at times, lacking in continuity, the more especially as the scene changes from England to India, and from India back to England, and I come into contact with Burmese monks and Tibetan incarnate lamas, involve myself with the ex-Untouchables, write books and poems, deliver lectures, hold seminars and, of course, found the Western Buddhist Order. Nonetheless, if we cast a backward glance over the developments I have described – if we cast a backward glance over a backward glance – I think we shall be able to perceive a definite thread of continuity running through them all.

My Going for Refuge began with an experience of the truth taught by the Buddha in the *Diamond Sūtra* and, to a lesser degree, by the Sixth Patriarch in the *Sūtra of Wei Lang* (*Huineng*). As a result of that experience I realized that I was a Buddhist, and always had been one, and two years later signalized the fact by formally taking the Three Refuges and Five Precepts from a Burmese monk in London. Being a Buddhist I wanted to live and work as a Buddhist. This was hardly possible in the army, into which I had by this time been conscripted, and with which I eventually travelled to the East; nor was it possible in any of the various Indian religious organizations and groups with which I became associated after leaving the army. Disillusioned with both them and worldly life, I therefore resolved to follow the personal example of the Buddha and renounce the household life for the life of homelessness. After 'Going Forth' in this way I spent two years as a freelance Buddhist ascetic, mainly in South India. The experience served to deepen my understanding of the Dharma and strengthened me in my conviction that I was a Buddhist, and I therefore decided that the time had come for me to regularize my position by taking formal ordination as a Buddhist monk. Returning to north-east India, I was ordained first as a *śramaṇera* or novice and then, a year and a half later, as a *bhikṣu* or full monk. By this time I had settled in Kalimpong, in the eastern Himalayas, but whether in Kalimpong or anywhere else being a monk had both its advantages and its disadvantages. On the one hand it meant that I was able to feel fully, and as it were officially, committed to the spiritual life. On the other, it meant that I was in danger of thinking that I was fully committed to the spiritual life just because I was a monk. I was in danger of confusing commitment with lifestyle, as I indeed did do for a while, at least to some extent. Moreover, I soon discovered that in becoming a monk I had become not a 'member' of a spiritual community but only a member of a particular socio-religious group, or a subdivision of such a group, so that an important element – that of *kalyāṇa mitratā* or spiritual friendship – was almost entirely lacking from my life. Nonetheless, the feeling of Going for Refuge was there underneath the ashes and blazed up whenever the 'eight worldly winds' happened to blow upon me more strongly than was their wont. Indeed, it blazed more brightly and more continuously with every year that passed. This was due not so much to the 'eight worldly winds' as to my increasingly close contact with Tibetan Buddhism, especially as represented by certain incarnate lamas and by the Nyingmapa version of the Going for Refuge and Prostration practice. As a result of that contact I came to have a better appreciation of the meaning and significance of Going for Refuge, that is to say, a better appreciation of the fact that Going for Refuge was not just a formality, nor even the means to the arising of the *bodhicitta*, but the central and definitive act of the Buddhist life, an act of which the *bodhicitta* was the altruistic dimension. At the same time, as a result of my contact with the newly converted ex-Untouchable Buddhists, and my taking bodhisattva ordination, I came closer to seeing that monasticism and spiritual life were not identical. Thus by the time I returned to England in 1964 I had realized that it was Going for Refuge that made one a Buddhist, that Going for Refuge was in fact 'the central act of the Buddhist life, from which all other [Buddhist] acts derive[d] their significance', that it meant organizing one's life round the Three Jewels, and that it constituted the fundamental basis of unity among Buddhists.

In England it did not take me long to discover that, although conditions there were favourable to the spread of the Dharma, a new Buddhist movement was badly needed. A movement was needed that would have as its heart and centre not a society but a spiritual community and which would be free from the infection of Theravādin pseudo-monastic triumphalism. On 7 April 1968 I therefore founded the Western Buddhist Order by conferring the *upāsaka/upāsikā* ordination, as it was then called, on nine men and three women; or rather, the Western Buddhist Order came into existence when nine men and three women committed themselves to the path of the Buddha by publicly 'taking' the Three Refuges and Ten Precepts from me in the traditional manner. The fact that they took the Refuges and Precepts from me, or were ordained by me, meant that their understanding of the meaning of Going for Refuge coincided with mine, at least to some extent. It meant, in other words, that I had in some degree succeeded in *sharing* my understanding of the meaning of Going for Refuge with them, and in the course of the years that followed I succeeded in sharing that understanding, directly and indirectly, with more and more people, so that not counting the three who have, unfortunately, died, and the twenty or so who have fallen away, there are at present in the world 337 members of the Western Buddhist Order or Trailokya Bauddha Mahasangha.

The language of conferring and taking, and even of sharing, should not be construed too literally. It should certainly not be construed in such a way as to suggest that in sharing my understanding of the meaning of Going for Refuge with the twelve original members of the Order I was sharing with them a certain fixed quantity of understanding, so to speak, which thereafter remained unchanged. After the founding of the Western Buddhist Order the meaning and significance of Going for Refuge became clearer to me than ever, and I started to perceive some of the deeper and more 'philosophical' implications of that central and definitive act of the Buddhist life. In particular, I saw that Going for Refuge took place within a context far wider than that of the individual's own personal existence, as well as on a number of different levels. I also saw the full extent of the difference between the 'old' (cultural and ethnic) Going for Refuge, as represented by the vast majority of south-east Asian Buddhists, and the 'new' (more conscious and individual) Going for Refuge, as represented by members of the Western Buddhist Order. Eventually, when the Order had been in existence for some fifteen or sixteen years, I saw that the majority of its members had organized their lives round the Three Jewels to such an extent that there was now little or no resemblance between them and the *upāsakas* or 'lay Buddhists' of the East. Indeed, it had become impossible to regard them as belonging to any of the traditional socio-religious categories. They were neither monks nor laymen, neither male or female novices nor male or female lay devotees. They were simply Buddhists, or individuals who had gone for Refuge to the Buddha, Dharma, and Sangha and who, as a means of giving expression to that act in their everyday lives, undertook to observe the ten precepts, that is, undertook to observe the ten great ethical principles that in fact constituted the *mūla-prātimokṣa* or 'fundamental moral code' of monks and laymen alike. For such 'mere Buddhists' – who were mere Buddhists in much the same way that the followers of the Yogācāra school were Cittamātrins or 'mere Consciousness-ists' – a new name was clearly needed, preferably one drawn from traditional sources. First in India and then in the West, therefore, it was decided that in future *upāsakas* should be known as *dharmacārīs* and *upāsikās* as *dharmacāriṇīs* – 'Dharma-farers' or 'practitioners of the Dharma'. That the change of nomenclature should originally have been adopted in India was perhaps not surprising for, as the writing of *Ambedkar and Buddhism* more than ever convinced me, our new Buddhist movement was a continuation of Ambedkar's own work for the Dharma, the great Untouchable leader having, in effect, asserted the fundamental unity of the Buddhist spiritual community no less uncompromisingly than I had insisted on the central importance of Going for Refuge.

This brings me down very nearly to the present day. It brings me down very nearly to the twentieth anniversary of the Western Buddhist Order, which we have gathered in (relatively) large numbers to celebrate. Now that I have traced the history of my Going for Refuge, however, where does this leave me? Where does it leave you? Where does it leave *us*? Quite simply, it leaves us, in a sense, exactly where we were twenty years ago, or whenever it was that we first committed ourselves to the path of the Buddha. It leaves us Going for Refuge. We do not, it is to be hoped, go for Refuge in quite the same way as we did then, or even as we did last year, or last month, or even last week. With every day that passes, in fact, our experience of Going for Refuge should gain in depth and intensity – should take place within a wider context, and on a higher level. With every day that passes we should have a more decisive realization of the fact that we are, each one of us, an arm, or a hand, of that Avalokiteśvara who is the embodiment of the cosmic will to Enlightenment and, therefore, the embodiment of the cosmic Going for Refuge.

At the beginning of this paper I said that, having traced the history of my Going for Refuge, it would also be appropriate for me to share with you some of my current thinking as regards my own relation to the Order and the relation of the Order itself to the rest of the Buddhist world. The tracing of that history has, however, taken me much longer than I expected and I shall, obviously, have to postpone my remarks on those subjects to some future occasion. The nature of my relation to the Order has, in any case, transpired to some extent in the latter part of the narrative. As regards the relation of the Order to the rest of the Buddhist world let me simply observe that it is a relation that subsists, essentially, with individuals, and that, on this the occasion of our twentieth anniversary, we are happy to extend the hand of spiritual fellowship to all those Buddhists for whom commitment is primary, lifestyle secondary and who, like us, go for Refuge to the Buddha, the Dharma, and the Sangha, repeating, whether in Pāli or any other language:

Buddhaṃ saraṇaṃ gacchāmi
Dhammaṃ saraṇaṃ gacchāmi
Saṅghaṃ saraṇaṃ gacchāmi

To the Buddha for Refuge I go
To the Dharma for Refuge I go
To the Sangha for Refuge I go.

now, and so long as life shall last
now, until the attainment of Enlightenment.

My Relation to the Order

INTRODUCTORY NOTE

Sangharakshita had planned to speak on the theme *My Relation to the Order* as part of *The History of My Going for Refuge* but the latter grew to such large proportions that the topic of his relation to the Order had to wait for two years before it was addressed. It was finally delivered as a paper to Order members on 8 April 1990 at Manchester Town Hall, the magnificent setting for that year's celebrations of the founding of the Western Buddhist Order and the Friends of the Western Buddhist Order, organized by the Manchester Buddhist Centre. *My Relation to the Order* was published the same year as a booklet by Windhorse Publications.

Sangharakshita writes about My Relation to the Order *in his 'Letter from Spain' in* Through Buddhist Eyes, *Windhorse Publications, Birmingham 2000, pp. 156–7 (*Complete Works, *vol. 24).*

Two years ago we celebrated the twentieth anniversary of the Western Buddhist Order, which was born in London on Sunday 7 April 1968. Marking as it did the completion of the first two decades of the Order's existence the occasion was an important one in many ways, and one that naturally gave rise to certain reflections on my part. Some of these reflections I communicated to you in a paper entitled 'The History of My Going for Refuge', in which I cast a backward glance over the various stages whereby the significance of that 'central and definitive act of the Buddhist life', as I called it, the *śaraṇa-gamana* or Going for Refuge, had become clear to me. On such an occasion as the present one, I declared in the opening section of the paper, when we had assembled in (relatively) large numbers to celebrate the twentieth anniversary of the spiritual community that formed the heart of our new Buddhist movement, it was no doubt appropriate that I should endeavour to trace the history of my Going for Refuge and that, having done this, I should share with you some of my current thinking as regards my own relation to the Order and the relation of the Order itself to the rest of the Buddhist world. As it happened, the tracing of that history of mine took much longer than I had expected, and in the concluding section of the paper I commented that I would obviously have to postpone my remarks on my own relation to the Order and on the relation of the Order itself to the rest of the Buddhist world to some future occasion. The nature of my relation to the Order had in any case transpired to some extent from the latter part of my narrative, while as regards the relation of the Order to the rest of the Buddhist world I would simply observe that it was a relation that subsisted, essentially, with individuals, and that, on this the occasion of our twentieth anniversary, we were happy to extend the hand of spiritual fellowship to all those Buddhists for whom commitment was primary, lifestyle secondary, and who, like ourselves, went for Refuge to the Buddha, the Dharma and the Sangha. These words were sufficient to indicate the tenor of my thinking, but they were by no means enough, and the time has now come for me to redeem my pledge of two years ago and deal more fully with the two topics that could not be dealt with properly then, viz. my own relation to the Order and the relation of the Order itself to the rest of the Buddhist world. I shall not be dealing with them at quite the same length as I dealt with the history of my Going for Refuge.

Before dealing with the twin topics of today's paper, however, I must take notice of the fact that in the two years that have elapsed since I endeavoured to trace the history of my Going for Refuge there have been some important developments within the Order, as indeed there have been in the world at large. In the first place, the Order has grown numerically. Two years ago there were 336 of us. Today there are 384: sixty men and women having been ordained during the last two years, two Order members having died, two others having resigned, and ten having had their names dropped from the Order register – in the case of the last a less happy development about which I shall have something to say later on. There has also been the increasing tendency for chapter meetings to take the form of 'spiritual workshops' (a not very expressive nomenclature for which I was, I believe, myself responsible), that is to say, for them to take the form of opportunities for the deepening of our spiritual life, and in particular of our Going for Refuge, by means of free and open communication and interaction of one kind or other.[626]

The most important development during the last two years, however, has been my handing over responsibility for conferring the *dharmacārī* ordination to Subhuti and Suvajra who, in the course of last year's Guhyaloka ordination retreat, between them ordained seven men as *dharmacārīs*.[627] Though a number of ordinations had been conferred in previous years by senior Order members acting on my behalf, so to speak, this was the first time anyone other than myself had received people into the Order entirely on their own responsibility, or without reference to me.[628] The occasion was thus one of the utmost significance for the future of the Order, and for me personally a source of the deepest satisfaction. It was moreover wholly appropriate that this particular development should have taken place in the very year that the Order attained its 'collective' majority.

But we must be on our guard against a possible misunderstanding. I have spoken of my *handing over* the responsibility for conferring ordination simply because that expression had somehow gained currency among us, but what has actually occurred is not so much a handing over as a *handing on*. In other words I have not handed over the responsibility for conferring ordination if one takes 'handing over' to mean that the responsibility in question, having been handed over, now no longer appertains to me but appertains instead to the two senior Order members previously denominated. Handing over does not mean *relinquishment*. Thus what has really taken place is not a handing over, or even a handing on, but rather a *sharing* of the responsibility for receiving people into the Order. In this connection there comes to mind the image of one lamp being lit from another, the first lamp 'transmitting' light to the other without thereby losing its own light. – I mention the matter not only to guard against possible misunderstanding – for the Māra of literalism is always lying in wait for us – but also because Mitras sometimes ask me whether I may still on occasion confer ordination myself. This question I always answer in the affirmative. Even though light – the light of ordination – is now being transmitted by new, brightly polished lamps with ardent flames, the old lamp burns on and is still capable, I trust, of lighting at least a few more lamps before the oil finally gives out.

Since this imagery of lamp and light seems to have caught my fancy let me extend it a little. The more lamps there are, especially brightly polished ones, the more brilliant will be the light and the greater the extent to which it will propagate itself. Similarly, my sharing of the responsibility for conferring ordination is not just the most important development to have taken place within the Order during the last two years; it is also a development that has been responsible for, or associated with, a veritable Indra's Net of new developments within the Order and, through the Order, within the wider Movement of which the Order is the heart. To begin with, the fact that they now share with me the responsibility for conferring ordination has moved Subhuti and Suvajra, as well as the other members of the men's ordination team at Padmaloka (and, no doubt, the members of the more *ad hoc* women's ordination teams),[629] to a more radical reappraisal of their own Going for Refuge. As Subhuti reported-in for the October 1989 issue of *Shabda*:[630]

> [Conferring ordinations] for me represents a far deeper level of responsibility than I have ever taken before. In witnessing someone else's Going for Refuge my own is called into question both by myself and by others. The whole effect of ordination derives from the fact that the one who is ordained has confidence in the integrity of the one who is ordaining. The ordinee feels a tremendous boost in confidence that his or her own Going for Refuge is genuine because the ordainer, being someone in whose Going for Refuge the ordinee has confidence, accepts and acknowledges that he or she is genuinely Going for Refuge. Indeed, the effect is that in expressing one's Going for Refuge in that context, for the first time one fully and effectively Goes for Refuge. From this point of view at least, the ordinee's Going for Refuge rests upon the ordainer's. That is the private aspect of the responsibility. From the public point of view, the Order and the movement at large accept that someone is a member of the Order because they have confidence in the ordainer and the process of selection and preparation. All of this is very exposing …

In witnessing someone else's Going for Refuge my own is called into question. This is the real crux of the matter, and it is the crux of the matter not just for those who have the actual responsibility for conferring ordinations; it is also the crux – the decisive point at issue – for all members of ordination teams and, indeed, for each and every individual *dharmacārī* and *dharmacāriṇī* who entertains an opinion, expressed or unexpressed (and such opinions *ought* always to be expressed), on the readiness or unreadiness for ordination of any Mitra or Friend who wishes to go for Refuge to the Three Jewels within the context of the Western Buddhist Order. In a sense it is ultimately the crux for the whole order, for it is the whole order which, indirectly if not directly, witnesses the ordinand's Going for Refuge and therefore the whole order whose Going for Refuge is ultimately called into question. This 'calling into question', whether by oneself or by others, is not tantamount to *doubting*. Rather does it constitute a process of self-interrogation – even of a (metaphorical) putting oneself to the question in the archaic judicial sense. It may also be described as a trying and testing, much as gold is tested on the touchstone or tried in the fire. In the course of this process, whether described in terms of self-interrogation or of trying and testing, one discovers to what extent one is speaking the truth when one asseverates '*Buddhaṃ saraṇaṃ gacchāmi*' or to what extent one's Going for Refuge is made of base metal, or mixed with impurities, rather than being solid twenty-four-carat gold. One discovers, perhaps, that without realizing it one has slipped from effective back to provisional or cultural Going for Refuge and that in assessing someone's readiness for ordination one in fact no longer relies on a strong sense of one's own Going for Refuge – a sense that enables one to detect a similar movement within another person's being – but rather relies on the formal application of criteria or on impressions, feelings, hunches, and intuitions. As Subhuti says, all this is very exposing.

A few moments ago I spoke of the new developments that have taken place within the Order, and, through the Order, within the wider Movement, as being a veritable Indra's Net.[631] But in Indra's Net, the marvellous jewels of which all mutually reflect one another, it is not always possible to say what is cause and what effect. This is particularly true of the new-style men's ordination process – as it has come to be called – at Padmaloka. I do not know whether it was my sharing of responsibility for conferring ordination that led to the emergence of this process, or the emergence of the process that led to my sharing the responsibility for conferring ordination, at least to the extent of its helping make such sharing a practical proposition. Be that as it may, there is no doubt that the new-style men's ordination process at Padmaloka is one of the most positive developments to have taken place in the course of the last two years and one whose repercussions have already been felt throughout the Movement in Europe and perhaps even farther afield. Subhuti has described the new-style process in his article 'The Men's Ordination Process' (*Shabda*, April 1989), which incorporates his 'Letter to Men Who Have Asked for Ordination', as well as giving a fuller (updated) description of it, from 'the request' to 'initiation' in his more recent lecture 'What is Ordination?'. Prominent features of the new-style men's ordination process are the series of five two-week long Going for Refuge retreats, at which are covered the five 'themes' dealing with the main areas of spiritual life within the Order,[632] the national gatherings of men who have asked for ordination, the Going for Refuge groups (the first of which I believe emerged spontaneously among Mitras quite independently of the 'official' ordination process),[633] the possibility of taking up the Going for Refuge and Prostration practice,[634] and the arrangements that are made from time to time for the ordination of the minority of men who, for *bona fide* reasons, are unable to go on the full length Guhyaloka ordination retreat.[635] Moreover, the *kalyāṇa mitra* system for men has been reconstituted on a somewhat new basis and made, in effect, part of the broader ordination process. As I made clear in my letter to you dated 2 January 1990 (*Shabda*, February 1990), *kalyāṇa mitras* will be available only to Mitras who have asked for ordination, and since being an effective *kalyāṇa mitra* requires qualities and circumstances which not all Order members at present possess it will be necessary for a proposed *kalyāṇa mitra* relationship to be discussed by the Order chapter(s) of the Mitra and the proposed *kalyāṇa mitras*, by the Mitra Convenors' Meeting and the Ordination Team. I myself will make the final decision as to whether the particular *kalyāṇa mitra* relationship is appropriate – a measure of the importance I attach to relationships of this kind.[636] As to the qualities and circumstances required to be an effective *kalyāṇa mitra*, I described these as follows:

> Kalyana Mitras should be relatively senior and experienced Dharmacharis in good contact with me, without difficulties or reservations with the Order and the FWBO, with good communication with members of the Ordination Team at 'Padmaloka', with proven abilities as kalyana mitras, with good Dharma knowledge and a consistent meditation practice, and with adequate opportunity to spend time with the particular mitra concerned.

Quite a formidable combination, but one that should not be beyond the reach of any Order member of ten or more years' standing or even less.

Thus, like my sharing of the responsibility for conferring ordination, the new-style men's ordination process has been responsible for, or associated with, a veritable Indra's Net of new developments. Some of these developments, such as the reinstatement of the *kalyāṇa mitra* system for men, are obviously of more direct concern to the men's wing of the Order as a whole than are others. Among the developments that are of greater concern and interest to the men's wing of the Order as a whole are the visits Subhuti has started paying to the different men's chapters and the series of lectures he and Aloka[637] have given on the Going for Refuge retreats and at the national gatherings of men who have asked for ordination. The purpose of Subhuti's visits is threefold: (1) to establish communication between the ordination team at Padmaloka and the chapters in order to ensure the future unity of the Movement; (2) to take all possible advantage of the chapters' advice and reflection; and (3) to be able to talk to chapter members about specific mitras. As for the lectures, they covered such vitally important topics as 'What is the Order?', 'The Refuge Tree', 'The Mythic Context', and 'Spiritual Friendship', and were both instructive and inspiring. So instructive and inspiring were they (judging from the minimally edited transcripts) that I would like to see them circulating more widely within the Movement or, at least, within the Order. I would also like to see the material that has been produced on the corresponding retreats for women circulating in the same way.[638]

But perhaps the most significant development for which the new-style men's ordination process has been responsible lies in the realm of ideas and ideals. Ideas and ideals form an integral part of the FWBO, even as they form an integral part of Buddhism itself, and it is therefore unfortunate that recent years have seen an increasing tendency, on the part of some Order members and mitras, to neglect certain of our Movement's most vital and characteristic ideas. These comparatively neglected ideas are now being reaffirmed as a result of the new-style men's ordination process.[639] One of the most important ideas to be reaffirmed in this way is that of the absolute centrality for the Buddhist life of the act of Going for Refuge, with its corollary of the necessity for a continual deepening of one's Going for Refuge or (if one prefers the language of ascent) a constant progression to higher and ever higher levels of Going for Refuge – from effective to real, and from real to absolute. In the case of mitras who have asked for ordination this means not screwing one's courage to the sticking point for a flying leap into 'ordination' so much as steadily deepening, or heightening, one's provisional Going for Refuge until it becomes effective Going for Refuge and can be 'witnessed' as such.

The act of Going for Refuge is of course an individual act, that is, the act of a (real) individual; but it is not an *individualistic* act. Going for Refuge has an altruistic dimension, as I have termed it, a dimension represented by what is known in the Mahāyāna as the *bodhicitta* or 'will to (Supreme) Enlightenment' not for one's own sake only but for the benefit of all living beings. As men and women who go for Refuge to the Buddha, Dharma, and Sangha, Order members therefore have an outward-going aspect to their lives as well as an inward-looking one. They seek to transform self *and* world. Indeed, they recognize that it is difficult to transform the one without transforming the other, at least to some extent. The medium through which we work together to transform the world is the loose network of organizations and institutions prominent among which are our (public) centres, our (residential spiritual) communities, and our (team-based right livelihood) co-operatives and their equivalent. This network constitutes the nucleus of the New Society as we call it, appropriating a term from current sociospeak and giving it a distinctive meaning of our own. The idea – and ideal – of the New Society is one of the comparatively neglected ideas now being reaffirmed as a result of the new-style men's ordination process.[640] Not that it is in need of reaffirmation throughout the Movement. Far from it. In India the idea of the New Society, as well as the related idea of the 'Dhamma revolution', has been consistently and powerfully affirmed from the very beginning of our work there. Only in the West, where it is so much easier for us to withdraw into a private world of purely personal concerns, has there been a tendency in recent years for this idea to be neglected and, therefore, a need for it to be reaffirmed. Without the idea – without the *vision* – of the New Society our Movement loses its cutting edge. As Subhuti wrote seven years ago, in *Buddhism for Today*:

> The purpose of the FWBO is not to find a corner for Buddhists in the midst of the old society. It does not seek to give Buddhism a place in the Establishment so that Buddhists can carry out their own colourful practices and hold their own peculiar beliefs. The FWBO is, to this extent, revolutionary: it wishes to change society – to turn the old society into the new.[641]

We would do well to remember these words. Without the idea of the New Society – without the idea of transforming world as well as self – our Going for Refuge is in danger of becoming an individualistic affair and, to that extent, in danger of being not truly a Going for Refuge at all.

Going for Refuge is sometimes spoken of in terms of *commitment* to the Buddha, Dharma, and Sangha, the word being perhaps most familiar to us in the aphorism 'commitment is primary, lifestyle secondary'. As I pointed out in *The Ten Pillars of Buddhism*, the fact that lifestyle is 'secondary' does not mean that it is 'unimportant', nor does it mean that 'lifestyle' represents some ethically neutral way of life that can be combined, without modification, with the pursuit of Enlightenment. There are both skilful and unskilful lifestyles, lifestyles that represent an expression of one's commitment to the Three Jewels and lifestyles that do not represent such an expression.[642] For those individuals who go for Refuge, or who seek to go for Refuge, the best lifestyle – circumstances permitting – is one that contains a strong single-sex element, either by virtue of the fact that one lives in a single-sex spiritual community and/or works in a single-sex co-operative or by virtue of the fact that one is a regular participant in single-sex retreats, study groups, etc.[643] This single-sex idea, as we rather inelegantly call it, is one of the comparatively neglected ideas and ideals now being reaffirmed as a result of the new-style men's ordination process. Closely connected with the single-sex idea are the ideas of deep and direct communication, of spiritual friendship, of 'Going Forth', and of psycho-spiritual androgyny. These ideas, too, are now being reaffirmed as a result of the new-style men's ordination process.

Another idea now being reaffirmed is that of the need for clearer thinking. Only too often our thinking is lamentably unclear and confused. It is therefore important that we should talk things out, or talk things through, to a much greater extent than we are in the habit of doing. It is in fact important that we should clarify issues generally, whether these issues happen to be of a practical or a theoretical nature and whether they relate to our personal lives, to the world at large, to the different fields of human activity, or to the basic teachings of Buddhism. In particular it is important that we should clarify issues relating to the meaning and significance of the Western Buddhist Order/Trailokya Bauddha Mahasangha, for unless we are clear about these issues ourselves we shall not be able to clarify them for mitras who have asked for ordination or, for the matter of that, for anyone else. Mitras who have asked for ordination have, after all, asked for ordination into the Western Buddhist Order – more often than not quite explicitly, as some of you will recollect doing yourselves. They have not asked simply to 'become Buddhists', or to 'be ordained' in some vague, general sense. They have asked to be allowed to take the most important step in their lives under *our* auspices and in the sense that *we* understand that step. It is therefore not enough for us to acquaint them with the meaning and significance of Going for Refuge and 'taking' the ten precepts. We have also to acquaint them with the meaning and significance – with the distinctive nature – of the Western Buddhist Order, so that they know on what principles the Order is based and can decide whether they do, in fact, want to be a 'part' of it – whether they do, in fact, want to be one of the thousand arms of Avalokiteśvara. All this calls for clear thinking. Without clear thinking on the part of Order members, especially on the part of those who are directly concerned with the ordination process, whether as chapter members or as members of a men's or a women's ordination team, it is difficult for a mitra who has asked for ordination to deepen his or her Going for Refuge to the point where provisional Going for Refuge begins to be transformed into effective Going for Refuge. Without clear thinking it is also difficult – perhaps even impossible – for an Order member to deepen his or her effective Going for Refuge to the point where, Insight arising, it begins to be transformed into real Going for Refuge. Lack of clear thinking is, indeed, one of the three principal reasons why Order members drift away from the Movement and eventually have to be dropped from the Order register, the two other reasons being the discontinuance of their daily meditation, especially the visualization and mantra-recitation practice they received at the time of ordination, and the disruption of their personal relationship with me.

This brings me, at last, to the first of the two topics I was unable to deal with two years ago, viz. my own relation to the Order. But first I want to say a few words about the dropping of names from the Order register. As I mentioned at the beginning of this paper, in the course of the last two years ten Order members have had their names dropped from the Order register (none were, I think, dropped before that). I need hardly say that for me the necessity of dropping someone's name from the register is an extremely painful one, the pain being perhaps more than commensurate with the happiness I felt at their ordination. I also need hardly say that no one's name has been dropped without a good deal of consideration on my part and without their having been out of touch with me, and out of touch with the Movement, for upwards of half a decade, as was the case with almost all those whose names have been dropped in the course of the last two years. At the same time I would like to make it clear that, painful as it is for me to drop an Order member's name from the Order register, I find it still more painful when the presence of someone's name on the register signifies a purely nominal membership of the Order on their part. There were several reasons why, twenty-two years ago, I took upon myself the onerous responsibility of founding the Western Buddhist Order. One reason was that I was dissatisfied with 'Buddhist' organizations whose membership was, for the most part, only nominally Buddhist – perhaps not even that. I wanted to have an organization that was genuinely Buddhist, which meant having one whose members were all Buddhists, that is, whose members all actually went for Refuge to the Buddha, Dharma, and Sangha. Thus it was that on Sunday, 7 April 1968, I founded not another 'Buddhist society' but a spiritual community or order – the Western Buddhist Order. You therefore can understand how disappointed I am when someone drifts away from the Movement and allows their membership of the Order to become purely nominal. You can understand why it is impossible for me to acquiesce in such a state of affairs indefinitely and why I eventually have to drop their name from the Order register. Though I would dearly love to have a big order, with tens of thousands, even hundreds of thousands, of Order members, I would much rather have a small order, *all* the members of which were real Order members, than have a big order that contained even a sprinkling of those whose membership of the Order was purely nominal. Having said this, however, I would like to say that Order members whose names have been dropped from the Order register can have them reinstated and can, if necessary, be re-ordained, as can Order members who have resigned. A *bhikṣu* is permitted to join and rejoin the monastic order up to seven times and we should not be less generous. But someone wishing to have their name reinstated on the Order register will have to clarify their thinking; they will have to resume their daily meditation practice, and they will have to renew their personal relationship with me.

Thus I am again brought to the topic of my relation to the Order, and to this we must now turn. The first thing that occurred to me, when I started preparing this paper, was that besides the question of my relation to the Order there was the question of the Order's relation to me – of *your* relation to me. But on second thoughts I realized that it was not really possible for me to share with you some of my current thinking as regards my own relation to the Order without, at the same time, sharing with you some of my current thinking as regards the Order's relation to me, if only by implication. My relation to the Order and the Order's relation to me were the two sides of a single coin. In sharing with you some of my current thinking concerning our mutual relation I shall, however, be speaking mainly in terms of my relation to the Order, leaving it to you to work out for yourselves what this implies in terms of your relation to me.

But first I must warn you that my current thinking about my relation to the Order is not particularly systematic. It is still very much 'work in progress'. Just how unsystematic my thinking was I realized only when, as my custom is before starting work on a lecture or paper, I jotted down my thoughts on the subject in the order in which they occurred to me. After half an hour I had several dozen such 'thoughts', and there did not seem to be much connection between them. As I gazed at the sheet of A4 on which I had jotted them down, however, they seemed – like the phenomena of mundane existence – to distribute themselves into five 'heaps'. In sharing with you my current thinking about my relation to the Order I shall, therefore, be speaking about (1) the *importance* of my relation to the Order, about (2) the *nature* of that relation, about (3) the *person* who has that relation, namely myself, about (4) the *ways* in which I relate to the Order, and about (5) the *future* of my relation to the Order – or my future relation to the Order, as I should perhaps put it. The order in which I have enumerated these five 'heaps' of thoughts is not necessarily the logical one (if indeed there is a logical one), and there may well be a certain amount of overlap between them, with some thoughts appearing in more than one 'heap'.

My relation to the Order is (1) *important*, that is, important to *me* (I leave aside for the moment the fact that it is important to you). It is important to me because you are important to me, both individually and collectively. You are important to me by virtue of the fact that you are human beings who live and must die, who experience pleasure and experience pain. You are important to me by virtue of the fact that you have gone for Refuge to the Buddha, Dharma, and Sangha. Above all, you are important to me because you have gone for Refuge with me as your 'witness', that is, because you have been ordained by me into the Western Buddhist Order/Trailokya Bauddha Mahasangha. (A growing number of you have, of course, been ordained by Subhuti and Suvajra acting on their own responsibility, but inasmuch as *their* Going for Refuge was 'witnessed' by me you are no less important to me than those whom I have ordained personally and my relation to you is no less important to me than is my relation to them.) Since you are important to me I follow the course of your spiritual – and worldly – careers (in the sense of *carya*) with the utmost interest. Your successes and failures are my successes and failures. Whatever concerns you concerns me. I read *Shabda* from cover to cover each month, usually as soon as it arrives, mainly because I want to know how you have been getting on – what you have been thinking, feeling, doing. Your contributions to *Shabda*, especially your respective reportings-in, are in fact my principal source of information about you, and I therefore feel very disappointed when month after month no word from Dharmachari X or Dharmacharini Y appears in its pages.[644] Besides reading *Shabda* from cover to cover, I read all your letters, picture postcards, and telegrams (not to mention your poems), which between them constitute a source of information about you second only to your contributions to *Shabda*. Nowadays I receive a good deal of mail (mitras and Friends also write, as do other people); but however much I receive I am always glad to hear from Order members, even though it is not always possible for me to reply. Some of you, I know, have wondered whether your letters actually reach me and, if so, whether I read them. I can assure you that they do reach me, wherever I happen to be, and that I *always* read them. Sometimes I read them twice.

Perhaps you are surprised that the Order should be important to me because *you* are important to me, and surprised that I should have emphasized the point in the way I have done. There are several reasons for the emphasis. In the first place, the Order really is important to me because *you* are important to me, and in sharing with you some of my thinking about my relation to the Order it was therefore hardly possible for me not to tell you how strongly I felt this. In the second place, the Order is growing numerically all the time. As I mentioned earlier, there are now 384 of us, sixty men and women having been ordained during the last two years. 384 is not really a very large number of Order members to have, especially when one considers how badly the world needs Order members; but I suspect that it is quite large enough for some of you to feel that you are in danger of getting 'lost in the crowd' – large enough for you to feel that in your individual capacity you do not count, that Bhante is too busy to take much notice of you, even that he does not care for you particularly. As I hope I have made clear, this is certainly not the case. So far as I am concerned you do count in your individual capacity (the only capacity that really matters), I am not too busy to take notice of you, and I do care about you. There are other reasons for my emphasizing that my relation to the Order is important to me – that *you* are important to me. The Order is now twenty-two years old. For the last twenty-two years I have put more of my energies into the Order than I have into anything else. Only my literary work and my friendships have represented anything like a comparable investment of my energies, and even these have increasingly subserved the needs of the Order (and the Movement), in the one case, and fallen within the compass of the Order in the other. For the last twenty-two years the Order has occupied the very forefront of my consciousness, there being hardly a day when my thoughts were not concerned with it, either directly or indirectly. The Order is my *chef-d'œuvre*, the principal work of my life, though by its very nature it is a work that could not have been accomplished without the co-operation of a number of people – without *your* co-operation. For these reasons, too, my relation to the Order is important to me, which means that *you* are important to me, both individually and 'collectively'.

One more point in connection with this particular 'heap' of thoughts. When I speak of my relation to the Order being important to me what I mean is that my relation to the whole, united Order is important to me. To the extent that the Order is not united it is not an order and I cannot relate to it as an order, that is, cannot relate to it as a whole, united order. (It would give me very little satisfaction to relate to a fragmented order.) Conflict and disharmony within the Order are extremely painful to me, even as they are damaging to the Order as a whole and detrimental to each and every individual Order member, especially to those immediately responsible for the conflict and disharmony. Conflict and disharmony represent a negation of the ideals for which the Order stands. They represent a negation of the Order's very existence. When conflict and disharmony arise within the Order, therefore, even to the slightest extent, they should be resolved as quickly as possible and peace and harmony restored.

By (2) the *nature* of my relation to the Order I mean its general character. That character is determined by the nature of the various particular relations in which I stand to the Order – relations which shade one into another and which are more easily distinguished than separated. Probably the most obvious relation in which I stand to the Order is that of founder, in the sense of being the one who, more than anybody else, was responsible for the Order's coming into existence. Closely connected with my relation to the Order as founder is my relation to it as preceptor, that is, as conferrer of ordination, for the Order came into existence, and I became related to it as its founder, only when – twenty-two years ago – I conferred the first *dharmacārī* and *dharmacāriṇī* ordinations as we now call them. Though closely connected with each other, however, the two relations are to some extent separable or, more precisely, are separable from a certain point in time onwards. As you know, last year I started sharing the responsibility for conferring ordination, and the point at which I did this was the point from which my relation to the Order as founder became separable from my relation to the Order as preceptor. The responsibility for founding the Order cannot be shared, of course, the founding of the Order being a unique historical event that took place once and for all and cannot take place again, at least not in the present world-period. From the fact that my relation to the Order as founder and my relation to the Order as preceptor are to some extent separable, that is, separable from the point at which I started sharing the responsibility for conferring ordination, it follows that while I stand in the relation of founder to the whole Order, or all Order members, I stand in the relation of preceptor only to a part of the Order, or some Order members. To that part of the Order to which I do not stand in the relation of preceptor I stand in the relation of preceptor's preceptor. Thus my relation to the Order as founder is in a way more fundamental.

A few minutes ago I spoke of myself as the founder of the Order in the sense of my being the one who, more than anybody else, was responsible for the Order's coming into existence. *More than* anybody else. The use of the comparative degree was deliberate. It signified my awareness of the fact that others, too, were responsible for the Order's coming into existence, albeit not responsible to the extent that I was nor perhaps in the same kind of way. Though I may have taken the initiative, even have played the leading part, I did not found the Order all on my own. I did not found the Order single-handed. Indeed it was impossible for me to found it single-handed. I could found it only by 'witnessing' the Going for Refuge of others and I could 'witness' their Going for Refuge only because they wanted me to 'witness' it. Or, I could found the Order only by ordaining people and could ordain them only because they wanted me to ordain them. Thus while I am the founder of the Order I am its founder only by courtesy of other people. I am its founder only because other people wanted the Order to be founded and wanted me to be its founder. It therefore would be no less true to say that they founded the Order with my co-operation than to say that I founded it with their co-operation.

But I am being a little paradoxical. I have overstated the case for my not having founded the Order all on my own, or single-handed. There is another side of the question – another factor to be taken into account. Though I indeed could found the Order only by 'witnessing' the Going for Refuge of other people, and 'witness' it only because they wanted me to, the nine men and three women whom I ordained on the occasion whose anniversary we are celebrating today all went for Refuge with a certain understanding of what was meant by Going for Refuge. That understanding coincided with my own understanding of what was meant by Going for Refuge, at least to some extent. It coincided with it because having studied and practised Buddhism under my guidance the men and women in question shared my views. In other words they were not just ordinands and I was not just their preceptor. They were also my pupils, my disciples, and I was their teacher; and because they were my disciples, and went for Refuge in the sense that I understood Going for Refuge, it would, after all, be truer to say that I founded the Order with their co-operation than to say that they founded it with mine.

Thus there is another relation in which I stand to the Order. Besides that of founder and that of preceptor (and preceptor's preceptor), I stand to it in the relation of teacher, that is, spiritual teacher or teacher of the Dharma. As I just now had occasion to mention, I was the teacher of the first twelve Order members, both before and after their ordination, and I have been, and still am, the teacher of the 384 existing

Order members. By this I do not mean that I have taught all Order members personally, or that even in the case of those whom I have taught personally I have necessarily taught them all they know about the Dharma. Senior Order members teach junior Order members, both before the latter's ordination and after (not that the picture is really as simple as that), which is why, incidentally, at the conclusion of the ordination ceremony the new Order member's 'formal' acceptance of the ordination includes the words 'with loyalty to my teachers'.[645] What I mean, when I say that I am the teacher of the Order, is that the Dharma studied, practised, and propagated by Order members is the Dharma as elucidated by me. This is not to say that I have elucidated the Dharma at every single point, only that I have elucidated it in certain fundamental respects. It is not to say that I have finished elucidating the Dharma. There may be many more elucidations to come. Moreover, the fact that the Dharma studied, practised, and propagated by Order members is the Dharma as elucidated by me does not preclude the possibility of an Order member elucidating points not elucidated by me, provided this is done in accordance with the spirit of my elucidations. Some Order members have, in fact, already started doing this. Others have started elucidating my elucidations. This is the way a tradition – a lineage – begins to develop.

The word 'elucidate' is from *lucidus*, bright, and means 'throw light on, explain'. It suggests the (metaphorical) bringing of something from obscurity and darkness into the light. It even suggests, we may say, the transferral of something from a place or realm of darkness to a place or realm of light. Thus to elucidate is also to *translate*, for the word 'translate' is the past participle of the very word from which we get the word 'transfer' meaning 'convey, remove, hand over, (thing etc. *from* person or place *to* another)'. The primary signification of 'translate' is 'express the sense of (word, sentence, speech, book, poem, etc.) in or *into* another language.' But there is language in the literal sense ('the languages of north India') and there is language in the metaphorical sense ('the language of art'). 'Translation' can therefore be either from one spoken or written tongue in or into another, or from one discipline, or set of ideas, or culture in or into another. As with 'translation' so with 'translator'. A translator can express the sense of a word, sentence, speech, book, poem, etc., in or into another language, or he (or she) can express the sense of one discipline, or set of ideas, or culture in or into the terms of another. In both cases something is brought from obscurity and darkness into the light. One who is literally a translator brings a word, sentence, speech, book, poem, etc. from the obscurity and darkness of an unknown tongue into the light of one that is known and understood. One who is a translator metaphorically brings a discipline, or a set of ideas, or a culture, from the obscurity and darkness of unfamiliar terms into the light of terms that are familiar. I myself am a translator because I elucidate, that is, elucidate the Dharma. It is because I am a translator, in the metaphorical sense, that when I visited Italy in 1966 I was so strongly drawn by paintings on the theme of St Jerome, especially by those paintings which represented him in his cell, or study, with an hour glass in front of him, a lion (which he had tamed) sleeping at his feet, his red cardinal's hat hanging on the wall, a large volume open before him, and a quill pen in his hand. As I wrote in 'The Journey to Il Convento', a paper I gave in the course of the fourth three-month pre-ordination course for men, held at Il Convento di Santa Croce in Tuscany during the winter of 1984:

> St Jerome is one of the four Fathers of the Latin Church. He lived in the latter half of the fourth and the first quarter of the fifth century, and was a contemporary of St Augustine, another of the Fathers of the Latin Church, with whom he had an acrimonious correspondence. When he was already middle-aged St Jerome left Rome and went to live in the Holy Land, at Bethlehem, and it is at this stage of his career that he is usually depicted in Christian art.... St Jerome was, of course, responsible for the production of the Vulgate, the standard Latin version of the Bible, which was in use throughout the Middle Ages, and when represented in his study he is generally understood to be engaged in this great work. Incidentally, he is represented as a very old man, with a long white beard.... Somehow this theme, or image, took hold of my mind. St Jerome was the Wise Old Man, and as you know the Wise Old Man is one of Jung's archetypes of the collective unconscious. That he was engaged in the work of translation, especially that of rendering the Word of God into ordinary human speech, meant that something hidden in the depths was being brought up to the surface, or brought from darkness into light. Thus St Jerome

> was the Alchemist – another embodiment of the Wise Old Man. His cell-study (sometimes depicted as a cave) was the Alchemist's laboratory. Indeed, it was the Alchemist's *limbec*, in which the Red King united with the White Queen, or his crucible, in which lead was transmuted into gold.

St Jerome was thus the translator both literally and metaphorically. In the next paragraph of 'The Journey to Il Convento' I tried to explain why I had been drawn to the image of St Jerome:

> No doubt I was drawn to the image of St Jerome partly because of my personal situation at the time. I was living in the desert. I had left the 'Rome' of collective, official, even establishment, Buddhism, and was seeking to return to the origins of Buddhism in the actual life and experience of the Buddha and his immediate disciples. Not only that. I was trying to teach Buddhism in the West, which meant I was trying to communicate the spirit of the Dharma in terms of Western rather than in terms of Eastern culture. I was thus a translator, with all that that implies in the way of seeking to fathom the uttermost depths of what one is trying to translate so that one may translate it faithfully, i.e. bring its meaning to the surface, or from darkness into the light. Thus I was drawn to the image of St Jerome, and was able to see that image as an embodiment of the archetype of the Wise Old Man as 'Translator' and Alchemist, because I had a personal affinity with that image, or because there was something in me that corresponded to that image.[646]

However, I have digressed. I have digressed due to my fondness for the figure of St Jerome, and must now return to my relation to the Order as teacher. As I said, I am the teacher of the Order in the sense that the Dharma studied, practised, and propagated by Order members is the Dharma as elucidated by me. In other words, the Dharma studied, practised, and propagated by Order members is the Dharma as 'translated' by me, that is, the Dharma as translated by me from the terms of Eastern culture into the terms of Western culture. But teaching is a form of communication, as is elucidation and 'translation', and since one cannot really communicate without friendliness (*maitrī*) one cannot really teach without friendliness either. One cannot, in fact, be a teacher without being a friend – cannot be a spiritual teacher without being a spiritual friend (*kalyāṇa mitra*). I therefore stand in yet another relation to the Order. I stand to it in the relation of spiritual friend. Between the Order and myself there exists the relation of spiritual friendship that is the sum total, so to speak, of all the different relations of spiritual friendship I have with individual Order members. The whole subject of spiritual friendship, both vertical and horizontal, has of course been much discussed within the Order, especially of late, and for this reason I do not propose to say anything about it now. Instead, let me refer you to the 'Spiritual Friendship' chapter in Subhuti's *Buddhism for Today* and to his nine Padmaloka lectures on the same inspiring theme.[647] I would also like to draw your attention to my own essay 'The Good Friend', written in Kalimpong in 1951.[648]

You may have noticed that I have said nothing about my standing to the Order in the relation of *guru*. According to a popular Indian etymology, *guru* means 'bringer of light', and the word may therefore be taken as having the same general signification as 'elucidator'. Nonetheless, I do not care to apply it to myself or to have it applied to me by others. In recent years the activities of so-called *gurus* have debased the meaning of the term to such a degree that the *Collins Dictionary of the English Language* (second edition, 1986) can attach to its secondary sense, 'a leader or chief theoretician of a movement, esp. a spiritual or religious cult', the connotative label *'often derogatory'*, implying that the connotation of the word is unpleasant with intent on the part of the speaker or writer. I showed signs of being not completely happy with the *guru* concept itself as early as 1970, when I gave the lecture 'Is a Guru Necessary?' In this lecture I did three things. Firstly, I tried to explain what a guru was not. He (or she – for there is a female of the species) was not the head of a religious group, not a teacher (that is, not one who imparts knowledge and information, not even religious knowledge and information), not a father- (or mother-) substitute, and not a problem-solver. Secondly, I tried to explain what a guru was. He was one who stood on a higher level of being and consciousness than we did, one with whom we were in regular contact, on whatever plane, and one between whom and ourselves there was an 'existential' contact and communication. Finally, I compared Eastern and Western attitudes towards the *guru*. In the East, I suggested, the *guru* was sometimes overvalued; in the West, usually undervalued. The proper course was to follow a middle way between the two extremes, simply recognizing that there were others more highly evolved than ourselves and that we could evolve through contact with them. What was required was not absolute faith but contact and receptivity. In this way did I attempt, in effect, to revise the *guru* concept and rid the word '*guru*' of its unpleasant connotation.[649] The tide was against me, and now, twenty years on, I would drop the *guru* concept and, as I said, preferably not apply the word '*guru*' to myself nor have it applied to me by others. We have in Buddhism the wonderful term 'spiritual friend' and this I am more than content to apply to myself and to have applied to me by others. Indeed, there are times when I think that 'spiritual friend' is almost too much and that just 'friend' would be enough. The English word 'spiritual' is in any case not the exact equivalent of the Indian word '*kalyāṇa*'. According to the *PTS Pāli-English Dictionary*, '*kalyāṇa*' means 'beautiful, charming, auspicious, helpful, morally good'.[650] Obviously I cannot claim to be beautiful, at least not in the literal sense, and I can hardly be described as charming, though I may be auspicious and helpful on occasion and morally good to some extent. Let me, therefore, be content with the appellation 'friend' and stand to the Order simply in the relation of friend.

Probably I have gone on about myself long enough, but I am afraid we have not yet finished with the subject, for having spoken about the importance of my relation to the Order, and about the nature of that relation, I must now speak about (3) the *person* who has the relation, that person of course being myself. Perhaps you are surprised to hear me speaking about myself in this connection. Perhaps you took it for granted that I would speak about my relation to the Order without explicitly bringing myself into the picture. After all, that is what we often do: we leave ourselves out; we omit the personal factor from the equation. Some would even say that we *ought* to leave ourselves out. We ought to leave ourselves out because, paradoxically, there is no self to leave out. There are relations but no *relata*. This is miserable sophistry – at least in the present connection, and on the level on which I am speaking. That it is I, and no other, who stands to the Order in the relation of founder, preceptor, and so on, cannot but make a difference, both to the relation itself and to the Order. So who is it that has the relation to the Order? Who am I? I must confess I do not know. I am as much a mystery to myself as I probably am to you. Not that I am a mystery to everyone, apparently. Quite a lot of people know exactly who and what I am (I am speaking of people outside the Movement). Quite a lot of people 'see' me. But they see me in different ways. This was very much the case when I lived in India. According to who it was that did the seeing, I was 'the English monk', 'a rabid Mahāyānist', 'a narrow-minded Hīnayānist', 'the Enemy of the Church', 'a Russian spy', 'an American agent', 'the Editor of the *Maha Bodhi*', 'an impractical young idealist', 'a good speaker', 'the invader of Suez', 'the guru of the Untouchables', and so on. More recently, here in England, I have been 'a good monk', 'a bad monk', 'the Buddhist counterpart of the Vicar of Hampstead', 'the author of the *Survey*', 'a crypto-Vajrayānist', 'a lecturer at Yale', 'the hippie guru', 'a first-class organizer', 'a traditionalist', 'a maverick', 'a misogynist', 'a sexist', 'a controversial figure', and 'an Enlightened Englishman'.

All these different 'sightings' have at least *some* truth in them, even though the people doing the 'seeing' may have looked at me from the wrong angle, in the wrong kind of light, through tinted spectacles, or through the wrong end of the telescope. They may even have had spots floating before their eyes. The reason why all these different sightings have at least some truth in them is that I am a rather complex person. (Not that I am so very unusual in this respect. Some of you, too, are rather complex, as I know only too well.) It is partly because I am a rather complex person that I am a mystery to myself, even if not to others. But though I am a mystery to myself I am not, I think, so much of a mystery to myself as to cherish many illusions about myself. One of the illusions about myself that I do *not* cherish is that I was the most suitable person to be the founder of a new Buddhist movement in Britain – in the world, as it turned out. I possessed so few of the necessary qualifications; I laboured under so many disadvantages. When I look back on those early days, and think of the difficulties I had to experience (not that I always thought of them as difficulties), I cannot but feel that the coming into existence of the Western Buddhist Order was little short of a miracle. Not only did the lotus bloom from the mud; it had to bloom from the mud contained within a small and inadequate pot. Perhaps it had to bloom just then or not at all, and perhaps this particular pot was the only one available.

Now, hundreds of lotuses are blooming, some of the bigger and more resplendent flowers being surrounded by clusters of half-opened buds. During the last twenty-two years a whole lotus-lake has come into existence, or rather, a whole series of lotus-lakes. Alternatively, during the last twenty-two years the original lotus plant has grown into an enormous lotus-tree not unlike the great four-branched Refuge Tree – has in fact grown into a whole forest of lotus-trees. Contemplating the series of lotus-lakes, contemplating the forest of lotus-trees, and rejoicing in the strength and beauty of the lotus-flowers, I find it difficult to believe that they really did all originate from that small and inadequate pot, which some people wanted to smash to bits, or cast into the dustbin, or bury as deep as possible in the ground. In brief, dropping the metaphor and speaking quite plainly, when I see what a great and glorious achievement the Order represents, despite its manifest imperfections, I find it difficult to believe that I could have been its founder. Not long ago, in connection with the dropping of names from the Order register, I spoke of my having taken upon myself the onerous responsibility of founding the Western Buddhist Order. I indeed took that responsibility upon myself, and it was indeed an onerous one. Nonetheless, there are times when, far from feeling that it was I who took on the responsibility, I feel that it was the responsibility that took on me. There are times when I am dimly aware of a vast, overshadowing Consciousness that has, through me, founded the Order and set in motion our whole Movement.

Before going on to speak about the ways in which I relate to the Order, I want to make just one more point. It concerns my own limitations as a person. That one is a person at all means that one has certain limitations. Apart from such obvious limitations as those of nationality, language, and class (or caste), there are the limitations imposed by the fact that one is of a particular temperament and experiences life in a particular kind of way. One can hardly be of all temperaments and experience life in every kind of way. One is either introvert or extravert, Hellenist or Hebraist, Platonist or Aristotelian, *śraddhānusārin* or *dharmānusārin*, *jñānin* or *bhakta*[651] – though it is a case, more often than not, of one's being predominantly rather than exclusively the one or the other. That it is I, and not someone else, who stands to the Order in the relation of founder, preceptor, and so on, thus cannot but make a difference, as we have seen. But though it makes a difference that difference should not constitute a limitation. I am by temperament inclined to the humanities, let us say, rather than to science, and in teaching the Dharma I tend to present it in terms of the humanities, that is, in terms of literature, philosophy, and the fine arts. But this does not mean that those Order members who are by temperament more inclined to science should not present the Dharma in terms of nuclear physics or biology. The important thing is that the Dharma should be communicated to as many people as possible and this means communicating the Dharma in as many different ways as possible – always assuming, of course, that it is in fact the Dharma that is being communicated. In other words – and this is the point I want to make – my own personal limitations should not be the limitations of the Order. The Order should not be simply Sangharakshita writ large. Avalokiteśvara has a thousand hands, and each of the thousand hands holds a *different* object. Similarly, Order members of particular temperaments have different talents, aptitudes, and capacities, and in making their respective contributions to the life and work of the Order they should allow – *you* should allow – those talents, aptitudes, and capacities full scope. The Order should be a rich and many-splendoured thing, with all kinds of facets. It doesn't have to be just a lotus-lake, or even a series of lotus-lakes. It can also be a rose garden, or a cabbage patch, as you prefer.

To relate means to communicate, and (iv) the *ways* in which I relate to the Order are simply the different means I employ to communicate with Order members, both individually and 'collectively'. My principal means of communication is the spoken and written word, as when I talk to you, whether live or on tape, or write a letter or an article. (That I am unable to communicate by means of visual images or musical notes is one of my own limitations.)[652] The other means I employ to communicate with Order members are, of course, non-verbal, but inasmuch as I make much less of them than I do of the spoken and written word I shall say nothing about them until I have spelled out the different forms taken by the spoken and written word as I communicate with you through that medium.

Communication by means of the spoken word takes the form of personal talks, public lectures, interviews, question-and-answer sessions, and study seminars, all of which can be, and except for personal talks usually are, recorded on tape. These tape-recordings can be transcribed and edited and even published in book form – which brings me to a point I would have made on the convention had not an indisposition prevented me from addressing you. Due mainly to the devoted labours of the Transcription Unit, more than half the many hundreds of thousands of words spoken by me over the years as I gave lectures and led seminars have been transcribed and made available in unedited form.[653] But not more than a hundredth part (my own rough estimate) of the words transcribed have been edited and published in book form, however inadequately. Hundreds of thousands of words remain untranscribed and, therefore, unedited and unpublished. Transcribed or untranscribed, collectively these words, the result of 200 lectures and 120 seminars, represent an enormous amount of material. They represent, in fact, an enormous amount of Dharma-teaching, even an enormous amount of 'translation', and since to teach is to communicate they also represent a communication. They are a communication not just to the audience or study group to which they were originally addressed but also, in principle, to Order members, Mitras, and Friends everywhere. But communication cannot be unilateral. Unless you hear me I cannot really speak to you. Unless you open and read my letters I cannot really write to you. I would therefore like my lectures and seminars to be accessible to as many Order members, Mitras, and Friends as possible, and to be accessible to them in book form. (Listening to tapes and reading unedited transcripts presents obvious difficulties, especially in the case of seminars.) This means that these lectures and seminars will have to be edited and properly published. We already have a small but heroic band of transcribers, the end of whose work is already in sight. What we now need is a bigger and even more heroic band of editors and publishers. I therefore appeal to all potential editors and publishers to come forward and offer your services, so that a work to which we ought to be giving a very high priority may be taken up without further delay and carried to a successful conclusion.[654]

Personal letters apart, communication by means of the written word takes the form of books. As of this present I have seventeen books in print, and by the end of the year may well have twenty. Only one of the seventeen is a *bona fide* book, in the sense of having been conceived and written as a book as well as published as such. (Not all that glitters is gold; not all that appears between covers is a book.) The others are either collections of essays, articles, and so on, or versions of three or more lectures, or *some* of the chapters of a book (the other chapters having been removed at the instance of the publishers), or contributions to encyclopedias. Even the *Survey*, which some of my friends consider my *magnum opus*, despite its 500 pages (in the original edition) was written up from the notes of four lectures. The only book I have actually conceived and written as a book, and had published as a book, is *Ambedkar and Buddhism*, which for this and other reasons occupies a special place in my affections. But whether conceived and written as books or not, like my transcribed and untranscribed lectures and seminars the seventeen 'books' that I have in print represent a communication – a communication by means of the written word. They are a communication not just to the readership for which they were originally intended (in the case of those published when I was living in India) but also, in principle, to Order members, Mitras, and Friends everywhere. They are particularly a communication to Order members, for it is Order members who, by virtue of their Going for Refuge, are able to understand me best, even in the case of those books that were written prior to the founding of the Order. Two of my more recent publications, namely, *The Ten Pillars of Buddhism* and *The History of My Going for Refuge*, were of course written as papers to be read on Order Day and as such are a direct communication to Order members. Recent or not so recent, however, all my books represent a communication and, in principle at least, a communication to *you*. I would like you to receive that communication. In other words I would like you to read my books, and to read them thoroughly, whether in the original English or in translation. (This reminds me that in addition to a heroic band of editors and publishers we need a heroic band of translators!)[655] Order members and others sometimes wish they had more contact with me. May I remind you that there is a great deal of me in my books, though not as much as I would like, and that when you read my books you are very much in contact with me.

At this point I would like to put in a good word for the Cinderella of my writings, that is, my poetry. Not that I expect you all to like my poetry. I am well aware that it can be characterized as traditional, neo-Georgian, and academic – though even as unacademic a person as Allen Ginsberg once assured me that in *his* view 'academic', as applied to poetry, was by no means a term of disparagement.[656] But regardless of how my poetry is to be characterized – even regardless of whether it is really poetry – like all my writings the poems collected in *The Enchanted Heart* and *Conquering New Worlds* represent a communication by means of the written word, and particularly a communication to Order members.[657] I would therefore like you to read my poetry, even to read it again and again. In my poetry, too, there is a great deal of me, perhaps more than there is in some of my prose writings, at least in certain respects. When you read my poetry you are not only very much in contact with me but in contact with me in a special kind of way. As I wrote in the preface to *The Enchanted Heart*, after acknowledging that not all the poems appearing in that collection were necessarily worth preserving as poetry:

> Many of them, if not the majority, have only a biographical – even a sentimental – interest. They give expression to passing moods and fancies as well as to deeper experiences and insights. They also reflect my response to my surroundings. As such they constitute a sort of spiritual autobiography, sketchy indeed, but perhaps revealing, or at least suggesting, aspects of my life which would not otherwise be known.[658]

There now remain only the non-verbal means I employ to communicate with Order members. I make much less use of these than I do of the spoken and written word, as I have already observed, and it is perhaps for this reason that I feel I cannot really say much about them. Perhaps the non-verbal means of communication should be dealt with non-verbally! Be that as it may, I do not, I think, make use of non-verbal means of communication in quite the same conscious and deliberate way that I make use of the spoken and written word, and may not always realize that I have made use of them until my attention is drawn to the fact. Some of you have told me that there are times when I respond to a question or remark with a significant silence, or a non-committal 'hmm', or a slight raising of the eyebrows. Apparently this can be quite disconcerting. But I have verbalized enough about non-verbal means of communication and will now go on to speak about my last 'heap' of thoughts on the subject of my relation to the Order. That is, I would go on to speak about it did it not suddenly strike me that in speaking about the non-verbal means I employ to communicate with Order members (and others) I have been guilty of a serious omission. No, I am not thinking of picture postcards, the visual message of which sometimes supplements the verbal message. I am thinking of film and video. Not that I am going to say anything about film and video. It is only quite recently that I have reluctantly acknowledged their existence and the possibility of my employing them as a means of communication – a means of communication which is simultaneously verbal and non-verbal, or both verbal and visual.[659]

Finally, there is (5) the *future* of my relation to the Order – or rather my future relation to the Order. Since I do not have a crystal ball, and probably would not be tempted to scry even if I did have one, this particular 'heap' of thoughts is the smallest of the five and I shall not be saying much more about my relation to you in the future than I have said about the non-verbal means of communication. In any case, my having a relation to you in the future depends upon my being around to have one, and since I do not know how much longer I shall be around I cannot be categorical on the subject. Young or old, strong or weak, we may die at any moment, as my mother's recent death served to remind me[660] (if indeed I needed a reminder), and as some of you will have been reminded yourselves by recent bereavements of your own.[661] Nonetheless, I propose to venture on a tentative and provisional forecast which, like all forecasts, may or may not prove correct.

The future being the outcome of the present, even as the present is the outcome of the past, my relation to the Order in the future will not differ so greatly from the relation I have to the Order now and the relation I have had to it previously. The Order will, of course, still be important to me – *you* will still be important to me, both individually and collectively. I shall continue to stand to the Order in the relation of founder and preceptor and preceptor's preceptor, though I shall not be actually conferring ordinations on a regular basis. One day, I hope, I shall stand to a large part of the Order in the relation of preceptor's preceptor's preceptor. I shall also continue to be the teacher of the Order and continue to elucidate and 'translate' the Dharma. I shall continue to be drawn to the image of St Jerome, though I must confess that nowadays I am being increasingly drawn to the figures of two other translators, in the fullest sense of the term: Marsilio Ficino and Thomas Taylor the Platonist.[662] St Jerome of course spent the latter part of his life in the Holy Land, at Bethlehem. It is unlikely that I shall go and live at Lumbini, or even at Dapodi,[663] but I shall continue to withdraw from organizational responsibilities and continue to spend much of my time in semi-retreat, whether in London or elsewhere.[664] There will be no withdrawing from *people*, however. I shall continue to be in personal contact with Order members, Mitras, and Friends – especially with Order members. I shall continue to communicate with you. Indeed, my having a relation to the Order in the future at all implies that I shall continue to communicate with the Order, for to relate means to communicate.

By what means I shall communicate with you (and others) I do not know. Very likely I shall communicate by the same means that I did before. I suspect, though, that while I may give the occasional lecture or lead the occasional seminar my *principal* medium of communication will be the written word. There are a number of things that I would like to write. On the 'autobiographical' front, I would like to finish writing the second volume of my memoirs, covering the period 1950–1957, or at least finish writing the first part of the second volume, covering the period 1950–1953. Staying on the 'autobiographical' front, I would like to write a volume of synchronic (as distinct from diachronic) reminiscences of my second seven years in Kalimpong. These reminiscences would cover the period 1957–1964, a period during which I was developing the Triyana Vardhana Vihara as a centre of non-denominational Buddhism, and would describe my contacts with my Tibetan teachers and with the ex-Untouchables, as well as describing some of the more remarkable people I came to know at that time. Leaving India for England, and continuing to be 'autobiographical', I would like to write a very personal account of the period 1964–1969. This was the period of my stay at (and eventual exclusion from) the Hampstead Buddhist Vihara, of my association with Terry Delamare, of my pilgrimage to Italy and Greece, and, of course, of the founding of the FWBO and WBO. These three 'autobiographical' volumes would not necessarily be written in the order of their chronological sequence.[665] I would also like to write a 'History of My Encounters with Christianity' (along the lines of *The History of My Going for Refuge*) and a substantial paper, at the very least, on Buddhism and Neoplatonism. Neoplatonism is the major spiritual tradition of the West, just as Buddhism is the major spiritual tradition of the East, and Buddhists can no more afford to ignore Neoplatonism than Neoplatonists (should there be any left) can afford to ignore Buddhism. Other literary projects include a supplement to the *Survey*, a commentary on 'The Veil of Stars', a commentary on the bodhisattva precepts, and a study on 'Reason and Emotion in English Literature'.

Mention of literature reminds me that I would like to do some purely creative writing. I would like to write a few more poems and stories. I would like, for instance, to write a long poem on the myth of Orpheus. Not that one can *decide* to write a poem. At best, one can only invoke the Muse and wait and see what happens. I would, in fact, like not only to do some purely creative writing but also to write in a new kind of way – in a way that was new for me at least. I would like to find a new literary form, or even a new medium of communication altogether. In the words of a poem I wrote in 1969:

I should like to speak
With a new voice, speak
Like Adam in the garden, speak
Like the Rishis of old, announcing
In strong jubilant voices the Sun
Moon Stars Dawn Winds Fire
Storm and above all the god-given
Intoxicating ecstatic
Soma, speak
Like divine men celebrating
The divine cosmos with divine names.
I should like to speak
With a new voice, telling
The new things that I know, chanting
In incomparable rhythms
New things to new men, singing
The new horizon, the new vision
The new dawn, the new day.
I should like to use
New words, use
Words pristine, primeval, words
Pure and bright as snow-crystals, words
Resonant, expressive, creative,
Such as, breathed to music, built Ilion.
(The old words
Are too tired soiled stale lifeless.)
New words
Come to me from the stars

From your eyes from
Space
New words vibrant, radiant, able to utter
The new me, able
To build for new
Men a new world.

But I have allowed myself to be carried away into the clouds and must return to earth. I must leave the topic of my relation to the Order and turn, at last, to the topic of the relation of the Order itself to the rest of the Buddhist world.

Extending the Hand of Fellowship

THE RELATION OF THE WESTERN BUDDHIST ORDER TO THE REST OF THE BUDDHIST WORLD

INTRODUCTORY NOTE

Extending the Hand of Fellowship was a paper delivered in April 1996 on the occasion of the twenty-eighth anniversary of the founding of the Western Buddhist Order which took place at Hopwood Hall College in the northern town of Rochdale. Like *My Relation to the Order* it was originally intended as a continuation of *The History of My Going for Refuge* but eight years elapsed before Sangharakshita was able to address the topic in a systematic way. *Extending the Hand of Fellowship* was published by Windhorse Publications that same year.

In April 1988, at a celebration marking the twentieth anniversary of the Western Buddhist Order, I read a paper in which I proposed to trace what I called the history of my Going for Refuge to the Three Jewels, as well as to share with my auditors some of my current thinking as regards my own relation to the Order and the relation of the Order itself to the rest of the Buddhist world. As it happened, the tracing of the various steps by which I had arrived at my understanding of the act of Going for Refuge as the central and definitive act of the Buddhist life took much longer than I had expected, and I was obliged to postpone my remarks on the two remaining subjects to some future occasion. Two years later, when the Order celebrated its twenty-second anniversary, I accordingly read a paper on 'My Relation to the Order'. But this, too, became longer than I had expected, with the result that I was unable to say anything about the relation of the Order to the rest of the Buddhist world. Now, six years further on, when we are celebrating the twenty-eighth anniversary of the Order, I hope to be able to deal with the subject, thus bringing my original undertaking to a belated conclusion. I shall take up the thread where I dropped it at the end of my paper on the history of my Going for Refuge. Having remarked that the nature of my relation to the Order had transpired to some extent in the latter part of the narrative, I continued:

> As regards the relation of the Order to the rest of the Buddhist world let me simply observe that it is a relation that subsists,

> essentially, with individuals, and that, on this the occasion of our twentieth anniversary, we are happy to extend the hand of spiritual fellowship to all those Buddhists for whom commitment is primary, lifestyle secondary, and who, like us, go for Refuge to the Buddha, the Dharma, and the Sangha.[666]

The three principles here laid down, at least by implication, provide me with a point of departure for what I have to say today. Before embarking on the subject of our – the Order's – relation to the rest of the Buddhist world, however, I want to make a few remarks of a more general nature.

Since I spoke on the history of my Going for Refuge eight years have passed. Eight years is a long time, especially when one considers that it represents nearly one third of the time for which the Order has been in existence. During those eight years quite a lot has happened. In 1988 there were 336 Order members world-wide. Two years later there were 384. Today there are 654. With the growth of the Order – and it has grown not only numerically but in 'collective' experience and maturity – there has been a corresponding growth in its – and the FWBO's – activities. New public centres and residential spiritual communities, and even team-based right livelihood businesses, have sprung up, while old ones have expanded and diversified. Books have been written, new magazines launched, and films produced. One might be forgiven for thinking that there was no end to what had happened, both externally and, what is no less important, in terms of the achievement, by individual Order members, of a deeper experience of Going for Refuge by means of ethical living, meditation, Dharma study, spiritual friendship, community life, and ritual and devotion. For me personally the most important thing to have happened in the course of the last eight years is that I have been able to hand on many of my responsibilities as founder and head of the Order to a team of some dozen Order members, especially those comprising the College of Public Preceptors.[667] Soon, I hope, *all* those responsibilities will have been handed on – at least to the extent that this is possible while I am still physically present among you. As you know, last year I celebrated my seventieth birthday, or rather you (and the rest of the Movement) celebrated it and I simply enjoyed the celebrations, and I feel it to be incumbent upon me, during such time as I have left, to do whatever I can to ensure the continuity, well-being, and growth of the Movement after my departure from the scene. This includes sharing with you my current thinking about the Dharma in general and our own tradition in particular, and this is one of the reasons I am addressing you today on the relation of the Order to the rest of the Buddhist world.

I have, of course, been anticipated by Subhuti, who in 1991 gave a talk on 'Relations with Other Buddhists'. In this talk he explored the subject under the three principal headings of the need for clarity, history of the FWBO's relations with other groups, and principles behind our contact with others, each of which enabled him to touch on a variety of issues and make a number of important points.[668] This paper will be much more limited in scope, as I shall be dealing with the relation of the Order, specifically, to the rest of the Buddhist world, as well as having more to say about that world itself. Subhuti's talk and my paper may therefore be regarded as complementary, and best read in conjunction with each other, even though there is a small amount of overlap between them. In any case, Subhuti has his style, and I have mine. Perhaps it is also relevant to observe that during the last four or five years I have had more personal contact with leading Western Buddhists, both European and North American, than I had in the course of the preceding twenty years.

But it is time I returned to the three principles that were laid down, at least by implication, in the remarks with which I concluded my paper on the history of my Going for Refuge and which provide me with a point of departure now. These three principles may be designated, for convenience, the principle of ecumenicity, as represented by the words 'the relation of the Order to the rest of the Buddhist world,' the principle of personal contact, as represented by the words 'it is a relation that subsists, essentially, with individuals,' and the principle of orthodoxy, as represented by the words 'we are happy to extend the hand of spiritual fellowship to all those Buddhists for whom commitment is primary, lifestyle secondary, and who, like us, Go for Refuge to the Buddha, the Dharma, and the Sangha.' For the sake of connectedness of exposition I shall be dealing with the second and third principles in reverse order.

THE PRINCIPLE OF ECUMENISM

It may not have escaped your notice that I spoke, in my paper on the history of my Going for Refuge, not of the relation of the Order to the Buddhist world but of the relation of the Order to the *rest* of the Buddhist world. The word was intended to emphasize the fact that the Order, and with it the FWBO, is a branch of the mighty tree of Buddhism which, for more than 2,500 years, has sheltered a considerable portion of humanity, and that the same vital juice that circulates in the older, bigger branches of that tree circulates in our younger, smaller branch too, even if it circulates in it a little more vigorously than it does in some of them. It is important that we should not only acknowledge this intellectually but also feel it. After all, our doctrinal teachings and methods of meditation, together with our terminology and our iconography, derive exclusively from traditional Buddhist sources, and we therefore might be expected to experience a sense of solidarity with the spiritual and cultural œcumene of which we form a part and with which, moreover, we might be expected to want to be in communication.

But what is this Buddhist world? Most certainly it is not a centralized world like that of Roman Catholicism, with its Pope and its Vatican, and its sacramental and catechetical uniformity. Notwithstanding the establishment of the World Fellowship of Buddhists in 1950, so few and so tenuous are the threads connecting the different parts of the Buddhist world that *effectively* no such thing as a Buddhist world really exists. Instead we have a number of sectarian Buddhist worlds which are divided one from another along doctrinal and other lines and which have – to revert to my previous metaphor – in some cases diverged so widely from the parent trunk that they have difficulty seeing themselves as branches of the same tree or feeling that an identical sap circulates through every one of them. According to the older Western writers on Buddhism there were two such worlds, that of Northern Buddhism and that of Southern Buddhism. In reality, however, the former consisted of two separate worlds, that of Northern Buddhism proper and that of Far Eastern Buddhism. Thus we may speak of there being, in the broadest sense, three Buddhist worlds, though these are such not only geographically and culturally but doctrinally and spiritually as well. Southern Buddhism is synonymous with the Theravāda, the School or Teaching of the Elders, which is found principally in Sri Lanka, Myanmar (Burma), Thailand, Cambodia, and Laos. Northern Buddhism corresponds to the Triyāna Buddhism of Tibet (I am ignoring present-day political realities),[669] Mongolia, and Bhutan, together with parts of Nepal, India, and Russia, wherein elements of the Hīnayāna and the Mahāyāna are subsumed in a synthesis the overall orientation of which is that of the Vajrayāna or Tantric Buddhism. Far Eastern Buddhism is that form of the Buddhist religion which predominates in (Han) China, Japan, Korea, and Vietnam. Here elements of the Hīnayāna and, though to a much more limited extent, of the Vajrayāna, are subsumed in a synthesis the overall emphasis of which is that of the Mahāyāna. All three forms of Buddhism, it should be noted, subsume substantial elements of local, indigenous ethnic culture, some of which are not always content to remain within the bounds prescribed for them.

It is also possible to speak of five Buddhist worlds and five forms of Buddhism, with one of the forms, the Theravāda, belonging to the Hīnayāna, and the remaining four to the Mahāyāna. This is what I have done, in effect, in *A Survey of Buddhism*, where having described the different characteristics of the Hīnayāna and the Mahāyāna in chapter 2, in chapter 3 I utilize the teaching of the five (spiritual) faculties or *indriyas* as a principle for the schematization of the Mahāyāna schools.[670] Applying this principle, I was able to arrive at a list of four movements within the Mahāyāna, which eventually crystallized into four schools. There was an intellectual movement that represented a development of the faculty of wisdom (*prajñā*) and found expression in the Madhyamakavāda or New Wisdom School; a devotional movement that represented a development of the faculty of faith (*śraddhā*) and found expression in the Buddhism of Faith and Devotion; a meditative movement that represented a development of the faculty of meditation (*samādhi*) and found expression in the Yogācāra-Vijñānavāda or Buddhist Idealism; and an activistic movement that represented the faculty of vigour (*vīrya*) and found expression in the Tantra, or Magical Buddhism. Mindfulness (*smṛti*), the fifth (spiritual) faculty, was represented in the history of Buddhism by the various syncretist movements which from time to time endeavoured to bring the different schools into harmony. Out of the four Mahāyāna schools here enumerated, three have not only survived in the East as distinct forms of Buddhism down to the present but also have been introduced in the West. Thus the Buddhism of Faith and Devotion appears in our midst as Pure Land Buddhism, Buddhist Idealism as Zen, and the Tantra as Tibetan Buddhism. The teachings of the New Wisdom School survive as an important element in both Zen and Tibetan Buddhism. As for the Theravāda, this has of course survived in the East as a distinct form of Buddhism down to the present and appears in our midst in various South-east Asian garbs.

In speaking of the relation of the Order to the rest of the Buddhist world one is therefore speaking of it as having, for all practical purposes, four separate relations, one to the Theravāda, one to Pure Land Buddhism, one to Zen, and one to Tibetan Buddhism, each of which inhabits a world of its own, with its distinctive manners and customs, even its distinctive atmosphere, and which more often than not is only vaguely aware of the greater Buddhist world to which, in principle, it belongs. In each case the nature of the relation will be determined, at least to an extent, by certain developments within the form of Buddhism to which the Order happens to be relating, as will transpire in the next section of this paper, when I deal with the principle of orthodoxy. Let me therefore conclude this section by saying something about the more general characteristics of the Theravāda, of Pure Land Buddhism, of Zen, and of Tibetan Buddhism, especially in so far as these characteristics constitute for us in the Order, as well as throughout the FWBO, a source of inspiration and spiritual guidance. First, however, I want to say a few words about the Buddhist world in the geographical sense.

In the course of my lifetime, at least, the portion of the earth's surface traditionally covered by Buddhism has shrunk dramatically. This fact is highlighted, with stark clarity, in an article published in a recent issue of *Tricycle*. Commenting on the undermining of Buddhism in Tibet, China, Mongolia, Vietnam, Laos, and Cambodia through the destruction of the monastic framework upon which the Buddhist community in those countries depended, Stephen Batchelor writes:

> Indeed, it is remarkable to compare the extent of the Buddhist world fifty years ago with what remains today. Never in human history has such a major world religion diminished in size and influence so rapidly. Three or four revolutions in the right places would more or less eliminate traditional Buddhism from the face of the earth.[671]

It is a sobering thought, especially when we consider that during the last fifty years both Christianity and Islam have expanded enormously (though not at the expense of Buddhism itself), with the result that

Buddhism is now the smallest and in certain respects the least influential of the three great world religions. The only bright spots in an otherwise quite gloomy picture are India, where up to ten million followers of the late Dr B. R. Ambedkar have become Buddhists in recent years, and Western Europe, the Americas, and Australasia, where the seed of the Buddha's teaching is steadily taking root in the hearts of thousands of practitioners. Even in those Buddhist countries which have not suffered under Communism, like Thailand and Japan, the demands of consumerism are eroding traditional values and the way of life based on them. Those values are also being eroded by the behaviour of some of their official custodians. On the very day I started writing this paper came the news that a Thai monk addicted to amphetamines had been charged with murdering and robbing a 23-year-old English woman solicitor missing for more than a month on a backpacking holiday. The monk confessed that three days before committing the murder he had raped another woman tourist. Giving details of the case, the South-east Asia correspondent of a leading daily wrote:

> Buddhism in Thailand has been rocked by a series of scandals in recent months. A revered abbot was charged with raping hill tribe girls in his care, a preacher was unfrocked amid allegations of sexual impropriety; a novice was arrested for roasting a still-born baby on a spit in a black magic ritual and six monks were charged with murdering a fellow monk.[672]

Scandals have also rocked the Tibetan diaspora in India, where there were unseemly dissensions between the supporters of rival candidates for the throne of the deceased Karmapa, the immensely wealthy head of the Karma Kagyu school. In the course of these dissensions acts of violence were committed, and an eminent lama died in what many regarded as suspicious circumstances.[673] While we must be careful not to extrapolate too freely from the facts, occurrences such as those reported from Thailand and the Tibetan diaspora suggest that, undermined as it is both from without and within, traditional Buddhism is in a state of decline, and that committed Buddhists everywhere need to give serious thought to the question of how best to preserve the Dharma for the benefit of future generations. One of the ways in which we of the Western Buddhist Order can help preserve the Dharma is by acquainting ourselves with the general characteristics of the Theravāda, of Pure Land Buddhism, of Zen, and of Tibetan Buddhism, especially in so far as these characteristics constitute a source of inspiration and spiritual guidance to us, and it is to the four schools and their scriptures that we must now turn.

The Theravāda is based on the Pāli Tipiṭaka or 'three baskets', that is to say, the Vinaya Piṭaka, the basket or collection of monastic discipline, the Sutta Piṭaka, the basket or collection of the Buddha's sayings and discourses, and the Abhidhamma Piṭaka, the basket or collection of further, i.e. more 'philosophical', teaching, as well as upon the various commentaries to these texts. So far, at least, we have tended to derive inspiration and guidance from what appear to be the older portions of the Tipiṭaka, especially from the *Sutta-Nipāta*, the *Udāna*, the *Itivuttaka*, the *Dhammapada*, and the *Thera-* and *Theri-gātha*, all of which belong to the Sutta Piṭaka, as do the *Dīgha* and *Majjhima Nikāyas*, select discourses from which are also a source of inspiration and guidance for some of us. The only non-canonical Theravādin text to which we have regular recourse is Buddhaghosa's *Visuddhimagga*, the second section of which, on *samādhi*, is particularly useful. All the texts I have mentioned inculcate harmlessness, non-attachment, tranquillity, contentment, forbearance, kindness, mindfulness, effort, and discrimination, and it is these which are the general characteristics of the Theravāda, at its best, as well as being among the essential, definitive qualities of the spiritual life. The same texts also give us, between them, a more vivid impression of the Buddha in his (enlightened) human, historical reality than do any other scriptures, with the possible exception of such portions of the Sanskrit counterpart of the Sutta Piṭaka as survive in the original language or in Chinese or Tibetan translation. This does not mean that the historical necessarily excludes the 'legendary'. As Reginald A. Ray has lately reminded us:

> Western and modernist notions of a demythologized individuality standing apart from and independent of symbol, cult, and legend have no relevance for the early Buddhist case. Gautama, in his own time and in subsequent times, was able to be the Buddha precisely because he was understood to embody, in an unprecedented way, the cosmic and transcendent. Far from being incidental to who he was, myth and cult defined his essential person, for his earliest followers as for later Buddhists.[674]

In my own words, commenting on Ray's assertion,

> we come closest to the historical Buddha precisely when we take the legendary and cultic idiom of his hagiographical tradition most seriously.[675]

That we are able to come close to the Buddha at all, and to derive inspiration and guidance from his personal example as well as from his actual teaching, is largely owing to the fact that we have access to the older portions of the Tipiṭaka, and we are accordingly grateful to the Theravāda for having preserved them. Various selections from the Pāli canon illustrative of the Buddha's life as well as of his teaching are available. One of the best of these is Bhikkhu Ñāṇamoli's *The Life of the Buddha*, which is well known to many of us, as is Dr B. R. Ambedkar's *The Buddha and His Dhamma*.[676]

The three remaining schools, being schools of the Mahāyāna, are all based, ultimately, on the Mahāyāna *sūtras*, though they may have a closer connection with some *sūtras* than with others. There are hundreds of Mahāyāna *sūtras*, by no means all of which have been translated into any European language. Those from which we have so far derived the greatest inspiration and guidance – and they happen to be among the most important Mahāyāna scriptures – are the *Prajñāpāramitā sūtras*, especially the *Diamond* and *Heart Sūtras*, the *Saddharma Puṇḍarīka Sūtra*, the *Vimalakīrti-nirdeśa*, and the *Suvarṇa-prabhāsa Sūtra*.[677] All these works are distinguished by universality of outlook, philosophical profundity, and a willingness, on the part of most of them, to communicate spiritual truths by non-conceptual means – all of which are general characteristics of the schools based on them. They all proclaim, moreover, the bodhisattva ideal, the ideal of absolute spiritual altruism, which in one form or other is the chosen ideal of all schools of the Mahāyāna.

Pure Land Buddhism is based on the two *Sukhāvatī-vyūha sūtras*, the *Larger* and the *Smaller*, and on the *Amitāyur-dhyāna Sūtra*. All three works describe Sukhāvatī, 'the Blissful', the Pure Land of the Buddha Amitābha, as well as describing Amitabha (or Amitāyus) himself and his two bodhisattva attendants.[678] A Pure Land, as distinct from one that is impure, is an archetypal realm which transcends conditioned existence and which apart from the presiding Buddha and his bodhisattvas is inhabited exclusively by gods and men. There are hundreds of thousands of such Pure Lands, but the most excellent of them is Sukhāvatī, the Pure Land of Buddha Amitābha, in which are concentrated all imaginable perfections of all imaginable Pure Lands. In other words what we are presented with, in these three *sūtras*, is the vision of an ideally beautiful Buddha in ideally beautiful surroundings. The contemplation of beauty gives rise to love, and when the beauty contemplated is the sublime beauty of Buddhahood, as manifested in the radiant figure of Amitābha, that love takes the form of faith and devotion, through which the devotee is assimilated to the object of his devotion and achieves, in the symbolic language of the *sūtras*, rebirth in Sukhāvatī. As yet, the Order as a whole has not paid much attention to the three Happy Land *sūtras* (as I have called them elsewhere), and therefore has not derived much inspiration and guidance from them, though I myself made a close study of them many years ago and at one time thought of lecturing on them, as I had done on other Mahāyāna sūtras.[679] But though we may not derive inspiration and guidance from this group of *sūtras* directly, in a way we do so indirectly. Many Buddhas besides Amitābha, as well as many bodhisattvas, have Pure Lands of their own, some of which are described in *sūtras*. Like the Happy Land *sūtras*, these texts establish a kind of pattern, in which a figure embodying the ideal of Enlightenment occupies the centre of a realm representing the conditions most conducive to the realization of that ideal. This pattern is exemplified in many of our *sādhanas*, in the course of which we visualize at the centre of a mandala of other divinities, or of the syllables of a mantra, a Buddha or bodhisattva who is the object of our faith and devotion and, at the same time, a source of inspiration and guidance. Some of us also derive inspiration from the various hymns in praise of this or that bodhisattva which, though they may not be a part of Pure Land Buddhism in the Japanese sectarian form in which we usually encounter this school in the West, are none the less a product of that Buddhism of Faith and Devotion of which Pure Land Buddhism, in all its forms, is itself a part.

Zen claims not to be based on any *sūtra* or group of *sūtras*. In the words of the well-known stanza in which it summarizes itself and defines its attitude, it is a special transmission *outside the scriptures*, does not depend upon words and letters, points directly to the mind, and points to the realization of Buddhahood by seeing into one's own nature.[680]

Historically speaking, however, Zen seems to have come into existence, in its original form as Chan, among a group of Chinese students of the *Laṅkāvatāra Sūtra*, though later the work was superseded by the *Diamond Sūtra* and, to a lesser extent, by the *Śūraṅgama Sūtra* and the *Vimalakīrti-nirdeśa*. For practical purposes, Zen bases itself on collections of anecdotes of the sayings and doings of ancient masters of the school such as the *Blue Cliff Record* and the *Gateless Gate*.[681] Despite its aversion to scriptural studies it has in fact produced a vast literature, little of which has been translated into any European language. Probably the classic Zen texts from which we in the Order have derived most inspiration are the *Sūtra of Wei Lang* (*Huineng*), otherwise known as the *Platform Scripture*, and Hakuin's 'Song of Enlightenment',[682] both of which are characterized by an emphasis on the necessity of direct realization of the highest spiritual truth. For some of us inspiration also comes from Zen by way of the poetry of Bashō and Ryōkan, with its appreciation of natural beauty, its sympathy for all forms of life, and its total disregard of unessentials, as well as by way of those other 'arts' which, under the influence of Zen, were transformed into paths to Enlightenment.[683] Nor must I forget to mention the words of the Tang dynasty master Baizhang which, after reverberating down the centuries and creating a distinctively Zen form of monasticism, have influenced our ideas about how the Movement and its activities should be supported – the famous words, 'A day of no working is a day of no eating.'[684]

Tibetan Buddhism is based on the Kangyur and Tangyur and, in the case of some of its subdivisions, on the *Rinchen Termo*, as well as on a variety of orally transmitted teachings. Broadly speaking, it represents a transplantation to the soil of Tibet of the entire heritage of Buddhist spirituality, thought, and culture as this existed in Northern India at the time of the Pala dynasty. Prominent among the works of Tibetan origin from which we in the Order have so far derived inspiration and guidance are the *Bardo Thödol*, better known as the *Tibetan Book of the Dead*, the biography and songs of Milarepa, the *Life and Liberation of Padmasambhava*, Gampopa's *Jewel Ornament of Liberation*, and the various texts translated in Geshe Wangyal's *Door of Liberation*.[685] It is noteworthy that two of these works, the *Tibetan Book of the Dead* and the *Life and Liberation of Padmasambhava*, are Nyingma *termas*, while the biography and songs of Milarepa and Gampopa's *Jewel*

Ornament of Liberation are of Kagyu provenance. Both the *Tibetan Book of the Dead* and the *Life and Liberation of Padmasambhava*, moreover, are characterized by extreme richness of imagery – a richness that characterizes Tibetan Buddhism as a whole, especially in its ritual and iconographic aspects. Probably it is in the archetypal images of Tibetan religious art, even more than in their literary counterparts in the two *termas*, that many of us find a great part of the inspiration we derive from Tibetan Buddhism. Be that as it may, there is no doubt that Tibetan Buddhist iconography is popular throughout the Euro-American wing of the Movement, though for my part I would like to see Japanese Buddhist art enjoying equal popularity.

Such, then, are the general characteristics of the Theravāda, of Pure Land Buddhism, of Zen, and of Tibetan Buddhism, especially in so far as these characteristics constitute for us in the Order, as well as throughout the FWBO, a source of inspiration and spiritual guidance. We derive that inspiration and guidance, however, not so much from these schools in the form in which they survive in the East, and have been introduced in the West, as from a selection of the scriptures on which, in principle, they respectively are based. As I pointed out when speaking of the Buddhist world, traditional Buddhism, undermined as it is both without and within, is in a state of decline. Actually it has been in a state of decline for a very long time, in that all four schools, in their different ways and in varying degrees, have tended to emphasize what is secondary in Buddhism at the expense of what is primary. This fact has an important bearing on the whole question of the relation of the Order to the rest of the Buddhist world, or rather, to the schools of which, for practical purposes, it consists so far as we are concerned. Which brings me to the second of my three principles.

THE PRINCIPLE OF ORTHODOXY

In 1957 I wrote an essay entitled 'The Meaning of Orthodoxy in Buddhism'.[686] I wrote it in response to the assertion, by a leading Pāli scholar, that the Theravāda was 'certainly the most orthodox form of Buddhism',[687] a description which effectively asserted, with equal decision, that the non-Theravādin schools were less orthodox, or unorthodox, or even positively heretical. In this essay, having pointed out that the exact literal equivalent of 'orthodoxy' (from the Greek *ortho*, right, true + *doxos*, opinion) was right view, I defined orthodoxy, in the Buddhist sense, as

> 1. Of right views (*sammādiṭṭhika*); hence, adhering to the Dharma of the Buddha as formulated in the stereotype formulas such as the four noble truths and the three characteristics (*tilakkhaṇa*) without inclining either to the extreme of eternalism (*sassatavāda*) or the extreme of nihilism (*ucchedavāda*); – opposed to wrong views (*micchā-diṭṭhi*), both in the wider sense of the erroneous beliefs of non-Buddhists and the narrower one of a misunderstanding of the Dharma by one who has taken the Three Refuges; as, an *orthodox bhikṣu*.... 2. According to, or congruous with, the doctrines of the scriptures common to all schools of Buddhism, especially as expressed in the stereotype formulas such as the four noble truths and the three characteristics (*trilakṣaṇa*) which are found in both the scriptures which are and the scriptures which are not common to all schools; as, an *orthodox* opinion, book, etc.... 3. Conventional, a matter not of natural (*pakati*) but of conventional (*paññatti*) morality; as, an *orthodox* prostration.[688]

This definition enabled me to vindicate the doctrinal and scriptural orthodoxy of the Mahāyāna and to show that the orthodoxy of the Theravāda was not a matter of so much certainty as had been supposed. It also enabled me to distinguish between an orthodox Buddhist and an orthodox Mahāyāna or Hīnayāna Buddhist and, by implication, between an orthodox Buddhist and an unorthodox Buddhist.

But what is an orthodox Buddhist? At the time of writing 'The Meaning of Orthodoxy in Buddhism' I did not realize the absolute centrality, in the genuinely Buddhist life, of the act of Going for Refuge, or rather, though I realized it to some extent I had not yet worked out its implications. I therefore did not connect the principle of orthodoxy with the fact of the absolute centrality of the act of Going for Refuge. Now, thirty-nine years later, the time has come for that connection to be made. To put it briefly, and in terms with which we are familiar, an orthodox Buddhist is one for whom Going for Refuge is primary, observance of the precepts secondary, or better still, one for whom Going for Refuge is primary, observance of the precepts (and practice of meditation etc.) secondary, and lifestyle tertiary. From this it follows that one for whom the act of Going for Refuge is not the central, definitive act of the Buddhist life is *not* an orthodox Buddhist, even though they may have formally 'taken' the Three Refuges and be professed adherents of orthodox Buddhism as defined in my essay. Indeed, going a step further and taking a plunge into paradox, it could even be asserted that there is in truth no such thing as orthodox Buddhism but only orthodox Buddhists, that is, Buddhists for whom Going for Refuge is primary, observance of the precepts secondary, and lifestyle tertiary. But paradox or no paradox, we have to take into account the fact that the followers of the four schools in connection with which, for all practical purposes, the question of the relation between the Order and the rest of the Buddhist world arises, are not, *in this sense*, orthodox Buddhists. They are not orthodox Buddhists because, for them, something other than Going for Refuge is of primary importance in the Buddhist life, at least in practice, and the fact that such is the case affects the nature of our relation to them as, indeed, it affects the nature of their relation to us.

At the beginning of this paper, quoting from the end of my paper on the history of my Going for Refuge, I spoke of our being happy to extend the hand of spiritual fellowship

> to all those Buddhists for whom commitment is primary, lifestyle secondary, and who, like us, go for Refuge to the Buddha, the Dharma, and the Sangha.

This might be taken to mean that we are happy to extend the hand of spiritual fellowship only to *orthodox* Buddhists. It was not my intention to impose any such limitation. There are degrees of spiritual fellowship, as we shall see when we come to the third of my three principles, the principle of personal contact. Meanwhile, we have to get to grips with the principle with which we are at present concerned, the principle of orthodoxy, and examine the different ways in which the Theravāda, Pure Land Buddhism, Zen, and Tibetan Buddhism, emphasize what is secondary in the Buddhist life at the expense of what is primary, or in other words, the different ways in which they are unorthodox rather than orthodox.

The Theravāda places its emphasis fairly and squarely on monasticism, on being a monk (*bhikkhu*) not a layman. It is the yellow-robed monk who is the real Buddhist, the white-clad layman or laywoman (and even the 'nun', whether Sinhalese *dasasilamata* or Thai *maechi*)[689] being at best only a second-class Buddhist whose principal duty is to support the monk. Thus the Theravāda's emphasis is on lifestyle, despite the fact that the traditional Refuge-Going formula is well known to all Theravādin Buddhists and is ceremonially recited, in Pāli, by monks and laity alike. Nor is that all. In actual practice, more often than not, it is not so much the spirit as the letter of monasticism which is emphasized, great importance being attached, in particular, to valid monastic ordination in the technical Vinaya sense, with the result that although some of the general characteristics of the true Theravāda certainly do shine through, here and there, today the school as a whole is vitiated by that very formalism of which the Buddha himself, according to the older portions of the Theravāda's own Pāli Tipiṭaka, was so persistently critical. I have given examples of this formalism in *A Survey of Buddhism* and, more recently, in *Was the Buddha a Bhikkhu?*,[690] and there is no need for me to enlarge upon the subject in this paper. Here I am concerned not so much with the Theravāda's emphasis on monasticism as with the way in which that emphasis affects our relation to this school and this school's relation to us. But before I turn to the relation of the Order to the Theravāda let me make a general point in connection with this question of formalism. Though I have tended, in my writings, to criticize only Theravādin formalism, it should not be thought that other forms of Buddhism are free from this canker. The reason for my criticizing Theravādin formalism, specifically, was that it was Theravādin formalism which, in my early days in India, I came across, not to say came up against. Subsequently I became aware that formalism, whether monastic or non-monastic, was a feature of much traditional Buddhism, almost regardless of school. It was, indeed, a danger that threatened the integrity of the religious life in all its forms and one against which even orthodox Buddhists needed to be on their guard.[691]

As the Theravāda places its emphasis on monasticism, even on monasticism in the merely formal sense, it sees the Buddhist community as being divided into two distinct groups. On the one hand there are the monks, who are the real Buddhists, on the other there are the laity (including the 'nuns'), who are the not-so-real Buddhists, as I once called them, who are expected to feed, clothe, and generally support the monks, and to observe in their dealings with them a protocol expressive of the profoundest veneration. But to which of these groups do members of the Western Buddhist Order/Trailokya Bauddha Mahasangha belong? So far as the Theravāda is concerned the answer is obvious. They belong to the second group, that of the laity, for not having received *bhikkhu* ordination (there is no question of *bhikkhunī* ordination, in the case of women Order members) they are not monks, and there is no other group to which those who are *not* monks *could* belong. Hence when a Theravādin monk meets an Order member – and it is usually a Theravādin monk, not a Theravādin layman, especially on 'official' occasions – he will automatically assume that, as the latter obviously is not a monk, he is a layman. As a layman he will therefore treat him, expecting that the Order member, in his turn, will treat *him* as a monk, with all that this implies. In these circumstances it is not surprising that there should sometimes arise situations which would be comical were they not based on a lamentable misunderstanding, on the part of the Theravādin monk, of a fundamental principle of the Dharma, the principle, namely, that spiritual attainment has little or nothing to do with socio-religious status, and that one is no more a *bhikkhu*, in the true sense, simply because one has been 'ordained' and wears a yellow robe, than one is a real Brahmin simply because one has been born into a 'Brahmin' family and wears a sacred thread. An Order member might even find himself (or herself) in the position of being condescendingly 'put right' as regards Buddhism by a globe-trotting career monk who obviously had no feeling for the spiritual life. On the other hand, it is important that when an Order member meets a Theravādin monk he (or she) should be open to the possibility that the monk is a real monk, even an orthodox Buddhist, and that it might be possible for one to relate to him not as though one was a 'layman', which would mean not really relating to him at all, but on the basis of one's being an Order member, that is, on the basis of one's Going for Refuge, effectively at least, to the Buddha, the Dharma, and the Sangha. Although there are incomparably more Theravādin monks in the East than there are in the West, an Order member probably stands a better chance of meeting a real monk, *and* of being able to relate to him on the basis of a common commitment to the Three Jewels, in the West than in the Theravādin lands of South-east Asia. In the latter the Theravāda is still firmly based on what Reginald

A. Ray calls the two-tiered model of Buddhism,[692] which makes it difficult for Buddhists who do not accept that model to extend the hand of spiritual fellowship either literally or metaphorically. How the difficulty might best be overcome we shall see in connection with the principle of personal contact.

Although the Theravāda places its emphasis on monasticism, in recent decades there has arisen within its fold a predominantly lay movement, generally known as the vipassanā or 'insight meditation' movement, which emphasizes what is secondary in Buddhism at the expense of what is primary in a different way. This movement, now well represented in the West, had its origins in Myanmar (Burma), in the efforts of a handful of monk and lay teachers to revive and popularize the practice of mindful awareness as taught by the Buddha in his discourse on the foundations of mindfulness. Nowadays, unfortunately, some of the movement's leading personalities not only emphasize meditation, in the sense of 'insight meditation', at the expense of Going for Refuge; they also ignore Going for Refuge completely. In extreme cases, having reduced meditation to '*vipassanā*', and *vipassanā* itself to a matter of mere technique, they take it out of its Buddhist context and seek to combine it with elements derived from other sources, so that it is no longer *vipassanā* in the traditional sense but something quite different. To the extent that one is a practitioner of this non-Buddhist '*vipassanā*' one is not a Buddhist, whether of the Theravāda or any other school, and there can be no question of an Order member relating to such a person on the basis of a common Going for Refuge, though he (or she) may relate to them positively in other ways.

The fact that the Order does not emphasize monasticism does not mean that there is no place for it within our ranks. There is certainly a place for Sūtra-style monasticism, as I have called it in *Forty-Three Years Ago*, though there is a place for it only as an *expression* of commitment to the Three Jewels, not as *constitutive* of that commitment, and I am glad to see that since I wrote that little book, three years ago, the number of Order members observing the training rule of chastity as *anagārikas* has doubled, from twenty-odd to forty-odd. Similarly, the fact that the Order does not emphasize meditation, in the sense of 'insight meditation', at the expense of Going for Refuge, does not mean that there is no place in it for *vipassanā* in the more traditional form which is common, in principle, to practically all schools of Buddhism.

Much less still does it mean that we do not regard the development of both calm (*śamatha*) and insight (*vipaśyanā*) as essential elements in our spiritual life.

If the Theravāda places its emphasis on monasticism, then the Jōdo Shinshū – the form of Pure Land Buddhism we are most likely to encounter in the West – goes to the opposite extreme and places it, in practice, on the laical life. This is not to say that it emphasizes the laical life in principle. In principle it places its emphasis on birth in Sukhāvatī through faith in the compassion of the Buddha Amitābha, especially as this finds expression in his famous eighteenth vow, according to which he would not gain Buddhahood unless those who had faith in him, and who wished to be born in his Pure Land, should be born there when he had gained it.[693] Since he has, in fact, gained Buddhahood, it follows that those who have faith in him are assured of such birth. Nevertheless the Jōdo Shinshū also distinguishes between the path of dependence on 'self power' (*jiriki*), which is the path followed by other schools, and the path of dependence on 'other power' (*tariki*), that is, on the power of Amitābha's vow, which is the path the Jōdo Shinshū itself follows. Monasticism, with its numerous rules, obviously belongs to the path of dependence on 'self power', and as such it has no place in the form of Pure Land Buddhism represented by the Jōdo Shinshū. Since there was no question of their being monks, followers of the school were lay people by default, as it were, for although Shinran Shōnin, the school's thirteenth-century founder, described himself as being neither a monk nor a layman, he married and raised a family and was in effect a layman. Rennyo, the eighth head priest in succession to Shinran, who is honoured as the second founder of the Jōdo Shinshū, married seven times and had twenty-seven children, his youngest son being born when he was in his eighty-fifth year. Thus there is in practice a definite emphasis on the laical life in the Jōdo Shinshū, even though there would appear to be nothing in the school's teaching to prevent its followers from living as monks (or nuns) out of gratitude to Amitābha for having assured them of birth in Sukhāvatī. In the Order we of course follow the path of dependence on 'self power', as the very fact of our going for Refuge to the Three Jewels and undertaking to observe the ten precepts indeed implies. This does not however mean that what may be experienced, in relation to the ego, as an 'other power', may not come into operation at a certain stage of our spiritual development.

It is well known that '*zen*' is the Japanese form of the Chinese word '*chan*', which is itself a corruption of the Sanskrit '*dhyāna*', usually rendered in English as 'meditation'. Thus the Zen school is the meditation school. Whether in the form of *zazen* or 'just sitting' practice favoured by its Sōtō branch, or in that of the koan practice favoured by its Rinzai branch, the emphasis of the Zen school falls unambiguously on meditation. According to tradition the Buddha gained Enlightenment while meditating beneath a peepul tree. Meditation is one of the three practices which he is represented, in the Pāli scriptures, as time and again recommending to his disciples during the last months of his life, the two other practices being right conduct (*śīla*) and wisdom (*prajñā*). Small wonder, then, that the Zen school should emphasize meditation. Unfortunately, it came to emphasize it at the expense of Going for Refuge, besides falling victim to formalism in the practice of meditation itself. Abbot Tenshin Anderson, a leading North American teacher of Zen, confesses:

> For many years at Zen Center I had never really noticed that I had taken refuge in Buddha, Dharma, Sangha.... This basic practice, this fundamental practice, which all Buddhists do, many Zen students never even heard about. It was said, but we didn't hear it, because it wasn't emphasized strongly enough. In some way our sitting practice is so essential, so profound, that we feel that we can overlook some of the more basic practices.[694]

That anyone should *not notice* that they had 'taken refuge' in the Three Jewels seems incredible, and the failure may well be connected with the fact that Abbot Anderson, like so many Western Buddhists, speaks of a *taking* rather than of a *going*. Be that as it may, a sitting practice so profound that one can 'overlook' something as basic as Going for Refuge is hardly profound in the Buddhist sense, particularly when basic means, in this context, not elementary but fundamental to the living of the Buddhist life in all its aspects and at every level. Moreover, the lack of emphasis on 'taking refuge' of which Tenshin Anderson speaks makes it all the more easy for 'Zen' to be detached from Buddhism and even taught by non-Buddhists, in which case it is no more truly Zen than non-Buddhist '*vipassanā*' is *vipassanā* in the traditional sense. Another leading North American teacher, Roshi Philip Kapleau, does not hesitate to cite 'the appropriation of fundamental elements of Zen training by psychotherapists ... teaching their patients meditation and equating it with spiritual liberation' as an example of the *real* corruption in Buddhism, nor to speak of 'Zen teachers sanctioning Catholic priests and nuns as well as rabbis and ministers to teach Zen' as being in many ways the most bizarre of all the threats to the integrity of Zen.[695]

Tibetan Buddhism is probably a richer and more complex phenomenon than any of the other schools with which, for all practical purposes, the Order's relation to the rest of the Buddhist world consists. In fact it comprises not one school but many, each with its own teachings, practices, and institutions. These schools all operate, however, within the framework of a common theoretical and practical schema, that of the three *yānas*, the three 'vehicles' or 'ways', i.e. the Hīnayāna, the Mahāyāna, and the Vajrayāna, to one or other of which all the different doctrines and methods of Tibetan Buddhism are systematically assigned. Thus Going for Refuge is assigned to the Hīnayāna, the arising of the *bodhicitta* or will to Enlightenment to the Mahāyāna, and *abhiṣeka* or 'Tantric initiation' to the Vajrayāna. As the three *yānas* are regarded not just as different levels of the Buddha's teaching but also as successive stages of the path to Supreme Enlightenment, the result is that for Tibetan Buddhism Going for Refuge is simply the means to the arising of the *bodhicitta*, and the arising of the *bodhicitta* the means to the receiving of *abhiṣeka*. In this way the arising of the *bodhicitta* comes to be emphasized at the expense of Going for Refuge, even as the receiving of *abhiṣeka* comes to be emphasized at the expense of the arising of the *bodhicitta*. In other words, Mahāyāna is emphasized at the expense of Hīnayāna, Vajrayāna at the expense of Mahāyāna. Although in theory the Buddhism of Tibet is a *triyāna* or 'triple vehicle' Buddhism, in practice it is predominantly Tantric in character, and it is as Tantric Buddhism that we usually encounter it in the West.

The fact that the arising of the *bodhicitta* is emphasized at the expense of Going for Refuge, and the receiving of *abhiṣeka* at the expense of the arising of the *bodhicitta*, makes it possible for individual Tantric teachings and practices to be emphasized at the expense of the Vajrayāna as a whole. Indeed, it makes it possible for them to be emphasized to such an extent that in the end they are taken out of the *triyāna* framework and detached, not from Tibetan Buddhism only but also, like '*vipassanā*' and 'Zen', from Buddhism itself. This is what has happened in the case of the Dzogchen or 'Great Perfection' teaching, the ultimate teaching of the Nyingma school, which according to some of its modern exponents has no essential connection with Buddhism. However else we may relate to them, obviously we cannot relate to such people on the basis of a common commitment to the Three Jewels.

Although Tibetan Buddhism regards Going for Refuge to the Buddha, the Dharma, and the Sangha simply as a means to the arising of the *bodhicitta*, within the Vajrayāna the Three Refuges have an esoteric counterpart known as the three roots. These are the lama or guru, the root of blessings, the *yidam* or chosen divinity, the root of accomplishment, and the Dharma protector, the root of activity. To the extent that the three roots represent a recognition, on the part of Tibetan Buddhism, of what may be termed the *principle* of Going for Refuge, as well as a recognition of the fact that at higher levels of spiritual experience this principle may exist in subtler forms, it is to be welcomed. None the less, in Tibetan Buddhism, at least as often encountered in the West, the teaching of the three roots can have, in practice, disastrous consequences. It can lead to the perversion of Tibetan Buddhism itself and the betrayal of some of the fundamental principles of the Dharma. To begin with, the importance of the lama, the root of blessings, is emphasized at the expense of that of the two other roots. The disciple is taught to see the lama as Buddha and to have unquestioning faith in him. Though such an approach may have a certain validity, when correctly understood, in practice it results, only too often, in the lama being regarded as infallible (and his behaviour therefore as beyond criticism), as well as in a surrendering, on the part of the disciple, of his (or her) intellectual independence and moral and spiritual autonomy. This is a far cry from the world of the *Kālāma Sutta* and from the Buddha's exhortation, as preserved in the Tibetan scriptures themselves, to test his words as the goldsmith tests gold in the fire.[696]

Moreover, the lama is the *Tantric* guru. He is the bestower of 'Tantric initiation'. Unfortunately for us in the West, when the tantras were translated into Tibetan the Sanskrit word *abhiṣeka*, signifying 'aspersion' or 'sprinkling with water', was rendered as *wangkur* or 'bestowal of power'. This has made possible the adoption of the fashionable term 'empowerment', with all its ideological connotations, as the standard term for *abhiṣeka* or Tantric initiation. Nowadays a lot of people feel deprived of power. But as they want power, and generally want something or someone to 'empower' them, it is not surprising that there should be a widespread demand for *empowerment*, Tantric and otherwise. Where there is a demand, there will be a supply. Tibetan Buddhism in the West would seem to be occupied, to a great extent, with the giving of Tantric initiations. Not only are these initiations advertised in the Buddhist and alternative press; they are open to anyone, Buddhist or non-Buddhist, who is in a position to pay for them, even though according to Vajrayāna tradition they are to be given only after one has gone for Refuge and developed the *bodhicitta*. Thus there is a wholesale commercialization and vulgarization of Tibetan Buddhism in general and the Vajrayāna in particular, a commercialization and vulgarization involving tens of thousands of people and millions of US dollars (it is usually US dollars). There is a lot more I could say on the subject, but I shall leave it for another occasion.

From this very rapid survey it should be evident that while the Theravāda, Pure Land Buddhism, Zen, and Tibetan Buddhism, all emphasize what is secondary in Buddhism at the expense of what is primary they do not all emphasize the same secondary thing. The way in which the Order relates to them will therefore vary, at least initially. Yet although they emphasize what is of secondary, even of tertiary, importance in the Buddhist life at the expense of what is primary, each school is based, ultimately, on scriptures and other works in which the centrality of the act of Going for Refuge is made sufficiently clear. It should therefore not be difficult for an open-minded follower of any school to appreciate the importance of that act, at least to an extent, and indeed there are cases where we actually find this happening. In his essay *The Threefold Refuge* the late Nyanaponika Thera explores the meaning of Going for Refuge from the standpoint of a liberal Theravādin, besides trying to find a way of reviving the practice of Going for Refuge as an act of individual commitment to the Three Jewels, as I and a group of Order members and Mitras discovered when we studied the essay at Padmaloka in the autumn of 1978.[697] Whether any present-day follower of Pure Land Buddhism emphasizes the centrality of Going for Refuge to the Three Jewels I do not know, but I notice that Rennyo, the 'second founder' of the Jōdo Shinshū, in his letters repeatedly refers to the fundamental importance of taking refuge in Amitābha.[698] I also gather, from personal correspondence, that in the Jōdo Shinshū there are two levels of ordination, in both of which the ordinand repeats (apparently in Chinese, with Japanese pronunciation) the standard threefold Refuge-taking formula. In view of the fact that Śākyamuni the historical Buddha and Amitābha the 'archetypal' or even transcendental Buddha are ultimately identical, and the fact that real Going for Refuge and the path of dependence on the 'other power' are in principle synonymous, it should therefore not be difficult for followers of the Jōdo Shinshū to recognize the absolute centrality for the Buddhist life of the act of Going for Refuge.

Followers of Zen should have no difficulty recognizing it either. I have already quoted Tenshin Anderson's moving confession that, astonishing as this might seem, he had never really noticed that he had taken refuge in the Three Jewels and that many Zen students had never even heard about this basic, fundamental practice. How, then, did he come to realize its importance? It was, he tells us, through the teaching and example of Dōgen, the founder (in Japan) of the Sōtō branch of Zen, the branch to which the American abbot himself belongs. Dōgen's last act as he was dying was to circumambulate a pillar on which he had written the words Buddha, Dharma, Sangha, saying as he did so,

> In the beginning, in the middle, and in the end, in your life as you approach death, always, through all births and deaths, always take refuge in Buddha, Dharma, Sangha.'[699]

The centrality of the act of Going for Refuge could hardly be more strikingly affirmed. Tibetan Buddhism can recognize the centrality of Going for Refuge only if it acknowledges that the latter is *not* simply a means to the arising of the *bodhicitta*, and we in fact do find at least one eminent contemporary lama coming close to just such an acknowledgement. In his commentary on the *Samādhirāja Sūtra* Thrangu Rinpoche appears to treat 'forming the bodhisattva resolve' and 'taking refuge in the Three Jewels' as *alternative* paths to the development of an extraordinary, as distinct from a mediocre, motivation for Dharma practice.[700]

In our attempts to relate to the Theravāda and the Jōdo Shinshū, Zen, and Tibetan Buddhism, we must, therefore, bear in mind that it is possible for each of these schools to come to an appreciation of the importance of Going for Refuge in the light of its own tradition. This brings me to my third and last principle, with which I shall be dealing more briefly than I have dealt with the principle of ecumenicity and the principle of orthodoxy.

In some of my writings and lectures I have spoken in terms of the group and the individual, and distinguished the individual (who is not the individual*ist*) from what I call the 'group member'.[701] One who goes effectively for Refuge is *ipso facto* an individual. Indeed only an individual *can* go for Refuge in this way, though a group member is of course capable of an ethnic or cultural Going for Refuge, which strictly speaking is not a Going for Refuge at all. Order members, by virtue of their (at least) effective Going for Refuge are individuals, and their 'membership' of the Order is therefore not a group membership. It is not a group membership because the Order itself is not a group but something for which we have no word in the English language but which may be termed a spiritual community, in the sense of a community united by what its 'members' have in common *spiritually*, that is, by their common commitment to the Three Jewels. When I speak of the relation of the Order to the rest of the Buddhist world, which in practice means its relation to the Theravāda, to Pure Land Buddhism, to Zen, and to Tibetan Buddhism, I am therefore not speaking of the relation of one 'Buddhist group' to other 'Buddhist groups'. In the words with which I ended my paper on the history of my Going for Refuge, and which I have already quoted at the beginning of this paper, the relation of the Order to the rest of the Buddhist world is a relation that subsists, essentially, with individuals.

This is not to say that the Order does not have relations, through the FWBO Communications Office and in other ways, with a number of different Buddhist organizations, even though these organizations do think of themselves as being 'Buddhist groups' and of the FWBO (the Order included) as being likewise a Buddhist group. The FWBO is in fact an active member of the European Buddhist Union, as well as being a member, through the Poona TBMSG, of the World Fellowship of Buddhists.[702] In relating to these bodies, however, we attach the greatest importance to personal contact. Those of us who have the responsibility of liaising with 'other' Buddhist groups therefore do our best to relate to them in our capacity *as individuals*, not just as faceless 'representatives' of the FWBO. It is as individuals – individuals who have gone for Refuge to the Three Jewels – that we extend to them the hand of spiritual fellowship, in this way seeking to place the relationship between the

Order and their organization on the basis of friendship between some at least of our respective members. Only on such a basis, I believe, is genuine co-operation between different parts of the Buddhist world really possible. None the less, we have not found it easy to develop the kind of friendship to which I have referred. Buddhist organizations, accustomed as they generally are to thinking of their relations with other Buddhist groups in collective, 'political' terms, find it difficult to grasp the idea of placing those relations on the basis of personal friendship between individuals or even to understand what the Order is getting at when it talks in this way. There is also the fact that in many parts of the Western world the ideal and institution of friendship, especially friendship between men, has lost much of its traditional significance and is even regarded with suspicion. All the same, we continue to extend the hand of spiritual fellowship to the representatives of such Buddhist groups as we are in contact with, in the hope they will reciprocate, as some of them have indeed already started doing.

In extending that hand there are a number of considerations that we have to bear in mind, both in justice to ourselves and out of respect for others. Subhuti has dealt with most of them in the third part of the lecture to which I have already referred, and there is no need for me to go over the same ground. In any case, I have promised to deal with the principle of personal contact more briefly than I have dealt with the two other principles. I shall therefore confine myself to making three points, which could perhaps be known as three points for Order members relating to the rest of the Buddhist world, which in practice of course means Order members relating to individual followers of the Theravāda, Pure Land Buddhism, Zen, and Tibetan Buddhism. Before I make these points, however, I would like to emphasize a point of a much more general nature, the importance of which should not be overlooked. As you know, in the Order we practise and teach – the *mettā bhāvana* or 'development of loving-kindness' meditation, in which feelings of ardent goodwill are successively directed to oneself, a friend, a neutral person, an enemy, and, eventually, to all living beings. But this does not mean that *mettā* is something one experiences only when seated on the meditation cushion. Far from it. *Mettā* or loving-kindness is an emotion which ideally the Buddhist should feel at all times (at least when awake), in all places, and with regard to every person – and every animal – with whom he (or she) comes in contact, irrespective of that person's nationality, race, religion, age, social position, or sexual orientation. Extending the hand of spiritual fellowship to other Buddhists thus does not exclude the possibility of friendship with those who are not Buddhists. In principle we extend the hand of friendship to all. Our deepest friendships, however, at least potentially, will always be with those who, like us, go for Refuge to the Three Jewels, especially when for them, too, the act of Going for Refuge is the central act of the Buddhist life. The important point of a more general nature having been made, now for my three points for Order members relating to the rest of the Buddhist world.

First point: Do not allow yourself to be put in a false position. According to the dictionary, a false position is 'a situation in which a person is forced to act or seems to be acting against his principles or interests' (*Collins*), or, more succinctly, 'one in which [a] person must seem to act against his principles' (*Concise Oxford*). An Order member is in a false position when he (or she) appears to behave as though he was not an Order member, that is, appears to behave as though he was not one who (at least) effectively goes for Refuge to the Three Jewels and for whom Going for Refuge is the central, definitive act of the Buddhist life. In other words, an Order member is in a false position when he (or she) appears to behave as though he was not, in fact, a real Buddhist and not one for whom, moreover, commitment is primary, lifestyle secondary. A simple and obvious example of the way in which an Order member may be put in this position is what happens when he meets a Theravādin *bhikkhu*. The Theravāda, of course, sees the Buddhist community as being divided into two distinct groups, that of the monks, who alone are the real Buddhists, and that of the laity, who are the not-so-real Buddhists. As the Order Member does not wear a yellow robe, and is not shaven-headed, the *bhikkhu* will therefore assume that, if he is a Buddhist at all, he is a lay Buddhist, and will treat him accordingly, as I have already pointed out when dealing with the principle of orthodoxy. He may, in all innocence, even ask the Order member how many times a year he visits the local (Theravādin) temple and makes offerings to the monks. This is like being asked whether one has stopped beating one's mother. The Order member will be able to 'answer' the *bhikkhu*'s question only by challenging his assumptions, which will necessarily involve going into such matters as the difference between commitment and lifestyle and the importance of *not* emphasizing the latter at the expense of the former. All this may well take time, especially if the *bhikkhu* finds it difficult to understand what the Order member is getting at, and in any case the Order member will be able to challenge the *bhikkhu* only if he is firmly established in his own Going for Refuge and has a thorough grasp of the principles on which the Order is based. But whether or not it takes time, and whether or not the *bhikkhu* has difficulty understanding what he is getting at, the Order member will conduct his side of the discussion with courtesy, tact, and good humour.

There are a number of other ways in which an Order member may be put in a false position, and appear not to be a real Buddhist. He (or she) may be asked if he practises 'insight meditation', the assumption being, in this case, that if one is not practising *vipassanā* in its modern 'Burmese' form one is not really meditating at all and has no spiritual life worth mentioning. Similarly, an Order member may be asked how many Zen *sesshins* he has attended or which Tantric initiations he has received from which Tibetan lamas. In these cases, too, he will 'answer' the question by challenging the assumptions on which it is based in the way I have indicated.

Second point: Look for the deepest common ground. Here the emphasis is on 'deepest'. Human beings have a lot of things in common. To begin with, they have in common the fact that they are members of the human race – that they are all risen apes or fallen angels or both. It is because human beings are basically one that it is possible, as I once told a Bombay audience I truly and deeply believed, for us 'to communicate with any other human being, to feel for any other human being, to be friends with any other human being.'[703] But there are levels of communication; there are levels of friendship. Ideally, an Order member should relate to the representative of a Buddhist group on the basis of what they have in common *as Buddhists*, rather than on the basis of a common interest in, for example, vintage motor cars or triangular postage stamps or on the basis of the fact that both parties happen to be parents or attended the same public school – though all these can, of course, serve as points of departure. What Buddhists have in common, as Buddhists, is the fact that they all go for Refuge to the Three Jewels. There are, however, a number of different levels of Going for Refuge: ethnic (or cultural), provisional, effective, real, and absolute. In relating to other Buddhists the Order member should try, initially, to ascertain the level of their Going for Refuge. In particular, he (or she) should try to ascertain whether it is ethnic or effective, all the time being open to the possibility that it is real. If their Going for Refuge is merely ethnic, or has a strong ethnic or cultural tinge, then it will be difficult, even impossible, to communicate and be friends with them as though they were true Buddhists. At best you and they will be able to relate as members of your respective 'Buddhist groups', whether larger or smaller, which means relating collectively and 'politically' rather than individually and spiritually. Should the Going for Refuge of the other Buddhists be effective, however, then between them and the Order member there will exist genuine common ground, and this common ground will be all the deeper if the other Buddhists are able to recognize not only that Going for Refuge is what all Buddhists have in common but also that it is the most important thing they have in common and central to the Buddhist life. One way an Order member can help other Buddhists recognize the importance and centrality of the act of Going for Refuge is by drawing their attention to passages in their own scriptures where this is made clear. Naturally, the Order member will be able to do this only if he (or she) has a good knowledge of those scriptures and is familiar, moreover, with the principal tenets of the school or schools to which the other Buddhists happen to belong.

Third point: Do not be misled by labels. In ordinary life labels are useful, even indispensable. But they can also be misleading, especially where human beings are concerned. Within the field of Buddhism the terms Mahāyānist and Hīnayānist are a case in point. A Mahāyānist or follower of the Great Way is not always dedicated to the salvation of all sentient beings, nor is a Hīnayānist invariably preoccupied with his own emancipation from suffering. 'Mahāyānists' may in actual fact be mean and selfish, 'Hīnayānists' warm-hearted and generous. For this reason it has been suggested that the terms Hīnayāna and Mahāyāna should be understood as referring not so much to schools and doctrines as to spiritual attitudes and orientations. Labels often take the form of styles and titles. In recent years the Buddhist world has witnessed the appearance on the scene of a perfect swarm of 'His Holinesses' and 'His Eminences', not all of them necessarily either holy or spiritually eminent. Originally, it seems, only the Dalai Lama was accorded the style of 'His Holiness' in international diplomatic usage, on the grounds that like the Pope he was both head of state and head of religion. The Panchen Lama was styled 'His Eminence', presumably because his position was analogous to that of a cardinal. In 1956, when the Indian government invited the two Grand Lamas to visit India, the Chinese insisted, as a condition of their allowing the visit to take place, that the same protocol should be observed for both and the Panchen Lama, too, be accorded the style of 'His Holiness'. The motive for this insistence on the part of the Chinese was, of course, purely political. Subsequently, the Karmapa started styling himself 'His Holiness',[704] with the result that such self-promotion soon became widespread, with more and more Buddhist teachers – not all of them Tibetan – calling themselves either 'His Holiness' or 'His Eminence'. Labels can also take the form of more traditional styles and titles such as 'Sangharaja' and 'Nayaka Maha Thera',[705] and these too can be misleading; nor must we forget that not everyone styling himself a 'meditation teacher' meditates and that a 'forest monk' may not actually live in the forest. Whatever the label may be, in relating to other Buddhists an Order member should do his (or her) best to relate not to the label but to the person behind the label, to relate on the basis of the Going for Refuge common to all Buddhists, and to relate on the deepest possible level of that Going for Refuge. Not that labels can be ignored completely, even if only because other people take them seriously; but if they cannot be ignored, they should at least not be allowed to mislead.

So much, then, for my three points. So much for the relation of the Order to the rest of the Buddhist world. Though issues already dealt with elsewhere have not been touched on, in this paper I have covered a good deal of ground. We saw that since I spoke on the history of my Going for Refuge, eight years ago, the Order has grown not only numerically but in 'collective' maturity and experience, while the FWBO's activities have expanded and diversified. I have therefore been able to hand on many of my responsibilities as founder and head of the Order, and hope soon to have handed them all on.[706] In connection with what I called the principle of ecumenicity we saw that instead of one Buddhist world there are a number of sectarian Buddhist worlds, and that for all practical purposes the Order has separate relations with the Theravāda, the Jōdo Shinshū, Zen, and Tibetan Buddhism. Each of these schools has its own general characteristics and its own scriptures, from all of which we in the Order derive inspiration and guidance. We also saw, in connection with this principle, that during the last fifty years the portion of the earth's surface traditionally covered by Buddhism has shrunk dramatically, so that, despite important accessions in India and the West, Buddhism was now the smallest and in certain respects the least influential of the three great world religions. The principle of orthodoxy enabled me, incidentally, to connect my earlier with my later teaching. An orthodox Buddhist, we saw, was one for whom Going for Refuge was primary, observance of the precepts (and practice of meditation etc.) secondary, and lifestyle tertiary. The Theravāda was not orthodox because of its emphasis on monasticism, the Jōdo Shinshū because of its emphasis on the laical lifestyle, Zen because of its emphasis on meditation, and Tibetan Buddhism because of its emphasis on Tantric initiation. None the less, as we also saw, all these schools were based on scriptures and other works in which the centrality of the act of Going for Refuge is made sufficiently clear. In connection with the principle of personal contact we saw that those of us who have the responsibility for liaising with 'other' Buddhist groups do so in our capacity as individuals, and that while our deepest friendships may be with those who, like us, go for Refuge to the Three Jewels, in principle we extend the hand of fellowship to all. I also had three points for Order members relating to the rest of the Buddhist world: do not allow yourself to be put in a false position; look for the deepest common ground; and do not be misled by labels. These points having been made, I have now finished sharing with you my current thinking about the relation of the Order to the rest of the Buddhist world. The promise of eight years ago has been redeemed.

Forty-Three Years Ago

REFLECTIONS ON MY BHIKKHU ORDINATION

INTRODUCTORY NOTE

Forty-Three Years Ago was written to coincide with the twenty-fifth anniversary of the founding of the Western Buddhist Order in 1993. Although the starting point for these reflections concerned the validity (or otherwise) of his *bhikkhu* ordination, 'it being technically correct or not pointed to something more radical which was of spiritual concern to me'. (Personal communication, 18 March 2018.) *Forty-Three Years Ago* was published by Windhorse Publications in 1993.

When I was twenty-five I received ordination as a *bhikkhu* or Theravādin Buddhist monk. The time was 24 November 1950, a full-moon day, the place the Burmese temple at Sarnath, only a few score yards from the spot where, 2,500 years earlier, the Buddha had taught his first five disciples. The ordination gave me immense satisfaction. As I wrote many years later:

> Whilst the ceremony was in progress I experienced an extraordinary sense of peace, satisfaction, fulfilment, acceptance, and belonging. It was a feeling such as I had not experienced before, and in subsequent years I was never surprised when an elderly monk told me that receiving the monastic ordination had been the greatest experience of his whole life.[707]

I had become a Buddhist, or rather realized that I *was* a Buddhist and in fact always had been one, some eight years earlier, after reading the *Diamond Sūtra* and the *Sūtra of Wei Lang*; had come to India (with the army) in 1944; had spent two years as a freelance wandering ascetic; had been ordained as a *sāmaṇera* or novice monk in Kusinagara, the site of the Buddha's 'great decease'; had studied Pāli and Buddhist philosophy in Benares; and finally in May 1950 had founded a Buddhist organization in Kalimpong, a town in the foothills of the eastern Himalayas, to which I was to return after my ordination and which would be my headquarters for the next fourteen years.[708]

Ordination as a *bhikkhu* was thus for me the culmination of a process of spiritual discovery and development that had been going on for a number of years, a process which may well have antedated not only my realization that I was a Buddhist but even my birth in South London in 1925. Yet if *bhikkhu* ordination represented the culmination of a process of spiritual discovery and development it was also, at the same time, the beginning of a further stage in that same process. After my return to Kalimpong I continued to meditate and study the Dharma, to write, to teach, to give lectures and, in short, to 'work for the good of Buddhism', as I had been directed to do by my teacher the Venerable Jagdish Kashyap, who was responsible for my being in Kalimpong in the first place and who had taken part in my ordination.[709] And of course I observed the Vinaya or monastic code as strictly as I could.[710]

In the autumn of 1956 I received a rude shock. I discovered that there had been a serious flaw in my ordination ceremony, that really I had not been ordained, and that technically speaking I was not a *bhikkhu*. According to the Theravādin Vinaya, in the Middle Country (i.e. north-east India) a *bhikkhu* has to be ordained by a chapter of at least ten *bhikkhus* (outside the Middle Country, at least five) and the ordination ceremony has to be conducted within a specially demarcated and dedicated area known as a *sīmā* (literally, 'boundary'). The *bhikkhus* constituting the ordaining chapter, and present within the *sīmā* and taking part in the ordination, have moreover to be *pārisuddha* or 'completely pure' in the sense of being guiltless of any major breach of the *sikkhāpadas* or rules of training, such as would render them liable to expulsion or suspension from the Order.[711] What I discovered that autumn was that one of the *bhikkhus* taking part in my ordination had rendered himself so liable, as at least some members of the ordaining chapter were aware. He had been guilty of a breach of the training-rule prohibiting intentional sexual intercourse, and in fact had a 'wife' and son living with him at his temple, the former being officially his cook.[712]

The discovery left me in a quandary. If the supposed *bhikkhu* was not really a *bhikkhu* then I was not really a *bhikkhu* either, his presence within the *sīmā* having invalidated the entire proceedings and rendered my ordination ceremony null and void. What should I do? It was not really open to me to seek re-ordination, since I would have no means of knowing whether the members of the re-ordaining chapter were *pārisuddha* or not and could hardly go round making enquiries. In any case, seeking re-ordination (or rather, again seeking to be ordained) would mean having to explain why I considered this to be necessary, and I already knew that questioning a *bhikkhu's* 'complete purity' was something that was rather frowned on in Theravādin monastic circles. In the event I did nothing about my discovery. I continued to meditate and study, continued to work for the good of Buddhism, and observed the Vinaya or monastic code to the best of my ability, just as though I *had* been validly ordained and *was* technically a *bhikkhu*. My confidence in the Theravādin branch of the monastic order may have been undermined, but my faith in the Dharma and the spiritual life, and in the monastic lifestyle, remained unshaken.

That I did nothing about my discovery meant that the memory of it came to be pushed to the back of my mind, and I ceased to think about it very much. Indeed I must admit that for a number of years I did not really allow myself to think about it. Eventually, however, after I had founded the Western Buddhist Order and developed my conception of Going for Refuge to the Buddha, the Dharma, and the Sangha as the central and definitive act of the Buddhist life, I not only allowed myself to think about it but started trying to fathom its implications. This has led to various reflections, some relating to me personally, others to the sangha or spiritual community in the widest sense. Now that the Western Buddhist Order is celebrating its twenty-fifth anniversary I believe the time has come for me to communicate these reflections to the WBO and FWBO and to the rest of the Buddhist world.

I

I do not regret being 'ordained' at Sarnath. Indeed I am glad there was a flaw in my ordination ceremony, glad that really I was not ordained, glad that technically I was never a *bhikkhu*, for in the long run this contributed more to my spiritual development, and more to my understanding of the Dharma, than any amount of correctness and technicality could have done. The *bhikkhu* who had a wife and son living with him at his temple may have been a bad monk, but he was a good Buddhist. He was kind to me, and took the trouble to help me, and I knew he had for many years striven, under difficult circumstances, to disseminate a knowledge of the Dharma. Later on, in the course of the eight years between my 'discovery' and my return to England in 1964, I came to know that most of the *bhikkhus* who had taken part in my supposed ordination were in much the same position as he was. They were either guilty, like him, of a breach of the training-rule prohibiting sexual intercourse, or guilty of a breach of one or more of the training-rules prohibiting actions of a sensual nature other than intercourse, and thus were permanently or temporarily self-excluded from the Order. Leaving aside the two Burmese *bhikkhus* from Rangoon,[713] with whom I had no contact after the ordination ceremony, the only *bhikkhu* in whose *pārisuddhi* I had complete confidence was my teacher Jagdish Kashyap, with whom I had lived for eight or nine months and who was a model of personal integrity. Yet though most of the *bhikkhus* who had taken part in my ordination were, like the *bhikkhu* with a wife and son, bad monks, they were, like him, good Buddhists. They looked after pilgrims, edited Buddhist magazines, published books on Buddhism, ran schools and dispensaries, organized Buddhist festivals, gave lectures, and received new converts into the sangha or Buddhist spiritual community, besides observing the basic ethical precepts and practising a little meditation. In the case of some of them, at least, these activities were the expression of a deep and genuine devotion to the Dharma, for whose sake they had, despite their sexual peccadilloes, made many sacrifices. I am therefore glad I was ordained by them, and in the case of two or three of them cherish fond memories of our subsequent association.

I am glad I was ordained by them not only because they were, in varying degrees, good Buddhists. I am also glad because they represented, between them, four different nationalities, two of them being Indian, three Burmese, one Nepalese, and the rest Ceylonese. All were Theravādins, but sitting outside the *sīmā* (since he belonged to a different tradition of monastic ordination) was a Tibetan, strictly speaking Ladakhi, *tulku* or 'incarnate lama' who was, of course, a follower of the Mahāyāna. My *bhikkhu* ordination not being a *bhikkhu* ordination at all, there was in reality nothing to exclude Kusho Bakula from the proceedings, despite appearances to the contrary, and it is therefore possible for me to rejoice in the fact that I was ordained by *bhikkhus* who represented, between them, the two major divisions of Buddhism.

II

Not all the *bhikkhus* in the ordaining chapter were really *bhikkhus*, technically speaking. The ceremony they performed was not really a *bhikkhu* ordination. What, then, did take place when, as I thought, I was being ordained as a *bhikkhu*? Were the words then spoken and the actions then performed no more than a sacrilegious mockery of the Vinaya, an empty charade, totally devoid of meaning and significance, so that the truth of the matter was that *nothing at all* took place and I was left in exactly the same position as before? The clue to the answer is in the words in which, writing many years later, I described the ceremony, and which I have already quoted:

> Whilst the ceremony was in progress I experienced an extraordinary sense of peace, satisfaction, fulfilment, acceptance, and belonging. It was a feeling such as I had not experienced before, and in subsequent years I was never surprised when an elderly monk told me that receiving the monastic ordination had been the greatest experience of his whole life.[714]

This feeling it is impossible for me to doubt or deny. Since reading the *Diamond Sūtra* and the *Sūtra of Wei Lang* some eight years earlier I had been very much on my own as a Buddhist. I had certainly been on my own as a Buddhist in the army, while my two years as a freelance wandering ascetic had been spent in a Hindu environment with a companion who was oscillating between Buddhism and Hinduism. In Benares I had been surrounded by Hindu orthodoxy, and in Kalimpong had founded a Buddhist organization the members of which were either Hindus sympathetic to Buddhism or more or less nominal, 'born' Buddhists. But now I was no longer on my own. I had been accepted into the sangha or Buddhist spiritual community, was a member of that community, belonged to that community. My heartfelt desire not just to be a Buddhist but to have the fact that I was a Buddhist recognized and appreciated by other Buddhists had at last been fulfilled. I felt satisfied and at peace.

At the time, and for six years afterwards, I was of course under the impression I had been ordained as a *bhikkhu*. I was under the impression that the sangha into which I had been ordained was not the sangha in the sense of the Buddhist spiritual community but the sangha in the much narrower sense of the monastic order, for I tended to identify the sangha with the monastic order. Only much later, after I had realized that the Going for Refuge was the central and definitive act of the Buddhist life, and that commitment to the Three Jewels was primary and lifestyle, whether lay or monastic, secondary, did it become possible for me, taking the feeling I experienced during my ordination ceremony as a clue, to understand what really happened and acknowledge to myself that I had been ordained not as a *bhikkhu* by *bhikkhus* but, in reality, as a Buddhist by Buddhists, and welcomed not into the monastic order but into the Buddhist spiritual community in the widest sense. I had been welcomed, moreover, not only by the yellow-robed and red-robed representatives of five different nationalities and the two major divisions of Buddhism but by their white-robed counterparts as well, who from their position immediately behind Kusho Bakula participated in the proceedings spiritually to no less an extent than anyone else did.

As I look back at my ordination in Sarnath over an interval of more than forty years, it strikes me that the feeling I experienced then was the kind of feeling experienced on the occasion of their 'public' ordination by members of the Western Buddhist Order, though the latter are much clearer about the significance of their ceremony than I was about the significance of mine. Would it be too fanciful to suggest that this is not the only parallel between my own spiritual journey and theirs? In 1943 or 1944 I 'took *pansil*' from the Burmese monk U Thittila in London.[715] The parallel to this in the FWBO is becoming a Friend, which one does simply by turning up at an FWBO centre and joining, perhaps, in the chanting of the Sevenfold Puja without understanding what it is all about, just as I found myself repeating the Three Refuges and Five Precepts in Pāli at a meeting of the Buddhist Society without a real appreciation of what I was doing. Six or seven years later, in a town in the Punjab hills, I 'went forth' from the household life into the life of homelessness.[716] Having left the army eight months earlier, I disposed of my remaining possessions, said goodbye to friends, and with a single companion set out on foot for the plains and, as it turned out, two years of wandering. A Friend parallels this 'Going Forth' of mine, it could be said, by becoming a Mitra, when he starts separating himself from conventional society and its values and turning in the direction of Enlightenment. He is one who has finished 'shopping around' other groups and religions and settled for the FWBO, who is willing and able to keep up regular contact with Order members, who meditates regularly, and who is willing to help Order members with the running of the local centre or some other aspect of the Movement to the best of his ability.[717] My 'Going Forth' fulfilled only two of these criteria, the first and the third, so that it is paralleled by a Friend's becoming a Mitra only to a limited extent, the limitation being entirely on my side. In May 1949 I was ordained as a *sāmaṇera* or novice monk in Kusinagara, the site of the Buddha's final teachings and 'great decease', my preceptor being the Burmese monk U Chandramani.[718] This is paralleled by a Mitra entering into a relation of *kalyāṇa mitratā* or spiritual friendship with two Order members, who take an active and sincere interest in the Mitra and his development and are able to give him any criticism, guidance, support, and advice that he may need. In my case there was only one *kalyāṇa mitra*, but a few months later I acquired a second in the person of Jagdish Kashyap, by whom, as was customary, I was in fact re-ordained as a *sāmaṇera* immediately prior to my *bhikkhu* ordination proper – a sub-ceremony paralleled by the 'private' ordination which in the case of members of the Western Buddhist Order precedes 'public' ordination. Being a *sāmaṇera*, and having U Chandramani and Jagdish Kashyap as my *kalyāṇa mitras*, enabled me to fulfil the two other requirements of FWBO Mitrahood. Besides having as much regular contact with them as I could, I helped U Chandramani by visiting his Newar disciples in Nepal and preaching to them, while at Jagdish Kashyap's behest I stayed in Kalimpong to 'work for the good of Buddhism'.[719] Thus there is more than one parallel between my own spiritual journey and the spiritual journey of members of the Western Buddhist Order, and it is not surprising that the feelings experienced in the course of those journeys should be of much the same kind.

On 12 October 1962, six years after my discovery that technically speaking I was not a *bhikkhu*, I received the bodhisattva ordination in Kalimpong from my friend and teacher Dhardo Rimpoche, a Tibetan 'incarnate lama' whom I regarded as a veritable embodiment of the bodhisattva ideal.[720] This ordination I took partly in order to give formal expression to my acceptance of the bodhisattva ideal, and partly as a means of progressing from the 'Hīnayāna', to which belonged the tradition (or rather, the traditions) of monastic ordination, to the less monastically orientated Mahāyāna. Though I did not fully acknowledge this to myself at the time, I also wanted to feel that I had a stronger formal connection with Buddhist tradition than was provided by an invalid *bhikkhu* ordination. Later I came to see that the Hīnayāna and the Mahāyāna are not, in fact, the lower and higher stages of a single path.[721] My experience of the bodhisattva ordination is therefore paralleled in the spiritual life of members of the Western Buddhist Order by the realization that the *bodhicitta* or will to (Supreme) Enlightenment for the benefit of all beings, the arising of which makes one a bodhisattva, according to the Mahāyāna,[722] is actually the altruistic dimension of the 'Hīnayāna' Going for Refuge to the Three Jewels. It is in this Going for Refuge, as recognized and formally acknowledged by the sangha or spiritual community of those who themselves go for Refuge, that *saṃvara* or ordination really consists.[723]

III

But what of the *bhikkhus* who ordained me at Sarnath? What did *they* think had taken place in the *sīmā* that morning in November forty-three years ago? A few of them no doubt thought that a valid ordination had taken place, that I was now technically a *bhikkhu*, and that the monastic order in India could congratulate itself on the accession of a new member to its ranks. Others, perhaps the majority, knew perfectly well that one of their number was not really a *bhikkhu*, and that his presence within the *sīmā* invalidated the proceedings, so that in fact no ordination had taken place and that 'the novice Sangharakkhita'[724] was no more a *bhikkhu* at the conclusion of the ceremony than he had been at the beginning. Did the *bhikkhus* deceive me, then? Did they connive at, indeed actively participate in, a conscious and deliberate imposture? I cannot really believe this to have been the case. From the evident satisfaction with which they participated in the proceedings, and the warmth with which they congratulated me afterwards, it was clear that they felt nothing but goodwill towards me, that they were ready to accept me as one of themselves, and that for them too that morning something had taken place, as I now believe, that was not explicable in terms of the letter of the Vinaya.

Not that they actually *thought* this. They did not think anything. Or if it did occur to them that at least one of their number was guilty of a major breach of the *sikkhāpadas* or rules of training, and that his presence within the *sīmā* at the time of my ordination vitiated the proceedings, then they automatically thrust the thought to the back of their minds. As I was to learn before I had been many months a *bhikkhu*, there were quite a lot of thoughts of this inconvenient nature that members of the monastic order thrust to the back of their minds. Happening to meet a very senior monk from Ceylon who was well known for his 'orthodoxy', i.e. for his strict adherence to the letter of the Vinaya, I asked him whether something could not be done about a certain prominent *bhikkhu* who, as I had known since long before my ordination, was notoriously guilty of major breaches of the *sikkhāpadas*. The monk, who had just been lamenting the shameful laxity of *bhikkhus* who took solid food after midday (actually a minor offence entailing simple confession), muttered something about it being none of his business, and changed the subject. Admittedly he belonged to another *nikāya* or 'family' of monks, and admittedly the guilty *bhikkhu* occupied a position of some influence in the Buddhist world, but even so I found the monk's unwillingness to do anything about a matter affecting the *pārisuddha* or 'complete purity', and hence the very existence, of the monastic order, rather surprising. What he was saying, in effect, was that it was simply 'not the done thing' to call a *bhikkhu*'s *pārisuddhi* into question. If one had doubts, one kept them to oneself.

Both before and after my ordination I had doubts, and more than doubts, about the *pārisuddhi* of quite a few of the *bhikkhus* with whom I was in contact, and though I kept these doubts to myself it was difficult for me not to think about them. Some *bhikkhus*, I was forced to conclude, were not *bhikkhus* at all, usually on account of their being guilty of the same major breach of the *sikkhāpadas* as the *bhikkhu* whose presence within the *sīmā* had, as I subsequently discovered, rendered my ordination invalid. Others, while still technically *bhikkhus* (assuming *their* ordinations to have been valid, which was quite a big assumption) had either rendered themselves liable to suspension or observed the letter of the Vinaya in the excessively formalistic manner I have criticized in *A Survey of Buddhism*, written during the year prior to my 'discovery'.[725] In those days I tended to think of all such *bhikkhus* simply as bad monks or, what amounted to the same thing, as laymen who were masquerading as monks for the sake of worldly advantage. Only many years later, after I had realized the supreme importance of Going for Refuge in the Buddhist life, and the *relative* unimportance of all lifestyles, including the monastic, did it become possible for me to adopt a more positive attitude and to think of some of them, at least, as good Buddhists rather than as bad monks. If they had also been good monks, in the true sense, it would have been better. But the fact of their being bad monks had not prevented them from being deeply and genuinely devoted to the Dharma, nor had it prevented them – as it had not prevented the *bhikkhus* who ordained me – from giving expression to that devotion in a variety of ways.

Yet though it is possible for me to think of some of them, at least, as good Buddhists rather than as bad monks, I sometimes wonder how they actually felt, those *bhikkhus* who were not really *bhikkhus*, and who, though wearing the yellow robe and receiving the offerings of the faithful, were living (in the case of the 'worst' of them) in a state of *de jure* expulsion from the monastic order. In particular I wonder how the *bhikkhus* who had taken part in my ordination felt, that is, those of them who were guilty of major breaches of the *sikkhāpadas* and who knew, somewhere at the back of their minds, that the ceremony in which they were so happily participating was not a valid ordination at all. Did they not have reservations about the part they were playing? Did they feel no uneasiness? Now that it is possible for me to think of them as good Buddhists rather than as bad monks, I believe I could go to them and raise the matter in a way that would have been inconceivable thirty or forty years ago. How did *you* feel, Venerable K——, when you had a wife and son living with you at your temple, only yards away; or you, Venerable D——, with your young wife in a distant city; or *you*, my old friend Venerable S——, whose exploits were eventually chronicled in the local press for months together, as you confided to me the last time we met? How did you and your colleagues in expulsion and suspension feel, sitting in the *sīmā* together on the morning of 24 November 1950, and ordaining, as it appeared, the young English Buddhist whose dearest wish was to be a *bhikkhu* and who had, in good faith and with implicit trust in your credentials, asked you to make him one? Alas! you are all long since dead, and unless you can revisit the Earth from some other realm of existence I shall never obtain an answer to my question.

But if I do not know, and may never know, whether or not the *bhikkhus* who ordained me in Sarnath had reservations about the part they were playing, or felt any uneasiness, there were certainly *bhikkhus* elsewhere in the Buddhist world who, both before and after that time, felt not just uneasiness but positive anguish at the thought that they were, or might be, living in a state of *de jure* expulsion or suspension from the monastic order. In *The Forest Monks of Sri Lanka*, which I read soon after its publication in 1983, there is a fascinating account of some of these *bhikkhus*. One of them, conscious that he had repeatedly violated the training-rules prohibiting actions of a sensual nature other than intercourse, went to great lengths to revive the complex and difficult procedure whereby one in his position could be purified of his offence and reaccepted into the monastic order, a procedure that had fallen into abeyance in the *nikāya* to which he belonged.[726] Another *bhikkhu*, convinced that the monastic order in Ceylon was utterly corrupt, and that no monk was 'completely pure', left the robe and took ordination at his own hands as a *tāpasa* or ascetic, just as the Bodhisattva or Buddha-to-be had done in the *Jātaka* tales.[727] In my own case, I eventually ceased to think in terms of monastic ordination. What *really* mattered was that one went for Refuge to the Three Jewels, after which, as an expression of that continuing act, one could live either as a 'monk' or as a 'layman'.

IV

After discovering that I was not really a *bhikkhu*, i.e. not a *bhikkhu* in the technical Vinaya sense, I could, theoretically, have sought re-ordination. Though there were practical difficulties, even if re-ordination was out of the question I could still have disrobed and gone to Burma or Thailand to seek ordination there. But this alternative was not really open to me. Whether in India, or Burma, or Thailand, or anywhere else in the Buddhist world, I had no means of knowing whether or not the members of the ordaining chapter were *pārisuddha* or 'completely pure' and no means of knowing, therefore, whether or not an ordination conferred by them was valid. Only one possessed of *paracittañāṇa* or '(telepathic) knowledge of the minds of others', the third of the five (mundane) *abhiññās* or higher knowledges,[728] had the means of knowing that. And even if all members of the ordaining chapter were *pārisuddha*, in the sense of being guiltless of any breach of the *sikkhāpadas*, this would not necessarily mean that they had been validly ordained and were, therefore, really *bhikkhus* and able to confer valid ordination. They might easily be in the same position that I had been in before making my discovery, i.e. might be non-*bhikkhus* without knowing themselves to be such. In order to be quite sure that I was receiving a valid ordination I would therefore need to know whether or not the members of the chapters which had ordained each of *them* were 'completely pure' and had been validly ordained – and so on back to the very beginning of the cenobitical monastic order. Logically speaking, I could not be sure that any *bhikkhu* was validly ordained unless I could be sure that all his predecessors in monastic ordination had been validly ordained. Nor was that all. Not only did the members of an ordaining chapter have to be 'completely pure'. Not only did they have to be validly ordained. The ordination itself had to be conducted in strict accordance with the requirements of the Vinaya, otherwise it was no ordination at all, and since these requirements extended to the minutiae of the ceremony mistakes – and disputes – could easily occur. In *The Forest Monks of Sri Lanka* there is an amusing example of the sort of thing that could happen. A certain plank, it was alleged, had impinged on the boundary of the *sīmā*, so that the ordinations conferred on that occasion were not valid, and those monks no monks at all.

> By the time this exercise in frustration petered out twenty years later, it had drawn into it chief monks from as far away as Burma and Thailand, most of whom tried to calm the contestants and bring them to an amicable settlement.[729]

All this goes to show that technically valid ordination is virtually impossible of attainment and that if one did, miraculously, obtain it, one could not know that one had done so.

Thus a *bhikkhu* can never really know that he is a *bhikkhu*. He can only believe that he is one, and the strength of his belief – considerations of temperament apart – will be in inverse proportion to the extent of his awareness of what it is necessary for him to know in order to be able to know that he is a *bhikkhu*. He can, of course, know whether or not he is observing the *sikkhāpadas* or rules of training; in the case of some rules, he is the only person who can know whether or not he is observing them. But even the strictest observance of the *sikkhāpadas* is not, by itself, sufficient to make him a *bhikkhu* in the technical Vinaya sense, though a major breach of the *sikkhāpadas* is enough to unmake him as a *bhikkhu*, assuming him to have been validly ordained in the first place. According to the *Dhammapada*, he is a *bhikkhu* (and a *brāhmaṇa* and a *samaṇa*) who, though well dressed (*alaṅkato*), is calm, controlled, assured (of release from mundane existence), and chaste (*brahmacārī*), and refrains from inflicting injury on anyone.[730] According to the Vinaya, however, he is a *bhikkhu* who is ordained, i.e. who has been accepted into the monastic order in the prescribed manner. Thus there is a tension, even a conflict, between Sūtra and Vinaya, or, as one might also express it, between the spirit of the Dharma and that *stressing* of the letter (not the actual letter itself) which constitutes legalism, in this case pseudo-monastic legalism, and which is ultimately self-defeating.

In practice the tension or conflict is not much felt. A *bhikkhu* generally *believes* he is a *bhikkhu* in the technical Vinaya sense, and he believes this not so much on account of his observance of the *sikkhāpadas* as because he has been accepted into the monastic order in the prescribed manner. That it is ordination, not observance of the *sikkhāpadas*, that really makes one a *bhikkhu* and worthy of the veneration of the faithful, is demonstrated by the kind of situation that came to my notice long before I discovered that my ordination was invalid and which gave me considerable food for reflection. A certain *bhikkhu* might be working as a college lecturer, drawing a salary and living with his servants in a bungalow equipped with every comfort and convenience. While avoiding any major breach of the *sikkhāpadas*, he might be worldly-minded and ambitious, having no real interest in the spiritual life. He might, furthermore, be ill-natured, abusive, and overbearing. Yet this *bhikkhu* would be treated with the utmost respect by the laity, who would prostrate themselves before him, spread white cloths for him to sit and even walk on, and address him, or refer to him, in a special honorific language. A certain layman, however, might be teaching meditation, accepting no remuneration and living alone in a simple hut. Though wearing a white robe, he might be observing the additional (*sāmaṇera*) precepts of abstention from non-chastity, from untimely meals, from dance, song, music, and unseemly shows, from personal adornment, and from handling gold and silver. He might, furthermore, be good-natured, courteous, and unassuming. Yet he would not be treated with the same profound deference as the worldly-minded *bhikkhu*. The *bhikkhu* has been *ordained*, and he has not. That it is ordination, and not the kind of life one leads, that really makes one a *bhikkhu*, is also demonstrated by what happens when a *bhikkhu* leaves the yellow robe, i.e. resigns his ordination, which the Vinaya allows him to do and for which there is a special procedure.[731] Even though there may have been no change in his way of life, the laity stop showing him any special respect, while he, for his part, now shows *bhikkhus* who had been his pupils the respect that formerly they had shown him. There is a third kind of situation that demonstrates how it is ordination, not the kind of life one leads, that makes one a *bhikkhu* (or a *bhikkhunī*), but this has come to my notice more recently and I shall deal with it separately later on.

If a *bhikkhu* does not know whether or not he is really a *bhikkhu*, and if his spiritual life depends on the fact that he *is* a *bhikkhu*, then his spiritual life has a very insecure foundation. Strictly considered, it has no foundation at all. As the author of *The Forest Monks of Sri Lanka* observes,

> The rigid separation of monk from layman is a bedrock on which the edifice of Theravāda spiritual life is founded.

What separates monk and layman (and monk and novice) is ordination, i.e. *bhikkhu* ordination, which the former has received while the latter has not. In Theravāda, however, though not in its own Pāli canon as a whole, the spiritual life is identified with monastic life, i.e. with being a *bhikkhu*, for, as the same author also points out,

> it is a firmly held view in Theravāda ... that only monks attain liberation.[732]

Since spiritual life is identified with being a *bhikkhu*, and since a *bhikkhu* is one who has been ordained, it follows that in Theravāda spiritual life is based on ordination. But if spiritual life is based on ordination, and if one does not, even cannot, know whether one is really ordained, one cannot know, either, whether or not one is really leading a spiritual life and moving in the direction of liberation. Spiritual life is based not on what one believes about oneself but on what one knows, even if what one knows is no more than the simple fact that one suffers. Unless it is so based there can be no question of our being self-reliant, and without self-reliance there can be no question of our being able to follow the

Buddha's dying exhortation to us to abide islands unto ourselves, refuges unto ourselves, taking refuge in none other.[733]

That a *bhikkhu* does not know whether or not he is really a *bhikkhu* has implications not only for his own spiritual life but also for the spiritual life, such as it is, of the laity. Not being a *bhikkhu*, i.e. not being ordained, a layman strictly speaking has no spiritual life. He does not seek to attain *vimutti* or liberation from mundane existence. Instead, he seeks to attain a state of greater happiness *within* mundane existence, both here and hereafter. Such a state is attained not by means of *paññā* or 'wisdom', which is the means to the attainment of liberation, but by means of *puñña* or merit. 'Making merit' thus comes to be the principal religious activity of the Theravādin layman, and the best and easiest way for him to make merit is by supporting the *bhikkhus*, in the sense of providing them with food, clothing, accommodation, and medicine (the traditional 'four requisites') and, in modern times, many other things besides. Supporting *bhikkhus* is the best and easiest way of making merit because *bhikkhus* are leading the spiritual life and because, according to tradition, the more spiritually developed is the person to whom offerings are made the greater is the merit that accrues therefrom. But the layman does not actually *know* that the *bhikkhu* is a *bhikkhu*. He only *believes* him to be such, his belief being based on the *bhikkhu*'s own belief that he *is* a *bhikkhu*. Thus the foundation of the layman's spiritual/religious life is doubly insecure. He is even less sure that he is actually making merit, and thus earning for himself a state of greater happiness within conditioned existence, than the *bhikkhu* is sure that he is really leading a spiritual life and moving in the direction of liberation.

Some lay people indeed seem to have an obscure awareness of how insecure is the foundation of their religious life. At any rate, they are anxious that the *bhikkhus* whom they support should be strict observers of the Vinaya, and keep as close an eye on them as possible. Should they come to know that a *bhikkhu* has been guilty of a breach of the *sikkhāpadas* (and lay people do not always know what constitutes a major and what a minor offence) they will feel extremely disappointed, even angry. They will feel disappointed not so much on account of the breach itself as because of what it means, namely, that the *bhikkhu* is not really a *bhikkhu* – and money spent supporting one who is not a *bhikkhu* does not make merit. It is money wasted. While such an attitude may not encourage *bhikkhus* to be actually hypocritical, it certainly encourages them to be more circumspect in their behaviour when under the surveillance of the laity than when they are on their own. A few *bhikkhus* may even flaunt the strictness of their own observance of the Vinaya, as compared with the laxity of the observance of other *bhikkhus*, in order to win the laity's favour. Generally speaking, however, *bhikkhus* are well aware that they are all in the same boat and are anxious not to rock it by drawing undue attention to one another's shortcomings. During the fourteen years I spent in India after my supposed ordination I did not once hear of a monk being actually expelled from the monastic order, though I did hear of a senior Thai *bhikkhu* being arrested and forcibly disrobed by the (Thai) police for the alleged possession of Marxist literature.

Whether or not because of the difficulty of being sure that a *bhikkhu* *is* a *bhikkhu*, in the strict Vinaya sense, in the Theravādin countries of south-east Asia the actual ordination *ceremony* has in practice come to assume, for *bhikkhus* and laymen alike, a quasi-magical character that gives it a kind of inherent validity of its own. A *bhikkhu* is a *bhikkhu*, for all practical purposes, because he has undergone this quasi-magical ceremony and himself assumed a quasi-magical character, something of which will remain with him should he ever choose to leave the robe, that is, leave it honourably or without having been guilty of a breach of the *sikkhāpadas*, as it is possible for him to do in Burma and Thailand. His quasi-magical character is reinforced by the highly ceremonious, even ritualistic, way in which he is treated by the laity, as well as by the fact that both he and the laity tend to regard the *sikkhāpadas* as taboos rather than as rules of training. The *bhikkhu* ordination ceremony proper, as laid down in the Vinaya Piṭaka, is far from possessing a quasi-magical character. Anything less 'magical' could hardly be imagined. The ordaining chapter, being of course 'completely pure', assembles within the *sīmā*. The chairman, as he may be called, puts to the monks the motion that the novice monk X wishes to receive the *bhikkhu* ordination from the chapter with the Venerable Y as his preceptor and that the chapter should, if it so wishes, grant him the ordination. Three batches of three monks (if the chapter consists of ten or more members, as is usually the case, even outside the Middle Country) then request the chapter to agree to the motion, each batch repeating the request in unison once. The chapter remaining silent, the motion is declared carried.[734] To outward appearances, at least, it is all much more like a board meeting than a religious ceremony.

V

In the early days of the Western Buddhist Order I was sometimes asked whether our ordinations were recognized by other Buddhists. The question was based on two assumptions. One assumption was that the 'other Buddhists' constituted a unitary, monolithic body, rather like the Roman Catholic Church, which had the power to grant – or not grant – formal recognition to new Buddhist groups. The other was that being so 'recognized' somehow conferred on our ordinations a validity which otherwise they would not possess. What form such recognition normally took was not made clear. If I thought the question was a *bona fide* one, and not simply an expression of hostility towards the FWBO, I would try to explain that Buddhists were in fact divided into as many different sects as Christians. Even monks were divided. To begin with, monks were divided into those who followed one or other of the different Sarvāstivādin versions of the Vinaya and those who followed the Theravādin version, the former being found in Mahāyāna countries such as China and Tibet, where monks combined observance of the Vinaya with commitment to the bodhisattva ideal, while the latter were found in Theravādin countries such a Sri Lanka, Burma, and Thailand. In each of the Theravādin countries the monastic order was divided into independent *nikāyas* or 'families' of *bhikkhus*, some of which had, over the years, given birth to *nikāyas* of their own. Thus the Amarapura *nikāya* of Sri Lanka, which had split off from the fifty-year-old Siyam *nikāya* in 1803, had since become divided into more than a dozen *nikāyas*. Which of these different sects and *nikāyas*, comprising at least six hundred independent bodies, was supposed to 'recognize' the WBO's ordinations? Did they *all* have to recognize them? Or would recognition by only a few of them suffice?

The fact is that these bodies do not always recognize one another. Leaving aside the sects, which are divided mainly along doctrinal lines, and leaving aside the Sarvāstivādin *nikāyas*, the Theravādin *nikāyas* do not recognize one another inasmuch as they do not recognize the validity, in the technical Vinaya sense, of each other's *bhikkhu* ordinations. This is hardly surprising, some of the later *nikāyas* having come into existence because their founders doubted the validity of the ordinations they had received from the earlier *nikāyas*. That the Theravādin *nikāyas* do not recognize one another, that is, do not recognize the validity of each other's ordinations in the technical Vinaya sense, certainly does not mean that they fight and quarrel among themselves, though tensions admittedly exist. What it means is that they do not take part in one another's *sanghakammas* or official acts of the monastic order (in effect, of the individual *nikāya*), since the presence within the *sīmā*, where all such acts take place, of one who according to them is not really a *bhikkhu*, would invalidate the proceedings. Otherwise, *bhikkhus* of different *nikāyas* associate freely for socio-religious purposes, separating according to *nikāya* only for their respective *saṅghakammas*.[735]

Should therefore a Theravādin *nikāya* refuse to recognize WBO ordinations it would be doing no more than it does when it refuses to recognize the ordinations of *bhikkhus* belonging to other *nikāyas* in its own country. *Nikāyas* are composed of *bhikkhus*, and *bhikkhus* can recognize – or refuse to recognize – only *bhikkhu* ordinations. Members of the Western Buddhist Order are not *bhikkhus* (or *bhikkhunīs*) and ordinations in the Western Buddhist Order are not *bhikkhu* ordinations, so that there is no more question of *nikāyas* being able to recognize WBO ordinations than there is of the WBO being able to recognize theirs. In the Western Buddhist Order *saṃvara* or ordination consists in effectively Going for Refuge to the Buddha, the Dharma, and the Sangha, and having that Going for Refuge formally recognized by others who themselves go for Refuge, that is, by existing members of the Order, as well as in undertaking to observe the ten precepts or *dasasikkhāpadas*, corresponding *not* to the ten *sikkhāpadas* of the *sāmaṇera* but to the ten *akusalakammapathas* or 'modes of abstention from unskilful behaviour'.[736] Thus ordination in the WBO is based on knowledge, that is, knowledge of one's own effective Going for Refuge and its recognition by others. It is not based on belief in the technical validity of one's ordination.

The fact that *saṃvara* or ordination consists in effectively Going for Refuge to the Three Jewels is closely connected with the fact that, in the Western Buddhist Order, Going for Refuge is seen as the central and definitive act of the Buddhist life, it being of secondary importance whether one lives as a monk or as a layman. In many parts of the Buddhist world Going for Refuge is not seen in this way. Particularly in the Theravādin countries of south-east Asia, where lifestyle is more important than commitment to the Three Jewels and where spiritual life is traditionally identified with monasticism, ordination as a *bhikkhu* has come to occupy the central place that really belongs to Going for Refuge. Theravādin lay people do 'take' the Three Refuges and Five (sometimes Eight) Precepts from a *bhikkhu* on special occasions,[737] but such taking does not constitute an ordination, as it does in those Mahāyāna countries where monks follow the Sarvāstivādin Vinaya and where, thanks to the universality of the bodhisattva ideal, there tends to be a distinction rather than a division between the monastic order and the lay community. Theravādin lay people thus do not receive (lay) ordination in the way that *bhikkhus* receive monastic ordination. They are in effect second-class Buddhists, their religious life consisting mainly in making merit for themselves by supporting *bhikkhus*.

This absence of lay ordination in the Theravāda presented a difficulty when, in October 1956, the ex-Untouchable Hindus of western and central India started converting to Buddhism in large numbers. As their scholarly leader, Bhimrao Ramji Ambedkar, well knew, one of the reasons for the disappearance of Buddhism from India, centuries earlier, was its over-identification with cenobitical monasticism. On the destruction of the great monastic establishments by the iconoclastic Turkish invaders there was nothing to prevent the Buddhist laity, who had been little more than supporters of the monks, from falling under the influence of Hinduism, by which they were eventually absorbed. Ambedkar did not want such a thing to happen again. His followers had to feel that they were *bona fide* Buddhists, not just supporters of monks and monasteries. They had to feel that they were full members of the Buddhist spiritual community. In order that they should feel this it was necessary for them to be formally accepted into Buddhism in the way that a monk was accepted into the monastic order. There had to be lay ordination. But within the Theravāda, at that time the only form of Buddhism with an effective presence in India, lay ordination was not available. Ambedkar met the difficulty by creating a ceremony of his own. Having taken the Three Refuges and Five Precepts from U Chandramani, who had made me a *sāmaṇera* six years earlier, and having pronounced twenty-two *pratijñās* of his own devising, he then himself administered all three – refuges, precepts, and vows – to the serried ranks of 380,000 of his followers, thus inaugurating the memorable and historic series of mass conversions of ex-Untouchables to Buddhism.[738] He thus did two important things at a stroke. By creating a conversion ceremony for his followers he in effect revived the tradition of lay ordination, and by conducting the ceremony himself, instead of allowing U Chandramani to conduct it, he placed the layman on an equal footing with the monk and lay ordination on an equal footing with monastic ordination.

Twelve years later, when I founded the Western Buddhist Order, I took the process a stage further. As originally envisaged, the Order comprised a hierarchy of different degrees of ordination, from *upāsaka* ordination up to *bhikkhu* ordination, corresponding to a hierarchy of different levels of commitment to the Three Jewels; but eventually, as I realized how necessary it was to emphasize that Going for Refuge is primary, and lifestyle secondary, these ordinations were all integrated into a single ordination, that of the *dharmacārī* (masc.) or *dharmacāriṇī* (fem.), an individual who goes for Refuge to the Three Jewels and who, as a means of giving expression to that continuing act in his or her everyday life, whether 'lay' or 'monastic', undertakes to observe the ten precepts.[739] No longer were lay ordination and *bhikkhu* ordination even placed on the same footing. There was only one principial Going for Refuge, one ordination, one spiritual community.

VI

Probably there is in the Buddhist world not a single Buddhist monk whose ordination would be recognized as technically valid by all other monks, or even by a majority of them. This certainly does not mean that there are no virtuous monks, that is, monks who are guiltless of any breach of the *sikkhāpadas*, whether major or minor, and deserving of the respect of all followers of the Buddha. Scattered throughout the Buddhist oecumene there must be thousands, perhaps tens of thousands, of such monks, many of them living in comparative obscurity, their merits known only to a tiny band of disciples and supporters. Yet impossible though it is for a monk to be a monk *without* observing the *sikkhāpadas*, even virtuous monks, and virtuous Theravādin monks in particular, believe themselves to be monks not on account of their observance of the (monastic) *sikkhāpadas*, which can in any case be observed by the layman without his ceasing to be a layman, but because they have received monastic ordination and believe that ordination to be technically valid. It is the same with those *bhikkhus* who are not so virtuous. They too believe that they are *bhikkhus*, not indeed on account of their observance of the *sikkhāpadas*, which may be quite lax, but because they have received *bhikkhu* ordination, at least in the sense of having undergone the ordination ceremony. This is by no means all. Those who have received monastic ordination not only believe themselves to be *bhikkhus*, but practically all of them, not excluding those whose observance of the *sikkhāpadas* is of the laxest, also believe that they are entitled to the support of the laity and should be treated with the utmost formal respect. In their eyes, only too often, the 'good Buddhist', i.e. the good lay Buddhist, is the one who is a lavish giver to the *bhikkhus* and treats them virtually like *arhants*.

This brings me to a point I regret having to make. During my fourteen years as a *bhikkhu* in India, I came to the conclusion that the extreme veneration shown to *bhikkhus* by the Theravādin laity is really quite bad for them. I am not saying that respect itself is a bad thing. Neither am I saying that the showing of respect to others is bad for one. On the contrary, I believe parents, teachers, elders, and the *truly* great, ought to be shown more respect than is customary nowadays. What I am saying is that the kind of veneration shown by the Theravādin laity to *bhikkhus*, by prostrating before them, seating them on a higher level, serving them on bended knees, and giving even the juniormost of them precedence over the highest lay dignitaries, has a negative rather than a positive psychological effect on them. The effect is somewhat less negative in the case of a few of the more conscientious *bhikkhus*, for whom such veneration acts as an incentive so to live as to deserve veneration. In the case of the majority the effect is very negative indeed, serving as it does to reinforce their sense of the superiority of the *bhikkhu* to the layman and giving them, in some instances, a quite inflated idea of their own importance and even of their own spiritual attainments. Indeed *bhikkhus* of long standing may have become so accustomed to being treated with the kind of veneration I have described, that they are unable to imagine being treated in any other way and unable to relate to the laity except on the basis of such veneration. Should Western converts to Buddhism, for example, happen to treat them with no more than ordinary politeness, they are liable to become uneasy, disconcerted, or even annoyed. 'These people have no faith,' they have been known to remark on such occasions, by faith meaning, really, faith in the superiority of *bhikkhus*.

In making this criticism, as I am afraid it is, I am referring specifically to Theravādin *bhikkhus*. I am not referring to those Chinese and Tibetan monks who follow one or other version of the Sarvāstivādin Vinaya, a Vinaya which is in substantial agreement with its Theravādin counterpart. Tibetan monks, in particular, are far less concerned to insist on the difference between the monk and the layman. They have no hesitation, for example, in returning the salutations of the laity, which Theravādin *bhikkhus* rarely if ever do. The reason for this difference may be that Tibetan monks are psychologically and spiritually more sure of themselves, or it may be that in Tibet the veneration that in Theravādin countries is shown to *bhikkhus* is (or was) directed towards the *tulkus* or 'incarnate lamas'. Most likely the main reason is that monk and layman alike accept the bodhisattva ideal, which has been described as the 'Presiding Idea' of Tibetan Buddhism.[740] Whatever the reason for it may be, the difference undoubtedly exists, Theravādin *bhikkhus* being not only more concerned to insist on the superiority of the monk but also more concerned that the layman should give practical recognition to that superiority by supporting the monk and venerating him. Often one of the first things to be taught by Theravādin *bhikkhus* working in India and in the West is 'how to pay proper respect to *bhikkhus*'. A senior Ceylonese *bhikkhu* once related to me, with every appearance of satisfaction, how he had taught the Muslim waiter in the five star hotel where he was staying to cut and offer him bananas in the approved manner and repeating the prescribed Pāli formula.

Justifications for the extreme veneration shown to *bhikkhus* by the Theravādin laity, and expected from the latter by the *bhikkhus* themselves, are by no means wanting. Respect is shown to the robe, one will be told, not to the wearer of the robe. But this is not very convincing. There is nothing about a piece of yellow cloth that makes it inherently worthy of respect. Whatever respect is shown it is shown on account of the ethical and spiritual qualities with which it has come to be associated. These qualities are human qualities, so that when one shows respect to the robe it is really these qualities one is respecting, not the robe itself. Should the wearer of the robe actually embody those qualities in his own person one ought to be able to respect him regardless of the colour of his dress; should he not so embody them, and even embody qualities of an opposite kind, one might as well hang a robe on a stick and show respect to that, without the necessity of supporting someone who wears the robe.

An important principle is involved here. It is natural that a particular colour, or cloth of that colour, should be associated with certain ethical and spiritual qualities, and as symbolism is an essential part of religion we need not regret this. It is also natural that there should be people who think that the wearing of a particular colour endows them with the ethical and spiritual qualities associated with that colour, and even people who adopt the colour for the sake of the material advantages to be gained from the respect shown to those qualities. At the same time – and this is the principle – there must not be too great a discrepancy between the qualities associated with a particular colour and the qualities actually possessed by the wearer of the colour, nor must such a discrepancy be allowed to become the norm, as it has become the norm in at least some parts of the Theravādin world. Should it become the norm, and remain the norm for too long a time over too big an area, the colour in question will inevitably lose its old associations and come to be associated with the actual qualities of the average wearer. The minority of conscientious *bhikkhus* might then find themselves in a rather odd position, with *dis*respect being shown to the robe, not to the wearer of the robe.

VII

Those who are ordained, in the technical Vinaya sense, are objects of extreme veneration to the Theravādin laity. Those who are not ordained, are not. The truth of these statements is borne out by the plight of the *maechis* of Thailand and their counterparts in the other Theravādin countries of south-east Asia.[741] *Maechis* are sometimes spoken of, in English, as 'nuns', but they are not nuns in the sense of being *bhikkhunīs*, the approximate female equivalent of *bhikkhus*. They are women who permanently observe the eight (or it may be the nine) precepts, who wear white (they are not allowed to wear yellow), and who devote themselves, to the extent that circumstances permit, to meditation and study and to the uplift of their lay sisters. Some *maechis* lead exemplary spiritual lives, practising the Dharma with a single-mindedness not equalled by all Thai *bhikkhus*. Yet many *maechis* – and there are tens of thousands of them – have to endure a good deal of hardship. Not being ordained, they are not venerated or supported by the laity in the way *bhikkhus* are (technically speaking, the *maechis* are laywomen), the reason for this being that supporting the unordained is less productive of merit than supporting the ordained. *Maechis* represent, if not money actually wasted, then a very poor investment. Usually they have to fend for themselves and find their own support, on occasion doing this by means of ordinary begging, as distinct from the *bhikkhu*'s ceremonious 'going for alms'. Not only are the *maechis* not supported by the laity in the way *bhikkhus* are. They receive little or no encouragement from the Thai monastic order, some of whose members regard them as a threat to their own livelihood.

The tradition of *bhikkhunī* ordination having died out in Thailand, as it has in the other Theravādin countries of south-east Asia, the *maechis* are unable to improve their lot by becoming *bhikkhunīs*. Unable, that is, to improve it by becoming *bhikkhunīs* within the Theravāda.[742] In theory they could become 'Mahāyāna' *bhikṣuṇīs*, the Sarvāstivādin (Dharmagupta) lineage of *bhikṣuṇī* ordination having survived in China and Korea as part and parcel of Mahāyāna Buddhism, but in practice this is not really an option. For Western women who become Buddhists and want to lead a monastic life there are no such difficulties. Not only do they not suffer the social and educational disadvantages of the *maechis*. It is open to them to take ordination as 'Mahāyāna' *bhikṣuṇīs*, as a handful of them have in fact done in recent years. Some Western Buddhist women, adherents of the Theravāda, would prefer to take ordination as Theravādin *bhikkhunīs*, and are trying to revive the tradition of *bhikkhunī* ordination. In my view the attempt is misguided, representing as it does the same unhealthy emphasis on ordination, in the technical Vinaya sense, that we find in the case of *bhikkhu* ordination. It moreover betrays a preoccupation with socio-religious status rather than showing a concern for monastic life as such. After all, there is nothing to prevent a woman from observing the appropriate *sikkhāpadas* or rules of training, even without being a *bhikkhunī*. That the attempt to revive the tradition of *bhikkhunī* ordination betrays a preoccupation with socio-religious status is evidenced by the fact that no Western Buddhist woman who wants to lead a monastic life ever seriously contemplates observing *all* the *bhikkhunī sikkhāpadas*. In particular, she does not contemplate observing those *sikkhāpadas* which subordinate the *bhikkhunī* sangha to the *bhikkhu* sangha and make the seniormost nun junior to the juniormost monk, with all that this entails in the way of making prostrations and giving precedence.[743] Thus the Western Buddhist woman's wish for *bhikkhunī* ordination is a desire, at least to an extent, for socio-religious status, especially for parity of status with the *bhikkhu*, and as such has its origins not in the idea of 'Going Forth' from home into the life of homelessness but rather in egalitarian notions that have nothing to do with Buddhism.

Western Buddhist women who want to lead a genuinely monastic life should stop thinking in terms of *bhikkhunī* (or *bhikṣuṇī*) ordination. Instead, they should emulate the *maechis* of Thailand, taking no precepts that they do not intend to observe, wearing simple clothing appropriate to their culture, and devoting themselves to meditation and study and other activities compatible with their vocation. It is unlikely that they will endure the kind of hardship the *maechis* have to endure (not that monastic life can ever be easy). Ideally, they will think of themselves not as nuns but as individuals who go for Refuge to the Three Jewels, and will see the monastic life as an expression of that Going for Refuge in terms of a particular lifestyle.

VIII

It has been said that Buddhism has been in decline for nearly a thousand years. This is an exaggeration, leaving out as it does important developments in Japan and Tibet, but it is an exaggeration of a truth. In the twentieth century the process of decline has accelerated. The greater part of Buddhist Asia is now under Communist control, while the rest of it is subject to the unhealthy pressures of capitalist consumerism. The only really bright spots in an otherwise almost uniformly dark picture are the revival of Buddhism in India and its spread to the countries of the West. Both of these, the revival in India no less than the spread to the countries of the West, are attended by serious difficulties. In the course of its twenty-five centuries of history Buddhism has accumulated an enormous amount of cultural baggage, most of which will have to be shed if the Dharma is to be really established – or, in the case of India, re-established – in the new environment, as distinct from a branch of one of its ethnic expressions being kept artificially alive under hothouse conditions. Much of that baggage is associated with the monastic order, which even in Asia is in need of a thorough reformation – not, indeed,

> A godly, thorough Reformation…
> As if religion were intended
> For nothing else but to be mended,[744]

but a reformation in the sense of a restatement of fundamentals and an expression of that restatement in more appropriate terms.

In the course of communicating these reflections on my *bhikkhu* ordination, forty-three years ago, I may have given the impression that I reject monasticism. This is by no means the case. What I reject is the identification of the spiritual life with the monastic life and the monastic life itself with pseudo-monastic formalism, an identification that has the effect of displacing the act of Going for Refuge from its central and definitive place in the Buddhist life, creating a division between the monastic order and the laity, and relegating the latter to the position of second-class Buddhists, besides seriously undermining the whole structure of Buddhism, both theoretical and practical. Far from rejecting monasticism, I have a very high regard for it, but as an *expression* of commitment to the Three Jewels, not as constitutive of that commitment. For the greater part of my own adult life I have lived as a monk, and despite the flaw in my ordination ceremony, and despite the fact that it took me a long time to realize that commitment is primary, lifestyle secondary, I have no regrets. Indeed I rejoice that I could live in this way, regretting only that I was not a better monk. I would like to see a revival of Sūtra-style monasticism throughout the Buddhist world. I would like to see more monks (and nuns) within the Western Buddhist Order, twenty-odd members of which already observe the training rule of chastity as *anagārikas*. But what *is* monasticism? What is a *monk*? Before saying anything more about WBO *anagārikas* I must deal briefly with this question.

A monk is one who is vowed to (a) chastity, (b) fewness of possessions, (c) simplicity of lifestyle, (d) careerlessness, and (e) community living.

(a) *Chastity*. This is what really defines a monk. Whatever other virtues one may possess, if one is not chaste one is not a monk, though it is, of course, possible to practise chastity without being a monk, i.e. without being *vowed* to chastity or living as a monk in other ways. Thus there can be no such thing as a 'married monk', the expression being a contradiction in terms, the more especially as the English word 'monk', like its equivalent in other European languages, derives ultimately from the Greek *monos*, alone. To speak of 'married Mahāyāna monks', as some have done, is quite inaccurate, and highly misleading. The traditional Buddhist term for chastity is *brahmacarya* (Pāli *brahmacariya*), and the vow or training-rule of chastity is couched, in terms that are grammatically negative, as 'abstention from non-chastity'. *Brahmacarya*, sometimes translated as celibacy (really the state of being unmarried, especially as consequent upon the taking of a religious vow of chastity), means a great deal more than abstention from sexual activity.[745] As I have explained elsewhere, *brahmacarya* means faring, practising, or living like Brahmā, that is, like one of those sublime spiritual beings who, transcending sexual dimorphism, occupy a range of celestial realms correlative to, and accessible from, the *dhyānas* or states of superconsciousness.[746] Since a Brahmā has no gross material body, there is no question of his having possessions, or lifestyle, or career. He moreover lives in company with other Brahmās. Similarly, one who practises *brahmacarya* or chastity will naturally tend to limit his possessions, to live simply, and to do without a gainful occupation. He will also naturally tend to live as a member of a spiritual community. Thus chastity not only defines the monk but is also the *fons et origo* of his other vows.

(b) *Fewness of possessions*. According to the Theravādin Vinaya a *bhikkhu* may possess only eight things: three *civaras* or 'yellow robes', an alms bowl, a razor, a girdle, a needle, and a water-strainer (the Sarvāstivādin Vinaya adds books and a few other items), though he also has a share in the use of the collective property of his monastery such as furniture and buildings. The modern monk will find it difficult to limit his personal possessions to the extent that a *bhikkhu* is (or was) required to do, especially if he happens to live in the West. He will also find it difficult to do without money.[747] Detailed legislation in this field is impossible, perhaps even undesirable. In principle the monk should limit his personal possessions to immediate necessities, resisting any temptation to accumulate, hoard, or save for the proverbial rainy day either belongings or money. He will bear in mind the example of the *bhikkhus* of old, who did not possess an extra robe, and who refused to keep salt from one day to the next. Perhaps he and his brother monks will be able to echo their song:

Happy indeed let us live, we who possess nothing.
Let us live feeding on joy, like the gods of sonant light.[748]

(c) *Simplicity of lifestyle*. Traditionally, this is covered by the sixth, seventh, eighth, and ninth of the ten precepts observed by the *sāmaṇera* or novice monk, relating, respectively, to abstention from untimely meals, from worldly amusements and entertainments, from personal adornment, and from luxurious living conditions.[749] The kind of spirit that pervades these four precepts is sufficiently obvious, and by no means to be regarded as limited to them. A monk living in our modern consumer society will formulate for himself hundreds of new precepts of this type, corresponding to the hundreds of different things he will have to give up if he wants to achieve simplicity of lifestyle. The simplicity of that lifestyle will not, however, be a sordid simplicity. It will be a refined simplicity, reflecting aesthetic as well as ethical and spiritual values, if indeed these can be separated. It will be a simplicity like that of a Greek vase painting or a Japanese 'Zen garden' of rocks and raked sand.

(d) *Careerlessness*. A career is 'a profession or occupation chosen as one's life work' (*Collins*) or 'way of making a livelihood and advancing oneself' (*New Oxford*). By careerlessness I therefore mean not having a gainful occupation that acts as the focal point of one's worldly ambitions and is the means by which one supports oneself and one's family. This is not to say that the monk does not work, or that (as in the Theravāda) he will necessarily be dependent on the 'laity', i.e. on those who do work. If his monastery is unable to support him he will either work at or from 'home' in the way Zen monks do ('a day of no working is a day of no eating')[750] or take an outside job of a kind that is not incompatible with his vocation. Should he take an outside job he normally will continue to live in the monastery and continue to be a full member of the community. The monk should never allow the monastic life itself to become a kind of career, as it has in many parts of the Buddhist world, with examinations, grades, titles, and financial incentives.

(e) *Community living*. The monk needs spiritual friends. This is not to suggest that those who are not monks do not need spiritual friends, but only that the monk will probably feel the need for them more acutely. Spiritual friends are best found, and spiritual friendship is best cultivated, within the context of a spiritual community, that is, a group of people having a common spiritual commitment and living and/or working together in order to help one another strengthen that commitment and give it more effective expression. Since the monk is one who gives expression to his commitment by vowing himself to chastity and so on, he needs not just spiritual friends but spiritual friends who are similarly vowed, and since spiritual friends are best found, and spiritual friendship is best cultivated, within a spiritual community, he also needs to live and/or work with other monks. He needs, ideally, to belong to a monastery, or at least to a 'closed' residential spiritual community, that is, one that does not admit visitors of the opposite sex.

The reason the monk will probably feel the need for spiritual friends more acutely than those who are not monks is that, vowed as he is to chastity, he has no occasion to experience the emotional warmth and intimacy which, even when they happen to be spiritually committed, are bound up, for those who are not monks, with their sexual relationship or relationships. For such warmth and intimacy he will depend on his spiritual friends, but especially on those who are themselves monks and who, being in the same position, feel the need for spiritual friends no less acutely than he does. Without spiritual friends the monk is in danger of drying up emotionally, as appears to have happened with so many of the Roman Catholic priests who, in recent years, have left the priesthood to get married – not, indeed, for the sake of carnal indulgence so much as for the sake of close human companionship.

The fact that a monk is one who is vowed to chastity, fewness of possessions, simplicity of lifestyle, careerlessness, and community living, does not mean that he is vowed only to these things. He is a Buddhist, and as a Buddhist he also observes the *sikkhāpadas* or rules of training undertaken by all Buddhists regardless of lifestyle, such as abstention from killing living beings, from taking the not-given, and from false, harsh, frivolous, and slanderous speech.[751] Chastity and the rest do not, in fact, constitute a set of additional, specifically 'monastic' vows, so much as a more thoroughgoing application of the principles underlying certain of the rules of training observed by the laity, i.e. observed by monks and laity in common. A Buddhist monk, it must be emphasized, is not a monk who happens to be a Buddhist but a Buddhist who happens to be a monk, and as such he has infinitely more in common with a Buddhist who is not a monk than he has with a monk who is not a Buddhist.

This brings me back to the subject of WBO *anagārikas*. Being a member of the Western Buddhist Order, a WBO *anagārika* observes the same ten precepts as other members of the Order – precepts which they all took when they were ordained. The only difference is that the *anagārika* observes the third precept not in the form of abstention from sexual misconduct (*kāmesu-micchācārā*) but in the form of abstention from unchastity (*abrahmacariya*). This more 'monastic' version of the third precept is taken some time after ordination (it may be a year or it may be twenty or more years after); it is taken formally, at a special ceremony in the course of which the new *anagārika* is given either a yellow robe or a yellow *kesa*, as he (or she) prefers, to replace the white *kesa* given at the time of ordination. The taking of a vow of chastity does not constitute an additional, higher ordination, and the status of the *anagārika* within the Order is no different from that of any other Order member. Whether in relation to one another or in relation to Mitras and Friends, all Order members have the same status, which is to say, they have no status, the concept of status being one that is meaningless from the spiritual point of view.

In the Buddhist world, however, and especially in the Theravādin part of that world, the (celibate) monk definitely does have status. He has a very high socio-religious status indeed, higher than that of even the most eminent layman. Consequently those who are desirous of status, but who are doubtful of their ability to achieve it by ordinary means, may be tempted to become monks, even though they do not really want to abstain from sexual activity. For them such abstention is the price that has to be paid for (monastic) status, just as for their counterparts in the Roman Catholic priesthood celibacy is 'part of the deal'. Since in the Western Buddhist Order no such status attaches to *anagārika*-hood, inasmuch as the taking of the vow of chastity does not constitute an additional, higher ordination, there can be no question of an Order member being tempted to take a vow of chastity for the sake of status. An Order member takes a vow of chastity, and becomes an *anagārika*, simply in order to deepen his experience of Going for Refuge and to help shift the locus of his being from the *kāmaloka* or world of (sensuous) desire to the *rūpaloka* or world of (archetypal) form, that is, to the *brahmā*-realms. He takes it, moreover, only after consulting with his spiritual friends and making sure that his living conditions will be conducive to its observance. Thus he is unlikely to break this, the 'monastic' version of the third precept, in the way that it was broken by so many of my old *bhikkhu* friends in India, who, while they may not have become monks for the sake of status, certainly were not strongly motivated to abstain from sexual activity.

Though the WBO *anagārika* takes the vow of chastity he is not vowed to fewness of possessions, simplicity of lifestyle, careerlessness, or community living, and is not, therefore, a monk in the sense in which I define the term. Chastity being the *fons et origo* of the other vows, however, the *anagārika* will have a natural tendency to live in the kind of way that is envisaged by these vows, simply because he is practising chastity. He will have a natural tendency to live as a monk. When I say that I would like to see more monks in the Western Buddhist Order it is the fact that *anagārika*-hood has this tendency that I have in mind, rather than the formal taking, by the individual *anagārika*, of (monastic) vows other than that of chastity.

IX

I am writing these reflections in the study of my flat in East London. Above the mantelpiece hangs a reproduction of Turner's *Bridge of Sighs, Ducal Palace and Custom-House, Venice*, with the pink and white façade of the Doge's palazzo gleaming from across the olive green water and the pink and white finger of the Campanile, in the centre of the painting, pointing into the pure cerulean sky.[752] It has been my companion for the last four years, bringing back memories of my two visits to Venice, in 1966 and 1983,[753] and serving to remind me that for hundreds of years Venice, the birthplace of Marco Polo, was Europe's gateway to the East.

Before the Turner I had a companion of a very different kind. This was Holman Hunt's *The Scapegoat*, described by a leading modern art critic as 'his most disturbing painting',[754] which hung above my mantelpiece for about ten years. Mine was a reproduction of a small study for this painting, which differs from the final version in that it includes a rainbow, the symbol of hope. Visitors were sometimes startled to see a picture of a goat occupying the place of honour in my study. Presumably they expected to see a picture of the Buddha. It is difficult to say why Holman Hunt's painting should have had such an appeal for me. Certainly I responded to the 'psychedelic' Pre-Raphaelite colour values of the work. But I must also have felt an inner connection with its subject matter, for shortly before purchasing my reproduction I wrote a poem entitled 'The Scapegoat: After Holman Hunt'. Indeed, looking through my files to check the date of the poem, I discovered that ten years earlier, in 1969, only one year after founding the Western Buddhist Order, I had written a poem on the same theme, though this first, much earlier 'Scapegoat' poem of mine was not 'after' the great Pre-Raphaelite artist in the way its successor was. Thus the image of the scapegoat, especially as mediated by Holman Hunt's powerful painting, must have been of particular significance to me during this period. The second of the two poems, written in 1978, is in sonnet form and reads as follows:

> Half hoof-deep in the salt-encrusted sands
> Of the Dead Sea, he stops and hesitates
> At last, perhaps because he understands –
> Far from the rancid herd-loves and herd-hates –
> What place it is his red eye contemplates
> With head half turned. Beyond the bottle green
> Of stagnant waters, mauve-pink hills serene
> Border, and yellow sky commensurates.
>
> but undismayed, his horned head bent,
> And threads of tell-tale scarlet on his brow,
> He halts before the staring countershape
> Of last year's victim, with salt sludge half blent.
> Green, mauve-pink, yellow glow intenser now
> And throb insistent. *There is no escape.*[755]

No escape for the unfortunate beast. He is the sacrificial victim. On the Day of Atonement the High Priest laid upon his head all the sins of the children of Israel and sent him into the wilderness to die. So now here he is, with all those sins upon him, waiting for death among the bones of the dead.[756]

When I wrote this poem I too was in the wilderness, as I had been when I wrote its predecessor, and the Western Buddhist Order was in the wilderness with me. Indeed it was my being in the wilderness that made it possible for me to found the Western Buddhist Order. I had been sent into the wilderness by ... but it does not really matter who sent me there. Unlike the goat in my poem I did not stop and hesitate: I did not die, as I was supposed to do. The wilderness is a wonderful place. In it many things become clear to one. What became clear to me was not the absolute centrality, in the Buddhist life, of the act of Going for Refuge to the Three Jewels (this had been clear to me for some time), so much as the need for the fact of that centrality to find 'collective' embodiment in a new Buddhist movement, and it was because this had become clear to me that I was led to found the Western Buddhist Order. What was less clear was the extent to which organizing one's existence round the Three Jewels, as one did when Going for Refuge became the central act of one's life, was a disruption of the 'normal' pattern of that existence, both individual and collective, and even of many 'traditional' Buddhist attitudes and practices. Just how disruptive it could be became clear, at least to an extent, as soon as Order members started making a serious effort to organize their existence round the Three Jewels, and especially as they started experimenting with different lifestyles. Not being a *bhikkhu*, in the technical Vinaya sense, and having in any case been sent into the wilderness, I too experimented with different lifestyles, sometimes living more like a monk, sometimes more like a layman. Whatever the lifestyle, the act of Going for Refuge remained central to my life, and I continued to spend the greater part of my time studying, writing, meditating, lecturing, and teaching.

The sending of the scapegoat into the wilderness is an act of betrayal. He does not know he is being sent to his death. Perhaps he thinks he is being taken to greener pastures. Sending me into the wilderness was an act of betrayal on the part of those who sent me there, for I trusted them, just as I had trusted those *bhikkhus* who, knowing that one of their number was not 'completely pure', had nonetheless gone ahead with the ordination ceremony and made me, as I believed for six years, a *bhikkhu* in the technical Vinaya sense. But betrayal has been described as an initiation into a new kind of consciousness.[757] There is a creative stimulus in it, and the betrayed one 'must somehow resurrect himself, take a step forward, through his own interpretation of what happened.'[758] Hence I do not regret being betrayed by those who sent me into the wilderness, for just as my betrayal by the *bhikkhus* contributed, eventually, to my spiritual development and my understanding of the Dharma, so my being sent into the wilderness led to the founding of the Western Buddhist Order.

Today I am not in the wilderness, neither is the Western Buddhist Order, except to the extent that the world itself is a wilderness. Working mainly through the different FWBOs, the 500-odd members of the Order seek to further the spread of Buddhism in the world by means of an organic network of ideas, practices, and institutions, as well as with the help of imagination and experiment.[759] As for me, I live as a monk, not because I have taken any vows but because that is the way I prefer to live, and with my Turner for companion devote myself mainly to literary work. The desert has been made to bloom as the rose. The promise of the rainbow has been fulfilled.

X

These reflections have been concerned with the past. But one also needs to look at the future. Not that the future can be predicted, but present trends may be indicative of possible future developments, and these can be encouraged if positive and discouraged if negative. According to a recent news item, the closest advisers of Jacques Delors, the President of the European Commission, believe there is now a spiritual void in Britain and other EEC countries and that Mr Delors should fill that void by subtly turning European federalism into a semi-religious crusade.

> Two internal commission reports lie on Mr Delors's desk, one of them strictly confidential. They are written in the baffling style, replete with diagrams, of a French seminarian. But the gist is clear.
>
> Ancient religious differences, say the authors, are at the heart of the conflict besetting the Maastricht Treaty on European Union; and religion – or at least some kind of peculiar new Euro-spirituality inspired by Brussels – is the answer to the Community's political crisis.
>
> 'We are not fascists,' says one of the authors, from his eyrie in Delors's personal think-tank, the 'Cellule de Prospective' charged with producing radical answers to the president's problems. 'We do not want to manipulate the soul of anybody.'
>
> But he believes only one cause is grand enough to transcend European popular disaffection with national political institutions; only one idea is big enough to restore faith in society: Europe – with spiritual knobs on.[760]

After referring to an encounter in Brussels between Mr Delors and the Archbishop of Canterbury, and to the rise of economic and political nationalism across the Community, the news item goes on to reveal that one of the reports on Mr Delors's desk, *Europe's Vocation*, drawn up by Mr Marc Luyckx, a full-time EC official, speaks of a 'crisis of democracy and a cultural change which has assaulted politics,' and a consequent 'hunger for spirituality'. Mr Luyckx concludes:

> Europe will be meaningful if it is seen by Europeans, and by the rest of the world, as having a contribution to make to the search for a meaning for human life at the end of the twentieth century.

The other report, *Churches and Ethics After Prometheus*, gives a detailed analysis of the religious and cultural reasons for strife between the 58 per cent of the [European] Community who are Catholics and the 28 per cent who are Protestant.

> Catholics tend to be 'vertical, hierarchical and centralised,' says the author; in other words, he says, they tend to be 'corrupt', 'autocratic', with more susceptibility to the mafia and maximum bureaucracy.
>
> Protestant countries, on the other hand – such as Britain and Denmark – tend to be more democratic and open, with less tolerance of centralised control.
>
> 'This is vital for understanding the Danish rejection of Maastricht,' says the official, 'They thought the Community was about trade, something they could understand. Now they feel trapped in a Community of Latins and continentals.'
>
> But these differences can be overcome, he says. The exact recipe, frankly, is vague.... The revolts against Brussels in 1992, then, were caused not by an overweening bureaucracy, but by the failure of Brussels to match the spiritual needs of the age.[761]

I do not know if economic and political union with the countries of continental Europe will be good for the United Kingdom.[762] I do not know if it will be good for those countries themselves, whether individually or collectively. But I am sure spiritual union would be good for both the United Kingdom and the countries of continental Europe, that is, good for all the people of Europe. For historical reasons, if for no others, neither Catholicism nor Protestantism can provide the inspiration needed for this kind of union, being in fact themselves – according to the author of the *Churches and Ethics After Prometheus* report – largely responsible for the differences within Europe that have to be overcome. They are part of the problem, not part of the solution. In effect, Christianity is part of the problem. What is needed, if the spiritual void in Britain and the other EEC countries is to be filled, and full economic and political union achieved (assuming this to be a good thing), is a spiritual 'third force'. That Buddhism could be such a force it would be rash and simplistic to assert. But I am confident Buddhism could make an important contribution to such a force; that it could help fill the void, help match the spiritual needs of the age.

The Buddhism that could do this is not the traditional Buddhism of south-east Asia and the Far East. It would have to be a Buddhism that was not identified with monasticism, and that had shed all unnecessary oriental cultural baggage. It would have to be a Buddhism in which commitment to the Buddha, the Dharma, and the Sangha was primary, and lifestyle secondary. It would have to be a Buddhism in which there would be no need for reflections such as these.

Was The Buddha a Bhikkhu?

A REJOINDER TO A REPLY TO *FORTY-THREE YEARS AGO*

INTRODUCTORY NOTE

Was the Buddha a Bhikkhu? is a response to an article by Bhikkhu Brahmavamso (also known as Ajahn Brahm), a British-born Theravādin *bhikkhu* and founder – later abbott – of Bodhinyana, a monastery in the Thai Forest tradition near Perth, Australia. His article was entitled 'On the Validity and Meaning of the Bhikkhu Ordination in Theravada'. An edited version was published in the British Forest Hermitage *Newsletter* in April 1994. Bhikkhu Brahmavamso's article was itself a response – to *Forty-Three Years Ago*. In *Was the Buddha a Bhikkhu?* Sangharakshita closely examines Bhikkhu Brahmavamso's assertions and shines a light on their deeper implications. It was published by Windhorse Publications in 1994.

A friend to whom I had written about his new book replied that he greatly appreciated my recognition of the book's value, adding, 'As you may have found yourself, publication is often followed by a disquieting silence.' I had indeed found that this was often the case. But not always. Publication, I had also found, was sometimes followed by a definite response. This has certainly been the case with *Forty-Three Years Ago*, subtitled 'Reflections on my Bhikkhu Ordination, on the Occasion of the Twenty-Fifth Anniversary of the Western Buddhist Order', which was published a year ago. The response to this little work has not been deafening, but there has certainly been a response, and with the exception of a single dissentient voice it has been welcoming and appreciative. One Buddhist correspondent – not a member of the FWBO – wrote to say that he found himself in agreement with more or less everything I said about the ambiguous status of the *bhikkhu* ordination. 'In a sense the whole issue is blindingly self-evident,' he concluded. 'As you point out, though, it is concealed by a huge conspiracy of Asian (and non-Asian) face-saving self-interest.' While agreement with what one says may be more pleasant, disagreement is often more useful. I shall therefore make no further reference to the welcoming and appreciative response that *Forty-Three Years Ago* has received, but concentrate, instead, on the criticisms of the single dissentient voice.

This dissentient voice made itself heard in the pages of the April 1994 issue of the Forest Hermitage *Newsletter*, edited by Phra Ajahn

Khemadhammo from Wat Pah Santidhamma, Lower Fulbrook, near Sherbourne, Warwick.[763] The voice is not that of Phra Ajahn Khemadhammo himself. It is that of Bhikkhu Brahmavamso, of the Bodhinyana Monastery, Perth, Australia.[764] 'While I was in Australia in January,' Ajahn Khemadhammo tells us in his editorial article,

> I discussed a certain booklet with my friend Phra Ajahn Brahmavamso and later I sent him a copy. About a month ago the fax machine disgorged a detailed, handwritten, three page response, with a note allowing me to edit it. In the interests of space, what appears in the next column and over the page has been much hacked about and is minus the references. The original could be made available on request.[765]

Having thus handed over the responsibility for replying to my booklet to his friend Brahmavamso, Khemadhammo turns to the more congenial business of telling his readers about the 'vastly improved car park and drive' his hermitage is soon to have.

Naturally I read the shortened version of Bhikkhu Brahmavamso's article with interest, and before long was able to lay my hands on a copy of the original, unedited version. (Strange to say, the April issue of the Forest Hermitage *Newsletter* never reached the Order Office,[766] though hitherto it had been received there regularly.) Whereas the shortened version is entitled 'On the Validity of the Bhikkhu Ordination in Theravāda,' the original is entitled 'On the Validity and Meaning of the Bhikkhu Ordination in Theravāda.' Unlike his friend Khemadhammo, Brahmavamso does not hesitate to mention either the title of the offending booklet or the name of the author. 'A recently published booklet *Forty-Three Years Ago*,' he writes, 'written by Sangharakshita, questions the validity and meaning of the *bhikkhu* ordination in Theravāda.' Of course I do very much more than that. The booklet deals with a number of topics; but obviously only one of them is of any interest to Brahmavamso.

> Basing his argument on his own bhikkhu ordination in India in 1950, Sangharakshita comes to the conclusion that 'All this goes to show that technically valid ordination (as a bhikkhu) is virtually impossible of attainment and that if one did, miraculously, obtain it, one could not know that one had done so.'

This is not quite correct. My argument that technically valid ordination is virtually impossible of attainment and that if one did, miraculously, obtain it, one could not know that one had done so, is not based on my own ordination, i.e. not based simply on the fact that one member of the ordaining chapter was not really a *bhikkhu*. As the preceding pages made clear, it is based mainly on the difficulty of knowing (1) whether all those conferring the ordination were really *bhikkhus* (i.e. had been validly ordained by *bhikkhus* who had themselves been validly ordained – and so on back to the beginnings of the cenobitical monastic order) and (2) whether the ordination ceremony itself had been conducted in strict accordance with the requirements of the Vinaya. My own ordination, or rather my discovery that not all those taking part in it were really *bhikkhus*, was the starting point of a series of reflections, not the first link in a chain of logical deductions, and my argument would still hold good even if all those taking part in my ordination had been really *bhikkhus* – not that I could actually have known this to be the case. Brahmavamso appears not to see this, and therefore continues,

> The misleading allegation that the bhikkhu ordination is practically invalid is so serious a charge that it deserves a serious reply,

as though I had come to the conclusion that *bhikkhu* ordination was technically invalid only on the basis of my own experience of ordination in India in 1950.

The allegation that *bhikkhu* ordination is practically invalid (I am assuming that Brahmavamso's 'practically' is equivalent to my 'technically') is indeed a serious one, especially in the eyes of those who are accustomed to think of their spiritual life, and their privileged status within the Buddhist community, as being dependent on their having been ordained in the technical Vinaya sense. It therefore is not astonishing that Brahmavamso should have considered my allegation, as he terms it, deserving of a serious reply. I appreciate his willingness to engage in dialogue in this way and only wish his reply could have been even more serious and have embraced some of the more fundamental topics – more fundamental than the question of the technical validity of *bhikkhu* ordination – dealt with in *Forty-Three Years Ago*.

He begins by going straight to what he sees as the main point.

> Unfortunately, Sangharakshita, though strong in many other areas of Buddhist scholarship, has only a limited understanding of the *bhikkhu's* Vinaya. His argument against the validity of the *bhikkhu* ordination crumbles because of a mistaken premise. On pages 8 and 9, he assumes his own *bhikkhu* ordination was invalid because of the presence of a 'sham monk', that is a layman in the guise of a *bhikkhu*. One of the members of the assembly, Sangharakshita later discovered, had committed a Pārājika (an offence entailing immediate and automatic return to the status of layman), had not yet owned up to the fault, and was thus technically a layman in the robes of a monk.

Whether I am strong in other areas of Buddhist scholarship is not for me to say, but I can freely confess that my understanding of the *bhikkhu's* Vinaya is (and was) a limited one. Few *bhikkhus* have more than a limited understanding of the Vinaya, which is probably why Khemadhammo had to go half way round the world to find someone who could attempt to reply (in English) to my charge that the *bhikkhu* ordination is technically invalid. Far from consisting of a few simple rules, the Vinaya (i.e. the Vinaya Piṭaka) is a complex and elaborate body of monastic law that occupies, in the English translation, six very substantial volumes, mastery of which, together with the extensive commentarial literature, is the work of half a lifetime of scholarly specialization.[767] The average Theravādin *bhikkhu* probably has no more understanding of the Vinaya *in this sense* than the average law-abiding English citizen has of Blackstone's *Commentaries on the Laws of England*.[768] Such understanding of it as he possesses he acquires by participating in the life of the monastic community, doing what other monks do, and not doing what they do not do. Thus he does not *know* that he is observing the Vinaya (in order to know this he would have to be personally acquainted with the appropriate texts); he only *believes* that he is observing it, and he is able to believe that he is observing it because he believes that there are monks who do know the Vinaya. Once again, spiritual life is based on belief rather than on knowledge, in this case not just on belief that one is a *bhikkhu*, in the technical Vinaya sense, but on belief that one is observing the Vinaya. As I point out in *Forty-Three Years Ago*, belief of this kind is not a very secure foundation for the spiritual life.[769] But perhaps there is no need for me to enlarge on this topic in the present connection. Brahmavamso continues:

> According to the Vinaya, the third of the Tipiṭaka dealing with the monastic rules and procedures, the assumption that the presence of a 'sham monk' invalidates the ordination ceremony is certainly wrong. There may be several 'sham monks' in the assembly conferring the bhikkhu status on a candidate, but as long as there are at least five bhikkhus (ten in the Ganges Valley of India) also present, then the ordination is valid (see Pali Text Society's 'Vinaya Pitakam', vol 1, p 319f; Mahavagga 9.3).[770]

Since Brahmavamso does not actually quote the passage to which he refers (Khemadhammo's shortened version does not even give the references, leaving the reader to take it on trust that the purport of the passage is as claimed), let me quote it in full. Before so doing, however, there is an ambiguity to be cleared up. In speaking of my ordination I did not distinguish, as perhaps I should have done, between what I called the ordaining chapter (Brahmavamso's 'assembly') and the quorum required for ordination in the Middle Country. My ordination was invalid not so much because there was a single 'sham monk' in the ordaining chapter as because the number of 'sham monks' (as I afterwards discovered them to be) in that chapter was such as to render it inquorate for the purpose of *bhikkhu* ordination. That such was the case should be evident from my comment that most of the *bhikkhus* taking part in my ordination were '*like the bhikkhu with a wife and son*, bad monks' (my present italics).[771] Now for the promised quotation from the Vinaya Piṭaka.

> 'If, monks, a fourfold Order, carrying out a (formal) act, should carry out the (formal) act with a nun as the fourth (member), then it is not a (formal) act and ought not to be carried out. If, monks, a fourfold Order, carrying out a (formal) act, should carry out the (formal) act with a probationer as the fourth (member) ... with a novice ... with a woman novice ... with a disavower of the training ... with one who has committed an extreme offence

> ... with one who is suspended for not seeing an offence ... with one who is suspended for not making amends for an offence ... with one who is suspended for not giving up a wrong view ... with a eunuch ... with one living in communion as it were by theft ... with one who has gone over to a sect ... with an animal ... with a matricide ... with a parricide ... with a slayer of ones perfected ... with a seducer of a nun ... with a schismatic ... with a shedder of (a *tathāgata's*) blood ... with a hermaphrodite ... with one belonging to a different communion ... with one staying in a different boundary ... with one standing above the ground by psychic potency ... with one against whom an Order is carrying out a (formal) act as the fourth (member), it is not a (formal) act and ought not to be carried out.'
>
> Carrying out by a Fourfold (Order).
>
> 'If, monks, a fivefold (Order), carrying out a (formal) act, should carry out the (formal) act with a nun as the fifth (member) ... with one against whom the Order is carrying out a (formal) act as the fifth (member), it is not a (formal) act and ought not to be carried out.'
>
> Carrying out by a Fivefold (Order).
>
> 'If, monks, a tenfold (Order), carrying out a (formal) act, should carry out the (formal) act with a nun as the tenth (member) ... with one against whom the Order is carrying out a (formal) act as the tenth (member), it is not a (formal) act and ought not to be carried out.'
>
> Carrying out by a Tenfold (Order).[772]

The first thing that strikes one about this passage (apart from its legalistic character) is that it does not support Brahmavamso's contention that there may be several 'sham monks' in the assembly conferring the *bhikkhu* ordination on a candidate. What it actually says, with regard to the carrying out of a (formal) act (such as ordination), by an Order of four, or five, or ten *bhikkhus*, is that such a (formal) act is not a (formal) act (i.e. is invalid) if the fourth, or fifth, or tenth member of the Order, as the case may be, is a nun ... down to one against whom an Order is carrying out a (formal) act. It says nothing about the presence of 'sham monks' in the assembly, as distinct from their (disallowed) membership of the quorum. The clear purport of the passage is to exclude 'sham monks' from the quorum, not to permit their presence in the assembly at the time of ordination or other (formal) acts of the Order. Why it is important to Brahmavamso, as apparently to the tradition to which he belongs, that the presence of 'sham monks' should not invalidate the ordination ceremony, as long as there are at least five *bhikkhus*, i.e. *bhikkhus* who are not 'sham monks', (ten in the Ganges Valley) also present, will transpire later. Meanwhile, by way of contrast to the passage from the Vinaya Piṭaka, let me quote a passage about the 'monastic' life from the Sutta Piṭaka.

> Good is restraint of sight. Good is restraint of hearing. Good is restraint of smell. Good is restraint of taste.
>
> Good is restraint in deed. Good is restraint in word. Good is restraint in thought. Good is restraint everywhere. The monk restrained in every way is freed from all suffering.
>
> He who is controlled in hand, foot, speech, and thought; he who delights in meditation, is composed, solitary and contented – him they call a monk.
>
> That Bhikkhu who is controlled in tongue, moderate in speech, is not puffed up, who explains the meaning and the text – sweet, indeed, is his speech.
>
> Abiding in the Teaching, delighting in the Teaching, pondering over the Teaching, calling to mind the Teaching – a Bhikkhu such as this does not fall away from the Teaching.
>
> A Bhikkhu should not despise what he has received, and look with envy upon the gain of others. The Bhikkhu who envies the gains of others does not attain concentration.
>
> Even if a Bhikkhu's gain be slight, yet let him not despise it. If pure of life and unremitting in effort, he is praised by the very gods.
>
> He who nowhere in the mind and body finds aught of which to say 'This is mine,' he who grieves not for that which he has not – he indeed is called a Bhikkhu.
>
> The Bhikkhu who abides in loving-kindness, whose joy is in the Teaching of the Buddha – that Bhikkhu attains the peace of *Nibbana*, the quiet happy ending of compounded existence.

Empty this boat, O Bhikkhu; emptied, it will go lightly with you. Cutting out lust and hatred, you will thereby go to *Nibbana.*

Cut away these five: (self-illusion, doubt, indulgence in rites and ceremonies, lust and ill will). Abandon these five: (desire for life in worlds of form, craving for formless realms, pride, restlessness of mind, and ignorance). Cultivate these five: (confidence, energy, recollectedness, meditation, and wisdom). The Bhikkhu who has gone beyond the five fetters is called 'Crossed-the-flood.'

Meditate, O Bhikkhu; do not be heedless. Do not let your mind revolve around the sensual pleasures. Do not, through negligence, swallow a ball of (red hot) iron. As you are burnt, do not cry 'O what torture.'

There is no concentration for him who lacks wisdom; nor is there wisdom for him who lacks concentration. In whom are found both concentration and wisdom – he, indeed, is in the presence of *Nibbana.*

To the Bhikkhu who has retired to a lonely abode, who has calmed his mind, who clearly perceives the Teaching – to him there arises a joy transcending that of men.

Whenever he reflects on the rise and fall of aggregates, he assuredly experiences joy and happiness. To the discerning, this is as nectar.

For the wise Bhikkhu, these are the first things to cultivate: sense-control, contentment, restraint through observance of the rules of discipline, association with noble and energetic friends whose livelihood is pure.

Let the Bhikkhu be hospitable, refined in conduct; full of joy he will thereby make an end of suffering.

Just as the jasmine sheds its withered flowers, so, O Bhikkhus, should you totally shed lust and hatred.

The Bhikkhu who is calm in body (or subdued in deed), calm in speech, calm in mind, well composed, emptied of all appetite for the world – such a one is called 'Tranquillized.'

By thyself rouse (or censure) thyself; thyself examine thyself. Thus self-guarded, mindful, the Bhikkhu shall dwell in happiness.

Oneself is one's own protector; oneself is one's own refuge. Control, therefore, your own self as a merchant, a spirited charger.

Full of joy, full of faith in the Teaching of the Buddha, the

> Bhikkhu will attain the Peaceful State, the happy stilling of the compounds of existence.
>
> Even a young Bhikkhu who devotes himself to the Teaching of the Buddha, illumines this world as does the moon freed from a cloud.[773]

In these two passages, one from the Vinaya Piṭaka and one from the Sutta Piṭaka, we breathe two different atmospheres, even find ourselves in two different worlds. One is the world of individual spiritual life; the other the world of highly organized corporate (cenobitical) existence. In one the emphasis is on the realization of principles; in the other, conformity to rules. Not that the two are mutually exclusive *in toto*. One of the *Dhammapada* verses speaks of the wise monk as cultivating restraint through observance of the rules of discipline (*pāṭimokkha*),[774] while the Vinaya passage's reference to a disavower of the training (*sikkhā*) implies the existence of an (ethical and spiritual) training to be disavowed. Nonetheless the distance between the two worlds is immense. There lies between them a process of development that extended over many decades, probably over two or three centuries, and that of course continued well beyond the Buddha's own lifetime. This process has been little studied, and so far as I know S. Dutt's *Early Buddhist Monachism* (1924) represents the only systematic attempt to apply the methods of the higher criticism to the Vinaya literature, as distinct from merely describing that literature. Indeed, since the pioneering work of C. A. F. Rhys Davids and G. C. Pande there has been little (in English, at least) in the way of application of the higher criticism to the literature of the Sutta Piṭaka either.[775] That application in its full rigour is still to come, and no doubt will affect our understanding of Early Buddhism in much the same way that the work of such figures as Eichhorn, Strauss, and Renan in the last century and Schweitzer in the first half of this century affected our understanding of the Bible and Early Christianity.[776] However, I am digressing. The fact that the Vinaya is not a unitary (originally oral) composition, with a single author, the Buddha, formed no part of my argument in *Forty-Three Years Ago*, though it could well have done, and I advert to it now because the assumption that the Vinaya is a unitary composition, the author of which is the Buddha, appears to underlie Brahmavamso's 'fundamentalist' attitude to *bhikkhu* ordination and needs, therefore, to be borne in mind. The contrast between the world of individual spiritual life, as represented by the *Dhammapada* verses, and that of highly organized cenobitical monasticism, as represented by the passage from the *Mahāvagga* of the Vinaya Piṭaka, also serves to illustrate what I meant when, in *Forty-Three Years Ago*,[777] I expressed a wish to see a revival, throughout the Buddhist world, of what I termed Sūtra-style monasticism – not of Vinaya-style monasticism. But to return to Brahmavamso and his article. Having, as he (wrongly) believes, shown that according to the Vinaya – at least according to the *Mahāvagga* passage to which he refers – there may be several 'sham monks' in the assembly conferring the *bhikkhu* ordination on a candidate, he continues:

> The bhikkhus included in the quorum do not need to be 'parisuddha or completely pure' as Sangharakshita mistakenly stated on p. 9. They just need to be bhikkhus, not laymen, and not under suspension imposed by the extremely rare act of the Sangha called UKKHEPANIYA-KAMMA (see Pali Text Society's 'Vinaya Piṭakam', vol 2, p 21-28; Cullavagga, chapter 1, vs 25–35).[778]

From the way the reference is given one would naturally think that *Cullavagga* 1, verses 25–35, contained a straightforward and unambiguous statement to the effect that the *bhikkhus* included in the quorum do not need to be completely pure. But such is not the case. In fact it deals, in a highly legalistic manner, and for ten whole pages together, with the procedures to be followed with regard to a monk who, having fallen into an offence, does not want to see the offence (as an offence). (*To begin with*, there are the forty-three observances connected with a (formal) act of suspension for not seeing an offence.) Opinions differ regarding what constitutes 'complete purity', both within the scholarly community and among *bhikkhus*. I have participated in at least one *bhikkhu* ordination, presided over by a very distinguished Sinhalese *mahāthera* (he may have had only a limited understanding of the Vinaya), prior to which we all 'confessed our sins' and purified ourselves – presumably so as to ensure that we conferred the ordination in a state of (complete?) purity. The *bhikkhus* whose presence within the *sīmā* at my own ordination rendered the assembly inquorate for the purpose of ordination, and my ordination therefore invalid, were certainly not 'completely pure' in the sense of not being *pārājika*. But

Brahmavamso is determined to pursue the question of quorum to the bitter end.

> Even if a bhikkhu has committed a gross offence such as Sanghadisesa, a group of offences next in severity to the Pārājika; such as for lustfully embracing a woman for example, then he may still make up the quorum for the ordination ceremony (Pali Text Society's 'Vinaya Piṭakam', vol 1, p 319f; Mahavagga, chapter 9, vs 4.1–4.4). Even if the preceptor (the UPAJJHAYA) is not really a bhikkhu but a layman appearing as a monk, then this still does not invalidate the ordination (Buddhaghosa's Vinaya Commentary, the Samantapasadika, Pali Text Society's edition, vol 14, p 868). A bhikkhu ordination only fails for 'lack of a quorum' (PARISA-VIPATTI) when there are less than five bhikkhus (ten in the Ganges Valley) among the assembly conferring the ordination. Sangharakshita does not say how many were present at his ordination ceremony in India in 1950, but if for example there were thirteen of which only three were later discovered not to have been bhikkhus, then his ordination would be valid and he would have been a bhikkhu.

As I have already explained, the number of 'sham monks' present at my ordination was sufficient to render it inquorate for the purpose of *bhikkhu* ordination, and although I appreciate Brahmavamso's openness to the possibility that I may have been validly ordained my ordination must therefore remain technically invalid and I must be content to be living, now, as a Sūtra-style monk rather than as a Vinaya-style *bhikkhu*. In any case, even though I came to know that some of the *bhikkhus* present at my ordination were really laymen appearing as monks, of the remainder (with one exception) I never knew that they were *not* laymen appearing as monks. Hence there was really never any question of my *knowing* that I was a *bhikkhu* in the technical Vinaya sense. I only believed myself to be such – mistakenly, as it turned out. The *Mahāvagga* passage to which Brahmavamso refers in support of his contention that a *bhikkhu* who has committed a gross offence such as *saṅghādisesa* may still make up the quorum for the ordination ceremony is the very passage to which he referred, earlier on, in support of his contention that there may be 'sham monks' in the assembly conferring ordination on a candidate. But again the passage does not support his contention. There is no straightforward and unambiguous statement to the effect that a *bhikkhu* who has committed a gross offence such as *saṅghādisesa* may still make up the quorum for the ordination ceremony. At best this can only be inferred from the fact that a *bhikkhu* who has committed a grave offence is not explicitly mentioned among the twenty-four kinds of person with whom as a fourth, or a fifth, or a tenth member a (formal) act of the sangha may not be carried out. But even if the passage in question is accepted as supporting Brahmavamso's contention, and if both 'sham monks' and monks who have committed a gross offence may be present in the assembly conferring ordination on a candidate, and even make up the quorum, this logically results in a very strange situation, as we shall see. The assertion by Buddhaghosa, who lived a thousand years after the Buddha, that a *bhikkhu* ordination is not invalid even if the *upajjhāya* or preceptor is not really a *bhikkhu* but a layman appearing as a monk is on a par with his assertion that even if a *bhikkhu* has twenty meals a day, provided they are all taken before midday he is still a 'one-mealer'.[779] Both assertions represent a *reductio ad absurdum* of the kind of legalistic understanding of the Vinaya to which Brahmavamso would seem to be committed.

From my ordination ceremony in India in 1950 Brahmavamso turns to his own nine years as a *bhikkhu* in Thailand.

> Sangharakshita then proceeds from his mistaken premise to question the validity of every bhikkhu ordination. Even if his own bhikkhu ordination in India does not turn out to be valid because there were not the required ten bhikkhus present, it is quite illogical to infer that all bhikkhu ordinations are invalid. Theravāda Buddhism in 1950s India is hardly representative of the Theravāda Buddhist World as a whole! In Thailand, where I spent nine years as a bhikkhu, bhikkhu ordinations require only five bhikkhus to complete the quorum, but usually there are at least twenty present, sometimes over a hundred. Among the many tens of thousands of monks in Thailand there will of course be some 'sham monks' who have committed a Pārājika and not owned up, but the vast majority would not have committed a Pārājika and would be bona-fide bhikkhus who can be counted to make up

> the quorum. One does not need a degree in statistical analysis to appreciate that, given the numbers usually attending a bhikkhu ordination in Thailand this century and considering the number of 'sham monks' as a percentage of the whole Bhikkhu Sangha, it is extremely unlikely that a bhikkhu ordination can fail for lack of a quorum.

In *Forty-Three Years Ago* I certainly do not infer that all *bhikkhu* ordinations are invalid from the invalidity of my own ordination. Such an inference would indeed be quite illogical, and I am astonished that Brahmavamso should be disingenuous enough to credit me with it. As I have more than once made clear, my argument that technically valid ordination is virtually impossible of attainment and that if one did, miraculously, obtain it, one could not know that one had done so, is not based on my own ordination, but on the difficulty of knowing (1) whether all those conferring the ordination were really *bhikkhus* and (2) whether the ordination ceremony itself had been conducted in strict accordance with the requirements of the Vinaya. My discovery that not all those taking part in my ordination were really *bhikkhus* was (to repeat myself) the starting point of a series of reflections, not the first link in a chain of deductions. It alerted me to the fact that a *bhikkhu* ordination could be seriously flawed, i.e. could be technically invalid, despite the sincerity of the candidate, and led me, eventually, to consider the likelihood of all *bhikkhu* ordinations being seriously flawed and the reasons for this being the case. If I proceeded from any premise, and if there was any logical inference, it was as follows: (1) In order to know that I was validly ordained and that I am, therefore, technically a real *bhikkhu*, I must know whether the assembly ordaining me includes a quorum of validly ordained, real *bhikkhus*. (2) I cannot know whether the assembly ordaining me includes a quorum of validly ordained, real *bhikkhus*, because in order to know them to be such I would have to know all their predecessors in monastic ordination to have been such, and obviously I cannot know this. (3) Therefore I cannot know that I was validly ordained and that I am, therefore, technically a real *bhikkhu*. All this has important implications for legalistic, Vinaya-style monasticism. As I point out in *Forty-Three Years Ago*, if a *bhikkhu*'s spiritual life depends on ordination, and if he does not know, even cannot know, whether he is really ordained, then his spiritual life – not to mention his socio-religious status – has a very insecure foundation. In fact it has no foundation, and if it is to have a real foundation then that foundation must be located in his observance of the *sikkhāpadas* and other ethical and spiritual practices of Sūtra-style monasticism.[780] (Not that Vinaya-style monastics do not observe the *sikkhāpadas*. They often do; but in their case spiritual life is not *based* on such observance. It is based on their belief that they have been validly ordained and are *bhikkhus* in the technical Vinaya sense.) As for Theravāda Buddhism in the India of the 1950s not being representative of the Theravāda Buddhist world, no doubt it was not – to its advantage in some ways. It was certainly not representative of 1950s Theravāda Buddhist Ceylon (as Sri Lanka was then known), where a *bhikkhu* assassinated the prime minister,[781] any more than it was representative, in the 1970s, of a Theravāda Buddhist Thailand where *bhikkhus* blessed tanks and guns and where Kittivaddho, the famous charismatic preacher, told mass audiences that it was no more a sin to kill a Communist than to kill a fish or a fowl to offer to a monk. Glittering golden spires, however beautiful, and royal or presidential patronage, however splendid, are not very reliable indicators of the spiritual health of a religion.

Nor, for the matter of that, does the number of those in yellow (or even in brown) robes constitute any such indicator. In Thailand, Brahmavamso reminds us, there are many tens of thousands of monks, and some of these, he admits, will be 'sham monks' who have committed a *pārājika* and not owned up, but the vast majority would not have committed a *pārājika* and would be *bona fide bhikkhus* who could be counted to make up the quorum. What he overlooks is the fact that it is not sufficient for the five *bhikkhus* completing the quorum not to have committed a *pārājika*. If they are to confer a valid ordination it is also necessary that they should have been validly ordained themselves, in the technical Vinaya sense, and that the *bhikkhus* making up the quorum that ordained *them* should have been validly ordained, and so on back to the very beginning of the cenobitical monastic order. Logically speaking, as I point out in *Forty-Three Years Ago*, and should not really have to point out again, one can be sure that any *bhikkhu* was validly ordained only if one can be sure that all his predecessors in monastic ordination were validly ordained.[782] Brahmavamso also overlooks the fact that, as I also point out, an ordination, to be valid, has not only to be performed by *bhikkhus* who have not committed a *pārājika*, and who have themselves been validly ordained; it has also to be performed in strict accordance with the requirements of the Vinaya, mistakes in meeting which can easily occur. Perhaps one needs a degree in statistical analysis after all, even given the numbers usually attending a *bhikkhu* ordination in Thailand this century, for one has to take into consideration not only the number of 'sham monks' as a percentage of the whole *bhikkhu* sangha, but also the percentage of invalid ordinations in the past, whether due to incomplete quorum, wrong procedure, or any other reason. Far from it being extremely unlikely that a *bhikkhu* ordination can fail for lack of a quorum, it seems extremely unlikely that it should *not* fail. Brahmavamso himself, perhaps inadvertently, only claims that such a failure is *unlikely* to occur. But unlikelihood is a very different thing from certainty, and the unlikelihood of there not being a quorum at one's ordination, and hence of one not really being a *bhikkhu*, in the technical Vinaya sense, is not a very secure foundation for a spiritual life based, as a *bhikkhu*'s spiritual life purports to be based, on a technically valid ordination.

Yet even assuming that one does not need a degree in statistical analysis and that, as Brahmavamso evidently believes, given the numbers usually attending a *bhikkhu* ordination in Thailand this century and considering the number of 'sham monks' as a percentage of the whole *bhikkhu* sangha, it is extremely unlikely that a *bhikkhu* ordination can fail for lack of a quorum, where does this in fact leave him? It leaves him in the strange situation to which I alluded earlier. Let us try to get the situation more clearly into view. Brahmavamso maintains that the presence of 'sham monks' in the assembly does not invalidate a *bhikkhu* ordination. He also maintains, following Buddhaghosa, that even if the preceptor is not really a *bhikkhu* but a layman appearing as a monk, possibly because he has committed a *pārājika*, then this still does not invalidate the ordination. Thus he asks us to envisage a situation in which a hundred monks, let us say, assemble in the *sīmā* for an ordination ceremony. An indeterminate number of them (Brahmavamso says 'several', but in view of the difficulty of knowing whether a *bhikkhu*'s predecessors in ordination were validly ordained this should surely be 'the majority' or even 'all') are, admittedly, 'sham monks', or laymen appearing as monks. How do we tell the 'sham monks' from the real monks? Do the former sit apart from the latter, for example? Apparently they do not. They are all mixed up together in the *sīmā* and we have no means of telling which are which. We do not have any means of telling whether the *upajjhāya* or preceptor is a 'sham monk' or a real monk – or the *ācariya* or instructor, or the first, or the second, or the third *kammavācā bhikkhus*. (Incidentally, if the *upajjhāya* or preceptor may be a layman appearing as a monk, as Brahmavamso maintains, then in theory at least he may be a layman appearing as a layman.)[783] Brahmavamso then asks us to envisage a situation – and this is the principal reason for its strangeness – in which the candidate presenting himself for ordination does not really know what percentage, if any, of the *bhikkhus* in the assembly are 'sham monks', whether the preceptor is a layman appearing as a monk, or whether the *bhikkhus* playing an active part in the ordination ceremony are really monks. In other words the candidate cannot know if he has been validly ordained and that he is, by virtue of that ordination, a *bhikkhu* in the technical Vinaya sense. He can only *hope* that he has been ordained, and is a real monk, on the grounds of its being – according to Brahmavamso – *unlikely* that there are not, scattered among the hundred monks assembled for the ceremony, five *bona fide* monks who can be counted to make up the quorum. Formalism could hardly go further than this! Surely it would be better to abandon the charade of technically valid ordination and base *bhikkhu* status (if there is to be such a thing) simply on the observance of the relevant *sikkhāpadas*. But it is doubtful if Brahmavamso, wedded as he is to the concept of a technically valid *bhikkhu* ordination, would be willing to do this. Monastic life is for him unthinkable apart from technically valid *bhikkhu* ordination, which is why he is prepared to defend such ordination at all costs and why it is important to him, as to the tradition to which he belongs, that the presence of 'sham monks' in the assembly at the time of ordination should not be regarded as invalidating the ceremony.

From Thailand this century Brahmavamso passes, perhaps with a sigh of relief, to seventeenth-century Siam.

> Even in the past it is highly unlikely that a significant proportion of the bhikkhus were 'sham monks': in 17th Century Siam '… if a monk is discovered having an affair with a woman, the law condemns him to be roasted alive over a slow fire. When I was in Siam this harsh sentence was carried out on two wretches who

had been convicted of this crime.' (From 'the Natural and Practical History of the Kingdom of Siam' by Nicolas Gervaise 1688, translated by John Villiers, Bangkok 1989, p 148f.) Not many bhikkhus would be game to risk such a fate, being fired from the Sangha, so to speak.

During the last three hundred years there would have been additional opportunities for breaches in the continuity of technically valid *bhikkhu* ordination (assuming this to have been still in existence at the beginning of the period). It therefore is obvious that it was less unlikely that *bhikkhu* ordinations failed for lack of a quorum in seventeenth-century Siam than in Thailand this century. But only less *unlikely*. That it is 'highly unlikely' that in the past a significant proportion of the *bhikkhus* were 'sham monks' is itself highly unlikely, especially in view of the difficulty of knowing, not only whether all those conferring the ordination were really *bhikkhus*, but also whether the ceremony had been conducted in strict accordance with the Vinaya. The quotation from Nicolas Gervaise makes horrifying reading. According to the Vinaya, the 'punishment' for a monk who breaks the first *pārājika* by having sexual intercourse with a woman is immediate and automatic return to the status of layman.[784] There is no other (religious) penalty. In seventeenth-century Siam, however, the law condemned him to be roasted alive over a slow fire, a sentence which the presumably Christian Gervaise characterizes as 'harsh'.[785] One can only speculate how, in an ostensibly Buddhist country, such a barbarous and un-Buddhistic punishment came to be decreed for such an offence, and it would be interesting to know when it was last inflicted. Brahmavamso seems to think the awfulness of the punishment acted as a deterrent, so that, as fewer monks were tempted to break the first *pārājika*, in the past it was more than likely that *bhikkhu* ordination did not fail for lack of a quorum. It is no less possible, of course, that in seventeenth-century Siam so many *bhikkhus* were guilty of breaking the first *pārājika* that in the end the lay authorities took draconian measures to stop the rot! But why should they have done this? Why should the punishment for a breach of the Vinaya, however serious, have been characterized by such extreme cruelty? The answer is probably to be found in section 4 of *Forty-Three Years Ago*, where I explain that should Theravādin lay people come to know that a *bhikkhu* has been guilty of a breach of the *sikkhāpadas* they will feel disappointed, even angry.

> They will feel disappointed not so much on account of the breach itself as because of what it means, namely, that the *bhikkhu* is not really a *bhikkhu* – and money spent supporting one who is not a *bhikkhu* does not make merit. It is money wasted.[786]

Thus it is not inconceivable that a medieval Siamese king, incensed by the discovery that he had been cheated out of the merit he supposed himself to have earned by the lavish support of *bhikkhus* who, having broken the first *pārājika*, were in fact not really *bhikkhus*, should not only have roasted the guilty parties alive over a slow fire but also have decreed that such, in future, would be the fate of any member of the monastic order who had an affair with a woman.

The idea of an unchaste *bhikkhu* being roasted alive over a slow fire Brahmavamso, it is to be noted, seems to find amusing, jocularly describing it as 'being fired from the Sangha'. The first time I saw the phrase I could hardly believe that a *bhikkhu*, or in fact any Buddhist, could be so insensitive as actually to make, on one of the most agonizing deaths imaginable, a silly schoolboy joke that is all too reminiscent of Mme Nhu's infamous quip about (Vietnamese) Buddhist monks 'barbecuing' themselves.[787] Some may object that I am making too much of what is really no more than a careless phrase, but I do not think the matter can be dismissed so lightly. Since the publication of Freud's *Jokes and their Relation to the Unconscious*, as well as of his *The Psychopathology of Everyday Life*, we have become accustomed to the idea that such things as jokes, and seemingly innocent slips of the tongue, may possess a deeper significance than the person responsible for them is aware.[788] Brahmavamso's rather perverted sense of humour suggests that there is an element of unconscious sadism in his psychological make-up or, alternatively, that his nine years as a *bhikkhu* in Thailand, and his preoccupation with the Vinaya, especially his concern for technically valid ordination, have had a deadening effect on his natural human feelings. Be that as it may, having made his little joke he proceeds, as he evidently believes, to bring his argument to a triumphant conclusion.

> Thus even in the past it is more than likely that *bhikkhu* ordinations did not fail for lack of a quorum. Indeed, there is no legitimate evidence at all to doubt the validity of the *bhikkhu*

ordination today. To suggest otherwise is to be misinformed or simply pernicious.

Here, it is interesting to observe, Brahmavamso becomes more categorical with every sentence, even though he adduces no fresh evidence in support of his position. It is as though the mere reiteration of that position is sufficient to increase his conviction of its rightness. At first it is only 'more than likely' that *bhikkhu* ordinations did not fail for lack of quorum even in the past. (The 'even' suggests that ordinations were more likely to fail for lack of quorum in the past than in the present, whereas statistically the contrary is the case.) Then 'there is no legitimate evidence at all to doubt the validity of the bhikkhu ordination today,' as though from the *unlikelihood* of ordinations not failing for lack of quorum in the past it was possible to deduce the *indubitability* of valid, i.e. quorate, ordination in the present. Brahmavamso does not say what he means by 'legitimate' as distinct from illegitimate evidence. Presumably illegitimate evidence is that which gives reason for doubting the validity of *bhikkhu* ordination. In any case, he appears to assume that it is the invalidity of *bhikkhu* ordination that has to be proved rather than its validity: an assumption which – in view of the opportunities there have been, in the course of twenty-five centuries, for breaches in the continuity of technically valid *bhikkhu* ordination – is very much open to question. Finally, Brahmavamso declares that to *suggest* – even to suggest! – that there is any legitimate evidence to doubt the validity of the *bhikkhu* ordination today is to be misinformed or simply *pernicious*. Thus he places before me, and anyone else venturing to doubt the validity of *bhikkhu* ordination today, two rather unpleasant alternatives. If we are not misinformed we must be pernicious, and if we are not pernicious we must be misinformed. There is, of course, always the possibility of one's being misinformed, or inadequately informed, or of one's giving a wrong interpretation of such information as one happens to possess. But pernicious? According to the dictionary, pernicious means: '1. wicked and malicious. 2. Causing grave harm; deadly.' As I cannot believe that Brahmavamso means to characterize me as either wicked or malicious for doubting the validity of the *bhikkhu* ordination today, I assume he believes that I cause grave harm by so doing, even that I am deadly. But to what or to whom do I cause 'grave harm', or am 'deadly'? Obviously to *bhikkhu* ordination, in the technical Vinaya sense, and those whose spiritual life, as *bhikkhus*, is based on their belief in the validity of such ordination. In his editorial, introducing Brahmavamso's article, Ajahn Khemadhammo comments that

> the Sangha, the Bhikkhu Sangha [sic!], is one amongst a number of things, such as traditional observances, methods of meditation, difficult and rather threatening teachings like that of No Self, that can really unsettle some people.

This is very true. People can certainly be unsettled, at least initially, by the idea of the (celibate) monastic life, whether Vinaya-style or Sūtra-style, by traditional observances like the Sevenfold Puja, by methods of meditation such as the six element practice, and by difficult and (ego-) threatening teachings like those of No Self and the Void. But if they are Theravādins, and especially if they are *bhikkhus*, they can also be unsettled, it would appear, by any challenge to the validity of the *bhikkhu* ordination, in the technical Vinaya sense – a challenge that not only strikes at the root of the *bhikkhu*'s spiritual and socio-religious status but also dismantles the whole machinery of 'merit-making'. As Khemadhammo goes on to observe,

> not enough is taught about kilesa (mental defilement) and the stepping back and paying attention to the effect that things have on one's mind.

Did Brahmavamso, I wonder, (or Khemadhammo himself, for that matter) step back and pay attention to the effect that *Forty-Three Years Ago* was having on his mind? Did he ask himself why the booklet had, as it would appear, 'unsettled' him, and why he felt compelled to reply to it in the way he did? In writing my 'Reflections on my Bhikkhu Ordination', I was concerned to explore the implications of a painful personal experience: the discovery that there had been a flaw in my ordination ceremony, that really I had not been ordained, and that technically I was not a *bhikkhu*. Brahmavamso is not concerned with this experience of mine, or what it might have meant for me, and he refers to it just in passing. Nor is he concerned with the true nature of ordination (*saṃvara*), with the difference between Vinaya- and Sūtra-style monasticism, with the negative effect on *bhikkhus* of the extreme veneration shown them by the Theravādin laity, with the plight of the *maechis*, or with any of the other important topics discussed in *Forty-Three Years Ago*. His sole concern is to safeguard the spiritual and socio-religious status of the *bhikkhu* by vindicating the validity, in the technical Vinaya sense, of the *bhikkhu* ordination today.

Having done this, at least in his own estimation, Brahmavamso proceeds to deal, briefly, with the *meaning* of Theravāda *bhikkhu* ordination.

> Enough has been said by me now on the technicalities of Vinaya which do in fact prove the validity of the Theravāda bhikkhu ordination, what now of its meaning? First it is worth emphasizing that no lay-scholar, nor part-time bhikkhu, can ever fathom the profundity of the bhikkhu ordination. They would be like someone on the outside peering through the window of a house thinking they can understand what goes on inside – the reality is that they miss too much. Only a bhikkhu of many years who has lived the lifestyle in a traditional context can ever really know the meaning of the bhikkhu ordination. You have to bite the mango to realize the taste.

Brahmavamso has indeed said a lot on the technicalities of Vinaya, even if not really enough to prove the validity of the Theravāda *bhikkhu* ordination, and it is not surprising that he should not want to leave us with the impression that Vinaya is simply a matter of technicalities. Hence the rather rhetorical 'what now of its meaning?' But what does he *mean* by 'meaning'? (The meaning of meaning has been the subject of much philosophical discussion, especially in the present century.) He does not say. Neither does he actually tell us what the 'meaning' of Vinaya is. He only tells us that the non-*bhikkhu* cannot know that meaning or, what apparently amounts to the same thing, cannot ever fathom the profundity of the *bhikkhu* ordination. There is, of course, an element of truth in this. The non-*bhikkhu* can no more know the meaning of *bhikkhu* ordination, in the sense of knowing what it is really like to live the traditional *bhikkhu* life for a long period of time, than the non-parent can know the meaning of parenthood, the non-artist the meaning of art (in the sense of creative activity), or the non-lover the meaning of love. These are all instances of the radical difference between subjective knowledge, in the sense of the knowledge a person has of himself *ab intra*, and objective knowledge, in the sense of the knowledge a person has of another person (or of a thing) *ab extra*, and there is in principle no more – and perhaps no less – reason to speak of the 'profundity' of the *bhikkhu* ordination than there is to speak of the profundity of parenthood, art, love, and so on. All personal experience, qua personal experience, is opaque to objective knowledge.

But Brahmavamso is not simply maintaining that one has to live as a *bhikkhu* in order to know what it means to live as a *bhikkhu*. By a kind of semantic sleight of hand he tries to maintain that one has to live as a *bhikkhu* in order to know that the *bhikkhu* ordination, in the technical Vinaya sense, is valid. Put in logical form, his argument would run: Personal experience is not accessible to objective knowledge. The meaning of the *bhikkhu* life is a matter of personal experience. Therefore the *bhikkhu* ordination, in the technical Vinaya sense, is valid today. What Brahmavamso overlooks, or ignores, or does not care to recognize, is that the technical validity of *bhikkhu* ordination is not a matter of personal experience. It is something that belongs to the sphere of objective knowledge, and the fact of its so belonging is not to be disguised by attempting to cloak *bhikkhu* ordination, in the technical Vinaya sense, in the 'profundity' that properly pertains to the living of the *bhikkhu* life, even as it pertains to all other forms of personal experience. Brahmavamso is indeed tacitly operating with two different meanings of the 'meaning' of *bhikkhu* ordination, and switches from one to the other without warning. One meaning is that of the actual experience of living the *bhikkhu* life. The other is the fact of one's being a *bhikkhu*, in the technical Vinaya sense. Contrary to what he seems to believe, or to want us to believe, what is true of *bhikkhu* ordination understood in the first sense, i.e. that such ordination, being a matter of personal experience, is inaccessible to objective knowledge, is by no means true of *bhikkhu* ordination understood in the second sense. Brahmavamso is able to make what is true of the one appear true of the other only by omitting to distinguish between the two different meanings of '*bhikkhu* ordination' and then employing them indiscriminately, which he is able to do because he does not tell us what he *means* by 'meaning', or by Vinaya and *bhikkhu* ordination, in the first place.

The two comparisons with which he seeks to clinch his argument are therefore beside the point, and serve only to underline its fallaciousness. Someone on the outside peering through the window of a house obviously cannot understand what goes on inside, but they certainly can see whether the window frame is rotten or whether there is a hole in the ceiling. *Bhikkhu* ordination in the sense of the living of the *bhikkhu* life corresponds to what goes on inside the house. It is inaccessible to objective knowledge, being a matter of personal experience. Bhikkhu ordination in the technical Vinaya sense corresponds to the house, or to part of the house. Not only is it accessible (in theory) to objective knowledge; it is not accessible in any other way, i.e. it cannot be a matter of personal experience. Similarly with the other comparison. You have to bite the mango to realize the taste because taste is a matter of personal experience. The technical validity of your *bhikkhu* ordination, however, is not something that can be experienced, so there is no question of your being able to 'realize', by means of personal experience, that you are validly ordained. What you can experience and realize are such things as your going for Refuge to the Three Jewels, your observance of the *sikkhāpadas*, and your stepping back and paying attention to the effect that things have on your mind – and surely that is a great deal!

But although you have to bite the mango to realize the taste you can, it seems, at least recognize it for a mango by seeing – and admiring – its beautiful golden skin. Brahmavamso makes the concession with the help of an ethnological concept.

> Nevertheless, the bhikkhu ordination can be known by everybody as a rite of passage whereby a Buddhist man, already gone for refuge to the Triple Gem, willingly undertakes a further commitment to a way of life personally designed by the Buddha as the most conducive, in the Buddha's view, to the realisation of Supreme Enlightenment (ARAHATTA-PHALA).

Someone on the outside peering through the window of a house cannot understand what goes on inside. However, he can see that *something* is going on and though he cannot, being outside the house, know the meaning of what is going on he can see what it is that it resembles in outward appearance. Thus the *bhikkhu* ordination can be 'known as' a rite of passage, for this is what it resembles when looked at 'through the window'. (I am reminded here of Plato's simile of the cave. The non-*bhikkhu* is no more able to know the meaning of the *bhikkhu* ordination than the prisoners in the cave are able to see the fire behind them. Just as the prisoners see only the shadows cast on the end of the wall by the light of the fire, so the non-*bhikkhu* knows the *bhikkhu* ordination only as a rite of passage.)[789] The *bhikkhu* ordination that is known as a rite of passage is, of course, *bhikkhu* ordination in the sense of the actual living of the *bhikkhu* life, the outward appearance of which can indeed be known, even though its meaning is a matter of personal experience. Since the meaning of *bhikkhu* ordination in the technical Vinaya sense cannot be understood, or its profundity fathomed, by the non-*bhikkhu*, *bhikkhu* ordination in this sense is not a rite of passage and cannot be known as such. It is what 'goes on inside', which no one peering through the window can understand.

Ordination in the technical Vinaya sense, the validity of which Brahmavamso is concerned to uphold, accordingly would appear to be a thing separate and distinct from 'the way of life personally designed by the Buddha as the most conducive … to the realization of Supreme Enlightenment', i.e. would appear to be separate and distinct from *bhikkhu* ordination in the sense of the actual living of the *bhikkhu* life. It would even appear to be separate and distinct from the acceptance of the *pāṭimokkha-sīla* and commitment to a life of renunciation, of which Brahmavamso goes on to speak, for these two, inasmuch as they appertain to *bhikkhu* ordination in the sense of the actual living of the *bhikkhu* life, are constitutive of what can be known as a rite of passage. As I point out in *Forty-Three Years Ago*, it is ordination in the technical Vinaya sense that really makes one a *bhikkhu*, not the observance of the *sikkhāpadas*, for it is possible to observe the *sikkhāpadas* without thereby being a *bhikkhu*.[790] Thus to Theravādins, as to all upholders of Vinaya-style monasticism, the validity of *bhikkhu* ordination in the technical Vinaya sense is crucial. It therefore is to be defended at all costs, and one way of defending it is to make it a matter of personal experience by removing it from the sphere of objective knowledge, where it really belongs, and surrounding it with a mystic aura of 'profundity'.

But I must allow Brahmavamso to continue.

> It is the acceptance of the Pāṭimokkha-Sīla, the rules for bhikkhus laid down by the Buddha in the Vinaya Piṭaka,

> which is the outward sign of the bhikkhu ordination [i.e. the bhikkhu ordination as known as a rite of passage, about which Brahmavamso is still speaking] (wearing a brown robe and never lay clothes is one of these rules), and it is the inner commitment to a life of renunciation (of the pleasures based on the five senses) which forms the internal meaning of the bhikkhu ordination.

In principle all this is common to both Vinaya-style and Sūtra-style monasticism. Both accept rules, though the number may vary and though Sūtra-style monasticism places more emphasis on the spirit than on the letter of their observance, and both are committed to a life of renunciation. Such acceptance and commitment are the outward sign and the internal meaning, respectively, of *bhikkhu* ordination not in the technical Vinaya sense but in the sense of the actual living of the *bhikkhu* life. The ordinations of both Vinaya-style and Sūtra-style monasticism can, therefore, be known as rites of passage. Both are separate and distinct from ordination in the technical Vinaya sense, even as ordination in this sense is separate and distinct from them. One who has received Vinaya-style ordination may, of course, *believe* himself to be ordained in the technical Vinaya sense (he cannot know this objectively) and may base his spiritual life as a *bhikkhu* and his socio-religious status on this belief, but that is a different matter. In the case of Sūtra-style monasticism, as described in section 8 of *Forty-Three Years Ago*, the monk (or FWBO *anagārika*) bases his observance of the additional 'monastic' precepts on his personal experience of Going for Refuge to the Three Jewels, whether effective or real. His observance of those precepts, like his observance of the precepts common to all Buddhists regardless of lifestyle, in fact is an expression of that Going for Refuge, as well as being a support for the continual deepening of his experience of the act of Going for Refuge itself.

But though conceding that the *bhikkhu* ordination can be known as a rite of passage, Brahmavamso is far from abandoning his conviction that the *meaning* of *bhikkhu* ordination can be understood only by a *bhikkhu*, i.e. by one validly ordained, in the technical Vinaya sense, and to this theme he now, in effect, returns. He returns to it, however, without mentioning – perhaps without even noticing – that while still speaking of '*bhikkhu* ordination' he is in fact no longer speaking of it as a rite of passage.

> It is not surprising that the bhikkhu ordination has been, will be, and is today, rightfully regarded with a sense of awed inspiration by most Buddhists, because it was established by the Buddha who was himself a bhikkhu, and because it has survived unchanged in whatever country it has gone to for over two thousand, five hundred years or so. Something which lasted so very long, something established by the Buddha, something praised by the Arahats of today and the past, SURELY IS DESERVING OF RESPECT!

The *bhikkhu* ordination spoken of in this passage is, of course, *bhikkhu* ordination in the technical Vinaya sense. What Brahmavamso has done is to switch from one meaning of '*bhikkhu* ordination' to another, and the fact that, having made the switch, he proceeds to wax rhetorical and speak of *bhikkhu* ordination in the technical Vinaya sense in such glowing terms means that the assertions he makes in this connection will have to be examined with particular care. There are six assertions: (1) *Bhikkhu* ordination (of course in the technical Vinaya sense) is regarded with awed inspiration by most Buddhists. (2) *Bhikkhu* ordination was established by the Buddha. (3) The Buddha was a *bhikkhu*. (4) The *bhikkhu* ordination has survived unchanged for over 2,500 years or so. (5) What has survived so long is deserving of respect. (6) *Bhikkhu* ordination is and was praised by the *arhants*. I shall comment briefly on each of these assertions, which bring Brahmavamso's short article very nearly to a close.

(1) *Bhikkhu ordination* (in the technical Vinaya sense) *is regarded with awed inspiration by most Buddhists*. The phrase 'awed inspiration' is a highly expressive one, and I cannot help wishing, as Oscar Wilde is said to have wished in connection with a saying of James McNeill Whistler, that I had thought of it myself.[791] To be awed is to experience overwhelming wonder, admiration, respect, and dread. It is the kind of emotion we feel when confronted by natural phenomena such as the Himalayas, Niagara Falls, the 'deep and dark blue ocean',[792] and the starry midnight sky, – by human artistic achievements such as the Parthenon, the ceiling of the Sistine Chapel, and Mozart's final symphonies, – by acts of supreme moral heroism and by religious images such as those of the Burning Bush, the Last Judgement, Arjuna's 'Vision of the Universal Form' (in the *Bhagavad Gītā*), and the prophet of Islam's Night Journey through the heavens to the Throne of God.[793]

Inspiration is the state of being stimulated or aroused in one's mind, feelings, etc., to unusual activity or creativity. One is stimulated or aroused by the divine, by God or the gods, and the inspired act or creation partakes of the divinity of its source ('It came from above!' declared Handel of *Messiah*, while Dante's *Commedia* came to be styled 'Divina').[794] When inspired one may feel carried out of oneself, or above oneself, or may even feel that one is possessed. Nietzsche's description of inspiration in this extreme sense is well known.[795] 'Awed inspiration' thus is the attitude of overwhelming wonder, admiration, respect, and dread one experiences in relation to the divine, or to a being of the divine order, as a result of which one is stimulated or aroused to unusual activity or creativity. According to Brahmavamso this is the attitude with which most Buddhists regard – and *rightfully* regard – technically valid *bhikkhu* ordination. Such ordination does not, of course, exist in the abstract; it exists, and can only exist, in the concrete, as embodied in the persons of ordained Buddhist men, i.e. *bhikkhus*. What Brahmavamso is really saying, therefore, is that most Buddhists regard – and rightfully regard – validly ordained *bhikkhus* with an attitude of awed inspiration.

Whether this is actually the case is extremely doubtful. Japan is a (predominantly) Buddhist country, but the vast majority of Japanese Buddhists, far from regarding valid *bhikkhu* ordination with feelings of awed inspiration have probably never heard of such a thing and never seen a validly ordained *bhikkhu* (except perhaps on TV). Even in China, Korea, and Tibet, and other parts of the Mahāyāna Buddhist world, where non-Theravāda (Sarvāstivāda and Dharmagupta) Vinaya-style monasticism is well known, the fact that monks also receive bodhisattva ordination and that monastic life itself is lived in accordance with the spirit of the bodhisattva ideal means that *bhikṣu* ordination does not possess the significance it possesses for Theravāda. (In Tibet whatever awed inspiration may be felt is directed towards the *tulkus* or 'incarnate lamas'.) This leaves us with the Buddhists of south-east Asia, not all of whom continue to show *bhikkhus* the kind of veneration described in section 6 of *Forty-Three Years Ago*. A Thai Buddhist scholar indeed goes so far as to characterize many Thai *bhikkhus* as 'simply uneducated farmers in yellow robes', a characterization hardly redolent of awed inspiration.[796] The fact is that however appropriate it may be to regard spiritual giants like Milarepa, Xuanzang, and Dōgen, and even figures like Michaelangelo and Beethoven, with an attitude of awed inspiration, it is ludicrously inappropriate to regard in this way one who just happens to have been ordained in the technical Vinaya sense. Even if he is a good monk, his being accorded what amounts to godlike status will, in any case, almost certainly have a deleterious effect on his mind.

(2) *Bhikkhu ordination was established by the Buddha.* The Buddha established a sangha or spiritual community, acceptance into which was marked by a rite of passage. At first that rite was very simple. The Buddha said 'Come, *bhikkhu*, live the spiritual life (*brahmacariya*) for the sake of the utter cessation of suffering,' whereupon the man thus addressed, whether homeless wanderer or householder, became a member of the community and 'ordained'.[797] Subsequently the rite became more elaborate, especially after the Buddha had entrusted the *bhikkhus* with the responsibility for accepting new members and conferring 'ordination', which they initially did by getting the candidate to shave off the hair of head and face, don yellow 'robes', and solemnly declare that he went for Refuge to the Buddha, the Dharma, and the Sangha. Exactly at what point in the history of the Order the *bhikkhu* ordination ceremony assumed its final and most elaborate form, as preserved (along with 'fossil' traces of the earlier forms) in the Vinaya Piṭaka, in the present state of our knowledge we cannot say; but it must have been after the *parinirvāṇa*, so that it is quite incorrect to speak of *bhikkhu* ordination *in that sense* as having been established by the Buddha.

(3) *The Buddha was a bhikkhu.* An Indian friend of mine who regarded himself as a follower of the Buddha but not (he was at pains to insist) as a Buddhist, once remarked to me that although the Buddha is represented, in the Pāli scriptures, as more than once describing himself as a Brahmin,[798] he is never represented as describing himself as a *bhikkhu*. While one would need to have a very extensive acquaintance with the Pāli scriptures to be sure that the Buddha *never* described himself as a *bhikkhu*, even a limited acquaintance with them is enough to show that he was generally known, to friend and foe alike, as Samaṇa Gotama. Indeed the idea of the Enlightened One's being known as 'Bhikkhu Gotama' seems faintly absurd. To disciples like Sāriputta he was the *Mahāsamaṇa* or '*Great* Samaṇa', a *samaṇa*, literally a '(spiritual) labourer', being a respected homeless, wandering, 'heterodox' *religieux*. If the Buddha was a *bhikkhu* at all he must have been a Sūtra-style *bhikkhu*, not a Vinaya-style one, for to be a Vinaya-style *bhikkhu* he

would have to have been ordained, in the technical Vinaya sense, and he could hardly have been ordained, in this sense, before the Vinaya came into existence, and there is no evidence for his having been 'ordained' afterwards.

That Brahmavamso should want to see the Buddha as a *bhikkhu*, in the technical Vinaya sense, is perhaps indicative of his whole outlook on Buddhism, the spiritual life, and monasticism. He wants to see the Buddha as a *bhikkhu*, in the technical Vinaya sense, because he is an upholder of the technical validity of *bhikkhu* ordination in Theravāda, and therefore seeks to buttress his case by arguing that such ordination was both established by the Buddha and exemplified by him in his own person. I am reminded of those Thai Buddhist paintings in which the Buddha, as well as his monk disciples, is depicted looking exactly like a Thai *bhikkhu*, complete with neatly laundered yellow robes and a shoulder bag, the only difference being that the Buddha is shown with an *uṣṇīṣa* or 'cranial protuberance'. Just as theists tend to anthropomorphize the deity so, it would appear, Theravāda *bhikkhus* tend to '*bhikkhu*-ize' the Buddha. In this connection I would like to invite Brahmavamso's attention to an interesting passage in the *Mahāparinibbāna Sutta* in which the Buddha describes to Ānanda how, before entering each of the eight 'assemblies' – of the nobles, of the Brahmins, of the householders, of the *samaṇas*, and of the four different kinds of gods – he adopts their (distinctive) appearance and speech, whatever it might be.[799] The passage is interesting on a number of counts. It is not simply that people – or beings – experience the Buddha as one of themselves: the Buddha actually transforms himself into their likeness. More interestingly still, though he transforms himself into a *samaṇa* to communicate with *samaṇas*, and even into a householder to communicate with householders, he does *not* transform himself into a *bhikkhu* to communicate with *bhikkhus*. Could it be, not only that the Buddha was not a *bhikkhu* but that, at the time of his describing to Ānanda his mode of entering the eight assemblies (which he may not have done immediately prior to his *parinirvāṇa*, the *Mahāparinibbāna Sutta* being a very composite work) there were no *bhikkhus*, at least not in the technical Vinaya sense, and that even if there were *bhikkhus* they were subsumed under the *samaṇas*?

(4) *The bhikkhu ordination has survived unchanged for over two thousand, five hundred years or so*. Monasticism is certainly a

permanent feature of most forms of Buddhism. Whether there has been an uninterrupted transmission of technically valid *bhikkhu* ordination, in the Theravāda or any other sect or school, is quite another matter. That it is highly unlikely that there has been such a transmission, that even if there had been we could not know it, and that a spiritual life based on the *belief* that there has been one therefore rests on a very insecure foundation, is the leitmotiv running through *Forty-Three Years Ago*, and there is no need for me to repeat myself here. I refer anyone who still thinks that *bhikkhu* ordination has survived unchanged through the centuries to S. Dutt's *Early Buddhist Monachism*, which I have already mentioned, as well as to its successor volumes *The Buddha and Five After Centuries* and *Buddhist Monks and Monasteries of India.*[800]

(5) *What has survived so long is deserving of respect.* Not necessarily. Evil ideas, institutions, and practices have sometimes survived for centuries, as a glance at world history will show, and these are certainly not deserving of respect. In any case did not the Buddha advise the Kālāmas of Kesaputta not to go by hearsay, nor by what was handed down by others, nor by what people said, nor by what was stated on the authority of their traditional teachings?[801] Such advice as this is not suggestive of respect for mere antiquity.

(6) *Bhikkhu ordination is and was praised by the Arahats. Arahats* are those who have realized Supreme Enlightenment (*arahata-phala*). While such exalted beings will certainly praise the spiritual life (*brahmacariya*), and even praise Sūtra-style monasticism, I for one find it difficult to imagine them praising *bhikkhu* ordination, in the technical Vinaya sense, as such, and it is ordination *in this sense* that Brahmavamso considers important, which he believes he and other *bhikkhus* possess, for the validity of which he is arguing, and of which, finally, he declares 'it SURELY IS DESERVING OF RESPECT!'

The concluding paragraph of Brahmavamso's article strikes an apologetic, even a defensive, note.

> In this article I have not meant to compare the *bhikkhu* ordination with any other rite of passage into any other order, nor to praise one group (the Bhikkhu Sangha) by putting down another group. I have written this article only to defend the validity and meaning of the Bhikkhu Ordination, and thereby to defend [a Freudian slip for 'attack' or 'rebut'?] the challenge to the integrity of the

> Theravāda Bhikkhu-Sangha. May all Buddhists grow and prosper according to the Dhamma, whether bhikkhu or otherwise.

I am sure we can accept the writer's protestation that in his article he has not meant to compare the *bhikkhu* ordination with any other rite of passage into any other order. Not that it might not be instructive to compare such rites of passage, provided the intention was not invidious, and it is presumably his meaning to compare them invidiously that Brahmavamso really is disclaiming. But though he may not mean to praise one group, the *bhikkhu* sangha, at the expense of another, this is what in effect he does and, given his fundamental position, cannot help doing. The *bhikkhu* sangha is the community of the validly ordained. It is the community of those who have received that ordination – in the technical Vinaya sense – which, according to Brahmavamso, is rightfully the object of 'awed inspiration' to all Buddhists, and who, as embodiments of that ordination, are in practice themselves rightly regarded with awed inspiration. *Bhikkhu* ordination, in the technical Vinaya sense, is even praised by the *arahats*, the Supremely Enlightened – a praise obviously implying praise of the recipients of the ordination, apart from whom such a thing as 'ordination' cannot exist. Non-*bhikkhus*, however spiritually developed, are not objects of awed inspiration. They are not praised by the *arahats*. It is therefore difficult to see how Brahmavamso can honestly claim that in praising one group, the *bhikkhu* sangha, he is not putting down another group, i.e. a group whose members are not *bhikkhus*, whether they are Jōdo Shinshū 'priests', Tantric lay *yogins* and *yoginis*, or even *dharmacārīs* and *dharmacāriṇīs* of the Western Buddhist Order. Surely all those who practise the Dharma to a superlative degree, whether living as monks or nuns, or as laymen or laywomen, or in any other way, are worthy of being regarded with awed inspiration! Surely the *arahats* – and bodhisattvas – will praise them unreservedly! Surely they will praise all those who go for Refuge – even if only 'effectively', as we say in the FWBO – in the knowledge that such have taken hold of the end of a golden string which, if they only can wind it into a ball, will lead them in at one or another of the three Gates of Liberation, built in the wall of the city of Nirvāṇa!

What we really need to defend is not technicalities of the Vinaya, or the validity and meaning of *bhikkhu* ordination, but the fundamental principles of Buddhism and the significance and value of the spiritual life (*brahmacariya*), both of which are currently under attack from so many quarters. What we need to defend is the integrity of the Dharma as the principial path to Supreme Enlightenment. If we can do that then all Buddhists, i.e. all who genuinely go for Refuge to the Three Jewels, in whatever degree, will indeed grow and prosper according to the Dharma. What is more, they will be in a position to help others grow and prosper according to the Dharma too.

APPENDICES

These five precepts are recognized and practised by Buddhists of all schools. There are many references to them in Buddhist literature. In the Pāli canon one example is to be found at *Aṅguttara Nikāya* 839 (iv.245). See Bhikkhu Bodhi (trans.), *The Numerical Discourses of the Buddha*, Wisdom Publications, Somerville 2012, pp. 1174–5.

The Five Precepts in Pāli

Pāṇātipātā veramaṇī sikkhāpadaṃ samādiyāmi
Adinnādānā veramaṇī sikkhāpadaṃ samādiyāmi
Kāmesu micchācārā veramaṇī sikkhāpadaṃ samādiyāmi
Musāvādā veramaṇī sikkhāpadaṃ samādiyāmi
Surāmeraya majja pamādaṭṭhānā veramaṇī sikkhāpadaṃ samādiyāmi

The Five Precepts in English

I undertake to refrain from taking life
I undertake to refrain from taking the not-given
I undertake to refrain from sexual misconduct
I undertake to refrain from false speech
I undertake to refrain from taking intoxicants

The Five Positive Precepts (recited in Triratna)

With deeds of loving kindness, I purify my body
With open-handed generosity, I purify my body
With stillness, simplicity, and contentment, I purify my body
With truthful communication, I purify my speech
With mindfulness clear and radiant, I purify my mind

THE EIGHT PRECEPTS

These precepts are observed in traditionally Buddhist countries by the laity on festival days. They are based on the ten *śrāmaṇera* precepts (see below) taken by the novice monk, but whereas the novice monk is expected to practise all ten all of the time, the eight are seen as an intensification of practice for festival days, bringing about a state of mind more conducive to meditation.

I undertake to refrain from taking life
I undertake to refrain from taking the not-given
I undertake to refrain from sexual misconduct
I undertake to refrain from false speech
I undertake to refrain from taking intoxicants
I undertake to refrain from eating at the forbidden time (i.e. after noon)
I undertake to refrain from song, dance, music, and indecent shows and the use of flower-garlands, scents, unguents, and ornaments
I undertake to refrain from lying on a luxurious sleeping place

The following ten precepts are taken by the novice monk or *śrāmaṇera* at the time of the lower monastic ordination. (The ten precepts taken by members of the Triratna Buddhist Order at the time of their ordination are explored in *The Ten Pillars of Buddhism*. They are listed on pp. 311–13 of this volume.)

I undertake to refrain from taking life
I undertake to refrain from taking the not-given
I undertake to refrain from sexual misconduct
I undertake to refrain from false speech
I undertake to refrain from taking intoxicants
I undertake to refrain from eating at the forbidden time (i.e. after noon)
I undertake to refrain from song, dance, music, and indecent shows
I undertake to refrain from the use of flower-garlands, scents, unguents, and ornaments
I undertake to refrain from lying on a high or luxurious sleeping place
I undertake to refrain from handling gold and silver (i.e. money)

1. I shall not consider Brahma, Vishnu, and Mahesh as gods, nor shall I worship them.
2. I shall not consider Rama and Krishna as gods, nor shall I worship them.
3. I shall not believe in 'Gauri', Ganapati, and any other gods and goddesses of Hinduism, nor shall I worship them.
4. I do not believe that god has incarnated.
5. I do not and shall not believe that Lord Buddha was the incarnation of Vishnu. I believe this to be sheer madness and false propaganda.
6. I shall not perform 'shraddha' nor shall I give 'pind-dan'.
7. I shall not act in a manner violating the principles and teachings of the Buddha.
8. I shall not get Brahmins to perform any ceremonies.
9. I believe that all human beings are equal.
10. I shall endeavour to establish equality.
11. I shall live according to the Noble Eightfold Path taught by the Buddha.
12. I shall practise the Ten *Pāramitās* taught by the Buddha.
13. I shall be compassionate towards all living beings and nourish and protect them.
14. I shall not steal.
15. I shall not tell lies.
16. I shall not commit sexual misconduct.
17. I shall not drink alcohol.
18. I shall lead my life bringing together the three Buddhist principles of wisdom, morality, and compassion.
19. I renounce Hinduism, which is detrimental to the fulfilment of human beings, and which considers human beings as unequal and degraded, and I embrace the Buddha Dhamma.
20. I firmly believe the Dhamma of the Buddha is the *saddhamma*.
21. I believe that I am taking a new birth.
22. Thus I vow to lead my life according to the Buddha's teachings.

Translated from Marathi by Mangesh Dahiwale and Dharmachari Lokamitra

THE BODHISATTVA'S *SAṂVARA-ŚĪLA* OR SIXTY-FOUR PRECEPTS

These sixty-four Bodhisattva Precepts from the Gelug Tibetan tradition of Tsongkhapa are here rendered into English by Sangharakshita according to the oral explanation of Dhardo Rimpoche. See *Precious Teachers*, Windhorse Publications, Birmingham 2003, p. 154 (Complete Works, vol. 22).

The Eighteen *Mūlāpattis* or Major Precepts

It is a bad thing:

1. To praise oneself and disparage others
2. To withhold the wealth of the Dharma from others
3. To punish and refuse to concede repentance
4. To give up the Mahāyāna while still pretending to belong to it
5. To steal what belongs to the Three Jewels
6. To renounce the Dharma
7. To forcibly remove the robes of a bad monk, or beat or imprison him
8. To commit the five heinous offences (such as wounding a Buddha)
9. To adhere to false views
10. To destroy villages
11. To instruct in the Doctrine of the Void someone not psychologically prepared for it
12. To discourage others from striving after Buddhahood and encourage them to aim at inferior goals
13. To give up the *prātimokṣa*
14. To disparage the Hīnayāna
15. To preach *śūnyatā* to one's disciples (indirectly praising oneself) by saying that if they practise according to one's instructions they will obtain what one has attained
16. To accept from another something really belonging to the Three Jewels, (as when a king imposes a fine on a monk knowing he will have to misappropriate the property of the Three Jewels in order to pay for it)
17. To impose troublesome regulations on the monks (of a monastery)
18. To give up the *bodhicitta*

The Forty-Six *Āpattis* (Minor Precepts)

It is a bad thing:

1. Not to worship the Three Jewels three times a day
2. To allow the mind to follow after lusts
3. Not to show respect for seniors (in bodhisattva ordination)
4. Not to reply to being asked a question (whether about religion or about oneself etc.)
5. Not to accept an invitation to teach the Dharma
6. Not to accept gold etc. if offered
7. Not to expound the Dharma to someone desirous of hearing (even if they ask with an evil motive)
8. To despise evildoers or anyone breaking his *śīla*
9. Not to exert oneself in such a manner that others may develop faith in one and listen to one's teaching
10. To be slack with regard to the welfare of others and refuse to accept extra monastic requisites from them even when they are happy to give them
11. Not to be prepared to break, out of compassion for others, the seven kinds of Vinaya rules
12. To gain anything by wrong livelihood
13. To laugh needlessly
14. To think that one will lead oneself alone to Emancipation
15. Not to take steps to put an end to slanders about oneself
16. Not to check evildoers out of fear of incurring their displeasure
17. To return abuse (or any of the three other kinds of wrong speech that may be used against one)
18. Not to pacify those who have become angry
19. Not to excuse those who have offended one and who ask for forgiveness
20. To indulge in angry thoughts
21. To have an entourage for personal aggrandisement
22. Not to dispel laziness
23. To waste time in idle talk
24. Not to search after the meaning of *samādhi*
25. Not to destroy the five hindrances at the time of meditation
26. To become attached to the experience of *samādhi*
27. To disparage the Hīnayāna

28. To be capable of practising the bodhisattva ideal yet abandoning it to follow the Hīnayāna
29. To abandon the study of the Dharma and devote oneself to the study of the works of the *tīrthikas*
30. To take delight in studying the works of the *tīrthikas* (as distinct from studying them for the purpose of controversy)
31. To renounce the Mahāyāna
32. To praise oneself and disparage others
33. Not to go (and preach etc.) for the sake of the Dharma
34. To abuse and despise a preacher of the Dharma and pay attention only to the letter and not to the spirit of what he says
35. Not to help those in need
36. To neglect the sick
37. Not to remove suffering
38. Not to exhort evildoers, warning them that in this and the next life they will have to experience the results of their actions
39. Not to return a good deed
40. Not to console those who are unhappy
41. Not to give to those who are desirous of riches
42. Not to work for one's circle of disciples
43. Not to adjust oneself to others (in doing religious work, taking their feelings into consideration)
44. Not to praise the good qualities of others
45. Not a take suitable action against those inimical to the Dharma
46. Not to terrify (the enemies of the Dharma) by means of supernormal powers

NOTES

(S) indicates a note supplied by the author. All other notes are written by the editor.

THE THREE JEWELS

1 From chapter 11 of the *Avataṃsaka Sūtra*. See Thomas Cleary (trans.), *The Flower Ornament Scripture*, Shambhala Publications, Boston and London 1993, pp. 315–6.

2 Quoted in T. W. Rhys Davids, *Buddhist Birth Stories*, revised edition, George Routledge and Sons, London n.d., p. 226, a translation of the *Nidānakathā*, the introduction to the *Jātakatthakathā*, a commentary on the Jātaka stories attributed to Buddhaghosa. See also Vinaya Piṭaka i.82 (*Mahāvagga* 1.54), I. B. Horner (trans.), *The Book of the Discipline*, part 4, Pali Text Society, Oxford 1996, p. 103.

3 N. Dutt, 'Survey of Important Books in Pali and Buddhist Sanskrit' in P. V. Bapat (ed.), *2500 Years of Buddhism*, Publications Division, Ministry of Information and Broadcasting, Government of India, New Delhi 1956, p. 144.

4 The Sanskrit *ātman* (Pāli *attan*) is generally translated as 'self'. and it is one of the most basic concepts of the Hindu tradition, in which the *ātman* is seen as the true self, the eternal essence of all beings. (This is a main theme of the Upanishads, for example.) By complete contrast, central to the Buddha's teaching is the idea of *anātman* or no fixed, unchanging self. *Punarjanman*

means reincarnation and is associated with the Hindu idea of a reincarnating soul.

5 T. W. Rhys Davids, *Buddhist India*, Motilal Banarsidass, Delhi 1971, chapter 11.

6 *Bhayabherava Sutta*, *Majjhima Nikāya* 4 (i.22). Bhikkhu Ñāṇamoli and Bhikkhu Bodhi (trans.), *The Middle Length Discourses of the Buddha*, Wisdom Publications, Boston 1995, p. 105; or I. B. Horner (trans.), *The Collection of the Middle Length Sayings*, vol. i, Pali Text Society, London 1976, p. 28.

7 See Francis Story, *The Case for Rebirth*, Buddhist Publication Society, Kandy 1959; and Francis Story, *Rebirth as Doctrine and Experience*, Buddhist Publication Society, Kandy 1975. Since this early book by a Westerner on the topic of rebirth, there have been many other studies collecting documentary evidence on this theme.

8 *Khāntivādijātaka, Pāli Jātaka* 313. See V. Fausböll (ed.), *The Jātaka*, vol. iii, Pali Text Society, Oxford 1990, pp. 39–43, reproduced with English translation in I. B. Horner (trans.), *Ten Jātaka Stories*, Luzac and Co., London 1957, pp. 43–9.

9 *Sivijātaka, Pāli Jātaka* 499 occurs in V. Fausböll (ed.), *The Jātaka,* vol. iv, Pali Text Society, Oxford 1991, pp. 401–12. Translations can be found on the Internet.

10 For a detailed account see *A Survey of Buddhism*, chapter 4 (*Complete Works*, vol. 1, pp. 445ff).

11 Ananda Coomaraswamy, *Buddha and the Gospel of Buddhism*, Asia Publishing House, Bombay 1956, p. 6 (after *Nidānakathā*).

12 The date of the Buddha's birth continues to be debated, scholars suggesting somewhere between 563 BCE and 480 BCE. His death is thought to have occurred between 480 BCE and 400 BCE.

13 This memory is recounted to Aggivessana or Saccaka, a Jain follower. See *Mahāsaccaka Sutta*, *Majjhima Nikāya* 36 (i.246–7). Bhikkhu Ñāṇamoli and Bhikkhu Bodhi (trans.), *The Middle Length Discourses of the Buddha*, Wisdom Publications, Boston 1995, p. 340; or I. B. Horner (trans.), *The Collection of the Middle Length Sayings*, vol. i, Pali Text Society, London 1976, p. 301.

14 *Aṅguttara Nikāya* i.145–6, in Bhikkhu Bodhi (trans.), *The Numerical Discourses of the Buddha*, Wisdom Publications, Somerville 2012, pp. 239–40; or F. L. Woodward, (trans.), *Gradual Sayings*, vol. i, Pali Text Society, Oxford 2000, pp. 128–9.

15 According to the *Ariyapariyesanā Sutta*, the Buddha described his own Going Forth in the following words:

While still young, a black-haired young man endowed with the blessing of youth, in the prime of life, though my mother and father wished otherwise and wept with tearful faces, I shaved off my hair and beard, put on the yellow robe, and went forth from the home life into homelessness.

See *Majjhima Nikāya* 26 (i.163) in Bhikkhu Ñāṇamoli and Bhikkhu Bodhi (trans.), *The Middle Length Discourses of the Buddha*, Wisdom Publications, Boston 1995, p. 256; or I. B. Horner (trans.), *The Collection of the Middle Length Sayings*, vol. i, Pali Text Society, London 1976, p. 207.

16 *Mahāsaccaka Sutta*, *Majjhima Nikāya* 36 (i.242–7). Bhikkhu Ñāṇamoli and Bhikkhu Bodhi (trans.), *The Middle Length Discourses of the Buddha*, Wisdom Publications, Boston 1995, pp. 337–40; or I. B. Horner (trans.), *The Collection of the Middle Length Sayings*, vol. i, Pali Text Society, London 1976, pp. 297–301.

17 Related in various *suttas*, for example *Bhayabherava Sutta*, *Majjhima Nikāya* 4 (i.21–3). See Bhikkhu Ñāṇamoli and Bhikkhu Bodhi (trans.), *The Middle Length Discourses of the Buddha*, Wisdom Publications, Boston 1995, pp. 104–7; or I. B. Horner (trans.), *The Collection of the Middle Length Sayings*, vol. i, Pali Text Society, London 1976, pp. 27–30.

18 The story of the haughty Brahmin occurs at *Udāna* 1.4. See John D. Ireland (trans.), *The Udāna and the Itivuttaka*, Buddhist Publication Society, Kandy 1997, pp. 15–16. The story is repeated along with the story of Tapussa and Bhallika at Vinaya Piṭaka i.2 and i.4 (*Mahāvagga* 1.2 and 1.4). See I. B. Horner (trans.), *The Book of the Discipline*, part 4, Pali Text Society, Oxford 1996, pp. 3–4 and 5–6.

19 The story of how the Buddha was inclined not to teach but was persuaded by Brahma Sahampati is told at Vinaya Piṭaka i.4–7 (*Mahāvagga* 1.4–6). See I. B. Horner (trans.), *The Book of the Discipline*, part 4, Pali Text Society, Oxford 1996, pp. 6–10. See also *Ariyapariyesanā Sutta*, *Majjhima Nikāya* 26 (i.167–170); Bhikkhu Ñāṇamoli and Bhikkhu Bodhi (trans.), *The Middle Length Discourses of the Buddha*, Wisdom Publications, Boston 1995, pp. 260–2; or I. B. Horner (trans.), *The Collection of the Middle Length Sayings*, vol. i, Pali Text Society, London 1976, pp. 211–13.

20 The story of Upaka occurs at Vinaya Piṭaka i.8 (*Mahāvagga* 1.6). See I. B. Horner (trans.), *The Book of the Discipline*,

part 4, Pali Text Society, Oxford 1996, pp. 11–12.

21 The story of the Buddha's meeting with the five ascetics is told at Vinaya Piṭaka i.8–12 (*Mahāvagga* 1.6), ibid., pp. 13–19.

22 The story of the conversion of Yaśa and his family and the sixty-one *arhants* is told at Vinaya Piṭaka i.15 (*Mahāvagga* 1.6–10), ibid., pp. 21–8.

23 Vinaya Piṭaka i.20–1 (*Mahāvagga* 1.11). Adapted from T. W. Rhys Davids and H. Oldenberg (trans.), *Vinaya Texts*, part 1, in M. Müller (ed.), *Sacred Books of the East*, vol. xiii, Motilal Banarsidass, Delhi 1974, pp. 112–13. See also I. B. Horner (trans.), *The Book of the Discipline*, part 4, Pali Text Society, Oxford 1996, p. 28.

24 The story of the thirty pleasure-seeking youths occurs at Vinaya Piṭaka i.23 (*Mahāvagga* 1.13). See I. B. Horner (trans.), *The Book of the Discipline*, part 4, Pali Text Society, Oxford 1996, pp. 31–2.

25 The story of the conversion of the Kāśyapa (Pāli Kassapa) brothers occurs at Vinaya Piṭaka i.24–34 (*Mahāvagga* 1.15–20), ibid., pp. 32–45. The 'Fire Sermon' occurs at Vinaya Piṭaka i.34–5 (*Mahāvagga* 1.21) ibid., pp. 45–6; and *Saḷāyatanasaṃyutta*, *Saṃyutta Nikāya* iv.19–20 (35.28), Bhikkhu Bodhi (trans.), *Connected Discourses of the Buddha*, Wisdom Publications, Boston 2000, p. 1143; or F. L. Woodward (trans.), *The Book of the Kindred Sayings*, part 4, Pali Text Society, London 1980, p. 10.

26 The story of King Bimbisāra and his gift of the Bamboo Grove occurs at Vinaya Piṭaka i.35–9 (*Mahāvagga* 1.22), ibid., pp. 46–52.

27 The story of the conversion of Śāriputra (Pāli Sāriputta) and Maudgalyāyana (Pāli Moggallāna) occurs at Vinaya Piṭaka i.39–43 (*Mahāvagga* 1.23–4), ibid., pp. 52–7.

28 Vinaya Piṭaka i.43 (*Mahāvagga* 1.24), ibid., pp. 56–7.

29 The story of the conversion of Anāthapiṇḍada (Pāli Anāthapiṇḍika) and his donation of the Jetavana, or Jeta Grove in Śrāvastī (Pāli Sāvatthī), is told at Vinaya Piṭaka ii.154–9 (*Cullavagga* 6.4). See I. B. Horner (trans.), *The Book of the Discipline*, part 5, Pali Text Society, London 1975, pp. 216–23.

The generosity – though not the purchase of a monastery – of Viśākhā, a lay-woman known as 'Migāra's mother' (Migāra was in fact her father whom she converted to the Buddha's teaching) is told at Vinaya Piṭaka i.290–4 (*Mahāvagga* 8.15). See I. B. Horner (trans.), *The Book of the Discipline*, part 4, Pali Text Society, Oxford 1996, pp. 413–20. The purchase of a monastery is told in the

Dhammapada Commentary (*Dhammapada Aṭṭhakathā* i.413). See E. W. Burlingame (trans.), *Buddhist Legends, Translated from the Original Pali Text of the Dhammapada Commentary*, part 1, Pali Text Society, London 1969, pp. 789–80.

30 See for example the *Pūralāsa* and *Māgha Suttas.* In the first, the Brahmin Sundarika-Bhāradvāja after his exchange with the Buddha goes forth and becomes a monk, eventually gaining Enlightnement. In the second, the young Brahmin, Māgha, becomes a lay disciple. *Sutta-Nipāta* 3.4 and 3.5. H. Saddhatissa (trans.), *The Sutta-Nipāta,* Curzon Press, London 1985, pp. 51–8. A striking example of a young Brahmin who meets the Buddha is Assalāyana. He is sent by 500 older Brahmins to argue against the Buddha's teaching of 'purification for all the four castes'. Assalāyana does his best but the shortcomings in his thinking are shown up and the *sutta* ends: 'From today let Master Gotama remember me as a lay follower who has gone to him for refuge for life.' *Assalāyana Sutta*, *Majjhima Nikāya* 93. Bhikkhu Ñāṇamoli and Bhikkhu Bodhi (trans.), *The Middle Length Discourses of the Buddha*, Wisdom Publications, Boston 1995, pp. 763–70; or I. B. Horner (trans.), *The Collection of the Middle Length Sayings*, vol. ii, Pali Text Society, Oxford 1994, pp. 340–9.

31 *Upāli Sutta*, *Majjhima Nikāya* 56 (i.375). Bhikkhu Ñāṇamoli and Bhikkhu Bodhi (trans.), *The Middle Length Discourses of the Buddha*, Wisdom Publications, Boston 1995, p. 480; or I. B. Horner (trans.), *The Collection of the Middle Length Sayings*, vol. ii, Pali Text Society, Oxford 1994, p. 40.

32 The story of Suddhodana's conversion is told in the *Nidānakathā*: T. W. Rhys Davids (trans.), *Buddhist Birth Stories,* George Routledge and Sons, London n.d., pp. 215–24. See also N. A. Jayawickrama, *The Story of Gottama Buddha* (*Jātaka-nidāna*), Pali Text Society, Oxford 1990, p. 124.

33 Ānanda, Devadatta, and other young Śākyans leaving home to join the order of monks is referred to by Aśvaghoṣa, *Buddhacarita* xix.39. See E. H. Johnston, *The Buddhacarita,* enlarged edition, Motilal Banarsidass, Delhi 1984, p. 46.

34 Rāhula's entry to the Order under Sāriputta is told at Vinaya Piṭaka i.82 (*Mahāvagga* 1.54). See I. B. Horner (trans.), *The Book of the Discipline*, part 4, Pali Text Society, Oxford 1996, pp. 103–4; and in J. J. Jones (trans.), *The Mahāvastu*, Luzac, London 1952, vol. ii, pp. 256–7.

The Buddha's admonitions to his son can

be found in, for example, the *Ambalaṭṭhikārāhulovāda Sutta*, *Majjhima Nikāya* 61; and the *Mahārāhulovada Sutta*, *Majjhima Nikāya* 62.

35 The story of Mahāprajāpatī (Pāli Mahāpajāpatī) and the eight *garudhammas* or 'special conditions' is told at Vinaya Piṭaka ii.254–5 (*Cullavagga* 10.1). See I. B. Horner (trans.), *The Book of the Discipline*, part 5, Pali Text Society, London 1975, pp. 354–5.

36 While references to Devadatta are scattered through the various *Nikāyas*, there is a connected account of the misuse of his psychic powers to further his ambition at Vinaya Piṭaka ii.184–203 (*Cullavagga* 7.2–4). See I. B. Horner (trans.), *The Book of the Discipline*, part 5, Pali Text Society, London 1975, pp. 259–84.

37 *Mahāparinibbāna Sutta*, *Dīgha Nikāya* 16 (ii.81). This translation is adapted from T. W. and C. A. F. Rhys Davids (trans.), *Dialogues of the Buddha*, part 2, Pali Text Society, London 1971, pp. 85–6. See also M. Walshe (trans.), *The Long Discourses of the Buddha*, Wisdom Publications, Boston 1995, pp. 234.

38 *Aṅguttara Nikāya* iv.15–21, in Bhikkhu Bodhi (trans.), *The Numerical Discourses of the Buddha*, Wisdom Publications, Somerville 2012, pp. 1009–13; or E. M. Hare (trans.), *Gradual Sayings*, vol. iv, Pali Text Society, Oxford 1995, pp. 10–13.

39 *Mahāparinibbāna Sutta*, *Dīgha Nikāya* 16 (ii.99–100): M. Walshe (trans.), *The Long Discourses of the Buddha*, Wisdom Publications, Boston 1995, pp. 244–5; or T. W. and C. A. F. Rhys Davids (trans.), *Dialogues of the Buddha*, part 2, Pali Text Society, London 1971, p. 107.

40 *Mahāparinibbāna Sutta, Dīgha Nikāya* 16 (ii.100–102). T. W. and C. A. F. Rhys Davids (trans.), *Dialogues of the Buddha*, part 2, Pali Text Society, London 1971, p. 108; or M. Walshe (trans.), *The Long Discourses of the Buddha*, Wisdom Publications, Boston 1995, p. 245.

41 *Mahāparinibbāna Sutta, Dīgha Nikāya* 16 (ii.119). T. W. and C. A. F. Rhys Davids (trans.), *Dialogues of the Buddha*, part 2, Pali Text Society, London 1971, p. 127; or M. Walshe (trans.), *The Long Discourses of the Buddha*, Wisdom Publications, Boston 1995, p. 253.

42 *Mahāparinibbāna Sutta, Dīgha Nikāya* 16 (ii.126–8 and ii.135–6). See Walshe, ibid., pp. 256–7 and 261–2; or Rhys Davids, ibid., pp. 136–9 and 147–8.

43 *Mahāparinibbāna Sutta, Dīgha Nikāya* 16 (ii.137–156). See Walshe, ibid., pp. 262–70; or Rhys Davids, ibid., pp. 149–173,

44 A rendering of *Mahāparinibbāna Sutta, Dīgha Nikāya* 16 (ii.156). See Walshe, ibid., p. 270; or Rhys Davids, ibid., p. 173.

45 Edward Conze (trans.), *The Perfection of Wisdom in Eight Thousand Lines and Its Verse Summary* (*Aṣṭasāhasrikā Prajñāpāramitā*), Four Seasons Foundation, San Francisco 1973, p. 172.

46 The *Mahāvaṃsa,* the fifth century CE epic poem, composed in Pāli, which tells of the origins of Sri Lanka, refers to three visits to that island by the Buddha. The *Sāsanavaṃsa* or *Thathanawin,* a history of the Buddhist order in Burma composed by the Burmese monk Paññāsāmi in 1861, refers to the oral tradition of visits of the Buddha to Burma (Myanmar).

47 The story of Yaśa (Pāli Yasa) can be found at Vinaya Piṭaka i.15–18 (*Mahāvagga* 1.7). See I. B. Horner (trans.), *The Book of the Discipline*, part 4, Pali Text Society, Oxford 1996, pp. 21–6. The same story of the sleeping dancing girls but told of the Buddha in *Nidānakathā*, T. W. Rhys Davids (trans.), *Buddhist Birth Stories,* George Routledge and Sons, London n.d., p. 171.

48 J. J. Jones (trans.), *The Mahāvastu*, Luzac, London 1952, vol. ii, pp. 154–5.

49 Aśvaghoṣa, *Buddhacarita* v.47–62. See E. H. Johnston, *The Buddhacarita,* enlarged edition, Motilal Banarsidass, Delhi 1984, pp. 70–1.

50 For example, the account by the Buddha in the *Ariyapariyesanā Sutta, Majjhima Nikāya* 26 (i.163). Bhikkhu Ñāṇamoli and Bhikkhu Bodhi (trans.), *The Middle Length Discourses of the Buddha*, Wisdom Publications, Boston 1995, p. 256; or I. B. Horner (trans.), *The Collection of the Middle Length Sayings*, vol. i, Pali Text Society, London 1976, p. 207.

51 J. B. Rhine (1895–1980) was an American botanist and founder of parapsychology. His book *Extra Sensory Perception* was published in 1934, reporting his experimental findings of ESP.

52 J. G. Jennings (ed. and trans.), *The Vedantic Buddhism of the Buddha*, Motilal Banarsidass, Delhi, 1947.

53 The Cock Lane Ghost was a haunting, widely reported in 1762, that was supposed to have occurred in a London lodgings. The ghost was said to have been Fanny, the common-law wife of one William Kent, who was supposed to have been poisoned. A commission that included Dr Samuel Johnson went on to prove the whole thing a fraud. The story survived in the Victorian imagination and is mentioned, for example, by Mrs Nickleby in Charles Dickens' *Nicholas Nickleby*.

54 Examples of all kinds of psychic powers exhibited by the Buddha occur, for example, in his encounters with the Kāśyapa (Pāli Kassapa) brothers: Vinaya Piṭaka i.24–34 (*Mahāvagga* 1.15–20). See I. B. Horner (trans.), *The Book of the Discipline*, part 4, Pali Text Society, Oxford 1996, pp. 32–45.

55 For example, Aśvaghoṣa, *Buddhacarita,* iii.1–61 and v.16–21. See E. H. Johnston, *The Buddhacarita,* enlarged edition, Motilal Banarsidass, Delhi 1984, pp. 32–42 (old age, disease, and death) and pp. 64–5 (the fourth sight).

56 Ossian was the purported Irish author of a cycle of epic poems published from 1760 by James Macpherson (1736–1796), a Scottish poet and politician who claimed to have discovered and translated them from the Gaelic. His claim was contested by Irish historians and by Samuel Johnson. He was unable to produce the originals to prove authenticity and it is generally thought that he created the poems himself based on fragments he collected.

The Decretal of Constantine, known also as the 'Donation of Constantine', is a forged imperial Roman decree, probably from the eighth century, in which Constantine the Great, Roman emperor 306–337 CE, appeared to transfer political authority over Rome and the western part of the Roman Empire to the Pope. It was used to support political claims by the papacy.

57 *Aṅguttara Nikāya* i.145–6. Quoted in E. J. Thomas, *The Life of the Buddha as Legend and History*, Routledge and Kegan Paul, London 1949, p. 51. See also F. L. Woodward (trans.), *Gradual Sayings*, vol. i, Pali Text Society, Oxford 2000, p. 129; or Bhikkhu Bodhi (trans.), *The Numerical Discourses of the Buddha*, Wisdom Publications, Somerville 2012, p. 240.

58 E. J. Thomas, *The Life of the Buddha as Legend and History*, Routledge and Kegan Paul, London 1949, p. 51.

59 See 'The Defeat of Māra' in the *Lalitavistara Sūtra*: G. Bays (trans.), *The Voice of the Buddha,* vol. ii, Dharma Publishing, Berkeley 1983, pp. 463–8.

60 *Udāna* 2.1. See John D. Ireland (trans.), *The Udāna and the Itivuttaka*, Buddhist Publication Society, Kandy 1997, pp. 23–4.

61 According to the *Lalitavistara Sūtra*, after his birth the Buddha-to-be takes seven steps in each of the directions, each time uttering words expressive of a great intention. See G. Bays (trans.), *The Voice of the Buddha,* vol. i, Dharma Publishing, Berkeley 1983, pp. 131–2.

62 For an exposition of the *trikāya* doctrine see *A Survey*

of Buddhism, in *Complete Works,* vol. 1, pp. 250ff.

63 'Body of Bliss' is a translation used by D. T. Suzuki, *Outlines of Mahayana Buddhism*, Schocken 1970, p. 65. 'Enjoyment body' is Conze's translation. See Edward Conze, *Buddhist Thought in India,* George Allen and Unwin, London 1962, pp. 233–4; also used in P. Williams, *Mahāyāna Buddhism,* Routledge, London 1989, pp. 177–8, where he refers to Hsüan-tsang's (Xuanzang's) *Cheng weishi lun* which tells of two aspects to the enjoyment body: the private aspect, enjoyed by the Buddhas themselves, and the enjoyment body for others where the Buddhas appear with their marks for the enjoyment and benefit of the bodhisattvas.

For more on the *sambhogakāya*, see *A Survey of Buddhism,* in *Complete Works*, vol. 1, pp. 261–4.

64 'The sphere of the Buddha's radiance envelops a billion world systems, each containing a billion worlds.' *Sūtra on the Visualization of the Buddha Amitāyus* (*Amitāyur-dhyāna Sūtra*), section 17 in Ratnaguna and Śraddhāpa, *Great Faith, Great Wisdom,* Windhorse Publications, Cambridge 2016, p. 312.

65 *Sutta-Nipāta* 6.6, verse 8. E. M. Hare (trans.), *Woven Cadences*, Oxford University Press, London 1945, p. 155. See also H. Saddhatissa (trans.), *The Sutta-Nipāta,* Curzon Press, London 1985, p. 123.

66 *Saṃyutta Nikāya* iii.118. See I. B. Horner (trans.), in Edward Conze (ed.) *Buddhist Texts Through the Ages,* Harper and Row, New York 1964, p. 106. See also F. L. Woodward (trans.), *The Book of the Kindred Sayings*, part 3, Pali Text Society, London 1975, p. 101; or Bhikkhu Bodhi (trans.), *Connected Discourses of the Buddha*, Wisdom Publications, Boston 2000, p. 936.

67 *Aggivacchagotta Sutta, Majjhima Nikāya* 72 (i.487–8). Adapted from I. B. Horner (trans.), *The Collection of the Middle Length Sayings*, vol. ii, Pali Text Society, Oxford 1994 p. 166. See also Bhikkhu Ñāṇamoli and Bhikkhu Bodhi (trans.), *The Middle Length Discourses of the Buddha*, Wisdom Publications, Boston 1995, pp. 593–4.

68 Edward Conze (trans.), *Vajracchedikā Prajñāpāramitā* 26a & b, in *Buddhist Wisdom Books*, Unwin Hyman, London 1988, p. 63. See also *Selected Sayings from the Perfection of Wisdom*, Buddhist Society, London 1955, p. 111; or *Vajracchedikā Prajñāpāramitā*, Serie Orientale Roma, Rome 1957, p. 89.

69 *Pañcaviṃśatisāhasrika* f. 505–6, in *Selected Sayings from the Perfection of Wisdom*, ibid., p. 113.

70 D. T. Suzuki, *Outlines of Mahāyāna Buddhism*, Schocken, New York 1970, pp. 222ff.

71 D. T. Suzuki (trans.), *Aśvaghoṣa's Discourse on The Awakening of Faith in the Mahāyāna*, Open Court Publishing, London 1900, pp. 100–1.

72 *Udāna* 6.4. See John D. Ireland (trans.), *The Udāna and the Itivuttaka*, Buddhist Publication Society, Kandy 1997, pp. 86–9.

73 Edward Conze, *Buddhism: Its Essence and Development*, Windhorse Publications, Birmingham 2001, p. 16.

74 For example, in the periodical *Buddhist World* the 'pure, pristine Dhamma' was synonymous with Theravāda Buddhism. See *Facing Mount Kanchenjunga*, in *Complete Works*, vol. 21, p. 246.

75 'The Truth is the whole.' G. Hegel (1770–1831), *The Phenomenology of Mind*, Preface, paras. 81–2 (*Phänomenologie des Geistes*, 1807).

76 *Tao-Teh-King* xxxv, in Lin Yutang (trans.), *The Wisdom of Laotse*, Random House, 1948.

77 See R. A. F. Thurman (trans.), *The Holy Teaching of Vimalakīrti*, Pennsylvania State University Press, University Park and London 1976, p. 77; and *The Inconceivable Emancipation* in *Complete Works*, vol. 16, pp. 549–50.

78 'Their wisdom was like the emptiness of space because with a great net of lights they had illuminated the Dharma-Realm.' David Rounds, https://davidrounds.wordpress.com/buddhism/sudhanas-quest-the-gandavyuha/ or Thomas Cleary (trans.), *The Flower Ornament Sūtra* (*Avataṃsaka Sūtra*), Shambhala Publications, Boston and London 1993, p. 1136: 'They had spacelike knowledge, pervading all universes with a net of lights.'

79 The Buddha speaks of the sixty-two wrong views all of which emerge from 'the feeling of those who do not know and see, the worry and vacillation of those immersed in craving'. See *Brahmajāla Sutta*, *Dīgha Nikāya* 1 (i.40). M. Walshe (trans.), *The Long Discourses of the Buddha*, Wisdom Publications, Boston 1995, p. 87; or T. W. Rhys Davids (trans.), *Dialogues of the Buddha*, part 1, Pali Text Society, London 1973, p. 53.

80 These similes occur as a description for a mind free from all the hindrances, for example: *Sāmaññaphala Sutta*, *Dīgha Nikāya* 2 (i.71–3). M. Walshe (trans.), *The Long Discourses of the Buddha*, Wisdom Publications, Boston 1995, pp. 101–2; or T. W. Rhys Davids (trans.), *Dialogues of the Buddha*, part 1, Pali Text Society, London 1973, pp. 82–4.

81 Just as the great ocean has one taste, the taste of salt, so also this Dhamma and Discipline has one taste, the taste of liberation.

Uposatha Sutta, Udāna 5.5. J. D. Ireland (trans.), *The Udāna and the Itivuttaka*, Buddhist Publication Society, Kandy 1997, pp. 74; or Vinaya Piṭaka ii.239 (*Cullavagga* 9.1) in I. B. Horner (trans.) *The Book of the Discipline*, part 5, Pali Text Society, Oxford 1992, p. 335.

82 *Alagaddūpama Sutta, Majjhima Nikāya* 22 (i.134–5). Bhikkhu Ñāṇamoli and Bhikkhu Bodhi (trans.), *The Middle Length Discourses of the Buddha*, Wisdom Publications, Boston 1995, pp. 228–9; or I. B. Horner (trans.), *The Collection of the Middle Length Sayings*, vol. i, Pali Text Society, London 1976, pp. 173–4.

83 *Atthārasarāsī Dīpanī,* published in Bangkok, Buddhist Era 2500 (i.e. 1957). No further information available.

84 For example the *Mahāmālunkya Sutta, Majjhima Nikāya* 64. For further references see T. R. V. Murti, *The Central Philosophy of Buddhism*, George Allen and Unwin, London 1955, p. 36, note 2.

85 In the *Anamataggasaṃyutta* the Buddha gives a number of similes to suggest the vastness of infinite space. A simile of grains of sand from the Ganges is at *Saṃyutta Nikāya* ii.182. See C. A. F. Rhys Davids (trans.), *The Book of the Kindred Sayings*, part 2, Pali Text Society, Oxford 1997, pp. 123–4; or Bhikkhu Bodhi (trans.), *The Connected Discourses of the Buddha*, Wisdom Publications, Boston 2000, p. 656.

86 'where this earth / Spins like a fretful midge', from D. G. Rossetti's poem 'The Blessed Damozel' (1850).

87 For example the *Vimalakīrti-nirdeśa.* See R. A. F. Thurman (trans.), *The Holy Teaching of Vimalakīrti,* Pennsylvania State University, New York 1990, chapter 10. (*Complete Works*, vol. 16.)

88 *Anamataggasaṃyutta, Saṃyutta Nikāya* ii.181 (15.5); see Bhikkhu Bodhi (trans.), *Connected Discourses of the Buddha*, Wisdom Publications, Boston 2000, p. 654; or C. A. F. Rhys Davids (trans.), *The Book of the Kindred Sayings*, part 2, Pali Text Society, Oxford 1982, pp. 121–2 where the 'solid mass' is stroked once every hundred years with a piece of 'Kāsi cloth'.

89 Buddhaghosa, *Visuddhimagga* 258–9 (viii.121). See Bhikkhu Ñāṇamoli (trans.), *The Path of Purification*, Buddhist Publication Society, Kandy 1991, p. 252. One such outraged person was a doctor

known to Sangharakshita in Kalimpong, India, as mentioned in a seminar on the *Satipaṭṭhāna Sutta*, held in Tuscany in 1982 (unpublished).

90 There is an exposition of Buddhist cosmology, including a list of the three *lokas* and thirty-one abodes in the introduction to M. Walshe (trans.), *The Long Discourses of the Buddha*, Wisdom Publications, Boston 1995, pp. 37–42. Vasubhandu describes in some detail the planes of existence and their inhabitants in his *Abhidharmakośa-bhāṣya*, trans. L. de la Valleé Poussin, translated into English by L. M. Pruden, Asian Humanities Press, Berkeley 1991, chapter 6, section 5, pp. 451ff.

91 'Experiences are preceded by mind, led by mind, and produced by mind…' See Sangharakshita (trans.), *Dhammapada,* Windhorse Publications, Birmingham 2001, p. 13. (*Complete Works*, vol 15.)

92 Nārada Thera, *A Manual of Abhidhamma* (*Abhidhammattha Sangaha*), vol. i, Vājirārāma, Colombo 1956, pp. 265–6.

93

> This mind of yours is inseparable luminosity and emptiness in the form of a great mass of light, it has no birth or death, therefore it is the buddha of Immortal Light. To recognise this is all that is necessary. When you recognise this pure nature of your mind as the buddha, looking into your own mind is resting in the buddha-mind.

Freemantle and Trungpa (trans. and eds.), *The Tibetan Book of the Dead*, Shambhala Publications, Boulder and London 1975, p. 37.

94 M. Eliade, *Yoga: Immortality and Freedom*, Princeton University Press, 2009, p. 235.

95 Junjirō Takakusu, *Essentials of Buddhist Philosophy*, Asia Publishing House, Bombay 1956, p. 37.

96 The five orders of conditionality, or *niyamas*, are enumerated by Buddhaghosa in his commentary on the *Dhamma-saṅgaṇi,* the first book of the Abhidhamma Piṭaka. See Pe Maung Tin (trans.), *The Expositor,* vol. ii, Pali Text Society, London 1921, p. 360; also in *Buddhaghosa's commentary on the Dīgha Nikāya*, ed. W. Stede, Pali Text Society 1920, p. 360 (not available in English translation). Sangharakshita's source is C. A. F. Rhys Davids, *Buddhism: a Study of the Buddhist Norm*, Williams and Norgate, London 1912, pp. 118–9.

97 For a detailed account see Junjirō Takakusu, *Essentials of Buddhist Philosophy*, Asia Publishing House, Bombay 1956.

98 *Dhammasaṅgaṇi*, Abhidhamma Piṭaka. C. A. F. Rhys Davids

(trans), *A Buddhist Manual of Psychological Ethics (Dhamma-saṅgaṇi)*, third edition, Pali Text Society, London 1974.

99 'Whosoever looketh on a woman to lust after her hath committed adultery with her already in his heart.' Matthew 5:28.

100 The story of the two monks and the girl is told in P. Reps, *Zen Flesh, Zen Bones,* Penguin, Middlesex 1971, p. 28. The story of the dog's tooth is told in Edward Conze, *Buddhism: Its Essence and Development*, Windhorse Publications, Birmingham 2001, p. 63.

101 *Cūḷa-kammavibhaṅga* and *Mahā-kammavibhaṅga Suttas, Majjhima Nikāya* 135 and 136 (iii.202–15). See Bhikkhu Ñāṇamoli and Bhikkhu Bodhi (trans.), *The Middle Length Discourses of the Buddha*, Wisdom Publications, Boston 1995, pp. 1053–65; or I. B. Horner (trans.), *The Collection of the Middle Length Sayings*, vol. iii, Pali Text Society, Oxford 1993, pp. 248–62.

102 At *Visuddhimagga* 103 Buddhaghosa writes that 'one of deluded temperament has formerly drunk a lot of intoxicants and neglected learning and questioning'. Bhikkhu Ñāṇamoli (trans.), *The Path of Purification*, Buddhist Publication Society, Kandy 1991, p. 102.

103 'Joy and woe are woven fine', W. Blake, 'Auguries of Innocence' (composed c.1803).

104 (1) The opening paragraphs of the *Sahasodgata Avadāna* (*Avadāna* 21) describes the Buddha's instructions for creating the *bhavacakra* or wheel of life. See article by C. A. Foley (later C. A. F. Rhys Davids), *Journal of the Royal Asiatic Society* 1894, p. 389). (2) In the *Rudrāyaṇa Avadāna* (*Avadāna* 37) it is said that the Buddha gave the first instruction for a drawing to be made for King Bimbisāra to send as a gift to King Rudrāyaṇa who, through studying the drawing, attained realization.

105 The worlds of the *asuras* and the *pretas* are sometimes transposed.

106 A. Schopenhauer (1788–1860), the German philosopher, published *Die Welt als Wille und Vorstellung* (*The World as Will and Representation*) in 1818. An expanded version elaborating his ideas appeared in 1844.

107 Junjirō Takakusu, *Essentials of Buddhist Philosophy*, Motilal Banarsidass, Bombay 1956, p. 30.

108 B. Shahn, *A Matter of Life and Death*, Ark Press, Marazion, Cornwall 1959, pp. 17–18.

109 A. F. Price and Wong Mou-lam (trans.), *The Diamond Sūtra and the Sūtra of Hui-Neng*, Shambhala Publications, Boston 1990. p. 91.

110 C. Luk (trans.), *The Vimalakīrti Nirdeśa Sūtra*, Shambhala Publications, Berkeley 1972, p. 13. See also R. Thurman (trans.), *The Holy Teaching of Vimalakīrti*, Pennsylvania State University Press, Pennsylvania 1976, p. 18.

111 As quoted by Edward Conze, *Buddhism: Its Essence and Development*, Windhorse Publications, Birmingham 2001, p. 131.

112 The 'vale of tears' is a translation of Psalms 84:6 and has often been used in the Christian tradition to describe the life of mortals on earth. In the Roman Catholic tradition the oft-recited Marian prayer 'Hail Holy Queen' (*Salve Regina*), dating back to the Middle Ages, speaks of our 'mourning and weeping in this vale of tears'.

> Think, in this batter'd
> Caravanserai
> Whose Portals are alternate
> Night and Day,
> How Sultan after Sultan
> with his Pomp
> Abode his destined Hour,
> ands went his way.

Verse 17 from Omar Khayyám, *Rubáiyát,* trans. E. Fitzgerald, fifth edition, 1889.

113 *Vajracchedikā Prajñāpāramitā* 26a & b. See Edward Conze (trans.), *Buddhist Wisdom Books*, Unwin Hyman, London 1988, p. 68.

114 See for example *Laṅkāvatāra Sūtra*, verse 412, in D. T. Suzuki, *The Laṅkāvatāra Sūtra*, George Routledge, London 1932, p. 257 where both *saṃskṛta* (conditioned) and *asaṃskṛta* (unconditioned) *dharmas* are likened to stars, an echo, things seen in a dream.

115 *Dhammapada* 277–9. See for example Sangharakshita (trans.), *Dhammapada*, Windhorse Publications, Birmingham 2001, pp. 95–6 (*Complete Works*, vol. 15).

116 At *Dhammapada* 368 and 381, Nirvāṇa is equated with ultimate peace. See Sangharakshita (trans.), *Dhammapada*, Windhorse Publications, Birmingham 2001, pp. 122 and 125 (Complete Works, vol. 15).

117 *Udāna* 3.2. I. B. Horner (trans.) in Edward Conze (ed.), *Buddhist Texts Through the Ages*, Harper and Row, New York 1964, p. 35. See also J. D. Ireland (trans.), *The Udāna and the Itivuttaka*, Buddhist Publication Society, Kandy 1997, pp. 35–9.

118 *Pāṭika Sutta, Dīgha Nikāya* 24 (iii.34–5). See F. L. Woodward (trans.), *Some Sayings of the Buddha*, Buddhist Society, London 1973, p. 139. See also M. Walshe (trans.), *The Long Discourses of the Buddha*, Wisdom Publications, Boston 1995, p. 382.

119 For example, see the extract, 'Twofold Agelessness and Emptiness' from the *Laṅkāvatāra Sūtra* in Edward

Conze et al (trans.), *Buddhist Texts Through the Ages*, Shambhala Publications, Boston and Shaftesbury 1990, pp. 211–2.

120 Sarvāstivāda means 'the doctrine (*vāda*) that all (*sarva*) exists (*asti*)'. The *locus classicus* for this doctrine is Vasubandu's *Abhidharmakośa* and his commentary, the *Abhidharmakośa-bhāṣya*, where it is stated that 'he who affirms the existence of the *dharmas* of the three time periods is held to be a Sarvāstivādin'. See *Abhidharmakośa* 5.25 in Leo M. Pruden, (trans.), *Abhidharmakośabhāṣyam of Vasubandhu translated into French by Louis de La Vallée Poussin*, Asian Humanities Press, Berkeley 1991, vol. iii, p. 808. The doctrine of *dharma*s existing in the three times was developed largely to deal with philosophical issues surrounding the theory of karma. Sangharakshita refers to the pluralistic realism of the Sarvāstivāda in *A Survey of Buddhism, Complete Works*, vol. 1, pp. 103 and 222ff. See also a useful paragraph in the commentary on the *Heart Sūtra* in *Wisdom Beyond Words*, Windhorse Publications, Birmingham 1993, p. 28 (*Complete Works*, vol. 14).

121 The word 'melioristic' can be defined as 'the belief that the human condition can be improved through concerted effort.' The term is thought to have first appeared in one of George Eliot's letters (1877).

122 D. L. Snellgrove, *The Hevajra Tantra*, Oxford University Press, London 1959, vol. i, p. 134.

123 Augustine of Hippo (354–430 CE), one of the foremost church fathers of Christianity, was a bishop in North Africa. His confessional autobiography *Confessiones* was written (in Latin) between 397 and 400 CE, amounting to some thirteen books. This quotation is from the opening verse of the first chapter of the first book.

124 J. W. Goethe (1749–1832), *Faust Part I*, lines 1699–1702. This translation by Beyard Taylor (1870–1).

125 The pact that Faust makes with Mephistopheles is that the devil can take his soul only

> When, to the Moment then, I say
> 'Ah, stay a while! You are so lovely!'

(*Faust I*, scene iv.) In the case of *Faust I*, the restlessness of the eponymous hero never ceases and the devil has no chance to seize his soul. However, in the final act of *Faust II*, Faust experiences a moment of bliss when he dedicates himself to helping the lives of others. As to what happens next, you will have to read it....

126 For example, Tsongkhapa's exhortation from *A Song of the Stages of the Path to Enlightenment* (Tibetan *Lamrim Nyamgur*), verses 13–14. A translation of these verses is included in Tsongkhapa, *The Principal Teachings of Buddhism,* trans. Geshe Lobsang Tharchin, Classics of Middle Asia, New Jersey 1998, p. 74. Another well-known translation whose source I have not been able to identify, runs

> The human body, at peace with itself,
> Is more precious than the rarest gem ... set your goal
> And make use of every day and night
> To achieve it....

127 D. Snellgrove in Edward Conze (ed.), *Buddhist Texts Through the Ages,* Harper and Row, New York 1964, pp. 246–8.

128 For a more detailed exposition of these categories see *Know Your Mind*, Windhorse Publications, Birmingham 1998 (*Complete Works,* vol. 17). This is Sangharakshita's exposition of Herbert V. Guenther's translation and commentary on the Tibetan text, *The Necklace of Clear Understanding*, by Geshe Gyaltsen (1713–1793) who was from the Gelug school, and who wrote in the tradition of the *Abhidharma-samuccaya* of Asaṅga.

129 Herbert V. Guenther, *Philosophy and Psychology in the Abhidharma*, Shambhala Publications, Berkeley 1976, p. 152.

130 For the eighty-nine *citta*s of the Theravādin Abhidhamma, see Bhikkhu Bodhi (trans.), *A Comprehensive Manual of Abhidhamma: the Abhidhammattha Sangaha of Ācariya Anuruddha*, BPS Pariyatti, Onalaska 2000, chapter 1. For the eight *vijñāna*s of the Yogācāra, see Asaṅga's *Yogācārabhūmi* as well as Vasubandhu's *Triṃśika* or *Thirty Verses.*

131 Jean-Paul Sartre, *Existentialism and Humanism*, Methuen, London 1948, p. 28.

132 See, for example, *Sutta-Nipāta* 4.5, verse 6; 5.4, verse 12; and 5.5, verse 8. H. Saddhatissa (trans.), *The Sutta-Nipāta,* Curzon Press, London 1985, pp. 95 and 122; or E. M. Hare (trans.), *Woven Cadences of Early Buddhists (Sutta-Nipāta)*, Oxford University Press, London 1945, pp. 120, 153, and 154.

133 For a more detailed exposition see *A Survey of Buddhism,* in *Complete Works,* vol. 1, pp. 114ff.

134 *Nidānasaṃyutta*, *Saṃyutta Nikāya* ii.30 (12.3). Bhikkhu Bodhi (trans.), *Connected Discourses of the Buddha*, Wisdom Publications, Boston 2000, pp. 553–6; or C. A. F. Rhys Davids (trans.), *The Book of the Kindred Sayings*,

part 2, Pali Text Society, Oxford 1997, pp. 26–7.

135 *Dhyana For Beginners*, chapter 1, in *A Buddhist Bible*, Dwight Goddard (ed.), Beacon Press, Boston 1970, pp. 442–3.

136 Herbert V. Guenther, *Philosophy and Psychology in the Abhidharma*, Shambhala Publications, Berkeley 1976, p. 51.

137 Pe Maung Tin (trans.), *The Expositor (Aṭṭhasālinī)*, Pali Text Society, London 1920, vol. i, p. 153.

138 Ibid., p. 154.

139 Ibid., pp. 155–6.

140 See for example *Mahāsaccaka Sutta, Majjhima Nikāya* 36 (i.247). Bhikkhu Ñāṇamoli and Bhikkhu Bodhi (trans.), *The Middle Length Discourses of the Buddha*, Wisdom Publications, Boston 1995, p. 341; or I. B. Horner (trans.), *The Collection of the Middle Length Sayings*, vol. i, Pali Text Society, London 1976, p. 302.

141 Lama Anagarika Govinda, *The Psychological Attitude of Early Buddhist Philosophy*, Rider, London 1961, p. 63.

142 *Vatthūpama Sutta*, *Majjhima Nikāya* 7 (i.37). Bhikkhu Ñāṇamoli and Bhikkhu Bodhi (trans.), *The Middle Length Discourses of the Buddha*, Wisdom Publications, Boston 1995, p. 119; or I. B. Horner (trans.), *The Collection of the Middle Length Sayings*, vol. i, Pali Text Society, London 1976, p. 47.

143 *Mahāsaccaka Sutta*, *Majjhima Nikāya* 36 (i.246–7). Bhikkhu Ñāṇamoli and Bhikkhu Bodhi (trans.), *The Middle Length Discourses of the Buddha*, Wisdom Publications, Boston 1995, p. 340; or I. B. Horner (trans.), *The Collection of the Middle Length Sayings*, vol. i, Pali Text Society, London 1976, p. 301.

144 *Ariyapariyesanā Sutta, Majjhima Nikāya* 26 (i.164–7). Bhikkhu Ñāṇamoli and Bhikkhu Bodhi (trans.), *The Middle Length Discourses of the Buddha*, Wisdom Publications, Boston 1995, pp. 257–9; or I. B. Horner (trans.), *The Collection of the Middle Length Sayings*, vol. i, Pali Text Society, London 1976, p. 207.

145 *The Philosophy of our People*, Presidential Address at the Indian Philosophical Congress, 1925. *Indo-Asian Culture*, New Delhi, vol. ix, no. 3, January 1961, p. 233.

146 See, for example, *Aṅguttara Nikāya* v.3. Bhikkhu Bodhi (trans.), *The Numerical Discourses of the Buddha*, Wisdom Publications, Somerville 2012, p. 1341; or F. L. Woodward (trans.), *Gradual Sayings*, vol. v, Pali Text Society, Oxford 1996, p. 4.

147 *Visuddhimagga* 652 in Bhikkhu Ñāṇamoli (trans.), *The Path of Purification*, Buddhist Publication Society, Kandy 1991, p. 675.

148 From the *Lam Gyi Gtso Bo Rnam Gsum* ('The Three Chief Paths [to Enlightenment'), verse 6. See Tsongkhapa, *The Principal Teachings of Buddhism,* trans. Geshe Lobsang Tharchin, Classics of Middle Asia, New Jersey 1998, p. 93.

149 *Mahāmaṅgala Sutta, Sutta-Nipāta* 2.4, verse 11. There are many alternative translations including E. M. Hare (trans.), *Woven Cadences of Early Buddhists (Sutta-Nipāta)*, Oxford University Press, London 1945, p. 40; or H. Saddhatissa (trans.), *The Sutta-Nipāta,* Curzon Press, London 1985, p. 30.

150 R. A. F. Thurman (trans.), *The Holy Teaching of Vimalakīrti,* Pennsylvania State University Press, University Park and London 1976, p. 77. (*Complete Works*, vol 16, pp. 549–50.)

151 Herbert V. Guenther, *Philosophy and Psychology in the Abhidharma*, Shambhala Publications, Berkeley 1976, p. 207.

152 *Jambukkhādaka-saṃyutta, Saṃyutta Nikāya* iv.251 (38.1), in Edward Conze (ed.), *Buddhist Texts Through the Ages,* Harper and Row, New York 1964, p. 94. See also see Bhikkhu Bodhi (trans.), *Connected Discourses of the Buddha*, Wisdom Publications, Boston 2000, p. 1294; or F. L. Woodward (trans.), *The Book of the Kindred Sayings*, part 4, Pali Text Society, London 1980, p. 170.

153 *Udāna* 8.3. I. B. Horner (trans.) in Edward Conze (ed.) *Buddhist Texts Through the Ages,* Harper and Row, New York 1964, p. 95. See also J. D. Ireland (trans.), *The Udāna and the Itivuttaka*, Buddhist Publication Society, Kandy 1997, p. 103.

154 Kenneth. W. Morgan, (ed.) *The Path of the Buddha*, Ronald Press, New York 1956, p. 178.

155 *Dhammapada* 203. See, for example, Sangharakshita (trans.), *Dhammapada*, Windhorse Publications, Birmingham 2001, p. 72 (*Complete Works*, vol. 15).

156 P. B. Shelley, *Adonais: An Elegy on the Death of John Keats*, canto 48 (1821).

157 T. W. Rhys Davids and W. Stede, *Pali–English Dictionary*, first Indian edition, Motilal Banarsidass, Delhi 1993, p. 558.

158 *Amitāyur-dhyāna Sūtra,* section 17. F. Max Müller (ed.), *Sacred Books of the East*, London 894, vol. xlix, part 2, p. 181. See also Ratnaguna and raddhāpa, *Great Faith, Great Wisdom,* Windhorse Publications, Cambridge 2016, p. 312.

159 Beatrice Lane Suzuki, *Mahāyāna Buddhism*, George Allen and Unwin, London 1959, p. 117.

160 Christmas Humphreys (ed.), *The Wisdom of Buddhism*, Michael Joseph, London 1960, p. 147.

161 The seven *bodhyaṅgas* in Sanskrit are *smṛti, dharma-pravicaya, vīrya, prīti, praśrabdhi, samādhi,* and *upekṣā*; and in Pāli, *sati, dhamma-vicaya, viriya, pīti, passaddhi, samādhi,* and *upekkhā.*

162 *Mahāparinibbāna Sutta, Dīgha Nikāya* 16 (ii.120). See M. Walshe (trans.), *The Long Discourses of the Buddha*, Wisdom Publications, Boston 1995, pp. 253; or T. W. and C. A. F. Rhys Davids (trans.), *Dialogues of the Buddha*, part 2, Pali Text Society, London 1971, p. 128.

163 This is a phrase that appears in the *Tiratana Vandanā* or 'Praises to the Three Jewels'. See Sangharakshita's commentary *Salutation to the Three Jewels* in *Complete Works*, vol. 15.

164 *Saddharma Puṇḍarīka (White Lotus) Sūtra*, chapter 16, 'Revelation of the [Eternal] Life of the Tatāgatha' in Bunnō Katō et al (trans.), *The Threefold Lotus Sutra,* Kosei Publishing, Tokyo 1975, pp. 249ff. (*Complete Works*, vol 16.)

165 See Edward Conze, *Buddhism: Its Essence and Development*, Windhorse Publications, Birmingham 2001, chapter 6.

166 T. R. V. Murti, *The Central Philosophy of Buddhism*, George Allen and Unwin, London 1955, p. 280.

167 *Kevaddha Sutta, Dīgha Nikāya* 11 (i.223). M. Walshe (trans.), *The Long Discourses of the Buddha*, Wisdom Publications, Boston 1995, pp. 179; or T. W. Rhys Davids (trans.), *Dialogues of the Buddha*, part 1, Pali Text Society, London 1973, p. 283.

168 *Ekakanipāta, Aṅguttara Nikāya* i.10. I. B. Horner (trans.) in Edward Conze et al (eds.), *Buddhist Texts Through the Ages*, Harper and Row, New York 1964, p. 33. See also F. L. Woodward (trans.), *The Book of the Gradual Sayings*, vol. i, Pali Text Society, Oxford 2000, p. 8; or Bhikkhu Bodhi (trans.), *The Numerical Discourses of the Buddha*, Wisdom Publications, Somerville 2012, p. 97.

169 *Sumaṅgala-Vilāsinī*, in *Indian Historical Quarterly*, II.i, p. 33.

170 'The triple world of existence is no more than thought-construction'. See the *Sagāthakam* of the *Laṅkāvatāra Sūtra*, verse 77, in D. T. Suzuki (trans.), *The Laṅkāvatāra Sūtra*, George Routledge, London 1932, p. 232.

171 'There is in God, some say, / A deep but dazzling Darkness…': lines from the seventeenth-century Welsh poet, Henry Vaughan's poem, 'The Night', a meditation on a verse from the gospel of St John. 'What is the Divine Darkness?' is the title of chapter 1 of *The Mystical Theology of Dionysius the Areopagite, translated from the Greek,*

The Shrine of Wisdom, Surrey 1923.

172 'He that findeth his life shall lose it: and he that loseth his life for my sake shall find it.' Matthew 10:39.

173 The unstruck sound or 'Anahad Shabd' is the divine, inner sound to which the great Indian mystic and poet Kabir (1440–1518) makes reference in his poetry.

174 In Chinese painting plum blossom is a symbol for winter, an orchid for spring, bamboo for summer, and a chrysanthemum for autumn.

175 See 'Factors in the Emergence of the Mahāyāna' in *A Survey of Buddhism*, *Complete Works*, vol. 1, pp. 219–36.

176 See 'The Positive Aspects of Nirvāṇa' in *A Survey of Buddhism*, *Complete Works*, vol. 1, pp. 80–8.

177 For a translation of the *Larger* and *Smaller Sukhāvatī-vyūha* or 'Array of the Happy Land' *Sūtras*, plus commentary, see Ratnaguna and Śraddhāpa, *Great Faith, Great Wisdom*, Windhorse Publications, Cambridge 2016.

178 Lama Anagarika Govinda, *Foundations of Tibetan Mysticism*, Rider, London 1969, p. 106.

179 Sangharakshita suggested (2018) the source of these ideas may have been Yogi Chen, from whom he learnt about and discussed meditation in the 1950s in Kalimpong. See *Precious Teachers*, Windhorse Publications, Birmingham 2007, pp. 142ff. (*Complete Works*, vol. 22).

180 See Edward Conze (trans.), *Buddhist Wisdom Books*, Unwin Hyman, London 1988, p. 103.

181 *Itivuttaka* 92. See J. D. Ireland (trans.), *The Udāna and the Itivuttaka*, Buddhist Publication Society, Kandy 1997, p. 217.

182 See, for example, *Itivuttaka* 100, in John D. Ireland (trans.), *The Udāna and the Itivuttaka*, Buddhist Publication Society, Kandy 1997, p. 226.

183 Sangharakshita came across this trinity in Nepal, probably in the iconography he saw there.

184 i.e. *bhikkhus, bhikkhunīs, upāsakas* and *upāsikās* or monks, nuns, laymen, and laywomen.

185 *Dhammapada* 62. See Sangharakshita (trans.), *Dhammapada,* Windhorse Publications, Birmingham 2001, p. 30 (*Complete Works*, vol. 15).

186 See under 'Arahant' in T. W. Rhys Davids and W. Stede, *Pali–English Dictionary*, first Indian edition, Motilal Banarsidass, Delhi 1993, p. 77.

187 For example: *Cūḷasīhanāda Sutta*, *Majjhima Nikāya* 11 (i.67–8). Bhikkhu Ñāṇamoli and Bhikkhu Bodhi (trans.), *The Middle Length Discourses of the Buddha*, Wisdom Publications, Boston 1995,

p. 163; or I. B. Horner (trans.), *The Collection of the Middle Length Sayings*, vol. i, Pali Text Society, London 1976, p. 90.

188 Edward Conze (trans.), *The Large Sūtra on Perfect Wisdom* (part 1), Luzac and Co. Ltd., London 1961.

189 'The Revaluation of all Values' was the working title for four volumes planned by Nietzsche of which only the first, *The Antichrist* (German original: *Der Antichrist,* 1885), was completed, in which he discusses transvaluation in terms of Christianity and Buddhism, the first being life-denying and the second life-affirming. For a study of Nietzsche by a Buddhist see R. G. Morrison (Dharmachari Sagaramati), *Nietzsche and Buddhism: A Study in Nihilism and Ironic Affinities*, Oxford University Press, Oxford 1997.

190 *Dhammapada* 178. See Sangharakshita (trans.), *Dhammapada*, Windhorse Publications, Birmingham 2001, p. 65 (*Complete Works*, vol. 15).

191 *Mahāparinibbāna Sutta*, *Dīgha Nikāya* 16 (ii.100). See M. Walshe (trans.), *The Long Discourses of the Buddha*, Wisdom Publications, Boston 1995, pp. 245; or T. W. and C. A. F. Rhys Davids (trans.), *Dialogues of the Buddha*, part 2, Pali Text Society, London 1971, p. 108.

192 Nyanatiloka, *Buddhist Dictionary*, Kandy 1988, p. 72.

193 Meister Eckhart (c.1260–c.1328) was German, a member of the Dominican Roman Catholic monastic order, a theologian and mystic, described sometimes as a Christian Neoplatonist. He was accused of heresy by the Roman Catholic Church.

St Teresa of Ávila (1515–1582) was a Carmelite nun renowned as a mystic, and as a reformer of her order. In her mystical writings she describes the ascent of the soul through four stages of devotion (the Devotion of Heart, of Peace, of Union, and of Ecstasy).

194 Milarepa (c.1052–c.1135) is a renowned figure associated with the Kagyu school of Tibetan Buddhism, a yogi, famed for his songs through which he communicated to his disciples and expressed his own inner realizations.

Tsongkhapa (1357–1419), one of the great figures of Tibetan Buddhism, is associated with the formation of the Gelug school, and founding the great Ganden monastery. He wrote a number of influential works, among them his renowned *Great Treatise on the Stages of the Path to Enlightenment* (*lam rim chen mo*).

195 N. Dutt, *Early Monastic Buddhism*, Calcutta Oriental Book Agency, Calcutta 1960, pp. 268–9.

196 The Buddha refers to a *bhikkhu* who is *ubhatobhāgavimutta* or freed in both ways in, for example, the *Kīṭāgiri Sutta*, *Majjhima Nikāya* 70 (i.477). Bhikkhu Ñāṇamoli and Bhikkhu Bodhi (trans.), *The Middle Length Discourses of the Buddha*, Wisdom Publications, Boston 1995, p. 580; or I. B. Horner (trans.), *The Collection of the Middle Length Sayings*, vol. ii, Pali Text Society, Oxford 1994, p. 152.

197 *Abhidharmakośa* vi.56. Vasubandhu, *Abhidharmakośabhāṣyam,* vol. iii, trans. L. de La Vallée Poussin, Asian Humanities Press, Berkeley 1988, p. 1000.

198 See e.g. *Kathāvatthu* i.2 in Shwe Zan Aung and Mrs Rhys Davids (trans.), *Points of Controversy*, Pali Text Society, London 1915, pp. 64–70.

199 See Nyanatiloka, *Buddhist Dictionary*, Buddhist Publication Society, Kandy 1980, p. 24. The list of the eight individuals, the four pairs of persons, i.e.

> the stream-enterer and the one who is on the way to realizing the fruit of stream-entry, the once-returner and the one who is on the way to realizing the fruit of once-returning, the non-returner and the one who is on the way to realizing the fruit of non-returning, the arahant and the one who is on the way to arahantship.

as given in Udāna 5.5 (*Uposatha Sutta*); see John D. Ireland (trans.), *The Udāna and the Itivuttaka*, Buddhist Publication Society 2007, p. 74.

200
> There lives more faith in honest doubt,
> Believe me, than in half the creeds.

Alfred Lord Tennyson, *In Memoriam A. H. H.*, canto 96.

201 The Ritualist controversies of nineteenth-century Anglicanism originated with the Oxford Movement or Anglo-Catholic revival of the mid-1840s. The controversies moved from theological debate to debates about ritual including the use – or not – of candles, incense, vestments, and so on.

202 Herbert V. Guenther, *Philosophy and Psychology in the Abhidharma*, Shambhala Publications, Berkeley 1976, p. 211.

203 Bimala Charan Law (trans.), *Designation of Human Types* (*Puggala-Paññatti*), Pali Text Society, London 1922, p. 104.

204 Vinaya Piṭaka i.20–1 (*Mahāvagga* 1.11). See I. B. Horner (trans.), *The Book of the Discipline*, part 4, Pali Text Society, Oxford 1996, p. 28.

205 This is further elaborated in *Was the Buddha a Bhikkhu?* in this volume.

206 Herbert V. Guenther, *Philosophy and Psychology in the Abhidharma*, Shambhala

Publications, Berkeley 1976, p. 232, note 2.

207 Ibid., p. 198, note 4.

208 Edward Conze (trans.), *The Large Sūtra on Perfect Wisdom* (part 1), University of California, Berkeley 1975, pp. 37–8.

209 *Saddharma Puṇḍarīka* or *White Lotus Sūtra,* chapter 2. See Bunnō Katō et al (trans.), *The Threefold Lotus Sutra*, Kosei Publishing, Tokyo 1975, pp. 58–9. See also the commentary in *The Drama of Cosmic Enlightenment,* chapter 2, in *Complete Works*, vol. 16.

210 Edward Conze (trans.), *The Perfection of Wisdom in Eight Thousand Lines and Its Verse Summary* (*Aṣṭasāhasrikā Prajñāpāramitā*), Four Seasons Foundation, San Francisco 1973, pp. 238–9.

211 A second-century CE image of Maitreya, 67cm high, from Ahicchatra (in modern day Uttar Pradesh, India, then part of the Kushan Empire). It is now in the National Museum of India, New Delhi. There is a black-and-white photograph in P. M. Lad, *The Way of the Buddha*, Ministry of Information and Broadcasting, Govt. of India, New Delhi 1956, p. 198.

212 Edward Conze (trans.), *The Perfection of Wisdom in Eight Thousand Lines and Its Verse Summary* (*Aṣṭasāhasrikā Prajñāpāramitā*), Four Seasons Foundation, San Francisco 1973, pp. 223–4; and Edward Conze et al (eds.) *Buddhist Texts Through the Ages*, Harper and Row, New York 1964, pp. 128–9.

213 Edward Conze et al (eds.) *Buddhist Texts Through the Ages*, Harper and Row, New York 1964, p. 131.

214 E. Conze (trans.), *Buddhist Wisdom Books*, Unwin Hyman, London 1988, p. 25.

215 D. T. Suzuki, *Essays in Zen Buddhism*, third series, Rider, London 1970, p. 172.

216 Ibid., pp. 178–80.

217 Ibid., p. 180–1.

218 Ibid., p. 170. See also Thomas Cleary (trans.), *The Flower Ornament Sūtra* (*Avataṃsaka Sūtra*), Shambhala Publications, Boston and London 1993, p. 324.

219 Herbert V. Guenther (trans.), *The Jewel Ornament of Liberation*, Rider, London 1959, p. 34.

220 Ibid., p. 35.

221 For more on the *bodhicitta* (or the 'awakening of the bodhi heart') see *The Bodhisattva Ideal*, chapter 2, in *Complete Works,* vol. 4.

222 Ibid., p. 114.

223 D. T. Suzuki, *Manual of Zen Buddhism*, Rider, London 1950, p. 14. An alternative translation appears in D. T. Suzuki, *Essays in Zen Buddhism*, third series, Rider, London 1970, p. 169.

224 A note by Rev. Bunyin Nanjio in F. Max Müller (ed.), *Mahāyāna Buddhist Texts*,

Sacred Books of the East, vol. xlix, Oxford and London 1894, part 2, p. 73. See also Ratnaguna and Śraddhāpa, *Great Faith, Great Wisdom*, Windhorse Publications, Cambridge 2016, p. 244.

225 For more on the *praṇidhicitta* or bodhisattva vow see *The Bodhisattva Ideal,* chapter 3, in *Complete Works,* vol. 4. See also the sixty-four bodhisattva precepts in the Appendix, pp. 657–9ff.

226 Sangharakshita explains the six *pāramitās* in more detail in *The Bodhisattva Ideal,* chapters 4–6, in *Complete Works,* vol. 4.

227 D. T. Suzuki, *Essays in Zen Buddhism,* third series, second edition, Rider, London 1970, p. 181.

228 Ibid., pp. 186–7. For an alternative translation of this passage see Thomas Cleary (trans.), *The Flower Ornament Sūtra* (*Avataṃsaka Sūtra*), Shambhala Publications, Boston and London 1993, pp. 1476–7. (The *Gaṇḍavyūha Sūtra* is the thirty-ninth chapter of the *Avataṃsaka Sūtra*.)

229 Edward Conze (trans.), *The Perfection of Wisdom in Eight Thousand Lines and Its Verse Summary* (*Aṣṭasāhasrikā Prajñāpāramitā*), Four Seasons Foundation, San Francisco 1973, p. 206.

230 Edward Conze (trans.), *Abhisamayālaṇkāra* iv.8, Serie Orientale Roma, Rome 1954, pp. 66ff. See also Edward Conze (trans.), *The Large Sūtra on Perfect Wisdom with the divisions of the Abhisamayālaṃkāra*, University of California Press, Berkeley 1975, pp. 388ff.

231 Edward Conze (trans.), *The Perfection of Wisdom in Eight Thousand Lines and Its Verse Summary* (*Aṣṭasāhasrikā Prajñāpāramitā*), Four Seasons Foundation, San Francisco 1973, p. 200.

232 For more on the Parable of the Burning House see *The Drama of Cosmic Enlightenment,* chapter 3, in *Complete Works*, vol. 16. The parable is from the third chapter of the *Saddharma Puṇḍarīka* or *White Lotus Sūtra.* See Bunnō Katō et al (trans.), *The Threefold Lotus Sutra*, Kosei Publishing, Tokyo 1975, pp. 85ff.

233 Edward Conze (trans.), *The Perfection of Wisdom in Eight Thousand Lines and Its Verse Summary* (*Aṣṭasāhasrikā Prajñāpāramitā*), Four Seasons Foundation, San Francisco 1973, p. 202.

234 Ibid., pp. 227–9.

235 In chapter 4 of the *Sūtra* the bodhisattvas express their reluctance to call on Vimalakīrti since he has in past encounters shown up their shortcomings. But in chapter 5 Mañjuśrī agrees to go and sets off with the other bodhisattvas and other members of the assembly, all eager to hear the

conversation between the two. R. A. F. Thurman (trans.), *The Holy Teaching of Vimalakīrti*, Pennsylvania State University Press, University Park and London 1976, p. 42. See also Sangharakshita's commentary in *The Inconceivable Emancipation*, *Complete Works*, vol. 16, pp. 518–34.

236 D. Snellgrove, *Buddhist Himalaya*, Bruno Cassirer, Oxford 1957, p. 57.

237 B. Bhattacharyya, *The Indian Buddhist Iconography*, K. L. Mukhaopadhyay, Calcutta 1958, pp. 100–23.

238 These verses are from the Mañjughoṣa *stuti sādhana* or visualization and recitation practice. Sangharakshita received initiation (Tibetan: *wangkur*) into this and three other *sādhanas* in October 1957 from Jamyang Khyentse Chökyi Lodrö (1893–1959), the great Tibetan lama of the Rimé tradition, in a ceremony held at Cooch Behar House, Darjeeling; afterwards receiving the written text which was translated by John Driver, an English scholar then living, like Sangharakshita, in Kalimpong. See *Precious Teachers*, Windhorse Publications, Birmingham 2007, pp. 14–16 (*Complete Works*, vol. 22). It is John Driver's translation that is quoted here and used by *dharmacāriṇīs* and *dharmacārīs* of the Triratna Buddhist Order who have taken up the practice of the Mañjughoṣa *stuti sādhana*, either taking it from their preceptor at the time of ordination, or afterwards.

239 *Saddharma Puṇḍarīka* or *White Lotus Sūtra*, chapter 25 of the Chinese version. See Bunnō Katō et al (trans.), *The Threefold Lotus Sutra*, Kosei Publishing, Tokyo 1975, pp. 319–321.

240 B. Bhattacharyya, *The Indian Buddhist Iconography*, K. L. Mukhaopadhyay, Calcutta 1958, pp. 124–44.

241 *Cakkavatti-Sīhanāda Sutta*, *Dīgha Nikāya* 26 (iii.76). See M. Walshe (trans.), *The Long Discourses of the Buddha*, Wisdom Publications, Boston 1995, p. 403; or T. W. and C. A. F. Rhys Davids (trans.), *Dialogues of the Buddha*, part 3, Pali Text Society, London 1971, pp. 73–4.

242 Jiddu Krishnamurti (1895–1986) was from present-day Andhra Pradesh. Around the age of fourteen, when the family had moved to Adyar, he was 'discovered' by theosophists Charles Leadbeater and Annie Besant and groomed to be the 'World Teacher', identified with Maitreya. He later rejected this role, nevertheless going on to give many lectures, and writing on religious and philosophical themes.

243 D. T. Suzuki, *Essays in Zen Buddhism*, third series, Rider, London 1970, p. 83.

244 Sir Charles Eliot, *Hinduism and Buddhism: An Historical*

Sketch, Routledge and Kegan Paul, London 1921, vol. ii, p. 24.

245 Xuanzang (602–664) in his *Xiyu Ji* or *Record of Western Countries* describes his travels from China through thirty-four kingdoms of central Asia until he reached India in 631. There he spent some years studying, including two periods at Nālandā, the great Buddhist monastic university, before finally returning to China with 627 Buddhist texts which he spent the rest of his life translating with the help of a translation team.

246 Kumārajīva (334–413 CE) was a great scholar and translator of the Madhyamaka school who, through his translations from Sanskrit, made Mahāyāna texts available to the Chinese, including the *Saddharma Puṇḍarīka* (*White Lotus Sūtra*), the *Vimalakīrti-nirdeśa*, and the *Aṣṭasāhasrikā-prajñāpāramitā Sūtra* (*Perfection of Wisdom in Eight Thousand Lines*).

247 Milarepa (1052–1135) is one of the great figures of the Tibetan Kagyu school, famed as a yogi and poet. See *Milarepa and the Art of Discipleship, Complete Works,* vols. 18 and 19; and note 194 above.

248 Tsongkhapa (1357–1419), one of the greatest figures of Tibetan Buddhism, is associated with the formation of the Gelug school. See note 194.

249 P. B. Shelley, *Adonaïs: An Elegy on the Death of John Keats,* canto 48 (1821).

250 Shōtoku Taishi (c.574–c.622 CE), renowned as a Buddhist, was appointed regent by the Empress Suiko during the Asuka period in Japan. He is thought to have written the first commentaries on Buddhist texts in Japanese.

251 Viśiṣṭacāritra or, in Japanese, Jōgyō (translated as Superior Conduct or Eminent Conduct) is one of the bodhisattvas whom the Buddha exhorts to uphold the Dharma in the future. See the *Saddharma Puṇḍarīka* or *White Lotus Sūtra* in Bunnō Katō et al (trans.), *The Threefold Lotus Sutra*, Kosei Publishing, Tokyo, 1975, p. 298.

252 Sarahapāda, often shortened to Saraha, meaning 'one who has shot with an arrow', flourished probably in the eighth century CE. He grew up in a Brahmin family in eastern India and attended Nālandā university. His tantric practices led him to overthrow social norms regarding caste and gender relations. He is recognized as the first of the great Mahāsiddhas of the Vajrayāna tantric tradition.

Tāranātha (1575–1634) was a scholar and lama of the Jonang school of Tibetan Buddhism and founder of a Jonang monastery in the Tsangpo valley. Foremost among his works is the monumental *History of Buddhism in India* (1608).

253 Kenneth. W. Morgan (ed.), *The Path of the Buddha*, Ronald Press, New York 1956, pp. 256–8.

254 Their 'spiritual emotions are the habitual centre of the personal energy'. See William James, *The Varieties of Religious Experience*, Dover Publications, Mineola N. Y. 2003, p. 271 (first published 1902).

255 S. Dutt, *Early Buddhist Monachism*, Kegan Paul et al, London 1924, chapter 2, especially pp. 68–9.

256 The four *pārājikas* (Sanskrit and Pāli) or 'defeats' are major breaches that render a *bhikṣu* liable to expulsion from the order, which include sexual intercourse, stealing, intentionally bringing about the death of a human being, and knowingly lying about spiritual attainment. They are the subject of the first four sections of the *Sutta Vibhaṅga* of the Vinaya Piṭaka. See I. B. Horner (trans.), *The Book of the Discipline*, part 1, Pali Text Society, Oxford 1996.

257 See *Dhammapada* 184–7 in Sangharakshita (trans.), *Dhammapada*, Windhorse Publications, Birmingham 2001, pp. 67–8 (*Complete Works*, vol. 15); and *Mahāpadāna Sutta, Dīgha Nikāya* 14 (ii.50) in M. Walshe (trans.), *The Long Discourses of the Buddha*, Wisdom Publications, Boston 1995, p. 219; or T. W. and C. A. F. Rhys Davids (trans.), *Dialogues of the Buddha*, part 2, Pali Text Society, London 1971, pp. 39.

258 See for example the group of young men who 'received the going forth in the Lord's presence', and joined the order of monks: Vinaya Piṭaka i.23–4 (*Mahāvagga* 1.14). See I. B. Horner (trans.), *The Book of the Discipline*, part 4, Pali Text Society, Oxford 1996, p. 32; and the Buddha's future chief disciples, the wanderers Sāriputta and Moggallāna, Vinaya Piṭaka i.43 (*Mahāvagga* 1.24), ibid., p. 56. To his future lay-follower Anāthapiṇḍika he also said simply, 'Come, Sudatta', using his given name, so that Anāthapiṇḍika felt 'joyful and elated'. Vinaya Piṭaka ii.156 (*Cullavagga* 6.4), I. B. Horner (trans.), *The Book of the Discipline*, part 5, Pali Text Society, London 1975, p. 219.

259 G. F. Allen, *The Buddha's Philosophy*, London 1959, p. 72.

260 S. Dutt, *Early Buddhist Monachism*, Kegan Paul et al, London 1924, pp. 82–3.

261 See W. Pachow, *A Comparative Study of the Prātimokṣa*, Motilal Banarsidass, Delhi 2007.

262 The story of Anāthapiṇḍada (Pali Anathapiṇḍika) and his donation of the Jetavana, or Jeta Grove in Śrāvastī, is told at Vinaya Piṭaka

ii.154–9 (*Cullavagga* 6.4). See I. B. Horner (trans.), *The Book of the Discipline*, part 5, Pali Text Society, London 1975, pp. 216–23. See also note 29.

263 The Second Buddhist Council that took place in Vaiśālī has been dated to 334 BCE. Aśoka's acceded to the throne of Magadha in 268 BCE.

264 This is the refrain to the 41 verses (as presented by E. M. Hare) of the *Rhinoceros Sutta* (*Khaggavisāṇa*), *Sutta-Nipāta* 1.3. See *Woven Cadences of Early Buddhists* (*Sutta-Nipāta*), Oxford University Press, London 1945, pp. 6–11; or H. Saddhatissa (trans.), *The Sutta-Nipāta*, Curzon Press, London 1985, pp. 4–7.

265 *Sutta-Nipāta*, 4.13, verse 6. E. M. Hare, ibid., p. 132; Saddhatissa, ibid., p. 105.

266 Referred to by S. Dutt, *Early Buddhist Monachism*, Kegan Paul et al, London 1924, p. 111. See also Bhikkhu Pesala (trans.), *The Debate of King Milinda*, Inward Path, Penang 2001, p. 117:

> It was said by the Blessed One: 'Fear is born from intimacy, Dust is from a house arisen. Homeless, free from intimacy, This is the sage's vision.' Yet he also said: 'Let the wise man have dwellings built and lodge learned men therein.'

267 S. Dutt, *Early Buddhist Monachism*, Kegan Paul et al, London 1924, p. 69.

268 N. Dutt and K. D. Bajpai, *Development of Buddhism in Uttar Pradesh*, Govt. of Uttar Pradesh, Lucknow 1956, p. 277. See also W. Pachow, *A Comparative Study of the Prātimokṣa*, Motilal Banarsidass, Delhi 2007.

269 The Siyama *nikāya* of Sri Lanka was established in 1753 when Upali Thera, a Thai (or Siamese) monk visited the then kingdom of Kandy and performed *upasampadā* for a group of local Buddhists. The Siyama *nikāya* came into disrepute when monks were implicated in a plot to place a Siamese prince on the throne, and when ordination was restricted to certain castes.

270 A. C. Banerjee, *Sarvāstivāda Literature*, D. Banerjee, Calcutta 1957, p. 118.

271 For details see W. Pachow, *A Comparative Study of the Prātimokṣa*, Motilal Banarsidass, Delhi 2007.

272 N. Dutt and K. D. Bajpai, *Development of Buddhism in Uttar Pradesh*, Govt. of Uttar Pradesh, Lucknow 1956, p. 277.

273 See W. Pachow, *A Comparative Study of the Prātimokṣa*, Motilal Banarsidass, Delhi 2007. See also note 387.

274 The Theravādin *bhikkhunī* tradition was revived when, in 2003, Thai Buddhist Chatsumarn Kabilsingh

received full ordination as Bhikkhuni Dhammananda. See also note 584.

275 Xuanzang (602–664) described his travels in his *Xiyu Ji* or *Great Tang Records of the Western Region*. See note 245.

276 S. Dutt, *Early Buddhist Monachism*, Kegan Paul et al, London 1924, p. 123.

277 A. C. Banerjee, *Sarvāstivāda Literature*, D. Banerjee, Calcutta 1957, pp. 187–8.

278 *Sāmaññaphala Sutta*, *Dīgha Nikāya* 2 (i.50). See M. Walshe (trans.), *The Long Discourses of the Buddha*, Wisdom Publications, Boston 1995, p. 92; or T. W. Rhys Davids (trans.), *Dialogues of the Buddha*, part 1, Pali Text Society, London 1973, p. 68.

279 *Udāna* 5.5. See J. D. Ireland (trans.), *The Udāna and the Itivuttaka*, Buddhist Publication Society, Kandy 1997, pp. 69–71.

280 Xuanzang (602–664) in his *Xiyu Ji* or *Record of Western Countries* describes his travels from China through thirty-four kingdoms of central Asia until he reached India in 631. There he spent some years studying, including two periods at Nālandā, the great Buddhist monastic university, before finally returning to China with 627 Buddhist texts which he spent the rest of his life translating with the help of a translation team.

281 *Visuddhimagga* 95. See Bhikkhu Ñāṇamoli (trans.), *The Path of Purification*, Buddhist Publication Society, Kandy 1991, p. 96.

282 *Visuddhimagga* 118–22, ibid., pp. 118–21.

283 *Dhammapada* 142. See, for example, Sangharakshita (trans.), *Dhammapada*, Windhorse Publications, Birmingham 2001, p. 54 (*Complete Works*, vol. 15).

284 *Aṅguttara Nikāya* ii.8 (4.7). See Bhikkhu Bodhi (trans.), *The Numerical Discourses of the Buddha*, Wisdom Publications, Somerville 2012, p. 394; or F. L. Woodward,(trans.), *Gradual Sayings*, vol. ii, Pali Text Society, Oxford 1995, p. 8.

285 Vinaya Piṭaka iv.13 (*Pācittiya* 4). See I. B. Horner (trans.), *The Book of the Discipline*, part 2, Pali Text Society, Oxford 1996, p. 190.

286 *Majjhima Nikāya* iii.261. See Bhikkhu Ñāṇamoli and Bhikkhu Bodhi (trans.), *The Middle Length Discourses of the Buddha*, Wisdom Publications, Boston 1995, p. 1112; or I. B. Horner (trans.), *The Collection of the Middle Length Sayings*, vol. iii, Pali Text Society, Oxford 1993, pp. 313.

287 Vinaya Piṭaka i.21 (*Mahāvagga* 1.11). I. B. Horner (trans.), *The Book of the Discipline*, part 4, Pali Text Society, Oxford 1996, p. 28.

288 In the *Pārāyana-vagga* the Brahmin Bāvari and his sixteen

Brahmin students, all teachers in their own right, visit the Buddha at the Rock Temple in Magadha and put to him a number of questions. After listening to his replies they are 'filled with pleasure by the clear-sighted vision of this Kinsman of the Sun' and 'settle down to a life of purity and goodness in the shelter of the precious wisdom of the Buddha'. See the Prologue to *Sutta-Nipāta* chapter 5; H. Saddhatissa (trans.), *The Sutta-Nipāta,* Curzon Press, London 1985, pp. 114ff.

289 See R. A. F. Thurman (trans.), *The Holy Teaching of Vimalakirti*, Pennsylvania State University Press, University Park and London 1976, pp. 56–8. See also Sangharakshita's commentary in *The Inconceivable Emancipation*, *Complete Works*, vol. 16, pp. 521–5.

290 E. J. Thomas, *The Perfection of Wisdom*, John Murray, London 1952, p. 58.

291 Philip Karl Eidmann, 'A Synopsis of the Sūtra of Brahma's Net of the Bodhisattva's Precepts', *Maha Bodhi*, vol. 66, December 1958, p. 392.

292 Sangharakshita took bodhisattva ordination, including the sixty-four bodhisattva precepts, from Dhardo Rimpoche on 12 October 1962. See *Precious Teachers,* Windhorse Publications, Birmingham 2007, pp. 151–4 (*Complete Works,* vol. 22). The sixty-four precepts are included in the Appendix, pp. 657ff.

293 But see notes 274 and 584.

294 Philip Karl Eidmann, 'A Synopsis of the Sūtra of Brahma's Net of the Bodhisattva's Precepts', *Maha Bodhi*, vol. 66, December 1958, p. 398.

295 Thotagamuwe Siri Rahula Thera (1408–1491) was a Buddhist monk famed for his erudition. He knew six languages and learned by heart the whole of the Tipiṭaka. He was of royal parentage and became the first *bhikkhu* of Ceylon to be appointed 'Sangharaja'.

For Milarepa see notes 194 and 247.

296 Aśvaghoṣa (c.80–c.150 CE) came from a Brahmin family of northern India and converted to Buddhism. He was the first great dramatist to write in classical Sanskrit. His epic poem on the life of the Buddha is the *Buddhacarita.*

297 Wu Daozi (680–c.760) was one of the great artists of the Chinese Tang dynasty. He drew mountain landscapes, flowers, and birds, and created murals in Buddhist and Daoist temples. There are many similar legends illustrating the brilliance of his art.

Kūkai (774–835), known posthumously as Kōbō Daishi or 'The Grand Master who Propagated the Buddhist

Teaching', was a Japanese Buddhist monk-scholar, calligrapher, poet, artist, and also engineer. He founded the Shingon school of Buddhism.

298 The *upasampadā-kammavācā* is the *bhikkhu* ordination ceremony. It was first translated from Pāli into English by Sir John F. Dickson as 'The Buddhist manual of the form and manner of ordering of priests and deacons' and published in 1875.

299 Edward Conze et al (eds.), *Buddhist Texts Through the Ages*, Harper and Row, New York 1964, p. 302.

300 Edward Conze (trans.), *The Perfection of Wisdom in Eight Thousand Lines and Its Verse Summary* (*Aṣṭasāhasrikā Prajñāpāramitā*), Four Seasons Foundation, San Francisco 1973, p. 104.

301 See for example the 'Great Crown' *dhāraṇī* at the end of the *Śūraṅgama Sūtra*. In Dwight Goddard (ed.), *A Buddhist Bible*, Beacon Press, Boston 1970, p. 272.

302 In 1962, when Chinese troops crossed the Indian border from Tibet, the authorities of the hill station, Kalimpong, where Sangharakshita then lived, requested that he and Dhardo Rimpoche, being highly respected by local people, would set an example by remaining in Kalimpong and so prevent a mass exodus. See *Precious Teachers*, Windhorse Publications, Birmingham 2007, pp. 157–8 (*Complete Works*, vol. 22).

303 A reference to Plato's *Symposium* (c.385–370 BCE) in which a number of men speak in praise of love or Eros. Socrates, when his turn comes around, explains that what he has to say he learnt from Diotima, a woman of Mantinea.

304 The Buddha specifically taught against astrology, divination, fortune-telling, and so on as means of livelihood. See *The Buddha's Noble Eightfold Path, Complete Works,* vol. 1, p. 547; and *Brahmajāla Sutta, Dīgha Nikāya* 1 (i.10–11); T. W. Rhys Davids (trans.), *Dialogues of the Buddha*, part 1, Pali Text Society, Oxford 1993, pp. 16–19; or M. Walshe (trans.), *The Long Discourses of the Buddha*, Wisdom Publications, Boston 1995, pp. 71–2.

305 That the Buddha did not recognize caste and in fact taught against it is illustrated in the Pāli canon itself, regarded as the authoritative word of the Buddha by the Theravāda. When someone joined the *bhiksu* or *bhikṣuṇī* sangha they no longer belonged to any caste (just as those who convert from Hinduism to Buddhism lose theirs). This is one of the eight wonderful qualities of the sangha described by the Buddha and recorded in the *Pahārāda Sutta,*

Aṅguttara Nikāya iv.202 (8.19); see E. M. Hare (trans.), *Gradual Sayings*, vol. i, Pali Text Society, Oxford 1995, p. 136; or Bhikkhu Bodhi (trans.), *The Numerical Discourses of the Buddha*, Wisdom Publications, Boston 2012, p. 1142–4; also *Udāna* 5.5 in John D. Ireland (trans.), *The Udāna and the Itivuttaka*, Buddhist Publication Society 2007, pp. 68–70. Elsewhere the Buddha explains to novice monks Vāseṭṭha and Bhāradvaja that no real distinction can be drawn between members of different castes, physical, moral, or spiritual. See the *Aggañña Sutta, Dīgha Nikāya* 27 (iii.80–4); M. Walshe (trans.), *The Long Discourses of the Buddha*, Wisdom Publications, Boston 1995, pp. 407–9; or T. W. Rhys Davids (trans.), *Dialogues of the Buddha*, part 3, Pali Text Society, London 1971, pp. 77–81.

306 Sir Charles Eliot, *Hinduism and Buddhism: An Historical Sketch*, Routledge and Kegan Paul, London 1921, vol. 1, p. xciv.

307 Sukumar Dutt, *The Buddha and Five After-Centuries*, Luzac and Co., London 1957, p. 169.

308 J. J. Jones (trans.), *The Mahāvastu*, Luzac, London 1952, vol. 2, p. 329.

309 *The Mahāvaṃsa*, Wilhelm Geiger (trans.), Pali Text Society, London 1912, chapters 18 and 19.

310 K. W. Morgan (ed.), *The Path of the Buddha*, Ronald Press, New York 1956, p. 131.

311 *Mahāparinibbāna Sutta, Dīgha Nikāya* 16 (ii.141). See M. Walshe (trans.), *The Long Discourses of the Buddha*, Wisdom Publications, Boston 1995, p. 264; or T. W. and C. A. F. Rhys Davids (trans.), *Dialogues of the Buddha*, part 2, Pali Text Society, London 1971, p. 154.

312 John Blofeld (1913–1987) was an English writer on Buddhism and Taoism. For some years he lived in China and travelled extensively in the East. He was a friend of Sangharakshita whom he came to know in Kalimpong and with whom he received the Vajrasattva *abhiṣeka* from Dudjom Rimpoche in April 1959. See *Precious Teachers*, Windhorse Publications, Birmingham 2007, pp. 114–17 (*Complete Works*, vol. 22). John Blofeld's *Wheel of Life : The Autobiography of a Western Buddhist* was published in 1978. Wutaishan (*shan* means 'mountain'), in Shanxi province, is one of the four sacred mountains of Buddhist China (the fourth sacred mountain is Jiuhuashan, associated with the bodhisattva Kṣitigarbha) and is regarded as sacred to Mañjuśrī. Many Buddhist monasteries and stupas are located there.

313 Edward Conze (trans.), *The Perfection of Wisdom in Eight Thousand Lines and Its Verse Summary* (*Aṣṭasāhasrikā Prajñāpāramitā*), Four Seasons Foundation, San Francisco 1973, p. 288.

314 Ibid., p. 289.

315 Wilhelm Geiger (trans.), *Cūḷavaṃsa*, part 1, Pali Text Society, London 1929, p. 167.

316 Sangharakshita experienced this himself when, after his *śramaṇera* ordination in 1949, he and his friend, Buddharakshita, took their begging-bowls from door-to-door to collect alms in the time-honoured way. See *The Rainbow Road from Tooting Broadway to Kalimpong, Complete Works,* vol. 20, pp. 415–18.

317 Wilhelm Geiger (trans.), *The Mahāvaṃsa*, Pali Text Society, London 1912, p. 223.

318 D. T. Devendra, *The Greatest Buddhist Festival* (*Vesak*), Kandy 1961, p. x.

319 Ibid., pp. 4 et seq.

320 Beatrice Lane Suzuki, *Mahāyāna Buddhism*, George Allen and Unwin, London 1959, p. 83.

321 These great figures of Japanese Buddhism are Dōgen Zenji (1200–1253) who founded the Sōtō Zen school; Kukai or Kōbō Daishi (774–835) who founded the Shingon school (see also note 297); Shinran (1173–1263) who was the founder of Jōdo Shinshū; and Nichiren Daishonin (1222–1282) the founder of a movement based on the *White Lotus Sūtra.*

322 Sīvali is mentioned by the Buddha as being chief among his disciples 'who receive offerings'. *Aṅguttara Nikāya* i.25. See F. L. Woodward (trans.), *Gradual Sayings*, vol. i, Pali Text Society, Oxford 2000, p. 18. Bhikkhu Bodhi's translation (*The Numerical Discourses of the Buddha*, Wisdom Publications, Somerville 2012, p. 110) is a little different. Sīvali is described as 'foremost among those who make gains'.

323 From 'Buddhism in Theravada Countries' by Balangoda Ananda Maitreyi, Chief Nayaka Thero of the Sudhamma Sect, Balangoda, Ceylon in K. W. Morgan, (ed.) *The Path of the Buddha*, Ronald Press, New York 1956, p. 137.

324 W. Y. Evans-Wentz, *The Tibetan Book of the Dead*, Oxford University Press, London 1957, pp. 18–28.

325 See ibid., p. 91 et seq.

326 Beatrice Lane Suzuki, *Mahāyāna Buddhism*, George Allen and Unwin, London 1959, pp. 82–3.

THE MEANING OF CONVERSION IN BUDDHISM

327 Sangharakshita settled in Kalimpong in the eastern Himalayas in 1950 and it

remained his base until his return to England in 1964. The lectures that make up *The Meaning of Conversion in Buddhism* were given in 1965–6 at the Hampstead Buddhist Vihara. Sangharakshita refers to the lectures, explaining why he gave them, in his memoir, *Moving Against the Stream*, Windhorse Publications, Birmingham 2003, p. 67 (*Complete Works*, vol. 23). There is also a section devoted to them in *The History of My Going for Refuge*, pp. 460ff.

328 Ghoom is situated some five miles south of, and 1,000 feet above, Darjeeling (and thirty miles south-west of Kalimpong). Sangharakshita first visited Ghoom and its monastery in 1945 as a young soldier on leave. See *The Rainbow Road from Tooting Broadway to Kalimpong, Complete Works*, vol. 20, pp. 133–4.

329 St Paul, also known as Saul of Tarsus, was at first a persecutor of Christians. On the road to Damascus he was stopped by a blinding light and a vision of the risen Christ and heard a voice asking him, 'Why do you persecute me?' As a result of this experience he became a Christian and one of the foremost influences on the early Christian church. See Acts chapter 9.

330 *Aṅgulimāla Sutta*, *Majjhima Nikāya* 86 (ii.97–105). Bhikkhu Ñāṇamoli and Bhikkhu Bodhi (trans.), *The Middle Length Discourses of the Buddha*, Wisdom Publications, Boston 1995, pp. 710–17; or I. B. Horner (trans.), *The Collection of the Middle Length Sayings*, vol. ii, Pali Text Society, Oxford 1994, pp. 284–92.

331 William Camden (1551–1623), best known for *Britannia*, the first topographical survey of Great Britain and Ireland, and his history of the reign of Queen Elizabeth I. The saying may have become well known through Dr Johnson. See J. Boswell, *The Life of Samuel Johnson* LLD, John Sharpe, London 1830, p. 543.

332 The classic study of religious experience within Christian culture is that of William James, see his *The Varieties of Religious Experience: A Study in Human Nature*, based on lectures given at the University of Edinburgh 1901–2 and published directly afterwards. A classic of modern psychology, it has never been out of print to date (2018).

333 Passages which identify the sangha or spiritual community with the monastic order need to be read in the light of Sangharakshita's realization that 'becoming a monk is of significance and value only to the extent that it is an expression of one's Going for Refuge'. (See *The History of My Going for Refuge*, section 5 above, p. 432.

334 In some languages, such as German, it is linguistically impossible to say 'I go for Refuge'. The word '*gehen*' = 'to go' cannot be used with '*Zuflucht*' = 'refuge'. The correct phraseological unit obliges one to speak of 'taking' refuge – '*ich nehme Zuflucht*'. This highlights the imperative of referring back to the original Pāli or Sanskrit to understand the subtler connotations of the Buddha's teachings.

335 *Udāna* 8.3. John D. Ireland (trans.), *The Udāna and the Itivuttaka*, Buddhist Publication Society, Kandy 1997, p. 103.

336 Jiddu Krishnamurti (1895–1986) was from present-day Andhra Pradesh. Around the age of fourteen, when the family had moved to Adyar, he was 'discovered' by Theosophists Charles Leadbeater and Annie Besant and groomed to be the 'World Teacher', identified with Maitreya. He later rejected this role, nevertheless going on to give many lectures, and writing on religious and philosophical themes. The incident Sangharakshita describes here is told in more detail in 'Some Bombay Friends' in *Adhisthana Writings, Complete Works*, vol. 26.

337 In his essay 'Tradition and the Individual Talent' Eliot remarks 'Only those who have personality and emotions know what it means to want to escape from these things.' T. S. Eliot, *The Sacred Wood: essays on poetry and criticism*, Alfred A. Knopf, New York 1921.

338 In the humourous *Kevaddha Sutta* Great Brahmā admits secretly that he is *not* all-knowing as people believe. See *Dīgha Nikāya* 11 (i.222) in M. Walshe (trans.), *The Long Discourses of the Buddha*, Wisdom Publications, Boston 1995, pp. 178–9; or T. W. Rhys Davids (trans.), *Dialogues of the Buddha*, part 1, Pali Text Society, London 1973, pp. 282ff. In the *Pāṭika Sutta* the Buddha explains to Bhaggava how the idea of a Creator is a wrong view and will hold him back along with other erroneous views about the origin of the universe. See *Dīgha Nikāya* 24 (ii.28–35) in M. Walshe (trans.), *The Long Discourses of the Buddha*, Wisdom Publications, Boston 1995, pp. 381–3; or T. W. and C. A. F. Rhys Davids (trans.), *Dialogues of the Buddha*, part 3, Pali Text Society, London 1971, pp. 25–32. The Buddha speaks more strongly about the unfortunate effects of believing in a Creator God at *Aṅguttara Nikāya* i.173–4. See Bhikkhu Bodhi (trans.), *The Numerical Discourses of the Buddha*, Wisdom Publications, Somerville 2012, pp. 266–7; or F. L. Woodward, (trans.), *Gradual Sayings*, vol. i, Pali Text Society, Oxford 2000, pp. 158.

339 In the Western Buddhist Order, founded in 1968, ordination is neither monastic nor lay, but based on effective Going for Refuge. This in a sense combines aspects of the second and third meanings of sangha described here, and avoids the lay–monastic split which has been in many ways a hindrance to the spiritual vitality of Buddhism in the East. (This note is reproduced from the first edition of *The Meaning of Conversion in Buddhism,* Windhorse Publications, Birmingham 1994 and may have been written by Sangharakshita.)

340 Alfred, Lord Tennyson, *In Memoriam* A.H.H. completed in 1849, a requiem poem for his friend, Arthur Haley Hallam.

341 D. T. Suzuki (trans.), *The Laṅkāvatāra Sūtra*, Routledge and Sons, London 1932, pp. 123–4. See also D. Goddard (ed.), *A Buddhist Bible,* Beacon Press, Boston 1970, p. 348.

342 See the discussion of the Buddha's fundamental law of conditionality in *A Survey of Buddhism, Complete Works*, vol. 1, pp. 89ff. See also note 374 below. In the *Mahānidāna Sutta* in which conditionality is the theme, the Buddha tells Ānanda it is through not understanding this doctrine that mankind has become 'like a tangled ball of string'. *Dīgha Nikāya* 15 (ii.55). M. Walshe (trans.), *The Long Discourses of the Buddha*, Wisdom Publications, Boston 1995, p. 223; or T. W. and C. A. F. Rhys Davids (trans.), *Dialogues of the Buddha*, part 2, Pali Text Society, London 1971, p. 50.

343 The spiral path is also discussed in Chapter 13 of *The Three Jewels*, pp. 101–19 above.

344 *Udāna* 1.10. John D. Ireland (trans.), *The Udāna and the Itivuttaka*, Buddhist Publication Society, Kandy 1997, pp. 19–22.

345 The twelve links of the spiral path are described in detail in *The Three Jewels*, chapter 13. See this volume pp. 101–11.

346 For more on confession see 'The Spiritual Significance of Confession' in *Transforming Self and World, Complete Works*, vol. 16, pp. 269–337. See also Subhuti, *Remorse and Confession in the Spiritual Community*, Madhyamaloka Publications, Birmingham 2001.

347 The myth of Sisyphus, king of Ephyra, comes from ancient Greece. Having offended Zeus and other gods, after his death he was made to endlessly roll a boulder up a steep hill.

348 That a Stream Entrant has no more than seven further rebirths is referred to in, for example, the *Ratana Sutta, Sutta-Nipāta* 2.1 (verse 9). H. Saddhatissa (trans.), *The Sutta-Nipāta,* Curzon

Press, London 1985, p. 25; or E. M. Hare (trans.), *Woven Cadences of Early Buddhists (Sutta-Nipāta)*, Oxford University Press, London 1945, p. 36; and in the *Saccasaṃyutta, Saṃyutta Nikāya,* Bhikkhu Bodhi (trans.), *Connected Discourses of the Buddha*, Wisdom Publications, Boston 2000, p. 1878; or F. L. Woodward (trans.), *The Book of the Kindred Sayings*, part 5, Pali Text Society, London 1979, p. 390.

349 The ten fetters are enumerated at, for example, *Saṃyutta Nikāya* v.61. See Bhikkhu Bodhi (trans.), *The Connected Discourses of the Buddha*, Wisdom Publications, Boston 2000, pp. 1565–6; or F. L. Woodward (trans.), *Kindred Sayings*, part 5, Pali Text Society, London 1979, p. 49. See also *Saṅgīti Sutta, Dīgha Nikāya* 33 (ii.234) in M. Walshe (trans.), *The Long Discourses of the Buddha*, Wisdom Publications, Boston 1995, p. 495; or T. W. Rhys Davids (trans.), *Dialogues of the Buddha*, part 3, Pali Text Society, London 1971, p. 225.

350 The Buddha has an exchange with the Brahmin Sundarika, who performs fire rites, and contrasts tending fires on altars with the light of inner practice. See *Brahmaṇasaṃyutta, Saṃyutta Nikāya* i.169. Bhikkhu Bodhi (trans.), *Connected Discourses of the Buddha*, Wisdom Publications, Boston 2000, p. 263; or C. A. F. Rhys Davids (trans.), *The Book of the Kindred Sayings*, part 1, Pali Text Society, London 1979, p. 212.

351 In his talk 'The Taste of Freedom', Sangharakshita discusses the first three fetters in terms of habit, superficiality, and vagueness. See *The Taste of Freedom*, Windhorse Publications, second edition, Birmingham 1997, pp. 19–22 (*Complete Works*, vol. 11).

352 See *A Survey of Buddhism, Complete Works,* vol. 1, pp. 85–8.

353 See *Aṣṭasāhasrikā Prajñāpāramitā Sūtra,* chapter 6. *The Perfection of Wisdom in Eight Thousand Lines and its Verse Summary,* Edward conze (trans.), Four Seasons Foundation, San Francisco 1973, pp. 124–34.

354 *The Treatise on Discourses about Giving Rise to the Bodhicitta: The Bodhicittotpādasūtra Śāstra of Vasubandhu,* trans. K. Crosby and A. Skilton, section 2, in *Western Buddhist Review*, vol. iv, at http://www.westernbuddhistreview.com/vol4/index.html

355 For more on themes discussed in this chapter see 'The Awakening of the Bodhi Heart' and 'The Bodhisattva Vow' in *The Bodhisattva Ideal*, Windhorse Publications, Birmingham 1999, pp. 31–86 (*Complete Works*, vol. 4).

356 The *Laṅkāvatāra Sūtra* was composed in Sanskrit, in the second half of the fourth century CE and first translated into Chinese c.443 CE. For a translation from the Sanskrit into English see D. T. Suzuki (trans.), *The Laṅkāvatāra Sūtra*, Routledge, London 1932. Selections from the *Sūtra* can be found in D. Goddard (ed.), *A Buddhist Bible,* Beacon Press, Boston 1970.

357 The doctrine of the *aṣṭa-vijñāna-kāya* or eight kinds of consciousness was developed by the Yogācāra school. See Vasubandhu's *Triṃśikā-kārikā* ('treatise in thirty stanzas') in *Seven Works of Vasubandhu*, Stefan Anacker (trans.), Motilal Banarsidass, Delhi 1984, pp. 186–9.

358 Jung first coined the term in his 1916 essay 'The Structure of the Unconscious', from when he continued to develop the idea, see C. G. Jung, *The Collected Works*, vol. ix, part 1: *The Archetypes and the Collective Unconscious*, Routledge and Kegan Paul, London 1968, pp. 42–53.

359 In his translation and studies of the *Laṅkāvatāra Sūtra* Suzuki refers to the *parāvṛtti* variously, sometimes as 'revulsion' or as a turning in 'our inmost consciousness'. See D. T. Suzuki, *Manual of Zen Buddhism*, Rider and Co., London 1974, p. 52.

Alan Watts uses the expression 'turning about in the deepest seat of consciousness' in *The Way of Zen*, Penguin, Middlesex 1962, p. 86.

360 Sangharakshita's visit to the ashram of Ramana Maharshi is related in his memoir, *The Rainbow Road from Tooting Broadway to Kalimpong, Complete Works,* vol. 20, pp. 336ff.

361 See Sangharakshita, *The Essence of Zen*, Windhorse Publications, fourth edition, Glasgow 1992, pp. 45–52 (*Complete Works*, vol. 13).

362 This is the theme of Nietzsche's book *The Antichrist,* first published in German in 1895. See F. Nietzsche, *Twilight of the Idols and The Antichrist*, trans. J. Hollingdale, Penguin, London 1990.

GOING FOR REFUGE

363 According to the commentaries, Mahākassapa was from a wealthy Brahmin family. How he met the Buddha and the effect on him of that meeting is told in the *Kassapasaṃyutta*, *Saṃyutta Nikāya* ii.221; see Bhikkhu Bodhi (trans.), *Connected Discourses of the Buddha*, Wisdom Publications, Boston 2000, p. 678; or C. A. F. Rhys Davids (trans.), *The Book of the Kindred Sayings*, part 2, Pali Text Society, Oxford 1997, p. 148.

One of the wanderers the Buddha met was Vacchagotta.

Their exchange is recounted in the *Aggivacchagotta Sutta, Majjhima Nikāya* 72 (i.484–5). Bhikkhu Ñāṇamoli and Bhikkhu Bodhi (trans.), *The Middle Length Discourses of the Buddha,* Wisdom Publications, Boston 1995, pp. 590–1; or I. B. Horner (trans.), *The Collection of the Middle Length Sayings*, vol. ii, Pali Text Society, Oxford 1994, pp. 162–5.

A story of the Buddha's encounter with a prince is told in the *Abhayarājakumāra Sutta*, *Majjhima Nikāya* 58 (i.392). Bhikkhu Ñāṇamoli and Bhikkhu Bodhi (trans.), *The Middle Length Discourses of the Buddha*, Wisdom Publications, Boston 1995, pp. 498–501; or I. B. Horner (trans.), *The Collection of the Middle Length Sayings*, vol. ii, Pali Text Society, Oxford 1994, pp. 60–4.

364 To give just one example from the Pāli canon of this much-repeated formula, see the end of the *Abhayarājakumāra Sutta*, cited in the previous note.

365 For example, the *Brāhmaṇasaṃyutta* at *Saṃyutta Nikāya* i.160–84 gives an account of ten Brahmins of the Bhāradvāja clan who individually meet the Buddha and, as a result of their exchanges with him, go forth from the home life, join the *bhikkhu* sangha, and become *arhants*. Ten further meetings are recounted of Brahmins who also, as a result of their meeting with the Buddha, go for Refuge to the Buddha, the Dharma, and the Sangha, asking that to be remembered as a lay-follower 'who from today has gone for refuge for life'. See Bhikkhu Bodhi (trans.), *Connected Discourses of the Buddha*, Wisdom Publications, Boston 2000, pp. 254–279; or C. A. F. Rhys Davids (trans.), *The Book of the Kindred Sayings*, part 1, Pali Text Society, London 1979, pp. 199–223.

366 Alfred, Lord Tennyson, from 'Guinevere' in *Idylls of the King,* published 1859.

367 Sangharakshita enlarges on this theme in his series of lectures, 'The Higher Evolution of Man' (1969) and 'Aspects of the Higher Evolution of the Individual' (1970). See *Complete Works*, vol. 12.

368 The threefold path is elucidated in detail in *A Survey of Buddhism*, chapter 1, sections 16–18, *Complete Works*, vol. 1. The six perfections are described in the same volume in chapter 4, section 5, and in *The Bodhisattva Ideal*, Windhorse Publications, Birmingham 1999, chapters. 4–6 (*Complete Works*, vol. 4).

369 *Aṅguttara Nikāya,* iv.279. E. M. Hare (trans.), *Gradual Sayings,* vol. iv, Pali Text Society, Oxford 1995, pp. 186–7; or Bhikkhu Bodhi (trans.),

The Numerical Sayings of the Buddha, Wisdom Publications, Somerville 2012, p. 1193.

370 According to Gampopa, the great Tibetan Kagyu teacher of the eleventh and twelfth centuries, when we are at the beginning of our spiritual career 'the greatest benefactor is a spiritual friend in the form of an ordinary human being'. See Gampopa, *The Jewel Ornament of Liberation,* trans. Herbert V. Guenther, Shambhala Publications, London 1986, p. 33.

371 Until 2010 the Friends of the Western Buddhist Order was known in India as Trailokya Bauddha Mahasangha Sahayaka Gana – 'Association of the Helpers of the Spiritual Community of the Three Worlds'. In 2010 the name Triratna was adopted by both Indian and Western wings of the Order and Community, a name suitable in all countries and one that pointed to what lay at the heart of that community: the Three Jewels. The movement is now known in English as the Triratna Buddhist Community, or the equivalent in local languages. For example, in India it is known as Triratna Bauddha Mahasangha. The Order is known as the Triratna Buddhist Order.

372 The first of the Buddha's disciples whose 'Eye of Truth' was opened was Kondañña, one of the five ascetics to whom the Buddha first taught the Dharma. See *Saccasaṃyutta*, *Saṃyutta Nikāya* v.423. Bhikkhu Bodhi (trans.), *Connected Discourses of the Buddha*, Wisdom Publications, Boston 2000, p. 1846; or F. L. Woodward (trans.), *The Book of the Kindred Sayings*, part 5, Pali Text Society, London 1979, p. 359.

373 Pāli sources referring to one or more of the five eyes are listed in the Pali Text Society's *Pali–English Dictionary*, T. W. Rhys Davids and W. Stede (eds.), Motilal Banarsidass, Delhi 1993, pp. 259–60. The five eyes are described in more detail in *Complete Works*, vol. 9, pp. 251–2.

374 In Pāli *Imasmiṃ sati, idaṃ hoti; imassuppādā, idaṃ uppajjati; imasmiṃ asati, idaṃ na hoti; imassa nirodhā, idaṃ nirujjhati.* This is found in the *Cūḷasakuludāyi Sutta, Majjhima Nikāya* 79 (ii.32). I. B. Horner (trans.), *The Collection of the Middle Length Sayings*, vol. ii, Pali Text Society, Oxford 1994, p. 229; or Bhikkhu Ñāṇamoli and Bhikkhu Bodhi (trans.), *The Middle Length Discourses of the Buddha*, Wisdom Publications, Boston 1995, p. 655. Also *Nidānasaṃyutta, Saṃyutta Nikāya* ii.28, in C. A. F. Rhys Davids (trans.), *The Book of the Kindred Sayings*, part 2, Pali Text Society, Oxford 1997, p. 23;

or Bhikkhu Bodhi (trans.), *The Connected Discourses of the Buddha*, Wisdom Publications, Boston 2000, p. 552.

375 The ten fetters are enumerated, for example, at *Saṃyutta Nikāya* v.61 (45.179–80). See Bhikkhu Bodhi (trans.), *The Connected Discourses of the Buddha*, Wisdom Publications, Boston 2000, pp. 1565–6; or F. L. Woodward (trans.), *Kindred Sayings*, part 5, Pali Text Society, London 1979, p. 224.

376 For a further discussion of the first three fetters in terms of habit, superficiality, and vagueness see *The Taste of Freedom*, second edition, Windhorse Publications, Birmingham 1997, pp. 19–22 (*Complete Works*, vol. 11).

377 For example, the ten Brahmins of the Bhāradvāja clan who, after meeting the Buddha, leave home and soon gain arhantship. (See note 365.)

378 For example Upāli the householder who, after hearing the Buddha, 'attained the Dhamma, understood the Dhamma, fathomed the Dhamma'. He renounced his Jain discipleship and declared he had 'gone over to discipleship under the recluse Gotama'. *Upāli Sutta*, *Majjhima Nikāya* 56 (i.380). Bhikkhu Ñāṇamoli and Bhikkhu Bodhi (trans.), *The Middle Length Discourses of the Buddha*, Wisdom Publications, Boston 1995, p. 485; or I. B. Horner (trans.), *The Collection of the Middle Length Sayings*, vol. ii, Pali Text Society, Oxford 1994, p. 46.

379 For a detailed exposition of the bodhisattva ideal see *Complete Works*, vol. 4.

380 See Śāntideva, *The Bodhicaryāvatāra*, K. Crosby and A. Skilton (trans.), Windhorse Publications, Birmingham 2002, especially chapters 1–3; and *The Bodhisattva Ideal,* chapters 2 and 3, in *Complete Works*, vol. 4.

381 In his 1978 lecture, 'Levels of Going for Refuge', Sangharakshita describes six levels: cultural, provisional, effective, real, ultimate, and cosmic. They are simplified here into four levels, the first two and the last two being combined. (For the 1978 lecture see *Complete Works*, vol. 12.)

382 In the lecture referred to in the previous note, Sangharakshita makes a distinction between 'cultural' (or 'ethnic') and 'provisional' Going for Refuge. He describes the provisional Going for Refuge as an appreciation of the Three Jewels, and the practice of the Dharma to some extent, but not yet expressing a full commitment. He equates this level with becoming a Mitra within the Triratna Buddhist Community.

383 For example *Dhammapada* 393 and 396. See

Sangharakshita (trans.), *Dhammapada*, Windhorse Publications, Birmingham 2001, p. 129. (*Complete Works*, vol. 15.)

384 In 2001 and afterwards changes were made to the Mitra system. Currently (2018) the request to become a Mitra involves making three declarations: (1) I consider myself to be a Buddhist; (2) I am trying to practise the five ethical precepts; and (3) The Triratna Buddhist Community is the context in which I want to deepen my practice.

385 For a full discussion of the *dharmacārī/dharmacāriṇī)* precepts see *The Ten Pillars of Buddhism* in this volume.

386 For a more detailed description of the *anagārika* in terms not only of commitment to celibacy, but also to the practice of simplicity of lifestyle, careerlessness, and community living, see *Forty-Three Years Ago*, pp. 604–9 in this volume.

387 The *pāṭimokkha* or code of conduct recognized by the Theravāda, and some other branches of the monastic sangha, consists of 227 rules for *bhikkhus* and 311 for *bhikkhunīs*. See I. B. Horner, *The Book of the Discipline*, parts 1–6, Pali Text Society, Oxford 1996–7. See also K. R. Norman, *The Pāṭimokkha*, Pali Text Society, Oxford 2001, which includes the Pāli in roman script beside the English translation. In the Mahāyāna tradition the *prātimokṣa* based on the *Dharmaguptaka Vinaya* has 250 rules for monks and 348 for nuns.

THE TEN PILLARS OF BUDDHISM

388 The Western Buddhist Order / Trailokya Bauddha Mahasangha was founded a year after the founding of the Friends of the Western Buddhist Order (FWBO). In 2010 it was renamed the Triratna Buddhist Order / Triratna Bauddha Mahasangha. See note 371.

389 *Itivuttaka* 1.3.7. See F. L. Woodward, *The Minor Anthologies of the Pali Canon*, part 2, Oxford University Press, London 1948, p. 130; or John D. Ireland (trans.), *The Udāna and the Itivuttaka*, Buddhist Publication Society, Kandy 1997, p. 169.

390 The legend of the sixteen *arhants* is known in Tibet, China, and Japan. They are frequently represented in Buddhist art and are depicted, for example, on the walls of Zen monasteries. See D. T. Suzuki, *Manual of Zen Buddhism*, Rider and Co., London 1950, pp. 168–71.

391 In the FWBO, or Triratna Buddhist Community, as it has been known since 2010 (see note 371), a Friend is anyone who has contact through a Buddhist centre

or in other ways with the Movement. A Friend becomes a Mitra by making three declarations (see note 384) and participating in a simple ceremony. Order members are those who effectively go for Refuge (see *Going for Refuge* in this volume, p. 302) and enter the Order in an ordination ceremony that takes place in the context of a retreat. (Where possible the retreat is of three or four months duration, though it may be as short as a few days in exceptional circumstances.)

392 The legal age of majority in the UK had changed from 21 to 18 in 1970 but 21 was still referred to as the age of obtaining 'the key of the door' and was still associated with 'coming of age'. In the USA there are even today (2018) some states in which the legal age of majority is 21.

393 The thousand-armed Avalokiteśvara represents the spiritual reality of the Triratna Buddhist Order.

394 It seems that no one was able to take on the responsibility of organizing the event that year. The first Order convention was held in 1974 since when conventions have been a regular part of the life of the Order. As the Order grew, regional conventions were organized in different parts of the world, while an international convention continued to take place every three years. From 2009 some international Order conventions have taken place at Bodh Gaya.

395 *Mahāparinibbāna Sutta*, *Dīgha Nikāya* 16 (ii.76). M. Walshe (trans.), *The Long Discourses of the Buddha*, Wisdom Publications, Boston 1995, p. 233; or T. W. and C. A. F. Rhys Davids (trans.), *Dialogues of the Buddha*, part 2, Pali Text Society, London 1971, p. 82.

396 From the very first ordinations conferred in 1968, the ordination ceremony included the recitation of the ten *kusala-dhammas* in Pāli, and the ten positive precepts in English in a rendering composed by Sangharakshita. As the Order became active in non-English speaking countries, the ten positive precepts were translated into local languages. In 2016, at the recommendation of Triratna Buddhist Order scholars, slight amendments were made to the Pāli to correct some grammatical errors. In addition, three of the positive precepts concerning speech were changed. Originally the speech precepts had been rendered: with truthful communication (fourth precept), with words kindly and gracious (fifth precept), with utterance helpful and harmonious (sixth

and seventh precepts). These became: with truthful communication (fourth), with kindly communication (fifth), with helpful communication (sixth), with harmonious communication (seventh). The change was made at the suggestion of Order members concerned that there should be four clearly separate positive speech precepts to correspond with the four 'negative' speech precepts. A number of versions were considered, including a version by Sangharakshita which, after some discussion by members of the College of Public Preceptors, with whom the final decision resided, was the one adopted. The use of the word 'communication' includes listening as well as speaking, and in fact includes communication beyond that of direct speech. The changes were formally adopted by the Triratna Buddhist Order at the Order's convention held at Adhisthana in August 2016.

397 John Milton (1608–1674), from *Comus: A masque presented at Ludlow Castle 1634*, lines 475–6.

398 W. Wordsworth, 'A Poet's Epitaph' included in *Lyrical Ballads,* 1800: 'you must love him, ere to you / He will seem worthy of your love.'

399 See *A Survey of Buddhism, Complete Works*, vol. 1, pp. 136–149; *The Buddha's Noble Eightfold Path*, chapter 4, 'Perfect Action: The Principles of Ethics', ibid., pp. 526–37; and 'Aspects of Buddhist Morality' in *The Priceless Jewel*, Windhorse Publications, Glasgow 1993 (*Complete Works*, vol. 11).

400 Maha Sthavira Sangharakshita, 'Aspects of Buddhist Morality' in *Studia Missionalia,* Rome 1978, vol. 27, pp. 159–80; and *The Priceless Jewel*, Windhorse Publications, Glasgow 1993, pp. 17–35 (*Complete Works*, vol. 11).

401 Members of the Triratna Buddhist Order (then the Western Buddhist Order) were known as *dharmacārīs* (masc.) and *dharmacāriṇīs* (fem.). See *Going for Refuge* in this volume, p. 305.

402 The *pāṭimokkha* or code of conduct recognized by the Theravāda, and some other branches of the monastic sangha, consists of 227 rules for *bhikkhus* and 311 for *bhikkhunīs*. See I. B. Horner, *The Book of the Discipline*, parts 1–6, Pali Text Society, Oxford 1996–7. See also K. R. Norman, *The Pātimokkha*, Pali Text Society, Oxford 2001, which includes the Pāli in roman script beside the English translation. In the Mahāyāna tradition the *prātimokṣa* based on the *Dharmaguptaka Vinaya* has 250 rules for monks and 348 for nuns.

403 By 'united' I mean spiritually united, rather than bound by

ties of mutual socio-economic dependence. (S)

404 *Kūṭadanta Sutta, Dīgha Nikāya* 5 (i.127–49). T. W. Rhys Davids (trans.), *Dialogues of the Buddha,* part 1, Pali Text Society, London 1973, pp. 173–85. See also M. Walshe (trans.), *The Long Discourses of the Buddha*, Wisdom Publications, Boston 1995, pp. 133–41.

405 *Sevitabbāsevitabba Sutta, Majjhima Nikāya* 114 (iii.45–61). Bhikkhu Ñāṇamoli and Bhikkhu Bodhi (trans.), *The Middle Length Discourses of the Buddha*, Wisdom Publications, Boston 1995, pp. 913–24; or I. B. Horner (trans.), *The Collection of the Middle Length Sayings*, vol. iii, Pali Text Society, Oxford 1993, pp. 94–104.

406 *Sevitabbāsevitabba Sutta, Majjhima Nikāya* 114 (iii.49–50). I. B. Horner (trans.), *The Collection of the Middle Length Sayings*, vol. iii, Pali Text Society, Oxford 1993, pp. 97–8; or Bhikkhu Ñāṇamoli and Bhikkhu Bodhi (trans.), *The Middle Length Discourses of the Buddha*, Wisdom Publications, Boston 1995, pp. 916–17.

407 *Aṅguttara Nikāya* (v.266–8). F. L. Woodward (trans.), *The Book of the Gradual Sayings,* vol. 5, Pali Text Society, Oxford 1996, pp. 178–80. In this edition the paragraph 'And how is cleansing by speech ... deliberate falsehood' is missing. The full version can be found in Bhikkhu Bodhi (trans.), *The Numerical Discourses of the Buddha*, Wisdom Publications, Boston 2012, pp. 1519–20.

408 In the *Aṅguttara Nikāya* the Buddha refers to the observance and non-observance of the ten precepts in terms of: (1) the hither and the further shore at v.253–254, (2) Dhamma and non-Dhamma at v.254–62, (3) the dark and light paths at v.281. See F. L. Woodward (trans.), *The Book of the Gradual Sayings,* vol. 5, Pali Text Society, Oxford 1996, pp. 172–3, 173–5, and 185. See also Bhikkhu Bodhi (trans.), *The Numerical Discourses of the Buddha*, Wisdom Publications, Boston 2012, pp. 1510–11, 1511–17, and 1527.

409 *Aṅguttara Nikāya* v.303–9, in Bhikkhu Bodhi (trans.), *The Numerical Discourses of the Buddha*, Wisdom Publications, Boston 2012, pp. 1544–7; or F. L. Woodward (trans.), *The Book of the Gradual Sayings*, vol. 5, Pali Text Society, Oxford 1996, pp. 197–8.

410 J. J. Jones (trans.), *The Mahāvastu*, vol. ii. Pali Text Society, Luzac and Co., London 1952. pp. 91–111.

411 Edward Conze (trans.), *The Perfection of Wisdom in Eight Thousand Lines and Its Verse Summary*, Four Seasons Foundation, San Francisco 1973, pp. 200–1.

412 See E. Lamotte (trans.), *The Teaching of Vimalakīrti*, (translated from the French by S. Boin), Pali Text Society, London 1976, p. 20; or R. Thurman (trans.), *The Holy Teaching of Vimalakīrti*, Pennsylvania State University Press, Pennsylvania 1976, p. 17.

413 Ibid., Lamotte p. 40; or Thurman p. 19.

414 Ibid., Lamotte p. 214; or Thurman p. 82.

415 R. E. Emmerick (trans.), *The Sūtra of Golden Light (Suvarṇabhāsottamasūtra)*, Pali Text Society, London 1970, p. 12.

416 Saddhaloka Bhikkhu (trans.), *The Giving Rise of the Ten Kinds of Mind of the Bodhisattva: The Discourse on the Ten Wholesome Ways of Action*, Yan Boon Remembrance Committee, Cameron Highlands Malaysia, n.d.

417 See *The Three Jewels*, chapter 5 in this volume, pp. 39ff. for a further elucidation of the *trikāya* doctrine.

418 Correlations with the five Buddhas are referred to in the *Guhyasamājatantra*. See A. Wayman, *Yoga of the Guhyasamājatantra*, Motilal Banarsidass, Delhi 1977, pp. 229–35. See also P. Williams, *Buddhist Thought*, Routledge, London 2000, p. 210–11 with a table showing correspondences between the five Buddhas and 'other sets of five'.

419 This 'well-known canonical formula' is found, for example, in the *Mahāparinibbāna Sutta, Dīgha Nikāya* 16 (ii.93). See M. Walshe (trans.), *The Long Discourses of the Buddha*, Wisdom Publications, Boston 1995, p. 241; or T. W. and C. A. F. Rhys Davids (trans.), *Dialogues of the Buddha*, part 2, Pali Text Society, London 1971, pp. 99–100. In the south-east Asian world, as well as in the Triratna Buddhist Community, the formula is recited to this day and is known as the *Tiratana Vandanā*, or 'Salutation to the Three Jewels' (explored in full in *Complete Works*, vol. 15). Another *locus classicus* for these words of praise of the Buddha is Buddhaghosa's *Visuddhimagga* 198–221. See Bhikkhu Ñāṇamoli (trans), *The Path of Purification,* Buddhist Publication Society, Kandy 1991, pp. 192–218; or Pe Maung Tin (trans.), *The Path of Purity*, Pali Text Society, London 1975, pp. 227–56.

420 The Buddha speaks of spiritual life in terms of training a mettlesome young horse in, for example, the *Gaṇakamoggallāna Sutta, Majjhima Nikāya* 107 (iii.2). See Bhikkhu Ñāṇamoli and Bhikkhu Bodhi (trans.), *The Middle Length Discourses of the Buddha*, Wisdom Publications, Boston 1995,

p. 874; or I. B. Horner (trans.), *The Collection of the Middle Length Sayings*, vol. iii, Pali Text Society, Oxford 1993, pp. 52–3. See also the *Kesi Sutta, Aṅguttara Nikāya* ii.112–13, in Bhikkhu Bodhi (trans.), *The Numerical Discourses of the Buddha*, Wisdom Publications, Boston 2012, pp. 492–3; or F. L. Woodward (trans.), *Gradual Sayings*, vol. ii, Pali Text Society, Oxford 1995, pp. 116–17. The Ox-herding pictures of the Zen tradition are described in D. T. Suzuki, *Manual of Zen Buddhism*, Rider and Co., London 1956, pp. 127–44.

421 For more on confession see 'The Spiritual Significance of Confession' in *Transforming Self and World, Complete Works*, vol. 16, pp. 269–337. See also Subhuti, *Remorse and Confession in the Spiritual* Community, Madhyamaloka Publications, Birmingham 2001, which draws on the *Bhaddāli Sutta, Majjhima Nikāya* 65. The taking of personal vows is discussed in *The Bodhisattva Ideal*, Windhorse Publications, Birmingham 1999, pp. 60–1 (*Complete Works*, vol 4).

422 R. C. Childers (1836–76), the British scholar who compiled the first Pāli–English dictionary (published 1872–5). For this translation of '*pāṭimokkha*' see T. W. Rhys Davids and W. Stede, *Pali–English Dictionary*, first Indian edition, Motilal Banarsidass, Delhi 1993, p. 450 where Childers is cited.

423 Asaṅga, *The Bodhisattva Path to Unsurpassed Enlightenment: A Complete Translation of … Bodhisattva Bhūmi,* A. B. Engle (trans.), Snow Lion, Boulder 2016, p. 240, note 683. Here the '*prāti*' in *prātimokṣa* would seem to be assimilated to *pratyeka* (= *prati* + *eka*), meaning 'for a single person, individual, personal', as in *pratyekabuddha*. (S)

424 A reference to the 150 rules of training occurs at *Aṅguttara Nikāya* i.231. See Bhikkhu Bodhi (trans.), *The Numerical Discourses of the Buddha*, Wisdom Publications, Boston 2012, p. 317; or F. L. Woodward, (trans.), *Gradual Sayings*, vol. 1, Pali Text Society, Oxford 2000, p. 211.

425 See note 387 and the discussion in W. Pachow, *A Comparative Study of the Prātimokṣa: On the Basis of its Chinese, Tibetan, Sanskrit and Pāli Versions,* Motilal Banarsidass, Delhi 2007.

426 The *prātimokṣas* for *śrāmaṇeras* and *śrāmaṇerikās* consist of ten precepts (different from those discussed in section 7, pp. 349–50 below).

427 For example, we find in verse 62 of the *sekhiyā* section of the *bhikkhu-pātimokkha* that monks are 'not to teach the Dhamma to one who is wearing sandals' see K. R. Norman, *The Pātimokkha*, Pali

Text Society, Oxford 2001, p. 105.

428 For example, some Order members are *anagārikas* and take the '*abrahmacarya*' precept or vow of celibacy signifying a deepening of their practice of the third precept. See see *Forty-Three Years Ago*, pp. 604–9.

429 *Aṅguttara Nikāya* v.213–5. See Bhikkhu Bodhi (trans.), *The Numerical Discourses of the Buddha*, Wisdom Publications, Boston 2012, pp. 1532–3; or F. L. Woodward (trans.), *The Book of the Gradual Sayings*, part 5, Pali Text Society, Oxford 1996, p. 186.

430 *Sevitabbāsevitabba Sutta*, *Majjhima Nikāya* 114 (iii.60). I. B. Horner (trans.), *The Collection of the Middle Length Sayings*, vol. iii. Pali Text Society, Oxford 1993, p. 104. See also Bhikkhu Ñāṇamoli and Bhikkhu Bodhi (trans.), *The Middle Length Discourses of the Buddha*, Wisdom Publications, Boston 1995, p. 924.

431 The three *skandhas* or 'groups' that constitute the factors of right living, the three *saṃpādas* or 'attainments', and the three *śikṣās* or 'trainings' all refer to the triad *śīla, samādhi, prajñā*, i.e. ethics, meditation, and wisdom. The three ways of skilful action are actions of body, speech, and mind.

432 These extra precepts can be found in the Pāli canon, for example in the *Brahmajāla Sutta*, *Dīgha Nikāya* 1 (i.6). M. Walshe (trans.), *The Long Discourses of the Buddha*, Wisdom Publications, Boston 1995, p. 69; or T. W. Rhys Davids (trans.), *Dialogues of the Buddha*, part 1, Pali Text Society, London 1973, p. 5.

433 Sangharakshita (trans.), *Dhammapada* 129–30, Windhorse Publications , Birmingham 2001, p. 51 (*Complete Works*, vol. 15).

434 George Bernard Shaw's 'golden rule' is the first of his 'Maxims for Revolutionists'. See *Man and Superman* (1903).

435 P. B. Shelley (1792–1822), from his essay 'A Defence of Poetry' written in 1821 and first published in *Essays, Letters from Abroad, Translations and Fragments* in 1840.

436 Śāntideva, *Bodhicaryāvatāra,* 8.90–4 and 8.110–17, in L. D. Barnett (trans.), *The Path of Light, rendered from the Bodhi-charyāvatāra of Śānti-Deva*, Butler and Tanner, London 1959, pp. 79–80. See also K. Crosby and A. Skilton (trans.), *The Bodhicaryāvatāra*, Windhorse Publications, Birmingham 2002, pp. 127–31.

437 From 'The Proverbs of Hell' in W. Blake, *The Marriage of Heaven and Hell*, composed 1790.

438 W. Whitman (1819–1892), 'Song of Myself', stanza 40 in *Leave of Grass,* published 1855.

439 This thirteen-verse poem, written by William Shakespeare, and originally untitled, was first published in Robert Chester's *Loves Martyr* (1601). The turtle is the turtle-dove.

440 A reference to one of the satirical poems of Horace (Quintus Horatius Flaccus, 65–8 BCE). The poem recounts the author being pestered by a chatterer who will not take the hint and leave. He justifies his fervent wish that he be left alone with a tale that it was prophesied by an old Sabine crone that a chatterer would be the cause of his death and therefore, 'windbags, if he recognizes them, he should shun; then he will reach old age'. Horace, *Sermones* 1.9, first published c.33 BCE.

441 'La propriété, c'est le vol!'. The slogan was coined by French anarchist Pierre-Joseph Proudhon (1809–1865). See his *What is Property? Or, an Inquiry into the Principle of Right and of Government* (1840).

442 W. Shakespeare, *Timon of Athens*, Act VI, Scene iii, line 26.

443 There is an exposition of Buddhist cosmology in the introduction to M. Walshe (trans.), *The Long Discourses of the Buddha*, Wisdom Publications, Boston 1995, pp. 37–42. Vasubhandu describes in some detail the planes of existence and their inhabitants in his *Abhidharmakośa-bhāṣya*, trans. L. de la Valleé Poussin, translated into English by L. M. Pruden, Asian Humanities Press, Berkeley 1991, chapter 6, section 5, pp. 451ff..

444 Sangharakshita here distinguishes between 'celibacy', meaning the unmarried, or, in modern western terms, the 'single' state, and 'chastity' by which he means abstention not just from sexual acts with another person but abstention from *all* sexual activity, both physical and that which is associated with speech or mind. To leave the world of sex behind in that way is to live in the higher or angelic worlds, without the painful tension of sexual polarization.

445 The question is often asked, 'What about people who are gay and not attracted to those of the opposite sex but to their own? Are not single-sex situations irrelevant to them?' Experience suggests that even when there is no sexual element involved, men and women tend to project more essentially onto members of the opposite sex, the opposite sex being more intrinsically 'other'. In addition, men and women tend to a somewhat different approach to life, and even spiritual life. Thus single-sex situations are relevant not only as a

support to the development of individuality but also to the development of spiritual friendship. It should be noted that the single-sex idea is *not* a 'principle', as it has sometimes, wrongly, been called. It is method, not doctrine. It is a means to an end, that end being the development of individuality which, as the next paragraph makes clear, in the end transcends identification with any one gender – or, indeed, with non-gender – altogether.

446 J. R. R. Tolkein, *The Lord of the Rings*, first published 1954–5.

447 *Dhammapada* 133 in Sangharakshita (trans.), *Dhammapada*, Windhorse Publications, Birmingham 2001, p. 52. (*Complete Works*, vol. 15.)

448 Sangharakshita elaborates on this theme in his essay *Buddhism, World Peace, and Nuclear War*, in *Complete Works*, vol. 11.

449 G. Orwell, *1984*, first published 1949. Newspeak is the language used by the controlling government in the fictitious country described in the novel.

450 *Analects* xiii.3. See W. E. Soothill (trans.), *The Analects of The Conversations of Confucius with his Disciples and Certain Others*, Oxford University Press, Oxford 1937, p. 129. See also D. Hinton, *The Analects of Confucius*, Counterpoint, Washington 1998, pp. 139f.

451 Quoted in F. Nietzsche, *Thus Spoke Zarathustra*, R. J. Hollingdale (trans.), Penguin, London 1969, p. 31.

452 *Dhammapada* 176. Sangharakshita (trans.), *Dhammapada*, Windhorse Publications, Birmingham 2001, p. 64. (*Complete Works*, vol. 15.)

453 For example in the chapter on 'Perfect Speech' in *The Buddha's Noble Eightfold Path*. See *Complete Works*, vol. 1, pp. 516–19.

454 *Saccasaṃyutta*, *Saṃyutta Nikāya* v.419–20. See Bhikkhu Bodhi (trans.), *Connected Discourses of the Buddha*, Wisdom Publications, Boston 2000, p. 1843; or F. L. Woodward (trans.), *The Book of the Kindred Sayings*, part 5, Pali Text Society, London 1979, pp. 355–6.

455 It is interesting to note that here Sangharakshita refers to the positive aspect of the sixth precept as 'meaningful speech', whereas the term used in the formal recitation of the positive precepts by Order members is 'helpful'. The relationship between what is meaningful and what makes something helpful is drawn out in this discussion.

456 A reference perhaps to G. K. Chesterton's story, 'The Song of the Flying Fish'. See chapter 4 of *The Secret of Father Brown*, published in 1927.

457 *Aṅguttara Nikāya* v.265. F. L. Woodward (trans.), *The Book of the Gradual Sayings*, vol. 5, Pali Text Society, Oxford 1996, p. 179. See also Bhikkhu Bodhi (trans.), *The Numerical Discourses of the Buddha*, Wisdom Publications, Boston 2012, pp. 1521.

458 See Sangharakshita, *The Purpose and Practice of Buddhist Meditation*, Ibis Publications, Ledbury 2012, pp. 472–95 on the six element practice; pp. 499–510 on the impurity of the body (*Complete Works*, vol. 5).

459 Garma C. C. Chang (ed.), *A Treasury of Mahāyāna Sūtras: Selections from the Mahāratnakūṭa Sūtra*. translated from the Chinese by the Buddhist Association of the United States, Pennsylvania State University Press, Pennsylvania and London 1983, p. 270.

460 See for example, *Aggivacchagotta Sutta*, *Majjhima Nikāya* 72 (i.487). Bhikkhu Ñāṇamoli and Bhikkhu Bodhi (trans.), *The Middle Length Discourses of the Buddha*, Wisdom Publications, Boston 1995, p. 592; or I. B. Horner (trans.), *The Collection of the Middle Length Sayings*, vol. 2, Pali Text Society, Oxford 1994, p. 164.

461 *Aṅguttara Nikāya* v.266. Bhikkhu Bodhi (trans.), *The Numerical Discourses of the Buddha*, Wisdom Publications, Boston 2012, p. 1520; or F. L. Woodward (trans.), *Gradual Sayings*, vol. 5, Pali Text Society, Oxford 1996, p. 178.

462 Sangharakshita, *The Purpose and Practice of Buddhist Meditation*, Ibis Publications, Ledbury 2012 (*Complete Works*, vol. 5) includes extracts from Sangharakshita's writings on the mindfulness of breathing (pp. 58–71), the recollection of the six elements (pp. 474–95), the contemplation of the twelve *nidānas* (pp. 511–15), the contemplation of the four kinds of *śūnyatā* (pp. 516–22), and the contemplation of the *lakṣana* of impermanence (pp. 463–70). All three *lakṣanas,* or characteristics of conditioned existence, are discussed in *The Three Jewels,* pp. 81–92 in this volume.

463 William Blake (1757–1827), the English visionary poet and engraver, one of Sangharakshita's five literary heroes. Martin Heidegger (1889–1976), the German philosopher whose writings concern the nature of 'being' and our relation to time. William Morris (1834–1896), the English designer, poet, and socialist, associated with the Arts and Crafts movement.

THE HISTORY OF MY GOING FOR REFUGE

464 J. Middleton Murry, *God: Being An Introduction to*

the Science of Metabiology, Jonathan Cape, London 1929, pp. 52–3.

465 The story of Sangharakshita's friendship with Terry Delamare is told in *Moving Against the Stream*, Windhorse Publications, Birmingham 2003 (*Complete Works*, vol. 23).

466 This picture can be seen in *Moving Against the Stream*, Windhorse Publications, Birmingham 2003, facing p. 329. There is also a reference to the first ordinations on p. 387 (*Complete Works*, vol. 23).

467 Stephen Parr (b. 1944) was one of the first twelve Order members ordained by Sangharakshita on 7 April 1968. He received the name 'Ananda'. Today (2018) he is the longest ordained member of the Triratna Buddhist Order. Ananda has devoted his life to poetry, and to writing as a spiritual practice. Through the 'Wolf at the Door' retreats he developed with his friend Manjusvara, he has inspired people from all around the world in this transformative practice. In the 1960s and 1970s he worked as a sound engineer for the BBC and was responsible for recording on his trusty reel-to-reel tape recorder Sangharakshita's early talks and lectures. Like the historical Ānanda, he has been a crucial part of the 'transmission' of the Dharma in the Triratna Buddhist Community.

468 Haslemere is a small, historic town 45 miles south-west of London. For Quartermaine see note 471.

469 From 'Six Poems Written in Retreat'. See *Complete Poems 1941–1994*, Windhorse Publications, Birmingham 1995, p. 261 (*Complete Works*, vol. 25).

470 Bush House is in Central London. From 1941 it was the headquarters of the BBC's World Service. (The final broadcast from Bush House took place in 2012.)

471 The Ockenden Venture was a charity founded after the Second World War dedicated to providing homes for refugee children. Keffolds was a large house on Bunch Lane, Haslemere, where refugee children were housed. Quartermaine was nearby on Franham Lane, and was the school attended by the children living at Keffolds. In the late 1960s the premises became available for the FWBO to hire for retreats.

472 And wisdom is a butterfly
And not a gloomy bird of prey.

From the poem 'Tom O'Roughley' by W. B. Yeats, included in his 1919 collection, *The Wild Swans at Coole.*

473 Shortly after I had written these lines another friend

pointed out that the chart was wrongly drawn. (S)

474 Sangharakshita began writing his memoirs in 1957 when he was living in Kalimpong in the eastern Himalayas, completing it only in 1973. When it was published in 1976 as *The Thousand-Petalled Lotus*, Heinemann, the publisher, omitted the first ten and part of the eleventh chapters which described his childhood and early youth. These were reinstated by Windhorse Publications when they published the memoir as *The Rainbow Road* in 1997. The *Complete Works* edition bears the title Sangharakshita originally intended: *The Rainbow Road from Tooting Broadway to Kalimpong, Complete Works*, vol. 20.

475 *The Rainbow Road from Tooting Broadway to Kalimpong, Complete Works*, vol. 20, p. 85. The words in parentheses were added by Sangharakshita to the original.

476 The *Diamond Sūtra* or, in the original Sanskrit, *Vajracchedikā Prajñāpāramitā Sūtra*, is generally regarded as one of the earliest Mahāyāna Perfection of Wisdom *sūtras*. The translation by William Gemmell, the first translation that Sangharakshita read, was published by Trench Trübner, London, in 1912. He went on to read a translation by Max Müller first published by the Oxford University Press in 1894 as part of the *Sacred Books of the East* series. The *Sūtra of Wei Lang* or 'Sūtra Spoken by the Sixth Patriarch on the High Seat of the Treasure of the Law' (also known as *The Sūtra of Hui Neng* or *The Platform Sūtra*) was translated into English by Wong Mou-Lam, and published in Shanghai by the Yu Ching Press in 1930. It was this edition that Sangharakshita read that summer of 1942. Both texts can now be found in A. F. Price and Wong Mou-lam (trans.), *The Diamond Sūtra and the Sūtra of Hui-Neng,* Shambhala Publications, Boston 1990.

477 'The three gems of our essence of mind, in which, Learned Audience, I advise you to take refuge'. See A. F. Price and Wong Mou-lam (trans.), *The Diamond Sūtra and the Sūtra of Hui-Neng,* Shambhala Publications, Boston 1990, p. 103.

478 In the *sūtra* (verse 14) we learn that 'the impact of the Dharma moved the Venerable Subhūti to tears.' See Edward Conze's translation, included in Sangharakshita's commentary on the *Diamond Sūtra* in *Wisdom Beyond Words*, Windhorse Publications, Glasgow 1993, p. 51 (*Complete Works*, vol. 14).

479 Although it regarded Buddhism as 'the most curious religion in the world', beautiful in some ways, but

also profoundly depressing, Harmsworth's *Children's Encyclopaedia* gave the young Dennis Lingwood a kind of introduction to the religions of the East, including Buddhism. Its sixty-one parts were given to him by kindly neighbours when, aged eight, he was confined to bed for two years with a diagnosis of valvular disease of the heart. It became his constant companion. See *The Rainbow Road from Tooting Broadway to Kalimpong*, *Complete Works*, vol. 20, p. 22.

H. G. Wells, *A Short History of the World*, was first published in 1922. It was based on his more substantial *Outline of World History*. Chapter 28 tells the story – in 1,700 words – of 'The Life of Gautama the Buddha'.

480 *The Rainbow Road from Tooting Broadway to Kalimpong, Complete Works*, vol. 20, p. 38.

481 Christmas Humphreys (1901–1983), was an English barrister, and later a judge, whose theosophical interests led him to Buddhism. He wrote many books, widely read at a time when there was little available in English on Buddhism. The Buddhist Lodge of the Theosophical Society was one of the first Buddhist organizations in Europe. In 1926, breaking with the Theosophical Society, it was renamed The Buddhist Society. Humphreys was its president until the end of his life. Its activities continue to the present day (2018).

482 See *The Rainbow Road from Tooting Broadway to Kalimpong* in *Complete Works*, vol. 20, pp. 102–3.

483 Sayadaw U Thittila (1896–1997) was ordained as a *bhikkhu* in 1916. He studied in India where he contributed to the revival of Buddhism in the south of the subcontinent. He went on to study English in London 1938–9, and to lecture on Buddhism in England and America, and later in many other countries. He held a number of responsibilities within the Burmese sangha. He produced the first English translation of the *Vibhaṅga* of the *Abhidhamma,* published by the Pali Text Society as *The Book of Analysis* in 1969.

484 ARP stands for 'Air Raid Precautions'. These were units organized by local councils during the Second World War that were made up mainly of volunteers. Duties included rescue work when under bombardment, as well as treatment of minor injuries, and getting civilians to places of safety.

485 *The Rainbow Road from Tooting Broadway to Kalimpong, Complete Works*, vol. 20, p. 102. The lines quoted are from chapter 9 of the memoir. At the time *The History of My Going for*

Refuge was delivered (1988) the memoir had been published by Heinemann. However they omitted the first ten chapters. See notes 474 and 665.

486 For more detail about what happened during those three years see ibid., chapters 10–23.

487 Ibid., pp. 224–6.

488 The Bengali friend was Robin Banerjee who was later ordained as Buddharakshita. The two met in Singapore where, the Second World War having ended, Sangharakshita spent a year awaiting demobilization. After leaving the army, he met up with Banerjee again in India (ibid., pp. 146–7 and 158ff.).

The Ramakrishna Mission was a Hindu organization that Sangharakshita first came across when stationed with his signals unit in Ceylon in 1944–5. The dedication of the Mission's swamis to the spiritual life greatly inspired him when, though in a Buddhist country, he was unable to find any really spiritually-minded Buddhists (ibid., p. 116–29). Its basic ideas were those of Advaita Vedanta. Sangharakshita's time in the Mission's Institute of Culture in Calcutta, and the reason for him leaving, is related in ibid. pp. 158–64.

The Maha Bodhi Society was founded in 1891 by Anagarika Dharmapala. Its original aim was to restore the temple at Bodh Gaya that had fallen into ruin, and to place the temple's management into Buddhist hands, as well as the restoration of other Buddhist shrines, and to propagate Buddhism. It was still the only active Buddhist organization in India when Sangharakshita arrived there in 1946. For more on the history of the Maha Bodhi Society, see 'Anagarika Dharmapala and the Maha Bodhi Society 1891–1952' in the editorial introduction to *Beating the Drum*, Ibis Publications, Ledbury, 2012, and *Anagarika Dharmapala: A Biographical Sketch*, Ibis Publications, Ledbury 2014 (both in *Complete Works*, vol. 8).

489 For the meeting with the old scholar 'Pandit-ji', and his project for the revival of the Dharma Vijaya Vahini; as well as the 'female ascetic', Anandamayi Ma, and her disciples; and disillusionment with both her and with the unscrupulous Pandit, see *The Rainbow Road from Tooting Broadway to Kalimpong*, *Complete Works*, vol. 20, chapters 18–24.

490 According to the *Ariyapariyesanā Sutta*, the Buddha described his own Going Forth in the following words: 'While still young, a black-haired young man endowed with the blessing of youth, in the prime of life, though my mother and father wished otherwise and wept

with tearful faces, I shaved off my hair and beard, put on the yellow robe, and went forth from the home life into homelessness.' *Majjhima Nikāya* 26 (i.163). Bhikkhu Ñāṇamoli and Bhikkhu Bodhi (trans.), *The Middle Length Discourses of the Buddha*, Wisdom Publications, Boston 1995, p. 256; or I. B. Horner (trans.), *The Collection of the Middle Length Sayings*, vol. i, Pali Text Society, London 1976, p. 207.

491 Again in the *Ariyapariyesanā Sutta*, at *Majjhima Nikāya* i.167, the Buddha recounts this experience to his disciples. Ibid., pp. 259–60 in Ñāṇamoli and Bhikkhu Bodhi, and p. 211 in I. B. Horner.

492 Taking accounts, for example, from the *Majjhima Nikāya,* we find examples of a whole range of responses to the Buddha and his teaching. There is Saccaka, 'a debater and a clever speaker regarded by many as a saint' who is highly impressed by the Buddha's response to his questions, but though 'delighted' he does not go for Refuge at all! See *Mahāsaccaka Sutta, Majjhima Nikāya* 36, Bhikkhu Ñāṇamoli and Bhikkhu Bodhi (trans.), *The Middle Length Discourses of the Buddha*, Wisdom Publications, Boston 1995, p. 343; or I. B. Horner (trans.), *The Collection of the Middle Length Sayings*, vol. i, Pali Text Society, London 1976, pp. 304–5.

Māgandiya is a wanderer who 'received the going forth' and the 'full admission' from the Buddha and went on to become one of the *arhants*. See *Māgandiya Sutta, Majjhima Nikāya* 75 (i.512–3). Ñāṇamoli and Bodhi, p. 617; Horner, pp. 919–2. Likewise Vacchagotta, also a wanderer (*Mahāvacchagotta Sutta, Majjhima Nikāya* 73 (i.496), Ñāṇamoli and Bodhi, p. 601; Horner, p. 175). In the *Mahāvacchagotta Sutta* the Buddha attests that among his disciples were many *bhikkhus* and *bhikkhunīs,* men and women who had gone forth and attained arhantship, as well as lay disciples, both men and women, who were well advanced on the path to Enlightenment, though not fully Enlightened. See *Majjhima Nikāya* 73 (i.490), Ñāṇamoli and Bodhi p. 596; Horner p. 168.

493 Sangharakshita's understanding of the emergence of the individual from the group is explored more fully in *What is the Sangha?* part 1, *Complete Works*, vol. 3, especially pp. 434–40.

494 'In the extravagance of our zeal for world-renunciation we had destroyed all our papers.' To the immigration officer enquiring after their nationality, they explained that

having renounced the world they had none! *The Rainbow Road from Tooting Broadway to Kalimpong, Complete Works*, vol. 20, p. 229.

495 Ibid., chapters 25–36.

496 Ibid., p. 302.

497 In the summer of 1987 Sangharakshita had received emergency treatment for prostate trouble.

498 Guhyaloka, or the 'secret realm', is a valley in the Sierra Aitana mountains of southern Spain, where four-month long – and some shorter – ordination retreats for men have been held annually since 1987. At the top of the valley is the retreat centre; a house for the resident community is at the bottom, while midway between the two is a bungalow where Sangharakshita stayed when he visited the valley.

499 *The Rainbow Road from Tooting Broadway to Kalimpong* in *Complete Works*, vol. 20, chapters 38–44.

500 Ibid., pp. 389–91.

501 This was Jagdish Kashyap with whom Sangharakshita went on to study Pāli, Abhidharma, and Logic at the Benares Hindu University. See ibid., pp. 394–5 and 442–56.

502 U Chandramani (1876–1972) was based at Kusinara from 1904. He campaigned for the restoration of viharas and stupas there and at Sarnath, Lumbini, and other Buddhist holy sites. He was regarded as the seniormost *bhikkhu* resident in India and for this reason Sangharakshita recommended he should be invited to conduct the conversion ceremony for Dr Ambedkar and his wife at the mass meeting held in 1956 after which the conversions for the gathered hundreds of thousands were then administered by Ambedkar himself. See section 21 pp. 494ff.

503 Sangharakshita's *śrāmaṇera* ordination, and his receiving the name 'Sangharakshita' is described in *The Rainbow Road from Tooting Broadway to Kalimpong, Complete Works*, vol. 20, chapter 45. For the ten *śrāmaṇera* precepts see Appendix p. 655.

504 Emily Brontë, 'No Coward Soul is Mine'. The poem first appeared in *Poems of Currer, Ellis and Acton Bell* in 1846.

505 The Mulagandhakuti Vihara was founded by Anagarika Dharmapala about whom Sangharakshita was soon to write a biographical sketch. See *Anagarika Dharmapala: A Biographical Sketch*, Ibis Publications, Ledbury 2014, especially pp. 63–5. For the indispensable financial contribution made by Mrs Mary E. Foster of Honolulu see pp. 74ff. (*Complete Works*, vol. 8).

506 This was U Kawinda Sayadaw 'a softly-spoken, mild-mannered man of about

fifty'. See *Facing Mount Kanchenjunga, Complete Works*, vol. 21, p. 107.

507 This 'unfinished continuation' was published three years later by Windhorse Publications, Glasgow 1991, with the title *Facing Mount Kanchenjunga*. See *Complete Works*, vol. 21. For an account of his *bhikṣu* ordination, including those present at the ceremony, see ibid., pp. 106–9.

508 See note 258.

509 Vinaya Piṭaka i.58 (*Mahāvagga* 1.30), See I. B. Horner (trans.), *The Book of the Discipline*, part 4, Pali Text Society, Oxford 1996, p. 75.

510 This was Kusho Bakula, a well-known Ladakhi, 'an aloof, mysterious figure ... with an expression of remarkable thoughtfulness and refinement.' *Facing Mount Kanchenjunga*, in *Complete Works*, vol. 21, p. 107.

511 Sangharakshita continued to compose new poems after 1988 although not as many as he had done in some of the previous years. Poems written after 1988 can be found in *Complete Poems 1941–1994*, Windhorse Publications, Birmingham 1995, pp. 363–95; *The Call of the Forest*, Windhorse Publications, Birmingham 2000, and *A Moseley Miscellany*, Ibis Publications, Ledbury 2015. *Complete Works*, vol. 25 includes all Sangharakshita's poetry to date.

512 *The Enchanted Heart* was printed on coloured paper and published by Ola Leaves, London 1980. The Preface, updated, was reproduced in *Complete Poems 1941–1994*, Windhorse Publications, Birmingham 1995, p. 7 (*Complete Works*, vol. 25).

513 'Taking Refuge in the Buddha' was composed in 1953. See *Complete Poems 1941–1994*, Windhorse Publications, Birmingham 1995, pp. 161–3 (*Complete Works*, vol. 25). See also *Facing Mount Kanchenjunga* in *Complete Works*, vol. 21, p. 429, where Sangharakshita describes how he came to compose the poem.

514 *Facing Mount Kanchenjunga*, in *Complete Works*, vol. 21, p. 7.

515 'Advice to a Young Poet' in *The Religion of Art*, Windhorse Publications, Glasgow 1988 (*Complete Works*, vol. 26).

516 Gampopa, *The Jewel Ornament of Liberation*, trans. Herbert V. Guenther, Shambhala Publications, London 1986, pp. 101–2. This translation first appeared in 1959.

517 Ibid., p. 102. Gampopa is quoting the *Thar.pa chen. po.mdo* or *Sūtra of Great Liberation*.

518 For the Pāli, and Sangharakshita's seminar on the text, see *Complete Works*, vol. 15.

519 *Grace Abounding to the Chief of Sinners,* a religious tract by John Bunyan, was written when he was serving a twelve-year prison sentence for preaching without a licence. It was published in 1666. 'Grace Abounding' is a reference to St Paul's Letter to the Romans 5:20 which states, 'Where sin abounded, grace did much more abound.'

520 *A Survey of Buddhism* is included in volume 1 of the *Complete Works.* Sangharakshita describes how he came to give the lectures on which it is based, and how he wrote up the lectures into a book, in *In the Sign of the Golden Wheel*, Windhorse Publications, Birmingham 1996, chapter 9. In subsequent chapters there are many references to his work of preparing the *Survey* for publication (*Complete Works*, vol. 22).

521 *A Survey of Buddhism, Complete Works*, vol. 1, p. 6.

522 Such limitations are discussed by Subhuti in his Foreword to the *Complete Works* edition. For example, where a later and more reliable translation of a text quoted in the *Survey* makes the illustration of a particular doctrinal point invalid. However, as Subhuti makes clear, although the illustration may be rendered invalid, the doctrinal point still stands. *A Survey of Buddhism, Complete Works*, vol. 1, pp. xiv–xv.

523 *A Survey of Buddhism, Complete Works*, vol. 1, pp. 6–7.

524 The sixth edition was published by Tharpa Publications, London 1987. The 'Introduction' was originally an article, 'A Bird's Eye View of Indian Buddhism' (see note 562).

525 The seven practices are: (1) *vandanā* (praise) (2) *pūjanā* (worship) (3) *deśanā* (confession) (4) *modanā* (rejoicing in merits) (5) *adhyeṣaṇā* (requesting the teaching) (6) *yācanā* (begging the Buddhas not to abandon beings) (7) *pariṇamanā* (dedication of merits). The Sevenfold Puja used within the Triratna Buddhist Community is based on verses from Śāntideva's *Bodhicaryāvatāra,* chapters 2 and 3. See introduction to these chapters in the translation by K. Crosby and A. Skilton, Windhorse Publications, Birmingham 2002, pp. 11–16. The Sevenfold Puja is included in *Complete Works*, vol. 11.

526 *A Survey of Buddhism*, in *Complete Works*, vol. 1, p. 408.

527 Ibid., p. 410.

528 See *Going for Refuge* in this volume, pp. 289ff. See also note 381 above.

529 *A Survey of Buddhism*, in *Complete Works*, vol. 1, p. 410.

530 See *Going for Refuge* in this volume pp. 300ff.

531 *A Survey of Buddhism*, in *Complete Works*, vol. 1, p. 397.

532 Ibid., p. 244.

533 Ibid., p. 11. In 2001 Shravasti Dhammika, an Australian who had been a Theravādin monk for twenty-five years, published online (and in 2006 as a book) a damning indictment of the Therāvadin monastic order as he had experienced it. See *The Broken Buddha: Critical Reflections on Theravada and a Plea for a New Buddhism*, Nimmala Group, 2006.

534
> We must be free or die, who
> speak the tongue
> That Shakespeare spake

from W. Wordsworth's poem, 'England' (1802).

535 'Buddhism in Tibet' by L. P. Lhalungpa in Kenneth W. Morgan (ed.), *The Path of the Buddha: Buddhism Interpreted by Buddhists*, Ronald Press, New York 1956. Jagdish Kashyap also contributed a chapter, 'Origin and Expansion of Buddhism'; and U Thittila a chapter on 'The Fundamental Principles of Theravada Buddhism'.

536 Ibid., pp. 275–6.

537 Ibid., p. 276.

538 Sangharakshita's *Ambedkar and Buddhism*, which was first published in 1986, is a concise, often gripping account of the life and career of Dr Ambedkar, indicating the principal milestones that led to his conversion to Buddhism. In chapter 2 he recounts his three meetings with Ambedkar. See *Complete Works*, vol. 9. These meetings are also recounted in his memoirs: the first meeting is in both *Facing Mount Kanchenjunga*, *Complete Works*, vol. 21, pp. 415–16, and *In the Sign of the Golden Wheel*, Windhorse Publications, Birmingham 1996, pp. 59–60 and 272 (*Complete Works*, vol. 22). The second and third meetings are recorded in *In the Sign of the Golden Wheel*, pp. 273–5 and 331.

539 At the second ceremony of mass conversion, held in Nagpur on 15 October 1956, Dr Ambedkar declared that through his conversion he felt that he had been delivered from hell, the hell of caste, and he wanted all his followers to share that experience. *Ambedkar and Buddhism*, in *Complete Works*, vol. 9, p. 134.

540 Gampopa, *Jewel Ornament of Liberation*, trans. Herbert V. Guenther, Shambhala Publications, London 1986, p. ix.

541 Atīśa (982–1054 CE) was one of the great Indian teachers who brought Buddhism to Tibet. 'First take the Three Refuges thrice', he exhorts the practitioner in the verses of his *Bodhipathapradīpa,* the text that lay the foundation

for the Lamrim tradition. See R. Sherburne (trans.), *A Lamp for the Path and Commentary*, George Allen and Unwin, London 1983, p. 5.

542 Sangharakshita relates his meeting with Jamyang Khyentse Rimpoche, and what happened afterwards, in *Precious Teachers,* Windhorse Publications, Birmingham 2007, pp. 12–15 (*Complete Works*, vol. 22).

543 Sangharakshita first encountered Padmasambhava in a Nyingma temple in Darjeeling in 1950. He wrote in his memoir, 'In seeing the figure of Padmasambhava I had become conscious of a spiritual presence that had in fact been with me all the time.' See *Facing Mount Kanchenjunga* in *Complete Works,* vol. 21, p. 93.

544 At the time this talk was given (1988), Order members still followed the Going for Refuge and Prostration practice as practised by Sangharakshita in India based on the *Tharpe Delam,* visualizing the Refuge Tree of the Nyingma school of Tibetan Buddhism for whom Padmasambhava is the central figure. Over the course of time, however, in keeping with the emerging culture of Triratna, a Going for Refuge and Prostration practice was created that reflected more essentially the myth and archetypes that held meaning and significance in the specifically Triratna tradition. The Buddha Śākyamuni became the central figure, with Padmasambhava taking a central place among the 'teachers of the past'. For a description of the Triratna Refuge Tree see Kulananda, *Teachers of Enlightenment*, Windhorse Publications, Birmingham 2000.

545 The formula recited when visualizing the Triratna Refuge Tree is simply 'To the Buddha for Refuge I go, to the Dharma for Refuge I go, to the Sangha for Refuge I go'.

546 The Going for Refuge and Prostration practice of the Buddha Śākyamuni is introduced to Mitras who have asked for ordination, i.e. men and women wishing to join the Triratna Buddhist Order, on their ordination training retreats. It is also practised on the ordination retreat itself, as well as at Order gatherings such as conventions. Some Mitras take up the practice under the supervision of, usually, a local Order member, undertaking to do it at least three times weekly in addition to their daily meditation practice.

547 Sangharakshita may be referring here to Dilgo Khyentse Rimpoche (1910–1991) and Dudjom Rimpoche (1904–1987), both great Nyingma scholars and teachers, from whom he himself received initiations,

including that of Amitābha from Dilgo Khyentse Rimpoche and Vajrasattva from Dudjom Rimpoche. See *Precious Teachers,* Windhorse Publications, Birmingham 2007, pp. 164–5 and 112–21 (*Complete Works*, vol. 22). Dilgo Khyentse married after many years of solitary meditation at the suggestion of his teacher. Dudjom Rimpoche was married twice and had many children. Short biographies of both can be found in Kulananda, *Teachers of Enlightenment,* Windhorse Publications, Birmingham 2000, pp. 257–9 and 259–63.

548 Included with other articles written in India in *Complete Works*, vol. 7.

549 Sangharakshita was later to revise this view of the three *yānas*, see Subhuti, *Sangharakshita: A New Voice in the Buddhist Tradition*, Windhorse Publications, Birmingham 1994.

550 *The Middle Way*, vol. 34, no. 3, November 1959, p. 98 (*Complete Works*, vol. 7).

551 Ibid., p. 101.

552 'Wanted: a New Type of Bhikkhu' and 'Wanted: A New Type of Upasaka' were published, among other places, in the *Maha Bodhi*, vol. 69, no. 10, October 1961, pp. 293–5, and vol. 70, nos. 3 & 4, March–April 1962, pp. 81–4. They are included as an appendix to *Beating the Drum*, Ibis Publications, Ledbury 2012. pp. 269–72 and 273–6 (*Complete Works*, vol. 8).

553 *Beating the Drum,* ibid., p. 269.

554 Ibid., p. 273.

555 *The Three Jewels*, in this volume, p. 8.

556 *The Eternal Legacy*, Windhorse Publications, Birmingham 2006 (*Complete Works*, vol. 14).

557 *The Three Jewels*, in this volume, p. 138.

558 *Dhammapada* 142. See for example, Sangharakshita (trans.), *Dhammapada*, Windhorse Publications, Birmingham 2001, p. 54 (*Complete Works*, vol. 15).

559 *The Three Jewels*, in this volume, p. 202–3. A *sutta* in which the Buddha places all four *vargas*, i.e. *bhikkhus, bhikkhunīs, upāsakas*, and *upāsikās* on an equal footing, can be found at *Aṅguttara Nikāya* ii.8 (4.7), in Bhikkhu Bodhi (trans.), *The Numerical Discourses of the Buddha*, Wisdom Publications, Somerville 2012, p. 394; or F. L. Woodward (trans.), *Gradual Sayings*, vol. ii, Pali Text Society, Oxford 1995, p. 8.

560 *The Three Jewels*, in this volume, p. 207.

561 'A Bird's-Eye View of Indian Buddhism' in *Complete Works*, vol. 7.

562 This Introduction was included in the fifth and all subsequent editions of the *Survey* up to and including the ninth

edition which was published by Windhorse Publications in 2001. For the *Complete Works* edition, i.e. the tenth, Sangharakshita's *magnum opus* has been restored to its original dimensions, see vol. 1. 'A Bird's-Eye View of Indian Buddhism' is included with other articles written in India in *Complete Works*, vol. 7.

563 'A Bird's-Eye View of Indian Buddhism', *Dhammamegha* 41 & 42, Sinhanad Publications, Pune 1987, p. 14 (*Complete Works*, vol. 7).

564 *A Survey of Buddhism*, ninth edition, Windhorse Publications, Birmingham 2001, p. 15 (*Complete Works*, vol. 1).

565 Upasika Chihmann (trans.), *The Two Buddhist Books in Mahāyāna*, H. K. Books, n.d., p. 7.

566 Śāntideva's *Śikṣā-samuccaya* is a compendium of quotations from Mahāyāna *sūtras*. The exact date of the work cannot be determined; Śāntideva is thought to have flourished in the seventh–eighth centuries CE. Sangharakshita found this volume in a cupboard in the Dharmodaya Vihara where he first took up residence after arriving in Kalimpong in March 1950. See *Facing Mount Kanchenjunga* in *Complete Works*, vol. 21, p. 23.

567 Chapter 4 is called simply 'The Bodhisattva Ideal' and the theme is explored in terms of: the ideal as a unifying factor in Buddhism, the bodhisattva ideal in comparison to the *arhant* ideal, the bodhisattva path, the *bodhicitta*, and the *pāramitās*. See *A Survey of Buddhism* in *Complete Works*, vol. 1, pp. 394ff. The articles in which Sangharakshita's inspiration for the bodhisattva ideal found expression include his editorials for *Stepping-Stones*, collected in *Crossing the Stream*, Windhorse Publications, Glasgow 1987, especially 'The Problem of Desire', 'The Simple Life', 'A Old Saw Re-sharpened' and 'Autumn Thoughts' (*Complete Works*, vol. 7). The poems on the same theme include 'The Bodhisattva', *Complete Poems 1941–1994*, Windhorse Publications, Birmingham 1995, p. 107 (*Complete Works*, vol. 25).

568 See *Facing Mount Kanchenjunga*, *Complete Works*, vol. 21, chapter 1.

569 Sangharakshita describes his bodhisattva ordination in *Precious Teachers*, Windhorse Publications, Birmingham 2007, pp. 152–4 (*Complete Works*, vol. 22).

570 The sixty-four bodhisattva precepts are included in the Appendix, pp. 657–9.

571 Sangharakshita writes about Dhardo Rimpoche and his contact with him in *In the Sign of the Golden Wheel*, Windhorse Publications, Birmingham 1996, especially pp. 180–2, 220–1, 311–13,

and 317–23 (*Complete Works,* vol. 22); and *Precious Teachers,* Windhorse Publications, Birmingham 2007, especially pp. 31–6 and 159–61 (*Complete Works,* vol. 22).

572 As related in *Precious Teachers,* Windhorse Publications, Birmingham 2007, p. 170, (*Complete Works,* vol. 22); and *Moving Against the Stream,* Windhorse Publications, Birmingham 2007, pp. 15ff. (*Complete Works,* vol. 23)

573 In a letter to his friend Dinoo Dubash dated 19 August 1963, he relates, 'I have accepted an invitation to go to England next year for a few months (lectures, of course)'. *Dear Dinoo* in *Complete Works,* vol. 21, p. 578.

574 The two years at the Vihara and the farewell tour of India are the subject of chapters 1–33 and 43–51 of *Moving Against the Stream,* Windhorse Publications, Birmingham 2007 (*Complete Works,* vol. 23).

575 The *Maha Bodhi* journal was founded by Anagarika Dharmapala in May 1892. Sangharakshita took over as editor in 1954, contributing a monthly editorial, as well as the occasional article or poem, and attracting articles from some of the leading Buddhist writers of the time. His editorials are collected in *Beating the Drum*, Ibis Publications, Ledbury 2012 (*Compete Works*, vol. 8).

576 Sangharakshita's experiences of Theravādin attitudes at the Hampstead Buddhist Vihara are told in his memoir *Moving Against the Stream*, Windhorse Publications, Birmingham 2003, especially chapter 3. The summer school tale is told in chapter 6 (*Complete Works*, vol. 23).

577 What follows here is a summary of those lectures, edited versions of which make up *The Meaning of Conversion in Buddhism*, included in this volume on pp. 237–85.

578 Two years later this idea found expression in the dedication ceremony that I composed for the opening of the Triratna Shrine and Meditation Centre [on 6 April 1967], the first home of the newly founded FWBO (S):

> Here seated, here practising,
> May our mind become Buddha,
> May our thought become Dharma,
> May our communication with one another be Sangha.

See *Puja: the Triratna Book of Buddhist Devotional Texts*, Windhorse Publications, Cambridge 2012, p. 37 (*Complete Works*, vol. 15).

579 *The Meaning of Conversion in Buddhism,* see this volume, p. 268.

580 See p. 403.

581 A striking example was the Maha Bodhi Society's

governing body which was dominated by caste Hindus. See *Beating the Drum*, Ibis Publications, Ledbury 2012, pp. 61–5 (*Complete Works*, vol. 8).

582 This is one of the six distinctive emphases of the Triratna Buddhist Community which Sangharakshita pointed out in a number of lectures given between 2002 and 2008. The six are: (1) Going for Refuge is central to a Buddhist life. (2) Triratna is a unified order, open equally to men and women, regardless of race, sexual orientation, caste, nationality, and so on. (3) Triratna is ecumenical, drawing on the whole Buddhist tradition. (4) The practice of spiritual friendship is recognized as being essential to spiritual life. (5) Team-based right livelihood is encouraged and supported as a means to personal transformation and the transformation of society. (6) The higher arts and culture can play a significant part in spiritual life.

583 Presumably Sangharakshita is here thinking of such functions as the chair of a Buddhist centre or retreat centre, or of Triratna businesses or charities; of Mitra convenors who are responsible for making sure the spiritual needs of local Mitras are met; of private preceptors who, in the first part of the ordination ceremony, witness the effective Going for Refuge of those they ordain, and of public preceptors who, in the second part of the ceremony, witness their Going for Refuge on behalf of the College, and welcomes them into the Order on behalf of all Order members. In all these cases those who are qualified, whether men or women, take equal responsibility.

584 In Buddhist traditions such as the Theravāda the *bhikkhunī* tradition died out many centuries ago so that only men were able to receive full ordination. As noted in *The Three Jewels*, even when women tried to live the life of a nun, because they were not technically *bhikkhunīs* they received little support from the lay people who preferred to support the fully ordained monks, believing that way they would gain greater merit. See pp. 214–15 above. Some twelve years after this paper was delivered the Theravādin *bhikkhunī* tradition was revived through the efforts of the Thai Buddhist Chatsumarn Kabilsingh, now Bhikkhuni Dhammananda, and others.

585 See previous note.

586 For more on Triratna's *anagārikas* and *anagārikās* see *Forty-Three Years Ago*, pp. 604–9 in this volume.

587 These themes are enlarged upon in *The Bodhisattva Ideal* in *Complete Works*, vol. 4.

588 The group, the individual, and the spiritual community are the subject of a number of Sangharakshita's lectures (*Complete Works*, vol. 12) as well as parts 1 and 2 of *What is the Sangha?* in *Complete Works*, vol. 3.

589 In 1973, six years after founding the FWBO, Sangharakshita spent six months in Cornwall. This not only gave him the opportunity of completing the first volume of his memoirs, which he had begun more than fifteen years previously when living in India, and left off midway through chapter 32; it also gave the young Order a chance to manage without him, to organize and teach classes, and so on. Thus it was a milestone in the growth of the Western Buddhist Order.

590 These lectures are included in *Complete Works*, vol. 12. It is interesting to note that Sangharakshita had already begun to think in evolutionary terms many years previously. See 'A Modern View of Buddhism', an article published in 1958 based on a lecture given in Singapore in 1946, in *Early Writings 1944–1954*, Ibis Publications, Ledbury 2013, p. 132 (*Complete Works*, vol. 7).

591 This fifth lecture in the series 'The Higher Evolution of Man' is called 'Buddhism and the Path of the Higher Evolution' (*Complete Works*, vol. 12).

592 Mahāprajāpatī was the Buddha's aunt and foster-mother on account of whose request the Buddha founded the Order of *bhikṣuṇīs*. On one occasion she came to him asking for clarification about what, in fact, was the Dharma that he taught. On this occasion he replied that it was whatever conduced to dispassion, contentment, solitude, frugality, and so on. See *Aṅguttara Nikāya* iv.280 (8.53), in E. M. Hare (trans.), *Gradual Sayings*, vol. iv, Pali Text Society, Oxford 1995, pp. 186–7; or Bhikkhu Bodhi (trans.), *The Numerical Discourses of the Buddha*, Wisdom Publications, Boston 2012, p. 1193.

593 The simile – or vision – of the lotus flowers in various stages of unfoldment is one that came to the Buddha directly after his Enlightenment. See *Saṃyutta Nikāya* i.138 in Bhikkhu Bodhi (trans.), *The Connected Discourses of the Buddha*, Wisdom Publications, Boston 2000, p. 233; or C. A. F. Rhys Davids (trans.), *The Book of the Kindred Sayings*, part 1, Pali Text Society, London 1979, p. 174; also Vinaya Piṭaka i.6 (*Mahāvagga* 1.5) in I. B. Horner (trans.), *The Book of the Discipline*, part 4, Pali Text Society, Oxford 1996, p. 9. The Parable of the Herbs and Plants (also called the Parable of the Rain Cloud) comes from the the *Saddharma Puṇḍarīka*,

or *White Lotus Sūtra* where the Dharma, or the Buddha's teaching, is likened to the rain that falls on all plants and herbs, allowing each to grow in its own particular way. See Bunnō Katō et al. (trans.), *The Threefold Lotus Sūtra*, Kōsei Publishing Company, Tokyo 1995, pp. 126–34.

594 For the twelve positive *nidānas* see Chapter 13, pp. 101ff. of *The Three Jewels* in this volume.

595 See *The Bodhisattva Principle: Evolution and Self-Transcendence*, Windhorse Publications, Glasgow 1983 (*Complete Works*, vol. 4), a lecture given at the Wrekin Trust's sixth annual 'Mystics and Scientists' conference in March 1983.

596 In his lecture, 'The Awakening of the Bodhi Heart', Sangharakshita says,

> We might, in fact – though here we have rather to grope for words – think of the *bodhicitta* as a sort of 'cosmic will' (I don't quite like to use this word 'will', but there's really no other) … a will at work in the world, at work in the universe, in the direction of what we can only think of as universal redemption: the liberation, the Enlightenment, ultimately, of all sentient beings.

An edited version of this lecture can be found in *The Bodhisattva Ideal*, Windhorse Publications, Birmingham 1999, p. 38 (*Complete Works*, vol. 4).

597 See *A Survey of Buddhism*, in *Complete Works*, vol. 1, p. 408.

598 As Nyanaponika explains: 'The Going for Refuge has two main divisions: it may be mundane or supramundane.' Nyanaponika Thera, *The Threefold Refuge*, Wheel Publication no. 76, Buddhist Publication Society, Kandy 1965, p. 3.

599 The 1978 lecture 'Levels of Going for Refuge' is included in *Complete Works*, vol. 12. As Sangharakshita goes on to explain in this section of his *History*, in his 1983 lecture on Going for Refuge given in Bombay (included in this volume), he spoke of four levels of Going for Refuge.

600 The language of refuge has been used in Buddhism since the earliest times. According to the Vinaya Piṭaka, the first two people to encounter the Buddha after his Enlightenment, merchants Tapussa and Bhallika, were moved to make him food offerings, and: 'We go for refuge to the Blessed One, and to the Dhamma.' Vinaya Piṭaka i.4 (*Mahāvagga* 1.4); see I. B. Horner (trans.), *The Book of the Discipline*, part 4, Pali Text Society, Oxford 1996, pp. 5–6. The refuge then became threefold, including not only the Buddha and his

Dhamma but also the Sangha. The declaration 'I go for Refuge…' occurs many, many times in the scriptures. Here is just one example: *Vekhanassa Sutta*, *Majjhima Nikāya* 80 (ii.44). Bhikkhu Ñāṇamoli and Bhikkhu Bodhi (trans.), *The Middle Length Discourses of the Buddha*, Wisdom Publications, Boston 1995, p. 665; or I. B. Horner (trans.), *The Collection of the Middle Length Sayings*, vol. ii, Pali Text Society, Oxford 1994, p. 239.

601 In his 1978 lecture, 'Levels of Going for Refuge', Sangharakshita explains the esoteric refuges as those that point one to one's own direct experience. In the Vajrayāna tradition the guru stands for the Buddha Refuge; the *deva*, here meaning the chosen Buddha or bodhisattva figure on whom one meditates, becomes in one's direct experience the Dharma Refuge; the *ḍākinī* is described initially as 'any member of the spiritual community with whom one is in close personal contact, who sparks one off spiritually, even inspires one' – not a kind of spiritual girlfriend but something more like what Blake called the 'Emanation'. It is communication on a higher spiritual plane. (This lecture can be found in *Complete Works*, vol. 12.)

602 Included in this volume. See pp. 289–306.

603 *Going for Refuge*, in this volume, pp. 300–1.

604 In the early years of establishing the Order and movement, Sangharakshita conducted many study seminars including many at Padmaloka, established in Norfolk in 1976 as the first FWBO (Triratna) retreat centre. Padmaloka means 'realm of the lotus'. For some years it was Sangharakshita's headquarters and as well as a large men's community, it housed the Order Office. With the development of the men's ordination process in the 1990s, Padmaloka became the main centre for training men who have asked for ordination and has held a mythic place in the life of many Order members.

605 The seminar was recorded, the recording transcribed, and the verbatim transcription edited by Sangharakshita. It was published as *The Threefold Refuge,* Windhorse Publications, London 1984 (*Complete Works*, vol. 15).

606 Nyanaponika Thera, *The Threefold Refuge*, Wheel Publication no. 76, Buddhist Publication Society, Kandy 1965, p. 9.

607 Ibid., p. 15.

608 Ibid., p. 4.

609 Ibid., p. 17.

610 Ibid., p. 25.

611 Lokamitra (b. 1947) was ordained by Sangharakshita in 1974. In 1977 he travelled

to India to visit the Buddhist holy places, Kalimpong (where Sangharakshita had lived for many years), and Pune, where he studied yoga with B. K. S. Iyengar. On his way to Pune he arrived in Nagpur on the very day that Dr Ambedkar's followers were celebrating the twenty-first anniversary of the mass conversion to Buddhism. He was so moved by what he saw that he decided to stay and work in India with Dr Ambedkar's Buddhist followers to create an Indian wing of the Order and movement that Sangharakshita had inaugurated. He has worked tirelessly for (to date) over forty years. For more on his life and work see 'TBMSG: A Dhamma Revolution in India' by Alan Sponberg (Dharmachari Saramati) in Christopher S. Queen and Sally B. King, *Engaged Buddhism*, State University of New York Press, Albany NY 1996, pp. 75–120; and *The Day That Changed My Life* and *Thirty Years in India*, two as yet unpublished talks by Lokamitra about his life and work in India. These can be downloaded as PDF files from freebuddhistaudio.com

612 During his 1981–2 tour of India Sangharakshita gave thirty-three talks and three question-and-answer sessions. Edited transcripts of these are gathered together in *Complete Works*, vol. 9. The Order meeting at which the change of nomenclature for Order members was proposed took place on 10 March 1982. See *Complete Works*, vol. 9, p. 539.

613 *Dhammapada* 168–9. See Sangharakshita (trans.), *Dhammapada*, Windhorse Publications, Birmingham 2001, pp. 62–3 (*Complete Works*, vol. 15).

614 A *brahmacārin* is one who is 'leading a pure life, chaste', or leading a divine life, the life of the *brahmās*. *Bhadracārin* means someone who practises what is good or auspicious. A *khecārin* is one who fares through space or the sky.

615 The term *bodhicarya* may be familiar as part of the title of Śāntideva's *Bodhicaryāvatāra*, translated, for example, by Stephen Batchelor as *A Guide to the Bodhisattva's Way of Life*.

616 The 'Last Vandanā' or, more properly, the *Dhammapālaṃ Gāthā* or 'Verses that Protect the Truth' includes the lines *Dhammacārī sukhaṃ seti / Asmiṃ loke paraṃhi ca*, meaning 'The Dharma-farer lives happily / Both in this world and the next'. See *Puja: The Triratna Book of Buddhist Devotional Texts*, Windhorse Publications, Birmingham 2012, p. 46 (*Complete Works*, vol. 11).

617 See *The Ten Pillars of Buddhism*, in this volume, p. 345.

618 *The Ten Pillars of Buddhism*, in this volume p. 346–7.

619 From 1981 to 1986 a three-month course for men was held at a former monastery of the Discalced Augustinian Order, Il Convento di Santa Croce, in Batignano, Tuscany, and after that at Guhyaloka in southern Spain (where in due course it was extended to four months). During the 1985 course twenty-three ordination ceremonies took place with Sangharakshita conferring ordinations as private and public preceptor (see note 628). The course was led by Dharmachari Vessantara with a team of Order members. Vessantara was to lead altogether seven men's ordination courses from 1983 to 1989). The 1985 course was notable in that one of those ordained (Mokshapriya) made a video film of the course. See *Through Buddhist Eyes*, Windhorse Publications, Birmingham 2000, pp. 34–5. (*Complete Works*, vol. 24.)

620 *Ambedkar and Buddhism* is included in volume 9 of the *Complete Works*.

621 *Ambedkar and Buddhism* in *Complete Works*, vol. 9, p. 131.

622 See Sangharakshita's lecture, 'Why Buddhism Disappeared from India and How it can be Prevented from Disappearing Again' given in Nanded, January 1982 in *Dr Ambedkar and the Revival of Buddhism I, Complete Works*, vol. 9, pp. 387–95, especially pp. 391 and 394.

623 The twenty-two vows are listed in the Appendix, pp. 656.

624 Sangharakshita read 'The Buddha and the Future of His Religion' when it first appeared in the Wesak edition of the *Maha Bodhi*, vol. 58, April–May 1950. Realizing the extent of the great political leader's interest in Buddhism, he wrote to Ambedkar, thus inaugurating their personal connection. The article is reproduced in Dr Babasaheb Ambedkar, *Writings and Speeches*, vol. 17 (part 2), Education Department, Government of Maharashtra, Mumbai 2003, pp. 97–108.

625 Quoted (in a slightly different version) in D. Keer, *Dr Ambedkar: Life and Mission*, third edition, Popular Prakashan, Bombay 1971, p. 498.

MY RELATION TO THE ORDER

626 A 'chapter' is a group of between three and ten or so Order members, usually of the same sex, who meet together regularly, usually weekly. Every chapter devises its own way of meeting but central to all is the reviewing of one's Dharma life, often including the practice of confession, as well as rejoicing in merits. Meeting regularly in this way, deeper trust grows so that, by confiding in one

another about the ups and downs of spiritual life, sharing inspiration, and exploring the deeper meaning of the Dharma, chapter meetings play an essential part in the life of Triratna Order members. Sangharakshita may have first used the term 'spiritual workshop' in a seminar on Gampopa's *Jewel Ornament of Liberation* held in Tuscany as part of the 1985 men's ordination course. 'I would like to see [chapter meetings] becoming more and more what I call spiritual workshops', he said. Unpublished seminar, p. 35 (see also p. 45 for a little more on the subject).

627 For Guhyaloka see note 498. Ordination courses were first held at Guhyaloka in 1987. That year and the following year Sangharakshita attended at least part of the course and performed the ordinations, but in 1989 he did not attend the course and the ordinations were conducted by Subhuti and Suvajra. For more on the significance of this see note 628. (From 1981 to 1986 the ordination courses had been held at a former monastery in Tuscany, Italy. See note 619).

Subhuti (b.1947) was ordained in 1973. He led the building team that established the London Buddhist Centre in Bethnal Green, becoming its first chairman and later its president. In 1980 he moved to Padmaloka, the men's retreat centre in Norfolk, England, then Sangharakshita's headquarters, to work as Sangharakshita's secretary. He went on to form, in 1988, the first men's ordination team, creating a systematic ordination training which was taken up for both men and women. He was instrumental in finding and helping to set up Guhyaloka retreat centre in the mountains of Spain where, since 1987, men's ordination retreats have taken place. He was a founding member and first chairman of the College of Public Preceptors, and one of the seven Order members to whom Sangharakshita handed on the headship of the Order in 2000. From 1995 he lived with Sangharakshita and members of the College and its Council at Madhyamaloka in Birmingham. In the mid-2000s he moved with Dharmacharini Srimala to a remote place in Wales: a base for periods of more solitary contemplation and for writing, though continuing for much of the year to be intensively active in the Triratna Buddhist Order and Community both in the UK and abroad. From 1990 to the present (2018) he has spent up to half each year in India supporting the growth of the movement and Order there. He is also active in Hungary among members of the Gypsy/Roma community inspired by the work of Dr Ambedkar. He has given numerous talks and lectures, and written a number of books, prominent among them his outstanding summary of Sangharakshita's thinking: *Sangharakshita: A New Voice in the Buddhist Tradition*, Windhorse Publications, Birmingham 1994.

Suvajra (b.1952) became a Buddhist at the age of sixteen and was ordained within the Western Buddhist Order in 1978. He was chairman of the Manchester Buddhist Centre from 1980 to 1989, moving to Padmaloka to join Subhuti and others to form the first men's ordination team. He was one of five senior Order members who, in 1993, at Sangharakshita's request, formed the College of Public Preceptors. From 1994 to 2010 he lived in India supporting ordination training for men, and from 2003 he was chairman of Bhaja Retreat Centre. In 2014 he moved to Adhisthana, Triratna's centre in rural Herefordshire, England, as one of the companions and helpers to Sangharakshita, from where he has continued to develop his keen interest in diverse aspects of the Buddhist tradition. He is the author of a biography of Dhardo Rimpoche: *The Wheel and the Diamond,* Windhorse Publications, Glasgow 1991.

628 Ordination within the Western Buddhist Order / Triratna Buddhist Order consists of two distinct ceremonies. The private ceremony takes place 'in private' when the private preceptor witnesses the effective Going for Refuge of the ordinand, the ordinand committing themself to the practice of the ten ethical precepts and a new meditation practice, and a new name is bestowed. The public ceremony follows at a later date – the time between often being in silence with longer periods of meditation. In the public ceremony ordinands are received into the Order.

In late 1985, at Sangharakshita's request, three senior Order members, Dharmacharis Subhuti, Suvajra, and Kamalashila, travelled from the UK to India and ordained thirteen men 'on his behalf', Subhuti and Suvajra as private preceptors and Kamalashila as public preceptor. In 1987 they again conducted ordinations in India 'on Sangharakshita's behalf'. Dharmacharinis Padmasuri, Srimala, and Ratnasuri were similarly asked to make the same journey and at Bhaja retreat centre, Maharashtra, Vimalasuri and Jnanasuri were ordained – the second and third women to be ordained in India. Padmasuri and Srimala acted as private preceptors, Ratnasuri as public preceptor. Accounts of their experiences can be found in: Padmasuri,

But Little Dust, Windhorse Publications, Birmingham 1997, pp. 176-85; and Srimala, *Breaking Free,* Windhorse Publications, Birmingham 1996, pp. 98–100.

The point being drawn out here is that in 1989, Subhuti and Suvajra were no longer acting 'on behalf' of Sangharakshita but themselves conferring the ordinations. In that same year Sanghadevi, Srimala, and Ratnasuri conferred ordinations on two different retreats at Taraloka women's retreat centre. Cittaprabha from Australia was ordained in August 1989, the first woman to be thus ordained by women, an historical event. Six others (including the editor of this volume) were ordained in September. All this was a crucial handing on.

629 For Padmaloka see note 604. Ordination training retreats were held at Padmaloka through much of the 1980s. A dedicated men's ordination team was formed in the late 1980s when Subhuti drew together a number of experienced Order members. They lived and worked intensively, running retreats for men who wished to deepen their Going for Refuge and join the Western Buddhist Order (now the Triratna Buddhist Order). On the women's side at this time (1990), ordination training retreats were held at Taraloka, the women's retreat centre on the Welsh borders that was founded in 1985. They were led by a more ad hoc group of women Order members who came together to run the retreat but did not yet live together. Tiratanaloka, the dedicated women's ordination training retreat centre, was founded in 1994 by the first full-time women's ordination team. As a result, many more women came to be ordained.

630 The first Western Buddhist Order newsletter was published in October 1973 and from January 1974 it was called *Shabda*, which can be translated as 'sacred sound'. It is a monthly newsletter written by and circulated among members of the Triratna Buddhist Order.

631 Indra is the Vedic king of the gods who is said to have a jewelled net that hangs over his palace. The image of Indra's Net in the Mahāyāna tradition illustrated the idea of the interpenetration of phenomena. See Thomas Cleary, *The Flower Ornament Scripture: A Translation of the Avataṃsaka Sūtra*, Shambhala Publications, Boston and London 1993, p. 925.

In the sixth century the idea was developed in the Chinese Huayen school. In the *Huayan Wujiao Zhiguan,* ('Calming and Contemplation in the Five Teachings of Huayan'),

TD 45, no. 1867:513 Indra's Net is described as 'made up of jewels. The jewels are shiny and reflect each other successively, their images permeating each other over and over. In a single jewel they all appear at the same time, and this can be seen in each and every jewel. Within the boundaries of a single jewel are contained the unbounded repetition and profusion of the images of all the jewels'. Quoted in W. T. de Bary, *Sources of East Asian Tradition: Premodern Asia*, Columbia University Press, New York 2008, p. 258.

632 The five themes for the retreats that formed ordination training at this time were Going for Refuge, Ethics, What is the Order?, Spiritual Friendship, and the Mythic Context.

633 The idea of Going for Refuge groups arose in the mid-1980s with Dharmacharini Vidyasri, then the women's mitra convenor at the London Buddhist Centre, in response to the needs of local women who had asked for ordination. She asked fellow Dharmacharini, Malini, to take on the idea and help set them up, which she readily did. The groups provided an opportunity for Mitras to talk about their Dharma practice, usually around a theme, and to deepen their connections with one another outside of formal study or, at a time when many Mitras worked in right livelihood teams, outside their working situation. The idea was soon taken up at other centres, and in due course by groups of men Mitras. Going for Refuge groups evolved to become a kind of proto-chapter in which members learn to come together on the basis of Dharma practice, to confess, confide, inspire, and encourage one another.

634 See notes 544 and 546.

635 From 1987 the annual ordination retreat for men ran for four months, from April to July. Other arrangements were made for shorter retreats at Padmaloka. Shorter retreats were also held at Guhyaloka, and locally in other countries, for men unable to attend the four-month retreat.

The training for women developed somewhat differently given the fewer resources there were at that time, far fewer women having been ordained, and energy having been put into establishing the first women's retreat centre, Taraloka (founded 1985), and the ordination training centre for women, Tiratanaloka (founded 1994). At the time this talk was given (1990) women's ordination retreats were being held at Taraloka. From 1995 they took place at Tiratanaloka. In 1999 a seven-week course was held for two groups of women ordained from two separate locations in Italy, one of which was Il Convento. With the founding of Akashavana in 2007, an ordination retreat centre for women located in the remote mountains of Aragón in northern Spain, annual three-month ordination retreats for women were established. For those unable to attend a long retreat, two-week retreats were held both at Akashavana and locally.

636 Originally, to become a Mitra one had to ask two Order members to become one's *kalyāṇa mitras*. Here Sangharakshita is making a significant change to the system.

637 Aloka (b.1948) is an artist and sculptor. He came into contact with Sangharakshita and the FWBO in 1974 and was ordained in 1976. From 1988 to 2000 he worked with the Padmaloka ordination team running retreats for men who have asked for ordination, and giving some memorable talks. He has lived the artist's life, his images (and his words) are known and have given inspiration to people throughout the Triratna movement, especially his paintings of Buddha and Bodhisattva figures and the Triratna Refuge Tree. From 2007 he worked on panelling the Padmaloka shrine-room with Buddhist images, and in 2012 a Buddha rupa sculpted by Aloka was inaugurated.

638 Transcripts of these talks by Subhuti were used for some years on both men's and women's ordination training retreats at Padmaloka and Tiratanaloka. In due course Tiratanaloka began producing its own materials, and both ordination teams revised their courses.

639 These essential ideas are explained by Subhuti in *Sangharakshita: A New Voice in the Buddhist Tradition*, Windhorse Publications, Birmingham 1994, p. 94 and especially chapter 7.

640 For Sangharakshita's ideas on the New Society see *Buddhism for Today – and Tomorrow*, Windhorse Publications, Birmingham 1996, and *Buddhism and the West,* Windhorse Publications, Glasgow 1992 (both in *Complete Works*, vol. 11); also Subhuti, *Sangharakshita: A New Voice in the Buddhist Tradition*, Windhorse Publications, Birmingham 1994, chapter 9.

641 Subhuti, *Buddhism for Today*, Windhorse Publications, Glasgow 1988, p. 174.

642 See *The Ten Pillars of Buddhism* in this volume, p. 351.

643 See the discussion of the third precept in *The Ten Pillars of Buddhism*, pp. 370ff. in this volume and note 445.

644 *Shabda*, the Order's confidential newsletter, began in 1974. At that time Order members gathered together once a month in London to report in about their lives. These reports formed the basis of the newsletter. As the Order expanded and it was no longer possible to gather together regularly in one place, reports were sent by letter. The newsletter developed and three or four times a year included articles. From 2005 *Shabda* was distributed electronically, although paper copies continue to be sent all over the world to those who prefer them.

645 'With loyalty to my teachers, I accept this ordination' is the first of the four 'lines of acceptance' with which the Triratna public ordination ceremony concludes. The key point here is that 'teachers' is plural, recognizing that although Sangharakshita stands as primary teacher, other Order members will have taught the Dharma and passed on the spirit of the Order to the new Order member.

646 'The Journey to Il Convento' in *The Priceless Jewel*, Windhorse Publications, Glasgow 1993, pp. 53–4 (*Complete Works*, vol. 26). Sangharakshita goes further into the imagery of St Jerome in 'St Jerome Revisited', ibid., pp. 67ff. (*Complete Works*, vol. 26)

647 Subhuti, *Buddhism for Today*, Windhorse Publications, Glasgow 1988, chapter 9. Subhuti's nine Padmaloka lectures on spiritual friendship were not published but circulated informally within the Order and Community. Some of the material is incorporated into: Subhuti with Subhamati, *Buddhism and Friendship*, Windhorse Publications, Birmingham 2004.

648 'The Good Friend' was originally published as an editorial in *Stepping-Stones* (vol. 2 no. 5, September 1951) the Journal of Himalayan Religion, Culture, and Education which Sangharakshita founded soon after his arrival in Kalimpong in 1950. These editorials were later included in *Crossing the Stream*, Windhorse Publications, Birmingham 1996 (*Complete Works*, vol. 7). 'The Good Friend' was written in anticipation of the visit to Kalimpong of a man Sangharakshita regarded as a kindred spirit: Lama Anagarika Govinda. See *Facing Mount Kanchenjunga* in *Complete Works*, vol. 21, p. 248.

649 'Is a Guru Necessary?' in *What is the Sangha?* in *Complete Works*, vol. 3, pp. 545–62.

650 T. W. Rhys Davids and W. Stede, *Pali–English Dictionary*, first Indian edition, Motilal Banarsidass, Delhi 1993, p. 199.

651 In the Hindu tradition a *jñānin* wins liberation through knowledge or wisdom, a *bhakta* through devotion. In the Buddhist tradition a *śraddhānusārin* is a 'faith-follower', a *dharmānusārin* a 'doctrine-follower'. See the discussion of the 'seven holy persons' in *The Three Jewels* in this volume pp. 141ff. The Buddha mentions these seven different kinds of followers (including the faith-follower and the doctrine-follower) at *Kīṭāgiri Sutta*, *Majjhima Nikāya* 70 (i.477). Bhikkhu Ñāṇamoli and Bhikkhu Bodhi (trans.), *The Middle Length Discourses of the Buddha*, Wisdom Publications, Boston 1995, p. 580; or I. B. Horner (trans.), *The Collection of the Middle Length Sayings*, vol. 2, Pali Text Society, Oxford 1994, p. 152. The seven holy persons are also described in Buddhaghosa, *Visuddhimagga* 659–60. See Bhikkhu Ñāṇamoli (trans.), *The Path of Purification*, fifth edition, Buddhist Publication Society, Kandy 1991, pp. 682–3.

652 Although Sangharakshita has not communicated the Dharma through visual images, when he was young he painted a good deal so that 'the feeling became general that I was going to be an artist' (*The Rainbow Road from Tooting Broadway to Kalimpong, Complete Works,* vol. 20, p. 28). In his essay – really a reverie-cum-reminiscence – 'And on his Dulcimer he Played', he recalls the part music played in his life, both as the creator of music and as listener. See *A Moseley Miscellany,* Ibis Publications, Ledbury 2015, pp. 136–43 (*Complete Works,* vol. 26).

653 Some transcribing began as early as 1973, and continued sporadically until a transcriptions unit was set up by Dharmacharis Cittapala and Silabhadra in 1983 with the aim of transcribing and digitizing all Sangharakshita's recorded lectures and seminars. This mammoth task, funded by generous donations, was very largely completed by 2004 through the work of these two and many volunteers, notably Dhivati and Amitaratna. From 2006 freebuddhistaudio.com made all the transcribed seminars available online.

654 The response to this appeal was swift. Already, lectures and extracts from seminars had been published in *Mitrata*, a bimonthly magazine produced by 'Lion's Roar', a team of women Order members and Mitras led by Dharmacharini Srimala. Windhorse Publications had published a number of small books based on talks and some seminars (now collected in *Complete Works*, vol. 11). Now (1990) Jinananda and Vidyadevi began the Spoken Word Project, whose aim was

to publish Sangharakshita's lectures and seminars in edited form. With the help of several other editors, they produced a wide range of books now collected together in the *Complete Works.* These include *Who is the Buddha?*, *What is the Dharma?*, and *What is the Sangha?* (vol. 3); commentaries on Mahayāna *sūtras* (vol. 16); *Wisdom Beyond Words,* a commentary on three Perfection of Wisdom texts (vol. 14); the Abhidharma-based commentary *Know Your Mind*, plus *Living Ethically* and *Living Wisely,* commentaries on Nāgārjuna's *Precious Garland* (vol. 17); *Living with Awareness*, *Living with Kindness*, and other commentaries on Pāli texts (vol. 15); *The Bodhisattva Ideal* and *The Endlessly Fascinating Cry* (vol. 4); *The Purpose and Practice of Buddhist Meditation* (vol. 5); *Tibetan Buddhism* and *Creative Symbols of Tantric Buddhism* (vol. 13). The Milarepa commentaries (vols. 18 and 19) were prepared especially for the *Complete Works.*

655 Sangharakshita's works have been translated into several Indian and at least twelve other languages.

656 Allen Ginsberg (1926–1997), the American poet best known for *Howl* (1956) and *Kaddish* (1961) was a central figure of the 1950s 'beat generation' of poets. He was also a social activist campaigning against militarism and for gay rights. In later life he was drawn to Eastern religion, both to Buddhism (through meeting Tibetan teacher Chögyam Trungpa) and the Hare Krishna movement. He first met Sangharakshita in Kalimpong in June 1962 when he was eager to discuss Tantric initiation. Sangharakshita took him to meet his teacher, Yogi Chen (see 'With Allen Ginsburg in Kalimpong, 1962' in *The Priceless Jewel*, Windhorse Publications, Glasgow 1993, pp. 215–20, and *Complete* Works, vol. 22). Three years later, Ginsberg visited Sangharakshita at the Hampstead Buddhist Vihara. A decade later he visited Sangharakshita at his flat above the London Buddhist Centre. On this occasion he sang a version of William Blake's 'The Tyger' whilst accompanying himself on finger cymbals. (See *Moving Against the Stream,* Windhorse Publications, Birmingham 2003, pp. 106–7, and *Complete Works*, vol. 23.)

657 To mark Sangharakshita's seventieth birthday Windhorse Publications published a beautifully bound hardback volume, *Complete Poems 1941–1994*. Further poems were published in a slim volume called *The Call*

of the Forest, Windhorse Publications, Birmingham 2000, and in *A Moseley Miscellany*, Ibis Publications, Ledbury 2015. For all Sangharakshita's poems see *Complete Works*, vol. 25.

658 *The Enchanted Heart,* Ola Leaves, London 1980, p. v. And, in a slightly updated form, in *Complete Poems 1941–1994*, Windhorse Publications, Birmingham 1995, p. 7 (*Complete Works*, vol. 25).

659 Dharmachari Mokshapriya, a trained film editor, then based in Manchester (where these words of Sangharakshita were uttered in the magnificent portals of the Town Hall) had already made a documentary film of his own ordination retreat (see note 619). He created Clear Vision in the late 1980s which over the next three decades made video recordings of all Sangharakshita's public lectures (as well as those of other Order members). From 1991 to 2003 Clear Vision created a six-monthly newsreel with news and stories from FWBO centres across the world. It also took on the production of educational resources on Buddhism which are widely used in schools in the UK and elsewhere. In 1992 another video maker, Suryaprabha, created Lights in the Sky, and set out to make a record of the early days of the Movement, creating a series of four documentary films.

660 Sangharakshita's mother, born Florence Ketskemety, died on 30 January 1990 at a hospital in Southend-on-Sea. In 'On the Edge of the Etheric' in *Adhisthana Writings, Complete Works*, vol. 26 Sangharakshita recounts how 'I suddenly *knew* that I had to see my mother that very day.' In 'The Young Florence Ketskemety' he tells something of his mother's younger life (also in *Adhisthana Writings*). There is more about his mother in the first chapters of his memoir, *The Rainbow Road from Tooting Broadway to Kalimpong, Complete Works,* vol. 20, and in his 'My First Eight Years' in *A Moseley Miscellany,* Ibis Publications, Ledbury 2015 (*Complete Works,* vol. 26).

661 The preceding sentence was the last sentence I wrote before learning a few hours later of the death of Dhardo Rimpoche (S). Dhardo Rimpoche died on 24 March 1990.

662 Both these men were Neoplatonists. Marsilio Ficino (1433–1499) was a Florentine, a protege of Cosimo de' Medici and, later, tutor to Lorenzo de' Medici. He was the first head of the Florentine Academy (modelled on Plato's Academy), and the first to translate Plato into Latin. He also translated the works of the Neoplatonists. He became

a Catholic priest and is known for his *Theologia Platonica de immortalitate animae* or *Platonic Theology* (1474).

Thomas Taylor (1758–1835) was the first translator into English of the complete works of Plato and Aristotle, as well as the writer of many original works. He published (1792) *A Vindication of the Rights of Brutes* (after Thomas Paine's *Rights of Man*, and Mary Wollstonecraft's *A Vindication of the Rights of Women*).

663 Lumbini, in southern Nepal, is the place where the Buddha-to-be is said to have been born, just as Jesus is believed to have been born at Bethlehem. Dapodi is the district in Pune which gave birth to TBMSG, as Triratna was originally known in India.

664 Sangharakshita undertook the process of handing on his responsibilities to his senior disciples over the course of many years, as he did so taking a step back from involvement with the organization he had founded.

665 The first volume of memoirs had been published by Heinemann – minus the chapters relating to Sangharakshita's childhood – as *The Thousand-Petalled Lotus* in 1976 (see note 474). Windhorse Publications published the full version in 1997 as *The Rainbow Road*. The *Complete Works* edition comes with the title originally envisaged by the author: *The Rainbow Road from Tooting Broadway to Kalimpong* (*Complete Works,* vol. 20). This covers the period 1925 to March 1950. After giving his talk on *My Relation to the Order* in 1990, Sangharakshita wrote four further volumes of memoirs all published by Windhorse Publications: (1) *Facing Mount Kanchenjunga,* covering the period March 1950 to early 1953, first published in 1991 (*Complete Works*, vol. 21), (2) *In the Sign of the Golden Wheel*, covering the period early 1953 to May 1957, first published in 1996 (*Complete Works,* vol. 22), (3) *Precious Teachers*, covering the period spring 1957 to summer 1964, first published in 2007 (also in *Complete Works,* vol. 22), (4) *Moving Against the Stream,* first published in 2003, covering the period August 1964 to April 1969 (*Complete Works,* vol. 23).

EXTENDING THE HAND OF FELLOWSHIP

666 *The History of My Going for Refuge*, in this volume, p. 502.

667 The College of Public Preceptors was founded by Sangharakshita in 1993. It comprised five senior Order members, Sanghadevi, Sona, Srimala, Subhuti, and Suvajra. As the Order and movement grew so did the

College and by 2018 there were more than forty public preceptors worldwide. The most essential responsibility of public preceptors is that of accepting people into the Order. The College also oversees the Triratna ordination process and works closely with others in the Triratna Buddhist Community holding key responsibilities, preserving, sustaining, developing, and communicating Sangharakshita's particular presentation of the Dharma.

668 Subhuti, *Relationships With Other Buddhists*, Padmaloka Books, Norfolk 1991.

669 A reference to the politically ambiguous status of Tibet which in 1951 had been forcibly incorporated into the People's Republic of China.

670 *A Survey of Buddhism*, *Complete Works*, vol. 1.

671 S. Batchelor, 'Creating Sangha' in *Tricycle: The Buddhist Review*, vol. 5, no. 2 (Winter 1995), p. 53.

672 S. Midgeley and P. Sherwell, *The Daily Telegraph*, Monday 15 January 1996, pp. 1–2.

673 K. Dowman, 'Himalayan Intrigue: The Search for the new Karmapa', in *Tricycle: The Buddhist Review*, vol. 2, no. 2 (Winter 1992), pp. 29–34.

674 R. A. Ray, *Buddhist Saints in India: A Study in Buddhist Values and Orientations*, Oxford University Press, Oxford 1994, p. 62.

675 Urgyen Sangharakshita, review of *Buddhist Saints in India*, in the *Times Higher Education Supplement*, 17 February 1995.

676 *The Life of the Buddha* was published in 1972 by the Buddhist Publication Society, Kandy. It is an anthology of extracts from the Pāli canon, arranged as far as possible in chronological order by British-born Bhikkhu Ñāṇamoli (1905–1960). Dr B. R. Ambedkar's *The Buddha and His Dhamma* was also published posthumously in 1957. He composed it, he explains in his Introduction, to answer a number of problems, including why the Buddha left home, the doctrine of karma and rebirth, and the existence of *bhikkhus.* In the course of eight 'books' or chapters Ambedkar covers the Buddha's life from before his Enlightenment ('How a Bodhisatta became the Buddha') and afterwards, and explains his principle teachings and their relevance.

677 Sangharakshita introduced these *sūtras* into the FWBO through seminars and lectures which were recorded, transcribed, and later turned into books. *Wisdom Beyond Words,* Windhorse Publications, Birmingham 1993, includes chapters on the *Heart Sūtra* (*Prajñāpāramitā-hṛdaya*) based on a lecture given in 1967, and the

Diamond Sūtra (*Vajracchedikā Prajñāpāramitā Sūtra*) based on a lecture given in 1969 and a seminar given in Tuscany in 1982 (*Complete Works*, vol. 14). He introduced (1) the *White Lotus Sūtra* (*Saddharma Puṇḍarīka*) in a series of eight lectures given in 1971 under the title 'Parables, Myths and Symbols of Mahāyāna Buddhism in the White Lotus Sūtra'. These form the basis for *The Drama of Cosmic Enlightenment*, published in 1993. (2) The *Inconceivable Emancipation*, published in 1995, is an introduction to the *Vimalakīrti-nirdeśa*, based on eight lectures with the same title given in 1979. (3) 'Transformation of Life and World in the Sūtra of Golden Light', a 1976 lecture series, introduces the *Suvarṇa-prabhāsa Sūtra* and forms the basis for *Transforming Self and World* (1995). These three titles are now published together in *Complete Works*, vol. 16.

678 For the texts of these *sūtras* and a commentary see Ratnaguna and Śraddhāpa, *Great Faith, Great Wisdom*, Windhorse Publications, Cambridge 2016.

679 Although Sangharakshita did not lecture on the Pure Land *sūtras,* there exists a recording of his reading aloud to Order members the *Larger Sukhāvatī-vyūha Sūtra.* The publication of *Great Faith, Great Wisdom* (see previous note), and Ratnaguna leading study retreats on the Pure Land *sūtras*, has led more recently (2018) to a growth of interest in the Pure Land teachings.

680 See *The Essence of Zen*, Windhorse Publications, Glasgow 1985 (*Complete Works*, vol. 13).

681 The *Blue Cliff Record* by Chan Master Yuanwu Keqin (1063–1135) is based on lectures on koan by a Chinese monk Xuedou Zhongxian (980–1052). It was translated into English by T. and J. C. Cleary, and first published by Shambhala Publications in three volumes in 1977. The *Gateless Gate* is a collection of forty-eight koan and commentaries by Chan Master Wumen Huikai (1183–1260), based on teachings given in 1228 at Longxiang monastery. See the translation by Kōun Yamada first published by Center Publications, Los Angeles 1979, and later by Wisdom, Somerville 2004.

682 For the *Sūtra of Wei Lang* see note 476. Hakuin Ekaku (c.1686–c.1769) was a key figure of the Rinzai Zen school of Japan, also an artist and poet. His 'Song of Enlightenment', also called 'Song of Zazen', begins: 'From the beginning all beings are Buddha. / Like water and ice, without water no ice...' Hakuin is one of the four

Japanese 'teachers of the past' on the Triratna Refuge Tree (see note 544).

683 Matsuo Bashō (1644–1694) is one the greatest Japanese poets, famed particularly as a writer of haiku. Ryōkan Taigu (1758–1831) was a Japanese Buddhist monk of the Sōtō Zen school who lived for many years as a hermit, composing poetry and practising calligraphy.

684 Attributed to Baizhang Huaihai (720–814), one of the early masters of the Chinese Chan (Zen) school. See T. Cleary, *The Sayings and Doings of Pai-Chang*, Center Publications, Los Angeles 1978.

685 1. *Bardo Thödol* means something like 'Liberation Through Hearing During the Intermediate State', i.e. the intermediate state after death and before rebirth. The text, regarded as a *terma* or hidden text, was revealed by the *terton* Karma Lingpa (1326–1386). It is known in the West by the title with which it was originally published in 1927 in an English translation by Lama Sumdhon Paul and Lama Lobzang Mingnur Dorje, edited by W. Y. Evans-Wentz: *The Tibetan Book of the Dead*. Sangharakshita gave a talk in 1967 on 'Psycho-Spiritual Symbolism in the Tibetan Book of the Dead' and led a seminar on the same text in September 1979.

2. Milarepa (1052–1135) is one of the great figures of the Tibetan Kagyu school, famed as a yogi and poet. From 1976 to 1980 Sangharakshita led a number of seminars on songs of Milarepa taken from Garma C. C. Chang's *The Hundred Thousand Songs of Milarepa* (1962). See *Milarepa and the Art of Discipleship, Complete Works*, vols. 18 and 19. Sangharakshita first came across a biography of Milarepa in 1945. 'As I read it my hair stood on end and tears came into my eyes.' See *The Rainbow Road from Tooting Broadway to Kalimpong, Complete Works*, vol. 20, p. 151.

3. The eighth-century Padmasambhava is known as the founder of the Samye monastery in Tibet. The story of his life has come down through the medium of myth, and is the subject of *The Life and Liberation of Padmasambhava*, a *terma* whose origin is traditionally ascribed to Padmasambhava's consort, Yeshe Tsogyal. A beautifully produced edition in an English translation by Kenneth Douglas was published by Dharma Publishing in 1978. The figure of Padmasambhava has been a key one for Sangharakshita since his first encounter with the 'Precious Guru' in Darjeeling in 1950 (*Facing Mount Kanchenjunga,*

Complete Works, vol. 21, p. 93. His lecture introducing the figure into the FWBO in 1979 has been described as 'electrifying'. See *Complete Works,* vol. 12. In 1987 he held question-and-answer sessions with a group of *dharmacāriṇīs* on cantos 37 and 38 of *The Life and Liberation of Padmasambhava.*

4. Gampopa (1251–1296) was one of Milarepa's foremost disciples. His *Jewel Ornament of Liberation* is one of the Kagyu Tibetan *lamrim* texts, that is, an exposition of the gradual path to Enlightenment. In the early 1980s, Sangharakshita led at least eight seminars on this text.

5. Geshe Wangyal (1901–1983), a monk of Kalmyk origin, studied in Tibet, worked in China, and accompanied Sir Charles Bell on his travels through Asia. In 1955 he moved to the USA where he established a monastery in New Jersey introducing many Western students to Buddhist teachings. His *Door of Liberation,* subtitled 'Essential Teachings of the Tibetan Buddhist Tradition' was published in 1973. Sangharakshita conducted a seminar on this text for a small group of men and women Order members in July 1975.

686 *The Meaning of Orthodoxy in Buddhism: A Protest,* Windhorse Publications, Glasgow 1987 (*Complete Works*, vol. 7).

687 I. B. Horner, 'Women in Early Buddhism' in *The Middle Way*, vol. 32, no. 1 (May 1957), p. 13.

688 *The Meaning of Orthodoxy in Buddhism,* Windhorse Publications, Glasgow 1987, pp. 15, 20, and 21 (*Complete Works*, vol. 7).

689 Since *bhikkhunī* ordination died out in the Theravāda tradition, women wishing to live as nuns committed themselves to observing the ten precepts (see Appendix, p. 655) of the novice monk or *sāmaṇera*. In Sri Lanka such women are known as *dasasilamata* ('ten precept nuns'). In Thailand they are known as *maechis*, living in monasteries or dedicated communities and observing eight precepts (see Appendix p. 654).

690 See, for example, *A Survey of Buddhism, Complete Works,* vol. 1, pp. 147 and 228; and *Was the Buddha a Bhikkhu?* in this volume, pp. 633ff.

691 Sangharakshita's concern to break through that formalism during the time he lived as a Buddhist monk in India is reflected in two pieces published in the *Maha Bodhi*, 'Wanted: a New Kind of Bhikkhu' and 'Wanted: A New Kind of Upāsaka'. See *Beating the Drum*, Ibis Publications, Ledbury, 2012, pp. 269–76 (*Complete Works*, vol. 8).

692 R. A. Ray, *Buddhist Saints in India,* Oxford University Press, Oxford 1994, chapter 1.

693 The Great Vow of Amitābha occurs in the *Longer Sukhāvatī-vyūha Sūtra*. See Ratnaguna and Śraddhāpa, *Great Faith, Great Wisdom*, Windhorse Publications, Cambridge 2016, p. 259. (There are differences in the numbering of the Chinese and Sanskrit texts; in this translation it is numbered 19.)

694 Abbot Tenshin Anderson, 'Speaking the Unspoken' Talk One, *Shambhala Sun*, (June 1993), p. 31.

695 'Life with a Capital "L": An interview with Philip Kapleau Roshi' in *Tricycle*: *The Buddhist Review*, vol. ii, no. 4 (Summer 1993), pp. 55–6.

696 To the Kālāmas of Kesaputta, the Buddha said:

> Come, Kālāmas, do not go by oral tradition, by lineage of teaching, by hearsay, by a collection of scriptures, by logical reasoning, by inferential reasoning, by reasoned cogitation, by the acceptance of a view after pondering it, by the seeming competence of a speaker, or because you think: 'The ascetic is our guru.' But when, Kālāmas, you know for yourselves: 'These things are unwholesome; these things are blameworthy; these things are censured by the wise; these things, if accepted and undertaken, lead to harm and suffering,' then you should abandon them.

Kālāma Sutta, *Aṅguttara Nikāya* i.188–93 (3.65) in Bhikkhu Bodhi (trans.), *The Numerical Discourses of the Buddha*, Wisdom Publications, Boston 2012, pp. 279–83. See also F. L. Woodward (trans.), *Gradual Sayings*, vol. i, Pali Text Society, Oxford 2000, pp. 170–5.

In the *Tattvasaṅgraha* of Śāntarakṣita, the eighth-century Indian scholar who brought the Sarvāstivādin monastic ordination to Tibet, the Buddha says:

> O Bhikṣus, my words should be accepted by the wise, not out of regard for me, but after due investigation – just as gold is accepted as true only after heating, cutting, and rubbing.

Ganganatha Jha (trans.), *The Tattvasaṅgraha of Śāntarakṣita*, Motilal Banarsidass, Delhi 1986, vol. ii, p. 1558, text 3588.

697 Nyanaponika Thera, *The Threefold Refuge*, Wheel Publication no. 76, Buddhist Publication Society, Kandy 1965. The seminar that Sangharakshita led on this text was recorded, transcribed, edited, and published as *The Threefold Refuge*, Windhorse

Publications, London 1984 (*Complete Works*, vol. 15).

698 See Gajin Nagao (trans.), *The Letters of Rennyo,* Hongwanji International Center, Kyoto 2000. Rennyo (1415–1499) was the eighth head monk of the Honganji temple in Kyoto established in 1321 on the site where, in 1263, Shinran, founder of Jōdo Shinshū, was buried. Through his work to clarify and articulate Shinran's teachings, Rennyo largely united the disparate Jōdo Shinshū sects so that it became one of the dominant Buddhist schools in Japan. His letters were collected and became the basis for study and recital in Jōdo Shinshū liturgy.

699 Abbot Tenshin Anderson, 'Speaking the Unspoken' Talk One, *Shambhala Sun* (June 1993), p. 31.

700 Thrangu Rinpoche, *King of Samadhi: Commentaries on The Samadhi Raja Sutra & The Song of Lodrö Thaye*, Rangjung Yeshe Publications, Boudhnath & Arhus, Hong Kong 1994, p. 39.

701 See *What is the Sangha?*, especially parts 1 and 2, in *Complete Works*, vol. 3.

702 The European Buddhist Union was founded in 1975. It is 'the umbrella association of national Buddhist unions and Buddhist organizations in Europe' with now (2018) nearly fifty member organizations from sixteen countries. Its mission statement is 'to facilitate international exchange and promote spiritual friendship amongst European Buddhists, to support social action and ideas motivated by Buddhist values, and to amplify the voice of Buddhism in Europe and worldwide.'

The World Fellowship of Buddhists was initiated by G. P. Malalasekara, and founded in 1950 with representatives of twenty-seven nations. Its headquarters are in Thailand but it has regional centres in thirty-five countries and members from all contemporary Buddhist schools.

703 'Dr Ambedkar's True Greatness: Buddhism Versus the Secular Philosophies of the Modern Age'. A lecture given in Bombay, 22 December 1983, recorded, transcribed, edited, and published by Triratna Grantha Mala, Pune as *Dhammamegha* no. 23 (*Complete Works*, vol. 10).

704 (1) The title 'Dalai Lama' comes from (a) *dalaiyin,* the Mongolian word for 'big' or 'ocean' and (b) the Tibetan 'lama' meaning master or guru. The title was first conferred on Sonam Gyatso (1543–1588) of the Gelug school of Tibet by the Mongolian leader Altan Khan (1507–1582) who, partly through his contact with Sonam Gyatso, adopted Buddhism as the Mongolian state religion.

The Dalai Lamas came to be seen as embodiments of the bodhisattva Avalokiteśvara. Sonam Gyatso was in retrospect designated third Dalai Lama. The 'great fifth' Dalai Lama, Ngawang Lobsang Gyatso (1617–1682), was the first Dalai Lama to have both spiritual and temporal power over all Tibet. The current and fourteenth Dalai Lama, Tenzin Gyatso (b. 1935), assumed his temporal (i.e. political) duties as head of state in 1950. Since the 1959 Tibetan uprising against the Chinese invasion of Tibet he has lived in exile in India.

(2) 'Panchen' comes from the Sanskrit *paṇḍita,* (from the Indian Buddhist tradition, a title awarded to scholars who had mastered the 'five sciences'), and the Tibetan *chen* meaning 'great'. The first Panchen Lama was tutor to the 'great fifth' Dalai Lama. He was given the title 'Panchen' by Altan Khan and the Dalai Lama in 1645. The Panchen Lamas came to be considered embodiments of the Buddha Amitābha. He is the head of the Tashilhunpo Monastery and hence sometimes referred to as the 'Tashi Lama'. He is strongly connected with the Dalai Lama being involved in the 'recognition' of a new *tulku*. The identity of the current Panchen Lama is disputed, the Tibetan government-in-exile and the Chinese government each having recognized a different man as holding the title.

(3) The Karmapa is the head of the Karma Kagyu, the largest sub-school of the Kagyu school of Tibetan Buddhism. The first Karmapa was Düsum Khyenpa (1110–1193), a disciple of Gampopa. The identity of the current, seventeenth Karmapa is disputed, two men having been enthroned as Karmapa, one in 1992, another in 1994.

705 The title 'Sangharaja' may be applied simply to the most senior monk in a monastery or locality; but in a number of Far East Asian countries the Sangharaja is appointed by the King, as for example in Thailand since 1782, and acts in association with the civil government in relation to the national monastic sangha. The title 'Nayaka Maha Thera' is associated primarily with Sri Lankan Theravāda tradition and is given to senior *bhikkhus* who head one of the *nikāyas,* or 'monastic fraternities'.

706 This talk was given in 1996. Sangharakshita had handed on some years previously his presidencies of FWBO centres, and, more recently, responsibility for the training and conferring of ordinations. (See *My Relation to the Order* in this volume, pp. 510–11. In a talk to the Order at its annual convention in 1999

he announced his intention of handing on the headship of the Order which he did formally the following year during his seventy-fifth birthday celebrations. He handed on the headship of the Order jointly to the five *dharmacārīs* and three *dharmacāriṇīs* who then made up the College of Public Preceptors. See Sangharakshita and Subhuti, 'Handing On' in *Madhyamavani*, issue 4, spring 2001, Madhyamaloka, Birmingham. However, in 2003, after many meetings, the College came to the conclusion that they would not use the term 'head of the Order' and an announcement to this effect was made in *Shabda*, the Order newsletter, in January 2004.

FORTY-THREE YEARS AGO

707 *Facing Mount Kanchenjunga*, *Complete Works*, vol. 21, p. 109. See also reflections on his *bhikkhu* ordination in section 6 of *The History of My Going for Refuge*, in this volume, p. 420.

708 The early years of Sangharakshita's life are related in his memoir *The Rainbow Road from Tooting Broadway to Kalimpong*, *Complete Works*, vol. 20. The organization he founded was the Young Men's Buddhist Association (Kalimpong).

709 How Sangharakshita came to be in Kalimpong is related in the final chapter of ibid., pp. 467ff.

710 Sangharakshita received his *upasampadā* or full ordination into the Theravādin monastic order in October 1950 (see *Facing Mount Kanchenjunga*, *Complete Works*, vol. 21, pp. 107–8). As a *bhikkhu* he undertook to follow the *pāṭimokkha* or rules of training laid out in the Vinaya Piṭaka. See the discussion in *The Ten Pillars of Buddhism* in this volume, pp. 342ff.

711 They must also be guiltless of any [minor] breach of the rules of training, but if necessary can purify themselves of such breaches, by confession, immediately before the ceremony. (S) For more on the four *pārājikas* or 'defeats': See note 256.

The rules for valid ordination in the Middle Country can be found at Vinaya Piṭaka i.319 (*Mahāvagga* 9.4). See I. B. Horner (trans.), *The Book of the Discipline*, part 4, Pali Text Society, Oxford 1996, p. 458.

712 Related in *In the Sign of the Golden Wheel*, Windhorse Publications, Birmingham 1996, pp. 313–16 (*Complete Works*, vol. 22).

713 The two Burmese *bhikkhus* were U Kawinda Sayadaw who acted as preceptor (U Chandramani, who had acted as preceptor at Sangharakshita's *sāmaṇera*

ordination, was unable to come due to illness) and Yetanapon U Zagaya, General Secretary of the Mahasanghas of Burma. For further details about these and others present at the ordination, see *Facing Mount Kanchenjunga*, in *Complete Works*, vol. 21, pp. 107–8.

714 See note 707.

715 See *The History of My Going for Refuge*, section 3, in this volume pp. 410ff. and *The Rainbow Road from Tooting Broadway to Kalimpong*, *Complete Works*, vol. 20, pp. 102–3.

716 See *The History of My Going for Refuge*, section 4, in this volume pp. 412ff. and *The Rainbow Road from Tooting Broadway to Kalimpong*, ibid., pp. 223–6.

717 These were the 'four criteria' for becoming a Mitra at this time. See Subhuti, *Buddhism for Today*, Windhorse Publications, Glasgow 1988, p. 137. The Mitra system was subsequently changed and currently (2018) Mitras are asked to make 'three declarations'. See note 384.

718 See *The History of My Going for Refuge*, section 5, in this volume pp. 417ff. and *The Rainbow Road from Tooting Broadway to Kalimpong*, *Complete Works*, vol. 20, pp. 408–11.

719 The teaching tour in Nepal that immediately followed his *sāmaṇera* ordination is related in *The Rainbow Road*, ibid., chapter 47. His obedience to Jagdish Kashyap's behest to 'stay here and work for the good of Buddhism' is the main topic of the next four volumes of memoirs which cover the years 1950–1964, during which Kalimpong was his headquarters.

720 See *The History of My Going for Refuge*, section 13, in this volume pp. 454ff. and *Precious Teachers*, Windhorse Publications, Birmingham 2007, pp. 151–4 (*Complete Works*, vol. 22).

721 See Subhuti, *Sangharakshita: A New Voice in the Buddhist Tradition*, Windhorse Publications, Birmingham 1994, pp. 39–44.

722 According to the Hīnayāna too, strictly speaking. For the Hīnayāna, however, the arising of the *bodhicitta* is a very rare phenomenon, and the bodhisattva a very exceptional kind of being, whereas for the Mahāyāna the bodhisattva ideal is, or can be, the spiritual ideal for all (Mahāyāna) Buddhists, who are, to that extent, (novice) bodhisattvas. (S)

723 See *Going for Refuge* in this volume, pp. 300–1.

724 At the time of his novice ordination he was given the name 'Sangharakkhita' (i.e. the Pāli form). However, from the beginning others called him Sangharakshita, the Sanskrit equivalent, which accorded more with pronunciation

in modern Indian languages. He therefore decided to use the name Sangharakshita when, for example, he published.

725 See *A Survey of Buddhism, Complete Works,* vol. 1, chapter 2, section 4, pp. 227–8.

726 M. Carrithers, *The Forest Monks of Sri Lanka*, Oxford University Press, Delhi 1983, pp. 147–54. The story is of one Ratanapāla. His eventual success in obtaining the necessary purification is to him 'a miraculous moment, like the dawn of my monk's life'.

727 Ibid., pp. 104–8.

728 The five mundane *abhiññās* are: (1) psychic powers such as walking on water and through walls (*iddhi-vidhā*); (2) divine ear or clairaudience (*dibba-sota*); (3) telepathic knowledge of the minds of others (*paracittañāṇa*); (4) the ability to remember one's past lives (*pubbe-nivāsanusati);* (5) divine eye or knowing the karmic destination of others (*dibba-cakkhu*). A sixth, transcendental *abhiññā* is often listed: the knowledge of the extinction of the *āsavas or* mental intoxicants (*āsavakkhaya-ñāṇa*). See *Sāmaññaphala Sutta, Dīgha Nikāya* 2 (i.78–83). M. Walshe (trans.), *The Long Discourses of the Buddha*, Wisdom Publications, Boston 1995, pp. 105–7; or T. W. Rhys Davids (trans.), *Dialogues of the Buddha*, part 1, Pali Text Society, London 1973, pp. 88–92.

729 M. Carrithers, *The Forest Monks of Sri Lanka*, Oxford University Press, Delhi 1983, p. 80.

730 *Dhammapada*, 142. See for example, *Dhammapada*, Sangharakshita (trans.), Windhorse Publications, Birmingham 2001, p. 54. (*Complete Works*, vol. 15.)

731 See Ṭhānissaro Bhikkhu, *The Buddhist Monastic Code: the Pāṭimokkha Training Rules Translated and Explained,* Metta Forest Monastery, California 1994, pp. 43–4.

732 Both quotations from M. Carrithers, *The Forest Monks of Sri Lanka*, Oxford University Press, Delhi 1983, p. 281.

733 *Mahāparinibbāna Sutta, Dīgha Nikāya* 16 (ii.100). See M. Walshe (trans.), *The Long Discourses of the Buddha*, Wisdom Publications, Boston 1995, pp. 245; or T. W. and C. A. F. Rhys Davids (trans.), *Dialogues of the Buddha*, part 2, Pali Text Society, London 1971, p. 108.

Sangharakshita added the following note: 'The Buddha also exhorts us to make the Dhamma our island and refuge, seeking refuge in the Dhamma and in none other. There is no contradiction. Abiding islands unto ourselves *is* making the Dhamma our refuge, the Dhamma being in principle the "cosmic" law that makes such abiding possible'. (S) This may refer to the *Attadīpā Sutta* of the *Khandhasaṃyutta*, *Saṃyutta Nikāya* iii.42. See Bhikkhu Bodhi (trans.), *Connected Discourses of the Buddha*, Wisdom Publications, Boston 2000, pp. 882–3; or F. L. Woodward (trans.), *The Book of the Kindred Sayings*, part 3, Pali Text Society, London 1975, p. 37, where the Dharma is translated as 'the Norm'.

734 Vinaya Piṭaka i.94–5 (*Mahāvagga* 1.76). See I. B. Horner (trans.), *The Book of the Discipline*, part 4, Pali Text Society, Oxford 1996, pp. 120–3.

735 Recent years have seen the occasional inter-*nikāya bhikkhu* ordination in Sri Lanka and India. My own *bhikkhu* ordination was, of course, an inter-*nikāya* one. (S)

736 See *The Ten Pillars of Buddhism*, in this volume.

737 For the five and the eight precepts traditionally followed by laypeople see Appendix, pp. 653 and 654.

738 See, *Ambedkar and Buddhism*, *Complete Works*, vol. 9, pp. 128–33. For the twenty-two *pratijñās* (vows) see Appendix, p. 656.

739 See Sangharakshita, *The History of My Going for Refuge*, in this volume, chapters 16 and 20.

740 See Marco Pallis, *Peaks and Lamas*, third edition (revised and enlarged), Woburn Press, London 1974, pp. 299 et seq.

741 See note 689.

742 But see note 584.

743 This reference is to the eight *garudhammas* (whose authenticity are often disputed) in which, on creating the order of *bhikkhunīs*, the Buddha laid down certain rules which made them subservient to the *bhikkhus*. See Vinaya Piṭaka ii.254 (*Cullavagga* 10.1). See I. B. Horner (trans.), *The Book of the Discipline*, part 5, Pali Text Society, London 1975, pp. 354–5.

744 S. Butler, 'Hudibras', a satirical poem in three parts composed during the English Civil War, published after the Restoration of Charles II in 1660.

745 For a distinction between chastity and celibacy see note 444.

746 See *The Ten Pillars of Buddhism*, in this volume, pp. 370ff.

747 This was Sangharakshita's own experience. After two years of living as an ascetic and *not* handling money he realized that to 'work for the good of Buddhism' in Kalimpong he would have to change this practice.

> The whole business of going into a shop, asking for what one wanted, and then handing over in exchange certain bits of paper and metal, seemed extraordinarily clumsy,

artificial, and unnatural, even slightly absurd, and it was several weeks before I became accustomed to it all.

Facing Mount Kanchenjunga, Complete Works, vol. 21, p. 42.

748 *Dhammapada* 200. The *ābhassara devas* are a class of Brahmās rendered here as 'gods of sonant light' and elsewhere as gods of radiant, brilliant, or shining light. See for example *Dhammapada*, Sangharakshita (trans.), Windhorse Publications, Birmingham 2001, p. 72 (*Complete Works,* vol. 15).

749 See Appendix, p. 655.

750 Attributed to Baizhang Huaihai (720–814), one of the early masters of the Chinese Chan (Zen) school. See T. Cleary, *Sayings and Doings of Pai-Chang,* Center Publications, Los Angeles 1978.

751 Sangharkashita here lists the first seven of the ten precepts which, in *The Ten Pillars of Buddhism,* section 6, he shows to be a *mūla-prātimokṣa* or fundamental code of ethics to be practised by all Buddhists whether their lifestyle be monastic or 'lay'. See this volume pp. 344ff.

752 This famous work by English painter J. M. W. Turner (1775–1851) was first exhibited in 1840. When *Forty-Three Years Ago* was first published in 1993, the cover designer, Dhammarati, used a detail from this painting, as well as a detail from a photograph of Sangharakshita taken after his *bhikkhu* ordination.

753 Sangharakshita's first visit to Italy was in 1966 with his friend Terry Delamare and included two days in Venice. See *Moving Against the Stream,* Windhorse Publications, Birmingham 2003, pp. 224–5 (*Complete* Works, vol. 23). He visited Venice again in 1983 with Prasannasiddhi when he had a notable experience in the Basilica di Santa Maria Gloriosa dei Frari, see *Through Buddhist Eyes,* Windhorse Publications, Birmingham 2000, p. 8 (*Complete* Works, vol. 24).

754 P. Fuller, *Theoria*, Chatto & Windus, London 1988, p. 82. W. Holman Hunt (1827–1910), one of the founding artists of the Pre-Raphaelite Brotherhood, spent time in Palestine in the mid-1850s when he made a number of paintings. He went out to paint in the desert to recreate the atmosphere of the Scapegoat. There are two versions of this painting, the smaller version with the rainbow in the Manchester City Art Gallery, the other in the Lady Lever Gallery, Port Sunlight, near Liverpool.

755 'The Scapegoat, after Holman Hunt' in *Complete Poems 1941–1994*, Windhorse Publications, Birmingham 1995, p. 321. The earlier

poem, called simply 'Scapegoat' begins,

How did it feel
To be left alone in the desert
Loaded down with the sins
Of a whole people?

Ibid., pp. 287–8 (*Complete Works*, vol. 25).

756 The scapegoat sent out into the wilderness bearing the sins of the people originated in the Jewish tradition and is referred to in Leviticus 16.22: 'the goat shall bear upon him all their iniquities unto a land not inhabited: and he shall let go the goat in the wilderness.'

757 J. Hillman, *Loose Ends: Primary Papers on Archetypal Psychology,* Spring Publications, New York and Zurich 1975, p. 67.

758 J. Hillman, Ibid., p. 75.

759 These are the 'Five Pillars of the FWBO' introduced in a talk given in 1991 (*Complete Works,* vol. 12). They should not be confused with the 'Ten Pillars of Buddhism' which are the ten ethical precepts.

760 Boris Johnson, 'Faithful urged to lead Euro crusade,' *Sunday Telegraph*, 28 February 1993.

761 Ibid.

762 The European Economic Community (EEC, more popularly known as the Common Market) was founded by the Treaty of Rome in 1957 with six founding countries. The United Kingdom first applied to join in 1961 but was vetoed. It finally joined in 1973. The European Union (EU) was created in November 1993 (half a year after this talk was given), incorporating the EEC, its purpose similarly to promote European political and economic union. By 2007 there were 28 member states. In a referendum held in June 2016, a majority of the voting public of the United Kingdom voted in favour of leaving the EU.

WAS THE BUDDHA A BHIKKHU?

763 The Forest Hermitage is a branch of Wat Nong Pah Pong in Thailand and has been developed after the tradition of the forest monasteries of North East Thailand. Ajahn Khemadhammo (b.1944) is British-born. He trained and worked as an actor, but went on to receive *bhikkhu* ordination in the Theravāda tradition in Thailand in 1972. For many years he worked to develop Angulimala, the Buddhist Prison Chaplaincy Service, for which he was awarded an OBE in 2003.

764 Bhikkhu Brahmavamso is today better known as Phra Ajahn Brahm. He was born in 1951 in London and ordained into the Thai Theravāda tradition at the age of twenty-three, going on to study with Ajahn Chah, who sent him to Australia to assist Ajahn Jagaro. The two founded the

Bodhinyana Monastery in 1983, a monastery after the Thai Forest Monks tradition. Today (2018) Ajahn Brahm is its spiritual director.

765 Despite my attempts to obtain a copy of the three-page original article by Bhikkhu Brahmavamso, or even the Forest Hermitage *Newsletter*, April 1994, in which the edited version of his article was published, I was not successful. Sangharakshita quotes from the original.

766 The Order Office was at this time (1994) located at Padmaloka, a Triratna men's retreat centre in Norfolk, and formerly Sangharakshita's residence.

767 The complete Vinaya Piṭaka was translated from the Pāli by I. B. Horner and published in six parts as *The Book of the Discipline* by the Pali Text Society from 1949 to 1966.

768 *Commentaries on the Laws of England* is a treatise on England's Common Law by the jurist, judge and Tory politician, Sir William Blackstone, originally published by the Clarendon Press, Oxford 1765–1769.

769 *Forty-Three Years Ago*, in this volume, pp. 592ff.

770 The number of monks that should be present at a 'formal act' is set out in Vinaya Piṭaka i.319 (*Mahāvagga,* 9.3). See I. B. Horner (trans.), *The Book of the Discipline*, part 4, Pali Text Society, Oxford 1996, pp. 457–8.

771 *Forty-Three Years Ago,* in this volume, p. 582.

772 Vinaya Piṭaka i.320 (*Mahāvagga* 9.4) in I. B. Horner (trans.), *The Book of the Discipline*, part 4, Pali Text Society, Oxford 1996, pp. 458–9.

773 *Dhammapada* 360–82. Buddhadatta Mahathera (trans.), *Dhammapadam: An Anthology of the Sayings of the Buddha*, Colombo (n.d.), pp. 96–102. For an alternative translation see Sangharakshita (trans.), *Dhammapada,* Windhorse Publications, Birmingham 2001, pp. 120–5. (*Complete Works*, vol. 15.)

774 *Dhammapada* 375. See, for example, Sangharakshita (trans.), *Dhammapada,* Windhorse Publications, Birmingham 2001, p. 124.

775 Caroline Augusta Foley Rhys Davids (née Foley) (1857–1942), studied psychology, philosophy, and economics. Her interest in Indian philosophy brought her into contact with Buddhist scholar and founder of the Pali Text Society, T. W. Rhys Davids, whom she married. She went on to hold lectureships in Indian philosophy and Buddhist studies in Manchester and London. She was Honorary Secretary and then President of the Pali Text Society from 1923 until her death. She was one of the first

to translate the Abhidhamma into English (published as *A Buddhist Manual of Psychological Ethics* in 1909) and the *Therīgāthā*, the songs of Buddhist nuns, published in 1909. She went on to complete many other Pāli translations, as well as publishing books and commentaries on Buddhist themes.

Govind Chandra Pande (1923–2011) was an Indian scholar in Hindu and Buddhist studies. He served as professor of ancient history and vice-chancellor at Jaipur and Allahabad universities. His *Studies in the Origins of Buddhism* was first published in 1957 and is currently (2018) in its third edition.

776 J. C. Eichhorn (1752–1827), a German theologist and Professor at Jena University. His *Introduction to the Old Testament* (*Einleitung in das Alte Testament,* in five volumes, Leipzig 1780–1783) was a foundation for the critical study of the Old Testament. It was followed twenty years later by a similar study of the New Testament.

D. F. Strauss (1808–1874), another German protestant theologian, published in 1835–6 *Das Leben Jesu, kritisch bearbeitet* (*The Life of Jesus, Critically Examined*) in which he attempted to give an historical portrayal of Jesus whose divine nature he denied. The book was translated into English by Marian Evans (more familiar under the pseudonym she adopted later, George Eliot) and published in 1846.

J. E. Renan (1823–1892) was a French scholar and historian, who became well known for his *Vie de Jésus*, 1863 (published in English, the same year, as *Life of Jesus*), in which he tried to show the historical Jesus as Man, and also Jesus as Christian purified of Jewishness.

A. Schweitzer (1875–1965) was a Lutheran doctor, musician, and writer, awarded the Nobel Peace Prize for his 'reverence for life' and humanitarian work in Africa. His *Geschichte der Leben-Jesu-Forschung* (published in English in 1910 as *The Quest for the Historical Jesus*) was a comprehensive review and critique of the previous findings of the Higher Criticism as applied to the New Testament and the life of Jesus.

777 See this volume p. 604.

778 The rules on the formal act of suspension of a monk are given in Vinaya Piṭaka ii.21–8 (*Culavagga* 1.25–35). See I. B. Horner (trans.), *The Book of the Discipline*, part 5, Pali Text Society, London 1975, pp. 31–40.

779 Buddhaghosa writes of the 'One-Sessioner's Practice' that an eating session counts as one meal so long as the diner has not got up from his seat. *Visuddhimagga* 71 (2.44); see

Bhikkhu Ñāṇamoli (trans.), *The Path of Purification,* Buddhist Publication Society, Kandy 1991, pp. 69–70.

780 *Forty-Three Years Ago,* in this volume, pp. 603ff.

781 S. W. R. D. Bandaranaike, Prime Minister of Ceylon 1956–1959, was shot by *bhikkhu* Somarama Thero who hid a revolver beneath his *bhikkhu* robes.

782 *Forty-Three Years* Ago, in this volume, pp. 589ff.

783 Readers of *Facing Mount Kanchenjunga* may recall that at my *bhikkhu* ordination in India in 1950 there was present a Ladakhi 'incarnate lama', Kusho Bakula. As he belonged to a non-Theravāda line of monastic ordination he sat outside the *sīmā*. According to Brahmavamso, he could have sat inside the *sīmā* and even acted as my preceptor. (S) See *Complete Works,* vol. 21, p. 107.

784

> Whatever monk should indulge in sexual intercourse is one who is defeated, he is no longer in communion.

Vinaya Piṭaka, *Suttavibhanga* 1.5. See I. B. Horner (trans.), *The Book of the Discipline*, part 1, Pali Text Society, Oxford 1996, p. 38.

785 Nicholas Gervaise (1662–1729) was a Roman Catholic cleric, who, in the course of his duties, spent time in Siam, the Caribbean and Latin America. He was made bishop by Pope Benedict XIII. His *Histoire naturelle et politique du Royaume de Siam* is in print even today (2018).

786 *Forty-Three Years* Ago, in this volume, p. 593.

787 Tr'ân Lệ Xuân (1924–2011) known as Mme Nhu acted as South Vietnam's First Lady during the premiership of her bachelor brother-in-law, President Diệm. Her husband, Ngô Đình Nhu, was his chief advisor. She became a Roman Catholic on her marriage. The brothers were assassinated in 1963 after which she lived in exile. Her infamous remark occurred when Buddhist monk Thích Quảng Đức publicly immolated himself in June 1963 to draw attention to the plight of Vietnamese Buddhists under Roman Catholic rule.

788 S. Freud (1856–1939) was the Austrian founder of psychoanalysis. In *Zur Psychopathologie des Alltagslebens* (*The Psychopathology of Everyday Life*) published 1901, and *Der Witz und seine Beziehung zum Unbewußten* (*Jokes and their Relation to the Unconscious*), 1905, his psychological theories that were based on his clinical work were applied to everyday life.

789 Plato, *The Republic*, Book 7. Plato's allegory is to show the effect of education on human nature. Through the literary device of a dialogue between

Glaucon and Socrates, he evokes a scene in which a group of people are chained inside a cave, facing a blank wall. They can only see shadows projected onto the wall from objects passing in front of a fire behind them. The prisoners believe the shadows are real. A philosopher is like a prisoner freed from the cave who comes to see that the shadows are not reality.

790 *Forty-Three Years* Ago, in this volume, p. 591.

791 J. A. M. Whistler (1834–1903), the American artist, known for his credo, 'art for art's sake'; and Oscar Wilde (1854–1900), the Irish playwright and poet. According to some sources Wilde said on one occasion, 'I wish I had said that' to which Whistler retorted, with reference to Wilde's habit of taking up Whistler's own views on art and so on, 'You will, Oscar, you will.'

792 Lord Byron, 'Childe Harold's Pilgrimage' (1812–1818), canto 179.

793 (1) The image of the Burning Bush occurs in Exodus 3. Moses hears God speaking from a bush that burns but which is not consumed by the fire, promising to lead the captive Israelites out of Egypt.

(2) The idea of a Last Judgement in which it is decided whether any soul shall dwell for ever with God in heaven or is destined for eternal damnation has for Christians biblical provenance. It is referred to in both the Old Testament and in the Gospels of Matthew and Luke, as well as Revelation 20:11–12. One of its most famous depictions is the fresco by Michelangelo covering one wall of the Sistine Chapel in Rome.

(3) Arjuna's Vision of the Universal Form is granted to him by Lord Krishna. See chapter 11 of the *Bhagavad Gītā*: 'Arjuna could see in the universal form of the Lord the unlimited expansions of the universe situated in one place although divided into many, many thousands.'

(4) The Prophet's Night Journey or '*Isra* and *Mi'raj*' is told first in the Koran, sura 17, in which Allah 'did take His servant for a Journey by night from the Sacred Mosque to the farthest Mosque'. The *Mi'raj* (literally 'ladder') refers to the account in the *Hadith* in which the Prophet is then taken by the angel Jibra'il (Gabriel) on a journey through the seven stages of heaven where he meets various prophets before finally meeting Allah. The Night Journey is commemorated annually all over the Muslim world.

794 G. F. Handel (1685–1759), the German-born composer who spent most of his adult life in London. The fifty-three movements of his oratorio *The Messiah* were composed in just over three weeks in 1741.

The words were taken from the Bible. Part 1 concerns the prophesy to redeem mankind by sending a Messiah. Part 2 is concerned with redemption through the Messiah's sacrifice; and with the power of God the Almighty that cannot be opposed.

Dante Alighieri (1265–1321), the Italian poet, originally called his great work simply *Commedia.* (It was Boccaccio who added 'Divina'.) A long, narrative poem in three parts, the *Divine Comedy* tells of a journey through Hell, (*Inferno*), Purgatory (*Purgatorio*), and Heaven (*Paradiso*) to the throne of God. It was completed in 1320.

795 A reference to Friedrich Nietzsche's writing on inspiration in *Ecce Homo* (1888) (paragraph 3 in the chapter, 'Thus Spake Zarathustra').

796 C. Kabilsingh, *Thai Women in Buddhism*, Parallax, Berkeley 1991, p. 83.

797 See note 258.

798 'Bhikkhus, I am a brahmin...' *Itivuttaka* 100. See John D. Ireland (trans.), *The Udāna and the Itivuttaka*, Buddhist Publication Society, Kandy 1997, p. 226.

799 *Mahāparinibbāna Sutta, Dīgha Nikāya* 16 (ii.109–10). See M. Walshe (trans.), *The Long Discourses of the Buddha*, Wisdom Publications, Boston 1995, pp. 248–9; or T. W. and C. A. F. Rhys Davids (trans.), *Dialogues of the Buddha*, part 2, Pali Text Society, London 1971, p. 117.

800 S. Dutt, *Early Buddhist Monachism* and *The Buddha and Five After Centuries,* were published by Luzac, London 1957, the second being the first critical buddhalogical study to appear. *Buddhist Monks and Monasteries of India* was published by Motilal Banarsidass, Delhi 1962.

801 See the *Kālāma Sutta, Aṅguttara Nikāya* i.188–93 (3.65). F. L. Woodward (trans.), *Gradual Sayings*, vol. i, Pali Text Society, Oxford 2000, pp. 170–5; or Bhikkhu Bodhi (trans.), *The Numerical Discourses of the Buddha*, Wisdom Publications, Boston 2012, pp. 279–83.

INDEX

Abhayarājakumāra Sutta 699n
Abhidharma (Pāli Abhidhamma) (Piṭaka) 150, 197, 203, 552, 672n, 755n
  beginnings of 328
  tradition 62, 67, 99
  worship of 225
Abhidharmakośa-bhāṣya 672n, 675n, 682n, 709n
Abhidharmakośa-vyākhyā 143
Abhidharmasamuccaya 676n
abhijñās (Pāli *abhiññās*) 15, 111, 589, 750n
abhimukhī 16, 170
Abhiniṣkramaṇa Sūtra 13
Abhisamayālaṃkāra 684n, 167
abhiṣeka 169, 442, 564–5; *see also* Tantric initiation
  compared with ordination (Sanskrit *saṃvara*) 447
  of Sangharakshita 442–3, 445, 692n
abortion 363
absolute
  ālaya 280–2, 464
  bodhicitta, *see bodhicitta*, absolute
  consciousness 96, 277
  Going for Refuge 482
  person 127–8
  reality, *see* reality, absolute, the Unconditioned
ācāryas (Pāli *ācariyas*) 81, 196–7, 421
Adhisthana xix, 704n, 732n, 797, 801
Āditta-pariyāya Sutta 24
Advaita Vedanta 715n
'Advice to a Young Poet' 424
Āgamas 69, 326
Aggañña Sutta 692n
Aggivacchagotta Sutta 44, 669n, 699n, 711n
Aggivessana 110–11, 662n
Ajanta 74, 212
Ajātaśatru 27–8, 200
Ajita 178
Ajñāta Kauṇḍinya 23
Ākāśagarbha 172, 181
Akashavana 735n
Akṣayamati 176
Akṣobhya xvi, 42, 172–3, 281
Alagaddūpama Sutta 671n
ālaya-vijñāna 43, 99, 279–82
alchemist 527
Allen, G. F. 188
alms 187, 189, 191, 421
  and householders 202, 204, 226, 451
  Sangharakshita and 693n
Aloka, Dharmachari 515, 735n
altruism 159, 208, 300, 553
  and individualism 463
altruistic dimension, of Going for Refuge 300, 431–3, 448, 452, 456, 465, 471, 474–5, 478, 483, 500, 516, 586
  and Gampopa 442
Amarapura nikāya 595
Ambalaṭṭhikārāhulovāda Sutta 666n

Ambedkar, B. R. 437–8, 490, 494–7, 551, 553, 794–5
The Buddha and His Dhamma 741n
and conversation ceremony 597–8, 717n
FWBO and 502
and Gypsy/Roma community 732n
Sangharakshita and 437–8, 494, 500, 720n, 729n, 730n, 746n
Ambedkar and Buddhism 437, 494–5, 497, 502, 534, 720n, 730n
amber, pillar of 380, 395
Amitābha 42, 163, 172–3, 177, 280, 566–7, 722n
and Panchen Lamas 747n
and Pure Land Buddhism 553–4, 562
vow of 562, 745n
Amitāyur-dhyāna Sūtra 125, 175, 180, 553, 669n, 678n
Amitāyus 42, 58, 404, 553, 669n
Amoghasiddhi 42, 172, 280
Anagarika Dharmapala 715n, 717n, 724n, 794
anagārikas 305, 469, 561, 604, 608–9, 643, 702n, 708n, 725n
Ānanda (historical) 26, 28, 29–30, 223, 647, 665n, 696n, 712n
and ordination of women 27
Ananda, Dharmachari 404, 712n
Ananda Maitreya 230
Anāthapiṇḍada (Pāli *Anāthapiṇḍika*) 25, 189, 204, 207, 664n, 687n
anātman (Pāli *anattā*), doctrine 15, 60–9, 144, 264, 661n
Anderson, Tenshin 563, 567, 746n
androgyny, spiritual 371–2, 517
angels 371, 372
Aṅgulimāla xvi, 238
Aṅgulimāla Sutta 694n
Aṅguttara Nikāya 35–6, 130, 203, 294, 330–1, 340, 347, 383, 391, 653, 662n, 666n, 668n, 677n, 679n, 689n, 691n, 693n, 695n, 699n, 700n, 705n, 707n, 708n, 711n, 722n, 726n, 745n, 758n
and the ten precepts 329–32, 705n
animitta 121
anitya (Pāli *aniccā*) 80, 82, 87–9, 144; *see also* impermanence
annihilationism 146; *see also* nihilism
antarābhava 76, 217
Anuruddha 114
apraṇihita (Pāli *appaṇihita*) 121–2
Ārāḍa Kāḷāma 20–1
Arapacana 174
archetypes 526, 556, 721n
arhants (Pāli *arahants*) 139–40, 141, 149–50, 155, 296
and *bodhicitta* 168
and bodhisattvas 154–5, 166, 168
first 23
sixteen 316, 702n
sixty-one 664n
wisdom-liberated and doubly-liberated 145
arhantship 145, 151, 160, 166, 204, 209–10, 716n
and the bodhisattva 160
and monasticism 204
Ariyapariyesanā Sutta 111, 662n, 663n, 667n, 677n, 715n, 716n
Arjuna 644, 757n
art
Buddhist 37, 68, 117, 176, 179, 316, 556, 702n
Chinese 131, 181, 213, 690n, 702n
Christian 372, 526
Japanese 181, 213, 556, 606, 690n, 743n
Vajrayāna 172
artists 212
arts 174, 197, 213, 316, 352, 424, 711n, 788, 790, 795
and FWBO 303, 532, 725n
and Higher Evolution 475
and Mañjuśrī 174
Zen and 555
arūpa-dhyānas 66, 73, 110–11
arūpaloka 66, 73, 78, 148, 370
Āryan Eightfold Path (Sanskrit *ārya-aṣṭāṅgika-mārga*), *see* Eightfold Path
āryas (Pāli *ariyas*) 115, 138
Āryasaṅgha 115, 138, 141–2, 151–2, 214, 294, 452
asaṃskṛta-dharmas 62, 80, 88, 674n
asaṃskṛta-śūnyatā 118
Asaṅga 81, 344, 676n, 707n
ascetics 181, 194
fire-worshipping 23–4
five 22–3, 24, 25, 664n, 700n
ordination 589
Sangharakshita as 751n
Aśoka 688n
time of 19, 190, 221–2
aspects of Buddhist Morality 319, 704
āśravas 22, 28, 111, 122, 139, 154, 476
destruction of the 22, 119, 122, 145
Aṣṭasāhasrikā-prajñāpāramitā (*Perfection of Wisdom in 8,000*

lines) 32, 156, 157, 167, 168, 216, 224, 333, 667n, 683n, 684n, 686n, 691n, 693n, 697n, 705n
astrology 219, 405, 691n
aśubha 80, 82–4, 144
aśubhabhāvanā 83
asuras 73–4, 77, 94–5, 253, 370, 372, 673n
Aśvaghoṣa 13, 33, 46, 213, 665n, 670n, 690n
Aśvajit 24
Atīśa 442, 720n
ati-yoga 443
ātman (Pāli *attan*) 14, 80, 99, 146, 661n; *see also anātman*
attainments
  spiritual 34, 152, 215, 247, 445–6, 599, 687n
    and status 560
  transcendental 138, 203–4, 451
Aṭṭhaka-vagga 188, 204–5
Atthārasarāsī Dīpanī 60, 671n
Aṭṭhasālinī 106, 107, 677n
Augustine, Saint 91, 526, 675n
austerities 21, 215
Avadānas 73–4, 673n; *see also Divyāvadāna, Mahāvastu Avadāna*
Avalokita Sūtras 175
Avalokiteśvara 65, 125, 172–3, 175–7, 178, 180, 224, 229
  and Dalai Lamas 182, 183, 747n
  and Western Buddhist Order 316, 404, 474–5, 502, 518, 532, 703n
  in wheel of life 74
Avataṃsaka Sūtra 5, 55, 78, 454, 661n, 670n, 683n, 684n, 733n
aversion (*dveṣa* Pāli *dosa*) 83, 115, 122, 146–8, 252, 256, 280; *see also* hatred
avidyā (Pāli *avijjā*) 28, 75, 149–50, 174, 253; *see also* ignorance
Awakening of Faith in the Mahāyāna, The 46, 670n
awareness, discriminating, *see vijñāna*
Axial, Vision 127, 140–1; *see also samyak-dṛṣṭi*

Bāhiya 257–8
bahujana 138, 204
Baizhang Huaihai 555, 743n, 752n
bāla 139
bala 16, 164; *see also* power
Bardo Thödol, *see Tibetan Book of the Dead, The*
Bashō, Matsuo 743n
Batchelor, S. 550, 729n, 741n
beauty 82–4, 554
becoming 75; *see also bhava*
betrayal 611
Bhaddāli Sutta 707n
Bhagavad Gītā 644, 757n
Bhaja Retreat Centre 732n
bhakti-mārga 143
Bhallika 22, 663n, 727n
Bhattacharyya, B. 174
bhāva 254
bhava 22, 28, 75; *see also* existence, conditioned and 'becoming'
bhavacakra, *see* wheel of life
bhāvanā 141, 204, 389
Bhayabherava Sutta 662n, 663n
bhikṣuṇīs (Pāli *bhikkhunīs*) 185, 192, 202, 247, 601, 602, 716n, 726n, 751n
  and arhantship 716n
  ordination 210, 469, 602–3, 688n, 689n, 725n, 744n
    'special conditions' (Pāli *garudhammas*) 666n, 751n
  possessions 605
  rules for 196, 702n
bhikṣus (Pāli *bhikkhus*) 185, 193, 202–3; *see also* monks
  'Come' 188, 687n
  expulsion of 687n; *see also pārājikas*
  first 23, 188
  ordination, *see* ordination, *bhikṣus*
  purity of (Pāli *pārisuddha*) 580, 587, 588–9, 628–9
    and laity 593–4
  resignation of 592
  rules of training, *see sikkhapādas*
bhūmis 16–17, 18, 164, 170–1, 175, 258
bhūmisparśa 181
biases, *see āśravas*
bīja-niyama 69
Bimbisāra, King 24, 25, 189, 664n, 673n
'A Bird's-Eye View of Indian Buddhism' 452, 453, 722n, 723n
Blake, W. 361, 393, 673n, 708n, 711n, 728n, 738n
bliss 20, 37, 46, 91, 107–8, 124, 260–1, 335; *see also sukha*
  four stages of 91
Blofeld, J. 224, 692n
Blue Cliff Record 555, 742n
'Blue Radiance' 42
Bodh Gaya 12, 223, 703n, 715n

bodhi 114, 126; *see also* Enlightenment, Nirvāṇa
Bodhicaryāvatāra 159, 360–1, 701n, 708n, 719n, 729n
bodhicitta 16, 126, 160–7, 300, 463–5
absolute (Sanskrit *paramārtha*) 162
as altruistic dimension of Going for Refuge 300–1, 431–3, 442, 448, 452, 456, 465, 471, 474–5, 478, 483, 500, 516, 586
arhants and 168
arising of xvi, 116, 165, 266–74
and *bhūmis* 171
and the Buddha 16
conditions for arising of 270–4
contradictory trends in 161–2, 271–2, 273–4
and conversion, 464
cosmic 478
as cosmic force or will 164, 727n
establishment aspect (Sanskrit *prasthānacitta*) 162, 164
in *Gaṇḍavyūha Sūtra* 165–6
and Hīnayāna 749n
practice (*mūla yoga*) 443
real and provisional 431
relative (Sanskrit *samvṛti*) 162
in Tibetan Buddhism 564–5
vow aspect (Sanskrit *praṇidhicitta*) 162–4
bodhicittotpāda 160, 266, 269
Bodhicittotpādasūtra Śāstra 697n
Bodhidharma 276
bodhipakṣyā-dharmas (Pāli *bodhipakkhiya-dhammas*) 60, 126
Bodhipathapradīpa 720n
bodhisattva
archetypal 172–82, 316
and *arhants*, compared 154–5, 166, 168
career of 16–17, 160–72
of the *dharmakāya* 171–2
eight 172, 180
five *dhyāni* 172
as hero 156–7
hierarchy 171–2
Hīnayāna view of 151–2, 749n
human and historical 181
ideal 155–72, 206–7, 299–300, 452–3
and arhant ideal 431
Dhardo Rimpoche as embodiment of 471, 585
and insight 156, 160
and Mahāyāna *sūtras* 553
and Pāli Tipiṭaka 209
Sangharakshita and 454–5, 585
in Tibetan Buddhism 600
as a unifying principle of Buddhism 432, 446, 452–3, 723n
irreversible 167–9, 171, 182–3, 333
of the Path 171, 182
precepts 208, 657–9
principle 477–8
spiritual community personifying 474
temptations of 168–9
and triple body (Sanskrit *trikāya*) 169–70
and universalism 183–4
Vinaya for all 207
vows (Sanskrit *praṇidhicitta*) 162–4, 274, 471, 684n; *see also* precepts
Bodhisattva Path to Unsurpassed Enlightenment, The 707n
Bodhisattva Principle, The 478, 727n
bodhisattva-śīla 208, 213
bodhi tree 36–7, 117, 219, 222–3, 251, 413
bodhyaṅgas (Pāli *bojjhaṅgas*), seven 60, 98, 126, 679n
bodies, three, see *trikāya*
body
of bliss, *see sambhogakāya*
of mutual enjoyment 41, 336; *see also sambhogakāya*
speech and mind 335, 337
of transformation 40, 46; *see also nirmāṇakāya*
of truth 43; *see also dharmakāya*
body-witness (*kāyasākṣin* Pāli *kāyasakkhī*) 143–5
Boin, S. 403, 404, 706n
Brahm, Ajahn, *see* Brahmavamso
Brahmā 370–1, 441, 605, 656, 695n
brahmacārin 491, 729n
brahmacarya (Pāli *brahmacariya*) 371, 605, 646, 648, 650
Brahmajāla-bodhisattva-śīla Sūtra 208, 213
Brahmajāla Sutta 392, 670n, 691n, 708n
Brahma Sahampati 663n
Brahmavamso 617, 620–49, 753n, 754n, 756n
brahma-vihāras 125, 170, 389, 392
Brahmins 415, 481, 560, 656, 663n, 665n, 686n, 690n, 697n, 698n, 699n
Buddha as 17, 646, 758n
Buddha on 302
Brontë, E. 418, 717n

Buddha 7, 43–4, 137, 567; *see also* Gautama, Śākyamuni, Siddhārtha, *Tathāgatha*
appearance and speech of 647
and *bhikkhu* ordination 646–7
biographies of 12–13, 24–5, 31, 332
symbolical 34–5
traditional 13, 31, 34–8
birth and early life 19–20, 38, 662n, 668n
birth day 226–7
as bodhisattva in previous lives 15; *see also Jātakas*
bodies
'created,' *see nirmāṇakāya*
three, *see trikāya* doctrine
characteristics of 26
on commitment and lifestyle 432
compassion of 22–3
on *dhyānas* 21, 110–11
Eternal 128
first sermons 22–3, 24
of the future 178–9
as the Goal 128
as a God 128–9
going forth of 20
historical perspective 11–12
image 219, 221–2, 229, 273
Laughing 182
and Māra 36
marks of a 41–2
myth and legend 13, 31–4, 38, 332, 552–3
parinirvāṇa 226–7
of the past 17
and pilgrimage 223–4
psychic powers of 34, 668n
as reality 43
recollection of the 44–5
as Refuge 242–3, 293, 303, 425, 461, 728n
Sangharakshita and 408–9
solitary or private, *see pratyekabuddha*
and teaching 291–2, 663n
as transcendental being 13, 38
and views 391
and Vinaya Piṭaka 627
and women 26–7
word of (Pāli and Sanskrit *buddhavacana*) 50–1, 243
Buddha and Five After Centuries, The 648, 758n
Buddha and His Dhamma, The 553, 741n
Buddhacarita 13, 33, 665n, 668n, 690n
Buddha-field 78, 154, 163, 334
Buddhaghosa 13, 65, 114, 115–16, 130, 178, 201, 484–5, 552, 629–30, 633, 661n, 673n, 706n, 755n
on Going for Refuge 485–7
on the *niyamas* 672n
on temperament 737n
Buddhahood 16, 96–7, 100, 117, 152, 173, 293; *see also* Enlightenment
and rebirth 17
Buddha-nature 100, 120, 125
Buddharakshita 693n, 715n
Buddhas
family protectors 173
five *dhyāni* 172, 280, 336, 706n
recollection of the 272
Buddha-to-be 668n
buddhavacana 243; *see also* Buddha, word of
Buddhayāna 168
Buddhism 7–8, 49–51, 244–5, 338, 551, 573, 735n
approaches to
encyclopedic 51–2
fundamentalist 50–1, 627–8
ideal 52
sectarian 49–50, 205, 548
basic teachings of 318, 493, 517
breadth and depth of 428
canonical literature of 32–3, 50, 209, 326
artificial form of 60
selective reading of 50
conversion to, *see* conversion
corruption of 220
cultural baggage of 603–4, 614
decline of 550–1, 556, 603–4
dynamic and static perspectives 87–8
early 344
understanding of 627
and existentialism 100
and the future 612–14
and Going for Refuge 323–4, 430
history xv
and legend 31–8
and interconnectedness 93–4
and labels 572–3
lowest common denominator in 324
magical aspect of 215–16
as 'melioristic' 90, 675n
and Neoplatonism 537
orthodoxy in 547, 556–8, 574
and other religions 243, 245–6, 337–8
not pessimistic 90
pragmatism of 242

Buddhism (*cont.*)
principles of 220, 436, 443, 649–50
schools of 101; *see also* individual schools
origin 50–1
and science 64–6, 86
as spiritual or transcendental experience 54
ten pillars of 395
as a training 343
triyāna 456, 548, 564
unifying factor or principle of 452
Bodhisattva Ideal as 432, 446, 452–3, 723n
Going for Refuge as xiii, xv–xvi, 428, 432, 439, 448
world of 548–51
Buddhism, Chinese 32, 128, 131, 175, 201, 209, 224, 243
Buddhism, Dr Ambedkar's 497
Buddhism, Japanese 126, 128, 131, 163, 175, 182, 201, 209, 225, 227–8
Buddhism, Northern and Southern 548
Buddhism, Tantric, *see* Vajrayāna
Buddhism, Tibetan 173, 182, 201, 252, 285, 434–5, 440, 447, 452, 548–50, 552, 555–6, 558, 574, 600, 686n, 721n, 747n
and Going for Refuge 435–6, 442, 445, 480, 500, 564–6, 567–8
Buddhism, Vajrayāna, *see* Vajrayāna
Buddhism, Western xi, 470
and monastic ordination xi–xii
Buddhism for Today 516, 528, 735n
Buddhism for Today – and Tomorrow 735n
Buddhist organizations
degeneration of 412–13, 467, 499, 519
as groups 568–9
Buddhist Publication Society 484
Buddhist Society, The 410, 457, 459, 584, 714n
Buddhist world 551
Bunyan, J. 426, 719n
Burma 32, 667n
Burning Bush 644, 757n
Bush House 404, 712n
Butler, S. 604, 751n

caittadharmas (Pāli *cetasika-dhammas*) 98
Cakkavatti-Sīhanāda Sutta 685n
cakṣus 295–6; *see also* eyes
Camden, W. 238, 694n
caste 437, 531, 686n
and *bhikṣu* ordination 193
Buddha and 665n
the Buddha and 25, 691n, 692n
and Maha Bodhi Society 725n
and mass conversion 437–8, 720n
in Sri Lanka 193, 219, 688n
and Triratna Buddhist Community 725n
celibacy 305, 371, 702n, 751n; *see also* *anagārikas*
and chastity 709n
vow of 305, 708n
Centre House 403, 466
cetanā 68; *see also* volitions
cetovimutti 145
chakras 37
Chan, or Dhyāna school 24, 32, 77, 131, 276, 555, 742n, 743n, 752n
Chandramani, Maha Thera, U. 417–18, 419–20, 437, 455, 495, 585, 597–8, 717n, 748n
change 87–8
Chapters, The, *see Skandhakas*
chastity 193, 371, 561, 591, 604–5, 607–9, 751n
and celibacy 709n
Chenrezig 175
Chesterton, G. K. 382, 710n
Chihmann, Upasika 454
Childers, R. C. 344, 707n
Christ 33, 87, 173, 179, 183, 694n
Christianity 11, 34, 53, 62, 85, 94, 104, 237–8, 260, 335, 457–8, 537, 614, 674n, 681n, 757n
Churches and Ethics After Prometheus 613–14
cintāmaṇi 181
citta 106, 130, 160, 268–9,
citta-mātra 130, 275–6
citta-niyama 69
cittas, eighty-nine 676n
clairaudience 33, 750n
clairvoyance 33, 296
clear thinking 517–18
cock 74, 77, 252
Cock Lane Ghost 34, 667n
college 741n
commitment
and doubt 264
levels of 301
and lifestyle 203, 299, 351–2, 411, 456, 570
and Dr Ambedkar 497

Sangharakshita and 499
and Theravāda monastic sangha 433, 597
at the time of the Buddha 186, 432, 558
and Western Buddhist Order xvi, 467–9, 611
and speech 382
communication
and believing others 377
between Enlightened and unenlightened mind 58–9
'existential' 528
levels of 571
mass- 393
as means to Enlightenment 382
and Sangha 247–8, 462
Sangharakshita and 532–6, 537–8
and single-sex idea 517
and speech 375
in ten precepts 704n
Communism, and Buddhism 550, 603, 632
compassion 116, 125–6, 389; *see also karuṇā*
absolute 74, 119
of the Buddha 22–3
Great (Sanskrit *mahākaruṇā*) 56–7, 125–6, 156
as ninth precept 389
and psychical continuity 94
and skilful means 164
and teaching 23
Uttarapāthakas and 152
and wisdom 128, 150, 159, 272, 274, 293
conceit (Pāli *māna*) 149–50
concentration 16, 109–13; *see also samādhi*
concepts 54, 58–9, 118, 121–2, 162, 268, 300, 337, 405–6, 431, 608, 634
conditionality 251–2, 255, 696n; *see also nidānas*, *pratītya-samutpāda*
Buddha's vision of 22
cyclic and progressive 102–3, 252, 255, 463; *see also nidānas*
five orders of, *see niyamas*
conditioned, and unconditioned
modes of awareness 265
non-duality of 56, 117–18, 121–2
conditioned co-production, *see pratītya-samutpāda*
confession 259–60, 334, 343, 696n, 707n
and monastic order 189, 199, 344
in Triratna Buddhist Order 730n
Confucianism 11
Confucius 243, 376, 710n
confusion 252, 256; *see also moha*
Conquering New Worlds 534
consciousness 75; *see also* mind, *vijñāna*
absolute 96, 277
activity- 46
and being 67, 77, 102
and betrayal 611
defiled mind, *see kliṣṭa-mano-vijñāna*
as a description of the Goal 129–30
discriminating (Sanskrit *vijñāna*) 97, 99
eight kinds of (Sanskrit *aṣṭavijñāna-kāya*) 698n; *see also vijñānas*, eight
phenomena-particularizing 46
and rebirth 94–6
relinking (Sanskrit *pratisandhi*, Pāli *paṭisandhi*) 75, 95
and space and time 63, 67
store, *see ālaya-vijñāna*
third order of 474–5
turning about in, *see parāvṛtti*
Universal 70; *see also ālaya-vijñāna*
which founded Western Buddhist Order 531
consecration (Sanskrit *abhiṣeka*) 169–71, 228
Constantine 35, 668n
consumerism 551, 603
contact (Sanskrit *sparśa*) 75, 254
contemplation
of decomposition 83
of idea of Nirvāṇa 262–3
of the twelve *nidānas* 392, 711n
of the virtues of the Tathāgatas 272, 273
contentment 370–1, 373
conversion 23, 140, 160, 237–85, 411, 460–5, 495, 720n, 795n
and arising of *bodhicitta* 160, 269
to Buddhism 285, 411, 462, 495, 720n
mass 437–8, 494–5, 497, 597–8, 717n, 720n, 729n, 794
and caste 691n
sudden 284
and gradual 461
within Buddhism 140, 263, 265–6, 275, 281, 285, 462–3; *see also* Stream Entry
conversion ceremony 717n, 720n
Conze, E. 50, 128, 669n

cosmology
Buddhist 62–3, 370, 373, 672n, 709n
and psychology 66–7, 371
Council, First 188
Council, Second 190, 192, 688n
covetousness (Pāli *abhijjhā*) 294, 312–13, 328, 385–90, 392, 468
and hatred (Sanskrit *dveṣa*) 388
meditation to eradicate 387
synonyms with 386
craving 75, 76, 102–4, 149, 252, 254–6, 258–60, 280, 305, 626, 670n; *see also* desire, *lobha*, lust, *tṛṣṇa*
for existence in the formless world (Pāli *arūpa-raga*) 149
for existence in the world of pure form (Pāli *rūpa-raga*) 149
and faith 259
as a fetter (*kāma-rāga*) 147–8
creativity 645
crystal, pillar of 319, 353, 373, 395
Cūḷa-kammavibhaṅga Sutta 71, 673n
Cūḷasakuludāyi Sutta 700n
Cūḷasīhanāda Sutta 139, 680n
Cūḷavaṃsa 225, 693n
Cunda 29, 330–1, 376, 391

ḍākinīs 172, 444
as esoteric Sangha refuge 481, 728n
Dalai Lamas 183, 572, 746–7n
dalits, *see* ex-Untouchables
dāna 16, 105, 164, 204, 207, 212, 214, 232, 293, 368
and merit 214–15
Dante Alighieri 645, 758n
darśana 55, 141, 263; *see also* seeing
Daśabhūmika Sūtra 170–1
death 662n
debt 367–8
Decretals of Constantine 35, 668n
Deer Park 22
Defence of Poetry, A 359, 708n
deities 66–7, 222, 441; *see also devas*, gods
hierarchy of 66
Delamare, T. 404, 537, 712n, 752n
delight (*prāmodya* Pāli *pāmojja*) 105, 107, 259–60
Delors, J. 612–13
delusion 86, 121, 392; *see also moha*
Designation of Human Types (Pāli *Puggala-Paññatti*) 150, 682n
desire 370; *see also* craving, *lobha*, lust, sensuous desire
for continued existence (Pāli *bhavāsava*) 119
plane of (Sanskrit *kāmaloka*) 66, 370
rationalization of 55–6
Devadatta 26, 27, 665n, 666n
Devamitra, Dharmachari 309
devas 33, 34, 83, 348, 444, 752n; *see also* deities, gods
and *dhyānas* 371
as esoteric Dharma refuge 481, 728n
devotion 485–6, 554
and the Goal 128, 243
of laity to monks 213–14
and monk-lay divide 451–2
popular 219
dhamma-kathā 381–2
Dhammapada 67, 81–2, 124, 139, 140, 187–8, 203, 359, 360, 374–5, 376, 432, 451, 491, 552, 606, 625–7, 628, 665n, 672n, 674n, 678n, 680n, 681n, 687n, 689n, 701–2n, 708n, 710n, 722n, 729n, 750n, 752n, 754n
definition of a *bhikkhu* 591
Dhammapālaṃ Gāthā, *see* 'Last Vandanā'
'Dhamma revolution' 516, 729n
dhāraṇīs 153–4, 216, 691n
Dhardo Rimpoche 434–6, 440, 443, 445, 455–6, 691n, 723n, 732n, 739n
and bodhisattva precepts 657
embodying the bodhisattva ideal 471, 585
and the *mūla yogas* 443
and Sangharakshita's bodhisattva ordination 455–6, 585, 690n
Dharma 7–8, 58, 60, 137, 243–6, 291, 339, 381, 674n, 675n
clarified to Mahāprajāpatī 476, 726n
elucidated or translated by Sangharakshita 525–7
and lists 59–61
and Mahāprajāpatī 294
original teachings of 50, 442
as path 293–4
as a raft 391
as Refuge 243, 246, 293–4, 425, 461, 728n, 750n
Sangharakshita and 408
special, of the Buddha 186, 187
teaching 23, 657–8
and words 51, 52, 59
worship of 224–5
Dharmacakra-pravartana Sūtra 22–3

dharmacārīs and *dharmacāriṇīs* xvi, 305, 323, 339, 449, 491, 501, 598, 729n
introduction of nomenclature 490–1
meaning of 491
dharmadhātu 43, 281, 464
Dharma Eye 296, 298, 300–1, 482–3
opening of Sangharakshita's 408
Dharmaguptika 13
Dharmākara 163
dharmakāya 43–6, 170–3, 221, 336, 425
static and dynamic aspects of 172
dharma-niyama 69
dharmānusārin 141–5, 152, 220, 531, 737n
dharmapālas 178, 444
dharmas 62, 88, 131, 674n, 675n
Dharmasaṅgīti Sūtra 125
Dharma Vijaya Vahini 412, 715n
Dharma-Vinaya 186, 188, 197, 200, 294
Dharmodaya Vihara 723n
Dhyāna, or Chan school, *see* Chan or Dhyāna school
dhyāna-pāramitā 41
dhyānas (Pāli *jhānas*) 66–7, 109–11, 164, 371; *see also* meditation
and *brahmacarya* 371, 605
Buddha, on 21, 110–11
and false views 392
formless 144; *see also arūpa-dhyānas*
and *karma* 72
and Nirvāṇa 145
and Zen school 563
dhyāni
bodhisattvas, five 172
Buddhas, five 172, 173, 280, 336, 706n
dialectics 42, 197
diamond, pillar of 319, 353, 358, 363, 395
'*Diamond Banner*' *Sūtra* 157–9
Diamond Sūtra, *see Vajracchedikā Prajñāpāramitā Sūtra*
Dickens, C. 667n
Dīgha Nikāya 28, 29, 30, 84, 110–11, 129, 187, 392, 552, 666n, 667n, 670n, 672n, 674n, 679n, 681n, 685n, 687n, 689n, 691n, 692n, 695n, 696n, 697n, 703n, 706n, 708n, 750n, 758n
and ten precepts 326–7, 705n
Dilgo Khyentse Rimpoche 721n, 722n
dimensions, *see* Going for Refuge, dimensions of
Dionysius 130, 679n
Diotima 218, 691n
Dīpaṅkara 17
disciples, and *ācāryas* 22, 25, 196, 248, 468, 524, 659
discipleship 211–12, 486–7
discipline 284–5, 526
disgust, *see nibbidā*
dispassion 117, 294, 726n; *see also virāga*
Divine Comedy 758n
divine eye (*divya-cakṣus* Pāli *dibba-cakkhu*) 295, 750n
Divyāvadāna 73–4, 179
doctrine-follower, *see dharmānusārin*
Dōgen Zenji 228, 567, 645, 693n
dog's tooth 71, 673n
Door of Liberation 555, 744n
dosa, *see dveṣa*
doubt 146–7, 264, 297; *see also vicikitsā*
'Dr Ambedkar's True Greatness' 746n
Drepung 191
Driver, J. 685n
dṛṣṭi 22, 28, 263; *see also* views
Dudjom Rimpoche 692n, 721n, 722n
duḥkha (Pāli *dukkhā*) 80, 85, 89–92, 98, 102, 103–4, 121–2, 144, 174–5, 477
and spiral path 258
duḥkha-nirodha 122
dukkhā, *see duḥkha*
Dutt, N. 12, 143, 195
Dutt, S. 186, 198, 627, 648
dveṣa (Pāli *dosa*) 70, 74, 83, 121–2, 388; *see also* aversion, hatred
Dzogchen 565

Early Buddhist Monachism 627, 648, 688n
Eckhart, Meister 143, 183, 681n
ecstasy, *see prīti*
ecumenism xii, xv, xvii, 245–6, 497, 547, 573, 725n
and inspiration 497, 550, 552, 554–6
and orthodoxy 557
principle of in FWBO 547–56
effort 111–12, 267, 273, 350; *see also* energy
egalitarianism 603
Eichhorn, J. C. 627, 755n
Eightfold Path 23, 30, 60, 112, 141, 218, 244, 258, 319, 375, 468, 656
and ten precepts 349–50
Ekakanipāta 130, 679n

elements (Sanskrit *mahābhūtas*) 97
Eliot, C. 220
Eliot, G. 90, 675n, 755n
Eliot, T. S. 244, 695n
emancipation 56; *see also* freedom, liberation, *vimukti*
of mind (Pāli *cetovimutti*) 145
temporary (Sanskrit *samayavimukti*) 145
of wisdom (Pāli *paññāvimutti*) 145
emerald, pillar of 387, 395
emotion 98, 148; *see also vedanā*
Axial (Sanskrit *samyak-saṅkalpa*) 141
positive 292
empowerment 565–6
Enchanted Heart, The 423, 534–5, 718n
energy 16; *see also vīrya*
and *bodhicitta* 160
and Buddha-nature 100
manifesting as sentient beings 93–4
and *nāgas* 37
and Nirvāṇa 125
and reality 86
and time, taking another's 366–7
English Sangha Trust 3, 235, 457, 466
enjoyment body, *see sambhogakāya*
Enlightenment, *see also bodhi*, Nirvāṇa
and absolute Going for Refuge 302–3
after- (Sanskrit *anubodhi*) 126
of the Buddha 21–2
Buddha's experience of 251
-factors (Sanskrit *bodhyaṅgas*) 98
and false views 392
and Going for Refuge 323
and Going Forth 413
immanent urge to 15
limbs or factors of, *see bodhyaṅgas* 55, 56–7, 96
prediction of (Sanskrit *vyākaraṇa*) 16, 163, 171, 179
seen as a mandala 132–3
seven factors of 60
sudden 284
thirty-seven wings of 60
three kinds of 266–7
reduced to two 463, 464–5
environment, concern for 363
equanimity 26, 41, 117, 126, 389; *see also upekṣā*
Eros 218, 691n
essentiality 43
eternalism (Pāli *sassatavāda*) 122, 146, 557
Eternal Legacy, The 450
ethical formalism 152, 366
ethics 71, 339–40, 350, 385; *see also* morality, precepts, *śīla*
and karma 70–2
meditation and wisdom 245; *see also* threefold path
European Buddhist Union xi, 568, 746n
European Commission 612
European Economic Community (EEC) 612–14, 753n
Evans-Wentz, W. Y. 231, 743n
evolution 261, 529
Evolution, Higher, *see* Higher Evolution
existence
conditioned 80–1, 100, 124, 148, 252
orders of 43, 65–6; *see also* levels, *lokas*, planes, realms, spheres, worlds
existentialism 100, 147
Expositor, The (Pāli *Aṭṭhasālinī*) 106, 107–8, 677n
Extending the Hand of Fellowship xvii, xix, 545–74
extra-sensory perception (ESP) 33, 667n
ex-Untouchables 437–9, 446, 455, 458–9, 482, 490–1, 494–5, 498, 500, 530, 537, 597–8
eyes, five (Sanskrit *cakṣus*) 295, 482, 700n
divine (Sanskrit *divya-cakṣus*) 295–6, 750n
of Truth (Sanskrit *dharma-cakṣus*) 295–6, 327, 482, 700n
of wisdom (Sanskrit *prajña-cakṣus*) 296
universal (Sanskrit *samanta-cakṣus*) 196

Face-to-Face, the, (Sanskrit *abhimukhī*) 170
faculties 127
five spiritual 549, 626
higher 40
prajñā as transcendental 92
faith xiii, 104–5, 477; *see also śraddhā*
-follower, *see śraddhānusārin*
-liberated one 143
schools of Buddhism 549, 554, 562
and spiral path 258–9
family protectors 173, 177
fatalism 69
Faust 91–2, 675n
feeling 97–8, 255; *see also* emotion, *vedanā*
Festivals 226–9
fetters
five 148, 370, 626

and holy persons 141–51
ten (Pāli *daśa-saṃyojana*) 146, 263, 297, 697n, 701n
three 146–7, 263–5, 297–8, 302, 463, 482–3, 697n, 701n
Ficino, M. 536, 739n
Fire Sermon 24, 664n
First Council 188
five eyes, *see* eyes, five
five 'heaps' 335; *see also skandhas*
five hindrances 626, 658, 670n
five *niyamas* 69–70
five pillars 612, 753n
five precepts, *see* precepts, five
five spiritual faculties 549, 626
Forest Hermitage 753n
Forest Hermitage *Newsletter* 619–20, 754n
Forest Monks of Sri Lanka, The 589, 590, 592, 750n
forgiveness 199, 658
Forty-Three Years Ago xiv, 575–614, 619
critique of, Sangharakshita's response 617–49
four *āryan* truths, *see* four noble truths
four great kings 67, 370
four noble truths 23, 60, 102, 122, 170, 244, 414, 557
four reliances 421, 455; *see also nissaya*
four sights 35–6, 186
fourteen inexpressibles (Sanskrit *avyākṛtavastus*) 63
freedom 56–7, 127; *see also* emancipation, liberation, *vimukti*
Freud, S. 636, 756n
friends 248; *see also kalyāṇa mitras*, spiritual friends
friendship xvii, 522, 569–70, 571, 736n; *see also* spiritual, friendship
levels of 571
Friends of the Western Buddhist Order, *see* FWBO
further shore 59, 132, 331, 705n
FWBO (Friends of the Western Buddhist Order) xi, 295, 303–6, 507, 700n, 789; *see also* Triratna Buddhist Community
and communication 462
films and videos 739n
founding of 724n
Friend(s) of 303–4, 584, 702–3n
and Going for Refuge 465
ideals and ideas 515, 517, 735n
five pillars of 612, 753n
six distinctive emphases of 725n
institutions xx, 516, 546, 612
and levels of Going for Refuge 481
Mitras of, *see* Mitras
as Movement set in motion 531
name change 700n
and New Society 516–17
relations with other groups 547, 568, 741n
Transcription Unit 533, 737n
and work 555

Gampopa 161, 162, 425, 440–2, 445, 555, 700n, 731n, 744n, 747n
Gaṇakamoggallāna Sutta 706n
Gaṇḍavyūha Sūtra 45, 161, 165–6, 173, 179, 670n, 684n
Gāndhāra 223
gap (Pāli *sandi*), between feeling and craving 255–6
Gateless Gate 555, 742n
Gautama 12, 15–17, 169, 175, 177, 408–9, 552; *see also* Buddha, Śākyamuni, Siddhārtha, *Tathāgatha*
Gelugpa School 178, 182, 445–6, 657, 676n, 681n, 686n
generosity 16, 105, 226, 341, 364–6, 368, 369, 386, 664n; *see also dāna*
Ghoom 237, 694n
gift
of the Dharma 26, 212
and giver 366
of material things 212
Ginsberg, A. 534, 738n, 801
giving 214, 268; *see also dāna*, generosity
goal, the 120–33, 204–5
God 42, 87, 245, 645, 695n
Buddha as a 128–9
gods 65, 73, 74, 95, 139, 370, 645; *see also* deities, *devas*
Goethe, J. W. 91, 675n
'Going for Refuge' xv, 482
Going for Refuge xii, 7–8, 240–9, 259, 292–306, 323, 325, 431
altruistic dimension of 300–1, 431–3, 442, 448, 452, 456, 465, 471, 474–5, 478, 483, 500, 516, 586
and *bhikṣu* ordination 421
centrality of xvi, xvii, 428, 431, 433, 439, 449–50, 471–2, 501, 515, 557, 566–7
embodied in Western Buddhist Order 611, 725n

Going for Refuge (*cont.*)
and conversion 461, 464
dimensions of xv–xvi, 34, 63, 66, 114, 248, 300–1, 516
Dr Ambedkar and 495–7
and ex-Untouchables 438–9
Gampopa on 441–2
and Higher Evolution 475–7, 482
and individual, act 473–4, 516, 568
and Jōdo Shinshū 566–7
levels of xvi, 301–5, 465, 479–82, 515–16, 701n, 727n
absolute 302
and communication 571–2
cosmic 482
cultural or ethnic 301, 480–1, 488, 701n; and ex-Untouchables, 490
effective 302, 305, 325, 429, 430, 465, 481, 487, 518, 568; and *dharmacārī/iṇīs*, 490
real 296–7, 302, 305, 465, 481–2
testing 513
loss of significance or undervaluation of xiii, 299, 324, 431–2, 479–80, 488
and monastic formalism 604
Nyanaponika Thera and 484–8
four modes of 486–7
and ordination 586; *see also* Going for Refuge, levels of, effective
and orthodoxy 557–8
and the precepts 305, 324–5, 336, 351, 557–8, 598
and Sangha 323, 450–1
Sangharakshita and process of understanding xiii, xv, 405–6, 413–14, 415–16, 418–19, 428, 430, 439, 443, 445, 452, 471, 498–502, 557, 584, 587–8, 598, 694n
and 'self' and 'other' power 562
and 'taking refuge' 241, 301, 563, 695n
three contexts of 473–8
and Tibetan Buddhism 435–6, 442, 445, 480, 500, 564–6, 567–8
at time of Buddha 188
as unifying factor or principle xiii, xv–xvi, 428, 432, 439, 448
and the Western Buddhist Order 405
witnessing of 512, 524
Zen and 563, 567
Going for Refuge and Prostration practice (*mūla yoga*) 442–5, 500, 514, 721n
Going Forth 186, 413–16
and becoming a Mitra of the FWBO 584
of the Buddha 20, 662n, 663n, 715n
Sangharakshita and 412–16, 499, 584
and single-sex idea 517
gold
as metaphor for practice 101, 246, 513, 527, 565, 745n
pillar of 319, 353, 369, 395
Golden Drum 309, 399
'The Good Friend' 528, 736n
gotrabhūs 142–3
Govinda, Lama 3, 108, 132–3, 736n
grace 426, 719n
Grace Abounding to the Chief of Sinners 719n
grasping 75–6, 255, 364, 366–7; *see also upādāna*
gratitude 367
gravitational pull 261, 263, 265
gravity, centre of 185, 250, 263, 304, 362
Great Treatise on the Stages of the Path to Enlightenment 681n
greed 70, 83–4, 121, 253; *see also lobha*
type (Sanskrit *lobhacaritra*) 83
group, the
and the individual 414–15, 568, 716n, 726n
and the spiritual community 415, 474, 499, 726n
Guanyin 175
Guenther, H. V. 106, 122, 147, 440–2, 676n
Guhyaloka 416, 717n, 730n
ordinations retreats or courses 510, 514, 731n, 734n
Guhyasamājatantra 706n
guilt 91, 105, 259–60, 485
gurus 142, 528–9
as esoteric Refuge 481, 565, 728n
Tantric 565–6
Guru Yoga (*mūla yoga*) 443

habit 697n
Hakuin Ekaku 555, 742n
Hampstead Buddhist Vihara 3, 235, 450, 457, 459–60, 537, 694n, 724n, 738n
Handel, G. F. 645, 757n, 758n
happiness 107–9; *see also sukha*
Haribhadra 167
harmony 248, 330, 384
Harmsworth's Children's Encyclopaedia 408, 714n
hate, type (Sanskrit *dveṣacaritra*) 83
hatred (*dveṣa* Pāli *dosa*) 121, 388–9

Heart Sūtra, *see Prajñāpāramitā-hṛdaya Sūtra*
heaven 77, 86, 132, 164, 214, 332–3, 370, 757n, 758n
of the Thirty-Three 83
tuṣitadevaloka 18, 179
Hegel, G. 50, 670n
Heidegger, M 393, 711n
hell 74, 77, 95–6, 156, 333, 370
of caste 438, 720n
and Kṣitigarbha 180–1
Hermetic Correspondence 96
Hevajra Tantra 675n
hierarchy
of grades of Enlightenment 267–8
spiritual or transcendental 115, 155, 247, 461
Higher Evolution 102, 293–4, 475–6, 482, 699n, 726n
Hīnayāna 60, 88, 131, 140, 149, 151–2, 161, 181, 204, 206, 208–11, 214, 549, 572; *see also* Theravāda, *yānas*
and *bodhicitta* 749n
in bodhisattva precepts 658, 659
emergence of 206
Gampopa and 441–2
and Going for Refuge 431–2
hindrances, five 626, 658, 670n
Hinduism 69, 143, 193, 335, 661n
and Buddhism 11, 58, 176, 223, 246, 597, 691n
and Dr Ambedkar 437–8, 495–6, 656
History of My Going for Refuge, The xiii, xix, xx, 397–503, 534, 543
Holman Hunt, W. 609–10, 752n
holy persons (*ārya-pudgalas* (Pāli *ariya-puggalas*) 141–6, 149–51, 232, 682n, 737n
homeless wanderers 20, 186, 203, 451, 646; *see also parivrājakas*
Horace 366, 709n
householders xiii, 203, 208, 451, 469, 647, 701n
Hsüan-tsang 669n; *see also* Xuanzang
Huayen 733n
Huayen school 733n
'Hudibras' 604, 751n
Huineng (Wei Lang) 77
humanitarianism 160
human life 94–6
Humphreys, C. 410, 714n
hungry ghosts, *see* pretas
Hymn to Avalokiteśvara 176
ideal, embodiment or personification of 103, 153
in spiritual community 474–5
idealism 130, 549
ignorance (Pāli *avijjāsava*) 76, 119, 139, 177, 252, 253, 254, 280; *see also avidyā*
Il Convento di Santa Croce 526, 730n, 735n
illumination 57–9, 172, 267
'The Illuminator' 42, 281; *see also* Vairocana
ill will 383, 388, 626
Imageless (Sanskrit and Pāli *animitta*) 121–2
images
language of 132–3
in Tibetan Buddhism 556
imagination 273, 278, 612
and empathy 360, 362
immanence 43
impermanence 85–6, 121; *see also anitya*
'The Imperturbable' 42, 281; *see also* Akṣobhya
India 223, 467, 489–90, 495, 516, 551, 597, 603, 700n, 715n, 729n, 730n, 731n, 732n, 740n, 744n, 794–5
individualism
and altruism 463
spiritual 116, 140, 270, 272, 274, 300
individuality 141
and single-sex idea 710n
individuals
and Going for Refuge 473, 516
and group 414–15, 716n
and Higher Evolution 482
and spiritual community 362, 473–4, 488
true 372, 381
and gratitude 367
Indra 733n
Indra's Net 511, 513, 515, 733n, 734n
'Infinite Life' 42, 58, 125, 175, 404; *see also* Amitāyus
'Infinite Light' 42, 180, 280; *see also* Amitābha
initiation 447–8, 455–6, 685n, 723n; *see also abhiṣeka*
insight 114–15, 121; *see also vipaśyanā*
and abandoning false views 393
arising of 262–5
and the bodhisattva ideal 156, 160
contemplative 143

insight (*cont.*)
and the five 'eyes' (Sanskrit *cakṣus*) 295–6
meditation movement 561
and real Going for Refuge 481–2, 518
and *samādhi* 145
and speech 382
and spiritual discipline 52
transcendental 139–40, 145, 160, 296, 370, 372
and Western Buddhist Order 561–2
inspiration 11, 243, 645, 758n, 789
awed 644–5, 649
and Deities of the Path 139
and ecumenism 497, 550, 552, 554–6
and *nāgas* 37
and united Europe 614
institutions 612, 648
insubstantiality, *see anātman*
integration 105, 112, 206, 260, 262, 367
intermediate state 217, 743n
intuition
as a faculty 40
and faith 104
Sangharakshita and 406
irreversibility (Sanskrit *avaivartika*) 166–71; *see also* Stream Entry
and the bodhisattva 160, 167–9, 171, 182–3
and the ten precepts 333, 705n
Islam 11, 53, 94
Itivuttaka 138, 315, 552, 663n, 668n, 670n, 671n, 674n, 678n, 680n, 682n, 689n, 692n, 695n, 696n, 702n, 758n

Jainism 68, 186
James, W. 185, 226, 687n, 694n
Jamyang Khyentse Chökyi Lodrö 440, 442, 685n, 721n
Japan 702n
Japanese 52, 131, 180–2, 209, 216, 227–8, 231, 404, 554, 563, 566, 645, 686n, 693n, 743n
jargon 376
Jātakas 13, 15–16, 210, 332, 477, 589, 662n, 665n
and ten precepts 332–3
Jātakatthakathā 661n
Jerome, Saint 526–7, 536, 736n
Jesus 12, 130, 237, 755n
Jetavana 664n
jewel, in a dunghill 126
'The Jewel-Born' 42
Jewel Ornament of Liberation, The 161, 425, 440, 442, 445, 555–6, 683n, 700n, 718n, 731n, 744n
jhānas, *see dhyānas*
Jizō 181
jñāna (Pāli *ñāna*) 16, 164, 278; *see also* knowledge, *vidyā*
and *prajñā* 164–5
jñānas, five 280–1, 336
jñeyāvaraṇa 56, 127; *see also* veils
Jōdo Shinshū 126, 149, 163, 231, 562, 566–7, 574, 649, 693n, 746n
John of the Cross, Saint 183
Johnson, S. 667n, 668n, 694n
'The Journey to Il Convento' 526, 527, 736n
joy 73, 252, 260, 626, 673n; *see also* delight, *prāmodya*)
sympathetic (Sanskrit *muditā*) 157, 389
Judaism 94
Jung, C. G. 132, 279, 526, 698n
just sitting 563

Kabir 130, 680n
Kachu Rimpoche 442–3, 445
Kagyu 700n
Kagyu schools 442, 551, 681n, 686n, 743n, 744n, 747n
Kālāmas 25, 648, 745n
Kālāma Sutta 565, 745n, 758n
Kalimpong 3, 579–80, 691n, 692n, 693n, 723n, 748n, 794
kalpas 64, 67
kalyāṇa xx, 529
kalyāṇa mitras 248, 585; *see also* spiritual friends
qualities and circumstances required 514
system 514–15, 735n
kalyāṇa mitratā 304, 387, 499, 585; *see also* spiritual friendship
kāma 22, 28, 147, 370; *see also* sensuous experience
Kamalashila, Dharmachari 732n
kāmaloka 66, 73, 78, 83–5, 105, 148, 370–1, 608
Kapleau, P. 563–4, 745n
Kāraṇḍa-vyūha Sūtra 176
karma 68–73, 102
and Abhidharma 76–7
and *dharmas* 675n
fourfold classification of 72
and the human state 95
misunderstanding of 68, 72

and rebirth 122–3
seven types of 70
karma-niyama 69–70
Karmapa 573, 747n
karma-phala 68
karma-vipāka 68–9, 95–6, 102
karuṇā 116, 125
Kashyap, Bhikkhu Jagdish (Kashyapji) 424, 455, 580, 582, 585, 717n, 720n, 749n
Kāśyapa (Pāli Kassapa) brothers 23, 664n, 668n
Kātyāyana 114
Kauṇḍinya 23
Kawinda Sayadaw, U 717n, 748n
kāyasākṣin (Pāli *kāyasakkhī*) 143–4
Keffolds 404, 712n
kesa 404, 608
Kevaddha Sutta 129, 679n, 695n
Khaggavisāṇa 688n
Khemadhammo, Phra Ajahn 619–20, 622, 623, 638, 753n
killing 357–9, 361
kings
four great 67, 370
four religious, of Tibet 183
Kīṭāgiri Sutta 682n, 737n
Kittivaddho 632
kleśas 77, 122, 175, 336
kleśāvaraṇa 55, 127
kliṣṭa-mano-vijñāna 99, 278, 280, 282
knowledge 16, 126, 127; *see also jñāna, vidyā*
path of (Sanskrit *jñāna-mārga*) 143
Knowledge and Vision of Things as They Are 113, 127, 140, 262; *see also yathābhūta-jñānadarśana*
Knowledge of the Destruction of the Biases (*āśravakṣayajñāna*) 119, 750n
Know Your Mind 676n, 738n
Kōbō Daishi (Kūkai) 213, 228, 690–1n, 693n
Kondanna 700n
Koran 65, 644, 757n
Krishnamurti, J. 179, 244, 683n, 695n
krodha 177, 388
kṣānti 16, 164
Kṣāntivādin 16, 662n
kṣetras 78
Kṣitigarbha 172–3, 180–1, 692n
Kūkai, *see* Kōbō Daishi
Kumārajīva 181, 686n
kuṇḍalinī 37
kuśala (Pāli *kusala*) 70, 317, 328, 340–1, 349
and *akuśala* 260, 328, 340, 391, 517
Kusho Bakula 421, 582, 584, 718n, 756n
Kusinārā (Kusinara, Kusinagaro) 12, 27, 29, 30, 223, 417, 418, 419, 717n
Kūṭadanta Sutta 326–7, 329, 705n
Kwannon 175

laity 202–17, 448, 449, 451, 496–7, 501, 559, 593, 607; *see also* lay followers, monk-lay divide, *upāsakas*
and donations 190, 226
Mahāyāna and 206–7
and precepts 324, 345
and veneration 599–600
lakṣaṇas 59, 114–15, 121, 392, 414, 463, 557
fourth 82
three 59, 80–92, 262, 711n
Lalitavistara Sūtra 12, 179, 668n
lamas
as esoteric Buddha refuge 444, 565
incarnate 182, 421, 436, 445, 498, 500, 645, 747n, 756n; *see also tulkus*
lamrim tradition 676n, 681n, 721n, 744n
language
and Buddhahood 97
of Buddhism, using 393
of images 132–3
limitations of 116–17, 123, 124, 474
literal and metaphorical 525
and literalism 501
and reality 88
and views 393
Laṅkāvatāra Sūtra 67, 173, 239, 251, 276–7, 279, 284, 463–4, 555, 674n, 679n, 696n, 698n
and meditation 81
and the turning about 276, 463–4, 698n
Laozi 183, 243, 670n
Last Judgment 644, 757n
'Last Vandanā' (Pāli *Dhammapālaṃ Gāthā*) 491, 729n
lay followers 29, 185, 229, 496; *see also* laity
and *dāna* 214–15
Dr Ambedkar and 496
Leaves of Grass 365

lectures 694n, 741n, 742n, 744n
Ledi Sayadaw 114
levels, of Going for Refuge, *see* Going for Refuge, levels
levitation 33
Lhalungpa, L. P. 183, 434–5, 720n
liberation 118–19, 592–3; *see also* emancipation, freedom, *vimukti*
entrances to, *see vimokṣa-mukhas*
individual 344, 346, 492
Life and Liberation of Padmasambhava 555, 556, 743n
Life of the Buddha, The 553, 741n
lifestyle
and commitment, *see* commitment and lifestyle
and ordination, *bhikṣus* (Pāli *bhikkhus*) 191, 591–2, 606
and precepts 351–3, 557–8
Western Buddhist Order and xvi, 467–9, 611
lineage
development of a 525
one who has entered the (Sanskrit *gotrabhū*) 142–3
lions 174, 180, 526
literalism 14, 17, 61, 87, 131, 501
Māra of 511
lobha 121–2; *see also* craving, desire, lust
Lokamitra, Dharmachari 490, 494, 656, 728–9n
Lokanātha 175
lokapālas, four 228
lokas 66–7, 672n; *see also* planes, spheres, worlds
Lokottaravāda 13, 221, 332
London Buddhist Centre 731n, 734n, 738n
Lord of the Rings, The 372
lotuses 20, 38, 107, 174–8, 180–1, 216, 404, 413, 444, 476, 530–1, 532, 726n, 728n
love 357–63; *see also mettā*
compared to compassion 389
and Enlightenment experience 57
and generosity 365
and Nirvāṇa 125
love mode, and power mode 361–3, 364, 368
loving-kindness 569, 625; *see also mettā*
Lumbini 18, 223, 228, 536, 717n, 740n
lust 36, 70, 74, 77, 93, 109, 252, 327, 386, 626, 658, 673n; *see also* craving, desire, *lobha*
Macpherson, J. 668n
Madhyamaka school 181, 686n
Mādhyamikavāda 549n
maechis 601–3, 639, 744n
Māgandiya Sutta 716n
Māgha Sutta 665n
magic 215–17, 230; *see also* miracles, powers, psychic or supernormal
quasi- 594
mahābhūtas 97
Maha Bodhi journal 452, 458, 530, 722n, 724–5n, 794
Maha Bodhi Society 412, 417, 421, 438, 715n, 725n
Mahā-kammavibhaṅga Sutta 71, 673n
mahākaruṇā 56, 125; *see also* Compassion, Great
Mahākārunika 175
Mahākassapa 698n
Mahāmālunkya Sutta 671n
Mahāmaṅgala Sutta 678n
Mahāmati 173
Mahānidāna Sutta 696n
Mahāpadāna Sutta 187, 687n
Mahāparinibbāna Sutta 28, 29, 30, 126, 223, 647, 666n, 667n, 679n, 681n, 692n, 703n, 706n, 750n, 758n
Mahāprajāpatī (Pāli Mahāpajāpatī) 19, 26–7, 294, 476, 726n
Mahārāhulovada Sutta 666n
Mahāratnakūṭa Sūtra 389, 711n
Mahāsaccaka Sutta 108, 110–11, 662n, 663n, 677n, 716n
Mahāsāṃghikas 13, 192, 205–6, 208, 221, 332
Mahāsaṅgha 138, 202, 207, 247, 347, 453, 492
Mahāsatipaṭṭhāna Sutta 225
Mahāsiddhas 686n
Mahāsthāmaprāpta 172–3, 179–80
mahāśūnyatā 118
Mahāvacchagotta Sutta 716n
Mahāvaṃsa 222, 226, 667n, 692n, 693n
Mahāvastu 12–13, 33, 175, 179, 332, 665n, 667n, 692n, 705n
Mahāvastu Avadāna 221
Mahāvihāra 191
Mahāyāna 131, 192, 206–7, 299–300, 442; *see also yānas*
and emptiness 118
and Going for Refuge 431
as inspiration and guidance 553–6
and laity 206–7
misunderstanding of 42

and monk-lay divide 211, 300
origins of 192, 206, 432
orthodoxy of 557
schools 114, 181, 275, 279, 336, 549, 553
and spiritual friendship 161
sūtras 44, 64, 96–7, 132, 153, 156, 170, 208, 213, 224, 333, 723n
as inspiration and guidance 553–4, 741n, 742n
and mind 67
and ten precepts 332, 333–4
and the twofold *nairātmya* 88
Vinaya 192, 207, 208–9, 452, 658
Mahāyāna-uttaratantra 425
Mahinda 228
Maitreya (Pāli *Metteyya*) 154, 156, 165, 172–3, 178–9, 182, 219, 230, 683n, 685n, 695n
Maitreya-vyākaraṇa 179
maitrī, *see mettā*
Majjhima Nikāya 44, 59, 108, 139, 347, 484, 552, 662n, 663n, 665n, 666n, 667n, 669n, 671n, 673n, 677n, 680n, 682n, 689n, 694n, 699n, 700n, 701n, 705n, 706n, 707n, 708n, 711n, 716n, 728n, 737n
and ten precepts 327–9
Malini, Dharmacharini 734n
Mallas 25, 27, 29–30
māna 149–50
mandala 96, 132–3
offering practice (*mūla yoga*) 443
personal 323, 324–5
Maṅgala Sutta 117
Mañjughoṣa 127, 173, 175, 404
Mañjughoṣa stuti sādhana 174–5, 685n
Mañjunātha 173
Mañjuśrī 54, 161, 172–4, 178–80, 182, 207, 224, 316, 684n, 690n, 692n
Mañjuśrī-Kumārabhūta 173
Mañjuśrī-mūla-kalpa 174
manomayā 67
mano-niyama, *see citta niyama*
mano-vijñāna 44, 66–7, 75–8, 80, 94–6, 98–9, 108–11, 129–30, 254–6, 278–82, 284, 335–6, 387, 474–6, 698n
mantras xv, 109, 127, 174, 176, 282, 443, 518, 554
Māra 36–7, 92, 117, 168–9, 511, 668n
of literalism 511
mārga 60, 102–3, 141–4, 146–7, 263; *see also* path
marriage 231, 445–6, 562, 605, 722n
mātṛkadharas 197
Maudgalyāyana (Pāli Moggallāna) 24, 26, 200, 664n, 687n
Māyādevī 18
Meaning of Conversion in Buddhism, The xv, 235–85, 460–5
Meaning of Orthodoxy in Buddhism, The 556
meditation 200–1, 261, 371; *see also dhyānas*
and ethics 349–50, 371, 385, 387
and five Buddha families 172
formalism in Zen school 563
and Going for Refuge 561–2
just sitting 563
mettā bhāvanā 569
mindfulness of breathing 392, 711n
and mind precepts 387
in monastic sangha 200–1
mūla yogas 443, 445
Going for Refuge and Prostration practice 443–5, 721n
sādhana 685n
sammā arahaṃ method 144
Sangharakshita on 711n
six element practice 387, 392, 711n
and techniques 112, 561
and temperament 83–4
vipassanā 561–2, 563–4, 571
visualization 273, 518, 669n, 685n
mental concomitants 98–9
mental events, *see* mental concomitants
mental perversities, *see viparyāsas*
mental states 14, 60, 79, 358
and false views 393
and Going for Refuge 477
unskilful, and false views 392
and worlds 79, 86
Mephistopheles 91–2, 675n
merit (*puṇya* (Pāli *puñña*)) 205, 214–15, 593, 602, 636
dedication or transference of 269–70
merits, rejoicing in 380, 389, 392, 719n, 730n
metaphors 250–1, 396
mettā (Sanskrit *maitrī*) 125, 315, 317, 361, 527, 569–70; *see also* loving-kindness
mettā bhāvanā 569
middle path 15, 34, 59–60, 246; *see also* Middle Way
Middleton Murry, J. 401, 711n
Middle Way (Sanskrit *madhyama-mārga*) 111–12, 470, 529

Middle Way, The 447
Milarepa 143, 181, 213, 273, 555, 645, 681n, 686n, 690n, 738n, 743n, 744n
Milinda, King 191, 688n
Milton, J. 319
mind 75, 98–9, 103, 106, 278; *see also* *citta*
absolute 67, 130, 277, 672n; *see also* *ālayavijñāna*
composed of (Pāli *manomayā*) 67
-consciousness
see mano-vijñāna
defiled, *see kliṣṭa-mano-vijñāna*
luminosity of 672n
One or Only, *see citta-mātra*
principal functions and family protectors 173–8
mind-determined (Pāli *manoseṭṭhā*) 67
mindfulness, movement and Going for Refuge 561
mindfulness of breathing 392, 711n
mind-preceded (Pāli *manopubbaṅgamā*) 67
miracles 34; *see also* magic, powers, psychic or supernormal
Mitras 304, 584–5, 701n, 702n, 703n, 735n, 749n
convenors 725n
and *kalyāṇa mitras* 514, 735n
and ordination 387, 512, 514–15, 517–18, 721n, 734n
and provisional Going for Refuge 301, 465, 481, 701n
and status 608
Mitrata 737n
Moggallāna (Sanskrit Maudgalyāyana) 24, 26, 200, 664n, 687n
moha 70, 74, 121–2, 390
Mokshapriya, Dharmachari 730n, 739n
monasteries 197, 213, 218, 228
monastic
code 192, 199–201, 209, 344, 580–1, 702n; *see also* *prātimokṣa*
breaches of, *see pārājikas*
formalism xii, xiv, 415, 432–3, 449, 459, 559, 604, 634, 744n
life 193–201
order, *see* order, monastic
monasticism 191, 192, 604
extreme 205–6
Mahāyāna 192
Sūtra-style 561, 604, 625–7, 628, 632, 638, 643, 648
and the Buddha 646
and Sangharakshita 629
and Tibetan Buddhism 446
Vinaya-style 628–9, 631–2, 638, 642–3, 645–6
and Sūtra-style compared 627
Zen 555
monk-lay divide xii, xiv–xv, 152, 211, 299; *see also* monks, and laity
and the Buddha 451
Dr Ambedkar and 597–8
Gampopa and 440
and Jōdo Shinshū 562
and Mahāyāna 211, 300
and monastic code 189
ordination and status 448
and respect 591–2
and Theravāda 558–60, 592
and Tibetans 600
monks 298, 558–60, 604–8; *see also* *bhikṣus*
'bad' 433, 530, 581, 588, 607, 657
becoming a 298–300, 413–15, 418–19, 432–3, 499, 694n
eight requisites of 198, 605
and girl, story of 71, 673n
and Going for Refuge 298
and laity 202–17, 345, 448–9, 451, 497, 501, 559, 607; *see also* monk-lay divide
and precepts 324, 345
and veneration 599–600
sham 622–5, 628–35
and socio-religious status 608–9, 638–9
Theravāda and Mahāyāna, shared lineage 192
and Western Buddhism xi–xii
moon, full-, and new- 187, 198–200, 226–7, 420, 579
moral codes, fundamental xvi, 492, 501; *see also* *mūla-prātimokṣa*
morality 16, 105, 164, 360; *see also* ethics, precepts, *śīla*
conventional 265
conventional and natural 557
moral rules, dependence, on (Sanskrit *śīlavrata-parāmarśa*) 146–7, 265, 297–8, 483
Morris, W. 393, 711n
Mucalinda 37–8
mudrās 42, 156, 177
Mulagandhakuti Vihara 420, 717n
mūla-prātimokṣa 320, 345–50, 492, 501, 752n
Mūlasarvāstivādins 195–6, 200

mūla yogas 443, 445
Murti, T. R. V. 129
My Relation to the Order xvii, xix–xx, 505–39

Nāgārjuna 179, 181, 738n
nāgas 37
Nāgasena 191
nairātmya 88
nairātmyatā 122
Nālandā 191, 201, 686n, 689n
Nanak 183
Ñāṇamoli 553, 741n
Nātha 175
Neoplatonism 11, 82, 335, 537, 681n, 739n, 740n
New Burmese Method of Satipaṭṭhāna 112
New Society 516–17, 735n
Newspeak 376, 710n
Nhu, Mme, *see* Xuân, Tr n L
nibbidā (Sanskrit *nirvid*, *nirveda*) 103, 115–17
Nichiren, sect 225
Nichiren Daishonin 182, 225, 228, 693n
Nidānakathā 13, 17, 33, 661n, 662n, 665n, 667n
nidānas 74–6, 255, 258
  contemplation of 392, 711n
  and Stream Entry 140
  twelve cyclic (wheel) 102–3, 253–5, 258, 463
  twelve positive (spiral path) 63, 101, 102–19, 140, 252, 258–63, 463, 727n
    and Eightfold Path 141
    and Higher Evolution 476–7
Nidāna-vagga 103
Nietzsche, F. 140, 284, 376, 645, 681n, 698n, 710n, 758n
nihilism (Pāli *ucchedavāda*) 122, 146, 557
niḥsvabhāva 89
nikāyas
  or 'families' of Theravādin *bhikkhus* 595–6, 747n
  of Pāli Tipiṭaka 326, 552
nimitta 121
nirmāṇakāya 40–1, 45–6, 170, 182–3, 225, 336
  tulkus as 182
Nirvāṇa 120–1, 169; *see also bodhi*, Enlightenment
  and bodhisattva 168–9
  contemplation of idea of 262–3
  as fourth *lakṣana* 82, 89
  as Goal
    negative description of 122–3
    positive description of 123–30
nirvāṇa, and *saṃsāra* 56, 119, 149, 159, 164, 166, 171
Nirvāṇa Sūtra 125
niśrayas (Pāli *nissayas*) 191, 194, 196, 421
  period 196
niyamas, five 69–70, 672n
non-duality 56, 91, 114, 164–5, 229
  and the bodhisattva 159
non-returner (Pāli and Sanskrit *anāgāmin*) 141, 148–9, 682n
non-violence (Sanskrit *ahiṃsā*) 341, 358, 361, 363
nuns 215, 345, 559, 604, 702n, 755n; *see also bhikṣuṇīs*, *maechis*, women and ordination
Nyanaponika Thera 484–8, 566, 727n, 745n
Nyingmapa School 178, 231, 443, 445–6, 500, 565, 721n
nymphs 82–3

offences, *see pārājikas*
Omar Khayyám 674n
once-returner (*sakṛdāgāmin* Pāli *sakadāgāmin*) 141, 147, 149, 682n
One Mind 130, 275–6
one-pointedness (Sanskrit *kauśalya-ekāgratā-citta*) 109
opal, pillar of 384, 395
oral tradition 51, 188–9, 197, 326, 667n, 745n
order
  conditions of the stability of the 317
  member 703n; *see also* Western Buddhist Order
  monastic 185–201; *see also* ordination, monastic
   and Going Forth 413–14
  Western Buddhist, *see* Western Buddhist Order
ordination
  bodhisattva (Sanskrit *bodhisattva-saṃvara*) 207–9, 455–6, 645
   and Western Buddhist Order 471
  and Going for Refuge 586
  and Going Forth 298
  and initiation (Sanskrit *abhiṣeka*) 447–8, 455–6, 685n, 723n

ordination (*cont.*)
into Western Buddhist Order, *see* Western Buddhist Order, ordination
lay 209, 597–8
monastic
bhikṣuṇīs 210, 469, 602–3, 688n, 689n, 725n, 744n
bhikṣus 189–90, 193–4, 421, 645; *see also upasampadā*; Brahmavamso defence of, 620–49; ceremony, 594–5, 646, 691n; inter-*nikāya*, 596, 751n; and lifestyle, 191, 591–2, 606; as rite of passage, 641–3, 646, 648–9; Sangharakshita reflection on, 580–609, 631; *sīmā*, xi, 580, 590; and status, 448; technical validity of, xii, 589–90, 620–5, 628–34, 636–7, 748n; who is fit to give, 196–7
śrāmaṇera (Pāli *sāmaṇera*) 414; compared to *kalyāṇa mitra* relationship, 585
and precepts 343
recognition of others' 595–6, 598
of Sangharakshita, *see* Sangharakshita, ordination of
self- 208, 589
and self-reliance 592–3
significance obscured 418–19
and status 448, 603, 608
temporary 210–11, 231
and the three *yānas* 447–8
'Ordination and Initiation in the Three Yanas' 447
Oriya Encyclopaedia 3, 8, 450
Orpheus 538
orthodoxy 547, 556–67, 574, 587, 744n
Orwell, G. 376, 710n
Ossian 35, 668n
'other power' (*tariki*) 562, 567
ownership 365, 368–9
Oxford Movement 682n

Padmaloka 484, 566, 728n, 734n, 754n
ordination, training 513–18, 728n, 733n, 735n, 741n
Subhuti talks at 528, 735n, 736n, 741n
Padmanarteśvara 178
Padmapāṇi 175
Padmasambhava 229, 743n
and Going for Refuge and Prostration practice 444, 721n
Sangharakshita and 442–5, 455, 721n, 743n, 744n
termas 555, 556
Padmasuri, Dharmacharini 732n
Pahārāda Sutta 691n
pain 85, 90, 95, 114; *see also duḥkha*, suffering
Pāli Tipiṭaka 13, 50–1, 326, 552
and bodhisattva ideal 209
as inspiration and guidance 553
and monastic formalism 559
and the word of the Buddha 50–1
pāmojja 103, 105; *see also prāmodya*
Pañcaviṃśatisāhasrikā 44–5, 669n
Panchen Lamas 572–3, 747n
Pande, G. C. 627, 755n
paññāvimutti 145
parables
of the Blind Men and the Elephant 49, 670n
of the burning house 168, 684n
of herbs or rain cloud 476, 726n
paradox 130–1, 132, 558
pārājikas 187, 194–5, 208, 622, 629–30, 632–3, 635–6, 687n, 748n
paramānanda 91
paramārtha 162
paramātman 130
pāramitās 16, 164, 207, 209, 293, 684n, 723n
and *bhūmis* 16–17, 170–1
and Dr Ambedkar 656
and ethics 319
and monk-lay divide 452
six 293, 699n
and spiral path 105
ten 41, 60
parāvṛtti 237, 239, 242, 248, 250, 275–85, 460–1, 463–5, 698n
Pārāyana-vagga 43, 188, 205, 690n
parinirvāṇa 12, 27, 30, 223, 226–7, 298, 317, 417, 647
parivrājakas (Pāli *paribbājakas*) 186, 188–9
Parr, S, *see* Ananda, Dharmachari
passaddhi, *see praśrabdhi*
path, *see also* Eightfold Path, threefold way
from *dāna* to *vimukti* 204
Deities of the 139
of devotion (Sanskrit *bhakti-mārga*) 143
and fruit (Sanskrit *mārga* and *phala*) 102
and goal 65, 121–2

gradual and sudden 256–8
of Higher Evolution 475–7
of knowledge (Sanskrit *jñāna-mārga*) 143
middle 15, 34, 59–60, 103, 246; *see also* Middle Way
in principle 101–3
of purity (Sanskrit *viśuddhi-mārga*) 82
of seeing 141, 146–7; *see also* path, of vision
spiral, *see nidānas*, twelve positive
threefold 28, 293, 699n
of transformation (Sanskrit *bhāvanā-mārga*) 141, 147–8
of vision (Sanskrit *darśana mārga*) 263, 463
'Path of Purity' 82, 487, 706n; *see also Visuddhimagga*
Path of the Buddha, The 434–5, 692n, 720n
patience 16, 26, 153–4, 161, 207; *see also kṣānti*
Pāṭika Sutta 84, 674n, 695n
pāṭimokkha xvi, 187, 200, 344, 627, 702n, 707n, 748n, 750n
Paul, Saint 238, 426, 694n, 719n
Pāvā 29
pearl, pillar of 378, 395
perception (*saṃjñā* (Pāli *saññā*)) 40, 46, 75, 97–8, 106, 121, 144, 328, 335–6
Perfection of Wisdom 118, 131, 159; *see also Prajñāpāramitā*
Sūtras, *see Prajñāpāramitā*, Sūtras
perfections, *see pāramitās*
Perfect Vision, *see samyak-dṛṣṭi*
phala 68, 102, 146, 641, 648
pig 74, 77, 252
pilgrimage 198, 216, 223–4, 537, 689n
pillars
five 612, 753n
ten 319, 353, 358, 363, 369, 373, 378, 380, 382, 384, 387, 389, 394, 395
pīti, see prīti
planes 73–4, 96, 109, 123, 133, 168, 274, 370–1, 528; *see also* levels, *lokas*, realms, spheres, worlds
of (subtle) form 66; *see also rūpaloka*
of archetypal form 370–1; *see also rūpaloka*
of desire 66, 370; *see also kāmaloka*
of existence, three 65–7
formless 66; *see also arūpaloka*
higher spiritual 82, 336, 728n
Platform Sūtra 555, 713n; *see also Sūtra of Wei Lang*
Plato 641–2, 691n, 739n, 740n, 756n, 757n
pleasure 90–1, 95–6, 102, 252, 255, 664n, 690n; *see also* happiness, joy
poetry 54, 168, 680n, 708n, 712n, 743n
paradox, and Nirvāṇa 132
of Sangharakshita 404, 423, 425, 455, 534–5, 538, 610, 718n, 723n, 738n, 753n
Zen 555, 742n, 743n
poets 40, 45, 85, 168, 184, 213, 365, 738n
power 16, 565–6; *see also bala*
self-, and other- 562
power mode, and love mode 361–3, 364, 365, 368
powers, psychic or supernormal 27, 33–4, 296, 659, 666n, 668n, 750n; *see also* magic, miracles
prajñā (Pāli *paññā*) 43, 82, 92, 114, 164, 593
Prajñāpāramitā 44, 170, 181
and Mañjuśrī 173–4
Prajñāpāramitā, Sūtras 224, 553
Aṣṭasāhaṣrikā-prajñāpāramitā (Perfection of Wisdom in 8,000 lines) 32, 156, 157, 167–8, 216, 224, 333, 667n, 683n, 684n, 686n, 691n, 693n, 697n, 705n
Large 140, 153–4, 681n, 683n, 684n
Prajñāpāramitā-hṛdaya Sūtra 133, 175, 317, 553, 675n, 741n
Vajracchedikā 669n, 674n, 713n, 742n
prajñās, five 172
prāmodya (Pāli *pāmojja*) 105, 259
praṇidhāna 16, 162, 164
praṇidhicitta 162, 164, 684n
Prasenajit 25
praśrabdhi 103, 106, 260, 679n
prātimokṣa (Pāli *pāṭimokkha*) 187, 344–50; *see also* monastic code
Gampopa on 441–2
prātimokṣa, in Mahāyāna tradition 704n
pratītya-samutpāda 74, 76–7, 103, 182, 251, 253, 414; *see also* conditionality, *nidānas*
formula 296, 700n
pratyekabuddhas (Pāli *paccekabuddhas*) 150–1, 168, 707n
preceptees, *see saddhivihārikas*

preceptors (*upādhyāyas* (Pāli *upajjhāyas*) 193, 194
  in monastic ordination 196–7, 629, 633–4
  and precepts 324, 343
  relationship with preceptee (Pāli *saddhivihārika*) 196
  of Sangharakshita 419, 420, 421, 455–6
  Sangharakshita as 523, 524, 529, 536, 730n
  in Western Buddhist Order, *see* Western Buddhist Order, preceptors
precepts 324–5; *see also* ethics, morality, *śīla*
  bodhisattva 208, 657–9
  of body 330, 357–73
  eight 204, 209, 227, 654
    and *maechis* 601, 744n
  as fetters 264–5
  five 411
    and laity (Sanskrit *upāsakas*) 193
    Sangharakshita 'taking' 410–11
  and formalism xiii, 410–11, 438, 486
  and Going for Refuge 305, 324–5, 336, 557–8, 598
  and lifestyle 351–3, 557–8
  of mind 331, 385–94
  and monks 345; *see also* monastic code, *prātimokṣa*, *sikkhāpadas*
  sixty-four bodhisattva 455, 657, 690n
  speech 330–1, 374–84, 385, 703n, 704n, 710n
  and Stream Entry 146
  ten, (Sanskrit *daśa-śikṣāpada*)
    in *Aṅguttara Nikāya* 329–32, 705n
    and *bhikṣu* ordination 193
    canonical sources of 326–34
    different terms for 340
    in English 312
    as ethical principles 346
    of novice monk (Sanskrit *śrāmaṇera*) 350, 418, 606, 655
    of 'nuns' (Pāli *dasasilamata*) 744n
    and ordination in Western Buddhist Order 305, 317, 468, 491–2; *anagārikas*, 608
    in Pāli 311
    as pattern of ethical behaviour 331–2
    as pillars 318–19
    positive 313, 330
    at the time of the Buddha 347–8
pretas 73–4, 94–5, 140, 168, 253, 370, 673n
prīti (Pāli *pīti*) 103, 105–7, 110, 260, 679n
Prophet's Night Journey 644, 757n
prostration 214, 444–5, 486–7, 603
protectors 173, 177, 181, 228, 565, 626
Proudhon, P-J 368, 709n
pṛthagjanas (Pāli *puthujjana*) 46, 115, 138–9
Psalms 674n
psyche-continuum (Sanskrit *citta-santāna*) 14–15, 478
psychic or supernormal powers 27, 33–4, 296, 659, 666n, 668n, 750n
psychological analysis 42, 71
psychology, and cosmology 66–7, 371
pudgalas 88, 99, 141
Puggala-Paññātti 150, 682n
puja 237, 273
  Sevenfold 343, 389, 392, 429, 470, 584, 638, 719n
Pukkusa 29
punarbhava 14
puṇya (Pāli *puññā*) 205, 214–15, 593
puṇya-kṣetra (Pāli *puññā-khetta*) 214–15
Pūralāsa Sutta 665n
Pure Abodes (*śuddhāvāsa* (Pāli *suddhāvāsa*)) 148–9, 370
Pure Land 78, 553–4, 562
Pure Land Buddhism 549, 550, 552–4, 556, 558, 562, 566, 568–9; *see also* Jōdo Shinshū
Pure Land *sūtras* 742n
purification 330
  seven stages of 258
purity
  and beauty 82
  path of, *see* path of purity

Quartermaine 404, 423, 712n

raft 59, 391, 425
rāga 147, 386; *see also lobha*
Rāhula 11, 26, 665n
Rāhula, S. 213
Rājagṛha 24, 27, 74
Ramakrishna Mission 412, 715n
Ramana Maharshi 282–3, 698n
rapture 105–7, 126, 252, 260–1; *see also prīti*
Ratana Sutta 696
Ratnapāṇi 172
Ratnasambhava 42, 117, 172, 281
Ratnasuri, Dharmacharini 732n, 733n

Ray, R. 552, 560–1, 741n, 745n
realism 87, 675n
reality, *see also* Unconditioned, the
  absolute 43, 45–6, 81, 408
  absolute *ālaya* as 279
  and bliss 108
  described in the *Udāna* 241
  empirical and ultimate 264
  and energy 86
  glimpsed in *samādhi* 262
  higher plane of 82
  and language 88
  non-dual 270; *see also śūnyatā*
  and *samādhi* 42
  spiritual, and factual truth 65
  unconditioned absolute, Buddha as 43
realms 123; *see also lokas*, planes, spheres, worlds
  brahmā- 608; *see also brahma-vihāras*
  'Contented' 18
  Nirvāṇa as a 132
  of truth 43
  in wheel of life 253
rebirth 14–15, 93–4, 231–2, 253–5, 662n
  and bodhisattvas 168, 182–3
  and Buddhahood 17
  and holy persons 141
  and karma 72–3
  and merit 214
  and Pure Land 554
receptivity 266, 485, 529
  to other traditions 245–6; *see also* ecumenism
recollection
  of the Buddhas 44–5, 272
  of death 387, 392
  of impurity 387, 392
  of previous abodes 15–16
  of the six elements 387, 392, 711n
Record of Western Countries (*Xiyu Ji*) 686n, 689n
reflection
  on suffering 271–2
  on Vasubandhu's four factors 272–4
refuge, language of 727n
Refuges
  only one 302–3
  and Precepts 240, 323–5
    and *bhikṣu* ordination 193, 421
    and Dr Ambedkar 437, 495–6; followers of, 438–9, 496
    and formalism xiii, 410–11, 438, 486
    and founding of Western Buddhist Order 405, 500
    recitation of 219
    relation between 323–4
    and Sangharakshita 'taking *pansil*' 410
    taking, *see* Going for Refuge, and 'taking refuge'
  Three (Sanskrit *tri-śarana*) 240, 241, 242, 303, 323, 425; *see also* Three Jewels
    and Buddhist unity 348
    esoteric 481, 728n
    and monastic ordination 193, 418–19
Refuge Tree 444–5, 515, 531, 721n
  Triratna 721n, 735n, 743n
reincarnation 182, 662n
rejoicing in merits 380, 389, 392, 719n, 730n
reliances, four 196, 421; *see also nissaya*
remorse 105, 259–60, 707n
Renan, J. E. 627, 755n
Rennyo 562, 566, 746n
renunciation 271, 642, 643
Republic, The 642, 757n
restlessness (*auddhatya* (Pāli *uddhacca*) 149, 150, 626
retreats
  FWBO study 484
  ordination 514–15, 717n, 734n
  rainy season 28, 187, 189, 199; *see also varṣāvāsa*
  single-sex 517
revenants, *see pretas*
reverence 176, 224, 226, 232, 294, 455, 755n
  of laity to monks 213–14
  Sangharakshita and 790
Rhine, J. B. 33, 667n
Rhinoceros Sutta (Pāli *Khaggavisāṇa*) 191, 688n
Rhys Davids, C. A. F. 627, 754–5n
  and *niyamas* 672n
right livelihood 489
  team-based 305, 387, 468, 516, 546, 725n, 734n
right understanding 127, 140
Rimé tradition 685n
rites 265
ritual 53, 105, 147, 222, 224, 546, 556
  dependence on 147, 264–5
Ritualist controversies 682n
robes 29, 190, 200, 411, 600–1, 608, 632
rock, splitting 283
rose-apple tree 20, 21, 110–11
Rossetti, D. G. 671n

ruby, pillar of 389, 395
rules of training 341–2; *see also* *sikkhāpadas* (Sanskrit *śikṣāpadas*)
rūpa 75, 97–8, 109, 144, 335, 370
rūpa-dhyānas 66, 73, 83–4, 110–11
rūpakāya 40, 221, 336
rūpaloka 66, 73, 78, 83–4, 105, 148, 608
Ryōkan Taigu 555, 743n

Saccaka 110, 662n, 716n
saddhā, *see śraddhā*
Saddharma Puṇḍarīka Sūtra 128, 155, 168, 173, 176, 178–9, 182, 216, 224–5, 553, 679n, 683n, 684n, 685n, 686n, 693n, 726–7n, 742n
saddhivihārikas 196
sādhana 554, 685n; *see also* visualization
sahāloka 63–4
Śākyamuni 7, 64, 128, 151–2, 272, 334, 444, 721n; *see also* Buddha, Gautama, Siddhārtha
śākyaputra- śramaṇas 25–6
Śākyas 19, 25
salt, taste of 56, 671n
Salutation to the Three Jewels (Pāli *Tiratana Vandanā*) 425, 679n, 706n
samādhi 109–13, 260–1
  Buddhaghosa on 552
  and human realm 96
  and insight 145
  and precepts 385
    of bodhisattva 658
  and reality 42
  and the *trikāya* 41
Samādhirāja Sūtra 567, 746n
Sāmaññaphala Sutta 200, 670n, 689n, 750n
Samantabhadra 172–3, 179–80, 224, 454, 477
Samantamukha 176
śamatha 562
śamatha-bhāvanā 204
sambhogakāya 41–3, 45–6, 78, 153, 170, 336, 669n
sambodhi 38, 111, 114, 116, 119–20, 124, 266–7; *see also* Enlightenment
saṃjñā (Pāli *saññā*) 75, 97, 98
saṃsāra, and *nirvāṇa* 56, 119, 149, 159, 164, 166, 171
saṃskāras (Pāli *saṅkhāras*) 67, 68, 75, 82, 97, 98–9, 253, 335
saṃskṛta-dharmas 62, 67, 80, 674n
saṃskṛta-śūnyatā 118
saṃvṛti 162
samyak-dṛṣṭi (Pāli *samma-diṭṭhi*) 127, 141, 390–1, 393, 557
samyak-samādhi (Pāli *sammā-samādhi*) 112, 141
samyak-sambuddha (Pāli *sammā-sambuddha*) 151, 293
samyak-saṅkalpa (Pāli *sammā-saṅkappa*) 141
Saṃyutta Nikāya 43–4, 103, 122, 664n, 669n, 671n, 676n, 678n, 697n, 698n, 699n, 700n, 701n, 710n, 726n, 751n
Sandhinirmocana Sūtra 67, 162, 683n
sangha 8, 137–8, 246, 248, 453, 694n; *see also* spiritual, community
  bodhicitta arising in 474–5
  bodhisattva 153–84
  and communication 247–8, 462
  early 23–6, 192
    four companies (*vargas*) of 202, 722n
  extreme views of 470
  as monastic order 185–201, 694n
    corporate acts of 198–200
    devotion towards 225–6
    expulsion from 194–5
    and monastic code 188
    and ordination 193–4
    stages of development 185–92
    in *The Survey* 432
  as Refuge 294, 425, 461–2, 728n
  Sangharakshita desire for 583
  schism in the early 192, 205, 452
  seven conditions of welfare 28
Sanghadevi, Dharmacharini 733n, 740n
saṅgha-karma (Pāli *sangha-kamma*) 193, 198–9, 596
Sanghamittā 222
Sangharaja 573, 690n, 747n
  of Ceylon 213
Sangharakshita 694n, 723n, 737n
  about himself 529–31, 737n
  autobiography 535, 537
  and bodhisattva ideal 454–5, 585
  and the Buddha 408–9
  desire for Sangha 583
  and *Diamond Sutra* and *Sūtra of Wei Lang* xiii, 407–8, 713n
  disciples of 524
  and Dr Ambedkar 437–8, 494, 720n, 729n, 730n, 746n
    followers of 438, 500

and Going Forth 412–16, 499, 584–5, 716n, 717n
'handing over' or 'on' 511, 536, 546, 573, 740n, 747n, 748n
on his books 533–4, 537–8
initiations (*abhiṣeka*) of 442–3, 445, 685n, 692n, 721n, 722n
lectures 235, 427, 460–1, 475, 532–4, 694n, 719n, 725n, 727n, 737n, 738n, 739n, 741–2n
and lifestyle 611
memoirs 404, 407, 413, 537, 694n, 698n, 713n, 713n, 720n, 721n, 726n, 739n, 740n, 748n, 796
mother 536, 739n
ordination of 499
bhikṣu 414–15, 420–1, 456, 589, 718n, 748n
bodhisattva 455–6, 500, 585–6, 690n, 723n
flaw in xiv, 580–1, 592, 596, 623
monks at 581–2, 586–7, 588
novice (*śrāmaṇera* 417–19, 585, 717n, 749n
preceptors 419, 420, 421, 455–6
poetry of 404, 423, 425, 455, 534–5, 538, 610, 718n, 723n, 738n, 753n
sabbatical in 1973 474, 726n
seminars 484, 728n
translation of 534, 738n
as translator 525–7, 533
and Western Buddhist Order
founding of xii, xv–xvi, xvii, 519, 523–4
relation to 523–4, 529, 531, 536, 730n
in the wilderness 610–12
Sangharakshita: A New Voice in the Buddhist Tradition 722n, 732n 735n, 749n, 797
Sangharakshita Library xix, 791
Saṅgīti Sutta 697n
Śāntarakṣita 745n
Śāntideva 125, 157, 159, 208, 360, 454, 723n
sapphire, pillar of 394, 395
Sarahapāda 182, 686n
Śāriputra (Pāli Sāriputta) 24, 26, 122, 204, 327–8, 347–8, 646, 664n, 665n, 687n
Sarnath 223, 417, 420, 579, 717n
Sartre, J-P 100, 676n
Sarvanivaraṇaviṣkambhin 172
Sarvāstivāda School 12, 74, 76, 88, 97–9, 145, 152, 192, 195, 222, 675n, 745n
Satipaṭṭhāna, New Burmese Method of 112
satkāya-dṛṣṭi 146, 263–4, 297
scapegoat 610–11, 753n
Scapegoat, The 609–10, 752n
scepticism 34, 142, 146, 148
scholasticism 142, 152, 156, 441
Schopenhauer, A. 76, 673n
Schweitzer, A. 627, 755n
science
and Buddhism 64–6
and Mañjuśrī 174
Second Vatican Council 457
seeds (Sanskrit *bījas*) 279–80, 282–3, 464
seeing (Sanskrit *darśana*) 55, 127
path of (Sanskrit *darśana-mārga*) 141, 146, 147
and sublimation of emotions 148
in terms of opposites 282
'things as they are' 55; *see also yathābhūta-jñānadarśana*
and views 390–1
self 86, 264, 661n; *see also ātman*
and bodhisattva ideal 159
empirical 283
-hood, spiritual 268–70, 463
and others
practice of equality of (Sanskrit *parātmasamatā*) 361
practice of substitution of (Sanskrit *parātmaparivartana*) 361
power (*jiriki*) 562
-reliance, and ordination 592–3
Supreme 130
-surrender, and Going for Refuge 487–8
-transcendence 477
-view, fixed, *see satkāya-dṛṣṭi*
and world, transformation of 516–17
sensuous desire (Pāli *kāma*) 22, 28, 139, 148, 370–1
bias towards (Pāli *kāmāsava*) 119
plane of, *see kāmaloka*
service 162, 361; *see also* altruism
seven factors of Enlightenment (Sanskrit *bodhyaṅgas*) 60, 98, 126, 679n
Sevenfold Puja 343, 389, 392, 429, 470, 584, 638, 719n
Sevitabbāsevitabba Sutta 327–9, 347–8, 705n, 708n
sexual dimorphism 371, 605
sexual misconduct, abstention from 312, 350, 370, 372, 387, 608
sexual polarization 372, 386, 709n

Shabda 512, 513, 514, 521, 733n, 736n, 748n
Shahn, B. 77
Shakespeare 58, 365, 369, 424, 434, 709n, 720n
Shaw, G. B. 359, 708n
Shelley, P. B. 359–60, 678n, 686n, 708n
Shingon Shū 213, 691n, 693n
Shinran Shōnin 228, 562, 693n, 746n
Shintoism 11
Short History of the World, A 408, 714n
Shōtoku Taishi 182, 228, 686n
shrines, household 229–30
Siam 634–5, 756n
Śibis, king of the 16
Siddhārtha 19–21, 35–6; *see also* Buddha, Gautama, Śākyamuni
sikkhāpadas (Sanskrit *śikṣāpadas*) 340, 342–3, 349, 591, 607
  breach of 580, 586–7, 589–90, 593–4, 598, 635
Śikṣā-samuccaya 125–6, 208, 454, 723n
śīla (Pāli *sīla*) 105, 147, 164, 642; *see also* ethics, morality, precepts
  samādhi, prajñā 28, 92, 349, 708n; *see also* threefold way
śīlavrata-parāmarśa (Pāli *sīlabbata-parāmāsa*) 146, 264–5
silence 51, 54
silver, pillar of 382, 395
sīmā xi, 580, 582, 590, 596, 756n
single-sex
  communities 607
  idea 517, 710n
  situations 372, 517, 709n, 710n
Sisyphus 261, 696n
Sīvali 229, 693n
six element practice 387, 392, 711n
Siyama *nikāya* 193, 595, 688n
Skandhakas (Pāli *Khandhakas*) 190, 192, 201
skandhas, Pāli *khandas*
  five 75, 97, 124, 335
  three 349, 708n
skilful (*kuśala* Pāli *kusala*), and unskilful, *see kuśala* and *akuśala*
skilful means (Sanskrit *upāya-kauśalya*) 16, 164, 218
snake 74, 77, 116, 177, 252
Snellgrove, D. 96
sobornost 474
Sona, Dharmachari 740n
Sōtō Zen 112, 563, 567, 693n, 743n
space, and time 63, 65–6, 67, 128
sparśa 75, 254
speech 374–84, 385
  precepts, *see* precepts, speech
spheres 66; *see also* levels, *lokas*, realms, worlds
  of extinction 43
  of infinite consciousness 110
  of infinite space 110
  of neither-perception-nor-non-perception 21, 110–11, 123
  of no-thing-ness 20–1, 110–11
spiral
  path, *see nidānas*, twelve positive
  and wheel 113, 239, 251–2, 255, 258–9, 265, 463; *see also nidānas*
spirit
  and letter 59, 155–6, 442, 659
    and precepts 343
    and truthfulness 377
  and letter and *bhikkhu* ordination 643
  and letter and monasticism 559
spiritual
  androgyny 371–2, 517
  attainments, *see* attainments, spiritual
  communities, residential 516–17, 546, 606–7, 802
  community 362, 366, 393, 414–15; *see also* sangha
    and the group 415, 474, 499
    and individual 473–4, 488
    and speech 375–6, 377
    and third order of consciousness 474
    unity of Buddhist 345–6, 496–7, 502
    Western Buddhist Order as 405, 568
  death 387
  development, and altruism 299–300
  discipline 52, 467
  faculties, five 549, 626
  fellowship 294–5; *see also* spiritual friendship
    and monk-lay split 446
    of Western Buddhist Order with others 502, 510, 545–6
  friends 160–2, 528–9, 606–8, 700n; *see also kalyāṇa mitras*
  friendship 486, 528, 546, 725n, 734n, 736n, 746n; *see also kalyāṇa mitratā*
    and community living/or working 606–7
    and kindly speech 380
    and ordination in Western Buddhist Order 488
    Sangharakshita and 499, 528

  and single sex idea 517, 710n
  vertical and horizontal 462, 528
 hierarchy 115, 155, 247, 461
 ideal 150, 206, 209–10, 292–3, 452, 461–2
 individualism 116, 140, 270, 272, 274, 300, 517
 life 276, 371, 392, 552, 592–3, 623, 627–8
  and false views 391–2
  identified with monastic life 203, 446, 592
  misunderstandings about 283–4
 rebirth 7, 387
 teachers 212, 242–3, 247–8, 461–2, 525, 528
 tension, and breakthrough 161–2, 271–2, 273–4
 tutelage 196; *see also* (*niśraya* (Pāli *nissaya*)
 workshops 510, 731n
spirituality, Euro- 612–14
śraddhā (Pāli *saddhā*) 103–5, 128, 243, 477, 549; *see also* faith
śraddhānusārin 141–5, 152, 220, 531, 737n
Srimala, Dharmacharini 399, 731n, 732n, 733n, 737n, 740n
śrīpāda (Pāli *siripāda*) 222–3
śrotāpanna (Pāli *sotāpanna*), *see* Stream Entrant
states
 human 95, 111, 173
 nine transcendental 60
 superconscious 20, 41, 66, 145; *see also dhyānas*
stealing 364
Stepping-Stones 723n, 736n
Sthaviravāda 192, 205–6, 209
store consciousness, *see ālaya-vijñāna*
Strauss. D. F. 627, 755n
Stream Entrant (*śrotāpanna* (Pāli *sotāpanna*)) 140–2, 146–7, 149, 171, 263–4, 297, 327, 481–2, 696n
Stream Entry (Sanskrit *śrotāpatti-mārga*) xvi, 115, 140–1, 250–65, 297–8; *see also* irreversibility
 and arising of *bodhicitta* 160, 300–1, 483
 and conversion 140, 263, 265–6, 275, 281, 285, 462–3, 464
 as metaphor 250
 and opening Dharma eye 296–8
 as real Going for Refuge 296–7, 300–2, 305, 465, 481–2
 and temperament 144
study
 in bodhisattva precepts 201, 392–3, 517, 659
 seminars 532, 728n
stupas 179, 220–1, 222, 223, 224, 228, 232, 692n, 717n
stuti 174, 685n
śubha 80, 82–3
Subhadra 30
Subhuti
 arhant 157, 159, 167, 333, 408, 713n
 Dharmachari 510, 511–13, 515–16, 521, 528, 547, 569, 696n, 707n, 719n, 722n, 731n, 732n, 733n, 735n, 736n, 740n, 741n, 748n, 749n
'suchness,' *see tathatā*
Suddhodana 19–20, 26, 665n
Sudhana 161, 165, 174
suffering 103–4, 258, 272, 477; *see also duḥkha*, pain
 cessation of 122–3
 reflection on 271–2
Sufism 11, 338
sukha (Pāli and Sanskrit) 80, 98, 103, 106–10, 260
Sukhāvatī 554, 562
Sukhāvatī-vyūha Sūtras 132, 163, 174–5, 553, 680n, 745n
Sumedha 17
śūnyatā (Pāli *suññāta*) 43, 89, 117, 121, 162; *see also* Void, the, voidness
 four degrees of 118–19, 392, 711n
 preaching 657
 Sangharakshita's response to 408
 as *vimokṣa-mukha* 121, 122
superconscious states 66, 145; *see also dhyānas*
superficiality 697n
superknowledges, *see abhijñās*
superman (Sanskrit *mahāpuruṣa*) 42, 45, 708
Śūraṅgama Sūtra 555, 691n
Survey of Buddhism, A 289, 427–33, 452–3, 455, 479, 533–4, 549, 559, 587, 696n, 699n, 719n, 722–3n
Sūtrāntikas 197
Sūtra of Golden Light (Sanskrit *Suvarṇa-prabhāsa Sūtra*) 334, 553, 706n, 742n
Sūtra of Hui Neng, *see Sūtra of Wei Lang*
Sūtra of Wei Lang 77, 408, 454, 555, 579, 583, 673n, 713n
 Sangharakshita and 407–8, 499, 579, 713n

sūtras (Pāli *Suttas*)
Mahāyāna 64, 67, 96–7, 132, 153, 156, 170, 208, 213, 224, 332, 723n; *see also* individual names
'Perfection of Wisdom,' *see Prajñāpāramitā*
schools based on 553–4
in *Śikṣāsamuccaya* 723n
translation of 333–4
Pāli Canon, *see* individual names, *Aṅguttara Nikāya*, *Dīgha Nikāya*, *Majjhima Nikāya*, *Saṃyutta Nikāya*, Sutta Piṭaka
Pure Land 742n
transition to *tantra* 174
Sutta-Nipāta 38, 43, 188, 191, 205, 552, 665n, 669n, 676n, 678n, 688n, 690n, 696n, 697n
Sutta Piṭaka 15, 326, 552, 625, 627
higher criticism of 627
and Vinaya Piṭaka 591, 627–8
Suvajra, Dharmachari 510, 512, 521, 731n, 732n, 733n, 740n
Suvarṇa-prabhāsa Sūtra 334, 553, 706n, 742n
Suzuki, B. L. 227–8, 232
Suzuki, D. T. 45, 160, 163, 179, 228, 277, 279, 669n, 698n, 702n, 707n
symbolism 34–5, 37–8, 67, 131–3, 172, 222, 229, 601
sympathetic joy (Sanskrit *muditā*) 157, 389
Symposium 218, 691n

Tagore, R. 112, 677n
Takakusu, J. 77
'Taking Refuge in the Buddha' 423–6, 718n
taṇhā, *see tṛṣṇā*
Tantra 174, 549, 675n, 706n
use of symbols 37–8, 67
tantras 67, 174, 565, 675n
Tantric initiation (Sanskrit *abhiṣeka*) 442, 564–5, 571, 574, 738n
Sangharakshita's 440
Taoism 11
tāpasa 589
Tārā 178, 229
Taraloka 733n, 734n
Tāranātha 182, 686n
Taste of Freedom, The 697n
taste of salt 56, 671n
Tathāgata 165, 272–3, 624
and ten precepts 334
tathāgatagarbha 43
tathatā 43, 89, 167–8
Tattvasaṅgraha of Śāntarakṣita, The 745n
Taylor, T. 536, 740n
TBMSG, *see* Trailokya Bauddha Mahasangha Sahayaka Gana
'TBMSG: A Dhamma Revolution in India' 729n
team-based right livelihood 305, 516, 546, 725n, 734n
temperament 83–4, 141–3, 191, 531, 590, 673n
or capacity and refuges 425
and five Buddha families 172
and liberation 737n
Sangharakshita's 531
and Stream Entry 144
and *vimokṣas* 144
and Western Buddhist Order 531–2
and *yānas* 168
Tennyson, A. 146–7, 248, 292, 682n, 696n, 699n
ten pillars 318–19, 352–3
individual correlations 358, 363, 369, 373, 378, 380, 382, 384, 387, 389, 394, 395
Ten Pillars of Buddhism, The xv, 309, 492, 517, 534
Teresa of Ávila 143, 681n
Tharpe Delam 443, 721n
Theosophical Society 410, 714n
Theosophists 151, 289, 482, 685n
Thera- and *Theri-gātha* 552
Theravāda 548–9, 552–3
'families' (Pāli *nikāyas*), of *bhikkhus* 595, 595–6, 747n
formalism of xii, xiv, 415, 432–3, 449, 459, 559, 604, 634, 744n
and Going for Refuge 299, 484, 488, 566, 597
and Maitreya 178
and monastic code 195, 196, 595, 702n, 704n
monasticism, *see* monasticism
and monk-lay split 211, 214, 558–60, 592–3, 599–601, 608
ordination, *see* ordination
and orthodoxy 556–7, 558–62
as 'pure' Dharma 50, 670n
relation of Western Buddhist Order to 490, 550, 556, 560–1, 567–8, 570, 573, 596
ritual and worship 147, 222, 225, 226–7, 229, 232
and Sangharajas 747n

Sangharakshita's criticism of 85, 152, 432–3, 449, 458–9, 495, 556–7, 558–61, 574, 599–600, 620, 630, 632, 639, 647
Therīgāthā 755n
Thittila, Sayadaw U. 410–11, 584, 714n, 720n
Thomas, E. J. 36, 668n, 690n
Thotagamuwe Sri Rahula Thera 690n
The Thousand-Petalled Lotus 413, 417, 420, 713n, 740n
Thrangu Rinpoche 567, 746n
three bodies, *see trikāya* doctrine
three characteristics, *see lakṣaṇas*
threefold path 28, 293, 563, 699n
Threefold Refuge, The 484–5, 566, 727n, 728n, 745n, 746n
The Three Jewels xiii, xv, 3–4, 7–232
Three Jewels xv, 7–8, 240–2, 292–5, 348; *see also* Refuges, Three
  becoming the 250
  in bodhisattva precepts 657, 658
  and Going for Refuge 259
  and precepts 318
  Sangharakshita and xiii
  and Stream Entry 146
  in Tibetan Buddhism 435–6
  and Triratna Buddhist Community 700n
three marks, *see lakṣaṇas*
three poisons 74, 121–2
three refuges, *see* Refuges, Three
three roots 565; *see also* Refuges, Three, esoteric
Tiantai school 105
Tibetan Book of the Dead, The (*Bardo Thödol*) 67, 76, 555–6, 672n, 693n, 743n
time
  and energy, taking another's 366–7
  and space 41, 63, 65–6, 67, 128, 317
Tiratanaloka 733n, 734n, 735n
Tiratana Vandanā 425–6, 679n, 706n
titans, *see asuras*
tradition, authority of xv
Trailokya Bauddha Mahasangha (TBM) 315, 317, 404–5, 490, 517, 700n, 702n; *see also* Western Buddhist Order
Trailokya Bauddha Mahasangha Sahayaka Gana (TBMSG) 289, 568, 700n, 729n, 740n, 795
Trailokyavijaya 172
tranquillity (Sanskrit *praśrabdhi* Pāli *passaddhi*) 106, 260
  as positive counterpart of covetousness 387
translation 525–7, 533
Trapuṣa (Pāli Tapussa) 22, 663n, 727n
trees
  bodhi 36–7, 117, 219, 222–3, 251, 413
  rose-apple 110–11
trikāya doctrine 39–43, 45–6, 128, 151, 160, 170, 182, 336, 435, 668n, 706n
Triṃśika 676n
Triṃśikā-kārikā 698n
Triratna Buddhist Community xii, xix, 289, 653, 721n, 725n, 728n, 736n, 740n, 754n, 796; *see also* FWBO
  change from FWBO to 700n
  dedication ceremony 462, 724n
  Friends of 702n, 703n
  Mitras of, *see* Mitras
  six distinctive emphases of 725n
Triratna Buddhist Order xvi–xvii, xix, 700n, 712n, 731n, 795, 802; *see also* Western Buddhist Order
Triyana Vardhana Vihara 537
tṛṣṇā (Pāli *taṇhā*) 75, 102–4, 254, 386
truth 21, 50, 96, 480, 555
  body of 43; *see also dharmakāya*
  Eye of 295–6, 327, 482, 700n
Tsongkhapa 116, 143, 182, 229, 657, 676n, 678n, 681n, 686n
tulkus 182–3, 225, 600, 645; *see also* lamas, incarnate, Dalai Lamas
Turner, J. M. W. 609, 612, 752n
'turning about' or 'around,' *see parāvṛtti*
tuṣitadevaloka 18, 179
twelve links, *see nidānas*, twelve, cyclic
twentieth blow 283
Two Buddhist Books in Mahāyāna, The 454, 477

Udāna 49, 82–3, 123, 241, 257, 552, 663n, 668n, 670n, 671n, 674n, 678n, 682n, 689n, 692n, 695n, 696n
Udraka Rāmaputra 21
Unconditioned, the 56, 84, 88–9, 92, 121–2, 149; *see also* reality
  and beauty (Sanskrit *śubha*) 82, 84–5, 486
  and conversion 250
  emptiness of 118, 122
  and faith (*śraddhā* Pāli *saddhā*) 104, 259
  and insight 262–3, 265
  insubstantiality of 88–9

Unconditioned, the (*cont.*)
and the *lakṣaṇas* 82
longing for 91–2, 161, 271
and non-duality 91, 114, 117–18, 122, 165, 229
Three Jewels as 259
and the *vipariyāsas* 80
and wheel of life 95–6
Unconscious, the 37, 105, 636, 698n, 756n
United Lodge of Theosophists 289
universalism 181, 183–4, 206
'Unobstructed Success' 42; *see also* Amoghasiddhi
Untouchables, *see* ex-Untouchables
upādāna 75, 254
upādhyāya (Pāli *upajjhāya*) 193–4, 196, 420
Upaka 22, 663n
Upāli 389, 701n
Upāli Sutta 665n, 701n
Upanishads 58, 661n
upāsakas (fem. *upāsikās*) 202, 453
ordination and status 448
and temporary monastic ordination 210
in Western Buddhist Order 468, 489
change to *dharmacārī/iṇīs* 490–1, 729n
upasampadā 187–91, 193–4, 198, 207, 216, 691n, 748n; *see also* ordination, monastic
lineage 192, 209
upāya-kauśalya 16, 164, 218–19
upekṣā 98, 110, 125, 150, 679n
uposatha, *see poṣadha*
Uposatha Sutta 671n, 682n
Uruvelā Kāśyapa 23–4
uṣṇīṣa 647
Uttarapāthakas 152

Vacchagotta 698–9n, 716n
Vagīśvara 173
vagueness 697n
Vaiḍūryaprabha 42
Vairocana 42, 172–3, 281
Vaiśākha (Pāli Vesākha, Sinhalese: Wesak) 226–7
vajra 157, 177
Vajrabhairava 178
Vajracchedikā Prajñāpāramitā Sūtra xiii, 44, 81, 159, 454, 553, 555, 579, 583, 673, 713n, 742n
Sangharakshita and xiii, 407–8, 499, 713n
Vajra-dhvaja 157
Vajraloka 371
Vajrapāṇi 172–3, 177, 180
Vajrasattva 443, 692n, 722n
Vajrayāna 91, 97, 118, 124, 147, 169, 172, 174, 177, 215, 442, 447–8, 564, 566, 686n, 728n 795; *see also yānas*
and Emptiness 118
and images 133
and magic 215
meditation 97
and worship 222
Vajrayudha 174
'vale of tears' 80, 674n
vargas 203, 205–9, 722n
varṣāvāsa 198–200
vase, sacred 179
Vasubandhu 81, 114, 672n, 675n, 676n, 682n, 698n, 709n
four factors 272–4, 697n
Vatthūpama Sutta 677n
Vaughan, H. 679n
vedanā 75, 97–8, 103, 106–7, 254, 335
Vedānta 108
vegetarianism 363, 468, 489
veils (Sanskrit *varaṇas*) 45, 56, 262; *see also jñeyāvaraṇa*, *kleśāvaraṇa*
Vekhanassa Sutta 728n
Venice 609, 752n
Vessantara, Dharmachari 730n
vicikitsā (Pāli *vicikicchā*) 146, 264, 297
vidyā (Pāli *vijjā*) 127; *see also* knowledge
Vidyasri, Dharmacharini 734n
view
non- 391
personality- (*satkāya-dṛṣṭi* (Pāli *sakkāya-diṭṭhi*)) 146
views, *see also dṛṣṭi*
extreme 14–15
false *mithyā-dṛṣṭi* (Pāli *micchā-diṭṭhi*) 390, 391–4
abstention from 312, 390, 393–4
and language 393
no 391, 393
sixty-two wrong 670n
viharas 189, 191, 420, 443, 537, 717n, 723n
vijñāna (Pāli *viññāṇa*) 75, 97–9, 254, 278, 280, 335, 463–4; *see also* consciousness
vijñānas, eight 99, 278, 280–1, 463, 676n
Vijñānavada 97, 99

Vimalakīrti 54, 118, 207, 334, 684–5n, 690n
Vimalakīrti-nirdeśa 78, 173, 553, 555, 670n, 671n, 674n, 678n, 685n, 686n, 706n, 742n
vimokṣa-mukhas (Pāli *vimokkha-mukhas*) 121
vimokṣas (Pāli *vimokkhas*)
  eight 143–4
  three 114–15, 122
vimukti (Pāli *vimutti*) 56, 96, 103, 118–19, 127, 204, 593; *see also* emancipation, freedom, liberation
Vinaya 30; *see also Dharma-Vinaya*, monastic code
  development of 13, 186, 190, 203, 627
  Mahāyāna and 192, 207, 208–9, 452, 658
Vinayadharas 197
Vinaya Piṭaka 552, 627
  (*Cullavagga*) 628, 664n, 666n, 671n, 687n, 688n, 751n, 755n
  (*Mahāvagga*) 23, 623–4, 628, 629, 661n, 663n, 664n, 665n, 667n, 668n, 682n, 687n, 689n, 718n, 726n, 727n, 748n, 751n, 754n
  (*Sutta Vibhaṅga*) 687n, 756n
  different versions of 595
  higher criticism of 627
  and ordination ceremony 580, 590, 591, 594–5, 622–3, 628–32, 635, 642–3, 646, 687n, 748n, 754n
Vinaya-saṅgīti 188
Vinayavastu 200
violence 358–9, 361–2
  and property 364, 368
  and speech 377
vipariyāsas 80–1, 90
Vipassin 187
Vipaśvin Buddha 176
vipaśyanā (Pāli *vipassanā*) 113–14, 127; *see also* insight
  meditation, and Going for Refuge 561–2, 563–4, 571
virāga 103, 117
vīrya 16, 156, 164, 293, 549, 679n
Viśākhā 25, 664n
vision
  -attained one 143
  Axial 127, 140–1; *see also samyak-dṛṣṭi*
  and Going for Refuge xii–xiii, 292
  of *lakṣaṇas* in *Dhammapada* 82
  path of 263, 463
  perfect 393
Viśiṣṭacāritra (Japanese: Jōgyō) 182, 686n
visualization 273
  and mantra recitation practice 518, 685n
  and Refuge Tree 444
Visuddhimagga 116, 178, 201, 487, 552, 671n, 673n, 677n, 689n, 706n, 737n, 755–6n
viśuddhi-mārga 82
Viśvapāṇi 172
Void, the 86, 121, 133, 168, 177, 408, 657; *see also śūnyatā*
  and *parāvṛtti* 276, 277
voidness 51, 91, 130, 166, 281
volitions (Pāli and Sanskrit *cetanā*) 68, 70–2, 74, 93–5, 123, 139, 335–6, 483, 485, 487
vows
  of Amitābha 562, 745n
  bodhisattva 470–1
  of bodhisattva *praṇidhicitta* 162–4, 274, 471, 684n
  of celibacy 305, 708n
  of chastity 605, 608–9
  four great 274, 471
  personal 347, 492, 707n
  of silence 375
  ten 468; *see also* precepts, Ten
  twenty-two, of Dr Ambedkar 437, 496, 597–8, 656

Wadia, B. P. and Mme 289
Wangyal, Geshe 555, 744n
'Wanted:
  A New Type of Bhikkhu' 448–9, 722n
  A New Type of Upāsaka' 448–9, 722n
Was the Buddha a Bhikkhu? xiv, 559, 615–50
Watts, A. 698n
Wei Lang (Huineng) 77
Wells, H. G. 408, 714n
Western Buddhist Order xx, 404–5, 696n, 702n, 789; *see also* Triratna Buddhist Order
  anagārikas 305, 469, 561, 604, 608–9, 643, 708n
  approach to sangha 470
  and Avalokiteśvara 316, 703n
  as Avalokiteśvara 474–5
  not a 'Buddhist society' 466–7, 519
  chapter meetings 510, 514–15, 518, 730n, 731n
  commitment and lifestyle xvi, 467–9, 611

Western Buddhist Order (*cont.*)
and communication 462, 527–8
conventions 317, 703n
dharmacārīs and *dharmacāriṇīs* xvi, 305, 323, 339, 449, 490–1, 501, 598, 729n
founding of 403–4, 466, 468, 471–2, 500–1, 519, 523–4, 530–1, 611–12, 702n
and Going for Refuge 324, 465, 487–8, 524, 611, 703n
not a group 568
in India 489–90; *see also* Trailokya Bauddha Mahasangha
and insight 561–2
meaning and significance of xii, xv–xvi, xvii, 517–18
and monasticism xi–xii, 347, 469, 560, 561, 570, 596, 604
newsletter 733n; *see also Shabda*
Order Office 620, 728n, 754n
ordination 304–5, 317, 387, 510–11, 696n, 732n
and *anagārikas*/*anagārikās* 469, 608, 725n
ceremony 305, 403–4, 703n, 712n
dharmacārīs and *dharmacāriṇīs* 469, 490–1
only one 346–7, 492, 598, 725n; *see also* unified order, below
original grades of 468–9, 471
private 494, 512, 585, 725n, 732n
public 304, 525, 584, 585, 725, 732n, 736n
re-ordination 519
retreats 717n, 721n, 730n, 731n, 734n, 735n, 739n
teams 512, 515, 518, 731n, 732n, 733n, 735n
training/process 513–18, 728n, 733n, 734n, 735n, 741n
and women xvi, 403, 467–8, 500, 512, 515, 725n, 733n, 735n
ordination ceremony 732n
preceptors 511, 512–13, 725n, 732n
College of Public 546, 704n, 725n, 731n, 732n, 740n, 741n, 748n
Sangharakshita as 523–4, 529, 531, 536, 730n
precepts of 325, 337, 346, 348, 655, 703n, 704n
register 510, 518–19
and rest of Buddhist world 502, 510, 545–6
relating to 547–56, 556–67, 568–73
Sangharakshita and, *see* Sangharakshita, and Western Buddhist Order
size of 500, 510, 519, 522, 546
and temperament 531–2
titles for members of 490–1; *see also dharmacārīs* and *dharmacāriṇīs*
original 468, 489; *see also upāsakas* and *upāsikās*
a unified order 467–8, 522–3, 725n
wheel
and Maitreya 179
and spiral 103–4, 113, 239, 251–2, 255, 258–9, 265, 463; *see also nidānas*
wheel of life (Sanskrit *bhavacakra*) 68, 73–4, 77–8, 85, 94, 96, 102, 122–3, 139, 252–4, 256, 258, 463, 673n
Whistler, J. A. M. 644, 757n
White Lotus Sūtra, *see Saddharma Puṇḍarīka Sūtra*
Whitman, W. 365, 708n
Wilde, O. 644, 757n
wilderness 610–12, 753n
Wille 76, 673n
will to Enlightenment, *see bodhicitta*
Williams, P. 669n, 706n
wisdom 16, 114, 127, 394; *see also prajñā*
and compassion 128, 150, 159, 272, 274, 293
Great (Sanskrit *mahāprajñā*) 125
-liberated one 145
of sameness or equality 117
as tenth precept 390–4
wisdoms, five (Sanskrit *jñānas*) 280–1
Wise Old Man 526–7
wish-fulfilling tree 181
wish-granting gem 181
women 25, 185, 305, 380, 453; *see also bhikṣuṇīs*, *maechis*
and arhantship 716n
and ordination 27, 602, 725n; *see also* ordination, *bhikṣuṇīs* Pāli *bhikkhunīs*
in Western Buddhist Order xvi, 403, 467–8, 500, 512, 515, 725n, 733n, 734n, 735n
and responsibility in Triratna 725n
Wong Mou-lam 408, 713n
Wordsworth, W. 319, 434, 704n, 720n
work, *see also* right-livelihood
monks and 606
World Fellowship of Buddhists 548, 568, 746n

worldly winds 499
worlds, *see also lokas*, realms, spheres
  formless 148–9, 370; *see also arūpaloka*
  and mental states 79
  of pure form 148–9, 370; *see also rūpaloka*
  'of tribulation' 63
  'triple' 679n
worship 29, 128, 178, 219–20, 221–2, 222–3; *see also* Puja, Sevenfold
Wu Daozi 213, 690n
Wutaishan 216, 224, 692n

Xiyu Ji 686n, 689n
Xuân, Tr n L 636, 756n
Xuanzang 181, 198, 201, 645, 669n, 686n, 689n

Yamaguchi, S. 124
Yamāntaka 178
yānas
  three 210, 447, 564
    Sangharakshita view of 447–8, 456, 586, 722n
    and Triratna Buddhist Order xvi
  ultimately converge 168
Yaśa 23, 33, 664n, 667n
yathābhūta-jñānadarśana (Pāli *yathābhūta-ñāṇadassana*) 55, 103, 113–15, 127, 262
Yeats, W. B. 405, 712n
yidam 565
yoga 37, 112, 303, 387, 443, 729n
yoga, ati- 443
yoga, mūla- 443
Yogācārabhūmi 676n
Yogācāra school 39–40, 42–3, 67, 201, 275–6, 278–9, 281–2, 285, 336, 463, 501, 676n, 698n
Yogācāra-Vijñānavāda 549
Yogi Chen 680n, 738n
Yorke, G. 3

Zen 112, 131, 256, 284–5, 549, 554–6, 563–4, 566–8, 673n, 693n, 742n, 743, 752n
  orthodoxy of 574
  and sixteen *arhants* 702n
  story of monk and girl 71, 673n
  and work 606, 752n
Zen School
  appropriation of 564
  and bodhisattva vow 163
  and formalism 433, 563
  and Going for Refuge 567
  monasticism 555
  'ox-herding pictures' 343, 707n
  Rinzai school 563, 742n
  Sōtō 112, 563, 567, 693n, 743n
  and *sūtras* 276, 554–5, 698n
Zhiyi 105
Zoroastrianism 337–8

A GUIDE TO THE COMPLETE WORKS OF SANGHARAKSHITA

Gathered together in these twenty-seven volumes are talks and stories, commentaries on the Buddhist scriptures, poems, memoirs, reviews, and other writings. The genres are many, and the subject matter covered is wide, but it all has – its whole purpose is to convey – that taste of freedom which the Buddha declared to be the hallmark of his Dharma. Another traditional description of the Buddha's Dharma is that it is *ehipassiko*, 'come and see'. Sangharakshita calls to us, his readers, to come and see how the Dharma can fundamentally change the way we see things, change the way we live for the better, and change the society we belong to, wherever in the world we live.

Sangharakshita's very first published piece, *The Unity of Buddhism* (found in volume 7 of this collection), appeared in 1944 when he was eighteen years old, and it introduced themes that continued to resound throughout his work: the basis of Buddhist ethics, the compassion of the bodhisattva, and the transcendental unity of Buddhism. Over the course of the following seven decades not only did numerous other works flow from his pen; he gave hundreds of talks (some now lost). In gathering all we could find of this vast output, we have sought to arrange it in a way that brings a sense of coherence, communicating something essential about Sangharakshita, his life and teaching. Recalling the three 'baskets' among which an early tradition divided the Buddha's teachings, we have divided Sangharakshita's creative output into six 'baskets' or groups: foundation texts; works originating in India; teachings originally given in the West; commentaries on the Buddhist scriptures; personal writings; and poetry, aphorisms, and works on the arts. The 27th volume, a concordance, brings together all the terms and themes of the whole collection. If you want to find a particular story or teaching, look at a traditional term from different points of view or in different contexts, or track down one of the thousands of canonical references to be found in these volumes, the concordance will be your guide.

1. FOUNDATION

What is the foundation of a Buddhist life? How do we understand and then follow the Buddha's path of Ethics, Meditation, and Wisdom? What is really meant by 'Going for Refuge to the Three Jewels', described by Sangharakshita as the essential act of a Buddhist life? And what is the bodhisattva ideal, which he has called 'one of the sublimest ideals mankind has ever seen'? In the 'Foundation' group you will find teachings on all these themes. It includes the author's *magnum opus, A Survey of Buddhism*, a collection of teachings on *The Purpose and Practice of Buddhist Meditation*, and the anthology, *The Essential Sangharakshita*, an eminently helpful distillation of the entire corpus.

2. INDIA

From 1950 to 1964 Sangharakshita, based in Kalimpong in the eastern Himalayas, poured his energy into trying to revive Buddhism in the land of its birth and to revitalize and bring reform to the existing Asian Buddhist world. The articles and book reviews from this period are gathered in volumes 7 and 8, as well as his biographical sketch of the great Sinhalese Dharmaduta, Anagārika Dharmapala. In 1954 Sangharakshita took on the editing of the *Maha Bodhi*, a journal for which he wrote a monthly editorial, and which, under his editorship, published the work of many of the leading Buddhist writers of the time. It was also during these years in India that a vital connection was forged with Dr B. R. Ambedkar, renowned Indian statesman and leader of the Buddhist mass conversion of 1956. Sangharakshita became closely involved with the new Buddhists and, after Dr Ambedkar's untimely death, visited them regularly on extensive teaching tours.

From 1979, when an Indian wing of the Triratna Buddhist Community was founded (then known as TBMSG), Sangharakshita returned several times to undertake further teaching tours. The talks from these tours are collected in volumes 9 and 10 along with a unique work on Ambedkar and his life which draws out the significance of his conversion to Buddhism.

3. THE WEST

Sangharakshita founded the Triratna Buddhist Community (then called the Friends of the Western Buddhist Order) on 6 April 1967. On 7 April the following year he performed the first ordinations of men and women within the Triratna Buddhist Order (then the Western Buddhist Order). At that time Buddhism was not widely known in the West and for the following two decades or so he taught intensively, finding new ways to communicate the ancient truths of Buddhism, drawing on the whole Buddhist tradition to do so, as well as making connections with what was best in existing Western culture. Sometimes his sword flashed as he critiqued ideas and views inimical to the Dharma. It is these teachings and writings that are gathered together in this third group.

4. COMMENTARY

Throughout Sangharakshita's works are threaded references to the Buddhist canon of literature – Pāli, Mahāyāna, and Vajrayāna – from which he drew his inspiration. In the early days of the new movement he often taught by means of seminars in which, prompted by the questions of his students, he sought to pass on the inspiration and wisdom of the Buddhist tradition. Each seminar was based around a different text, the seminars were recorded and transcribed, and in due course many of the transcriptions were edited and turned into books, all carefully checked by Sangharakshita. The commentaries compiled in this way constitute the fourth group. In some ways this is the heart of the collection. Sangharakshita often told the story of how it was that, reading two *sūtras* at the age of sixteen or seventeen, he realized that he was a Buddhist, and he has never tired of showing others how they too could see and realize the value of the '*sūtra*-treasure'.

5. MEMOIRS

Who is Sangharakshita? What sort of life did he live? Whom did he meet? What did he feel? Why did he found a new Buddhist movement? In these volumes of memoirs and letters Sangharakshita shares with his readers much about himself and his life as he himself has experienced it, giving us a sense of its breadth and depth, humour and pathos.

6. POETRY, APHORISMS, AND THE ARTS

Sangharakshita describes reading *Paradise Lost* at the age of twelve as one of the greatest poetic experiences of his life. His realization of the value of the higher arts to spiritual development is one of his distinctive contributions to our understanding of what Buddhist life is, and he has expressed it in a number of essays and articles. Throughout his life he has written poetry which he says can be regarded as a kind of spiritual autobiography. It is here, perhaps, that we come closest to the heart of Sangharakshita. He has also written a few short stories and composed some startling aphorisms. Through book reviews he has engaged with the experiences, ideas, and opinions of modern writers. All these are collected in this sixth group.

In the preface to *A Survey of Buddhism* (volume 1 in this collection), Sangharakshita wrote of his approach to the Buddha's teachings:

> Why did the Buddha (or Nāgārjuna, or Buddhaghosa) teach this particular doctrine? What bearing does it have on the spiritual life? How does it help the individual Buddhist actually to follow the spiritual path?... I found myself asking such questions again and again, for only in this way, I found, could I make sense – spiritual sense – of Buddhism.

Although this collection contains so many words, they are all intent, directly or indirectly, on these same questions. And all these words are not in the end about their writer, but about his great subject, the Buddha and his teaching, and about you, the reader, for whose benefit they are solely intended. These pages are full of the reverence that Sangharakshita has always felt, which is expressed in an early poem, 'Taking Refuge in the Buddha', whose refrain is 'My place is at thy feet'. He has devoted his life to communicating the Buddha's Dharma in its depth and in its breadth, to men and women from all backgrounds and walks of life, from all countries, of all races, of all ages. These collected works are the fruit of that devotion.

We are very pleased to be able to include some previously unpublished work in this collection, but most of what appears in these volumes has been published before. We have made very few changes, though we have added extra notes where we thought they would be useful. We have had the pleasure of researching the notes in the Sangharakshita Library at 'Adhisthana', Triratna's centre in Herefordshire, UK, which houses his own collection of books. It has been of great value to be able to search among the very copies of the *suttas*, *sūtras* and commentaries that have provided the basis of his teachings over the last seventy years.

The publication of these volumes owes much to the work of transcribers, editors, indexers, designers, and publishers over many years – those who brought out the original editions of many of the works included here, and those who have contributed in all sorts of ways to this *Complete Works* project, including all those who contributed to funds given in celebration of Sangharakshita's ninetieth birthday in August 2015. Many thanks to everyone who has helped; may the merit gained in our acting thus go to the alleviation of the suffering of all beings.

Vidyadevi and Kalyanaprabha
Editors

THE COMPLETE WORKS OF SANGHARAKSHITA

I FOUNDATION

VOLUME 1 A SURVEY OF BUDDHISM / THE BUDDHA'S NOBLE EIGHTFOLD PATH
A Survey of Buddhism
The Buddha's Noble Eightfold Path

2 THE THREE JEWELS I
The Three Jewels
The Meaning of Conversion in Buddhism
Going for Refuge
The Ten Pillars of Buddhism
The History of My Going for Refuge
My Relation to the Order
Extending the Hand of Fellowship
Forty-Three Years Ago
Was the Buddha a Bhikkhu?

3 THE THREE JEWELS II
Who is the Buddha?
What is the Dharma?
What is the Sangha?

4 THE BODHISATTVA IDEAL
The Bodhisattva Ideal
The Endlessly Fascinating Cry (seminar)
The Bodhisattva Principle

5 THE PURPOSE AND PRACTICE OF BUDDHIST MEDITATION
The Purpose and Practice of Buddhist Meditation

6 THE ESSENTIAL SANGHARAKSHITA
The Essential Sangharakshita

II INDIA

7 CROSSING THE STREAM: INDIA WRITINGS I
Early Writings 1944–1954
Crossing the Stream
Buddhism in the Modern World: Cultural and Political Implications
The Meaning of Orthodoxy in Buddhism
Buddhism in India Today
Ordination and Initiation in the Three Yānas
A Bird's Eye View of Indian Buddhism

VOLUME 8 BEATING THE DHARMA DRUM: INDIA WRITINGS II
Anagarika Dharmapala and Other 'Maha Bodhi' Writings
Dharmapala: The Spiritual Dimension
Beating the Drum: 'Maha Bodhi' Editorials

9 DR AMBEDKAR AND THE REVIVAL OF BUDDHISM I
Ambedkar and Buddhism
Lecture Tour in India, December 1981–March 1982

10 DR AMBEDKAR AND THE REVIVAL OF BUDDHISM II
Lecture Tours in India 1979 & 1983–1992
Other Edited Lectures and Seminar Material

III THE WEST

11 A NEW BUDDHIST MOVEMENT I
Ritual and Devotion in Buddhism
The Buddha's Victory
The Taste of Freedom
Buddha Mind
Human Enlightenment
New Currents in Western Buddhism
Buddhism for Today – and Tomorrow
Buddhism and the West
Aspects of Buddhist Morality
Buddhism, World Peace, and Nuclear War
Dialogue between Buddhism and Christianity
Buddhism and Blasphemy
Buddhism and the Bishop of Woolwich
Buddhism and the New Reformation
Great Buddhists of the Twentieth Century
Articles and Interviews

12 A NEW BUDDHIST MOVEMENT II
Previously unpublished talks

13 EASTERN AND WESTERN TRADITIONS
Tibetan Buddhism
Creative Symbols of Tantric Buddhism
The Essence of Zen
The FWBO and 'Protestant Buddhism'
From Genesis to the Diamond Sūtra

IV COMMENTARY

VOLUME 14 THE ETERNAL LEGACY / WISDOM BEYOND WORDS
The Eternal Legacy
The Glory of the Literary World
Wisdom Beyond Words

15 PĀLI CANON TEACHINGS AND TRANSLATIONS
Dhammapada (translation)
Karaṇīyamettā Sutta (translation)
Living with Kindness
Living with Awareness
Maṅgala Sutta (translation)
Auspicious Signs (seminar)
Salutation to the Three Jewels (translation)
The Threefold Refuge (seminar)
Further Pāli Sutta Commentaries

16 MAHĀYĀNA MYTHS AND STORIES
The Drama of Cosmic Enlightenment
The Priceless Jewel (talk)
Transforming Self and World
The Inconceivable Emancipation

17 WISDOM TEACHINGS OF THE MAHĀYĀNA
Know Your Mind
Living Ethically
Living Wisely
The Way to Wisdom (seminar)

18 MILAREPA AND THE ART OF DISCIPLESHIP I
The Yogi's Joy
The Shepherd's Search for Mind
Rechungpa's Journey to Enlightenment

19 MILAREPA AND THE ART OF DISCIPLESHIP II
Rechungpa's Journey to Enlightenment, continued

V MEMOIRS

20 THE RAINBOW ROAD FROM TOOTING BROADWAY TO KALIMPONG
The Rainbow Road from Tooting Broadway to Kalimpong

VOLUME 21 FACING MOUNT KANCHENJUNGA
Facing Mount Kanchenjunga
Dear Dinoo: Letters to a Friend

22 IN THE SIGN OF THE GOLDEN WHEEL
In the Sign of the Golden Wheel
Precious Teachers
With Allen Ginsberg in Kalimpong (essay)

23 MOVING AGAINST THE STREAM
Moving Against the Stream
1970: A Retrospect

24 THROUGH BUDDHIST EYES
Travel Letters
Through Buddhist Eyes

VI POETRY AND THE ARTS

25 COMPLETE POEMS
Complete Poems 1941–1994
The Call of the Forest
Other Poems

26 APHORISMS AND THE ARTS
Peace is a Fire
A Stream of Stars
The Religion of Art
In the Realm of the Lotus
The Journey to Il Convento
St Jerome Revisited
A Note on the Burial of Count Orgaz
Criticism East and West
Alternative Traditions
The Artist's Dream and other Parables
A Moseley Miscellany
Adhisthana Writings
Urthona Articles and Interviews

27 CONCORDANCE AND APPENDICES

WINDHORSE PUBLICATIONS

Windhorse Publications is a Buddhist charitable company based in the UK. We produce books of high quality that are accessible and relevant to all those interested in Buddhism, at whatever level of interest and commitment. We are the main publisher of Sangharakshita, the founder of the Triratna Buddhist Order and Community. Our books draw on the whole range of the Buddhist tradition, including translations of traditional texts, commentaries, books that make links with contemporary culture and ways of life, biographies of Buddhists, and works on meditation.

To subscribe to the *Complete Works of Sangharakshita*, please go to: windhorsepublications.com/sangharakshita-complete-works/

THE TRIRATNA BUDDHIST COMMUNITY

Windhorse Publications is a part of the Triratna Buddhist Community, an international movement with centres in Europe, India, North and South America and Australasia. At these centres, members of the Triratna Buddhist Order offer classes in meditation and Buddhism. Activities of the Triratna Community also include retreat centres, residential spiritual communities, ethical Right Livelihood businesses, and the Karuna Trust, a UK fundraising charity that supports social welfare projects in the slums and villages of India.

Through these and other activities, Triratna is developing a unique approach to Buddhism, not simply as a philosophy and a set of techniques, but as a creatively directed way of life for all people living in the conditions of the modern world.

For more information please visit thebuddhistcentre.com